FULL & AUTHENTIC REPORT

OF THE

TILAK TRIAL

FULL & AUTHENENTIC REPORT
OF THE
TILAK TRIAL.

(1908.)

BEING THE

CALIFORNIA HINDI STUDENTS ASSOCIATION

ONLY AUTHORISED

VERBATIM ACCOUNT OF THE WHOLE PROCEEDINGS WITH INTRODUCTION AND CHARACTER SKETCH OF

AUTHOR:

BALGANADHAR TILAK

TOGETHER WITH PRESS OPINION.

EDITOR : N. C. KELKAR

GYAN

Published by

Gyan Publishing House
5, Ansari Road
Daryaganj, New Delhi-110002
Phone: 011-47034999, 9811692060
E-mail: books@gyanbooks.com

Distribution Network
gyanbooks.com
India, USA, Canada, UK, Australia, France

ISBN : 978-81-212-9590-1 (PB)
First Published, 1908

2nd Impression 2023

Printed at: Gyan Press, Delhi.

FULL & AUTHENTIC REPORT OF THE TILAK TRIAL
Author: BAL GANGADHAR TILAK

FULL & AUTHENTIC REPORT

OF THE

TILAK TRIAL.

(1908.)

BEING THE

ONLY AUTHORISED

VERBATIM ACCOUNT OF THE WHOLE PROCEEDINGS WITH

INTRODUCTION AND CHARACTER SKETCH OF

Bal Gangadhar Tilak

TOGETHER WITH PRESS OPINION.

September 1908.

PRINTED AT

THE INDU-PRAKASH STEAM PRESS, BOMBAY.

The Tilak Case.

CONTENTS.

PREFACE.

I need, I think, make no apology for presenting this full and authentic account of the Tilak trial to the public. The case is of course one of great importance from the point of view of Mr. Tilak himself; but it is perhaps even more important from the point of view of the Indian public. The record in the case is bound to take rank as a part and parcel of the constitutional history of India in the beginning of the 20th century. While the trial was going on at Bombay there was hardly anything that was being talked of more than its proceedings throughout the length and breadth of the country. And since its termination the appearance of a number of more or less incomplete accounts of the case in various languages has testified to the fact that the people would very much like to be helped with the means of keeping an accurate memory of the great State Trial which had cut a niche in their mind. The present account of the proceedings, being prepared from short-hand notes and embodying all the papers and documents used in the case, will, it is hoped, serve that purpose to some extent.

I must acknowledge my thanks to those workers who voluntarily and cheerfully helped me in my work. I must also thank the men of the *Indu Prakash* Press for their loyal co-operation.

I am painfully conscious of the typographical errors which have successfully avoided the corrector's vigilant eye. But the book had to be brought out within what was in effect a 'time-limit;' and the reader would, it is hoped, forgive those errors in consideration of the high pressure under which the whole work had to be done.

Bombay, 15th September 1908. N. C. KELKAR.

Character Sketch

OF

Mr. Bal Gangadhar Tilak, B.A., LL. B.

Mr. Tilak belongs to a race that has already made a mark in the Maratha history. He is a *Chitpavan* Brahmin, and was born at Ratnagiri on 23rd July 1856. His father, Mr. Gangadhar Ramchandra Tilak, was at first an Assistant Teacher at Ratnagiri and then Assistant Deputy Educational Inspector at Thana and Poona. Gangadharpant was a very popular teacher of his time, and had published works on Trignometry and Grammar. He did not, however, live long to superintend the education of his son. By the death of his father in August 1872 young Bal was left an orphan at the age of 16. He was, however, able to continue his studies without interruption and passed the Matriculation four months after his father's death. He joined the Deccan College, passed the B. A. with honours in 1876, and took the degree of LL. B. of the Bombay University in 1879. While studying law he made the friendship of the late Mr. Agarkar, afterwards the Principal of the Fergusson College, and the two youths passed many a sleepless night in deliberating upon the best scheme they could construct for benefitting their countrymen. They eventually formed a resolution never to accept Government service, but to start a private High School and College for the purpose of imparting cheap and healthy education to the younger generation. They were, of course, laughed at by their fellow-graduates for their Utopian ideas, but neither ridicule nor external difficulties could damp the ardour of the youthful enthusiasts. About this juncture, an older man of congenial spirits came on the scene. The late Mr. Vishnu Krishna Chiplunkar, popularly known as Vishnu Shastri, had just resigned Government service because he could not pull on with his superiors, and had come to Poona with a firm determination to start a private High School. The son of an illustrious father, he was also already famous as the best Marathi prose writer of the time. Messrs. Tilak and Agarkar, having heard of Mr. Chiplunkar's plan, conferred with him, and the trio were soon joined by another man possessing remarkable energy and intelligence, the late Mr. M. B. Namjoshi. Messrs. Chiplunkar and Tilak, with the aid of Mr. Namjoshi, started the Poona New English School on 2nd January 1880. Mr. V. S. Apte M. A. joined them in June and Mr. Agarkar at the end of the year after passing his M. A. The five men did not confine their activity to the School alone. Simultaneously with the School, two newspapers the *Mahratta* and the *Kesari*, were started, and they at once made their mark in the field of Native journalism. Mr. Vishnu Shastri Chiplunkar also established two printing presses, the *Arya-Bhushan* for the use of the two news-papers, and the *Chitrashala* for the purpose of encouraging fine arts. With these various undertakings the five men had enough to do for some time, and they pushed these on manfully. The New English School soon attained the first rank among the Poona schools ; the *Kesari* and the *Marhatta* became the leading papers in the Deccan.

This band of patriotic workers, however, had soon to pass through an ordeal. The *Kesari* and the *Mahratta* published some articles severely criticising the treatment given to H. H. Shivajirao, the late Maharaja of Kolhapur, and the then Karbhari of the State Mr. M. W. Barve, consequently prosecuted Mr. Tilak and Mr. Agarkar as editors of the *Mahratta* and the *Kesari* respectovely for defamation. To add to the troubles, while the case was pending Mr. V. K. Chiplunkar died, and soon after his death Messesrs. Tilak and Agarkar were convicted and sentenced to simple imprisonment for four months. The Kolhapur trial only served to increase the popularity of the School and the two papers. Willing assistance came from all sides. After Mr. Chiplunkar's death, Mr. Tilak was, for a long time, the guiding spirit and Mr. Namjoshi the active member of this small band. In the latter part of 1884 they resolved to give themselves a statutory existence, and with that view they formed the Deccan Education Society of Poona, with themselves as its first body of life-members. They were soon joined by the late Professor V. B. Kelkar, Professor Dharap, and Professor M. S. Gole, while later on came Prof. Gokhale, Prof. Bhanu, and also Prof. Patankar. In 1885 the Fergusson College was eatablished under the auspices of the Deccan Education Society, and all the life-members agreed to serve in it as Professors for 20 years. The Society's institutions soon became prosperous. They purchased the Gadre Wada and the Knabutarkhana play—ground. The Nana Wada was later on handed over to them by Lord Reay in accordance with a promise of Sir James Fergusson's Government and they erected a splendid structure near the Chaturshingi for the accommodation of the College. Mr. Tilak's connection with the School and College, however, ceased in 1890. The causes that brought about this disruption were many and various, and this is not the place to go into them. The process of disintegration had, in fact, begun long before. The Chitrashala had become an independent concern even in the life-time of Vishnu Shastri. About the year 1888 differences of opinion on social and religious questions between Mr. Tilak and Mr. Agarkar led to the latter's resigning his editorship of the *Kesari* and starting a paper of his own, the *Sudharak*. It was then found that the interests of the School and the College could not be identical with those of the papers, and so a partition was effected by which the *Arya-Bhushan* Press and the two papers became the private property of Mr. Tilak, Professor Kelkar, and one Mr. H. N. Gokhale, Professor Kelkar being the editor in charge of the two papers. This state of things lasted till the end of 1890, and might have continued indefinitely if fresh differences had not tended to increase the rupture. The differences chiefly related to the principles which should regulate the conduct of the life-members and the management of the School, and were brought to a head by Professor Gokhale's appointment to the Secretaryship of the Poona Sarvajanik Sabha in 1889. Mr. Tilak was from the first strongly in favour of a Jesuitical mode of life, and insisted upon an absolute rule that life-members should devote all their time and energy to their proper function as teachers. The majorty of his colleagues, however, did not agree with him, and consequently he severed his connection with the Society by sending in his resignation in November 1890. As a Professor, Mr. Tilak was very popular. He was permanent Professor of Mathematics, but he also acted at intervals as Professor of Sanskrit and Science. Originality and thoroughness was his motto; and whatever was the subject he took in hand, his pupils had never any cause for complaint. As a mathematician he was unrivalled, and often reminded his pupils of the late Professor Chhatre, of the Deccan College, Mr. Tilak's own Guru. His resignation was a heavy loss to the College in more ways than one.

After freeing himself from the drudgery of school, Mr. Tilak resolved to devote most of his time to a life of public usefulness. Having obtained more leisure just at the time when the Age of Consent Bill was brought before the Viceroy's Council, Mr. Tilak rushed into the controversy with his wonted ardour. Not that he was ever opposed to the principle of social reform, but he disliked reform by coercion. The Age of Consent Bill, however laudable its aims and objects might have been, was virtually an attempt to force reform on Hindu society by Government interference; and even many sincere advocates of social reform were consequently opposed to it. Mr. Tilak's attitude in this matter at once brought about a division of Poona society into two camps, the Orthodox and the Reformers, and the rupture between the two widened as new differences led to fresh quarrels. After resigning his place in the College, Mr. Tilak started a Law Class, the first of its kind in this Presidency, for the purpose of preparing students for the High Court and District Pleadership examinations. He also took over charge of the *Kesari*, while Professor Kelkar remained editor of the *Mahratta* till about the end of the year. Professor Kelkar, however, had soon to discontinue his connection with the papers altogether, and Mr. Tilak became the editor of both. A year later there was a partition between them of the press and the papers, and Mr. Tilak became the sole proprietor and editor of the *Kesari* and the *Mahratta*, while Professor Kelkar and Mr.

Gokhale remained owners of the *Arya-Bhushan* Press. Such were the vicissitudes through which the two papers had to pass since their birth. The *Kesari* especially has steadily risen in popularity since Mr. Tilak took it in hand, and its circulation now far exceeds that of any other English or Vernacular paper in this country.

Mr. Tilak was not a man to waste the whole of his time in ephemeral writing. He now resolved to turn his leisure to some account and devoted himself to his favourite books the "Bhagavadgita" and the "Rigveda." As a result of his researches in the chronology of the Vedas, he wrote a paper on the antiquity of the Vedas as proved by astronomical observations. He sent a resume of this paper to the International Congress of Orientalists, which was held in London in 1892, and published the whole paper next year in a book form under the title 'The Orion; or the Researches into the Antiquity of the Vedas.' Mr.Tilak in this book traces the Greek tradition of Orion and also the name of that constellation to Sanskrit Agráyana or Agrahâyana ; and as this latter word means the beginning of the year, Mr. Tilak concludes that all the hymns of the Rigveda containing references to that word or the various traditions clustering round it must have been composed before the Greeks separated from the Hindus and at a time when the year began with the Sun in the constellation of Orion or Mrigashirsha, *i. e.*, before 4,000 B. C. It is impossible to do justice to his wide research and masterly argument in a sketch like this, but everybody who has a curiosity on the subject ought to go through the book himself. The book was highly praised by European and American scholars, and Mr Tilak's conclusions may now be said to have met with universal acceptance. Many Orientalists, such as Max Müller, Weber, Jacobi, and Whitney have acknowledged the learning and the originality of the author. After the book was published, Mr. Tilak carried on for some time a friendly correspondence with Prof. Max Müller and Weber on some of the philological questions discussed by him, and the result was that both parties agreed that there was much to be said on each side. Professor Whitney of America, only a short time before his death in 1894, wrote an able article in the Journal of the American Oriental Society in which he highly eulogised Mr. Tilak's theories. Similarly Dr. Bloomfield, of John Hopkins University, in an anniversary address, spoke about Mr. Tilak's book in these terms :—

'But a literary event of even greater importance has happened within the last two or three months—an event which is certain to stir the world of science and culture far more than the beatific reminiscences. Some ten weeks ago I received from India a small duodecimo volume, in the clumsy get-up and faulty typography of the native Anglo-Indian press. It came with the regards of the author, a person totally unknown to fame

I had never heard his name; Bal Gangadhar Tilak B. A. LL. B. Law Lecturer, and Pleader, Poona. The book is published by Mrs. Radhabai Atmaram Sagoon, Bookseller and Publisher, Bombay. The title is 'Orion or Researches into the Antiquity of Vedas.' It will be understood that the entry of the little volume upon my horizon was not such as to prejudice me in its favour, and secondly, I placed it where it might be reached without too much effort in the drowsy after-dinner hour, to be disposed of along with much second class matter, such as reaches a scholar through the channels of the Postal Union. Nor was the preface at all encouraging. The author blandly informs us that the age of the *Rigveda* cannot be less than 4, 000 years before Christ and that the express records of the yearly Hindu antiquity point back to 6, 000 before Christ. Having in mind the boundless fancy of the Hindu through the ages and his particularly fatal facility for 'taking his mouthful' when it comes to a question of numbers, I proposed to myself to continue to turn the leaves of the book with the amused smile of orthodoxy befitting the occasion. But soon the amused smile gave way to an uneasy sense that something unusual had happened. I was first impressed with something leonine in the way in which the author controlled the Vedic literature and the Occidental works on the same; my superficial reading was soon replaced by absorbed study and finally having been prepared to scoff mildly, I confess that the author had convinced me in all the essential points. The book is unquestionably the literary sensation of the year just before us; history the chronic readjuster shall have her hands uncommonly full to assimilate the results of Tilak's discovery and arrange her paraphernalia in the new perspective.'

It would have been well if Mr. Tilak had immediately followed the same line and tackled the many questions which he had left unsolved in this book on Orion; but the profession he had chosen, namely, that of a Law-lecturer and a Journalist, would not allow him the time to concentrate his attention on questions of philology and chronology.

In 1894 Mr. Tilak had to busy himself with an important case, partly in the interest of a personal friend and partly in the larger interests of the Baroda State. This was the well-known Bapat Case in which a Special Commission was appointed to try Rao Sahib W. S. Bapat, the *de facto* head of the Settlement Department, for a number of charges of corruption. The case arose out of a conspiracy against the Department, which was practically headed by the British Political department; and Mr. Bapat's trial had certain special features of interest inasmuch as it was timed to be held behind the back of the Maharaja who was then on a tour in Europe, and the revelations in the trial were expected by the enemies of the Maharaja to cast a damaging slur on at least one aspect of his administration. It was not the unpopularity of the Settlement Department alone but the unpopularity of many high personages, whom we need not here mention, which brought the matters to a head. Mr. Bapat, it was evident, was going to be made a scapegoat and to be punished not only for his own sins, but vicariously for the sins of others also. The prosecution was conducted by the Hon. P. M. Mehta and afterwards by Mr. Branson, Bar-at-Law, and the defence was conducted by the late Mr. M. C. Apte and Mr. D. A. Khare. But Mr. Tilak had the lion's share of the work of the defence, and the splendid results of the searching cross-examination of witnesses for the prosecution, and the masterly argument for the defence stand out as a monument to his industry and ability.

Mr. Tilak's activity in contemporary politics was not, however, left in abeyance. He had now ceased to be the Secretary of the Deccan Standing Committee of the National Congress; but as the Secretary of the Bombay Provincial Conference he organized its first five sessions, the fifth of which, held at Poona in 1892, under the Presidency of the Hon. Mr. P. M. Mehta, was a splendid success. The next year, with its deplorable riots between Hindus and Mahomedans, and the many new questions suggested by them, brought about a great change in the political atmosphere, and Mr. Tilak was again to the front. Never before did he place himself in such direct antagonism with the apparent policy of some Anglo-Indian officials and never before did those officials realize so well his influence over the masses. Mr. Tilak's attitude with respect to this riot question, whether right or wrong, was clear and unmistakable. He attributed those manifestations of racial prejudice mainly to the secret instigation of some short-sighted Anglo-Indian officers. The policy of 'Divide and Rule,' initiated by Lord Dufferin, was, according to him, at the bottom of all the mischief; and the only effective way, he contended, to check these riots was for Government officials to observe strict neutrality between Hindus and Mahomedans. He made, in fact, a direct charge against a certain class of officials and they naturally resented it. Both Lord Harris, the Governor, and his Secretary, Mr. Lee-Warner, were anything but favourably disposed towards him; but Mr. Tilak was not a man to be cowed down by official frowns. Through his paper the *Kesari* he exercised an immense influence over the masses, and it is this influence that is mainly responsible for the infusion of a new spirit among the people. His influence with the educated class was also great. He was twice elected a member of the local Legislative Council and also a Fellow of the Bombay University. In 1895 he headed the poll at the general elections to the City Municipality of Poona and won the esteem of his colleagues as a sound practical worker.

The new spirit had hitherto manifested itself chiefly in a return towards the veneration of indigenous institutions. The most noticeable instance of this was the revival of old religious worship in the form of the Ganpati and the Shiwaji festivals, and Mr. Tilak's name has come to be indissolubly connected with both these movements. Mr. Tilak firmly believed that a healthy veneration of the old gods and the national heroes would best infuse a true spirit of nationality aud patriotism. The run for spurious imitations of foreign ideas and customs and the consequent spirit of irreligiousness among the younger generations were, in his opinion, exerting a disastrous influence upon the moral character of the Indian youth ; and if things were allowed to drift in this way, the ultimate result, Mr. Tilak believed, would be a moral bankruptcy from which no nation can ever hope to rise. It was a very grave problem, and even the Government of India had turned their attention to it at that time. The official panacea, however, was the teaching of moral text-books in Indian schools, which Mr. Tilak in several articles in the *Mahratta* severely criticised. Mr. Tilak thought that to make Indian youths more self-reliant and more energetic, they must be taught greater self-respect, and that could only be done by making them respect their religion and their forefathers. Excessive and aimless self-debasement may perhaps be a good thing in an asetic or a philosopher, but it does mischief in practical life. Superfluous patriotism may sometimes lead to excesses, but it will also do some good; while self-denying abjectness will only lead to lethargy and death. This is, in brief, Mr. Tilak's social and political philosophy ; and however opinions may vary as to its correctness, nobody can deny that he has followed it consistently. Mr. Tilak has often been accused of hypocracy and inconsistency in matters of social reform. He is a practical reformer in his own way. He has educated his daughters, postponed their marriages till the utmost limit sanctioned by the Shastras, advocated relaxation of caste restrictions, and generally sympathized with the social reform movement; and yet he attacked the social reform party. Superficial observers are staggered at this strange incongruity of behaviour, while his opponents attribute it to a desire to gain cheap popularity. The fact is, his conduct in this matter was entirely the result of his strong convictions. He desired social reform, but did not believe in the men or the methods that were then employed in carrying it out. The so-called social reformers of the past generation were not, in his opinion, the men who possess the aptitude or the moral qualities requisite for a successful reform movement. Hence his critcisms are generally directed to the men and not to the object aimed at. This is the real key to Mr. Tilak's attitude as regards social reform. His principle of criticism is in fact the same with respect to political as well as social questions. He may approve of a Government measure and yet criticise the conduct of officials who carry it out; similarly he may desire a particular reform and yet srongly condemn those who want to pose as its ministers.

In 1895 Mr. Tilak came to be associated with the Shivaji Commemoration movement. A stray article of his in the *Kesari* of 23 April 1895 gave such an impetus to the public desire to subscribe for the repair of Shivaji's tomb at Raigad fort in the Kolaba district Rs. 20,000 were in a short time collected, mostly from small contributions. Festivals also began to be celebrated at many places since that time on Shivaji's birthday or coronation day. When it was resolved to hold the eleventh National Congress in Poona, in the Christmas of 1895, Mr. Tilak was, by the united voice of all parties in Poona, chosen its Secretary, and had as such to do almost the whole work of organization in the beginning. He worked till September, when differences as to whether the Social Conference was to be held in the Congress pandal led to bitter party quarrels and compelled Mr. Tilak to retire from the work. He did not, however, cease to take interest in the Congress, but on the contrary did much from outside to make it the great success it was.

The year 1896 saw one of the severest types of famine in this Presidency, and Mr. Tilak was again to the front. He urged upon the Bombay Government to carry out the provisions of the Famine Code and made various suggestions which, if adopted, would have considerably alleviated the sufferings of the people. In Poona he succeded in preventing famine riots by opening cheap grain shops just in time. When he heard of the distress of the weavers in Sholapur and Nagar he went on the spot, and, in consultation with the local leaders, framed a scheme by which local committees were to cooperate with Government to provide suitable relief to that class. The scheme was similar to the one adopted by the Lieutenant Governor of the North-Western-Provinces. Unfortunately, owing to the unsympathetic attitude of the Bombay Government on this question, the scheme was not accepted; and what is more, the Bombay Government got the provision sanctioning such schemes amended. The wrath of Government was apparently caused by the persistent agitation of the Poona Sarvajanik Sabha, of which Mr. Tilak was supposed to be the leading spirit, to acquaint the people with the concessions allowed to them by law during famine times, and to inform the Government of the real wants of the people. This agitation was of course not much to the taste of officials. The Sabha sent several memorials to Government but received curt or no replies, and ultimately it came to be proscribed altogether. All this of course was indirectly meant for Mr. Tilak, who fearlessly pursued his own way.

Mr. Tilak's next service to his countrymen was the part he played in the campaign against the plague. As soon as the plague appeared in Poona he started the Hindu plague hospital and worked for days together to collect the necessary funds. While most of the so-called leaders in Poona had run away, he remained at his post, moved among the people, accompanied the search parties as a volunteer, managed the hospital, established a free kitchen in the segregation camp, and was often in communication with Mr. Rand and His Excellency the Governor on the subject of hardships suffered by the populace. In his papers he strongly supported the various measures adopted by Government for the suppression of the plague, but advised their being carried out in a humane and conciliatory spirit. He advised the people not to make useless resistance, and took the Poona leaders to task for flying away at a time of distress.

But his public services did not save him from prosecution and persecution by Government. The story of his first prosecution for sedition in 1897 may be briefly told as follows :—

In 1895 a movement was set afoot for repairing the tomb of Shivaji at Raighur, which at last in 1896 took the shape of a festival in honour of Shivaji on his birthday. In 1897, owing to the plague, the festival was not held on the birthday of Shivaji but on his coronation day, which happend to fall on the 13th of June. On that day, and on the previous and subsequent days, a long programme of prayers, hymn-singing, sermon-preaching or *Puran* and lecturing was gone through. A very condensed report of the proceedings, with a hymn sung on the occasion, was published in the issue of the *Kesari* of the 15th of June.

On the 22nd of June Mr. Rand and Lieutenant Ayerst were murdered by some unknown person, which created intense excitement, especially in the Anglo-Indian community of Poona and Bombay. The Bombay Government gave sanction to prosecute Mr. Tilak on Friday the 26th July, and Mr. Baig, the Oriental Translator, laid information before Mr. J. Sanders Slater, the Chief Presidency Magistrate of Bombay, on the 27th July. Mr. Tilak was arrested the same night in Bombay and placed before the Magistrate the next day. An application was made to the Magistrate for bail soon after, which was strenuously and successfully opposed by Government. On the 29th a similar application was made to the High Court, which was disallowed, with permission to apply again. The case was committed to the High Court Sessions on the 2nd of August and an application for bail was again made to Mr. Justice Budrudin Tayabji, the presiding Judge, in Chambers by Mr. Davur of the Bombay Bar, instructed by Messrs. Bhaishankar and Kanga. The application was, of course, very strenuously opposed by the Advocate-General. The Judge, however, admitted Mr. Tilak to bail.

The case came on for hearing in due course on the eighth of September and lasted for a week. Mr. Pugh, of the Calcutta Bar, assisted by Mr

Garth, defended Mr. Tilak, and the Hon'ble Mr. Basil Lang, the Advocate-General, conducted the prosecution. Mr. Justice Strachey presided at the trial; and the Jury consisted of five European Christians, one European Jew, two Hindus, and one Parsee. The six Europeans returned a verdict of guilty, and the three Native jurors of not guilty. The Judge accepted the verdict of the majority and sentenced Mr. Tilak to eighteen months' rigorous imprisonment. When the Jury had retired to consider their verdict, an application was made to the Judge on behalf of the accused to reserve certain points of law to the Full-Bench, which was refused. A similar application to the Advocate-General, subsequently made, met the same fate. On the 17th of September 1897 an application was made to the High Court for a certificate that the case was a fit one for appeal to the Privy Council. This application was heard by Sir Charles Farran, C. J., and Candy and Strachey, JJ. and leave was refused.

An appeal, however, was made to the Privy Council and the Right Honourable Mr. Asquith, who is now the Prime Minister of England, argued the appeal on behalf of Mr. Tilak on the 19th of November 1897. Lord Halsbury, the Lord Chancellor, who was then a member of the Cabinet went out of his way to preside over the Council, though it was well-known that the State Secretary for India, another member of the Cabinet, had sanctioned the prosecution. Mr. Asquith laid great stress on the misdirection of the Jury by Mr. Justice Strachey; but the Privy Council, taking the whole summing-up together, saw no occasion for correcting anything therein; and consequently they rejected the application for leave to appeal.

The judicial avenues to Mr. Tilak were thus closed. But the events had made a deep impression on the British public, and Professor Max Muller and Sir William Hunter, with the large-heartedness which usually characterised them, took the lead in presenting an influentially signed petition to the Queen, praying for mercy to Mr. Tilak on the ground that he was a great scholar and that there was much to be said in favour of his release. This petition, among other things, had its effect, and after negotiations Mr. Tilak was persuaded to accept certain formal conditions (Vide page 14 Magisterial Proceedings) and he was released by order of His Excellency the Governor of Bombay on Tuesday 6th of September 1898.

Mr. Tilak having lost enormously in physique by his imprisonment, he spent the next six months in recouping his health. First he spent some days at the Sinhgad sanitarium and after attending the Indian National Congress at Madras in December he made a tour to Ceylon. The next year or two he spent in taking up the threads of the movements which he had already in hand, but the work in connection with which was suspended owing to his imprisonment. A grand Shivaji festival was celebrated on the Raygad Hill Fort in the year 1900 : and the cause of perpetuating the memory of Shirvaji by a monument was pushed on appreciably further thereby. But more important than any other was the work that he undertook of developing his idea about the antiquity of the Vedas which was, as it were, haunting him persistently ever since he published his book on the 'Orion'. Much of his spare time during the preceding ten years, he says in his introduction to the new book 'The Arctic Home in the Vedas', had been devoted to the search of evidence which would lift up the curtain through which a deeper peep could be taken into the misty antiquity of the Vedas. He then worked on the lines followed up in the 'Orion', and by a study of the latest researches in Geology and Archaeology, bearing on the primitive history of man, he was gradually led to a different line of search and then finally the conclusion was forced on him that the ancestors of the Vedic Rishis lived in an Arctic home in inter-glacial times. The enforced leisure in the Jail he turned to account in developing his theory with the assistance of the complete edition of the Rig Veda, which Prof. Max Muller had sent him and the use of which was allowed to him in the Jail. The first manuscript of the new book was written at Singhgad at the end of 1898, but Mr. Tilak deliberately delayed the publication of the book as he wanted to consult Sanskrit scholars in India and as the lines of investigation had ramified into many allied sciences. The book was actually published in March 1903 and it was very favourably received everywhere. We will quote only one important testimony, that by Doctor F. W. Warren, the President of the Boston University and the author of 'Paradise Found', which is published in the *Open Court Magazine* Chicago for September 1905.

"Within the limits of this article no summary of the author's argument can be given. Suffice it here to say that in the judgment of the present writer the array of the evidences set forth is far more conclusive than any ever attempted by an Indo-Iranian Scholar in the interest of any earlier hypothesis. Absolute candor and respect for the strictest methods of historical and scientific investigation charcacterize the discussion throughout. This results in part no doubt from the fact that the author's own attitude of mind was at the outset highly sceptical. He says :— "I did not start with any preconcevived notion in favour of the Arctic theory; nay, I regarded it as highly improbable at first; but the accumulating evidence in its support eventually forced me to accept it." It is hard to see how any other can-did mind can master the proof produced without being mastered by it in turn. Twenty years ago, in preparing my work on the broader problem of the cra dle-land of the whole human race, I went through all the Vedic and Avestic texts so far as existing translations would then permit, reaching at the end the same conclusion that Mr. Tilak has now reached. Incidentally, in my argument a new light was thrown upon various points in the mythical geography and cosmography of the ancient Iranians,—light which the foremost Iranist of his time, Professor Spiegel, generously acknowledged. Incidentally, I also arrived at a new interpretation of the Vedic myth of the captive waters, and of other Vedic myths. Especially gratifying, therefore, is it to me to find in Mr. Tilak a man in no degree dependent on translations, yet arriving not only at my main conclusion, but also at a number of minor ones of which I had never made public mention. I desire publicly to thank this far-off fellow-worker for the generosity of his frequent references to my pioneer work in the common field, and for the solidity and charm of his own, in certain respects, more authoritative contribution. Whoever will master this new work, and that of the late Mr. Jhon O' Neill on *The night of the Gods*, will not be likely ever again to ask, where was the earliest home of the Aryans? "

But by the time Mr. Tilak's new book was issued to the public, he was already in the vortex of another prosecution at the instance of the Bombay Government. This was the well-known Tai Maharaj Case which has taken up a big slice out of Mr Tilak's time since 1901 and which, besides subjecting him to far more excruciating physical trouble and mental torture than any State Prosecution for sedition is capable of, actually involved him in a loss of several thousands of rupees.

The story of this case briefly is as follows:—

Mr. Tilak was the principal among the four trustees and executors of the estate of the late Shri Baba Maharaja, a first class Sardar of Poona and a particular friend of Mr. Tilak. Baba Maharaj died on 7th of August 1897, a couple of days after Mr. Tilak was released on bail by the High Court in the State Prosecution for Sedition against him in 1897. Misfortunes never come singly; and, by a curious co-incidence, on the very day on which Mr. Tilak returned from Bombay after his release, he was called to the death-bed of his friend who insisted upon Mr. Tilak accepting the office of an executor under his last will and testament; and Mr. Tilak agreed to take the heavy responsibility in the hope that by doing so he might be the means of regenerating the Maharaj family, one of the old aristocratic families of the Deccan—by freeing it from debts and handing an unencumbered estate to an heir who might be educated and brought up under his personal supervision. Till sometime after Mr. Tilak's release from jail, he could not apply his mind to the administration of the estate. But as soon as he could take up the work he found two matters urgently waiting for disposal. One was the liquidation of debts and the curtailment of expenditure as the only and necessary means to that end, and the other was the giving of a boy in adoption to Tai Maharaj, as owing to plague, then raging in Poona, human life had become uncertain in the city, and Tai Maharaj was of course the only person who could adopt a son to her husband. Both these matters unhappily contained the germ of the future dispute. The liquidation of debts meant the curtailment of expenditure, and this could not be very agreeable to Tai Maharaj. And the young widow, well aware of the beneficent intentions of Mr. Tilak, at first cheerfully accepted her position as the titular representative of the estate the real and effective ownership being vested in the trustees appointed by her husband's testament. But the lady was soon got over by her favourite Karbhari and was taught to fancy herself to be the equitable owner of the estate and to regard her possible divestment by an adopted boy as a legitimate grievance. There were also harpies who fed on her, had made themselves more or less dear to her as the objects of idle amusement in her widowed leisure, and who gradually and slyly nestled into her confidence as counsellors that whispered agreeable words and made pleasant suggestions. They magnified to her eyes the sad points in her future plight as a mere pensioner and a dependant upon the estate when, if she had but the will, she had also a way to remain independent for ever or at any rate make terms with the boy who would like to sit in her lap and take the estate even as conditioned by her with a far-sighted eye to the welfare of herself and her most favourite and actively co-operating counsellor. But even such a limited and conditioned estate may be a fortune to many boys who were comparatively poor as they were, and would gladly seek adoption or be persuaded thereto by their brothers, for instance, who, in the event of such an adoption, might find their own means appreciably augmented by at least one lawful sharer being cleared out of the way to the ancestral estate. And all this did happen in the case of this unfortunate lady. The cutting down of the budget caused her alarm, and the machinations of the unscrupulous party, led by one Nagpurkar and Pandit Maharaj of Kolhapur, who entered into a conspiracy to get Tai Maharaj to adopt Bala Maharaj, Pandit's brother, were encouraged by her fitful moods. But neither the lady nor Nagpurkar had courage enough to openly oppose the trustees, the former having all along a deep-rooted conviction that the trustees would do nothing that should either benefit themselves personally or compromise the posthumous welfare of her late husband. And at any rate there was admittedly no disagreement between them and her upto the 18th of June, 1901, the day when they all finally started for Aurangabad where eventually a boy was given in adoption to her from the Babre branch of the Maharaj family.

But on her return from Aurangabad she again fell into the hands of evil counsellors and Tai Maharaj was induced by her advisers of evil to get the probate of her husband's will cancelled in the belief that she would be then quite free and her own mistress. The application was made to Mr. Aston, District Judge, Poona on 29th July 1901.

The proceedings in this application lasted from that date to the 3rd of April 1902. Altogether about thirty-four sittings were held, out of which so many as 14 were taken up by the cross-examination of Mr. Tilak under the united battery of Mr. Aston and Tai Maharaja's Pleaders. The principal noticeable point in these proceedings is that the Aurangabad adoption, though not raised to the status of a distinct issue, was forced in by Mr. Aston as almost the principal question to be decided; and a whole flood of documentary and oral evidence bearing on it from the side of Tai Maharaj was let in, in spite of Mr. Tilak's challenge and protest to the contrary, through the wide floodgates of Mr. Aston's ideas of the Law of Evidence on the point of relevancy. The specific issues raised were only whether the grant of Probate to Mr. Tilak and others had become useless and inoperative and whether the executors had become unfit to act in the Trust so as to make the appointment of new trustees necessary. On these issues Mr. Aston decided in the affirmative, held the Aurangabad adoption disproved, revoked the Probate and ordered the costs, *as in a suit*, to be borne by Mr. Tilak and Mr. Khaparde personally. The judgment is a lengthy document of about 40 printed foolscap pages, but 90 per cent of it is devoted to findings and criticism upon facts relating to wholly irrelevant matters such as the alleged confinement of Tai Maharaj at Aurangabad, the Aurangabad adoption, the alleged ill treatment of Tai Maharaj at Poona—matters which, it must be remembered, Mr. Tilak had protested against as irrelevant, and relating to which he did not put in a single scrap of evidence except by his own answers given under compulsion, and upon which he instructed his pleader to let him severely alone in examination by him. Obviously, therefore, there was only a one-sided account of all these matters before Mr. Aston, and yet he did not scruple to draw conclusions and make criticisms as if he had all the possible evidence from Mr. Tilak's side before him. The whole was a regular Inquisition, Mr. Aston himself acting the part of a 'Devil's Advocate' against Mr. Tilak.

As the result of the Inquistion over which he presided, Mr. Aston found that Mr. Tilak had not only deserved discredit by revocation of Probate, but had committed a number of offences in the transactions brought to his notice, and he crowned the improper, illegal and harassing proceedings in his Court as a Civil Judge by taking action under 476 of the Cri. Pro. Code, and committing Mr. Tilak to the City Magistrate to be dealt with according to law. The criminal charges formulated against him were seven and as follows:–(1) Making false complaint for breach of trust against Nagpurkar. (In this connection Mr. Aston even went out of his way to induce Nagpurkar to put in an application for sanction under sec. 195 Cr. P. C.) (2) Fabricating false evidence for use by making alteration and interpolation in the accounts of the Aurangabad trip. (3) Forgery in connection with the above. (4) Corruptly using or attempting to use as genuine evidence—evidence known to be false or fabricated in connection with the attesting endorsement of Tai Maharaja on the adoption deed. (5) Corruptly using as true or genuine evidence the said adoption deed. (6) Fraudulently using as genuine the adoption deed containing his interpolation over Tai Maharaj's signature. (7) Intentionally giving false evidence by ten sentences which were grouped under three sub-heads relating to (*a*) the fact of adoption at Aurangabad, (*b*) Tai Maharaj's confinement in the Wada at Poona, and (*c*) use of force to Bala Maharaj in the same Wada. This in itself is a formidable list. But to make the thing complete we may as well state here that not content with a commitment on these charges, Mr. Aston had suggested to Government an investigation in certain other collateral charges arising out of the same transaction such as giving false information to the Police, cheating, unlawful assembly, riot, &c., &c.

Repeated appeals were made to the High Court which, if it had given one stich in time would have saved nine which it had to give afterwards. But while upsetting Mr. Aston's order for the revocation of Probate as wrong, the High Court allowed in a light-hearted fashion the criminial proceedings against Mr. Tilak to go on. As regards the charge of false complaint, Mr. Beaman refused to uphold the sanction for prosecution against Mr. Tilak which fell through. But after a prolonged trial Mr. Clements, Special Magistrate, convicted Mr. Tilak on the charge of perjury and sentenced him to rigorous imprisonment for eighteen months, admitting that Mr. Tilak was not actuated by selfish motives but condemning him as a man who was demented and whose mind was unhinged by obstinacy and love of power.

The fair weather region, however, began with the decision of Mr. Lucas, the Sessions Judge, who in appeal, reduced the sentence to six months after completely vindicating Mr. Tilak's motives and intentions. Mr. Lucas's judgment for conviction was top-heavy and insupportable and Mr. Tilak came out triumphant and with flying colours in the High Court on the 4th of March 1904. The charge of perjury was knocked down on the head and Government out of very shame withdrew all the other charges; and so Mr. Tilak emerged from the fiery ordeal without a stain on his character.

The judgment of Sir Lawrence Jenkins was for all practical purposes a judgment on the adoption suit itself. For the party of Tai Maharaj, having fallen to the temptation of using Mr. Aston to the fullest extent possible, had sown the wind by getting Mr. Tilak to be committed on a charge of perjury relating to the factum itself of adoption; and they must thank themselves for having to reap the whirlwind in that the adoption itself was indirectly pronounced upon by the High Court. The crash of course came late, but it was complete when it did come; and the conspirators against Mr. Tilak realised that they had really dug the grave for themselves though meant by them for Mr. Tilak. It was of course extraordinary that the issue of an adoption should be decided like this in a criminal case, but it was made inevitable by Mr. Aston for the good of Tai Maharaj and for the ruin of Mr. Tilak. But Mr. Aston now found himself hoisted with his own petard! The case took nearly all Mr. Tilak's time from May 1901 to March 1904. A calculation shows that these proceedings occupied about 160 sittings, Mr. Tilak having to appear in Court for most of these days in person. The aggravating feature of the prosecution was that in prosecuting Mr. Tilak the Bombay Government were indirectly seeking the fulfilment of their animus against him. They were fighting the battles of Tai Maharaj on the ground of adoption. It was an evil combination of official animus and a woman's self-interest; and we for one cannot decide what was the real fact, namely, whether Tai Maharaj was a tool in the hands of Government or Government were a tool in her hands! The probability is that each of them used and was actually used in turn as a tool by the other to a certain extent, though it is to be pitied that in all this the Government so far forgot their dignity as to debase and put themselves on the mean level of an illiterate, selfish and misguided young widow! All this took the public interest in the case far beyond the personality of Mr. Tilak, though he was no doubt the central figure therein.

How Mr. Tilak behaved during all these troubles; how he could not only keep the serenity of his mind so as to pursue his ordinary avocations without detriment; how even in his darkest hours when expressions of hope from others were only likely to have sounded as hollow mockeries or premature consolations, he not only maintained cheerfulness enough for himself and to spare for others and proved a source of intellectual inspiration to his own legal advisers; how he could command isolation of mind even amidst his deep-rooted and worrying anxieties, only intensified by the death of his eldest son, in order to pursue his favourite literary studies to issue his latest book "the Arctic Home in the Vedas" a few days after his commitment by Mr. Aston—these are all matters on which perhaps it is not for us to dwell at any length.

Mr. Tilak has since won the civil case for adoption in the Court of Original Jurisdiction at Poona which has completely vindicated his word and his action.

The next year Mr. Tilak spent in organising his private affairs, specially relating to the papers and the press. The enormous circulation of the *Kesari* required the importation of a big machine for printing it, and the generosity of the Maharaja Gaikwad who sold to him the Gaikwad Wada at Poona for only a fair price, enabled him to give his papers and the press the much needed permanent local habitation. With his well-known versatility he also applied his mind to the casting of a new kind of Marathi type with a view to adapt it to a Marathi lino-type machine, and in this matter he has achieved remarkable success. Lino-type makers in England have approved of his design of the new type, but the actual importation of lino-type machines fitted with Marathi type has been delayed owing to the fact that there are very few printing houses in the country who could afford to use Devanagari lino-type machines and that consequently the lino-type makers in England cannot be persuaded to lock their capital in the casting of the new machines till that time.

Since the year 1905 Mr. Tilak has been deeply engrossed in active political agitation. The Bengal Partition led to a sudden upheaval of national sentiment throughout the country and to the inauguration of the movements of Swadeshi, Boycott, National Education and Swarajya. The Benares Congress was the beginning of an organised and strong expression of public opinion in the country; and the story of the Calcutta and the Surat Congresses is too fresh in the minds of our readers to need reiteration. It has been acknowledged that Mr. Tilak was by far the ablest leader of the new party of Nationalists and that it was owing to him that the lamp of nationalistic feeling, according to the new lights, was kept burning in Western India since the partition.

Mr. Tilak's has been a most eventful life. He is a man of originality which is surpassed only by the glow of his fiery spirit and by his untiring activity. He scorns ignoble ease and is particulary happy when he is face to face with an undertaking in which the odds are manifestly against him. Then again most of his acts have a real altruistic aspect. His ambition has been to strive for the good of the people; and it is admitted that he has been able to realise his ambition in a pre-eminent degree. These two things go to make up the secret of his success as a man who, more than any other of the present or the past few generations, has touched the imagination of millions of his countrymen. The unprecedented popularity and esteem which Mr. Tilak enjoys and deserves needs no description. He combines ability, industry, enterprise and patriotism in such a degree that the British Government think they have always to be mindful of him. And many of Mr. Tilak's friends will, we suppose, be content to accept the attitude of the Mighty British Government towards him as perhaps the most eloquent testimony to his worth.

---

* The first portion of this character sketch has been taken from the book of the Tilak Case of 1897 with a few alterations.

INTRODUCTION.

This book contains a full and authentic account of the proceedings of the great *Tilak Trial* which was held at the third Criminal Sessions of the Bombay High Court from the 13th to the 22nd July 1908.

The present is the second State prosecution for sedition against Mr. Tilak, the first one being in 1897. In both the cases Mr. Tilak was prosecuted in his capacity as the publisher of certain alleged seditious matter in his paper the *Kesari*. Mr. Tilak was even in 1897, as of course he is to-day, the most popular Mahratta in India. And the *Kesari* which now enjoys the largest circulation of all newspapers, Indian or English, in this country was even eleven years ago the most widely circulated newspaper in the Bombay Presidency. In the back-ground of both the prosecutions there was a scene of great popular unrest due to the operation of a repressive policy on the part of the Government resulting in political murders. Both the cases were tried by a Judge of the Bombay High Court with the aid of a Special Jury, a large majority of which was made up of Europeans, and which found Mr. Tilak guilty of sedition on both the occasions by a majority in exactly the same proportion which the European element bore the Indian in that body. It only remains to be added that in both the ca[illegible] the Indian public by an almost unanimous voice adjudged the prosecut[illegible] to be ill-advised and the conviction unjust.

The genesis of the present prosecution could be traced to the abortive session of the Surat Congress, in December 1907, which marked the culminating point of the unpleasant relations between Mr. Tilak as the leader of the New Party and the Moderate school of Indian politicians; and these relations might be taken as being in a way the reflection of the relations between Mr. Tilak and the New Party on the one hand and the Government on the other. The out-burst of sentimental violence and political crime in Bengal had for some time past helped to accelerate the process of disintegration in the body of political workers in this country. And the news of an attempt on the life of Mr. Allen, the Collector of Dacca, only a couple of days previous to the session of the Surat Congress was universally regarded as calculated to complete the fermentation of the political situation which was yeasty and uncomfortable enough already. When the Congress dispersed at Surat on that memorable 27th of December 1907 and the components of that unusually large gathering went away to their homes in different parts of India, carrying with them bitter memories and sullen thoughts, it looked as if glowing sparks from a fearful furnace had been driven by a malignant wind and spread broad-cast among magazines full to the brim with combustibles. The first few weeks after the Congress witnessed the course of futile but aggravating recrimination between different Congress camps, while Government were wisely replenishing their resources of repression with a view to deal an effective blow at the New Party. The bomb outrage at Muzzafurpore towards the end of April 1908 offered Government the psychological moment for inaugurating an era of arrests, searches, prosecutions and persecutions to which not even a distant parallel could be found throughout the whole course of the history of India under British Rule.

In these affairs Bombay had of course its own share; and the Government never concealed their belief that whatever might or might not happen in Bengal or else where, Mr. Tilak was the source of all political activity and that no campaign of repressive prosecutions could be ever complete unless it involved this towering leader of the New Party. Since his return from Surat Mr. Tilak had, moreover, shown unusual activity. He organised the District and the Provincial Conferences and brought the Temperance agitation in Poona to a head. The organised picketting at liquor shops was looked upon by Government officials as the first object-lesson in the training of national volunteers; and as Mr. Tilak began to extend his lecturing tours to places even outside Poona, Government must have concluded that it was no longer safe to keep Mr. Tilak free. By the time the Bombay Legislative Council met at poona on the 20th of June, Government had apparently decided to strike the blow at him ; and when His Excellency Sir George Clarke, the Governor of Bombay, remarked that certain persons who possessed influence over the society were in the habit of exciting feelings of hatred and contempt against Government and feelings of animosity between classes of his Majesty's subjects, that these persons were only playing with fire and that Government would not be deterred by anything to put the law in motion against them, there was hardly any one who had any doubt in his mind as to the real objective of those remarks. Already four Native newspapers in the Presidency were on their trial for sedition; and there could possibly be no mistake as to the personage who was now specially meant to be honoured with the pregnant minatory prouounce-ment referred to above. A week before this, Mr. S. M. Paranjape, the editor of the *Kal* and a friend of Tilak, was committed to the High Court Sessions; and when he shifted his camp from Poona to Bombay to assist Mr. Paranjape in his defence, Mr. Tilak himself had a sort of premonition that he could not return to Poona for a considerably long time. Two days after the Governor's speech the official sanction for Mr. Tilak's prosecution was signed at Bombay, and on the next day, that is to say, on the 24th of June at about 6 P. M. Mr. Tilak was arrested at the *Sardar Griha* where he was putting up at the time. The same evening his house and press at Poona were locked by the Police where the next day they conducted a search under a warrant by the Chief Presidency Magistrate of Bombay. By an extention of the warrant authorised by the District Magistrate of Poona, the Police also searched, on the same day, Mr. Tilak's residence at the hill-fort sanitarium *Singh Garh*, following the unusual procedure of breaking open windows and conducting a search behind the back of any recognised representative of the owner. The *search at both the places resulted in nothing of importance being found except a post-card, with the names of two books on explosives written thereon, which was made so much of at the trial.

On the 25th of June Mr. Tilak was placed before Mr. Aston, the Chief Presidency Magistrate, who rejected an application for bail and remanded him to jail. While Mr. Tilak was in jail it somehow dawned upon the Bombay Government that it was risky to stake Mr. Tilak's ruin upon the article of the 12th of May alone, (See Exhibit C), and another sanction to prosecute Mr. Tilak, for publishing the leading article in the *Kesari* of the 9th of June, was signed at Bombay on the 26th of June. A fresh information was thereupon laid before Mr. Aston who issued a fresh warrant which was executed on Mr. Tilak in jail. On the 29th of June some formal evidence was recorded, and Mr. Aston committed Mr. Tilak to the third Criminal Sessions of the Bombay High Court on two sets of charges under Section 124 A and 153 A, by two separate orders of commitment.

The day next after his arrest, Mr. Tilak was lodged in the Dongri jail at Bombay. Here as an under-trial prisoner he was allowed the use of food, bedding and clothes supplied to him from his home. But Mr. Tilak had to suffer from a grievance which was worse than any physical discomfort. He was practically handicapped in the preparation of his defence.

On the 2nd of July an application was made by Mr. Jinnah, Bar-at-Law, to Mr. Justice Davar, who presided at the third Criminal Sessions, for Mr. Tilak's release on bail, and the rejection of this application together with its surrounding circumstances conclusively showed the way the judicial wind was blowing.

Notice had been by this time served on Mr. Tilak's Solicitor that the Crown would make an application to the Court for directing that a Special Jury should be empanelled to try Mr. Tilak. It was most unfair to make such an application as Mr. Baptista's able argument against it (vide page 18) shows. But Government was lucky enough to be able to run on the innings merrily in their own favour entirely from the beginning, and the hearing of the application for a Special Jury on the 3rd of July resulted in its being granted.+

---

*All the papers taken in custody were either necessary for a formal proof of Mr. Tilak's connection with the *Kesari* or mere innocent curiosities of a miscellaneous nature. The second kind of papers were put in by the defence itself to show the kind of company in which the card was found. As regards the card it was successfully explained away by Mr. Tilak, and eventually both the Judge and the Advocate-General had nearly to admit that it could not carry the proof of the charge of Sedition against Mr. Tilak any further than the incriminating articles themselves could do.

+It may be noted that one could easily know how to interpret the language of Mr. Justice Davar when in disposing of the application he remarked that "it was in Mr. Tilak's own interest that he should have the benefit of being tried by a Jury selected from the citizens of Bombay from a higher class of citizens."

Between the day of the rejection of the application for bail and the day of the trial Mr. Tilak had slightly over a week within which to prepare his defence. The jail authorities had of course given him certain facilities in this repect ; but after all only a very limited number of friends could go and see him during a limited number of hours of the day. And eventually such defence as Mr. Tilak could actually prepare was not because of the facilities which were given to but in spite of the restrictions which were imposed upon him. The speech which Mr. Tilak delivered in his defence occupies nearly a hundred pages of this book and bristles with references to legal and literary works. That shows in a way the great resourcefulness and the power of Mr. Tilak's mind and memory.

The trial opened on the 13th of July, and attention was centred on the first day on the ruling the Judge might give on the question of the amalgamation of the two cases in one trial and on the constitution of the Jury. In the first matter Mr. Tilak's objection was over-ruled ; the two cases were amalgamated ; and as many charges were put together as the Judge then thought he might combine so as to be technically within the law. Mr. Tilak objected to the amalgamation both on the ground of law and of the prejudice which might be caused to him by the confusion in his own mind as well as in the minds of the Jury in respect of the different charges, which really deserved to be separately tried if the requirements of justice were to be satisfied. The evil effects of this amalgamation were not long in being realised; for, as will be seen from the proceedings, practically one single article was made the ground of three convictions and sentences on three different charges. As regards the constitution of the Jury, the Judge in granting the application of the Crown for a Special Jury had expressed an expectation that the panel summoned would be such that, making allowance for the challenges, there would be a fair representation of the different Indian communities on the Jury as actually empanelled in the box. But far from that being the case the Jury was made up of seven Europeans and two Parsis.

The recording of the evidence for the Prosecution, which was more or less of a formal character, occupied the Court for about two and a half days. The only witness that was cross-examined, with any degree of keenness on the part of Mr. Tilak, was Mr. Joshi who was put into the box to identify certain official signatures, to put in the incriminating and other articles, and to certify to the correctness of the translations which not he himself but some one else had made. Mr. Joshi could thus be cross-examined not as one responsible for the translations himself, but more or less as an official expert who could take liberties with the questions put to him in the cross-examination or give answers with a certain sense of irresponsibility. The record of this cross-examination, which was searching and creditable to the Marathi scholarship of a man like Mr. Tilak, will show that Mr. Tilak completely succeeded in establishing the merits of the objection which he subsequently dwelt upon in his speech, namely, that though not purposely distorted the mistranslations were numerous enough and calculated to create a wrong notion in the reader's mind about the spirit of the Marathi articles.

Out of the fifteen exhibits put in for the Prosecution seven were articles from the *Kesari*, two were Government sanctions for the prosecution, two more were Mr. Tilak's formal declarations as press owner, printer and publisher, and two others were the search warrants; one was the copy of the Panchanama of the search in which were noted sixty three documents which were seized by the Police! And the remaining exhibit was the post card. Of these Mr. Tilak objected to the admissibility of the articles other than the charge articles and to the post-card. But his objections were over-ruled. As regards the Panchanama, with the exception of the post-card, one portion of the papers included therein were not put in at all by the Prosecution, but were returned to Mr. Tilak. The remaining portion was bodily put in as a whole bundle by Mr. Tilak along with his written statement. This bundle Mr. Tilak had to put in only for the purpose of showing the character of the papers and the conditions in which the post-card was found. But the putting in of these papers even for that limited purpose was regarded technically as amounting to giving evidence for the Defence, and that cost Mr. Tilak the right of reply which is extremely precious to an accused person, especially in a trial by Jury. Having lost the right of reply, Mr. Tilak decided also to put in a number of newspapers which were calculated to prove his contention that his articles were written in a controversy, and as replies to the points, as they arose in the controversy, between the Anglo-Indian papers on the one hand and the Indian papers on the other. Mr. Tilak's statement (See page 69 Sessions Proceedings) was a simple and a brief one in which he asserted that he was not guilty and described the real character of the incriminating articles.

Mr. Tilak opened his speech for the defence at about 4 P. M. on Wednesday, the third day of the trial; and with the exception of Saturday and Sunday following he occupied the time of the Court up to about the noon of Wednesday, the 8th day of the actual sitting of the Court. It would, we think, be superfluons to say anything about the speech which is undoubtedly a memorable one from many points of view. Mr. Tilak did not command 'eloquence' as the word is usually understood. But it amply served the purpose which Mr. Tilak really meant to serve by undertaking to defend himself in person. And whatever the verdict they gave, the Jury must have, during the days of the speech, acquired an intimate knowledge with the master mind of the man on whom they were called upon to sit in judgment. The speech lasted, as the Judge himself was careful enough to note for a purpose of his own, for twenty one hours and ten minnutes and no Jury, constituted of average men, could fail to perceive that whatever Mr. Tilak's faults as a speaker, they could not have much fault to find with him as a man. And on the hundreds of highly educated people who crowded the Court every day and thousands who read the reports outside, the speech had undoubtedly a greatly elevating effect.

As the speech is one of extraordinary dimensions, it may be worth while just to briefly summarise the principal points made by Mr. Tilak in order to facilitate its comprehension by the reader. The amalgamation of two cases, the joinder of four charges, and the subsequent dropping of one of them only to make the trial good, was illegal, and likely to cause prejudice. The admission of articles other than the incriminating ones to prove intention was improper. The post-card (Exhibit K) was inadmissible. The translations of the articles instead of the originals were made the basis of the charges. The whole of the articles were embodied in the charges and the particulars of the manner in which the offences were committed were not specified by setting out particular words or sentences alleged to be seditious under Section 124 A or criminal under 153 A. Mr. Tilak practically gave a discourse upon the law of Sedition in England and the law of Sedition in India and made some interesting new points about the construction of sections 124A and 153 A. With regard to Section 124 A Mr. Tilak pointed out that the first portion of the Section did not apply to him at all, because that contemplated the fact of an actual excitement of disaffection, and there was in this case no evidence given whatever to show that Mr. Tilak's writings resulted in such actual excitement of disaffection. What was proved in the case was only the words of the published articles and the identity of their publisher. The real character of the words of the articles was a matter for the Jury; but no evidence was given to show to the Jury, who did not know Marathi, that the words were really capable of the meaning which the Prosecution sought to attribute to them. What remained of Section 124A, therefore, was only an attempt to excite disaffection. Mr. Tilak elaborately discussed the meaning of the word 'attempt'. He contended that the word could not be taken in its ordinary meaning but that it had a special meaning of its own. An act under the Section must be an intentional and premeditated act with the definite object of exciting disaffection, which must be proved to have failed in accomplishment by causes not dependent upon the will of the man making the attempt but operating quite independently of his control. There was here no evidence of the success of the attempt, or of the failure being due to something operating independently of Mr. Tilak's will. As regards the object of the attempt, even supposing that the words of the articles were likely to create disaffection, the creation of that disaffection was not the object with which the articles were written. Even when a writing may be violent or reckless and even when there may be a likelihood of disaffection being caused thereby, the writer could not be punished for an attempt under 124A, if he has no criminal intention. The question of intention was therefore the principal one to be considered; and in deciding this question it was improper and unsafe to follow the maxim of civil law, namely, that every man must be presumed to *intend* the natural consequences of his acts. This intention could not be a matter of presumption, nor could it be proved only by the character of the words or inuendoes in writing. Criminal intention must be positively proved by the evidence of surrounding circumstances. The motive or object with which an act is done is of course not identical and ought not to be confounded with intention; but this motive or object is necessarily one of the most reliable indications in an inquiry as to intention. His real object or motive in writing the articles, Mr. Tilak contended, was to give a reply to the theories and suggestions, which were controversial enough, of Anglo-Indian and other critics who took the opportunity of the bomb-outrages merely for recommending to Government an aggravated policy of repression. The surrounding circumstances showed that; and to prove this one circumstance Mr. Tilak had to put in seventy-one newspapers, Indian or Anglo-Indian, a perusal of the articles in which would show how big was the controversy that was raging. Mr. Tilak's intention could not be to excite disaffection because the articles showed that they were written with the express purpose, mentioned in so many words in the articles themselves, of giving advice and a warning to Government. The construction put upon the words of the articles by the Prosecution was unjustifiable. In the first place the words relied on were mistranslations, some of them very gross ones, calculated to mislead the mind of the Jury. The translator himself was not put into the witness box, but an official expert who generally certified to the correctness of translations which he himself had not made. Even when the necessary corrections were made, there remained the inuendoes ascribed to the writer. No specific inuendoes were charged and therefore no inuendoes could be found or supplied by the Jury. But the Prosecution affected to find an inuendo in every word, as it were, on the gratuitous assumption that the writer was actuated by a criminal intention. This intention they had not proved. As for the language of the articles, it had to be remembered that in writing on high political thesis, the writer had to labour under the disadvantage of the Marathi language not yet being able to cope with the progress in the political life of the country. Even the official expert had to use antiquated dictionaries in the witness box to translate certain sentences put to him in the cross examination; and even when he had the help of those dictionaries he could not help making himself ridiculous by making queer translations of sample words and sentences. That should give an idea as to the hard task a leading newspaper writer has to perform, as he has to write on all manner of subjects without long notice and sometimes on the spur of the moment. Moreover the words and ideas for which Mr. Tilak was now being sought to be held responsible were not invented by him. They formed a part of the political controversy which had been raging in India for over thirty years past between the official and the pro-official party on the one hand and the popular party on the other. If the language of the articles was properly understood in the light of these considerations, then the Jury would have no difficulty in acquitting him. Something more than the mere objectionable character of certain words had to be proved to bring home the charge to him; and the Prosecution not having done so, the Jury had no option but to acquit him. He appealed to to the Jury to regard the question as one not of an individual, much less that of a man who was not a *persona grata* with Government, and who might be regarded as their political opponent, but as one involving the liberty of the Press in India. He appealed to them to bear in mind the traditions of their fore- fathers, who fought for their liberty of speech and opinion, to regard themselves as guardians of the Press even in India, to stand between the Press and the Government, and to temper the operation of hard laws. He told them that they were not bound by the direction the Judge would give them as to the facts and reminded them that in India today, as has been the case in England since Fox's Libel Act of 1792, the Juries are the sole Judges of the merits of a seditious libel. The vigilance of the Juries in England saved the liberty of the Press and rendered the prosecutions for sedition rare in England; and he begged of the Jurymen that they in India too would be actuated by similar public-spiritedness.

Mt. Tilak finished his address to the Jury at about 12-30 noon on the eighth day which also proved the last day of the trial. The address of Mr. Branson, the Advocate General, was conceived in a satirical spirit and at times he indulged in language to which strong objection could have been taken. This address lasted for about four hours, but was apparently hurried up to a close. At about 5 P. M. mysterious movements and consultations began among the Government party, and the Judge declared his intention of finishing the case that very day though they might have to sit till late at night. Mr. Tilak was taken by surprise and it affected him particularly in this way that he could not hold the consultation with his friends and relations which he had intended to hold that evening and the next morning, in view of the eventuality of his conviction. The net was somewhat surreptitiously woven round his life in the closing vesper hours of that memorable day. After the close of Mr. Branson's speech the Judge delievered a strongly adverse charge. The Jury retired at 8-3 P. M. and returned at 9-20 P. M. On all the three charges they, by a majority of seven to two, found Mr. Tilak guilty, and the Judge, accepting the verdict, sentenced Mr. Tilak to six years transportation and a fine of one thousand rupees, but not before he addressed him bitter words of reproach which Mr. Tilak had a right to regard as only insult added to injury. Mr. Tilak, however, had an occasion to tell the Judge as well as the public what he thought about it all; and when asked whether he had any thing to say he uttered in a solemn and piercing tone the following words from the dock:—

"All I wish to say is that in spite of the verdict of the Jury I maintain that I am innocent. There are higher Powers that rule the destiny of things and it may be the will of Providence that the cause which I represent may prosper more by my suffering than by my remaining free."

For the couple of hours since the Jury retired to consider their verdict the big Court room was possessed by a solemnity of feeling which was marked on every face. The dim gas-light in the hall only added to the effect of the dead silence on the part of the spectators who were looking from the Judge to Mr. Tilak and from Mr. Tilak to the Judge. The whole thing over, Mr. Justice Davar rose at 10 P. M. and all rose with him; and Mr. Tilak was spirited away in the twinkling of an eye.

It was not till about 7 P. M. that evening, that the news about the Judge's determination to finish the case that night leaked from the High Court, which was kept specially guarded in all directions. And yet within a couple of hours thousands of people gathered at the entrances to the High Court and were anxiously waiting to know the result of the trial. Heavy showers of rain were at intervals falling, and the dim light in the streets combined with the murky weather spread a pall of gloom which could not but affect the minds at least of those who were absorbed in imagining what must be passing in the Court house to which all access was completly prohibited. At about 10 P. M., the secret was out ; there was bustle and commotion all round the High

Court buildings; the mounted police were galloping in every direction to disperse the crowd; and the sad news of Mr. Tilak's conviction and sentence was conveyed from soul to soul almost by a process of telepathy. The Police and the Judge thus successfully prevented what might have been a monster demonstration. But the next morning when the news of the doings of the previous night spread like wild fire through the city the people felt aggrieved, as it were, at the smartness of the authorities and they commenced demonstration with a vengeance. The effect of the news of Mr. Tilak's conviction and transportation, especially upon the masses, was something tremendous. The great millhand population was determined to strike work in honour of Mr. Tilak and by a spontaneous movement the Bazars in several quarters in the city were closed for business. The streets, however, were kept alive by the cries of newspaper boys, for in the course of that half week Mr. Tilak's pictures, newspapers giving accounts about him and leaflets containing songs composed in his honor were sold by tens of thousands. The popular feeling about Mr. Tilak was manifested in a hundred other ways in private and public places in the great metropolitan City. The Police and some other people who were endowed with a larger measure of blind loyalty to Government than tact, discretion or common sense, most unwisely interfered with the passive demonstration. Some of the millhands also went out of their way in trying to coerce those, whom they regarded as the black-legs among them, into stopping work. The general result of all these contributory factors was that the mob mind got out of control and there was rioting in several parts of the city; the military had to be called out and firing resulted in the deaths of 15 and the wounding of 38 people. For nearly six days business was at a standstill and a reign of terror prevailed in many parts of the city. These unusual demonstrations completly proved the great depth to which the roots of Mr. Tilak's popularity had penetrated in a population which is generally regarded as the least homogenous in formation and the least susceptible to political sentiment.

That is the story in brief of this great trial. The case is yet *sub judice* so far as the Privy Council is concerned. Mr. Tilak's appeals to Mr. Justice Davar, to the Advocate General and to the Appelate Bench of the High Court for a consideration of the objections urged by him on the ground of law have been rejected more or less summarily. But he still hopes to get justice at the hands of the Privy Council which is the highest tribunal of appeal in the British Empire.

NOTE—The rejection of Mr. Tilak's application for his release on bail was universally regarded as unjustifiable. Curiously enough it so happened eleven years ago that Mr. Justice Davar was engaged as Counsel for Mr. Tilak in the sedition case of 1897, and he successfully got out Mr. Tilak on bail as the result of an application made to Mr. Justice Badruddin Tayabji. Mr. Tayabji's judgment proved an epoch-making judgment so far as the question of bail in cases of sedition was concerned. For eleven years afterwards, the Tilak case was quoted as a conclusive ruling in support of the release of under-trial prisoners on bail. With Mr. Davar changing the Gown for the Wig, or it should rather be said the Bar for the Bench, the whole course of law was to be changed; and Mr. J. Davar's judgment in the Tilak case of 1908 has already been widely quoted and acted upon to support the rejection of applications for bail. Below in three parallel columns we quote important sentences from Mr. J. Tayabji's judgment in 1897, Mr. Davar the Barrister's argument in 1897, and Mr. Davar the Judge's ruling in 1908 in respect of the same subject matter, namely, the principles on which bail may be granted or refused to an under-trial prisoner especially in cases of sedition.

TAYABJEE J. (1897)	BARST. DAVAR. (1897.)	JUDGE DAVAR. (1908)
All legislation in regard to the release of accused parties on bail was based upon the anxiety of the Legislature to *secure the attendance* of the accused at the time the trial came on. The leading principle of jurisprudence was that a man was not to be presumed to be guilty until he had had a fair trial and was found to be guilty. But at the same time another leading principle that the Judges had to bear in mind was that there ought not to be any miscarriage of Justice by the accused absconding or not appearing when the case was called on for hearing. If it was absolutely or morally certain that the accused would be forthcoming at the trial it would be contrary to the principles of Justice to keep him in jail till the trial came	Mr. Davar, Counsel for Mr. Tilak applied for bail on the following grounds. He was perfectly prepared to urge that this was eminently one of those cases in which the accused person was entitled to be bailed out on more grounds than one. It was *absolutely necessary* that the accused should *personally* give instructions to his Solicitors. Mr. Davar also laid stress on the ground that the Jail rules required the presence of the Jail authorities even when the accused was giving instructions to his Solicitors, and that the difficulty of defending the accused would be still greater. He relied very strongly on the Bangobasi case and on what took place in connection with the case, which was the only precedent which would guide his Lordship in the present case particularly on the question of bail. It would be argued in the present case that this was a most serious case and it was a matter in which punishment was for transportation for life though the alternative punishment did not exceed three years. The only evidence in the present case of the article being of such a nature, as would cause disaffection among the people, was that of Mirza Abbas Beg, the Oriental Translator, who said that the words and expressions were of an ex-	Section 498 Cr. Pr. Code left the Judge unlimited discretion. It was a judicial discretion and it must be judicially exercised and with care and caution. I am not in accord with the statement broadly made that the only consideration which ought to guide the Court in deciding whether bail should or should not be granted, was the consideration that the accused would appear to take his trial. It was by no means the only consideration or the main one. It might be one of the considerations or an important one. But in considering applications in serious cases there were many circumstances that must be weighed before coming to a conclusion. It would be wise under the present circumstances not to give any reason or enter

off. In order to ascertain whether he would be forth-coming or not it was material to consider the three leading questions; first, as to the gravity of the offence with which the accused was charged ; second, as to the nature of the sentence with which he might be punished; and third, as to the evidence which was before the Court to see whether it was of such an over-whelming character as that the accused must necessarily be convicted and that in order to avoid the punishment he might not be forth-coming.

tremely, objectionable inflamatory character such as were calculated to excite feelings in British India. That was the whole of the evidence recorded by the Magistrate to prove that the articles published were likely to inflame and excite disaffection and it was to say the least *worthless*. He ventured to submit that anybody who had *any* knowledge of the Marathi language and who read the original articles, *if he was not blinded by passion or prejudice*, would come to the conclusion that they were not calculated to excite disaffection in the minds of the people. *The only ground on which this application could be opposed would be an apprehension that the accused might not be forthcoming for his trial.* Another ground being that the accused being at liberty, might try to do away or tamper with the evidence for the prosecution. In this case there was no fear of that. "I ask your Lordship accordingly to exercise your discretion vested in you, and make an order which will show, that the accused is not prejudged by the tribunals that administer justice and law, &c. &c."

into a discussion of the considerations weighing with him in refusing the application for bail.

THE TILAK CASE.

The Magisterial Proceedings.

The prosecution against Mr. Bal Gangadhar Tilak was set in motion by his Excellency the Governor in Council Bombay ordering the institution of a complaint against him and thus sanctioning the prosecution. The sanction to prosecute is as follows:—

The first case.

Government sanction.

(Before me)

A. H. S. Aston

Chief Presidency Magistrate

Bombay 24-6-08.

Under Section 196 of the Code of Criminal Procedure 1898, His Excellency the Governor in Council is pleased to order Herbert George Gell, Commissioner of Police Bombay or such Police officer as may be deputed by him for this purpose, to make a complaint against Bal Gangadhar Tilak, editor and proprietor of the " Kesari " , a weekly vernacular newspaper of Poona, in respect of an article headed "The country's misfortune", printed at columns 4 and 5, page 4 and columns 1 and 2 page 5 of the issue of the said newspaper dated the 12th May 1908, under Section 124 A of the Indian Penal Code and any other Section of the said Code (including section 153 A) which may be found to be applicable to the case.

By order of his Excellency the Governor in Council

(Sd.) H. O. Quin

Dated 23 June 1908 Bombay. Acting Secretary to Government.

Judicial Department

Pursuant to withinwritten order I hereby depute Superintendent Sloane of the ' K ' Division, Bombay City Police, to make the complaint therein referred to.

(Sd.) H. G. Gell.

Head Police Office Bombay. Commissioner of Police, Bombay.

24th June 1908.

In pursuance of the sanction, Superintendent Sloane, of the Bombay Police, laid the following information before Mr. A. H. S. Aston, Chief Presidency Magistrate, Bombay:—

Information of Superintendent Sloane.

The information of William Sloane taken upon oath before me Arthur Henry Southcote Aston Esquire, one of his Majesty's Justices of the Peace for the Town and island of Bombay and the Chief Presidency Magistrate Bombay on Tuesday the 24th day of June 1908.

1. "I am informed and verily believe that Bal Gangadhar Tilak of Poona is the editor, printer and publisher of the "Kesari" a weekly Marathi Newspaper and that the said newspaper is printed and published at his press called the Kesari Press situated at 486 Narayan Peth Poona.

2. That the Kesari Newspaper dated the 12th May 1908 which is now produced and shown to me and marked A contains an article printed in the 4th and 5th columns of page 4 thereof and columns 1 and 2 of page 5 thereof and headed (as translated into English) " The country's misfortune. "

3. That a translation of the said article is also produced and shown to me and marked B.

4. I verily believe that the said Bal Gangadhar Tilak has by the publication of the said article in the 'Kesari' newspaper dated the 12th of may 1908 brought or attempted to bring into hatred and contempt and has excited or attempted to excite disloyalty and feelings of enmity towards His Majesty and the Government established by law in British India.

5. I am informed and verily believe that several numbers of the 'Kesari' newspaper dated the 12th of May 1908 were forwarded to subscribers to that newspaper in Bombay and were received in Bombay by such subscribers and that I am advised that there has been publication of such newspaper containing the said article within the jurisdiction of this Court.

6. That I accordingly charge the said Bal Gangadhar Tilak, as being responsible for the publication in Bombay of the said article in the Kesari newspaper dated the 12th day of May 1908, with committing offences punishable under Sections 124 A and 153 A of the Indian Penal Code and I pray that process may be issued against the said Bal Gangadhar Tilak.

7. That an order under section 196 of the Criminal Procedure Code dated the 23rd of June 1908 directing this complaint to be made is now produced and shown to me and marked C.

The Magistrate thereupon issued a warrant of arrest against Mr. Tilak on 24th June 1908 and it was executed on his person the same evening at Bombay.

The Magistrate also issued a warrant on the same day for a search being made of the residence of Mr. Tilak at Poona, and for the seizure of certain documents &c. The following is the text of the warrant and the endorsements on it will show the manner in which it was executed.

Magistrates warrant.

Case No. 421 of 1908.
Complainants' name.
Superintendent sloane.
Address—Bombay.
(Fee-free)

No. of 190

To

The District or City Magistrate Poona, the Superintendent of Police division, and all constables and other His Majesty's officers of the Peace for the Town of Bombay.

Whereas information has been laid before me of the commission of the offence of sedition and promoting enmity between classes, and it has been made to appear to me that the production of the files of the newspaper Kesari, registers of subscribers, drafts, proofs, manuscripts, correspondence, books of account and other documents, relating to the said Kesari newspaper is essential to the inquiry about to be made into the said offence.

This is to authorise and require you to search for the said books, documents, writings and newspapers in the residence of Bal Gangadhar Tilak, situated at Poona and if found to produce forthwith the same before this Court, returning this warrant with an endorsement certifying what you have done under it immediately upon its execution.

Given under my hand and the seal of the Court this 24th June 1908.

(Sd.) A. S. ASTON.

Chief Presidency Magistrate.

Forwarded to the District Superintendent of Police, Poona, for execution.

(Sd.) H. F. CARVALHO,

24-6-08. City. Magistrate

Poona.

Returned duly executed

Davies.

25-6-08. District Superintendant of Police, Poona.

Returned to the D. S. Police, Poona. The warrant cannot be considered to be fully executed until the residence of Bal Gangadhar Tilak at Singhgad has been searched. This search should now be made.

(Sd.) E. CARMICHAEL,

25-6-08. D. M. Poona.

Executed. — Nothing found at Singhgad.

Davies

D. S. Police Poona.

Returned to the Presidency Magistrate Bombay.

(Sd.) E. CARMICHAEL

25-6-08. D. M. Poona.

The Panchanama (Vide Ex. L in Appendix page 49-50) will show the results of the search made in the residence of Mr. Tilak at Poona.

On the 25th of June Mr. Tilak was produced before the Presidency Magistrate and the following proceedings took place in his Court.

IN THE COURT OF THE CHIEF PRESIDENCY

MAGISTRATE BOMBAY.

Case No. 421 W of 1908.

Superintendent Sloane..Complainant.

VS.

Bal Gangadhar Tilak .... Accused.

Charge—Sedition and promoting enmity between classes......
Sections 124 A 153A I. P. Code.

Accused present in Custody.

Mr. J. D. Davar Bar-at-law and Mr. Bodas M. A. LL. B. High Court Pleader for Accused.

WILLIAM SLAONE. sworn said:—

I identify the Accused as the person named in the information. The Kesari is published and sold in Bombay. I have been purchasing it for several months. I purchased the issue of the 12th in Bombay.

Mr. Davar:—I am willing to admit publication and ask that the case may be tried forthwith.

Mr. Bowen:—It is necessary to prove publication. The case for he Crown is not ready and I apply for an adjournment in order to call evidence. I have not all my witnesses here and I have a case this afternoon in the 3rd Presidency Magistrate's Court.

Order—Postponed to June 29th at 3-30 p. m.

Mr. Davar applies for bail.

Mr. Bowen opposes.

ORDER.—The application is refused. The offence in question is not bailable and I am of opinion that there are reasonable grounds for believing that accused has committed the offence of which he is charged.

(initialled) A. H. S. A.

25. 6. 08.

Mr. Davar to have permission to take copies of information and translations.

Mr. Dikshit and Mr. Bodas and Mr. W. S. Gandhy to have permission to interview accused, also Mr. W. S. Bapat and Mr. Baptista and also Hon'ble Mr. Khare in the Police Court lock-up.

Accused to be detained in the Police Court lock-up.

Copy ordered to be furnished to accused forthwith.

(Initialled) A. H. S. A.

25-6-08.

(TRUE COPY)

A. H. S. Aston

Chief Presidency Magistrate,

and Revenue Judge, Bombay.

SECOND CASE.

On the 26th of June His Excellency the Governor in Council instituted another prosecution against Mr. Tilak by authorising the Secretary of the Judicial Department to direct another complaint being laid against Mr. Tilak, while the latter was in custody.

The following is the second Sanction to prosecute Mr. Tilak.

SANCTION TO PROSECUTE.

(A. H. S.

27-6-08.)

Under section 196 of the Code of Criminal Procedure 1898 His Excellency the Governor in Council is pleased to order Herbert George Gell, commissioner of Police Bombay, or such Police officer as may be deputed by him for this purpose to make a complaint against Bal Gangadhar Tilak, editor and proprietor of the *Kesari*, a weekly Vernacular newspaper of Poona in respect of an article, headed "These remedies are not lasting" printed at columns 2, 3 and 4 of page 3 of the issue of the said newspaper dated the 9th June 1908 under section 124 A of India Penal Code and any other Section of the said Code (including Section 153 A.) which may be found to be applicable to the case.

By order of His Excellency

the Governor in Ccuncil.

Dated Bombay }
the 26th June 1908. }

(Sd.) H. O. QUINN.

Acting Secretary to Government,

Judicial Department.

P. T. O.

Pursuant to the withinwritten order, I hereby depute Superintendent Sloane of the K. Division, Bombay City Police, to make the complaint therein referred.

(Signed) H. G. GELL,

Commissioner of Police,

Bombay.

Head Police office,

Bombay, 27th June 1908.

In pursuance of the above Sanction Superintendent Sloane instituted the following complaint against Mr. Tilak before Mr. Aston, Chief Presidency Magistrate Bombay.

INFORMATION OF WILLIAM SLOANE.

The information of William Sloane Superintendent of Police, Bombay taken upon oath before Arthur Herry Southcote Aston Esqr, one of His Magesty's Justices of the Peace for the Town & Island of Bombay, and the Chief Presidency Magistrate Bombay, on Saturday the 27th day of June 1908:—

I am informed and believe that Bal Gangadhar Tilak of Poona is the publisher, Proprietor and Editor of the " Kesari " a weekly Marathi Newspaper and that the Newspaper is printed at his press called the Kesari Press situated at 486 Narayan Peth at Peona.

2. That the issue of the Kesari newspaper dated the 9th of the June 1908 now produced and shown to me marked A contains an article at Columns 2 to 4 on page 4 thereof, which is headed (as translated into English) "These remedies are not lasting."

3. That a translation of the said article is also produced and shown to me and marked B.

4. I verily believe that the said Bal Gangadhar Tilak has by the publication of the said article in the Kesari newspaper dated the 9th day of June 1908 brought or attempted to bring into hatred and contempt and has excited or attempted to excite disaffection disloyalty and feelings of enmity towards His Majesty and the Government established by law in British India and has also attempted to promote feelings of enmity and hatred between the English and Indian subjects of His Majesty.

5. I am informed and verily believe that several numbers of the Kesari newspaper dated the 9th day of June 1908 were forwarded to subscribers of that newspaper in Bombay and were received in Bombay by such subscribers and that I am advised that there has been publication of such newspaper containing the said article or articles within the jurisdiction of this Court.

6. That I accordingly charge the said Bal Gangadhar Tilak as being responsible for the publication in Bombay of the said article in the Kesari newspaper dated the 9th day of June 1908 with committing offences punishable under Section 124A and 153A of the Indian Penal Code and I pray that process may be issued against him.

7. That an order under Section 196 of the Criminal Procedure Code dated the 26th day of June 1908 directing this Complaint to be made is now produced and shown to me and marked C.

(sd.) William Sloane
Superintendent of Police.

(Before me,)
(sd.) A. H. S. Aston
Chief Presidency Magistrate.
27-6-08. Bombay.

Mr. Aston thereupon issued a warrant for the arrest of Mr. Tilak which was executed on his person in Jail on the morning of the 29th June.

On the 29th of June the following proceedings took place in the Court of the Presidency Magistrate.

Proceedings.

Deposition of Mr. B. V. JOSHI—

(FOR THE CROWN.)

"I having made solemn affirmation state that my name is Bhaskar Vishnu Joshi. My calling 1st Assistant Oriental Translator to Government.

I see a copy of the Kesari newspaper dated 9th June 1908. It contains an article entitled "These remedies are not lasting" on page 4 Columns 2 to 4. I have made a translation of it. My translation is correct. Newspaper and translation put in Exs. D & Dl.

Taken on solemn affirmation. (sd.) Bhaskar Vishnu Joshi.

This 29th day of June 1908.

Before me.

(Sd.) A. H. S. Aston.

Chief Presidency Magistrate, Bombay:—

Deposition of Mr. N. J. DATAR—.

I having made solemn affirmation state that my name is Narayan Jugannath Datar, my calling Clerk Customs Reporter General's Office.

I also do business of distributing the Kesari and other papers. I receive about 3000 copies of the Kesari a week. Some of them go to subscribers and others to non-subscribers. Copies of the issue Ex. D of the 9th June were distributed by my agency in Bombay.

Taken on solemn affirmation. (Sd.) N. J. Datar.

this 29th day of June 1908.

Before me,

(Sd.) A. H. S. Aston.

Chief Presidency Magistrate, Bombay.

The statement of the accused was then taken and was as follows.

STATEMENT OF ACCUSED.

I state as follows:-

My name is– Bal

,, father's name–Gangadhar

,, age about– 52 years.

,, caste– Brahmin.

,, Occupation– Editor.

I wish to reserve my statement. (Sd.) Bal Gangadhar Tilak.

I certify that this examination was taken in my presence and hearing and contains a full and true account of the statement made by the Accused.

(Sd.) A. H. S. Aston.

Chief Presidency Magistrate,

Bombay.

Order of Commitment.

The Magistrate after recording the above depositions committed Mr. Tilak to the Sessions. The following are the orders of commitment in the two cases:—

C. P. C. 273

No. Case No, 421/w of 1908.

Charge (Secs, 521, 221, 223 C. P. C,)

A. H. S. Aston Esqr.

(Altered by my charges this 2nd day of July 1908. Sd. M. R. Jardine. C. C.)

I Chief Presidency Magistrate at Bombay hereby charge you Bal Gangadhar Tilak as follows: —

That you on or about the 12th day of May 1908 at Bombay by words intended to be read brought or attempted to bring into hatred or contempt or excited or attempted to excite feelings of disaffection towards the Government established by law in British India by publishing in a vernacular newspaper entitled the "Kesari", of which you were the Printer and Publisher an article as translated into English " The Country's misfortune" and thereby committed an offence punishable under Sectiou 124A of the Indian Penal Code.

2ndly. That you on or about the 12th May 1908 at Bombay by words intended to be read promoted or attempted to promote feelings of enmity or hatred between different classes of His Majesty's subjects by publishing in a vernacular newspaper entitled the "Kesari" of which you were the Printer and Publisher an article as translated into English "The conntry's misfortune" and thereby committed an offence punishable under

Section 153 A of the Indian Penal Code and within the cognizance of the High Court and I hereby commit you to the said High Court to be tried on the said charges.

29th day of June 1908.

(Sd.) A. H. S. Aston.
Chief Presidency Magistrate
and Revenue Judge Bombay.

No. Case No. 435,w of 1908.

Charge (Secs. 221–222–223 C. P. C.)

A. H. S. Aston Esquire,

(Altered by my charges this 2nd day of July 1908. (Sd.) M. R. Jardine. C. C.)

I Chief Presidency Magistrate at Bombay hereby charge you Bal Gangadhar Tilak as follows :—

That you on or about the 9th day of June 1908 at Bombay by words intended to be read brought or attempted to excite feelings of disaffection towards the Government established by law publishing in a vernacular newspaper entitled the " Kesari " of which you were the Printer and Publisher an article as translated into English " These remedies are not lasting " and thereby committed an offence punishable under Section 124 A of the Indian Penal Code.

2ndly. That you on or about the 9th day of June 1908 at Bombay by words intended to be read promoted or attempted to promote feelings of enmity or hatred between different classes of His Majesty's subjects by publishing in a vernacular newspaper entitled the " Kesari " of which you were the Printer and Publisher an article as translated into English " These remedies are not lasting. "

And thereby committed an offence punishable under Section 153 A of the Indian Penal Code and within the cognizance of the High Court and I hereby commit you to the said High Court to be tried on the said charges.

29th day of June 1908.

(Sd.) A. H. S. Aston
Chief Presidency Magistrate
& Revenue Judge Bombay.

BAIL PROCEEDINGS IN THE HIGH COURT.

On the 2nd day of July Mr. Tilak applied through Counsel to Mr. Justice Davar presiding over the third Criminal Sessions of the High Court for his release on bail; but the application was refused.

In connection with the bail application the following affidavits and counter affidavits were made.

(1) Affidavit of Mr. Bodas.

I, Mahadeo Rajaram Bodas M. A. LL. B. of Bombay Brahmin Hindu inhabitant, High Court Pleader of this Hon'ble Court residing at Girgaum outside the Fort, solemnly affirm and say as follows:—

1. That on the 25 th June I appeared with Messrs. J. D.Davar, Barrister-at-Law, and S. M. Dikshit for the abovenamed accused before the Chief Presidency Magistrate Bombay in the case instituted against him under Sec. 124 A and 153 A of the Indian Penal Code.

2. That on a complaint filed by Mr. Sloane, Superintendent Criminal Investigation Department Bombay, Bal Gangadhar Tilak B. A. LL. B. Editor and Proprietor of the Newspaper "Kesari" the abovenamed Accused was arrested on Wednesday the 24th June at 6-30 P. M. at Sirdar Griha in the Sitaram Buildings, near the Crawford Market, and was placed the next day on the 25th day of June before His Worship A. H. S. Aston Esquire the Chief Presidency Magistrate for the city of Bombay, who remanded him to custody. An application for bail was then made to the Chief Presidency Magistrate who refused it.

3. That the said Accused was on Monday the 29th instant charged with offences under Secs. 124 A & 153 A Indian Penal Code before His Worship A. H. S. Aston Esquire the Chief Presidency Magistrate for the city of Bombay.

4. That on the 29th day of June after the evidence of the Prosecution was recorded the learned Magistrate on the application of the Public Prosecutor committed the Accused to take his trial at the present Criminal Sessions of the Bombay High Court on charges under Secs. 124 A and 153 A of the Indian Penal Code.

5. That the said Accused, Bal Gangadhar Tilak, is at present in custody and has been in custody as an under-trial prisoner in the Dongri Jail since the 24th June.

6. I submit that the release of the Accused on bail is absolutely necessary for the proper conduct of his defence and I therefore pray that this Hon'ble Court will be pleased to order his release on bail. The grounds on which this application has been made are as under:—

1stly. That I am of opinion that the Accused has a good defence and that if he is not released on bail the Accused will not be able to properly instruct those whose help he wants to secure for his defence.

2ndly. That the Accused has been suffering from diabetes for some time past and was under medical treatment when he was arrested.

3rdly. The said articles are too lengthy to allow the Accused to send instructions thereon from Jail and official translations of the said articles used in the proceedings before the Magistrate are incorrect and misleading, that the Counsel will not be able to make a proper defence unless the Accused had himself an opportunity of explaining the correct meaning and spirit thereof to his Counsel.

4thly. That the Accused is a B. A. LL. B. of the Bombay University, a well-known author, was a Professor of Mathematics in the Fergusson College Poona, and sometime member of the Bombay Legislative Council and occupies a very high position among the educated Hindus of the Deccan.

5thly. That the question whether the said articles come within the meaning of Secs. 124 A and 153 A Indian Penal Code is a matter to be decided by a Jury and till that question is determined the Accused should be released on bail.

Solemnly affirmed at Bombay aforesaid this 30th day of June 1908. } (Sd.) M. R. Bodas.

Before me.

(Sd.) E. J. Davar.

Commissioner.

---

(2) Affidavit of Mr. Bowen.

I, John Guthbert Crenside Bowen residing at Malabar Hill Bombay, Acting Solicitor to Government make oath and say as follows :—

1. That I have read a copy of an unaffirmed affidavit of Mahadeo Rajaram Bodas which was furnished to me on the 29th June 1908.

2. In September 1897 the abovenamed Accused, Bal Gangadhar Tilak, was tried in this Court for an offence punishable under Sec. 124A of the Indian Penal Code in respect of the publication of certain articles in his newspaper the "Kesari" and was convicted and sentenced to 18 month's rigorous imprisonment on the 6th of September 1898. The Local Government remitted, subject to certain conditions, remainder of the punishment to which the said Bal Gangadhar Tilak had been sentenced. A copy of the order of Government and of the said conditions are annexed hereto and marked A.

3. I crave leave to refer to the articles in the issue of the "Kesari" dated the 12th May 1908 which is headed (as translated into English) "The Country's misfortune" for which the Accused has been committed to take his trial at the Sessions for offences punishable under Secs. 124A & 153A of the Indian Penal Code and I am informed by the first assistant to the Oriental Translator to Government and verily believe that in the issue of the Kesari, dated the 2nd of June 1908, another article has been printed which is headed (as translated into English) "The secret of the Bomb" and he has sent me a translation of that article. The writer of that article referred to the murder of Mr. Rand in 1897 and the explosion of the Bomb at Muzzafarpur and stated that considering the matter from the point of view of daring and skill in execution the Chaphekar brothers take a higher rank than the members of the club of the Bomb in Bengal and that considering the end and the means the Bengalees must be given the better commendation. The writer further stated in the said article that bombs explode when the repressive policy of Government becomes unbearable.

4. I also crave leave to refer to the article headed "These remedies are not lasting" which is printed in the issue of the "Kesari" dated the 9th June 1908 and which is the subject of the charge against the said Bal Gangadhar Tilak in case No. 435 of 1908 in which he has also been committed to take his trial at the Sessions.

5. With reference to the allegations in paragraph 6 of the said affidavit that in the opinion of the deponent the Accused has a good defence I crave leave to refer to the said articles in the issue of the "Kesari" dated the 12th of May 1908 and to the said articles in the issues of the 2nd & 9th June.

6. With reference to the allegations in the said affidavit that the translations of the articles in the issue of the Kesari of the 12th May 1908 before the Magistrate are incorrect and misleading I say that a translation of the said article is being made by one of the Translators of the High Court which will be used at the trial of this case.

7. I further say that I am informed by the Local Government through one of their Secretaries that if the Accused is released on bail the Local Government believe that he will use his liberty to excite feelings of disaffection and hatred against Government and that it would be dangerous to release him.

Sworn at Bombay aforesaid,

this 30th day of June 1908

Before me,

E. J. Dovar.

Commissioner.

Appendix to Mr. Bowe'ns Affidavit.

In exercise of the power conferred by sec. 401 of the Code of Criminal procedure 1898 the Governor of Bombay in Council is pleased hereby to remit, subject to the conditions hereafter set forth, the remainder of the punishment awarded to Bal son of Gangadhar Tilak and a convict in the Yerrowada Central prison No. 1445 at present undergoing a sentence of eighteen months rigorous imprisonment.

The conditions are these:—

That he will not countenance or take part directly or indirectly in any demonstration in regard to his release, or in regard to his conviction or sentence.

That he will do nothing by act, speech or writing to excite disaffection towards the Government.

Judicial Department,
6th September 1898.

By order of the Governor of Bombay
in Council

(Sd.) S. W. Edgerley
Secretary to Government.

I hereby accept and agree to abide by the above conditions understanding that by the speech or writing referred to in the second condition is meant such act, speech or writing as may be pronounced by a Court of Law to constitute an offence under the Indian Penal Code and I acknowledge that should I fail to fulfil those conditions or any portion of them the Governor of Bombay in Council may cancel the remission of my punishment whereupon I may be arrested by any Police officer without warrant and remanded to undergo the unexpired portion of my original sentence.

Dated the 6th September 1898.

Bal Gangadhar Tilak
Prisoner.

Certified that the foregoing conditions were read over to the prisoner Bal Gangadhar Tilak and accepted by him under Sec. 401 of the Code of Criminal Procedure in my presence.

J. Jackson
Surg. Captain.
Superintendent.

Witness. Harry Brewin
D. S. of Police.
Dated the 6th September 1898.

(3) Affidavit of Mr. Sullivan.

I, Peter Sullivan of Bombay, residing at Maharbowri Police Station Inspector Bombay Police, make oath and say as follows :—

1. The information in this case was filed on the 24th June 1908 and a Search Warrant was issued by the Chief Presidency Magistrate and I proceeded to Poona with the said Warrant. On the 25th of June 1908 the District Superintendent of Police of Poona searched in my presence the office, press and residence of the abovenamed Accused Bal Gangadhar Tilak at No. 486 Narayan Peth Poona and a memo was found amongst the papers which were then found and it contained the following particulars viz.—

Hand book of Modern explosives by M. Eissler

(publ. Crossby Lockwood & Sons)

Nitro—Explosives

By P. Gerad Sandford.

I was informed by Mr. Kelkar, the Editor of the Mahratha Newspaper, and verily believe that the said memo is in the handwriting of the said Accussd.

2. The said memo was found in a drawer in a writing table in the Accused's residence and it has been put in and marked as an exhibit in the proceedings in the Magistrate's Court.

Sworn at Bombay aforesaid }
this 30th day of June 1908. }

(4) Affidavit of Mr. Bodas.

I, Mahadev Rajaram Bodas of Bombay, Hindu inhabitant, High Court Pleader, residing at Churni Road outside the Fort solemnly affirm and say as follows:—

1. I have read the copy of the unaffirmed affidavit of John Cuthburt Orenside Bowen Acting Solicitor to Government, served on the Accused's Attornies Messrs. Raghavaya, Bhimji & Nagindas yesterday.

2. With reference to para 2 of the said affidavit I say that no previous conviction could be referred to at this stage under section 310 of the Criminal Procedure Code and such reference is highly objectionable as it seems to be intended to prejudice the Court against the Accused.

3. With reference to the third para of the said affidavit I say that the article referred to therein as "Secret of the Bomb" is not in evidence and can not therefore be referred to. The contents of the article have no bearing on the present application and the Marathi heading has been mistranslated as " Secret of the bomb ".

4. With reference to para seventh of the said affidavit I submit that the statement made by the deponent on the alleged information of an unnamed Secretary of the Local Government is unauthenticated, irrelevent and inadmissible in evidence. I also submit that the allegation contained in the said para is not supported by any reason or evidence.

I have also read the copy of the unaffirmed affidavit of Peter Sullivan of the Bombay Police served on Messrs. Raghavayya Bhimji and Nagindas yesterday and with reference thereto I say that the alleged memo referred to in para 1 therein was objected to by the Counsel for the Accused in the Chief Presidency Magistrate's Court as being irrelevent and not proved but was allowed to be exhibited merely as an article found during search. I therefore submit that the contents of the memo are irrelevent to the present application and ought not to be referred to.

Solemnly affirmed at Bombay aforesaid this 1st day of July 1908. } (Sd.) Mahadeo Rajaram Bodas.

Before me,

(Sd.) G. A. DAVAR.

Commissioner.

Mr. N. C. Kelkar, editor of the *Mahratta* also made an affidavit stating that the allegation, that he (Mr. Kelkar) informed Mr. Sullivan that the card found in the search of Mr. Tilak's house was in the handwriting of Mr. Tilak, was untrue.

The following proceedings took place in Court in connection with the bail application referred to above:—

Mr. M. A. Jinnah appeared to make the application on behalf of Mr. Tilak and Mr. R. E. Branson, Advocate-General, Mr. J. D. Inverrarity and Mr. B. B. Binning, appeared to oppose the application.

In opening his case Mr. Jinnah briefly reviewed the progress of the case up to Mr. Tilak's committal by the Chief Presidency Magistrate to take his trial at the Bombay High Court Criminal Sessions. His reasons, he said for making that application were that he was of opinion that the Accused was in custody as an under-trial prisoner, and his release was absolutely necessary for the proper conduct of his defence. Accused has a good defence, but he would not be able to instruct those whose help he wanted for his defence if he was not released on bail. He also suffered from diabetes and was under medical treatment for it. The translations of the articles charged to him were incorrect and misleading; therefore, he wanted to instruct Counsel in order to give the spirit in which those articles had been written. He was a B. A., and an LL. B. : he was an author; was a professor in a College for sometime; he was for a period a member of the Legislative Council; and a well known man in the Deccan. To this affidavit, added Mr. Jinnah, there was a reply-affidavit.

Mr. Justice Davar: I have read every one of the affidavits before coming to Court. I see in the affidavit of Mr. Bodas that he objects to certain statements in the affidavit of Mr. Bowen, and for the matter of that, in the affidavit of Mr. Sullivan. These may contain statements which will prejudice the case for the Accused at the trial, and some of which perhaps may not be held to be legally admissible. Having regard to the publicity that is given to the proceedings in this Court, it is very undesirable to go into these statements, also to give publicity to these statements beforehand. Therefore, I should like to hear you as if you were making this application "*ex parte*," as if you were making it independent of any opposition from Government.

Mr. Jinnah said that his application was that Mr. Tilak be released on bail. His Lordship was aware of the two sections in question, and he had to deal with this very question not long ago when the application to release Paranjape, the Editor of the "Kal" newspaper, was made. The whole point of bail was then placed before the Court and thoroughly threshed out. There was absolutely no ground whatever for refusing bail to Tilak. The whole question was whether Mr. Tilak would be forthcoming to stand his trial and to take his sentence, if any be passed against him. That had been laid down over and over again. His Lordship knew of the well-known judgment of the late Mr. Justice B. Tyebji. The arguments in the case took a long time, and Mr. Justice Tyebji thought all legislation in regard to the release of accused parties on bail was based upon the anxiety of the Legislature to secure the attendance of the accused at the trial. The leading principle of jurisprudence was that a man was not to be presumed to be guilty until he had a fair trial and was found to be guilty (Bom. L. J. Vol VIII, p. 254). So the whole question was in a nutshell. Was there any suggestion or any shadow of hint that there was any apprehension that Tilak would not come forth to stand his trial? There was no suggestion of this sort made in the affidavits; therefore, he asked for Tilak's release on bail; they were perfectly willing to furnish substantial security to any amount.

Mr. Branson: I appear—

Mr. Justice Davar: I will not trouble you, Mr. Advocate-General.

Mr. Branson: Very well, my Lord.

Mr. Justice Davar, in disposing of the application, said:—Ever since he was informed that in these two cases Mr. Tilak was charged under Sections 124 A and 153 A, and an application for bail was going to be made to the High Court, he had given to the question his most anxious consideration. If it was only a question of personal feelings he would be most unwilling to keep a prisoner, who was under-trial, in custody before his trial: unless there were reasons why the unfettered discretion, which was vested in the High Court under Section 498 of the Code, should not be exercised in favour of the accused. There was no doubt that Section 498 left the Judge of the High Court unlimited discretion, unfettered by any condition, and gave him power to release an accused person on bail, pending his trial. That was a judicial discretion; a discretion, that must be judiciously exercised; and exercised with care and caution. Mr. Jinnah had relied on the judgment of the late Mr. Justice Tyebji. His Lordship was very familiar with that judgment, and with all that had preceded it, and the arguments made use of by both the sides by the then Advocate-General Mr. Lang, and by Mr. Tilak's Counsel. He was by no means in accord with the statement, broadly made, that the only consideration, which ought to guide the Court in deciding whether bail should or should not be granted, was the consideratiou that an accused would appear to take his trial. It was not by any means the only consideration, or the main one; it might be one of the considerations or an important one. But in considering applications in serious cases there were many circumstances that must be weighed before coming to a conclusion. As he had said before he had very anxiously thought over the question, and had considered the reasons and circumstances which guided him in making the order he proposed to make. He was most anxious that the Accused should have a perfectly fair and an unprejudiced trial. Accused would be tried before a Jury, and in view of the publicity that was widely given to everything said in this Court, it was eminently desirable that nothing should be said before the trial that would in any way prejudice either the case for the Prosecution or for the Accused. He, therefore, thought that it would be wise under the present circumstances, not to give any reason, or enter into a discussion of the considerations weighing with him in refusing the application. He came to this decision with much regret but he was constrained to refuse bail, pending the trial.

SPECIAL JURY APPLICATION.

On the 3rd July 1908, the Crown applied for a Special Jury being ordered to be empanelled to try Mr. Tilak. Mr. Tilak, through Counsel, opposed the application; but Mr. Justice Davar granted it.

The following proceedings took place in Court in connection with this application.

On Friday, the 3rd July at the Criminal Sessions of the High Court, presided over by the Hon'ble Mr. Justice Dinshah Davar, the Hon'ble Mr. Branson, Acting Advocate-General, instructed by Mr. Bowen, Public Prosecutor, appeared for the Crown in the case of Emperor vs. Bal Gangadhar Tilak and applied for the trial of the Accused by a Special Jury on the ground that the case was one of great importance and a Special Jury would be eminently fitted to try the case.

Mr. Baptista, Bar-at-law, appeared for the Accused and in the following able speech opposed the application for a Special Jury.

MY LORD:—This is a prosecution instituted by Government for a political offence under the special sanction of Government. It therefore comes with a force and recommendation naturally calculated to overwhelm the defendant. Under the circumstances we are entitled to the utmost consideration of the Court and the most scrupulous fairness from the Prosecution. We, therefore, ask the Prosecution not to press this application and we ask your Lordship not to grant it. We are perfectly convinced, and I submit, there is and there can be not a scintilla of doubt, that a Special Jury would prove most detrimental to the defence if it is empanelled in the ordinary way. I am, therefore, constrained to oppose the application for a Special Jury.

In the benevolent theory of the Law the Jury is designed chiefly, if not exclusively for the benefit and protection of the accused. If therefore we had made the application your Lordship would have good reason to entertain it favourably. But we do not want it. As a matter of fact we are afraid of the proffered gift. *Timeo Danaos dona ferentes.* Why then should it be forced upon us against our will? But if the Prosecution insists, we are willing to yield provided the Prosecution consents that the majority on the Special Jury consists of Indians conversant with the language in which the indicted articles are written, viz Marathi. I submit, the Prosecution can have no reasonable objection whatever to a Jury thus constituted. This can be secured if my learned friend exercises the right of challenge against Europeans and I shall assist him in that direction. If the right of absolute challenge is exhausted, special objection can bet aken and allowed by consent on the ground that the Juryman does not understand the language of the articles.

This will give the Prosecution the Special Jury they seek, and the defendant a Jury of fit judges composed of his countrymen, which is, after all one of the fundamental essentials in a Trial by Jury, a form of trial which the genius of the English people has devised as one of the bulwarks of the liberty of the people. If my learned friend deliberately refuses such a fair and just proposal I must oppose the application on the following grounds.

1. In the first place, my Lord, it must be remembered that Mr. Tilak resides in Poona, the *Kesari* is printed in Poona, and the language of the *Kesari* is Marathi. Ordinarily Mr. Tilak should have been tried in Poona. Had he been tried in Poona he would have been committed to the Poona Court of Sessions. I am aware, my Lord, that the recent amendment of the Criminal Procedure Code has given jurisdiction to inferior Magistrates who are empowered to try and, do actually, the charge of sedition without any Jury whatever. But considering the position and personality of Mr. Tilak there can be little doubt but that he would have been committed to the Sessions in Poona as he is committed to this Court. Had he been committed to the Sessions in Poona he would have the advantage of being tried by a Judge who knows the language well and who would have been assisted by Assessors who would unquestionably be Marathas. If he were tried by a Jury he could under Sec. 275 claim, as a right, that the majority should consist of persons who were neither Europeans nor Americans. He would thereby obtain that very kind of Jury which a trial by Jury really contemplates *viz. men taken from the place and from the people who know the language and the accused and would therefore be the fittest judges.* This is a privilege that cannot be too highly prized. Your Lordship is aware that the Jury by their right and power of returning a general verdict have really become the sole judges both of fact and law as Lord Mansfield and Lord Fitzzerald declared in the cases reported in 21 State Trials, page 951, and 11 Cox Criminal cases, page 44. The privilege therefore is of supreme importance to the Accused, but unfortunately he has been deprived of that privilege by the prosecution. They issued a warrant for the arrest of Mr. Tilak from Bombay as they were technically entitled to do. In this way they have given jurisdiction to this Court. But even here Mr. Tilak would be tried by a Common

Jury. If a Common Jury were empanelled the majority would be non-Europeans judging from the list of Jurors. The list mentions 569 Europeans and 1673 non—Europeans. The probabilities are therefore in favour of a Jury of non—Europeans in proportion of one to three. This might not be as good as a Poona Jury, but it is far more preferable to the Special Jury. But this application seeks to deprive us even of that limited advantage. As the Jury is for our benefit why should we be deprived of the Jury which the law allows and we desire under existing circumstances? There is absolutely no reason for the refusal of my offer. On the contrary a Special Jury would be prejudicial to a fair trial for the following reasons:—

(a) A Special Jury means that the majority shall consist of Europeans, judging from the list of Jurors. This list shows that there are 242 Europeans against 156 Indians. In all probability, therefore, the majority in the Jury would be Europeans. That was the case in the last Tilak trial and that was the case in all sedition trials in this Court.

(b) Europeans would not make fit Jurymen on the present occasion, as they would be handicapped on account of their inability to understand the language of the alleged incriminating articles. They would therefore be compelled to judge of any possible tendency of these articles to excite disaffection towards Government through the medium of an official translation. Now, it is a notorious fact that translations by the best of scholars are not very satisfactory. Why then insist upon an imperfect medium when it is avoidable and when a Jury of competent men is available. This is prejudicial to the Accused.

(c) Europeans would be compelled to accept official translations as correct although their accuracy is impeached. The Indians could bring their own knowledge of the language to bear upon the translations. Indeed no translations would be needed. *Is this not conducive to justice and should this be deliberately discarded?* Erroneous translations would make an impression which it would be difficult to remove, specially as these translations have already been published in the Anglo-Indian Journals. There are no risks of a false impression upon Jurors who know the language and therefore no danger of misjudging.

(d) In this case a Jury have to determine the effect of these articles upon the readers of the *Kesari* in exciting disaffection against Government. Obviously Marathi knowing Jurors would be by far the best judges of this—men taken from the very class to whom these articles are addressed. *But by a special Jury Europeans would have to judge of the effect of Marathi articles upon people who differ from them constitutionally in a thousand ways.* This is condensed in the formula "*East is East and West is West.*" It is an extremely difficult and delicate task, and there is great danger of misjudgment. For example an article on cow killing would excite Indians to a riot. It would fall flat on Europeans. On the other hand articles advocating seriously Bureaucratic Government in England such as we enjoy or an attempt to abolish Trial by Jury, would lead to rebellion in England, but it would fall comparatively flat in India. Therefore Europeans would be bad judges of the effect of these articles and yet the innocence of tha accused would be in their hands when it is avoidable.

(*e*) Lastly, my Lord, it is impossible to close one's eyes to the fact that these political offences and press prosecutions are really a struggle between the rulers and the ruled for political rights and privileges, which can be obtained from the rulers alone. Now Englishmen belong to the ruling class. There must exist some political and patriotic bias against Indian aspirations. Moreover Englishmen at the present moment are rather inflamed on account of the assassinations in Muzaffarpur. There is therefore a real danger that Englishmen would be unconsciously biased against the Accused to his great prejudice. These are the objections to a Special Jury on a charge of Section 124 A. *But there is a second charge under Sec. 153 A.* Under that charge Mr. Tilak is accused of exciting the feelings of Indians against the Europeans. Practically therefore the Europeans are the accusers, and yet they will sit in judgment upon the accused. The result is this :—On the charge under 124 A the Rulers will sit in judgment upon a subject for his alleged rebellious spirit, and under Sec. 153 A the accusers will sit in judgment upon the accused for exciting hostility against themselves. This is opposed to all the fundamental principles of justice and jurisprudence. I must therefore ask your Lordship to reject the application especially after the suggestion I have made for empannelling a Special Jury composed of the majority of special Jurymen who are conversant with the Marathi language and would therefore be the fittest Judges in a case of this descrirption.

His Lordship, after hearing the arguments, in disposing of the application, said :—

Under Section 276 of the Criminal Procedure Code a Special Jury is necessarily summoned in all offences punishable with death, and under the same section in any other case in which the Judge of the High Court so directs a Special Jury is called. Now the settled practice of these Courts is that in all important cases where the interests of the parties concerned required that a Jury consisting of men who are selected from a higher sphere of life, and consequently supposed to bring better intelligence to bear on the cases before the Court are necessarily to be empanelled, the application is made to the Judge and, if the Judge thinks it right, he grants the application. There is no doubt whatever that the cases against Mr. Tilak are important cases from his own standpoint, and I feel in his own interest he should have the benefit of being tried by a Jury selected from the citizens of Bombay, but from the higher class of citizens.

Yesterday I had a murder case before me tried by a Special Jury in which the Jury consisted of three Parsees, two Hindus and four Europeans. On the previous days I had common juries which, on two occasions at least had a European majority. The panel summoned for a Special Jury is summoned under certain regulations fixed by Sir Michael Westropp, and ordinarily consists of a small majority of Europeans, but the Native community is fairly represented. In the panel that was originally fixed for these Sessions, that was before the Sedition cases were contemplated or came to this Court, twenty-seven Jurymen were empanelled, out of which there are four Parsees, five Hindus and two Mahomedans and Jews.

The rule under which the Special Jury is empanalled is Rule 832. So there is no question that the Sheriff has no option when he is fixing the panel of a Special Jury that he must have at least half the number Europeans.

Having regard to the exigencies of the Sedition cases and the probability of a large number of challenges, it does appear to me that the panel of twenty-seven out of which two or three have already been chosen, is in adequate; and therefore an additional panel of Jurymen is to be summoned; and I will see that in the panel that is made up for the Sedition cases the rule shall be adhered to, but it is possible that we shall have a greater proportion of Natives than we have now. We have now sixteen and eleven, and eight more have been summoned so that there is a proportion of five and four. The names are picked out without having regard to the Europeans or Natives as they are called. So the chances are if there is not a majority of Natives, then at all events there will be a fair representation of Natives; but that is a matter entirely more or less to the extent as to how the Jury is selected. You have the Jury list fixed, and they are selected according to the rules obtained in this Court for many years.

I hardly think that there is much substance in the arguments addressed as to the knowledge of the language. Of course if it comes to a conflict, then the Court must necessarily accept the translations of its authorized translators. At the same time if there is any glaring mistake or mistranslation, and if it is pointed out by Counsel for the accused, it is the bounden duty of the Judge presiding at the Sessions to see that the translation is correctly placed before the Jury, and if there is a mistake or mistranslation that ought to be corrected.

I promise to give my most careful attention to anything pointed out during the trial. As I have said, I think it is a mistake to resist the formation of the Special Jury, under these circumstances. These cases are of importance, and so far there has been no precedent where in important cases Special Jury is asked and refused except on very special grounds.

I have very carefully considered Mr. Baptista's arguments addressed to me. I think on the whole, the interests of Justice will be gained if these cases should be tried by a Special Jury. I am quite sure that any member of the Special Jury will come in and take his oath to administer justice and will leave out all prejudices if he has any and all extraneous circumstances entirely out of his consideration,

His Lordship fixed Monday, the 13th instant, for the hearing of the caes.

In the second case also in which Mr. Tilak was charged with Sedition, on the application of Mr. Binning, his Lordship ordered the trial to be by a Special Jury.

The Sessions Proceedings.

(Bombay High Court Third Criminal Sessions.)

Commencing on Monday, the 13th July 1908, and concluding on Wednesday the 22nd July 1908 at 10 p. m.

Before Mr. Justice D. D. DAVAR.

Mr. Branson, acting Advocate General, with Mr. Inverarity and Mr. Binning for the Crown.	Mr. Tilak appeared in person to conduct his own defence.

1st day—Monday 13th July 1908.

Mr. Justice Davar having taken his seat on the bench, the Advocate General Mr. Branson said :—Your Lordship will allow me to mention this case. I appear for the Prosecution with my learned friends Messrs. Inverarity and Binning, and I apply that the charges might be tried together.

His Lordship :—In both cases ?

Advocate General :—Yes my Lord.

Advocate General :—I propose to put up the Accused on both charges at the same trial. In this case there have been two charges and two committals made by the Magistrate on the same day in respect of articles appearing in the *Kesari* dated 12th May and 9th June 1908 respectively.

His Lordship :—Do you apply for that ?

Advocate General :—No My Lord, I say that I am entitled to do so. It is not a question of amending the charges. Under Sec. 234 Criminal Procedure Code and the subsequent Sections, your Lordship will find it stated that " where a person is accused " (Reads Section). That is the Section.

I also call your Lordship's attention to Sec. 233 which provides (Reads the Section). Section 234 is the Section which is directly applicable to the facts of the present case. The offences are exactly the same. They are committed within three weeks of each other and under Sec. 234 the Crown is entitled to see that although there are two separate committals the Judge shall try the two cases together. From the point of convenience there can be no question that it would be more convenient to have them tried together rather than by two separate Juries at an unascertainable distance of time. Your Lordship will look at Sec. 235 (Reads Section). It is quite true that the Allahabad High Court, according to I. L. R. 26 Allahabad, page 195 has held that there must be a separate charge for each offence. So there is. There is a separate charge for each offence in this case. Look at the wording. Your Lordship will see there are two charges (Reads). Now under Sec. 235 I submit we can do this. It is exactly the wording of that section. Section 239 will not apply. It refers to cases where more than one person is charged.

His Lordship :—Sec. 235 in the first paragraph states that the charges must refer to the same transaction.

Advocate General:- That expression has been the subject of various rulings of the Bombay High Court, and your Lordship will find the words interpreted in 16 Bombay. Your Lordship will also find the expression dealt with by the Allahabad and Calcutta High Courts. 16 Bombay page 414 will supply your Lordship with all that is necessary. That is the case of Varjivandas and at page 234 Prinscep's Edition we find (Reads) Your Lordship would find that (has Your Lordship got the articles there?) the articles impeached and the articles upon which we rely to prove intention of the party begin from 12th May 1908. This paper being a weekly paper published in Poona from week to week up to the 9th June has published a series of articles which form the subject matter of the charges viz the articles of 12th May and 9th June and a series of intervening articles upon which we rely as showing that they were all intended for the purpose of one transaction, that of creating disloyalty, disapprobation and disaffection towards Government established by Law in India. There is sufficient authority for this. Here are cases reported in the Allahabad and Calcutta High Courts of the same sort. Your Lordship will find them mentioned at page 234 of Princep's Commenary. One, perhaps a stronger case, is to be found in 10 Bombay page 234 (reads). This is a very different case, because there may be very considerable time between making a false charge and making false evidence in support of that charge. Your Lordship will find two or three cases cited in the Notes at page 203 & 204 of Mr. Justice Princep's book. To this it is not necessary to refer until I hear what Mr. Tilak has to say as to the applicability of Sec. 234.

His Lordship:—The only applicability of Sec. 234 is that we have two cases but they can not be consolidated into one because there are four charges.

Advocate General:—No, My Lord, but under Sec. 153 A I do not propose to put the Accused up.

His Lordship: Do you mean with regard to the charge under Sec. 153A with regard to each article ?

Advocate General:—Only with reference to the second article. I propose to put him up under two charges under Sec. 124 A and on one charge under Sec. 153A. Section 233 provides that at any stage &c. (reads) Therefore in order to avoid the possibility of finding ourselves within the ruling of the Calcutta and Punjab High Courts and the Privy Council as reported in 25 Madras I think this would be the safest course to adopt, in order to answer any suggestion that we have done something or proposed to do something that is not within the words of the Act. That is all I have to say with regard to the joinder of the Charges.

Accused:—With regard to the law applicable here I think Sec. 227 is the one to be taken here.

Sections 233, 234 & 235 are the Sections under which the charges are laid in the first instance before the Magistrate (Reads the Sections. Section 233 applies when the charge is first framed by the Magistrate. There is no provision in the Section by which the different charges can be amalgamated as it is proposed at present. That is my objection on the law point. Secondly, what I have to urge is that I think the two offences may not be regarded as the same transaction. They form different subjects altogether. It would be more convenient to me to have each of them tried separately. The two articles refer to different subjects and if they are tried together it might make confusion, if not in the mind of the learned Counsel prosecuting, at all events in my own mind. I do not think I shall be able to conduct the defence of both cases together. Sections 234 & 235 are permissive but Sec. 227 is imperative. These articles are really separate, dealing with different aspects of the same question. On these grounds I object to the joinder of the charges.

Advocate General:—I have pointed out my Lord that this is not the case of amending the charges. If it were, if Your Lordship will look at 226 and the next Section, your Lordship will find that it gives powers of mending or adding to the charges. Here the two charges remain unaltered and I propose on behalf of the Crown to try them both together. The only question is whether Sec. 234 applies in this instance. If your Lordship will look to Sec. 227 you will find that the Court may alter or add to the charges at any time (Reads Sec. 227). Now that Section has been held to justify a High Court first of all in framing a charge and then withdrawing it. I refer my Lord to 12 Allahabad page 551. A still stronger proof of the powers of the Court to deal with these charges, as I propose to deal with them, is to be found in Sec. 230 which provides that (Reads Sec.). It shows that although you may not have had the previous sanction of Government which is necessary in 196 of the Criminal Procedure Code, still if the Court found it was necessary to add a charge the only result of 230 would be that that charge could not be gone into until Government have given their sanction. Section 235, one would have thought, is plain enough for any one to understand who wanted to understand (Reads Sec.) I should have thought it a matter beyond argument. But it seems from experience that one finds arguments are raised on points which are as clear as daylight.

His Lordship:-Have you given notice of this application to the Accused?

Advocate General:-My Lord. I have given notice of the application to the other side. This is not an application, I say I am entitled to do what

I propose. Sec. 235 will dissipate all difficulty. The charges under 124A and 153A, my Lord, will be treated as being alternative charges, (Reads) in which case either offence may or may not be proved. In this case there will not be four charges but in order to avoid having any difficulty or doubt which may arise hereafter I propose to proceed under Sec. 233 and say that for the present I will not proceed under Sec. 153A on the first charge and that will result in stay of the proceedings and discharge of the Accused but not in acquittal.

His Lordship:-With reference to this application I gathered from the Gujarathi newspapers that this application will be made to me to-day ; and having considered the possibility of hearing such an application made to me I have devoted considerable thought to the subject. In this case two separate informations were laid before the Magistrate and the Magistrate held two separate inquiries and made two separate committments. The question now is whether these two cases can be taken together and tried at one trial. It would be extremely desirable from my point of view and in the interest of the Accused that there should be one trial and before one Jury. The Accused is entitled under Sec. 233 to be tried separately unless Sec. 235 to 239 come into operation. I have grave doubts about Sec. 235 applying to this case. It seems to me that there would be considerable convenience if newspaper articles written from time to time can be considered as coming within the section. I have no difficulty however in ordering one trial under Sec. 234 provided that the charges do not exceed three. There are four charges in these two cases; but the Advocate General under Sec. 233 proposes to stay proceedings on one of the four charges. I am quite willing to allow him to make use of that section and hold over for the present any one of the charges. I do not wish the Advocate General to be taken by surprise and I feel it would only be fair to the Accused and the Crown if under the powers vested in me under the same section I order that such stay of proceedings may amount to an acquittal. It is not fair that the Accused should have that charge hanging over him and I will order these charges to be tried in the same trial provided there are not more than three charges. It will be for the Advocate General on which of the charges he means to proceed.

Advocate General :—I have already stated to your Lordship that I do not intend to proceed under more than three charges. I do not propose to proceed under Sec. 153A in the case of the article appearing in the *Kesari* of 12th May 1908.

His Lordship :—I think it is only fair to the Acused that he should be discharged from that charge.

Advocate General :—I am dealing with that question. I can select any three charges and proceed on them and ask for a stay of proceedings on the other.

His Lordship :—But that stay should be final.

Advocate General :—That might lead to a serious question whether it does not amount to *Autrefois Acquit*.

His Lordship :—That would not affect the other charges on the other articles. It will apply to this article on which you propose to hold over the charge; that would not affect the other charges.

Advocate General :—I can see perfectly well how it may be ingeniously argued that it can. That is why I ask Your Lordship not to pass such order till the case is over.

His Lordship :—Have you to make that application before the case is over or after?

Advocate General:—I have made the application so far it is an application now. I am not applying, I am stating that it is my proposal to put the Accused up on three separate charges.

His Lordship :—So long as there are only three charges I order that the charges be tried at one trial. You will undertake Mr. Advocate General to apply for the stay and that such stay shall be final.

Advocate General :—I simply undertake that I will not further prosecute. I am entitled to do that.

His Lordship :—That will be the application.

Advocate General:—Yes, when the three charges are over I shall tell the Court as I have already adumbrated before the Court that I do not intend to proceed further.

His Lordship:—My present order then will be that the Accused will be tried on three charges,that is one charge in case No. 16 and two charges in case No. 17.

Advocate General:—My Lord, My learned friend Mr. Inverarity will open this case before the Jury.

The Clerk of the Crown "Mr. M. R. Jardine" commenced to read the charges when Accused said:,

Accused:—My Lord, the objectionable passages on which the prosecution is laid are vague and are not specified so that I can not properly conduct my defence.

Clerk of the Crown :(Reads first chage) Do you plead guilty or not guilty ?

Accused:—I plead not guilty.

Clerk of the Crown:—You are further charged (Reads second case) Do you plead guilty or not guilty ?

Accused:—I plead not guilly. But I think the words on the articles on which the prosecution rely should be specified.

Mr. Inverarity:—As the whole lot of the words are objected to I ask your Lordship to amend the charges by putting in the whole articles into the charge. It is usual to give notice of charges to the Accused by giving him reference to page and column of his newspaper as it appears this is not sufficient I apply for the whole of the articles to be put in, in order that there may be no chance of any difficulty arising there afterwards.

His Lordship:—What is it you apply for?

Mr. Inverarity:—That the whole of the articles be included in the charges.

His Lordship:—This means that the whole article will have to be read to the Jury.

Accused:—Yes, My Lord.

His Lordship:—That is what you apply for?

Accused:—What I complain of is that the charges are vague and that the whole article can not be contended to be seditious.

His Lordship:—If you think that you have not sufficient of what you are charged with, Mr. Inverrarity will put in the seditious passages.

Accused:—I do not ask your Lordship to do that.

His Lordship:—Mr. Inverarity says he puts in the whole article? Do you wish that read?

Accused :— yes.

His Lordship :—It may waste half a day.

Accused :—It may happen that first the Prosecution relies on certain passages and then—

His Lordship :—I understand Mr. Inverarity to say that the whole of the articles must be put in.

His Lordship to Accused :—You must understand exactly the order I am making. I am now making an order on your objecting to the charges that the subject matter of the charge should be set forth in the charges themselves. That will be done and you will now understand that you are charged with the whole article of May 12, 1908 and the whole article of June 9, 1908 as seditious, and you are on trial on the whole of these two articles. You will also understand that I have made an order that you will be tried in one trial for three charges which are made against you.

Clerk of the Crown :—The charges in the first case will now be read (reads).

Clerk of the Crown.—The charges in the second case will now be read (reads).

Accused :—The second article may be taken as read. My objection is only to the translations.

Clerk of the Crown :—On these charges as amended do you plead guilty or not guilty?

Accused : I claim to be tried.

The Jury were then called.

The names of the jurymen present were then called by the Clerk of the Crown:—

James M. Mair (Challenged by the Accused)

Nair Nissim (Challenged by the Accused)

Bhimrao Atmaram (Challenged by the Accused)

F. G. Wood.

John Greig.

Bertram Glass Hilliard.

Palonji Dadabhoy Davar.

Chundulal Sitalal (Challenged by the Crown).

G. J. C. Hodson.

Shapurji Sorabji.

Claude Ureriam Biddell (Challenged by the Accused).

Rustamji F. Wadia (Challenged by the Crown).

Edwin Yeo (Challenged by the Accused).

S. Hempson.

G. H. Mc. Causland (Challenged by the Accused).

Wiliam C. Anderson.

J. G. Martin.

Mr. W. C. Anderson was appointed Foreman of the Jury.

The Jury were then sworn.

His Lordship to Accused:—Do you wish the whole of the articles to be read to the Jury in the course of the charge to the Jury?

Accused :—No, my Lord, they may be taken as read.

His Lordship :—Of course they will be read later.

The Clerk of the Crown then read to the Jury the charges against Mr. Tilak which were as follows:—

IN THE HIGH COURT OF JUDICATURE AT BOMBAY..

CASE No. 16.

Crown Side **Bombay**, to wit. You Bal Gangadhar Tilak are charged by the Clerk of the Crown as follows:—

Firstly:—That you on or about the 12th day of May 1908 at Bombay, then and there being the Printer and Publisher of a certain vernacular newspaper and entitled the "*Kesari*", by printed words brought or attempted to bring into hatred or contempt or excited or attempted to excite feelings of disaffection towards the Government established by law in British India, to wit, by publishing in Bombay in the issue of the said newspaper of the 12th May 1908 in columns 4 & 5 of page 4 and in columns 1 and 2 of page 5 thereof, an article headed with words having (when translated) the following effect viz "The countrys' misfortune" and proceeding, (when translated) as follows:—"No one" &c.

And that you thereby committed an offence punishable under Section 124 A of the Indian Penal Code and within the congnizance of the High Court.

Given under my hand this 13th day of July 1908.

(Sd.) M. R. JARDINE

Clerk of the Crown.

Crown Side Bombay, to wit. You Bal Gangadhar Tilak are charged by the Clerk of the Crown as follows:—

Secondly:—That you on or about the 12th day of May 1908 at Bombay, then and there being the Printer and Publisher of a certain vernacular paper entitled the "*Kesari*", by printed words promoted or attempted to promote feelings of enmity or hatred between different classes of the subjects of his Majesty the King Emperor, to wit, by publishing in the issue of the said newspaper of the 12th May 1908 in columhs 4 and 5 of page 4 and columns 1 & 2 of page 5 thereof an article headed with words having (when translated) the following effect viz. "The country's misfortune" and proceeding (when translated) as follows:—

"No one" &c.

And that you thereby committed an offence punishable under Section 153A of the Indian Penal Code and within the cognizance of the High Court.

Given under my hand this 13th day of July 1908.

(Sd.) M. R. JARDINE.

Case No. 17

Crown Side Bombay, to wit. You Bal Gangadhar Tilak, are charged by the Clerk of the Crown as follows:—

Firstly:—That you on or about the 9th day of June 1908 at Bombay, then and there being the Printer and Publisher of a certain vernacular newspaper entitled the " *Kesari* ", by printed words brought or attempted to bring into hatred or contempt or excited or attempted to excite feelings of disaffection towards the Government established by Law in British India, to wit, by publishing in Bombay in the issue of the said newspaper of the 9th June 1908 in columns 2 to 4 of page 4 thereof an article headed with words having (when translated) the following effect viz, " These remedies are not lasting " and proceeding (when translated) as follows:— " From this "

And that you thereby committed an offence punishable under Section 124A of the Indian Penal Code and within the cognizance of the High Court. Given under my hand this 13th day of July 1908.

(Sd). M. R. JARDINE

Clerk of the Crown.

Crown Side Bombay, to wit. You Bal Gangadhar Tilak are charged by the Clerk of the Crown as follows :—

Secondly.—That you on or about the 9th day of June at Bombay then and there being the Printer and Publisher of a certain vernacular newspaper entitled the "*Kesari*", by printed words promoted or attempted to promote feelings of enmity or hatred between different classes of the subjects of His Majesty The King Emperor, to wit, by publishing in Bombay in the issue of the said Newspaper of the 9th June 1908 in Columns 2 to 4 of page 4 thereof an article headed with the words having (when translated) the following effect viz "These remedies are not lasting" and proceedings (when translated) as follows :—"From this" &c.

And that you thereby committed an offence punishable under Section 153A of the Indian Penal Code and within the congnizance of the High Court.

Given under my hand this 13th day of July 1908.

(Sd.) M. R. JARDINE

Clerk of the Crown,

OPENING ADDRESS FOR THE PROSECUTION.

MR. INVERARITY, Barrister-at-Law then began his opening address which was as follows:—May it please your Lordship and gentlemen of the Jury. My learned friend Mr. Branson, the Advocate General, has had to go away to attend to a case in another court. Therefore the duty of stating this case devolves upon me. The Accused is charged as you have heard with offences under two sections of the Penal Code in respect of two articles which appeared in the *Kesari* newspaper. The *Kesari* is a Marathi newspaper printed and published at Poona and also published in Bombay, where it has a large circulation and is sold for three pice per copy. The first Section under which he is charged and which I have read to you is section 124A. I. P. C. (Reads Section). There are three explanations to the section (Reads the explanations). This Section, you see gentlemen, gives full effect to what is the law of all civilised countries. It gives the press and any person who chooses to write in the press full liberty to say anything on any action of the Government, but it does not allow them to use these comments as a vehicle for defaming Government. There is a definition here as to defaming private persons and of bringing them into contempt and hatred. You may comment on the administrative measures of Government; but when you go further and charge Government with bad motives, of acting with disregard to the interests of the people and of acting with regard to Europeans, only that is not allowed by the law. There are several pronouncements of these Courts, some in judgments and some in the form of summings up to the Jury. I do not propose to read them to you as his Lordship is perfectly familiar with them. The Section appears to be perfectly clear in itself; it distinctly states that (Reads). Well, there has been some controversy as to the meaning of the word disaffection, but the first part of the section says (Reads Section). That is not an exhaustive definition; but I submit to you that we can very easily get over that by citing from the indictment in England, the definition of what is meant by Seditious Libel (Reads).

That is the form of indictment of libel in England. It is set out in Archibald's Criminal Indictments page 729. (reads again.) That appears to me to put one of the matters to be included in the term disaffection and it is summed up in the phrase attempting to create disloyalty. I am going to refer to the charges separately. The first article is dated 12th May 1908. Before reading it to you I will state very shortly what the Prosecution submit as the effect of that article. We don't want you to take separate parts of that article. It begins with a comment upon what is known as the Muzufferpore bomb outrage which is described in the paper as an attempt by some Bangalis to bomb with the intention of killing an official; the bomb was thrown in a wrong carriage and two unfortunate ladies were killed. You will find that all stated in the article as being what the Muzufferpur outrage was. The whole of the article is devoted to stating that the whole cause of this outrage is the iniquitious character of the oppressive and tyrannical rule of the British in this country. That we submit to you is the effect of that article. It speaks of the Country's Misfortune. What is meant by the country's misfortune? It will be for you to say if it means that it is the country's misfortune to be ruled by the British or whether it is that India is coming to the same state as that in Russia, or the state the Accused says Russia is in. I shall hand you copies of the articles as soon as they have been proved. It is sometimes difficult to follow an article without it being before you. But you will have ample leisure hereafter to study them. It begins "The Country's misfortune" (Reads down to "white official class.") In that passage the writer describes the details of the Muzuffarpur outrage and ascribes this to the perversity of the white official class. I think you will have no doubt in finding that the oppressive white official class means the British Government. (Reads down to "Mr. Kingsford.") That was the gentleman on whom the attempt was intended. (Reads down to "occur even in Russia"). As I said before, you have to see what the real state of Russia is. He describes the affairs in Russia and says oppressions have exasperated the people till thay have begun to throw bombs. (Reads down to "is gaining ground"). I will pause there and try and impress on you what the writer is there trying to point out. He says that British rule is entirely governed by self-interest except in so far as it is bounded by the necessity of avoiding exasperating the people of the country. That I say is a gross libel on the Government of India and of Great Britian. It goes on to say that such power must be taken out of the hands of Government and put into "our own hands." Our own hands there means the hands of the Natives. (Reads down to "the rights of Swarajya"). That is a word that means one's own rule and may mean Self-Government or imperial or autocratic. There it is said that the Government of India are only induced to go on exactly as they choose by these considerations. The lesson being a rise like that of Japan in the recent war with Russia, lesson of history. (Reads to "horrible deeds recklessly"). There is a phrase used which explains the meaning of Swarajya. We have it defined by himself in another article in the paper. He says the people are growing stronger and stronger and they want Swarjya. Well, Swarajya is translated by the translator as literally one's own rule or Government, Self-Government. We have the Accused's own definition of Swarajya. Judge between the two. Well then, gentlemen, there is the *Kesari's* own definition of Swarajya and it apparently means that whenever the people like to upset the Government they are entitled to do so. (Reads to "methods of the Russian subjects,"). According to this the *Kesari* had on previous occasions warned the Government that Russian methods would be imitated by the people of India if they were not careful. I think there can be no doubt that the Russian methods must be the throwing of bombs. (Reads down to "beyond certain limits"). These words are put into the mouths of the Anglo-Indian Officials. (Reads down to "the whole country"). There the writer represents 30 crores of people in India burning with indignation and says it is impossible not to expect some of them to commit outrages induced by the oppressive system of Government. (Reads down to "occasions"). That, gentlmen, is a most defamatory statement against Government that it is their desire to benefit their own contry at the expense of the Natives of India (Reads down to "stop this traga".) Traga is interpreted to mean inflicting upon one's own person some injury in order to bring evil or blame upon another.

That last page that I have read is a good illustration of what the law allows. It is particularly fair comment to make whether bomb-throwing should be suppressed by repressive means or other means are quite justified.

But what the Government say is that these articles are a direct attack on Government alleging that it is unscrupulous to say that it is the strong desire of Government to benefit itself to the loss of the Natives, and in an earlier part it likens the people of this country to a cat. The article compares the Government to the man who confines a cat with such cruelty that it leaps at him and tries to kill him. You will see from the observations whether it is or it is not a transgression of the elements which the law allows to be discussed ot Gcvernment measures. On that part of the case I would like to quote you some passages from Lord Ellenborough's judgment, in the case of King *Virsus* Lambert reported in II Campbell, page 298 in which there is a seditious libel against George III tried over a hundred years ago, in 1810. Lord Ellenborough in that case said (reads) Just apply the words to this article here. Does it say that Government is actuated by good motives and is being merely misled into errors or is it going a step further and insinuating that Government says (Reads from " We shall practiee" to "beyond certain limits"). If they do that it would be most libellous. Further on Lord Ellenborough says at page 402 (Reads) and at page 304 he says (Reads down to " convey ".) That really is a test of what the words convey. What were those words intended to convey and what the probable effect that it would have on the minds of the men who read them. Then later on at page 405 he says (reads down to propogate and to libel). Just apply those words to this article. Don't you think that this article is intended to convey to readers that the only thing which comes between the people of India and the blessings of this country is the English rule ? So much for the first article.

The second article is dated 9th June 1908. I may mention to you we mean to put in and rely on the first article which you will remember is dated May 12th and we are going to rely on another article of May 12th and on an article of May 19th and another article of May 26th and two other articles dated 2nd and 9th June 1908. I do not propose to read them to you *in extenso* though they will be read to you *in extenso* if you wish it. I shall only read such passages as will show you what was in the mind of the Accused. You will know that the articles which have been selected for this charge are only part of a series showing the writer's inquisitious characterisation of the methods of Government. In the first article the writer repudiates all sympathy with the throwing of bombs for subverting British rule. In the next article, it is a most extraordinary article with regard to bomb—throwing, it points out, and it is a most mischievous thing to do, that people in other countries have obtained what they want by bomb—throwing. It points out that Government cannot prevent the manufacture of bombs, they are easy to make, they only require a few chemicals. It suggests in a veiled manner that other countries have got advantages by the use of bomb and foul murders, and that bombs can be very easily made in India. I will read you that article. (Reads article in "*Kesari*" dated 9th June 1908 headed " These remedies are not lasting" down to " rights of Swarajya"). Well, we call your attention to this passage and ask you to say whether it is or is not defamatory to the English Government? Then it is alleged that British Rule has been based on self interest and Government carry it on as they like, or as it is put " a selfish administration." This means an administration devoted to the benefit of the people by whom it is carried on and not of the people of India. (Reads down to " not got as much generosity as the Moguls "). Then again it says Government after all is enriching England at the expense of India. (Reads down to "English in India not being permanent"). You see he says were it not for this bomb—coming Government would have been able to pursue their object of enriching England at the expense of India.

But the bomb has come in and prevented such a state of things becoming permanent. (Reads to " it is a charm, an amulet"). What is the meaning of that? How does a bomb become a witchcraft, or amulet or charm, unless it is intended to be used? (Reads from "it is not necessary" down to "violent turn—headed persons"). Quite apart from any reference to bombs you will find that Government is described in the same manner there as the people who have a grievance to bring to the notice of the people of England. You will see this for yourselves when you read the articles themselves. There are two paragraphs to the same effect that British Rule is a curse to the country, and if that is really the case they must expect to have the same state of affairs in India as, the writer says, exists in Russia. The writer actually refers to the murder of the King of Portugal as resulting in having the desired effect. Does it not appear to you that it was a threat to the Government of India and a suggestion to the people of India that British Rule cannot be allowed to go on as it is at present, and that it is impossible to suppress the making of bombs because they are so easy to make and only want a few chemicals to make them? The second article is under section 124A I. P. C. and also under Section 153A I. P. C. Only three charges can be tried at one trial, and in this case there are two charges under section 124A and one charge under section 153A. (Reads Section and explanations). You see that is a Section which makes it an offence to write matters which stir up racial feelings between Natives and Europeans. This article comes within this Section. Well, I have read the passages to you and it will be for you to say whether these passages are, or are not calculated to stir up racial feelings. You will find that the intention of the writer can be gathered from the other articles. You will see that in his first article he frequently alludes to the alien rulers being white. What is the object of the reference to the rulers being alien, and being white? It can only be intended to stir up racial feeling between Europeans and Natives of the country by pointing out to them that the white class is acting in India in a manner which is directly hostile to the interets of the natives. With regard to the other Articles, I am not going to read the whole of them to you. you will be able to say if they are unfairly selected, because they will be put before you. I only propose to read any of those particular passages to show that the object of the writer was only to attack the actions and measures of Government, or the policy of the Government itself.

Accused :—I don't think those articles can be put in to show intention, until such time as the other Articles are put in and admitted.

Mr. Inverarity :—Under section 13 of the Evidence Act they are admissible. If the Accused thinks the articles cannot be admitted in evidence at this point I will not read them now. The Advocate General will read them to you in summing up the case. There is no charge against him in respect to these articles. They are only used as showing what was in the mind of the printer and publisher of these Articles when he published them. Section 14 of the Evidence Act is the one under which we shall tender them and we shall ask you to use them in this way. Section 14, says (Reads Section 14). We say that this Article is one of extreme hostility to the Government as a Government. You will find the illustration to that Section is exactly to the point (Reads illustration E.). There are many other illustrations which are also appropriate, but that is the one which is most appropriate. Here is a writer who is charged with defaming Government and I have referred to one article as showing what is Accused's idea of what is "Swarajya." Gentlemen, I have not been too long. I have refrained from reading long judgments and long summings up. I will leave those to my learned friend the Advocate General and to His Lordship. There are three charges which will claim your attention. Two of them under Section 124A. and one under 153A. It might be convenient to you to have with you copies of these two Sections. With his Lordship's permission I will hand to each of you, gentlemen of the Jury, copies of these two Sections so that you will be able to see for yourselves what the words really are. The words are so clear that I don't think you will want anyone to explain to you what they mean.

Advocate General :—I tender, my Lord, the sanction to prosecute in this case. (Exhibit A.)

The Advocate General :—We will now call the witnesses for the Prosecution and my learned friend Mr. Binning will examine them.

Mr. Bhas ker Vishnu Joshi was then called.

EVIDENCE FOR THE PROSECUTION.—

First Witness: BHASKAR VISHNU JOSHI

Examined by Mr. Binning, Bar-at-Law.

Q. What is your name?—Bhaskar Vishnu Joshi. Q. You are first assistant to the Oriental Translator?—Yes. Q. You are a B. A. of the University of Bombay?—Yes. Q. Do you recognise the signature of this document? —Yes. Q. Whose is it?—It is that of Mr. H. O. Quinn, Acting Secretary to Government Judicial Department. Q. It is the sanction to prosecute in the first case?—Yes. Mr. Binning: My Lord, I put that in. His Lordship: (to acccused) Have you any objection to this going in?-No, my Lord; I have no objection to its going in. (Ex. A.)

Q. You see this other document giving sanction for the other prosecution?—Yes. Q. Is that the signature of Mr. Quinn?—Yes. It is dated 16th June 1908. Mr. Binning: I tender it. (Ex. B.)

Mr. Binning:—I want to show him the signature at the end of both the documents and ask him to prove Mr. Gell's signature. To witness: Do you recognise that signature?—Yes. It is that of the Commissioner of Police. Q. You produce this newspaper-the *Kesari* of the 12th May 1908?—Yes. Q. On page 4 and 5 you see an article, which you translated?—Yes. Q. You also see the official translation?—Yes, I do. His Lordship: You received that newspaper in the course of your duty?—Yes, my Lord. Mr. Binning: I tender the newspaper and translation. (Ex. C.)

His Lordship : You translated the article. How is it headed ?—It is headed 'The Country's Misfortune '. Mr. Binning: You see the other article in the *Kesari* of the 9th June; did you get it in the course of your duty as assistant to the Oriental Translator to Government ?—Yes. Mr. Binning: Will your Lordship direct that if there are any witnesses in this case in Court they should be asked to leave ? Mr. Inverarity: If there is any witness assisting the Accused in his defence in Court, I have no objection to his remaining. It was stated that Mr. N. C. Kelkar was helping the Accused and was witness. Mr. Inverarity : I have no objection to his remaining. (Ex. D.)

Mr. Binning : You see columns 2 and 4 of the article headed ' These remedies are not lasting ' in the issue of the 9th June ?—Yes. Q. You produce the *Kesari* of the 12 th of May ?—Yes. Q. You see an article in column 3 of the page 5 ?—Yes. His Lordship : Where are they ?—They came under the ' Editor's Stray Thoughts ' and they are 3 and 4 of these notes. The articles begin with " Since the commencement of the bomb affair ". Mr. Binning : I tender this my Lord. The Accused : I object to the articles going in as proving intention. They may go in as showing the circumstances under which the article was written. I refer your Lordship to Mayne's Criminal Law page 522. In the last *Kesari* case many articles were put but not as showing intention. What I say is that these articles can go in to show the surrounding circumstances under which the article was written but they cannot be put in to prove intention.

His Lordship : This question has been argued in previous cases, and I shall admit them for the same purpose for which they have been admitted in previous cases. (Ex. E.)

Mr. Binning to witness : Do you produce the *Kesari* of the 19th May and do you see a Marathi Leader on page 4 Columns 4 & 5 and Column 1 of page 5 ?—Yes. How is it headed ?—A double hint. His Lordship: Is it an article?—No, my Lord, it is the leader. Mr. Binning : I tender the article and translation. (Ex. F.)

Q. Do you produce the *Kesari* of the 26th May 1908 ?—Yes. Q. Do you see columns 3, 4, & 5 of page 4 and do you find a Marathi leader in these columns headed " The Real Meaning of the Bomb."—

Yes. Mr. Binning:—My Lord, each paper goes in with the foot note showing that it was printed and published by the Accused. (Ex. G.)

Continuing after lunch Mr. Binning proceeded with the examination. Q. Do you produce a copy of the Kesari dated 2nd June 1908?—Yes. You see there in columns 3, 4 and 5 of page 4 a leader entitled 'The Secret of the Bomb'?—Yes. Q. That came to you in the course of your duty?—Yes. Mr. Binning: I tender that, my Lord, with the official translation. (Ex. H.)

Mr. Binning: There is only one more. I show you Ex. D in this case. The Kesari of the 9th June and in the 2nd and 3rd Columns of the pages 5 do you see an article?—Yes. Q. is it a leading article?—No, it is amongst "Stray thoughts of Editor." Q. What note is it ?—It is note No. 11 and begins "the English are openly an alien Rule". Mr. Binning: I put in the article and translation. (Ex. I.)

His Lordship :—Does the Accused wish to ask the witness any question?

CROSS-EXAMINATION OF THE WITNESS BY MR. TILAK :—

The translations that you have put in, have you made them yourself ?—They are High Court Translations. Can you vouch for their accuracy ?—The originals are not here but I can vouch for their accuracy. Have you compared them yourself with the original ?—Yes, I have. His Lordship : All of them ?—No my Lord, One I did not get. His Lordship : Which was that ?—That was of the 26th of May. Excepting that one I compared them all. His Lordship : That is Ex. G. Q. Did you translate all of them before ?—Yes. Q. Did the two translations differ ?—My translations differ in minor respects from those of the High Court. You have before you the High Court translation. Is it to be preferred to yours ?—Yes in most cases. Q. Have you got your own translations with you ?—No. Mr. Branson intimated that they had been sent for. His Lordship to Accused : Which translation do you want ?—The original translation of the article of 12th May. Q. Now take the original translation Ex. H dated 2nd June 1908. Is that the official translation ?—Yes. Q. Can you give us the date of the translation ?—I cannot remember. Q. You have said that you have translated. Can you not give the date ?—No, I do not remember. Q. Can you tell me that that was the translation before Government when Government gave sanction to prosecute?—No, I can not say that. Q. At all events it was prepared before the case came before the Magistrate ?—I am not authorised to say anything about that. Q. You put a translation in the Magistrate's Court ?—Yes. Q. So it was made before the 25th of June ? That was the date of the Magistrate's proceedings. So it was prepared before that date. (The original translation made by Mr. Joshi was handed to him and Mr. Tilak continued his cross-examination.) How do you translate देशाचें दुर्दैव ?—The country's misfortune. How do you translate गोऱ्या स्त्रिया ?—European Ladies. In the Official translation what is the translation of innocent white ladies ?—गोऱ्या. Q. What does गोऱ्या mean in Marathi ? Can it be translated in any other way ?—I do not know. Q. Does it apply to complexion or colour ?—I do not understand the difference. Q. Could you say गोरी

सफेती दिली आहे ?—No. Q. Which translation would give the sense better ? " White " or " European " ladies ?—Both would convey it better. Q. Better ? Equally. The only thing is that the word white is more comprehensive. Q. How can white be more comprehensive ?—I cannot answer that question. Q. Then you translate it yourself as European ?—Yes. I put in the marginal note that it literally means white. Q. You translate the word गोऱ्या with a marginal note showing that the literal meaning is white ?—Yes. Q. In your official capacity you are required to read the vernacular papers ?—Yes. Q. In expressing current political ideas many new words have to be coined in Marathi ? His Lordship: In expressing what ?—The accused: Modern Political Ideas; (to witness) and sometimes in order to clear up the meaning newspaper writers insert the English words after the Marathi translation ?—Yes. Q. Just a few lines below that phrase, you find, (reads from the Marathi). After using the word अधिकारी वर्ग it is the practice to write afterwards " Bureaucracy " ?—Yes. Q. What does that English word stand for according to you ?—अधिकारी वर्ग. Not for white Official Class ?—No. What does अधिकारी वर्ग mean in English ?—Official Class. And if you have to join the idea to ' ruling class ' could you express it if you say राज्यकर्ता अधिकारी वर्ग ? Will that do ?—Yes; it may mean English Official Class. If you want a synonym for अधिकारी वर्ग will it do if you express it by English ?—It will express the idea in constructive manner. It will not be a synonym, for it will express the matter in another way. Q. In another way ?—Yes. We say (1) गोरा अधिकारी वर्ग (2) सरकारी अधिकारी वर्ग (3) इंग्रजी अधिकारी वर्ग (4) राज्यकर्ता अधिकारी वर्ग do they mean Bureaucracy ?—No, not bureaucracy. His Lordship: There are four expressions: do they mean the same thing or different things ?—They mean the same thing but not bureaucracy. His Lordship : Then what do they mean ?—They mean (1) Ruling Official Class (2) White Official Class (3) English Official Class & (4) Official Class in power. Q. You have said, you have rendered bureaucracy by सरकारी अधिकारी वर्ग ?—No, the adjective is superfluous. Q. Class of officials merely ?—The (British) Class of officials. Q. What is the meaning of the latter syllable in the word राज्यकर्ता अधिकारी वर्ग ?—I am not well practised in terminology. Q. Does it mean ruling Official Class ?—No. Q. The word bureaucracy, does it not convey the idea of ruling Class ?—No, I do not think so. Q. You do'nt know ?—No. Q. In the word Aristocracy does 'cracy' convey any idea of ruling class? I cannot tell you the meaning of Aristocracy. Q. My question is, does this convey the idea of the ruling Class ?—No. Q. Does the word Plutocracy convey the idea of ruling ?—I do not know. Q. Do the word अधिकारी वर्ग convey the idea of both Europeans and Natives?-अधिकारी "Officials",and वर्ग "Class."Q.Do the words include both Europeans and Natives ?—Yes. Q. If you want to confine it to Europeans it would have to be qualified by an adjective ?—Yes. Q. How do you translate the word Despotism ?—जुलमी राज्यपद्धती. Q. How do you translate the word tyrannical ?—जुलमी. Q. How do you translate the word oppressive ?—जुलमी Q. How do you translate the word coercive ?—Where does it occur ? I do not want to be examined in English words. His Lordship: Do you not know the Marathi meaning of the word Coercive ?—Yes. "Then give it." Witness :—Coercive also means जुलमी. Q. How would you translate the word repressive ?—I cannot give meanings of all kinds of words off hand. I will be able to give them better with a dictionary. There are shades of differences in meanings. His Lordship: Give the meaning if you know and then you can refer to the dictionary. What is the Marathi word for repressive ?—There may be different words ; I may give one of them.

His Lordship: Give the ordinary meanings of the word repressive. Witness: दडपशाही is the noun, and दडपशाही, दडपशाहीचा the adjectives. Q. This is a newly coined word ?—Yes. His Lordship: You say, it is a new word ?—Yes my Lord, it is a coined word. Q. You say " Julmi " can be rendered by tyrannical, despotic or oppressive ?—Yes, but in every context we must choose. It may be in different contexts. Q. Not except according to the context ?—That you may do if you like. Q. Now in describing the situation of a country in what sense is the word despotic used ?—Where it is ruled by a despot. His Lordship: How ? —When it is ruled by a despot or by despotic officials. Q. Is there any difference between despotic officials and tyrannical officials or between despotic monarch and tyrannical monarch ?—There may be, I am not aware of these minute differences. Q. According to your opinion despotic monarch is the same as tyrannical monarch ?—Yes, as far as I can say. I have no dictionary with me. Q. Have you ever come accross the expression " A despotic rule need not necessarily be tyrannical" ?—I have not. His Lordship: What ?—I do not remember to have come accross any such expression. Q. Now suppose I give you that expression. Will you translate it in Marathi ? " A despotic rule need not be necessarily tyrannical "—जुलमी राज्यपद्धती जुलमाचीच असली पाहिजे असें नाहीं. Q. How will you translate Aristotle's dictum " Tyranny is the perversion of Monarchy " ?—जुलमी राज्यपद्धती ही राजसत्ताक पद्धतीचा विपर्यास आहे. Q. I will take the words aristocratic, absolute, arbitrary. How are these words rendered in Marathi ? Absolute, translate that ?-अनियंत्रित. Q. Arbitrary ?—I cannot give you one word for that. Q. Never mind, give your rendering ?—Should I not be allowed to use my dictionary ? I may otherwise be giving incorrect meanings. I can explain the word arbitrary better in English than in Marathi. His Lordship: Give what you know. Witness: I cannot give one word. His Lordship: Explain it in Marathi. Witness: I can explain it better in English. I may have to give more than one word. His Lordship: Give them. Witness: ज्याला निर्बंध नाहीं असा or स्वैर. स्वैर is the Sanskrit word. His Lordship: Now we have autocratic ?—It is also अनियंत्रित. What is uncontrolled ?-It is also अनियंत्रित. What is irresponsible ?—बेजबाबदार. There is one more word. How will you translate imperialistic ?—बादशाही बाण्याचा. Now how will you translate a sentence like this ?—His Lordship: I do not wish to hamper your Cross Examination but I want to know if in the articles there is a description of despotic rule and the question is how are these things to be translated. Do you dispute the translations ? Accused—Yes my Lord, these words have been mistranslated and even the official translation is wrong.

Q. How will you translate ?—" The Government of India is a despotism tempered by public opinion in England" ?—हिंदुस्थानसरकार विलायतेंतील लोकमतानें सौम्य झालेलें जुलमी पद्धतीचें राज्य आहे. Q. What is the translation of the word माथेफिरू ?-Turnheaded. How will you translate the word fanatic ?—There is not one word. Q. Supposing you want to coin a word ?—I can give you a hundred words which would convey the same idea ; the word is Ghazi. Q. Even if it is different from its regular meaning ?—I have translated as Ghazi.

Q. Deprived of its religious significance how will you translate?-I do not know. His Lordship : What do you say of a man who is called a fanatic ?—माथेफिरू or वेडा might do. Will you translate आततायी ?--Violent-headed man. Do you know that आततायी is a felon ?—I have not come accross that. Q. Can you give us the meaning of the word in Sanskrit : who are called आततायी in Sanskrit ?—I do not know. Accused : There is a Sanskrit dictionary. Witness : What do you want to know ?—You will find in the persons mentioned there that felons are one of these ?—There is the phrase given there. Q. I want to know what are आततायी. There are six classes mentioned in dictionaries. Poisoners, persons infatuated with weapons, persons crazy with wealth, persons who deprive a man of his wife. —Yes these may be known as आततायी. His Lordship : What dictionary is that ? Sanskrit into English by Waman Shivaram Apte. Q. Then आततायी is a stronger word than माथेफिरू ?—Yes. Q. It might be borrowed in Marathi ?—Yes, but not necessarily in the same sense that most people use it. Molesworth gives the word आततायी as a violent turnheaded man. Q. You have said in one place that Molesworth's is an antiquated dictionary ? If we want a stronger word than the Marathi form then we go to Sanskrit. The one is stronger than the other ?— (No reply from witness). His Lordship : Is one form stronger than the other ?—I would with due respect ask your Lordship to decide it yourself. Q. In ordinary writing आततायी conveys the more forcible idea ?—Yes. But very few people will understand the word आततायी. It is not Marathi. Q. Do you know we often quote this verse आततायिनं &c., Manu VII. 41 ?—It is generally quoted. I am not aware that this is frequently quoted. Q. In this country the word is rendered felon ?—Yes, along with some other words. Q. Is not felon a stronger word than fanatic ?—I cannot judge of these fine distinctions. It would be very risky to judge. Q. You know that in writing on modern political matters we have to coin different words to express different meanings ?— Yes. Q. Sanskrit words have to be borrowed to coin suitable words for English expressions as there are no Marathi equivalents ?—For the matter of that in industrial and scientific departments very many words have to be coined. Q. How will you express in Marathi the following words, State ?—राज्य or सरकार. Government ?—सरकार, शासनपद्धति or if the abstract meaning is intended राज्यपद्धति. I cannot give the equivalents of each of these words. I cannot go into the subtle differences of these words. Q. Can administration be referred to as सरकार ?— No. Q. Rule is ?—राज्य. Q. Sway is ?—राज्य or अंमल. Q. Take these three English words, (1) Manliness (2) Vigour & (3) Sense of honour, as qualities of a living or ruling nation. How would you translate Manliness ?—मर्दानीपणा or पौरुष. Vigour ?—सामर्थ्य. Sense of honour ?—अभिमान. Q. Is not तेज the abstract word for sense of honour ?—No. तेज means a different thing altogether ? Q. Is it never used for sense of honour ?—I have not heard it so used. Q. Neither in Sanskrit nor in Marathi ?—I do not know Sanskrit. Q. And you won the Jagannath Shankarset Sanskrit Scholarship ? How would you render this : न तेजस्वी साहे ?—I am not aware that it means sense of honour. I would translate it energy, spirit. Q. One who would not brook insult. तेजस्वी is a man who would not brook insult ?—I would translate it as a spirited man. Q. Will you please render this न तेजस्तेजस्वी प्रभृतमपरेषां प्रसहते &c. ?—I cannot translate that. His Lordship : What do you understand ? Witness : I understand the meaning and know the construction, but can not translate it. Q. Then you know it ?—That is another matter. Witness:—Your Lordship will know that it is a Sanskrit sentence. I may translate it to-morrow if you give me time. Q. You can translate Marathi sentences, can you not ? How do you translate this न तेजस्वी साहे प्रकट परतेजोबलमदा ?—That is also Sanskrit. It is full of Sanskrit. Q. I have given you Marathi words ?—I know that it is a Marathi rendering of the Sanskrit. Q. Do you know that it occurs in the 4th Standard Reading Book ?—I can not say. His Lordship : You can ask necessary questions but do not ask unnecessary questions. Q. How will you render the word संताप ?—Indignation. Q. How will you render the words : दुःखानें संतप्त ?—Afflicted with sorrow. Q. Not indignant by sorrow ?—No. Afflicted with sorrow. Q. How would you render the word त्वेष —Passionate anger. That is the meaning given in the dictionary I am using. Q. You must stick to the dictionary whether it suits context or not ?—No. I do not mean that I am guided by the dictionary. Q. How will you render the word आवेश ?—Vehemence. It also means angry passions, passions of rage. Mr. Tilak : I do not want you to read from the dictionary. Witness : I have made the translations of these myself from the dictionary. Mr. Tilak : I think that might go down in the evidence. Q. To which dictionary do you refer ?—I have used three dictionaries for the rendering of the words of this article namely Molesworth, Candy, Apte and Monier Williams but the latter very rarely. Accused—Apte's is the dictionary I gave you just now ?—Yes. Q. Of the renderings you have given in translations from the dictionaries you selected the best ?—Yes. Q. New meanings are being assigned to words, did you take care to look to that ?—Who is assigning them ? Mr. Tilak : the writer. Q. If the writer wanted to assign new meanings to the words you do not care about that ?—I do not know the writer's mind. I do not care about it. Q. And yet you know that good many words have to be coined in Marathi to express new ideas ?—Yes, I know that. Q. Take the article of 9th June in the original. How will you translate this in Marathi ?—"The Evil Genius haunting the man" दुष्ट बुद्धि, माणसाच्या पाठीमागें भुतासारखी लागलेली. Q. Evil Genius is दुष्ट बुद्धि, भूत. How will you translate the words ?—Evil Genius means भूत. His Lordship:—How did you translate first ?—दुष्ट बुद्धि. Q. Genius in the sentence is spirit, e. g. the one that followed Socrates ? Please give the definite meaning of this साकेतिसाच्या मागें भूत लागलेलें होतें ?—A fiend haunted or pursued Socrates. Q. In the translation would an evil genius haunted Socrates be better ?—What evil genius? Ordinary evil genius or his own evil genius ? His Lordship:—Can it be translated like that ?—Yes, it may be translated as evil genius. Q. In the scond sentence in the article we have दडपशाहीचें भूत पांच दहा वर्षांनीं &c. can that sentence be rendered "The evil genius of repression seizes the Government of India every five or ten years?"—Seizes is a free translation, it means catches hold of. Q. of What ? The body of Government ?—It is a free translation. Q. How do you translate seize in Marathi?—धरतें. Q. पछाडतें is not seized ?—It is a fabricated meaning. Q. Two or three lines below we find खुद मांत्रिक व्रतभ्रष्ट झाले. What does मांत्रिक mean ?—Do you want the literal meaning or the intended meaning? It is not used in its literal sense but in its suggestive sense. It may mean haunted persons. Literally it means one versed in incantations or one who recites charms. Q. Refer to the official translation; it is stated in the marginal note that a Mantra is a Vedic text?—Yes versed in incantations also means one versed in Charms or Vedic Mantras. Q. In what sense does the writer use it, Vedic Mantra or Charm?—It means a reciter of Charms or the Vedic Mantras. Q. Here it does not mean that? Translate व्रतभ्रष्ट?—Who has fallen from his vows, or his observances. Q. Does it mean that you have to keep up this in order that the Mantra may by effective?—Yes. Q. In the official translation it is "abjured their ideals?"—It is the suggestive sense. Q. Is it correct according to the context? Does it correctly represent the context?—Yes, I think it does. Q. After the same line we have सुळसुळाट. What is your rendering of that?—Fiends swarming everywhere. Q. In the Marathi it is सुळसुळाट and refers more to action than to numbers?—To both. Q. According to the context to both? How can that be?—I can not say. Q. Can not it be rendered actively ardent or ardently active?—It is very far-fetched. Q Is it not correct in a far-fetched manner? Down below you have the word बुद्धिभ्रंश. What does that mean?—Infatuation of the mind. Q. How would you render in Marathi "error of judgment"?—I shall have to coin a word. it will take some time. His Lordship:—If you were asked to translate error of judgment in Marathi how would you do it?—I must take some time to think. The idea is very complicated. There is no Marathi word for "Judgment." "Error" I can translate, but Error of judgment is without care, thought and deliberation; I can not translate. Q. If we can not find a real word for that we have to use a coined word for it. We newspaper writers can not wait. Suppose you have to write an article in a hurry would you be able to spare time to find a word?—I am not a writer of articles. Q. Will you be able to give us the word to-morrow?—Yes, I shall try. Q. A few lines below you find चळली. How will you render बुद्धि कशी चळली?—Became fatuous. Q. Use the verb for the word चळली; do not translate it by two words, use the verb?—The literal meaning is "discharged from its place." Not moved in a wrong direction?—No, I can not say that. Q. Now I put it to you, can it not be erred in their judgment?—No. Q. How do you render the word "Decentralization of power"?—अधिकारविभागणी. Q. On the other page just about the middle we have राजकीय सत्तेचा कोणचाही भाग पृथक करून ते लोकांचे हातीं देण्यास तयार होत नाहींत. It is in the second column. The English translation at the bottom of page 2, seven or 8 lines from the bottom. Can it not be rendered by decentralization?—No "Decentralization" would not suit the context. Q. I have said विभागणी and not वांटणी. What is the difference between the two?—The difference between the two is that विभागणी has been used in the sense of general decentralisation but not वांटणी. Q. Is decentralisation used here as a coined word?—Yes. His Lordship: What is the coined word अधिकारविभागणी. It is a coined word. Q. It can never be rendered अधिकाराची वांटणी?—I can not say. His Lordship: It cannot be rendered by the word?—No, I do not think so.

(Case adjournod till Tuesday 14th July).

2nd day Tuesday 14th July 1908.

The Jury having answered to their names, Mr. Tilak addressed His Lordship and said:—

May I mention a matter, Your Lordship ? Some compositors and printers have been summoned here from my press at Poona and I believe they are required to give evidence as to my being Printer and Publisher of the Kesari. I have already admitted that before the Magistrate. These men have to get the Paper out and if they are summoned for me and not for some other purpose I suggest that they might be discharged.

His Lordship:— I have no doubt the Advocate General will release them as soon as he can.

Mr. Branson:—The accused has not admitted in the Magistrate's Court or anywhere else that he is Printer and Editor of the "Kesari". If he will do so now it will save a lot of time.

His Lordship:—I do not think it advisable to have that statement made before the proper time.

Mr. Branson:—If I get the names of these particular witnesses, I will call them as soon as I can.

Accused:—Offered to supply the names. Examination of witness Joshi continued:—

You remember you told us yesterday that the Marathi in the original for Decentralisation could not have meant Decentralisation. I show you an article in the Kesari dated 17th March on Decentralisation.

Advocate General:—Do you propose to put it in ?

His Lordship to accused:—I ought to tell you what the result of your doing so will be. If you put in anything that you have used during the course of cross-examination you will be deprived of the right of replying to the Counsel for the prosecution.

Q. Take the following sentence :—अधिकाराची विभागणी....वांटणी do the words convey the same meaning ?

No answer from the Accused.

His Lordship :—Are they used there in the sense of decentralisation of power ?

A. It means I think apportionment of power.

Q. It does not mean decentralisation ?

A. I cannot say now.

His Lordship:—Why cannot you say now? Will you say what you think?

Witness :—They are used both as apportionment of power and decentralisation of power.

Advocate General to Accused:—You are reading from the same article? I do not want to raise any unnecessary objections but you must not make use of the article, it is something not before the Court.

His Lordship:—He is using the writing for the purpose of cross-examination.

Advocate General:—With due deference to your Lordship, I do not think he can do it in that way.

His Lordship:—Supposing he proposes to show some of his writings to the witness for the purposes of cross-examination is he not entitled to use the article ?

Advocate General:—I am not aware of any provision of the Evidence Act or of any law which entitles him to do that.

His Lordship to accused :—Perhaps it will be as well to put the witness suppositious sentences and examine him on them.

Accused:—Yes my Lord I will put hypothetical ones.

Q. If you have a sentence like this what does it mean : प्रांतिक सरकार व हिंदुस्थान सरकार यांमधील अधिकाराची वांटणी ?

A : The apportionment of power between the Provincial Government and the Supreme Government.

Q. Take the Official translation of the article of the 12th of May and the original. In the original you see देशाचें दुर्दैव. How do you translate it ?

A. The Country's Misfortune.

Q. Now come to the 5th line of the translation. You find the words "inspire many with hatred," how do you translate hatred ?

A—तिटकारा.

Q—And how do you render द्वेष?

A—It means hatred or enmity.

Q—Is there any difference between तिटकारा and ?

A—There is no difference? One is a Sanskrit word.

Q—And the other मराठी ?

A—That is a Marathi word.

Q—Does not तिटकारा mean disgust in Marathi?

A—I cannot say. I have not referred to the dictionary in making your translation?

Q—But did not you refer to the dictionary?

A—I cannot remember.

Q—Refer to the word तिटकारा at page 379 of Candy's Dictionary, is the meaning given there as hatred ?

A—No.

Q—While "disgust" is; "a feeling that produces disgust."

A—The words scorn or scorning also appear.

Q—It produces equally dislike or disgust?

A—You are reading the adjective not the verb.

Q—What is your edition when was it published, in 1857 ?

A—Yes.

Q—We are both looking at the same edition. You do not read it as feeling of disgust?

A—No.

Q—Look 3 or 4 lines further down "the obstinacy and perversity of the white official class." What is the original word for obstinacy in Marathi?

A—हट्ट.

Q. And for pervesity ?

A. दुराग्रह.

Q. Then हट्ट and दुराग्रह are the original words. Are not these words synonymous and used to make the sentence more emphatic ?

A. I cannot say.

Q. There are two words which are nearly synonymous and are used for the purpose of emphasis, do you admit that ?

A. No, there is the conjunction "and" between the two words; otherwise it should have been " or ".

Q. You say, हट्ट cannot be rendered as stubbornness or obstinacy ? Cannot it be translated as stubborness ?

A. No the word cannot be used in the sense of stubbornness or obstinacy.

His Lordship:—Can it be rendered stubbornness ?

Q. What would be necessary to make it stubbornness ?

A. I cannot say.

Q. Suppose I add the words हट्ट किंवा दुराग्रह then would it mean stubbornness?

A. No.

Q. Could the meaning of the line हट्टानें किंवा दुराग्रहानें read stubbornness o perversity ?

A. I do not think so.

Q. Please look at the article of 19th May headed "A Double Hint" see the translation on page 3, 25th line "when several.........attempts."

Q. Turn to the article of 12th May, see the words "But the dispensations of God are extraordinary". What do you make extraordinary in Marathi ? A. वरचा नेमानेम. Q. What do you make नेमानेम ? A. Appointment or determination or destination. Q. How is it derived ? A. It is derived from नियम. Q. It is a reduplication of नेम-नियम ? A. That is not the meaning here. Q. You don't think it can be better rendered by rules ? A. Rules will not do. Q. Can it be rendered by the ways of God are strange ? A. Yes, it would do equally good. Q. Better ? A. I do not say better but equally. Q. What is the meaning of उर्मट ? A. Overbearing. Q. Rude ? A. Yes. Q. It is used as insulting, can we say impatiently ? A. Yes it might, I cannot say. Q. Not impudently=उर्मटपणें ? A. I cannot say offhand ; it may do. Q. You said just now impatiently would do ? A. I said I could not say offhand. I do not know the shades of meaning. Q. Look at the sentence "patience of humanity" would "human patience" do ? A. it might. Q. What is मनुष्यमात्र? A. It may be used as humanity. Q. Would you say the humanity of the English ? A. It is either an abstract or collective noun. Q. It may be equally well represented that way? A. But not literally. Q. What is क्षुब्ध? A. Excited, agitated or exasperated. Q. How did you translate it? A. As exasperated. Q. Turn to the sentence "inebriated with the insolence of authority" what is मद ? A. Insolence. Q. And धुंद ? A. Inebriated. Q. Does धुंद mean blind or inebriated? A. I do not know without looking at the dictionary. Q. What is धुंद ? A. Blind or dimmed or dulled vision; intoxication is the second meaning. Q. What is मद ? A. Arrogance, haughtiness, Q. What is the primary meaning? A. I do not know. I know that it means arrogance and haughtiness literally. Q. How do you render अधिकार-मदानें धुंद ? A. Blinded by the intoxication of power. Q. How do you render Monopoly ? A, एकट्यानें मक्ता घेतलेला. Q. Would सर्व मक्ता do ? A. Yes it would be a free rendering, but it would not express the meaning properly or accurately. Q. How do you render सर्व मक्ता ? A. Whole control. Q. How do you render असें झाल्याखेरीज रहणार नाहीं ? A. This cannot fail to happen. Q. It cannot but be so will be a proper translation ? A. It would be a free rendering. Q. How do you render असें असल्याखेरीज रहाणार नाहीं ? A. This cannot but be so. Q. His Lordship: What is the correct translation ? A. 'This cannot fail to be so.' Q. Give me the Marathi for Embark. It occurs in the sentence "cannot fail to embark" on page 2 ? A. प्रवृत्त होणें. Q. Is not "embarking" high flown rendering for प्रवृत्त होणें? A. It is the dictionary meaning. Q. How do you render जसें पेरावें तसें उगवतें ? A. As you sow so it grows or germinates. Q. Translate यथा बीजं तथांकुरः ? A. As the seed so is the sprout. Q. How do you translate शिरजोरपणा ?

Q. How would you translate ही बायको शिरजोर झाली आहे ? A. This woman is something of termagant. Q. In this sentence is not the word शिरजोर domineering ?

A. I cannot say without referring to the dictionary. Q. How do you translate this शिरजोर, बेहजद मनुष्य ? A. Headstrong, reckless, termagant. Q. How do you translate this (reads from Molesworth.) अधिकारी शिरजोर झाले.आहेत ? A. the authorities have become reckless. Q. Reckless or domineering ? A. No, not domineering. Q. Take this अरेरावी & शिरजोरपणा how would you render शिरजोरपणा ? A. Blustering, boasting, headstrong. Q. And अरेरावी ? A. High handedness, as in the High Court translation. Q. Take शिरजोर ? has that an allied meaning ? A. I cannot say; it has an allied meaning to अरेरावी. Q. Translate domineering into Marathi. A. हुकुम चालविणारा. Q. Domineering would not be अंमल गाजवणारा ? A. No, that would be different. Q. Is शिरजोरपणा Lording it over ? A. I do not know. Q. Will you translate Lording it over ? A. प्रभुत्व or अंमल चालविणारा. Q. साप साप म्हणून मारणें is म्हणून 'saying' or 'mistaking ?' A. The literal meaning is saying. Q. Mistaking will do for म्हणून ? A. No the meaning is saying and not mistaking. Q. सर्परज्जुदृष्टांत is a common illustration in Sanskrit or Marathi ? A. It may in Sanskrit but not in Marathi. Q. Translate त्यानें साखर म्हणून मीठ खाल्लें A. He ate salt thinking he was eating sugar. Q. Translate चोर म्हणून मला मारूं नका A. Do not beat me thinking I am a thief. Q. It would not mean "mistaking" me for a chief ? A. It may mean, in a far fetched way, "under the belief" or "mistaking for." Q. सहस्ररश्मी is omitted from the High Court translation; it is used to show intensity ? A. It is only an eloquent expression. I have not translated it. *His Lordship* :—Are those words omitted. A. Yes my Lord. *Accused* :—The words are omitted my Lord. They mean a "thousand-rayed" sun. Mr. Joshi has vouched for the High Court translation but now he says he is not responsible for it. Is the H. C. translator coming to depose ? *His Lordship* :—That is for the Prosecution to say. Advocate General : No my Lord we do not intend to call him. *His Lordship*:—It is not usual to call him; the High Court translation is generally accepted as a correct translation. Q. At page 4, line 9 of the translation you find the word King has a capital "K"? A. That is due to the Printer's devil. Q. राजा व प्रजा, what does it mean ? A. Ruler and ruled ? Q. Below again the capital K is used, is that also due to the printer's devil ? A. Yes, it should be a common noun. Q. राजा व प्रजा were the original words; what do they mean ? Q. King and subject. *His Lordship*:—It is a common noun ? A. Yes my Lord. *Accused*: Yes my Lord it is a common expression in Marathi राजा & प्रजा. It means ruler and ruled. Q. Would राजा mean many rulers ? A. No. Q. Turn to page 4, eighth line from the bottom "*regardless of its own life after all means of protection have become exhausted.*" The original word there is बचावाचे मार्ग, that means means of escape ? A. No, means of protection. Q. बचाव, would be protection ? A. No, it may mean protection, escape or resort according to the sense. Q. That is merely the simile of a stag at bay ? A. Yes. Q. How do you translate Political Science into Marathi and Science of Politics. A. Witness : I cannot at once. Q. राजनीतीचें शास्त्र and राजधर्माचें शास्त्र would that do ? A. Yes, it might. Q. How do you render Science laying down the duties of kings. A. राजधर्मशास्त्र. Q. Could we say असें राजधर्मशास्त्र कंठरवानें सांगत आहे ? A. Yes ? Q. You have said this means settled conclusions of the science ot politics ? A. It would be a paraphrase of the rendering. Q. Now let us turn to Exhibit E in the original. Look at the translation of the 3rd note, page 5 column 3. कलकत्त्याचें Statesman पत्र

मिशनऱ्यांच्या तंत्राचें असून how do you render that? A. Controlled by missionaries. Q. Not following the missionary policy? A. No. Q. Does तंत्र never mean policy? A. It means "subservience." Q. Never policy? A. I cannot say. I shall see the dictionary. Q. Have you consulted the dictionary? A. Yes, it means subservience; line of conduct, according to Molesworth. Q. What is आमचें तंत्र वेगळें, तुमचें तंत्र वेगळें? A. It means line of conduct. Q. In the 4th note the words राष्ट्रवध appear, how do you render them? A. National Assassination. It occurs in two places, which do you refer to? Q. In both. A. *Rastra* is nation and वध means to kill. Q. What does वध mean?—Assassination. Q. It means killing a nation? A. No. Q. Not killing nationality? A. No, assassination of a nation. Q. Then it may mean killing a nation? A. Yes, it may. Q. Then why did you say the word means "assassination" instead of killing. A. I have already told you it is not my translation. Q. Turn to the article of 2nd June; how do you translate हूल उठविणें? A. Raise a false report. Q. And according to Molesworth हूल means alarm or outcry? A. Yes. Q. Turn to page 2, line 49, you see the word "world" there, how do you translate that? A. It is a mistranslation or the translator has misread the original जगत or जगत्. Q. Then it is a mistake and the meaning is changed? A. Yes. Q. The translator has misread the original? A. Yes. Q. Look at Exhibit "D" the *Kesari* of 9th June, the second incriminating article. Take मुसलमानांची कडवी जात, How will you translate it? A. Savage. Q. Would you use the word fierce for कडवा instead of savage? A. Yes, savage, fierce, harsh would do. Q. Would it do to substitute stern or relentless? A. Yes. Q. How do you translate पौरुष? A. Manliness. Q. Is there no distinction between manhood and manliness? A. Yes, there may be a difference. Q. Take the dictionary and tell me. A. In Molesworth's dictionary there is "manhood". Q. In Apte's Dictionary there is "manhood?" A. No, Apte gives manliness, valour, courage, strength, power. Q. Do you still maintain that it means manhood? A. Yes, I maintain that पौरुष means that; here manhood is the proper word according to Molesworth. Q. How would you translate "When once the Indian people become emasculated it will be long before you can get them to recover their manliness and vigour?" A. एकदा हिंदुस्थानच्या लोकांचें मर्दानीपण नाहींसें झालें म्हणजे पुन्हां त्यांचें पौरुष आणि तेज परत त्यांना प्राप्त करून देण्यास पुष्कळ वेळ लागेल. Q. For what English word have you used पौरुष in the sentence? A. Manliness. Q. Now refer to the word emasculate in Candy's dictionary; what do you find? A. खसी करणें. Q. That is not different खसी & खची करणें? A. No. Q. What is the ordinary expression? A. खची करणें? Q. In the original passage the words are एकदा खची करणं & पौरुष. Which words do you translate as emasculation and manliness. A. In the original the words are castration and manhood. *His Lordship to Mr. Joshi*:—What are the original words in the Marathi. A. खची करणें & पौरुष. *The Advocate General*:—I understand my witness to say that it is correctly translated by the High Court translator in the official translation. Q. Take the sentence about the Empire of Delhi, the word रडत कडत may mean 'lingering death'? A. No, lingering in a wobbling manner. Q. What is in the original for the word heedless? A. बेगुमानपणानें. Q. Would it be better translated 'in an irresponsible way' A. No. Q. What is गुमान?. A. Heed or regard. Q. What is another equivalent? A. खातरें, पर्वा. Q. It may mean regard? A. Yes, regard or heed. Q. It means regard in this context? A. I cannot say. Q. How do you render "migratory bureaucracy" the words used by Burke?

A. उपरी अधिकारी वर्ग, not having a permanent residence. Q. उपरी अधिकारी would do ? A. It would be crude. Q. Will you accept migratory bureaucracy ? A. It might do, though it would not be the literal meaning. Q. Now look at the words "nose string" in ninth line of page 3, the original word is वेसण which means bridling in English ? A. Yes, the corresponding English idea is bridling. Q. What is नाहक in English ? A. Gratuitous, I am giving it offhand. Q. नाहक, what does that mean ? A. Literally it means causeless. Q. How do you translate बोलून चालून ? A. Openly, avowedly. Q. Not admittedly ? A. Yes but that would be stretching it further still. Q. Admittedly or avowedly would do in that case ? A. It goes without saying that it will mean those words. Q. Now take up the article of the 26th May. What is the real meaning of हितशत्रु ? A. One who is adverse to the weal of others. Q. Do You take षष्ठी तत्पुरुष ? A. I did not know the word. I referred to the dictionary for it. Q. You have translated it as welfare? A. Yes. Q. Is it not हितश्च शत्रुश्च ? would that be false ? A. Indirectly. Q. Do you mean to say that the words do not convey the meaning of a false friend ? A. I am not prepared to give an opinion. Q. Can it be rendered as an enemy in the garb of a friend ? A. I have not seen it rendered in that light before. I hesitate to say so in the face of Molesworth. Q. Is the word हित used for friend ? A. No, it is used for welfare. Q. Does वक्रदृष्टि mean evil glance ? A. Literally it means cross glance. Q. Does it not mean disfavour ? A. That may be its remote meaning. Q. How would you translate त्यांची आमच्यावर वक्रदृष्टि झाली आहे ? A. He is looking with an evil glance at me. Literally he is looking at me with an evil eye or with disfavour. Q. Look at page 2 and the third line, you see there 'look with disfavour upon the people ?' A. Yes. Q. Look at page 2 line 3 " malignant eye." A. It can be made 'disfavour' but that would be a remote meaning. Q. How do you translate गळ्याला मिठी मारणें ? A. To throw one's arms round another's neck; to embrace. Q. On the same page 2, 3rd line, the rendering is to catch him by the neck. A. The more literal translation is to throw one's arms round the neck. His Lordship.—Then that is not the correct translation ? A. It is rather uncouth but correct. Q. Then the difference between embracing and catching by the neck is only uncouthness ? A. Catch is used in its literal sense.

At this stage the Court adjourned for lunch.

On the Court re-assembling Mr. Tilak was about to recommence the cross-examination of Mr. Joshi when his Lordship remarked, that he had noticed certain remarks in the *Bombay Gazette*, which were not only untrue but objectionable and he warned the press.

The passage to which his Lordship took exception was the following :—

The accused complained tnat the official translation did not give the correct equivalents in English. And that was the burden of his complaint. He was allowed to cross-examine the writness at further length, as though the witness was competing at a prize competition.

Application was then made for the use of books of reference in the High Court Library for the purposes of Mr. Tilak's defence.

His Lordship said he would allow the legal advisers of Mr. Tilak to see him at all times but the Bar Library was not under his control.

The cross-examination of Mr. Joshi was then continued by Mr. Tilak.

Q. What is the meaning of एकमुखी ? A. The dictionary meaning is 'one-sided.' Q. In what sense is it used in this article ? A. I have translated it autocratic. Q. It is a coined word? A. Yes. Q. Do you know that the word सनदशीर is used in the article? It means constitutionally? That is a coined word, is it not? A. Yes. Q. अडवणूक translate that. A. It means literally resistence. Q. It is a new word used by journalists and means passive resistance? A. It means obstruction. His Lordship: Is it now used by journalists in the sense of resistance? A. Yes. Q. Similarly बहिष्कार is the word used in sense of boycott? A. Yes. Q. It is a new meaning given to the word? A. Yes, it has a different meaning in the common sense. Q. These meanings cannot be found in Molesworth, Candy's or Apte's Dictionaries? A. No, I do not think so. Q. All these words have new meanings which have come into use during recent times? A. Yes. Q. The dictionaries would be no good in assertaining the meanings of these words? A. No. Q. Much in the same way as Johnson's Dictionary is useless for modern scientific terms. A. I am not an expert in English. Q. Let us take an old English dictionary published thirty years ago for determining the modern political terms. A. They would be of no use. Q. I asked you yesterday to bring me your translation of the word "error of judgment" the Marathi of which you took time to compose; have you got it with you? A. Yes, it may be translated विवेकविभ्रम. Q. Is that from current Marathi literature? A. No, it is a coined word. Q. You have just coined it? A. No. Yasterday. Q. You have coined it because there has been no reason to express the idea before in Marathi A. I coined it yesterday as there is no expression for it in Marathi so for as I know. Q. Is the word बुद्धि used in the sense of विवेक in Sanskrit? A. Yes, it is used in Sanskrit. Q. मन is distinct from बुद्धि? You have a passage in the Bagwat Gita—मनसस्तु पराबुद्धिः; now can the word बुद्धि be substituted for विवेक? A. Yes. Q. In विवेकविभ्रम the word बुद्धि may be used for विवेक. A. Yes. Q. How would you translate विवेकभ्रष्टानां भवति विनिपातः शतमुखः? A. One who has fallen from his judgment, one whose judgment has been destroyed. Q. It may mean one who has erred in his judgment? A. No. Q. विवेकभ्रष्ट would be milder? A. Yes. Q. भ्रंश primarily means to fall, and भ्रष्ट fallen,-not destroyed. A. Yes. *His Lordship*: Does the word बुद्धिभ्रष्ट mean suffering from aberration of the intellect? A. Yes. Q. बुद्धिभ्रष्ट is the same as विवेकभ्रष्ट? One whose intellect has sufferred aberration, one who has fallen from his बुद्धि? A. Yes. Q. In your official capacity I suppose you have to read the Marathi newspapers? A. Yes. Q. And it may be taken that you are well acquainted with the general thought of those papers? A. Yes. *Witness to Court.* Am I being taken into confidential matters? *His Lordship.* No. I don't think so. Q. You are acquainted with the general trend? A. Yes, in my official capacity Q. Can you tell us if there are any parties amongst the Marathi newspapers? A. I do not think I can answer that question. *His Lordship:*—You are asked whether there are parties? A. I wish your Lordship to decide whether I should give an answer in my private or official capacity. *His Lordship:*—Do you read the papers in two different ways, one as an official, and the other as a private individual? Well, reading the Marathi papers as you read them are these newspapers divided as classes agianst one another? A. Yes, There are parties and I will give that answer in my private capacity. *His Lordship*: Have you a different opinion in your official capacity? A. There are parties. Q. How many? A. I cannot say exactly how many. Q. About? A.

Three or four parties. Q. Can you give us the leading exponent of each of the 3 or 4 parties ? A. Of the Anglo-Marathi and Marathi party the *Kesari* is the leading exponent of one party. *His Lordship*: Did you say leading exponent ? A. Yes, my Lord. Q. And the next ? A. The *Indu Prakash* is the leader of another party, the *Shudharak* is of another party and the *Subodha Patrika* of the other party. Q. You have given four parties, have you left no political party out of your enumeration ? A. No. This closed the cross examination of Mr. Joshi. The Advocate General then re-examined Mr. Joshi.

Re-examination.

Q. With re-ference to the articles and words which have been referred to in this case and the lengthy cross-examination, can you from your own knowledge of those articles, can you tell me what would be the effect of those articles on the minds of the ordinary subscribers to the *Kesari ? Accusd* :—My Lord, does this arise out of cross-examination? It is a matter of opinion to be formed by the jury. *His Lordship*: It is a legitimate question arising out of your cross examination. *Advocate General.* I wanted to know the opinion of the ordinary reader. Q. You have been ten years Oriental translater to Government ? A. Yes. A. Having gone through the offiicial translation made by High Court are you satisfied that these translations are correct ? A. Yes. I am. Q. Except one word जग which should have been जग and not उग्र ? A. Yes. Q. What is the vernacular word for stubbornness ? A. दुराग्रह. Q, That might be interpreted into the English word stubbornness in the article of 12th May 1908 ? Is something wanted in the translation of the English expression ? A. Yes. Q. Can you supply the missing part ? A. Obstinate retention of a wrong opinion. Q. Now you were asked about the word " embark. " Will you give me the vernacular for that word ? A. प्रवृत्त. Q. Is that correctly translated in 'embark? A. Yes. Q. See the bottom of page and top of page three; do you see the word ' Indignation ?' Is that correctly translated ? Q. Yes. Q. Then you were asked also about the word " assassination", which appears in more than one place of the articls of 12th May ? Q. Yes. Q. What is the Vernacular expression for the word ? A. वध. Q. Does that correctly translate the English word assassination? A. yes. Q. I think it was suggested to you that the word 'kill' is probably more correct representing 'to slaughter' than 'to assassinate'? A. I do not agree with that. *His Lordship*: You say 'kill' is not the right expression? A. No. Advocate-General:-Will you tell his Lordship and the Jury whether assassintion is the proper meaning and whet her you prefer it to killing ? *His Lordship* : Why do you think assassination is more proper than killing? A. नारायणराव पेशव्याचा वध-That menas the assassination of Narayenrao Peshwa; गोवध means slaughter of cows. वध-means assassination. *His Lordship*: Then the word वध is translated killing, slaughter or assassination according to the context ? A. Yes. Q. Now you were asked about parties in the native press. You said the *Kesari* was one ; is it the leading papet ? A. Yes. Q. To what party does the paper belong ? A. The party known as the Extremists are the Nationalist party. Q. Do you know who is editor of the paper ? A. Yes Q. Who is it ? A. The accused. Q. Do you know who is the proprietor ? A.

Yes, the accused. *His Lordship* :—I don't think that arises out of the cross-examination. *Advocate General* :—The object was to prove that there are parties in the native press and we have to show that the *Kesari* represents the extremists and that the accused is Editor and proprietor. *His Lordship* :—The accused did not ask about the Editors of the other papers.

Advocate General:—Well, if your Lordship thinks it is not permissible I will not press it. There are other materials which will prove the Proprietor and publisher of the *Kesari* ; and that he is editor also.

His Lordship:—I have no admission of his editorship before me.

Advocate General:—He described himself before the Magistrate as an editor. He did not say he is editor of the *Kesari*. I propose to put in his declarations made under Act. 25 of 1867 and a copy of this declaration is permissible as evidence. It was for the purpose of convinience and saving time I asked the witness whether accused was Editor and proprietor of the *Kesari*.

His Lordship:—Of course the court has a right to ask any question but I do not wish to do so.

Advocate General:—I quite understand the delicacy of your Lordship's position and the way you have directed the witness. I only thought perhaps it would be much better for the accused to admit this.

His Lordship:—If the accused wishes to make that statemant of course I'l hear him.

Advocate General:—If I have gone further than I ought in pressing this it was only to save time. I will put in the two declarations in due course.

Accused:—We are not going to dispute that point. I am Editor, Publisher and Proprietor of the *Kesari*, and I accept full respensibility of the articles in question.

His Lordship:—You admit this?

A. Yes. My Lord.

His Lordship.—And you accept responsibility for all the Exhibits from C to I ?

A. Yes, My Lord.

Advocate Generel:—As a mere matter of form I will put in the declarations of the accused dated 1st July 1867 both dated the same day. They are declarations befor the first calss Magistrate of Poona and the certified copies here are evidence under section 7 and the following sections of Act. 25 of 1867.

That will save considerable time and that will set free Mr. Tilak's compositers. I do not wish to detain them here as their services are required at Poona.

Mr. Joshi: —Am I done with Your Lordship ?

His Lordship :—Yes, you may go.

Advocate General :—We have two short witnesses to prove publication in Bombay and as I do not apprehend that they will be cross-examined we may be able to put up the witness who searched the house.

NARAYAN JUGANNATH DATAR.

Examined by Mr. Binning:—

Q. You are a clerk in the Customs Reportor General's Department ?

A. Yes.

Q. Where do you live ?

A. Kandewadi.

Q. In addition to your occupation do you do any other business ?

A. Yes.

Q. What is it ?

A. The agency of the *Kesari* and the *Maratha.*

Q. During the period 12th May and 9th June 1908 ?

A. Yes.

Q. Where is your agency. ?

A. In Bombay.

Q. When did you begin to be agent to the *Kesari* ?

A. Off and on I have been connected with the agency of the *Kesari* for the past 25 years.

His Lardship: since when did you last become agent ?

A. Since 1886.

Q. Were you agent in 1908.

A. yes, up till July 4th,

His Lordship:—When did you begin the last time to be agent ?

A. About 1900.

His Lordship :—And you gave it up on the 4th of July 1908.

A. Yes.

Q. As agent of the *Kesari*, what had you to do ?

A. I kept accounts and made clerks do the work.

Q. Kept accounts of what ?

A. How many copies were sold.

Q. How many copies did you receive each week ?

A. About 3000; the number has been changing this year.

Q. Now generally you got about 3000 copies in May ?

A. Yes, sometimes a hundred or two less.

His Lordship :—About 2800 in May ?

Q. How many subscribers are there in Bombay ?

A. 1250.

Q. Do you read the paper yourself ?

A. Yes.

Q. See Exhibits C and D, did you read these articles ?

A. Yes.

Q. And were copies of these sent to you at Bombay ?

A. Yes.

Q. Do you see Exhibits C to B. 19, 26 May and 2 June ? did you receiv those issues in Bombay ?

A. Yes.

Q. You supplied them to subscribers ?

A. Yes.

Q. Every week ?

A. Yes.

Q. What is the cost of subscription ?

A. Rs. 1-12 per year in Bombay.

Q. And to non-subscribers.

A. 3 pice (9 pies).

His Lordship :—Mr. Tilak, do you wish to cross-examine ?

Accused :—No, my Lord.

His Lordship to Witness :—You say, you kept copies and your accounts, did you return unsold copies ?

A. They were sold here.

Q. What was the honorarium paid to you ?

A. It was fixed.

Q. How much ?

A. Rupees 30 per month.

Q. Did you supply a copy to the Translator's office ?

A. I do not remember.

Rupat Rama was called but was not present.

Balvant Krishnaji was called but was also not present.

Advocate General :—I wont waste time in asking for warrants.

His Lordship :—What were they to prove.

Advocate General :—That they were sold in the street.

His Lordship :—Please recall the last witness.

His Lordship to Witness :—Besides sending 1250 copies to subscribers 1600 or 1700 copies were left, how did you sell those ?

A. I sold them to the news boys.

Q. what do they pay?

A. $\frac{1}{2}$ anna per copy.

Q. The news boys make 1 pice (three pies) on each copy?

A. Yes.

Peter Sullivan (Bombay Police) examined by Mr. Binning.

Q. Your name is Peter Sullivan?

A. Yes.

Q. You are an Inspector of the Bombay Police?

A. Yes.

Q. Now in this case did you get a warrant for Execution in Poona?

A. Yes.

Q. Was it for the search of the house of Mr. Tilak

A. Yes.

Q. For the press and office?

A. Yes.

Q. You got it from the Chief Presidency Magistrate, Bombay?

A. Yes.

Q. Who was it executed by

A. By Mr. Davis, District Superintendent of Police, Poona.

Q. Were you present when the warrant was executed?

A. I was.

Q. And when the premises of Mr. Tilak were searched were you there?

A. Yes.

Q. That is to say press and office and house searches. Were you present at all?

A. Yes, I was.

Q. Who actually conducted the search of the office and press?

A. The search was conducted in the presence of the District Superintendent of Police assisted by myself and Deputy Superintendent Power and other police officers.

His Lordship:—Give me the names.

Q. Mr. Daniels—Assistant Superintendent, Mr. Power—Deputy Superintendent and Mr. King—City Inspector, myself and some native officers.

A. Mr. Davis D. S. P. was also there?

Q. Yes, my Lord.

Mr. Binning.—And was Mr. Kelkar there ?

A. He was present.

Q. Did you yourself find anything in the course of the search ?

A. I did.

Q. What did you find ?

A. Amongst other things. I found a post card with some writing upon it.

Q. Is this the card you found ?

A. Yes.

Q. Where was it found ?

A. In the top right hand drawer of the writing table in a room in Mr. Tilak's residence apparently used as an office.

His Lordship:—I understand that you tell me that the press, residence and office are in the hame house ?

A. No, my Lord, they are joined. The residence is on one side.

His Lordship:—Are the places separate or joined ?

A. The press is separate, the other places are joined.

Q. And this was found in a room in Mr. Tilak's residence apparently used as an office ?

A. Yes.

Mr. Binning;—Now when you found that card what did you do with it ?

A. I showed it to Mr. Davis and Mr. Power and also to Mr. Kelkar.

Q. Did you hand it over to any body or did you keep it yourself ?

A. I did.

Q. Did you produce it before the Magistrate in Bombay ?

A. I did.

Q. Having kept the card till now you produce it ?

His Lordship.—Were you entrusted with it all the time till you produce it ?

A. I was, my Lord.

Mr. Binning:—Did Mr. Kelkar initial it ?

Accused;—Mr. Kelkar is here and what he said is not evidence.

His Lordship:—I was watching for that, Mr. Tilak.

Accused:—Mr. Kelkar initialled it, what has that got to do with it ? Is it relevant ?

Advocate General:—Of course if:—Accused says it was found in his drawer there is no need to go any further. This is all very informal, my Lord, I now tender it as evidence against the accused as showing thas it was in his possession. Whether it carries the case further or not is another matter. That depends upon the evidence. But the fact is that it was found in his residence, in a drawer in a table in the room occupied by him.

I would draw your Lordship's attention to the case decided by Lord Campbell and Chief Justice Pollock, in Crown V Bernard, reported in Forster and Findlayson at Page 240. I point to this case as having a very direct bearing on this.

His Lordship:—His Lordship directs against.

Advocate General:—Yes, my Lord.

Advocate General:—The other case, my Lord, I will refer to very shortly but this case is so absolutely on the point that I shall draw your Lordship's attention to it first. The facts are stated in page 386 of Russell on Crimes, the latest edition:—(Reads " when a trial for murder &c. " to" admissable.") Your Lordship will see directly, that there is the writing of the person on this card. Of course in the case under reference the letter was written by a third person and here is Russell's comment on it:—(Reads from " all the person") I think I must state what the contents are in order that you may consider the question of law in regard to the admission.

His Lordship:—I would rather you did not state them.

Advocate General ;—If your Lordship thinks I ought not to, I will not. Will your Lordship take a look at it ? (Hands card up to court) Your Lordship is, no doubt, familar with the case in England, which differed to a certain extent from the present case where the accused were charged with murder and among other items of evidence produced by the prosecution were entries in the handwriting of the accused showing that he had been stocking poisons including the poison with which the crime was committed. (Reads from 387 of Forester and Findlayson. In this case entries were admitted in evidence. Your Lordship will find (Reads from same page from "if the papers" to "that of the person") That my Lord is a case in Crown Pleas Chapter 11, page 119. Now I do not wish to say what is on the card, till his Lornship decides whether it may be admitted. But there can be no question that it has a very close application to the charges which are framed and more especially those which my learned friend Mr. Inverarity referred to towards the close of his adress. I will not say any thing more upon it until the admissibilty of the card is considered. It wont take the Jury two minutes to see what the contents are.

His Lordship to accused:—Do you wish to say anything ?

Accused:—The only thing I would point out is that if it is relevent in the case your Lordship may admit it. I leave it to you, the only question is a relevancy;

His Lordship:—But what is the point you urge ?

Accused:—That the contents are not relevant. I do not wish to deny possession of the card though it was found behind my back.

His Lordship:—I do not follow you.

Accused:—The contents are not relevant to the facts of the case. That is my only objection.

His Lordship:—This is a document found in the possession of the accused in the course of a search under a warant and I have no option but to admit the card.

Advocate General:—The card is one of those folding ones. On one side you have

" Hand book of modern explosives " by M. Eissler published by Crosby and Lockwood 13/6; " Nitro Explosives " by Gerard Sanford 9/—" and on the other side ' Modern Explosives ' by Esiel Explosives " by Crosby and Lockwood. I tender it my Lord,

(Exhibit)

This was passed round to the jury.

Inspector Sullivan Cross Examined by accused.

Q. Did you find any other papers in the search ?

A. Yes.

Q. Can you get those here ?

A. No, they were taken to the Court and are in possession of the Magistrate.

His Lordship:—You brought them to Bombay ?

A. Yes, my Lord.

Q. You have not brought them here ?

A. No,

His Lordship to acucsed:—Do you want any of them sent for ?

Accused:—Yes all of them, My Lord.

His Lordship:—Will you see Mr. Advocate General that they are produced tomorrow ?

Accused:—I may ask those questions tomorrow.

His Lordship:—You want to ask him some questions on those papers ?

A. Yes.

His Lordship:—You may ask them tomorrow.

The Advocate General;—These papers are in the custody of the Cleark of the Crown, we have nothing to do with them. We can show a list of all that was found. Do you want the list or papers, Mr. Tilak ?

Accused:—I want the papers themselves.

His Lordship:—Can you go on with the witness now, excepting those matters relating to the papers ?

Accused:—Yes.

His Lordship:—Well, go on with him now.

Q. Did you go into my Library ?

A. I don't know, we went into several rooms in the house with the D. S. P. Poona. I don't know if one of them was the library.

Q. All the other papers were found in the same desk ?

A. I don't know how many of the other papers were found.

His Lordship:—Were they found in the same drawer ?

A. I think so my Lord.

Q. Was the drawer locked ?

A. No it was open.

Q. Do you know if anyone searched the library ?

A. They might have, I dont remember.

Q. You did not do so yourself ?

A. No.

Q. Where did you find this card ? Lying at the top or did you have to search it ?

A. The card was amongst the other papers.

Q. Was it down deep ?

A. I do not think that it was at the top. I was looking at the papers to examine them.

Q. You got down all the papers from the drawer on the floor ?

A. No, I brought them out one by one on the top of the table. I took some and Mr. Power took some.

Q. The papers were taken out and placed on the table and then examined.

A. No they were taken out one by one and examined.

Q. How many papers were there in the drawer ?

A. I cannot tell you, I did not count.

Q. About how many ?

A. I really cannot tell.

Q. 10, 20, 50 ?

A. I suppose there were some hundreds.

Q. How many other papers did you take from the drawer?

A. I have a list here of the papers I took.

His Lordship:—Have you a list of all the papers you brought to Bombay ?

A. Yes, my Lord, I put them in a small envelope.

Q. Can you produce the list ?

A. I produce the *panchnama* and a copy in English. The original is written in Marathi.

His Lorbship:—May I see the English Copy?

Q. You have the list and copy

A. Yes.

Advocate General:-There is the *Panchnama* in Marathi conning the effects of the Search and the things found.

Accused:—I do not want the Panchnama, I only want the list. You don't remember how many other papers were taken from the drawer?

A. So far as my memory serves me there were cuttings from I think American papers. They are all here in the possession of Magistrate.

Q. How many papers were there in the drawer ?

A. I do not remember.

Q. Now just try to remember whether there were 10, 20 or 50. I do not ask you how many papers there were, in the drawer, I want to know how many were taken out.

A. That I cannot say.

Q. In the whole search how many papers were taken?

A. The panchnama was written in Marathi I have only a copy. 63 items appear on the list.

Q. I am not talking about the panchnama. You gave some evidence from memory now. I want you to tell me in the same way, how many papers, about were taken from my house.

A. I cannot.

Accused.—I ask my Lord that the further examination of this witness may be left till to-morrow as I must have those papers.

His Lordship :—You wanted some books, have you asked your Solicitor to give you a list of the books ? I will try to see that you have them.

His Lordship :—Gentlemen of the jury, before you come to-morrow, I would be glad if you devoted some little time to the articles before you. You will have to go into 7 articles, Exhibits "C" to "I." I will be glad if you will be good enough to read those articles carefully before you come here tomorrow and then you will be in a better position to hear both sides.

The Court then adjourned till Wednesday 15th July 1908.

Proceedings of the Third Da;

Wednesday 15th July 1908.

Cross Examination of Inspector Sullivan continued:—

Mr. Tilak:—Have you got the papers which you were asked yesterday to produce this morning? A, Yes, I believe they are here. Q. All the papars that you found in the search? A. Yes, as far as I know, I have not seen them.

His lordship:—Do you want them ?

Accused:—Yes, in fact these papers were got behind my back. I was not there.

His Lordship:—Would you like to see them?

Accused:—Yes, before I put any in.

His Lordship—You may go round there and look at them.

After Examinning some bundles, accused returned to his place of the table and said:—My Lord, they have got a few books here. The other papers, taken from my desk are not here.

His Lordship:—Are all the papers taken, here, Mr. Sullivan ?

Inspector Sullivan:—Apparently not, my Lord. There are some newspaper cuttings and letters which are not here.

His Lordship:—Yesterday accused asked for these papers and they should have been here.

Advocate General:—They are not in the Police custody.

His Lordship:—But surely the Magistrate should have sent them all on.

Advocate General:—I believe that a man from the Clerk of the Crown has gone to fetch the other papers.

His Lordship to Accused:—You can go on with the Cross-examination, and when the other papers come I will let you have them.

Accused to witness:—

Q. Did you go to Singhad to search my house there ? A. Yes. Q. Had you a warrant ? A. Yes, a warrant-issued by the Chief Presidency Magistrate, Bombay and endorsed by the City Magistrate of Poona. Q. To search my house at Singhad Specifically ? A. To search the house there. Q. At Singhad or at Poona ? A. At Singhad. Q And for the Poona house there was a separate warrant ? A. No. the same one. Q. Was Sinhgad specifically mentioned therein ? A. By the district Magistrate, yes. Q. The Presidency Magistrate did not mention it. A. He mentioned your residences. Q. The Presidency Magistrate did not mention Singhad.

A. But the Disttict Magistrate did.

Witness to His Lordship:—It must be remembered that I only assisted in the execution of the warrant.

Q. You have signed the warrant? A. Yes. Q. Then you can tell me who added Sinhgad in the warrant. A. The warrant was not entrusted to me but to the District Superintendent of Police, Poona.

His Lordship :—The question is was Sinhagad mentioned in the warrant.

A. Not to my recollection.

His Lordship :—Do you recollect when the District Magistrate at Poona added Singhad to the warrant?

A. I don't know when, but I believe he had. Q. Have you got the warrant here now? A. It was returned in the ordinary course to the Presidency Magistrate. Q. I want to know from you if it is among the many miscellaneous papers which have been brought here from the Magistrate's Court.

Advocate General :—The clerk has, I believe, gone to the Magistrate's Court for all the papers.

Accused :—I request your Lordship to order it to be brought from the Magistrate's Court.

His Lordship :—I should like to know your point with regard to this search warrant.

Accused :—I wish to know about the manner of the search. I am coming to that, my Lord.

Q. Did you take any of my men to Sinhagad? A. No, you had a watchman there. Q. I think you should answer my question. You did not take any of my men or my clerk or relation to Sinhagad. A. No. Q. Did you open the door yourself or did the servant? Q. No, the servant opened it for us. Q. And the cupboards, I believe you opened them and broke the locks without the servant's permission. A. We had no keys and we opened them. Q. In spite of his remonstrance? A. No, he did not remonstrate.

Inspector Sullivan :—I should like to state that there were two cupboards opened.

Accused :—Cupboards in the wall?

A. Yes. Q. You have stated that you did not take any of my men from Poona, did you inform them that you were going to Sinhagad? A. No, I did not. Q. Did you get anything from Sinhagad? A. No, nothing. Q. You left the broken locks as they were? A. The locks were not broken, hinges were loosened. Q. The hinges were loosened and you searched the cupboards? A. Yes. Q. And it did not occur to you to put then in order again. A. No I could not. Q. Now about these papers, have they come? A. No.

His Lordship:—If there are any questions you desire to ask when the papers come, you can have Mr. Sullivan recalled.

Advocate General:—I will now put in the statement of the accused made before the magistrate.

His Lordship;—That is all the evidence for the Prosecution.

Clerk of Crown:—The accused Bal Gandhar Tilak was asked by the magistrate if he wished to make a statement before him. His reply in case No 16 was:— "I wish to reserve my statement for the Sessions Court.

In Case No 17 his reply was:—" "I wish to reserve my statement"

His Lordship :—Under section 289 C. P. C. now I would be entitled to examine you. I do not purpose to ask you any questions. You are entitled to make any statement you like now, in order to enable you to explain any of the evidence brought against you. If you are not going to enter any evidence you will have the right of reply after the Advocate General has spoken.

If you wish to bring evidence then you can adress the Jury now.

Accused:-I wish to make a statement. There are certain facts in the papers which I want to incorporate in my statement as evidence. I cannot do without the papers.

His Lordship:—You understand at present in this case the prosecution made no use of any of your papers except the post card.

Accused:—Yes, but I cannot explain the post card unless I have the papers.

Advocate General:—I make no objection, I understand the accused wishes to examine the papers which have been left behind. He and his advisers have been supplied with a list of these papers.

His Lordship:—Are the papers which have been left behind in the list?

Advocate Gen.:—Mr. Tilak says they are. There are 63 bundles of papers mentioned.

His Lordship:—They asy some of these papers are not here.

Advocate General:—I do not know but I believe it is correct.

His Loprdship:—Such omission should never have taken place.

Advocate General:—Well that has nothing to do with us. Your Lordship must quarrel with the magistrate.

His Lordship:—The accussd gave notice last evening of all that he wanted and the papers should have been here. If that had been done, all this waste of time of the court and of the jury would not have taken place.

Advocate General:—That has really nothing to do with us, My Lord.

His Lordship:—I think that as the prosecution you are assisted by the police and it should have been seen to that these papers were brought to the Court.

Advocate General:—They have passed them on to the Poona Magistrate, my Lord.

His Lordship:—But surely if the magistrate had been told, he would have sent all the papers here.

Advocate General:—Perhaps the accused can't say which of the 63 bundle he wants.

Accused:—All those papers brought here, My Lord, were taken from my office. We want the papers which were taken from my residence.

His Lordship:—to Advocate General (after some considerable time had been spent waiting.) Don't you think it would be desirable to send a responsible officer to the police court to hurry up the papers?

Advocate General:—I am told one has already gone, my Lord.

Accused:—My Lord, in order to utilize the time, will your Lordship allow me, in anticipation of my statement, to put in certain papers which I wish to use in my defence ?

His Lordship:—Do you want to put them in as Exhibits ? I suppose you know that course gives the Advocate General the right of reply.

Accused:—Yes, we have decided upon that course although it gives the right of reply to the other side.

His Lordship:—You have considered that ?

Accused:—Yes.

His Lordship:—I cannot proceed further till you tell me whether you wish to make a statement now.

Accused:—Yes I do, but I cannot yet decide what papers are to go in as Exhibits among the missing papers.

His Lordship:—I cannot proceed further till you make that statement.

Advocate General:—I have the warrants here now my Lord; the other papers might be checked with the list to see what we have.

His Lordship:—Perhaps some one will check them on behalf of the accused and Inspector Sullivan on behalf of the Police.

Mr. Kelkar on behalf of Mr. Tilak and Mr. Sullivan on behalf of the police then checked the papers in court.

Accused:—On comparing the Panchanama of papers with the papers which are here, I think it is only the papers which were found in the office that are here. The papers were in my desk in the drawers, viz. telegrams, letters, are not here. Those that were marked and initialled are not here.

His Lordship:—(Reads a letter from the Police Magistrate.) My information is that there are no other papers in the Presidency Magistrate's office. The accused's complaint is that items 19 to 52 are not here.

Advocate General:—I will just ask Mr. Sullivan if he knows anything about it. I put in the original Panchanama. It has been produced. Where is the man from the Magistrate's office ?

His Lordship:—It seems to me that the Magistrate's clerk was in charge of the papers; the papers were not in charge of the Crown officers. The man was told not to leave but he is apparently not here.

Advocate General:—I am told that the Magistrate's clerk was told in the presence of the Crown officials that he might go and search for the missing paper.

His Lordship:—Has he gone back to his office ?

Advocate General:—Yes my Lord and Mr. Sullivan has gone also.

Advocate General:—I understand that Mr. Tilak and his advisers wish to state deliberately that there is something in these papers of which they wish to make use. From Nos. 19 to 52.

His Lordship:—Yes from 19 to 52, except No. 46. The note I have taken is that accused says he will make a statement when those papers which are not here are produced.

Advocate General:—Your Lordship has a list from 19 to 52. It will be curious hereafter to see how this allegation as to whether there are seriously any papers amongst these papers is supported.

Accused:—I made no allegations. Certainly there are some papers which may throw some light upon matters.

His Lordship:—You say you cannot make any statement till you have these papers.

Accusd:—I must make some explanation. I cannot explain the post-card without seeing what there is in the papers; perhaps the papers will throw some light upon that.

Advocate General:—It will be hereafter significant to point out how many of those papers are found to be necessary for the purpose of the defence.

Accused:—I make no allegation. I have not yet seen the papers.

Advocate General:—I understand Mr. Tilak to say that he has not seen the papers. Will your Lordship look at the list?

His Lordship:—Has Mr. Sullivan been sent for?

Advocate General:—Yes, my Lord.

After some lapse of time Inspector Sullivan returned.

Advocate General:—I put Mr. Sullivan back in the witness-box, my Lord.

Q. Do you produce the original Panchanama in Marathi?

A. I do.

His Lordship:—You produce the original Panchanama made on 26th May when the search warrant was executed?

Q. Yes my Lord.

Q. Are these the warrants of which you have been speaking?

A. Yes.

His Lordship:—Are there two?

A. Yes my Lord. Two different warrants.

His Lordship:—Of two different dates?

A. No. For two different places. One is for the *Kesari* press and the other for the residence.

Advocate General:—I put in the warrants and Panchanama.

Q. Have you translations of the Panchanama, dated 25th June 1908? A. Yes.

His Lordship:—Is it an official translation? A. No, it is made by a Police Officer in Bombay.

Advocate General:—We can have official translations made if your Lordship thinks it necessary and Mr. Tilak's advisers think it is necessary.

At 1-15 P. M.

His Lordship :—Have the papers been found Mr. Advocate General ?

Advocate General :—Yes, my Lord, they have been found.

His Lordship :—Let them be opened and examined ?

After the papers had been examined by Mr. Tilak.

At 1-45 P. M.

His Lordship :—Do you wish to ask Mr. Sullivan any questions ?

Advocate General :—Will your Lordship take a note that all the rest of the papers have been produced and shown to the accused ?

Cross-examination of Inspector Sullivan was then continued by Mr. Tilak.

Q. Can you say whether the papers now produced were found on the top of the table or in the drawers ? A. Some were found on top and some in the drawers.

Q. You cannot say which were found in the drawer and which on top ? A. So far as my recollection goes the large Mss. were found on top and the smaller papers such as newspaper cuttings were found in the drawers. Q. Can you point them out taking the list in your hand. A. I might do one or two but not all, because we had to go through four hundred papers.

Accused :—The search warrants have been put in my Lord. May they be given to the witness ?

Q. Look at that search warrant, turn to the endorsement on the back. A. To which are you alluding.

His Lordship :—To the Magistrate's endorsement.

Q. It is the signature of the City Magistrate ? A. Yes. Q. It was not taken to the District Magistrate ? A. When I got to Poona it was late in the evening and the District Magistrate was not at home, so I went to the City Magistrate, that being addressed to either the District or City Magistrate.

His Lordship :—The District Magistrate was not at home so you carried it to the City Magistrate ?

A. Yes, my Lord. Q. On what date was it endorsed by the City Magistrate ? A. On the 24th of June. Q. Do you know when, morning or evening ? A. Yes, in the evening. Q. When did you go to my residence ? A. I went the following morning. Q. At 2 A. M. ? A. No, at daybreak. Q. When did you return it executed ? A. I did not execute the warrant. It was returned on 25th June executed. His Lordship:—The warrant against the residence ?

A. Yes, my Lord. Q. When did you finish your search ? A. Which search ? Q. The search of the residence ? A. Where ? Q. At Poona ? A. At 9-30 or 10 A. M. Q. Say between 9 & 10 a. m ? A. Yes. Q. When did you start for Sinhagad ? A. At about 12 noon. Q. Who went with you ? A. Mr. Davis, District Superintendent of Police of Poona and Mr. Power, Deputy Superintendent of Police. Q. Now between 9 & 12 noon it was returned to the District Magistrate and a further endorsement to search the house at Sinhagad was obtained? A. Not to my knowledge. His Lordship: You don't know yourself? A. No, my Lord. Q. Was the warrant with you when you went to Sinhagad? A. It was with the District Superintendent of Police Mr. Davis to whom it was entrusted. Q. Did you see it with him? A. Yes, I saw it with him. Q. Now the papers found in the residence did you see if they tallied with the list given in the Panchanama. A. To which are you referring? Q. To Poona. A. House?

His Lordship:—What you took at Poona was it in the course of what you were ordered to search?

A. Yes, my Lord I believe so.

Accused:—I ask, my Lord, that the papers should be bundled up as one bundle and exhibited as one Exhibit in the case.

His Lordship:—All the papers that were last brought in?

Accused:—Yes, my Lord, those that were last brought in.

His Lordship:—You want to put in the whole of them?

Accused:—Yes.

His Lordship:—I will let you do that when the time comes.

His Lordship:—Just look at those papers Mr. Sillivan. Does this bundle of papers contain papers that were found in and on the desk at the residence?

A. Yes, my Lord.

His Lordship:—They were found either in the drawers or on the desk?

A. Yes, my Lord.

His Lordship:—Including this book?

A. No my Lord, the book was found, so far as I can remember, in the offiice.

Accused:—Then it cannot be put in. It was not found at the residence.

His Lorsdhip:—Do you wish to put in all these collectively?

Accused:—Yes, my Lord, collectively as one Exhibit.

The papers were then bundled up and marked (Exhibit O.)

His Lordship:—Do you wish to ask any other questions?

Accused:—No, my Lord.

His Lordship to Advocate General:—Then that is your case?

Advocate General:—Yes, my Lord.

Clerk of the Crown then again read the statement made by Accused before the Magistrate.

His Lordship to accused:—Now, do you wish to make your statement?

Accused:—Will the court allow me a little time by rising now? The statement is ready but some alterations have to be made in connection with the papers just put in.

His Lordship :—The only difficulty is that the Jury's tiffin will not be ready till 3-30 P. M. I cannot ask them to go without that.

Accused :—Then we might meet as usual at 3-30 P. M.

Foreman of Jury :—The Jury are prepared to chance it about their tiffiin being ready.

His Lordship :—Very well, we will rise now.

After Lunch at 3 p. m. Wednesday 15th July.

His Lordship :—Have you any written Statement?

Accused :—My statement is ready, my Lord. I will read it.

Mr. Tilak then read the following statement to which was attached an Appendix of 71 Exhibits.

MR. TILAK'S STATEMENT MADE TO THE COURT.

I, Bal Gangadhar Tilak, Accused in this case do hereby state as follows :—

1. I am Editor, Printer, Publisher and Proprietor of the *Kesari*, a weekly Marathi journal published at Poona every Tuesday morning, and as such do admit all legal responsibility in respect of the articles forming the subject matter of the charges.

2. Marathi terminology in the discussion of Political subjects not being settled, I have used the following Marathi expressions for the English equivalents put against them :—

गोरा अधिकारी वर्ग
सरकारी अधिकारी वर्ग
इंग्रजी अधिकारी वर्ग
राज्यकर्ता अधिकारी वर्ग
} Bureaucracy.

जुलमी = Despotic. माथेफिरू = Fanatic. तेज = Mettle or spirit. आवेश = Enthusiasm. त्वेष = Intensity of feeling. चीड = Wounded self-respect or sense of honour. एकमुखी = Absolute. अनियंत्रित = Uncontrolled. अडवणुकीचा मार्ग = Passive resistance. भूत = Evil Genius. मतभ्रष्ट = Fallen from observances. बुद्धिभ्रंश = Error of judgment. आततायी = Felonious. कडवी = Stern. पौरुष = Manliness. पृथक वांटणी = Decentralization.

There are some more words and phrases of similar kind but these are not inserted in this statement to save space.

3. My views in regard to the Political reforms required in India at the present day are, as stated by me in March last in my evidence before the Decentralisation Commission, as follows:—

"The mere shifting of the centre of power and authority from one official to another is not, in my opinion, calculated to restore the feelings of cordiality between officers and people prevailing in earlier days. English education has created new aspirations and ideals amongst the people and so long as these national aspirations remain unsatisfied it is useless to expect that the hiatus between the officers and the people could be removed by any scheme of official Decentralization, whatever its other effects may be. It is no remedy-not even palliative-against the evil complained of, nor was it put forward by the people or their leaders. The fluctuating wave of Decentralization may infuse more or less life in the individual members of the Bureaucracy, but it cannot remove the growing estrangement between the rulers and the ruled, unless and until the people are allowed more and more effective voice in the management of their own affairs in an ever expansive spirit of wise liberalism and wide sympathy aiming at raising India to the level of the self-governing country."

4. The charge-Articles are a part of a controversy in which I have endeavoured to maintain and defend the above views.

With reference to Exhibit K. I have to explain that after the Explosives Act was passed I wished to criticise it and especially the definition of explosives in the same. For this purpose it was necessary to collect materials and the names of the two books on the card were taken down from a catalogue in my library with a view to send for them in case they could not be found in any of the Poona or Bombay Libraries. The Article of 9th June is intended to point out the futility of repressive measures alone in preventing the recurrence of bombs. In support of what is stated above in para 4 I produce along with this statement papers as per list annexed. The charge Articles embody my honest convictions and opinions. I state that I am not guilty of any of the charges brought against me and pray that I may be acquitted.

His Lordship:—Do you wish to produce any evidence?

Accused:—No, my Lord.

His Lordship:—You do not want to call any evidence or witnesses?

Accused:—No, my Lord.

His Lordship—I presume Mr. Advocate General, the accused having put in Exhibits you will ask him to proceed.

Advocate General—Yes, I shall have to reply. I notice in this statement that there is a list of 71—

His Lordship:—Newspaper articles ?

Advocate General:--I don't quite know how they can be admitted. I take it that what the Accused intends to do, instead of putting in those articles or tendering them, is to read extracts from them showing his own views. But would that be relevant, what somebody else has written? Can it show what he did or intended to do?

His Lordship.—That would depend on what the Accused wishes to read to the Jury; we can thus decide. It would be very much the same liberty as counsel would have of quoting before the Jury in his behalf from other articles.

Advocate General:—How could counsel have liberty to quote from a newspaper to show what some one else wrote. Here there are Calcutta papers. Madras papers, &c. &c.

His Lordship:—I do not quite know what the Accused proposed to do. We must wait till we see what he does. It may be that in those articles he produces that certain bad advice is given to Government as in the *Times of India* and the *Pioneer*.

Advocate General:—The only paper which he says offers bad advice to Government is the *Pioneer*.

His Lordship:—But he makes other statements.

Advocate General:—I ask at this stage my Lord, whether he is to be allowed to take into his defence articles for the purpose of explaining what he has said by reference to what somebody else has said in any part of Inida.It is apprently an attempt to prolong this trial indefinitely. That is a matter which I won't say anything more about. How can it be relevant for the defence of the Accused to those particular charges to be allowed to put in extracts from papers written in different parts of India. The question is what is the meaning of his language and from the meaning of his language what intention ought to be imputed to him. Not what is the meaning or opinion of a hundred other newspaper writers. How can you allow him to drag into his defence in this case matters of this sort.

His Lordship:—Up to the present there has been no attempt to prolong this trial indefinitely. If in the course of his defence he transgresses you will no doubt draw my attention to it. The list is annexed and we will wait and see what he proposes to do.

Advocate General:—I have not had the advantage or disadvantage of consulting all those papers.

His Lordship:—Accused does not perhaps intend to read them.

Advocate General:—Still he is allowed to put them in as his defence.

His Lordship:—We will see what use he does make of them and we will then be in a better position to judge.

Advocate General:—I submit I am entitled to a ruling. The apalling notion of having to read these apalling extracts is enough to terrify one out of his life.

His Lordship to accused:—Now you can adress the Jury in any way you like in your defence.

Accused:—I think that in the opening address for the prosecution nothing was said but that the whole article should go in and I do not know specifically the points upon which I have to reply. It would be more convenient if the prosecution summed up the case now and I replied afterwards.

Advocate General:—I do not want to weary the Jury.

His Lordship to accused :—I warned you yesterday that if you put in documents you would loose the right of reply. The Advocate General is not bound to anything more. You may address the Jury on the whole of the articles or on such portion of the articles as you think the prosecution rely upon.

Accused :—Then it will be a very long address as I must go over the whole course.

His Lordship :—You are quite at liberty to do that.

Accused :—Then I will begin now.

Mr. Tilak then addressed the Jury in his defence as follows :—

Mr. Tilak's Speech.

My Lord, and Gentlemen of the Jury! The Case for the Crown has been placed before you by the Learned Advocate General in an eloquent and able manner and though I cannot command that eloquence and ability I take it upon myself to represent my case to you in the hope that the personal explanation that I shall be able to give to you may be found satisfactory. The Charges are rather vague. Whole Articles have been included in the Charges and this throws upon me the responsibility of referring to every portion of the Articles likely to be pressed against me. I do not know definitely on what portions the Prosecutionr elies. The opening Address of the Learned Counsel for the Crown contained only a few remarks. The net consequence will be that I shall have to cover wider ground and detain you longer than I meant to do. I am not a practising Barrister in this Court and it is likely that my address will not be so argumentative and close as you might expect from a Barrister parctising long in this Court. I therefore request that you would show me that indulgence that is usually shown to parties pleading their own cause especially in criminal matters. The case for the Prosecution is that there are certain Articles which have been read to you and you are asked to draw certain inferences from the wording of those Articles and by acting upon the maxim that a man intends the natural consequences of his acts and return a verdict against me. A Case of Sedition divides itself into three parts. (1st) There is the publication of the Article; (2ndly) there are certain insinuations and inuendoes and lastly the question of intention. The publication I have already admitted. I have taken full responsibility of the publication of those articles. I may mention that one of the points namely insinuation and inuendoes should not be based on the translations of that Article. They are not the original. The original has got perverted in the translations and any insinuations based upon these translations would be likely to be unsafe. The only evidence of intention produced by the Prosecution is the Card, besides the Articles. They ask you to rely upon the translations of the two incriminating Articles and the other three which have been produced before you to prove intention. They say you have to judge from the writings themselves whether they are seditious or not. I think the matter is not so simple as that. The question of intention is the main question in this case; and I hope to show that by reading the Articles by themselves you cannot form any judgment as to my guilt or innocence. It is unsafe, nay dangerous to adjudge me guilty merely because the words, as conceived by you from the wrong translations, are in your opinion calculated to produce feelings of hatred and contempt in a community of which probably you know nothing. It amounts to something like this: You are asked to sit in judgment on an Article written in Freneh and translated into English. you are asked to judge of the effect this French Article will probably produce upon the French population in England. This is a case of that kind. I shall have to refer later on to the inconvenience caused by this procedure but I want to point out that the Article is written in Marathi and addressed to the Marathi knowing population. you have to judge what effect this Article is likely to produce, i. e. what is the tendency of the words employed and what effect they would probably produce on the minds of the Marathi-speaking population. The *Kesari* is only read by Marathi-speaking people. It is not read all over India. You have not to say what the effect would be in Bengal. You have to judge what effect these words would have on the minds of the readers of the *Kasari*, solely from the facts that the words complained of had a particular meaning and the sentences conveyed particular insinuations. No other fact or piece of evidence has been placed before you except the Articles themselves; and the general point upon which I shall address you when I take up the question of Law will be that this is a very unsafe method. In fact it is not sound to rely exclusively on this one maxim *viz.* that a man intends the natural consequences of his own act or actions. That was the question much discussed before English Juries about a hundred years ago when there was a controversy raised in England in the time of Grorge III. before Fox's Libel Act was passed in 1792. That doctrine as embodied in the maxim is now much discredited. It is an exploded theroy; and English Juries now-a-days draw their own conclusions not merely from the character of the writing itself but from all the surrounding circumstances. What those surrounding circumstances are I shall show from the papers I have put in. You know the way Juries are charged in this Country. They are told-" Take the whole Article, do not take a particular phrase or draw inferences from a single sentence, look to the context;" but nothing more is said. It is always unsafe to draw any inference by reading an Article alone. That is the doctrine in force now in England and that constitutes the main bulwark of the liberty of the Press in England. The Law is the same here as in England so far as the law of Sedition goes. It is the same in both countries. There was some difference 10 years ago, but by an amendment in 1898 the Law has been made the same as in England. In fact it has been brought into harmony with the English Law, and now there is no question as to what 'disaffection' means, but there is this difference, viz. that though the Law may be the same in England, English Juries use wider powers and they have fought for them even against the direction from the Judges. They have insisted upon their right to discuss the questions for themselves and return a verdict of common sense. The question is, "Has the Jury in India the same power as the Jury in England?" If it has, I ask you to exercise that power and draw your conclusion in the same way as an English Jury would do. For that purpose I will first read to you the Sections. They have been read to you already. They are Sections 124A and 153A; and they have been read to you by the learned Counsel for the Crown and I will read them to you and explain them in my own way. It is for His Lordship to say finally what the Law is, but it is a mixed question of fact and Law and I cannot avoid referring to it in my address to you.

Section 124A reads: " Whoever by words either spoken or written or by visible representation or otherwise brings or attempts to bring into hatred or contempt, or excites or attempts to excite disaffection towards His Majesty or Government established by Law in British India, shall be punished with transportation for life or any shorter term to which fine may be added or with imprisonment &c. to which fine may be added or with fine. " The charges which are framed against me are under Sections 124A and 153A. There are two charges under 124A; so I am taking that Section first. It has three Explanations, but we will come to that afterwards. If you examine Section 124 A you will find that it is divided into two parts; The 1st part is "whoever by words either spoken or written *brings into hatred or contempt* His Majesty etc etc." There is no question of intention but of the effect produced. If the hatred or contempt is produced by the writing no proof of intention is necessary. That is the first part. But it seems to me that the Prosecution does not mean to proceed under that part of the Section. There is no evidence adduced before you that any excitement has been caused by the Articles in question, so my case does not come within the first part of the Section. Had there been the least evidence to show that excitement was caused by these Articles, the question would have been different. There is absolutely no evidence before you. This is the reason why I asked that the charges should be made clearer. The whole Section is also put down there. They do not say whether I am charged with causing disaffection or with attempting to cause it. It would have been much better if a particular charge had been imputed. There is an alternative charge and so I have been obliged to refer to the first part of the Section. The charge is put under both parts of the Section. The 1st part of the Section is evidently not applicable and was never intended to apply to this case. Well, the charge was so framed by the Magistrate. The 2nd part of the Section reads "*attempts* to excite disaffection etc." Disaffection is a positive feeling meaning alienation of allegiance. The Explanation shows that it is a positive feeling and not a negative one. I will now read to you the Explanation. The first Explanation is "The expression 'disaffection' includes disloyalty and all feelings of enmity." So whoever attempts to excite disloyalty or attempts to bring Government into contempt is punishable under the latter part of the Section. The expression "attempts to bring" introduces the legal term "attempt." We must know what an attempt means. The words are not merely " knows as being likely to". The words are "attempts to excite" and they mean premeditation. I shall read from the charge of Mr. Justice Batty in the Bhala

Case, (B. L. R. Vol. VIII. Pages 438 to 439). There is a quotation from the charge of the Chief Justice. I now pass on to discuss the word 'attempt.' You will observe as has already been pointed out to you by the learned Councel, that it is not necessary in order to bring the case within the section that it should be shown that the attempt was successful. Attempt does not imply success. It is merely trying. Whether the intention has achieved the result is immaterial. I read to you a passage from the observations of the Chief Justice in a case tried in 1900 in this Court. "An attempt is an intentional premeditated action which if it fails in its objects, fails through circumstances independent of the person who seeks its accomplishment. If its failure is to be attributed to something which he cannot control, its failure is no excuse."

That is the meaning of the word 'attempt'. Attempt is actually an offence minus the final act of crime. When it fails it is only an attempt at the crime. There must be everything necessary to make it an offence except success under the particular circumstances. It must be shown that if I have failed in this attempt, it was from circumstances beyond my control. Now that kind of evidence has not been put before you. The mere fact of the publication of the Article, the mere fact that a certain Article is published, will not make it an attempt when attempt is so defined. Attempt definitely means that a man intends to do something ; the act must be present to his mind. This has been stated by Justice Stephens in his History of the Criminal Law of England Vol. 2 page 221 where he says (Reads). A crime must first occur to the mind, it must then be considered and determined upon, preparations more or less extensive must, in most cases, be made for it and it must be carried into execution. The execution may either be prevented or may be fully carried out, in which case it may either accomplish, or fail to accommplish, the full object which the criminal proposed to himself. That is attempt. It is not 'attempt' when it is fully carried out and accomplished. The subject has also been discussed in Mayne's Criminal Law and you will find at page 511 the following. Mere preparation is not punishable under this Section. If the man make certain preparations, and if those preparations fail from reasons ontside his control, then only is it an 'attempt' under this section and not otherwise. Now the illustrations are very curious and I will read to you some of them. (Reads page 932-933 Mayne's Criminal Law).

You must have pushed your preparation or activity so far, that success was prevented only by some thing beyond your control or irrespective of your will. The legal definition is something more.

There is a case given of a man with a sword running after another man, and though he is not far behind him, he cannot be said to be attempting murder. There is another illustration given, and still a further one. There is also a very curious case in 3 Bengal Reports Criminal Appeal page 45. You will find how the legal term 'attempt' is defined there. In that case Mr. Justice Mitra was right in saying that it was not an attempt, though you may punish him under any other Sections of the Penal Code. A transaction must be carried to such a point that you must consider that an attempt has been committed. The act here adduced is publication and publication alone. Publication is brought in to show intention, but I maintain that mere publication cannot prove any intention. Intentiou is to be proved in this case not merely by the fact of publication but by something else which would show that the publisher really did intend to excite disaffection. The article is before you. It was read to you by Clerk of the Crown. Now if publication alone were sufficient to constitute an attempt then the Clerk of the Crown could have been indicted for Sedition ! The Article has been published in every newspaper in India. Is every newspaper in India therefore guilty of attempting to commit Sedition in publishing that article ? No, and why ? Because publication was made merely to give information to the public. You have to take the intention with which it was done. You must have some act of definite intention. Lord Cockburn's exposition of the present Law is contained in column 2 page 2 as follows :—

"The mischief done or attempted *mals animo*. Besides being actual, the mischief must be done or attempted *mals animo*."

The guilt of Sedition is not contracted by the mere publication of language calculated to excite disaffection or disorder , for this may be done by a lunatic, or a Clerk of Court reading an indictment, or the speaking of machine. There must be a *criminal mind*. This state of mind is usually described by saying that the mischief for which the publication was calculated, must have been intended, because such an intention is usually the fact. But it is not meant by this, and it is certainly not necessary, that the accomplishment of that particular mischief should form the exact motive. A criminal indulgence in even a good motive will do ; as if a person should inflame the rabble from love of power, or of applause. And there may be a *culpable indifference of consequences*, in which absence of motive there may be as much wickedness as in the operation of motive. All these, and many other, mental conditions are states of *malus animus*. The great error to be avoided is the error of supposing that Sedition can ever consist in *the mere use of the language, abstracted from every other consideration*. Such a principle would be inconsistent with the right of public discussion. Not that the *malus animus*, that is the wickedness, must always be established *as a substantive fact by separate evidence*. It may be inferred from the whole circumstances, and especially from the words, or the act or acts, charged. It is a fair presumption that people mean what they say, and intend what they do. But it is competent to the Accused to exclude the application of this presumption. And consequently since it is a matter of evidence, it is for the Jury to decide it.

This shows that the mere publication of an article, whatever the context, whatever the surrounding circumstances, is not an offence. The Jury has to make up its mind not by reading the Article alone. I do not mean that it is not evidence. It is some evidence, but if I were to attribute to it a pecuniary value I wonld say the financial value of the article is merely one Anna in the Rupee; you have to find 15 Annas worth of evidence elsewhere and when this is done you must look to the other circumstances. Of course if the defence does not urge other circumstances perhaps it may be justifiable to return a verdict cf guilty by reading the article alone. But, when there are other circumstances which are shown to exist, then it is the bounden duty of the Jury to take all the circumstances into consideration and then to decide whether certain intention was in the mind of the accused or not. That is what I wanted to draw your attention to in the beginning. The Section does not say whoever publishes anything *likely* to create disaffection; that is not the wording of the Section. The Section says whoever "attempts" to excite, and if that is proved you can truly say a man is guilty. If you find an ounce of opium with a man would you say that he had intended to commit suicide ? The possession of the opium would not be an indication of intention; he may have been an habitual opium-eater. If you saw a man leaping into a tank would you say it is necessarily an *attempt* to commit suicide ? He may be a good swimmer and may want to enjoy a plunge. Of course it would be argued that it is for the defence to bring evidence to prove the contrary; that the burden of it lies upon the Accused. That again is wrong law and wrong doctrine. It is not sanctioned by the Evidence Act. It is the duty of the prosecution to prove every thing including intention. According to the Evidence Act you have to presume first that the accused is not guilty; it is for the prosecution to show by reliable evidence that every element of the crime that enters into the definition is made out. I ask you what have they proved in this case ? They have merely shown you some articles, and would appear to say "Don't you think they are sedetious ? Return a verdict of guilty. Here is the article; we have got it translated from the original. We place it before you; you can see that some of the words are very strong and likely to excite disaffection, therefore as a matter of legal inference the Accused is guilty; so return a verdict of guilty and go away." That is the whole case; absolutely nothing else. To them it makes no difference what the cricumstances were, when the article was written. The burden of proving all that is thrown upon the defence. They do not take into consideration the fact that this article was written in the heat of controversy, that this article was intended as a piece of advice, and that it is written in reply to certain criticisms already published. These are the principal circumstances under which the article was written. But the prosecution says " it is no business of ours to inquire into these circumstances. We only place the article before you and if the Accused does not reply, the best course for you, and the only legal course for you possibly, is to return a verdict of guilty. " Now Section 124 A has three Explanations and not exceptions. The Explanations are as follows:—

Explanation 1.—The expression " Disaffection " includes disloyalty and all feelings of enmity.

Explanation 2.—Comments expressing disapprobation of the measures of the Government with a view to obtain their alteration by lawful means, without exciting or attempting to excite hatred, contempt or disaffection, do not constitute an offence under this section.

Explanation 3.—Comments expressing disapprobation of the administrative or other action of the Government without exciting or attempting to excite hatred, contempt or disaffection do not constitute an offence under this section.

They explain the words in the main part of the Section. They explain ' disloyalty ' '(Reads). I think that ought to have been proved by the prosecution in the first instance that the Explanations to the section are satisfied as well as the Section itself. The burden of proof is not on the defence. The prosecution have not discharged this duty and have wrongly thrown the burden upon the defence. They ought to have shown by substantial proof that the writer has exceeded the limits of fair expression of opinion, fair comment, and fair disapprobation. I know that you will be told " we do not object to the liberty of the press, but we don't want that liberty to descend to license. " But you have to define what that may mean to yourself. Where does liberty cease and where does license begin ? That has to be defined by the common sense of the Jury. That is your duty. The law is very strict but it is the Juries in England that have stood between the strictness of the law and the liberty of the press, and you have to perform the same duty in this case. I mean to place before you all the circumstances under which the article was written and it is important to show what my intention was in writing that article. Whether I meant to excite disaffection or attempted to do so or whether that was not my intention. Intention is not a physical fact ; no one can see the heart of another man. If I have to judge of your intention, I must judge it from your overt acts. I cannot dive into your heart and know what is passing there. Intention has always to be gathered by inference; but the question here is whether inference is to be judged from one fact or from several surrounding circumstances. The fact of publication alone is not sufficient; you must take into consideration all the surrounding circumstances. I maintain, and several learned persons in England have maintained, that you must take into consideration the surrounding circumstances and give them their proper evidentiary value in law and you must arrive at your verdict by taking into consideration every fact that is before you. It would be unwise to say that the character of the writing may be *prima facie* inferred from the words themselves; and if you were to go on sending to prison every man who only writes particular words you would have to send to jail every writer of a dictionary. Webster's Dictionary e.g. contains all possible seditious words.

Then I must refer you to another case. It is from Erskine's speeches Vol.1. page 1867 and is known as the Dean of St. Asaph's case.In the speech for the defence the following words occur. Suppose the Crown were to elects some passage from Locke upon Government as for instance "that the sre wa no difference between the King and the Constable when either of them exceeded their authority. " That assertion under certain circumstances if taken by itself, without the context, might be highly seditious and the question therefore would be *quo animus* it was written. Perhaps the real meaning might not be discoverable by the immediate context without a view of the whole chapter-perhaps of the whole book.

Then I will read to you another passage from Erskine Vol. I. page 386. This refers to the Bible and says that if only the words " There is no God " were read and their context omitted, even the Bible would be a blamphemous work. You will have to look to the circumstances. In order to do this effectually, the Jury is selected from the people, the Jury is thus likely to know their circumstances. You, of course, have not that advantage here; there can be no comparison between an English Jury and the Jury in India, in this respect. It is a matter to be decided by twelve men drawn *from among the people*. Intention is to be decided by twelve men and, mark you, they must be unanimous. That is not the case here. In England if one man out of the twelve disagrees, the Jury is discharged, and another Jury is empannelled; and if this happens two or three times the man is ultimately acquitted. Of course in charging the Jury it is the custom to say you should look to the article and to the surrounding circumstances, but I believe it is the duty of the Prosecution to point out whether there are any exculpating circumstances and I have no doubt His Lordship will direct acccrdingly. Now there are other points of the Section to which I wish to draw your attention. What does " Excite " mean ? It is from *exciter;* it is to inflame, to create what does not exist, to raise to a higher degree what exists already. If there is no hatred or contempt already existing, to ' excite ' is to create it. If it does exist it is to highten it, to increase it. Now I will make myself clear by an illustration. Suppose there is unrest, and Government sends an officer to inquire into the reasons thereof and that officer makes a report to the Government that the unrest is due to certain causes and it could be easily remedied by Government; would you charge that officer with disaffection ? The man only describes the feelings of the people and represents them. He makes a report upon them. He does not go beyond that and is certainly not doing a seditious act. To excite feelings of disaffection means that by your act you must heighten feelings of disaffection when they exist or create them when they do not. If you do not do anything to excite feelings, if you merely express, if you merely report, if you only express sentiments which exist at the time, surely your act does not come under Section 124 A. Nay, more, you may create a feeling of disapprobation. I can say with impunity something is bad; it ought to be remedied. I have to write; I have a right to do that and if I find fault it is only natural that some ill-feeling is created. We are not all saints. So in disapprobation some ill-feeling is necessarily implied. That is the meaning of Explanation 2 to the Section; it refers to "Comments expressing disapprobation of the measures of the Government." When I say that Government is going wrong, evidently I say something which the authorities may not like. That is not sedition; if that were so, there could be no progress at all and we shall have to be content at the end of the 20th century with what we have at present. True progress comes of agitation; and you are bound to consider the defects pointed out and discussed and the reforms proposed and to look to the real intention of the man. I say the 'real intention' and not the 'fictitious intention' which is inferred from the legal dictum that every man intends the natural consequences of his acts. This then is the conclusion reached. If the intention is really to reform Government it is not seditious. "Sedition" has never been properly defined. The Explanation to the Section is as follows:-

I cannot conceive of disapprobation being expressed without exciting some bad feeling in the minds of the hearer about the person against whom that comment is made. It is impossible to do it. That is what the Explanation there refers to. It is to show either that so much liberty is allowed to the press or it has no meaning, at all. I request you to take it that it has a meaning and that the legislature intended it to have that meaning. The Explanation was not meaninglessly introduced. If it has a meaning, the only meaning it can have is that a certain amount of unpleasant feeling is allowed to be created by law. It is impossible to define the limit where liberty and disapprobation end and license and sedition begin. It is not to be decided merely as a legal inference; you have to decide as men of commonsense.

Lord Kenyon has said; "if any twelve men of my countrymen unanimously say that a particular Article or writing deserves to be condemned that is sedition. No definition can give you any correct idea about it". It is a doctrine laid down by a very learned and respected Judge. He gives up the attempt to define and says "bring twelve men from among the people and ask them if I have exceeded the limits and if they say yes, then convict me." That is why that definition of sedition has been very often quoted. It is the popular definition. I will now read a passage to you from Lord Kenyon's Charge to the Jury from Paterson on the "Liberty of the Press". That is the simplest definition that can be given. It lays down the limit between liberty and license and between legitimate disapprobation of Government and Sedition.

According to the phraseology of Law "act" is different from action. Act is something done; action is abstract and may include a policy of Government. Then there is another expression to which I wish to draw your attention; and it is " Government established by law in British India" ' Government ' here does not mean the Executive or the Judiciary but it means Government in the abstract. The word ' Government ' is defined in the Indian Penal Code and includes any officer, even a police constable. It does not mean that if I say a police man is not doing his duty then I am guilty of sedition. Go up higher. If certain Officials have not been doing their duty I have every right to say that these officials should be discharged; there should be stricter supervision and that particular departments should be altered. So long as the word " Government " is qualified by the words " established by Law, " how can it have the meaning given to it by a definition of the word ("Government") in a particular part in the Penal Code ? The qualifying phrase makes it a quite different thing. It is " Government established by law." We shall have to come afterwards to the question whether Bureaucracy is Government or not ? Whether the British Government is solely dependent upon the Bureaucracy? Can it not exist without it? The Bureacracy may say so, it may be very flattering to them to say that the services of certain officers are indispensable to them but is it the meaning conveyed by the expression "Government established by law in British India"? Does it mean a " form of administration" and is it consistent with that meaning? So far as ideals are concerned they do not come under the Penal Code. I may say that a certain system of administration is better suited to the country and may try to spread that opinion. You may not agree with me but that is not the point. I have to express my opinion and so long as I do not create any disaffection I am allowed to express it freely. There can otherwise be no progress; progress would be impossible unless you allow intelligent gentlemen the right to express their opinion, to influence the public and get the majority of the public on their side. See the wording of the Section. The words are "Government established by Law in British India." I think Justice Batty in the "Bhala" case (the same case from which I have already quoted to you) says that you have to consider the tendency of the writing etc. The passage says that it is quite allowable for a man to say that the particular form of Government should not exist. That does not imply any hostility to Government. Now if we were philosophically discussing the point, and Section 124 A were strictly applied, every philosopher in the world to whom we owe all this progress will have to be sent to Jail.

Supposing a man in England were to write that constitutionl monarchy is not good for England, it has been stated that it is not seditious to express that view. I will read in this connection from Morley on Compromise, page 224. He says :—"Again take the case of the English monarchy. Grant if you will that this institution has a certain function and that by the present chief magistrate this function is estimably performed. Yet if we are of those who believe that in the stage of civilisation which England has reached in other matters the monarchy must be either obstructive or injurious or else merely decorative and that a merely decorative monarchy tends in diverse ways to engender habits of abasement, to nourish lower social ideals, to lessen a high civil self-respect in the community; then it must surely be our duty not to lose any opportunity of pressing these convictions. To do this is not necessarily to act as if one were anxious for the immediate removal of the throne and the crown into the museum of poltical antiquities."

That has been the pronouncement of a statesman and not merely of a legal authority. I want to be a millionaire; will you infer from it that I want immediately to commit a dacoity? All that I want is to earn money. So if I say Bureaucracy should be changed or modified it is not fair to infer that my intention is to raise a rebellion and create feelings of hatred against the Government. Why should you infer that my intention is really to raise a rebellion and create feelings of hatred? You must be very careful in inferring intention from words especially when you have to infer the feelings of the community in which you do not move. If you take the writing, reading it alone is not sufficient; you will have to judge the effect the writing will produce on Marathi-speaking people. It is a very difficult task. There is always the possibility of misunderstanding. We very often misunderstand each other. If I draw an inference as to your intention without knowing the state of your society it is not likely to be correct. In the same way if you wish to draw an inference from the Marathi writing as to the effect it would produce on the Marathi-knowing community you have to consider the feelings and the general state of that community. Without doing that you cannot say whether the writing will excite any particular feelings or not. Take the instance suggested to me by my learned friend Mr. Baptista. You write upon the cow-question. If you write in a particular way the Mahomedan community may not be offended but the Hindu community may be. The question of effect in that case does not, depend only upon the writing but also, and more especially, upon the state of the mind of the people to whom it is addressed and the particular time at which it is addressed; upon the particular state of society and the stage of its development at the time it is addressed. What may cause disaffection to-day may not have excited disaffection 20 years ago, and what appears horrible to-day may appear quite different 10 years hence. It is a threefold question. The question of the writing is one factor, the state of the society to which that particular writing was addressed at that particular time is another factor, and the time at which it is addressed is the third factor. It is an example of an equation involving three unknown quantities. You can't find the value of the equation by knowing the value of only one of them. The Prosecution have stated to you the value of only one factor, and have left you to evolve that of the other two from your inner consciousness. You are judging of human individuals-of the Natives-of whom you have little knowledge. It is quite a different thing when the writing is in the language which you understand and the community to be judged by you is the one to which you belong. The question is very peculiar under Sec. 153 A. You have to decide questions between communities. India is not yet a nation in the sense in which it is understood in western communities. You have to judge whether feelings of animosity may be created between Hindus and Mahomedans, Parsees and Jews, or Jains and Buddhists. How are you to judge? Simply by the possible effect of the writing itself? That will evidently be a lame, incorrect, unsafe and dangerous way of doing it. The Prosecution ought to have produced evidence before you to show what the state of the Marathi speaking people is and how are they likely to be affected. They have produced no evidence to show what may be the probable effect. I do not blame any body. You, gentlemen, are all shrewd business men. You can form your opinion on facts and if the Prosecution did not place these facts before you who is to be blamed? Don't think that in any circumstances you are bound to return a verdict of guilty. You can say you can give no verdict as there is no evidence. If there is not evongh evidence it does not mean that from whatever evidence you have you must give a verdict of guilty. It is open to you to say you cannot make up your minds. Sec. 153 A reads as follows :—" Whoever by words, either spoken or written, or by signs, or visible representations, or otherwise promotes or attempts to promote feelings of enmity or hatred between different classes of His Majesty's subjects shall be punished with imprisonment which may extend to two years, or with fine, or with both." Then there is this expression in the explanation :—" It does not amount to an offence within the meaning of this section to point out, *without malicious intention* and with an honest view to their removal, matters which are producing or have a tendency to produce feelings of enmity or hatred between different classes of His Majesty's subjects. " It is the malicious intention on which you have to decide. You are not to presume that intention. Thus Sedition consists in *intention;* it does not consist in the act of publication. Sedition does not consist merely in the character of the writing. It consists in an evil mind and that evil mind is to be proved and it must be proved by facts from which you can infer that evil intention. That is the reason why that subject is left to the Jury. Otherwise there is no reason for the Jury to sit in Judgment. Any one could pick up an article and say this is seditious. I do not think that that requires much intellectual power. Where is the necessity of a Jury and of its being unanimous. ? The doctrine is that if 12 men taken from the people come to the honest conclusion that malicious intention does exist then the accused is guilty and not otherwise. Is there any malicious intention? Is there any criminal intention? Is there any evil motive in publishing these articles? Is there any evidence as to what I had really intended? If you have no materials before you, you must return a verdict of not guilty. The mere character of the writing may be *prima facie* evidence of the intention but intention must always be inferred from overt acts. Tilak or no Tilak is not the question. The question is, do you really intend as guardians of the liberty of the Press to allow as much liberty here in India as is enjoyed by the people of England.? That is the point that you will have to very carefully consider. I wish to show you that mine is an Article written in controversy as a reply to an opponent. It was penned to defend the interests of my community. You may not agree with me in my views. Different communities have different views. And every community must have opportunity to express its own views. I have not come here to ask you any grace. I am prepared to stand by the consequences of my act. There is no question about it. I am not going to tell you that I wrote the article in a fit of madness. I am not a lunatic. I have written it believing it my duty to write in the interest of the public in this way, believing that that was the view of the community. I wanted to express it, believing that the interests of the community would not be otherwise safeguarded. Believe me when I say that it was both in the interest of the people and Government that this view should be placed before them. If you honestly go to the question like that it will be your duty to give a verdict fo not guilty, whatever may be your opinion about me, even if you dislike me as much as you can. I know I am not a *persona grata* with the Government; but that is no reason why I should not have justice. My personality is not the question. The question is one of intention and that is what *you* have to decide, not his Lordship. Juries in England have returned verdicts against the directions of Judges. You might think that Government has launched this prosecution, and sometimes lower officers consider a sanction as tantamount to a mandate. I think that that view will not be taken in this case. I am sure of it; and I am sure his Lordship will so direct you. Government for its own purposes likes certain things to be done and certain things not to be done, but the Government policy is not always justified by the principles of Law and Justice. Here it is not a question of convenience, it is not a question of expediency, but a question of Justice pure and simple. If you look at the question from this standpoint then much of the misunderstanding, much of the dust that is likely to be raised by the Prosecution about this question, will be cleared up. The matter is to be looked at from one standpoint and one standpoint only. And that stand point is to do justice. I ask whether in your own heart of hearts, under the circumstances, you think that you would not have written like this. If you were placed in my position and if you had been impelled by my circumstances to take up the defence of your community what would you have done? As I told you it is a question like, that; you must place yourselves in my position and then judge of my motives and my intention. If you find by going over the whole of the incidents that my intention is pure, there is no other course open to you but to return a verdict of not guilty. I shall presently show you that the translations that are placed before you are wrong,—I will not say intentionally wrong, but I will say that they are wrong and very highly prejudicial to the Defence. I am not going to say that the translator was actuated by any bad motive. I cannot say that; but the result is there and it is ruinous to the Defence. Whatever the words may mean, it is a question of intention. You ought to be very careful in ascribing intention to any one. If the results are not harmful it is your bounden duty to suppose that the intention is good ; even in the case where they are harmful you cannot say that the intention was necessarily bad. I will read to you from Stephens, History of Criminal Law in the case of the Dean of St. Assaph. What do you find in this case ? Killing may be an offence ; it may amount to culpable homicide not amounting to murder ; or it may be caused by a rash act. If it is proved to you that a man A has merely killed B, you cannot return a verdict of murder. Mere killing is not murder and merely taking away a purse is not theft. The circumstances under which the man takes away the purse are materially relevant or necessary to be taken into consideration. It is the duty of the Jury not to infer intention merely from the taking of the purse. The Jury must know that he took it with a wicked intention. Of course in this case no discontent or disaffection has been proved to have been caused and the procedure here is slightly different. The Penal Code has now defined all crimes ; so there is no necessity to infer wicked intention. When the Sections are named that serves the purpose. There has been no evidence placed before you that any discontent has been brought about. You have to infer it from the writing. That procedure is I think not legal nor equitable nor moral. " The maxim that a man intends the natural consequences of his acts is usually true; but it may be used as a way of saying that because recklessness to probable consequences is morally as bad as an intention to produce those consequences, the two things ought to be called by the same name, and this is at least an approach to a legal fiction. It is one thing to write with a distinct intention to produce disturbances and another to write violently and recklessly matter likely to produce disturbances. " p. 360 Stephen. So the two things are not the same. Those are the words stated there. You cannot infer any intention from the writings themselves. As I said before give it a scale value ; and if the total accumulating evidence comes to sixteen Annas in a Rupee convict me. The publication is only one factor in judging of a criminal intention. There must be a distinct criminal intention to justify a verdict of wicked intention. So what I have said amounts to this that this intention can not be inferred from merely the fact of publication but from surrounding circumstances ; and between these two lies the Liberty of the Press, the whole Liberty of the Press.

The Liberty of the Press is not guarded by the Section. The Law says always infer intention from the publication, but then there would be no liberty. Liberty means that you must take all the circumstances into consideration. It is upon you that the Liberty of the Press depends.

The Court Adjourned till Thursday.

FOURTH DAY.

Thursday, the 16th July 1908.

Proceedings commenced at 11-30 A. M.

Mr. Tilak said :-Before we begin today I would like to make a request to your Lordship about the books and papers which have been put in and those which have not been put in. I request that the other books and papers which have been retained may, if the Prosecution has no objection, be returned as they are wanted at Poona in the office for the purpose of continuing the paper.

Mr. Branson:—I have no objection, my Lord; we have no wish to retain any papers and books that have not been put in, just as I stated yesterday that the compositors might go back to Poona.

His Lordship:—They may be restored to the Accused.

Mr. Tilak continuing his address then said:—

My Lord and gentlemen of the Jury, I explained to you yesterday what my view of Sec. 124 A was and it becomes necessary in view of the difficulty placed in my way to anticipate some of the objections which might probably be raised by the Prosecution because I shall not have the right of replying afterwards. In anticipating these objections perhaps I may state something which the Prosecution might not have in its mind. But I cannot help that. I have to state the case in full and as I have no right of reply I have to anticipate the objections and reply to them also. Had the learned Advocate-General summed up the case before I began to address you, the difficulty might have been removed. But the law allows that privilege to the Prosecution and this difficulty has been created not entirely by the Prosecution, but by the law that obtains. I stated yesterday that the word 'attempt' is not defined. It is the most important word. The general plea is that in Sedition cases it is enough to look at the intention and pretend that the intention should be gathered from the legal maxim that a man intends the natural consequences of his acts. I will try to show you that that is not the case. The word 'attempt' necessarily postulates the idea of a premeditated action having a definite end in view. In a case tried in this Court in 1900 before the Chief Justice, he said that an attempt implies an end in view. So also we have Justice Stephen saying that a crime must be in view. It is a contradiction in terms to say that a man attempted to do what he had never in view. To prove an attempt there should be direct evidence of the end and object in view. The object in view goes by the name of motive. The man must intend it and that must be his end in view. There is also another factor which has to be kept in mind viz. that an attempt, legal attempt, is only complete when success is prevented from any cause external to the will of the man. He must be prevented from carrying out his object by causes beyond his control and perhaps which he never anticipated. In the present case there has been no evidence to show that this attempt failed on account of some thing else. I think in a Sedition case it is absolutely necessary to give this evidence. There ought to be some evidence before you to that effect. Did the attempt fail ? All the elements of an offence must be proved and it must be proved that the attempt failed from certain causes not in the control of the man who made it. Absolutely no evidence has been brought by the Prosecution to show that this attempt failed because the Government interfered or because the people were not willing to listen to what I had to say. It is seriously urged in such cases that the attempt need not be successful. I take this to be a very meaningless direction. You charge a man with having excited disaffection, or with the alternative charge of having attempted to excite disaffection. You are told that if there is no success you may commit him under the latter part of the Section. I told you yesterday that the first part of the Section is not applicable to this charge and I claim acquittal on that part. Attempt includes both intention and motive. Without an end in view there can be no attempt. I will explain it to you by taking a common illustration. I *intend* to go to the Bori Bunder station and my *end in view* is to go to Poona. Object is the ultimate end in view. That is motive; and my first contention is that the word attempt includes both intention and motive and both have to be considered in coming to a conclusion as to whether a man has made an attempt. The motive and intention, it is eventually urged, must be looked at in the light of the maxim that a man intends the natural consequences of his acts. Of course it is a beautiful maxim, but it is not a reliable guide. As I explained yesterday I take attempt to mean all acts including motive, including intention and all acts which would have led to the commission of an offence, had the person committing the offence not been prevented by an extraordinary agency from carrying his intention into practice. There are of course certain cases which show that an attempt need not be carried so far that success would have followed had something else not interfered at the last point, i. e. up to the penultimate point; that it may be short of penultimate. To illustrate, say there are ten stages in an act. It is not necessary to carry the attempt to the ninth stage; it is quite enough if it is carried to the sixth stage. There are certain decisions on this point which are likely to be quoted against me and for that reason I must explain. I will read to you a case before I give my explanation. It is the case that I referred to yesterday, the case of Varjivandas reported in No. 30 Punjab Law Reports page 225. This is a case of attempting to kill. A man ran after another man with an axe in his hand; he was only four paces behind. The defence was that being four paces off he might have been induced to give up his intention and the accused placed in *locus penitentie*.

Mr. Branson:—May I ask who were the Judges ?

Accused:—The Judges are not given here. It is on page 735 of the Fourth Edition. (Reads down to "inteference from without.") There are certain Sections in the Indian Penal Code which make an attempt punishable as the crime itself. There is Section 511 under which the punishment is much less, about half the length of the term assigned for the offence. There are two kinds of attempts punishable under the Indian Penal Code; one is the full attempt and the other is something less. In a case of murder how are we to distinguish between the two, whether the attempt is a full attempt or something less. Now the test for distinguishing between the two is this. A man does a thing or only attempts that thing and yet the person may be equally punishable. Where the punishment is thus equal the attempt must be carried to the ultimate stage; but where the punishment is less (half or quarter) then you might say that the attempt may not be carried to the last point. For instance Sec. 124 A speaks of 'attempt' but it does not say that a man may escape from the consequences if it is only half made. A man may be charged with an attempt to commit an offence under Sec. 124 A. The meaning of the word attempt in that Section however is quite different from its meaning in Sec. 511. Section 511 is somewhat wider (quotes the Section. " Whoever attempts to commit an offence punishable by this Code with transporation or imprisonment or to cause such an offeuce to be committed, and in such attempt does any act towards the commission of the offence, shall, where no express provision is made by this Code for the punishment of such attempt, be punished with transporation or imprisonment of any description provided for the offence for a term of transporation or imprisonment which may extend to one half of the longest term provided for that offence or with such fine as is provided for the offence or with both.") There you have distinctly a lower state of attempt, an attempt not carried to its utmost limit. No act may be carried in its preparation to the final stage or even to the penultimate stage to make it an attempt under 511. Under Sec. 124A that definition cannot be adopted; there the attempt must be a full attempt. A man must be prevented from carrying out his object by some extraordinary agency as it is said here. (Reads from Bengal Law Reports 30.) Hence the Prosecution must show that but for some extraneous act the attempt would have succeeded. They have failed to show that; and having failed to show that they cannot ask you to find me guilty under Sec. 124A. There is no evidence before you to show that I did not succeed because some one came in my way. I am going to show you further on that my motive was quite a different one. In this case, taking the case as it is, the charge mentions only an attempt, and the Prosecution is not entitled to succeed unless it shows that this attempt would have leen carried on and would have developed into an offence but that it was prevented by extraneous causes. There are cases in which it is held that an attempt need not be carried to its last point; but that is under Sec. 511. If you want to convict a man under 124A it must be shown to have been carried to the last stage. I am not charged under Sec. 511. It may be a mistake but there it is. I am charged under Sec. 124A and not under Sec. 511. Another point is also very important; they will say that I am making a confusion and muddling up intention and motive; and that by thus confounding the two I am giving all false law to the Jury. That is the purport of the objection raised by Stephens against Erskine in the Dean of St. Asaph's case (Reads—"If you ask the Jury to take motive into consideration.")

His Lordship:—The reference to the Punjab Case was wrong. I find the Volume is 39 and not 30.

Accused:—It may be wrongly quoted here.

His Lordship:—The case is quoted here.

Mr. Branson:—The reference is quite right, you would see that the case is 30 but the volume is 39.

His Lordship:—I see; it is case No. 30, volume No. 39.

Mr. Tilak continuing said:—Now it is urged, gentlemen, that in such cases the jury ought to find intention and motive separately. The motive of the man may be good. A man may be good. A man may become a thief with the object of giving the money in charity. His intention, however, was to commit theft although his motive was good. There is no reason why the man should not be convicted of theft. That is exactly the argument used on page 360 in the History of Criminal Law in England, Volume 2. The second objection that may be urged is that you would confound intention and motive, but the objection is unfounded. I do not ask you to consider any of them alone. Take the two together and you are sure of arriving at a correct decision. Stephens is one of the writers who do not like the present state of the law in England, and observes as follows in his History of Criminal Law:—

"A further objection to referring to the defendant's intention in any case, and especially in defining the crime of libel with reference to it, is that a confusion is sure to occur between intentions and motives. Indeed in the many trials for seditious libel which followed the passing of the libel Act, I have not found an instance in which the distinction was pointed out. The words are constantly used as if good motives and good intentions were convertible terms. It is, however, obvious as soon as the matter is mentioned that the two are distinct. A man may be led by what are commonly regarded as pure motives to form seditious or even treasonable intentions, and to express them in writing, just as he might be led to commit theft or murder by motives of benevolence. If a man who steals in order to give away the stolen money in charity, or a man who kills a child in order to save it from temptations of life, is not excused on account of the nature of his motives, why should a man who writes a libel calculated and intended to produce a riot be acquitted, because his motive was generous indignation against a real grievance? By making the intention of the writer, the test of his criminality a great risk of this result is incurred. A Jury can hardly be expected to convict a man whose motives they approve and sympthize with, merely because they regard his intention with disapproval. An intention to produce disaffection is illegal, but the motive for such an intention may be one with which the Jury would strongly sympathize and in such a case it would be hard even to make them understand that an acquittal would we against their oath."

I do not ask you to take into consideration merely motive or merely intention. But do not inferthe intention merely from the fact that the Article contains certain words that are likely to be construed in a peculiar way. What I say is, do not infer intention by an abstract principle of law but from fact. That is my point. I do not want to confuse you. Motive is an element to be considered in arriving at the intention. What is intention? Unless you consider the motive fully you cannot know the intention fully. Intention may be inferred from the legal fiction that a man intends the natural consequences of his acts. But if there are circumstances before you to show that the motive of the man was different, then surely you would not be justified in returning a verdict of guilty. Intention and motive are both to be considered. I am going into the the history of the Law directly. The word in the Section is "attempt" (Reads Sec. 124A). The words are not "whoever publishes" but "whoever attempts". It does not say merely "publishes." If it did, it would then have the legal addition that whoever publishes must mean the natural consequences of his acts. 'Attempt' means the act carried to its fullest extent, short only of success. Of course you need not trouble yourself about the success, but you must show that there is that kind of attempt. If there is an inferior attempt you must charge me under Sec. 511. I am not charged under Sec. 511, but under Sec. 124 A. So what we have to consider in this case is whether the word attempt includes both intention and motive. That is the idea in the illustration I gave you about the man who commits theft with the best motive. If intention and motive are right at the two points the act lies evenly between them. If the motive and intention are the same, it is a straight act. When an offence and an attempt are punishable with a similar punishment, the attempt must be carried to its fullest extent. About motive and intention I contend we are bound by the law as it exists. The word attempt is not defined and unless the Legislature takes it into its mind to modify the law, as it did in 1897, the Sec tion must continue to mean a full attempt. It may be contended that I am explaining to you a new doctrine and that it is inappropriate and far-fetched, and it is likely to be said that it only arises from a certain imagination of mind which the Legislature never intended. I have quoted the definition of Sir Lawrence Jenkins and of Justice Batty in Bhala Case, from the Bombay Law Reporter of 1900. The word attempt is defined by the learned Chief Justice as follows (Reads). This is the explanation of attempt given to the Jury by the learned Chief Justice in a case of sedition.

It is also quoted by Mr. Justice Batty who says that an attempt is a premeditated act short of accomplishment. These are the three definitions given by the learned Judges and all of them have been given in connection with the recent sedition cases. So that, gentlemen of the Jury, what I have stated is the correct view of the law. It is not distorted by me or drawn by me but it is a correct view of the law taken by responsible and learned Judges and so explained to the Jury in trials where the charge has been of Sedition. I do not wish to strain the law in my own interest in an excited state of mind, but it is the correct law of the land and so long as the word attempt remains there it will be the law of the land and must be so interpreted.

Now having fortified my position in reply to a possible objection by the Prosection, I shall place before you the history of the trouble which has brought about the change of Law in England and I will show you the way how Juries in England have been acting. It is often said that English and Indian Law is the same. The learned Counsel for the Crown says that Sec. 124A is the law as it exists in both countries. I quite agree with him, but it is not administered in the same way. And I want to show you it is with you, gentlemen of the Jury, to administer the law properly. The fault will not be of the law but will be of the Jury in this case if the law is not properly administered. The entire question is left to you for your decision. Don't think that you have not the power. We often speak of a Judge-made law but there is also the Jury-made law, though that distinction is not yet to be found in law books. The liberty of the Press is under the Jury-made law. It is not the law made by Legislature, it is not made by Judges, it is entirely a Jury-made law. Juries have frequently to refuse to take a particular view of the case inspite of the Judge's charge to the contrary. Juries have an independent position, they have certain prescribed rights, and they must exercise them. They will fail in their duty if they do not do so and deprive the subjects of the protection against the arbitrary use of power. Juries are the bulwark of our liberty. I want to explain to you by what this result has been achieved as I think you will be the better able thereby to discharge your functions as Jurors in this case. The question, gentlemen of the Jury, first arose in 1792, in what is known as the Dean of St. Assaph's case. It is also known as the Shipey case. It was in fact a remarkable struggle between Jurors, Lawyers, Statesmen and others. They wanted more freedom for the Press and Public Meetings, but the law would not allow it. You, gentlemen, who are Englishmen know that your ancestors fought for this Liberty. During the reign of James II he issused a Writ of Indulgence to seven Bishops who refused to accept it. They were tried and the Jury persisted in returning a verdict of 'not guilty.' The Judges did not like it; there was a row and eventually the law of the land prevailed. There is another case of the same type. But I am not going to trouble you with all the cases. The case of the Dean of St. Asaph was the first case in which this point was raised. The old Law of England was this. There were three things to be considered in a Seditious Libel case and with two of these, publication and inuendoes, the Jury had to deal; and the Judges insisted that the Jury had nothing to do with intention. They said if a Jury was satisfied that the writings were published and that the inuendoes were correct it was for them to say so, and that it was for the Judges to infer intention; and their formula was that 'every man intends the natural consequences of his acts.' The Jury said "that is a wrong procedure, we don't agree with you and we cannot convict the man." There was a fight; the Jury's cause was espoused by Lord Erskine and the Judges were represented in this controversy by Lord Mansfield. Those were very troublesome times in 1792 during the period of the French Revolution and the contagion had spread through all parts of Europe. It was an exciting time. I think that it was in 1792 that the French Republic was established and it was in 1792 that Fox's Libel Act was passed. That was the general condition of the country when the Dean of St. Asaph was charged. It was a very peculiar case. The objections in that case, and the arguments of Lord Erskine in moving for a Writ of Impeachment and a new trial, are regarded as a master-piece of eloquence and learning combined. I think the times here in India are exactly the same as they were in England in 1792. There is unrest. That is admitted. And with the object of stopping it Government thinks that some people must be prosecuted and deported if possible to the Andamans or to Australia. It is not convenient, in their opinion, to have some persons at large. The case is exactly of the same type as the cases which were tried in England between 1792 and 1800, or a few years before 1792. I put it down as 1780. There was then a regular age of prosecutions, a great crop of prosecutions for Libel and Sedition just as we have it in India now. A number of cases for Sedition were being tried there as they are now being tried here. The parallel is exact, and the lesson which I wish to draw from it is very important. The trouble arose at that time in this way. You know Sir William Jones, the great transtator of Shakuntala. He was a Judge of the High Court at Calcutta and was afterwards a Judge of the Supreme Court. He wrote a pamphlet in which, in the form of a dialogue between a farmer and a gentleman, the political relations between the Government and the people were discussed. He sent it for publication to his brother-in-law the Dean of St. Asaph from Calcutta. There are some extracts from the pamphlet given in Erskine's Speeches Volume 1 pages 97,98 and 99. I am not going to read to you the whole dialogue and take up your time; but there is one important point in it. I will read one paragraph (Reads—" In the year 1783, soon after the conclusion of the calamitous war in America, the public attention was very warmly and generally turned throughout this country towards the necessity of a reform in the representation of the people in the House of Commons. Several societies were formed in different parts of England and Wales for the promotion of it; and the Duke of Richmond and Mr. Pitt, then the Minister, took the lead in bringing the subject before Parliament. To render this great national object intelligible to the ordinary ranks of the people, Sir William Jones, then an eminant barrister in London, and afterwards one of the Judges of the Supreme Court of Judicature at Bengal, composed a dialogue between a scholar and a farmer as a vehicle for explaining to common capacities the great principles of society and government, and for showing the defects in the representation of the people in the British Parliament. Sir William Jones having married a sister of the Dean of St. Asaph, he became acquainted with and interested in this dialogue, and recommended it strongly to a committee of gentlemen of Flinlshire who were at that time associated for the object of reform, where it was read, and made the subject of a vote of approbation. The Court party, on the other hand, having made a violent attack upon this committee for the countenance thus given to the dialogue, the Dean of St. Asaph, considering (as he himself expressed it) that the best means of justifying the composition, and those who were attacked for their approbation of it, was to render it public, that the world might decide the controversy, sent it to be printed &c." The object of this dialogue was to show that the people were not properly represented in Parliament, that Parliament required to be reformed. This was before the Reform Act was passed. The question was whether Parliament ought to be reformed or not. That phamplet was placed before a committee formed for the purpose of reforming Parliament and was published. This was regarded as a seditious procedure. The whole case came before a Judge and Jury of the day. The Judge was Mr. Justice Buller, the Counsel for the defence was Mr. Erskine. The whole case was argued and the Judge said that it was for him to say whether the intention was seditious or not and for the Jury to say if it was published and if the inuendoes were correct. He said it was for the Judge to say whether it was libel or no libel. That was in 1792. The Jury was asked in that case to return a verdict of guilty because the pamphlet was published and because there were certain insinuations in it which cast reflections on the then Government of England and the Judge thought there was a particular insinuation which showed seditious intention. Mr. Erskine defended the accused very strongly. He said the doctrine was absurd. He went into the history of the Criminal Law of England and treated Sedition just like murder. It was not merely a question of law. The question before the Court was whether there was seditious intention which was not a question of law, but of mixed law and fact, or of pure fact. It was entirely a question for the Jury; you cannot take it from the Judge. Lord Erskine urged that they should not return the verdict just as the Judge asked them to do. What did the Jury do? They returned a verdict of "not guilty of seditious intention", but, they said, if you want the word "guilty" in the verdict, we will say "guilty of publication only". There was an interesting conversation between Lord Erskine and the Jury as follows:—

Associate:—Gentlemen, do you find the defendant guilty or not?

Foreman :—Guilty of publishing only.

Mr. Erskine :—You find him guilty of publishing only?

A Juror :—Guilty only of publishing.

Mr. Justice Buller. I believe that is a verdict not quite correct. You must explain that one way or the other as to the meaning of the innuenuendoes. The indictment has stated that G. means Gentlemen, F. Farmer, the King the King of Great Britain, and the Parliament the Parliament of Great Britain.

One of the Jury :—We have no doubt of that.

Mr. Justice Buller :—If you find him guilty of publishing, you must not say the word only.

Mr. Erskine :—By that, they mean to find there was no sedition.

A Juror. We only find him guilty of publishing. We do not find anything else.

Mr. Erskine. I beg your Lordship's pardon with great submission. I am sure I mean nothing that is irregular. I understand they say, 'We only find him guilty of publishing.'

A Juror. Certainly; that is all we do find &c. &c.

It is an historical dialogue. That was a very interesting case. It was a struggle between Juries and Statesmen on the one hand, and lawyers and judges on the other. Now although that verdict was returned by the Jury, the Judge found the accused guilty and convicted the man. This was considered to be a wrong judgment in that case. There were other cases but I am not going to take up your time because I have to refer to cases since 1792. In the case just referred to, Lord Erskine moved for a new trial and to set aside the judgment. The matter came before Lord Mansfield who heard Lord Erskine's arguments but refused the application. He, however, directed the notice of parliament to the matter and that was how the Fox's Libel Act was passed in 1792. It was taken up in the House of Commons and the House of Lords. The popular argument was that the state of the mind in a case of Sedition as in cases of murder and theft must be left to the Jury to decide. Judges have certain formulœ. It saves the Judge much trouble if he has a ready made maxim or legal formula such as "a man must intend the natural consequences of his acts." It is like a doctor prescribing mixture No. 1 or No. 2. But then what is left for the jury? They have only to say whether the writing is published or not and if so whether the innuendoes are correct or not. Out of the three questions two were left to the Jury and one was left to the Judge. Erskine argued that this was not sound law. It is not in accordance with British Justice or tradition. Again where there was struggle between Government and the people, the Jury in England had to be unanimous. It does not matter whether a Jury is unanimons or not in a case of theft, because the interests involved are the interests of a particular person. But as between Government and the people the method of trial by Jury is most important. It is, therefore, that you are the bulwark of the liberty of discussion, and of the Press. Judges are bound down by precedent. The Judge ignores the importance of the matter and follows the precedent in order to keep up the current of the decisions of his predecessors; and they maintain these decisions because they say uniformity of practice must be maintained. They say it is the law of the land; we cannot change it. As you know, in England, after a time, the law became fixed and the legislature had to come in. Till then the Jury must take it into their own hands. Judges may not know when this stage is reached, and that is really how the Court of Equity in England came to be established. The special Court of Equity has the matter placed before it now-a-days, and eventually the matter is taken to Parliament. Before that, in 1792, the state of things was entirely different. The people had to struggle against this doctrine and when they had struggled in very many cases, they refused to say that a man had been guilty of seditious intention. They said publication and inuendoes were proved, but as regards intention they did not say anything. It was not a verdict of guilty. It was a verdict of publication only. The matter was eventually taken to Parliament. Lord Mansfield represented the views of the Judges in the house of Lords while Mr. Erskine took up the cause of the people in the House of Commons. The Act was passed in 1792 and is consists of four sections. It was stated that it was not the Judge who was to decide intention from the article, and in consequence of the Act the Jury had to decide upon it. Now that is Act 32 of George IV. Chapter 360 and the enactment can be found in Erskine's speeches. I will read the Act to you. It is only a short Act, containing 4 clauses. (See Appendix.) It is to be found in the Statute Book and in other works of Criminal Law. The controversy that the jury should decide the question of intention is the chief point of the 1st clause. Now the jury had to give a verdict on the whole matter, including intention, finally taking intention to be a question of fact and not of law. So you see in a clear legislative enactment that you will not be charged to find the prisoner guilty. It is left to your discretion. You will not be charged by the Judge to say by reading the documents or acting on the maxim that a man intends the consequences of his deeds that the accused is guilty or not guilty in this case. You must take the surrounding circumstances. The Judge may give you his opinion or not. In England it is the practice not to express an opinion. Of course you must be guided by him. He must give you his assistance. This Act is not intended for the purpose of exciting Juries to rise against the Judges. It is not intended to excite disaffection between Judges and Juries. But you cannot be asked by the Prosecution or Judge to find that since the maxim is an accepted maxim, a man must be presumed to intend the consequences of his act. There you need not go any further than this Act. It was all decided by Fox's Act of 1792. Pitt was Prime Minister at that time, and Hansard's Parliamentary report for that time is very interesting reading in regard to this matter. The Act leaves discretionary power to the Judge. The Act says that a Judge may or may not give his opinion. For some time the practice was for Judges to give their opinion. Afterwards they thought that it was a discretionary matter and it was better in the interests of justice not to give an opinion. That is the law in England. Those times were exciting times, and unrest prevailed in England, and in every other country in Europe. It was the time of the French Revolution. Of course this struggle was very keen and it was an act of wise statesmanship to solve the matter in the interests of the people, and the Parliament took the matter in hand and passed the law which has been in force from 1792 upto the present time. I will refer to a few cases after that in order to show how that Act was administered and was carried out in general practice. Since that day it is now entirely in the hands of the Jury to return a verdict of guilty or not guilty. If you think the man is not honest, that a man is not writing in the interest of the public, and is a fanatic, and that he goes against the current of public opinion, then return a verdict of guilty; but if you are convinced, not merely by publication but by considering all the surrounding circumstances, if you come to the conclusion that by anything the man says his real object has been contrary, you must return a verdict of not guilty. You move among the people, you know what is going on. As Mr. Erskine said, it is impossible for a Jury to misconceive the motives of the accused. The authorities may, the Executive Government may misconceive, but it is impossible for the Jury to do so.

So therefore you can never be dependent upon the support of an arbitrary Government. What is the real safe-guard of liberty in England? The Jury. If any 12 men taken at random from my countrymen say that my conduct is blamable certainly I have no right to complain. I am living amongst them, and if the people around me don't like my writings or my views, I have no right to force them down their throats. That was the provision of the English Statute enacted by the Jury Act of 1792, and that Statute safeguards the liberty of the English people in matters of speech, in matters of meetings, of public discussion, and of public writings. The whole test is this and that is what is laid down by Lord Kenyon who says the law of sedition in England is that you can write anything or say anything that 12 of your countrymen approve of. The unanimity of the Jury is another safeguard. Happily for India the law is the same here in Bombay. I am glad in one sense that the case has been brought to Bombay, and that it is to be tried by Judge and Jury, and not by a Magistrate. One of the undesirable reforms of 1898 is that the offence of sedition is triable by a First Class Magistrate. That is the law and I knew that the Presidency Magistrate could have tried me. And it is exactly for this reason that the law should be administered upon a more equitable basis, that these cases are brought before the High Court, or a Sessions Court and tried by a Jury or Assessors. And if there is any safeguard for the people it is because their own countrymen are empanelled upon the Jury and asked to say if the writings are seditious or not. If you libel a private individual it is defamation; if you libel Government it is sedition. That is the necessary qualification.

Now the first case that arose in England after 1792 is the case of Regina vs. Lambert and Perry in 1793. It is the case which has been referred to by Counsel for the Crown and was the 2nd case against these gentlemen. That case was reported in 22 State Trials, Col. 9 85. It is reported also in Erskine Vol. 1, page 405. There was a second case against the same men referred to by Counsel for the Crown. That was at the end of 1810, and is reported in State Trials on p. 305. Now gentlemen, the facts of the case are that these men were Editors and Proprietors of the "*Morning Chronicle.*" It is a Newspaper case (Reads). The trial was the first after Fox's Act of 1792. Now there are certain statements here veiy similar. Reform of Government was asked for (reads down to "we say that the expenses mnst be reduced.") The first demand is for economy, just as we are demanding it here. (Reads down to "dignity of the nation"). We are complaining of the same thing here. It is no use extending the limits of British India, while famines and poverty are ruling in the land. (Reads down to " Military extravagance"). That is one of the complaints made at the Congress in India today. In the same strain this goes on to ask for reforms in a peaceful and constitutional way. Now there is a summary of this in Stephens' History of Criminal Law Vol. 2 P. 367 (Reads). That was matter published in 1793, immediately after the passing of this Libel Act. What do you think would have been the result of such publication before 1792? Every Judge in England would have pronounced it seditious. Fortunately the Act had been passed and was a few months old. Mr. Erskine appeared for the defence and made a very eloquent speech (reads–" Mr. Erskine repeated the very arguments which he had used on the previous occasions "). These were exciting times. It was the time of the French Revolution. The jury returned a verdict of guilty of publication. Lord Kenyon would not receive it. He said " that is not a verdict I shall accept from you ". The first verdict amounted to 'guilty with no malicious intent'. Finally the Jury returned a verdict of not guilty. The case is reported in No. 22 State Trials, Col. 985. This is how the proceedings are reported here (Reads from " the jury then withdrew " down to " a verdict of not guilty "). That was the first case after the Act of 1792 was passed. Another very interesting case of sedition was Rex. Vs. Reeves, reported in 26 State Trials Col. 530. It is also referred to in the history of Criminal Law in England by Stephens, p. 367. " The immediate effect of the Libel Act was, as appears from these cases to make the Juries *ex post facto* censors of the press. " It is written in a despondent tone. He did not approve of the law as it was. I might remind you that it was Stephen who framed the Penal Code Code for India in 1870, and he framed Section 124 A under which I am charged. He also framed the Contract Act and he was a great writer and a learned man. He was of the old Tory type. He did not approve of government by the people. He believed the old direct government was the best. He looked upon Monarchy as a tree, and the House of Lords, and the House of Commons as only branches, or ornamental foliage of the tree. Mind, it was a prosecution made by the sanction of the Parliament. It was an observation against Parliament and its institutions. (Reads down to " return this verdict "). Lord Ellenborough was the Attorney prosecuting, and Lord Kenyon was the presiding Judge. In fact the Jury did not agree with the view which was propounded in the pamphlet, but they thought it was the right of every Englishman to plainly express his view, the motive being of a reformation of the English Constitution. He was himself the author of a Histroy of English law. That being his motive the Jury said he was not guilty. So you see what the right of a Jury had been since 1792. I was talking to you of intention and motive; if you are convinced that the motive is good, that it honestly asks for the reform of certain institutions it is not seditious. You may not like these views or those reforms. You might have quite different views from the writer; that is immaterial. You cannot find him guilty on that. The question is not difference of opinion which you have to decide. Today I am in the dock for opinions which I have promulgated. If you want reform, you might be in the dock tomorrow! You have not to decide whether you accept my views or not; you may consider it to be an absurd view, a view that ought not to have been put in that way. That is a different question altogetner. What I say is what liberty I have now you will have tomorrow; what liberty you would deprive me of by your verdict will be denied to you tomorrow. It is a question of the rights of individuals to propound certain views; whether those views are right or wrong, you must consider this from the point of view of a common citizen–whether every citizen should or should not have the right to express his views. We have to try to convert the majority to our views. We try to create and keep up public opinion. If it is in the direction of reform and progress you are bound to return a verdict of not guilty. You may be quite prejudiced against the man in society. If it were a case of having a dinner with the man it would be a different matter. But this is a question of the right of public discussion,to which you are equally entitled as myself, and it is from that point of view that you have to decide the question.

Another case to which I will refer you is Rex Vs. John Burns in 1886 reported in 26. State Trials Col. 596 (Reads from "in this case the prisoner was charged with sedition"). This was about a meeting for a political purpose, for advocating certain political reforms. Now at that meeting the defendant was reported to have said that it was the object to obtain reform "by fair means if possible" (Reads down to "would shed his blood on the field or on the scaffold"). The speaker, gentlemen, is today the President of the Board of Trade in the English Cabinet. He said that they were moving in a perfectly constitutional manner but–(reads "if the Government continues obstinate" down to "scaffold"). I am quite sure that if this case had occured in 1792, the Judge would have said "this is sedition, and the man must be deported". But the Jury knew the man and for what purpose the Association to which he belonged was established. It was for the liberty of the people that they were fighting. They knew the state of the country at the time. Language like that was held innocent, and not likely to excite feelings of disaffection. I will read to you the verdict. It is a verdict of not guilty. I will now refer you to another case taken up in 1810, and a passage from which was read to you by the learned Counsel for the Crown. It was the second case against Lambert and Perry. I read to you an abstract from the summing up of Lord Ellenborough, who defined what are the elements of the liberty of the Press, and the license of the Press. The extract was quoted to you to show what was the liberty of the Press according to Law and what was license. But there is no use in quoting from the summing up of a Judge; you want to know what the verdict of the Jury is. The liberty of the Press depends upon the commonsense view and not the view of the law. The Jury has not to decide merely from the summing up of the Judge. The Judges have to take the verdict of the Jury. This is the safeguard of liberty. You are the law-makers in this case. As I have said it is Jury-made law, and not Judge-made law. In 1810, just a hundred years ago, the "Manchester Chronicle" was charged for the second time (Reads down to "total change of system"); just the same as we have been asking for. If Bureaucracy be a Policy, Bureaucracy is not the Government. It is a system of Government. (Reads on down to "the whole course of his policy"). That is the dictum of Lord Ellenborough. If we say that a king is mistaken in his policy, that is not Sedition (Reads verdict of jury; also reads Lord Ellenborough's charge down to "degrades his Majesty".) It is a question of intensity. There are errors and deficiencies in Government, there is nothing seditious in saying it. There would be no progress otherwise. England would not have been what she is but for the liberty of the Press. (Reads down to "Rebellion".) The jury immediately pronounced them not guilty. Gentlemen, I wish that the Counsel for the Prosecution had quoted the paragraph that I have just read to you. Never mind; now we will proceed to the charge of Lord Ellenborough. I shall read it to you. (Reads). The same view of the Law prevails upto now. There have been other cases where the prisoners have been convicted. I don't want to conceal that from you; possibly the Prosecution might read to you some of them. The principle is established in England and, gentlemen, I ask you to put it into practice in India as the net consequence of the word "attempt" in section 124A. I have read this passage to you with the object of informing you that the word won't stand alone if you value the meaning which I have suggested. There are cases since the publication of the Fox's Libel Act in 1792 and the same law is followed here. I shall presently read to you some findings of the Jury in libel cases. These are tried by means of a Jury and a Judge. I think it is the practice in this Court to leave the whole matter to you. That means that the law here is the same as in England since 1792. That means that the Judge will sum up and leave the whole matter to you. That means that you will not act on the direction that a man is to be presumed "to mean the consequences of his act." The Jury has the right to decide not merely from the legal fiction but from a general consideration of the whole. There are various other circumstances. What is the motive of the publication, what are the other facts which influence the writer? If his motives are good, if he is trying to secure constitutional rights of the people, trying in a fair way and a persevering manner, he is entitled to express his views fully and fearlessly. It would not be fair to obstruct him in expressing these views. It would be coming in the way of the progress of the country to do so. These are your traditions. We admire them. So long as we admire them you are pleased, but as soon as we begin to imitate them you call it seditious. That is what English education has done for the community. What does Government say here? Well, since you try doing things that way it is rather inconvenient to the men in power. They have long enjoyed absolute arbitrary power. We are fighting against it. It is a great struggle between the bureaucracy and the people. We want you to support it. We want you to support us here in the same way as the Juries did in England. I have read to you the views of the English Juries in 1792. It took a long time for the juries to establish this principle that it is for you (juries) to say what is sedition and what is not. Make the law as strict as you can. The law will take care of itself. We are not so concerned with the law as with the rights of the Jury. So long as we have our own people in the Jury we are quite certain that the law may be of itself rigid, but that will not avail in the administration of justice. That is why you are called the guardians of the liberty of the Press. I will read to you from Cox's Criminal Law, page 51, the charge of Lord Fitzgerald in the case Rex Vs. Sullivan (Reads down to "arbitrary power"). "Arbitrary power" that is the expression I used some time ago. You are the protectors of the press. It is a sacred duty which you have to perform. You have to judge of the motives of the man. When a power is arbitrarily exercised you must protect him if you can (Reads down to "Guardians of the press"). You must not take a criminal view but must put an innocent interpretation upon it if you can. It is a principle of Law that every man is considered innocent till he is proved guilty. That is the law that they followed in this case. In the summing up the Judge said (Reads from the charge). We have a right to complain if India is to be governed in a completely arbitrary manner. But India is governed by a nation having respect for the liberty and the freedom of the Press, which sacrificed some of its best men for it. Although the Bureaucracy here may feel the inconvenience of the principle, it is your duty, gentlemen, to stand between us of the press and those people and protect us. You are the guardians of our liberties. I say we want local self-Government, local Home-rule, whatever you may call it. Government at once says 'there they are; they are discontented and they want a share in the Government. They are acting disrespectfully.' Is it not derogatory to our self-respect and prestige? And if the matter is to be considered like this and the law of sedition is to be considered so rigidly as this, in every case the accused will be found guilty. We had better not have trials at all. It will remain in the hands of Government to send a man to the Andamans without trial. It is not sedition to complain to Government and to ask for a share in its powers. It is not seditious to find fault with or to advocate the reformation of the administration. If that is the law in England it is also the law here. If the English Juries take this view of the law I request you to act in the same spirit and take the same view and say that although you have come out to India, you have the same view and respect for the same traditions that the English Juries have. Further on you will find (Reads "province of the Press" "down to protection from the jury"). There are some who say that juries have nothing to do with motive, whether the writing was intended for publication and whether the writer was actuated by a desire to further the cause of the people. I say that they don't understand the law on the subject of the liberty of the Press. This much is allowed. I have not come here to ask an indulgence of any kind at your hands. If you think that I am writing, that I am fighting, for the liberty of the people, for a change in the constitution, for a reform of Government, then it will be your duty to return a verdict of not guilty.

Whether you approve of my views or not, so long as you are convinced of my good motive you need not depend on the legal fiction which I have referred to previously. It is not your business to depend upon this fiction of the law which has been adopted in a number of convictions, as there are also a number of exceptions to it. Finally I refer you to the case of Rex. Vs. Burns, Hyndman and Ors, which is reported in Vol. 16 of Cox's Criminal Cases at page 365. It was tried by Justice Cave and his charge to the jury is given here. —

The direction of the Judge on this point was as follows:—" I am unable to agree entirely with the Attorney General when he says that the real charge is that though these men did not incite or contemplate disorder, yet, as it was the natural consequence of the words they used, they are responsible for it. In order to make out the offence of speaking seditious words, there must be a criminal intent upon the part of the accused; they must be words spoken with a seditious intent; and although it is a good working rule, to say that a man must be taken to intend the natural consequences of his acts, and it is very proper to ask a Jury to infer, if there is nothing to show the contrary, that he did intend the natural consequences of his acts, yet, if it is shown from other circumstances that he did not actually intend them, I do not see how you can ask a jury to act upon what has then become a legal fiction. × × × × The maxim that a man intends the natural consequences of his acts is usually true, but it may be used as a way of saying that, because reckless indifference to probable consequence is morally as bad as an intention to produce those consequences, the two things ought to be called by the same name, and this is at least an approach to a legal fiction. It is one thing to write with a distinct intention to produce disturbances and another to write violently and recklessly matter likely to produce disturbances." Now, if you apply that last sentence to the speaking ot words, of course it is precisely applicable to the case now before you. It is one thing to speak with a distinct intention to produce disturbances, and another thing to speak recklessly and violently of what is likely to produce disturbances (R. v. Burns 1886) (16 Cox C. C. 366.) The Jury returned a verdict of *not guilty*.

The next case to which I wish to draw your attention is a case in America recorded by Stephens in his History of the Criminal Law. What happened in England happened in America. This legal fiction was taken from England to America by the settlers. It occured in 1735. The Americans had not yet established their Independence and the Colonial Government there tried to carry out this fiction from old records. The same arbitrary power characterised the Government in America. The case was that of Zenger reported in 12 American State Trials page 675 in the year 1735. I have not got that book here but I will read to you a passage from that trial as quoted in a newspaper here from Booth's History of New York. The facts of the case are very interesting (Reads "In 1734 Cressby, then Governor of New York" &c. Vide Defence Exhibit no.) The acts of Government were very severely criticised. It was not a republican form of Government then, but a Colonial form of Government. Hamilton occupied the same position in this case as Erskine in England. Hamilton fought for the Liberty of the Press in America as Erskine fought for it in England. This was a case that depended upon innuendoes, not so much upon direct attack on the Government, but it was contended that certain innuendoes introduced into the articlas or invented or whatever you may call it were intentional. Then the doctrine it laid down was that " A libel was so much more dangerous if true. Don't take the person into account nor the state of society into account; don't take the motives into account. Take the writings and upon them convict him." (Reads " in this case the Governor became the representative of the Crown "). For that purpose the Government is represented by the Crown. In this country every policeman calls himself a representative of the Crown. (Reads down to " libel is not sedition"). Innuendoes go for nothing, that is what Erskine contended in the Dean of St. Asaph's case. And there are besides other authorities such as Locke on Government, which say that taken by themselves they are not seditious. There is a passage in the Bible which says "there is no God etc." If you leave out "the fool hath said in his heart" then it is held to be blasphemy. If a man writes a pharse like that from the Bible there are people who would bring a charge of blasphemy against him and ask the Jury to give a verdict of guilty. Hamilton's argument was similar to that (Reads on down to "there's the innuendo"). So by the help of these innuendoes innocent words in any writing can easily be converted into a seditious libel.

The Court then rose for tiffin.

(Resumed after tiffin on Thursday).

My Lord and Gentlemen of the Jury, I think that I have sufficiently laid before you my view of the meaning of Sec. 124 A and I am not going to try your patience further on the point. It is a delicate matter, and his Lordship would direct you on this point in summing up the case. There are some questions which I should like to call your attention to, and there are some points of 153 A which I think I ought to go into at once as they are points which I desire to raise in my defence. My view of the law as I have stated is that you cannot merely read the Articles, apply the legal fiction and give a verdict. There are a number of circumstances to be considered. For what purposes were the articles written? Were they written for the purpose of exciting disaffection ? If you think that they were written with the motive or object of exciting disaffection then you are entitled to return a verdict of guilty. If I succeed in showing, which I hope to do, that these Articles were written for a definite purpose, a purpose which is perfectly legitimate, then you are bound to return a verdict in my favour. Let us come to that point. I have already given you the history of the Law of Libel in England during the last hundred years and I think the law in England and India is the same. The Jurymen are the real Judges. This is the fact that has made libel actions so rare in England. If you take that view and enter the same spirit as the jurymen in England I dare say that libel actions will be as rare in India as in England.

In the case which I quoted to you yesterday—case of the Dean of St. Asaph-the question was what was the purpose for which the pamphlet was published ? Mr. Erskine told the Jury that if that purpose was proved there was no reason to doubt that. Now in the articles before you there are clear indications of the purpose for which these articles have been written. I say clear indications. The first article states the reason for which I have written it. It is Ex. C in this case and is dated 12th May 1908 and at page 5 at the bottom of the page you will find it stated. There is a clear indication at the bottom of the article of the purpose for which the article has been written. Why should you disbelieve it ? What evidence has been produced by the Prosecution to show that this is not really the reason for the writing of this article ? Absolutely no evidence except the legal fiction. There is no reason for you to suppose that a man has any other end in view. It is clearly stated in the article itself. You find that on the first page line 28. I would come to the question of the translations afterwards. They are faulty. You see that I am answering the objections raised in the Anglo-Indian Press. Then you will see on page 3,line 13th a clear statement. Then again there is a reference in the article showing that the article is written for the purpose of refuting some of the articles which appeared in the Anglo-Indian Press and for the purpose of giving correct advice, according to my view, to Government at this time. You may think that if I have advice to give I should go and say this to the officers; but that is not the duty of the newspaper man. Whatever I have to say I say in my newspaper. I am notpaid for visiting officers and I do not know how my visits would be received. I express my views on public matters of interest frankly; and that would be expressing the views of my community. When I have done that I have done but my duty. Newspapers, as I have said, stand between the arbitrary power and and the people, and the press represents public opinion to Government and this is particularly necessary in the administration of the country. Government may have their officials to represent the view of the people to them, but the view of the situation from the official stand—point necessarily gets corrupted.

An opinion must be represented in an independent spirit if it his to have any value. Now place yourself in my position. Bomb-outrages take place at the beginning of the twentieth century in Bengal. I represent a large portion of the community in my paper ; Khudiram Bose has just been sentenced; and I have to express myself on the subject; that is my duty, whether the times are excited or peaceful ; and if the times are times of unrest, it becomes the duty of a newspaper man to impress upon Government the causes of that unrest. It is a very hard duty—a very thankless duty and sometimes a very risky duty. I understand it very well, but it has to be done. If the newspaper is to go on for the benefit of the people and the interest of the Government, you cannot allow any other consideration to interfere with your duty. We have not started these papers to earn money only. We have started them to discuss current topics and public questions and for creating public opinion in the country. Whether what we say be palatable or unpalatable to the people, or palatable or unpalatable to the Government, we have to make up our judgment on the spur of the moment. If the incident takes place to-day and my paper is published to-morrow I am bound to give my view upon it to-morrow. Perhaps it may not be correct. Man is liable to err, especially the man who writes on the spur of the moment. There are party papers that take a different view of the same matter and people learn to find out which view of the case is right. It is said that this can only be done by public discussion and agitation; well, that is exactly what the newspaper writer has to do, I suppose. These articles were written in the performance of that duty and not for the purpose of exciting disaffectien against Government. That is my point; and if I write in discharge of my public duty you cannot say that the Articles contain here and there expressions which in peculiar circumstances might be considered as likely to give rise to disaffection. Stating the case and writing one's views on a political question of the day is very different from sedition; a critic may find fault with you; but to question the writer's motive is extremely ungenerous. I am not infallible; man is liable to err; but to drag me out for sedition and for punishment for malicious attempt is, gentlemen, to say the least, ungenerous—exceedingly cruel; you might or might not have experience of my position and it is for this purpose that I have to create around my articles, by reading certain extracts from other papers, the atmosphere in which I worked at the time I wrote those articles. It is quite necessary for you to realise my position at the time and see for yourself what was the atmosphere created around me and what *you* would have done uuder the circmstances. That is the proper way of judging the motives of a man, and the intention of a man; and the several papers that I have put in are papers which were lying before me at the time when those articles were written and each of them contains arguments to which I had to reply at that time. In a homogeneous country like England, there are parties like Conservatives, Liberals, Radicals and Nationalists; each man takes his own view of public events. Take, for instance, the Boer war; there were people who disapproved of it, though they were a very small minority. The majority of the nation determined upon going to war and the war did take place. Those who represented the view of the minority used arguments in favour of the Boers, they were called the pro-Boer party; the others used arguments against the Boers. So there was public opinion discussed on both sides and from both points of view. That is the beauty of a free press, which allows discussion in this way to the people of the country upon a particular subject. Now to come to the point, if the deplorable incident at Muzzafarpore had happened in England the people would have been able to discuss their views freely. There was no difference of opinion here as to the character of that deplorable event but the question for Government to decide was how to prevent a reccurrence. What was the cause of it? This was a question which was perfectly legitimate as a subject for discussion. Something very extra-ordinary takes place; something that appeals to you as quite out of the way and public discussion is sure to take place. You must realise what my position was and I am going to prove that position by reading to you extracts from Anglo-Indian newspapers of the time at which I was writing. Of course his Lordship has ruled that if we put in certain papers we shall lose the right of reply. I do not care for the right of reply, I care for truth. The whole history of this matter must be before us. That is why I explained the law of intention to you yesterday at such length. Suppose I say something in a club before the members in a discussion at the club in which members were taking part. I make some observations. If you consider my observations without taking into consideration what was said by the other members also you are sure to carry away some wrong impression. The whole discussion must be taken into consideration. Thus to form your opinion about this Article, you must read the whole article. This is admitted by the prosecution so far, but when we try to put in the papers they object. Am I not entitled to put in a single contribution to the controversy? I have read the views of other people, and have taken part in the controversy on a certain incident; I have had to modify my views and where I disagreed with them I have had to say so. It is for that reason that the freedom of the press is protected. When communities takepart in a dis cussion, Anglo-Indians, Mahomedans, Hindus, and Parsees each discuss the matter in their own way. in England, in every civilized country, there are parties. In India which is divided into communities public opinion is not represented by parties formed on principles, but parties formed more or less by different communities. Now take the Bomb incident. What was the cause of it? English papers rang on one note that the true cause of it was the agitation carried on by journalists of different shades of opinion. The "*Pioneer*" wrote about the "Cult of the Bomb" I wrote about the "Secret of the Bomb." Whether my view is correct or the *Pioneer's* view is correct is not the point. Perhaps you will accept my view. Others will accept the *Pioneer's* view. When this was happening it was my duty to write about it. I move in a community which has a particular view, and being one of them find that by consulting them I can see what my community itself thinks of it. I do not say I take votes to decide the matter but I am living amongst the members of the community which I represent and I am in constant touch with them and know the view they take. Necessarily therefore I have to express the view of my community upon this important question of the day. If I do not express my view in my own journal I do not know why I should continue to be the Editor and Proprietor of a Newspaper. I shall have to give up my post and make room for others. That being the case, while there are different views formed as to the cause of this regrettable incident, I have called it "A misfortune of the Country." It is the heading of my article. It is not that I am now asked for an opinion about the regrettable incident but I have said it is the very hinge of my article on this great misfortune. Well, and there are also other expressions which I will have to point out to you. Now this misfortune having occurred we were faced with two different kinds of views. One view was that it was due to political agitation, from the Congress downwards or upwards. The argument was something like this. The leaders of the Congress expressed their own opinion merely, and the Congress was not a legislative assembly. On the other side it is stated more strongly that the nationalist party is to blame. An attempt was made to show that the Bombs were the latest outcome of the agitation of these people; and they said, "Well, if that is the cause put a stop to the Congress and everything of the kind. This should no longer be tolerated". That was the view put forward by the *Pioneer*,

Englishman, *the Times of India*, and even by the London *Times*. I need not name the other papers. That was one view of the case. That was the chain of the reasoning; and what was the Government to do? Why to put a stop to everying with a high-hand. Now I ask you, Gentlemen of the Jury, if you were the representatives of your community as I am of mine, what would you have done? Evidently you would have done what I did. The learned Advocate General said that if you put any thing frankly, that is no offence. It was no offence to show that the following was the view of my community. My view was the view of the Marathi-speaking people and of the Hindoos every where. You charge me with exciting public feeling. If I show you that I did not excite the people but only expressed public opinion and simply stated the public feeling and put that down in writing for the purpose of replying to the arguments on the other side and for the information of the Government how can you hold me to be guilty of sedition? It is but my duty. Secondly I am expressing public opinion and putting forward new ideas which may not be approved of by every community or which are peculiar to this province. That is my defence and you have to judge of my defence from that point of view. Our view evidently is that the *Pioneer* was referring only to a certain number of the links of the chain. What is the Congress agitation really for? For the reform of the bureaucracy! I follow the line of argument of the *Pioneer*. I say you only discuss some rungs of the ladder. I say that there is a hidden rung which I bring to the public view. There is an old story; something like this. Ten men were sitting round a table; each one was asked "how many are you here"? Each man replied 'nine,' forgetting to count himself. This case is something like that. The bureaucracy forgets to count itself with the rest, putting it very benevolently here. That is the view on one side. What is the view on the other? It is this; we do accept your chain of reasoning and go a little further on, we find that the constitution of the Congress is due to certain defects in the bureaucracy. If you want to stop bombs now it will not do to put down the Congress agitation; but you ought to put down the bureaucracy first or reform it. I know that some of you may not like this. That does not matter. I have not come here with the object of forcing my view upon you. The solution of the question ultimately rests with Government. Government may take one view or other or favour one view or favour the other. The Judge has to decide in a different manner altogether. I know that when bureaucracy is not taken to task they like it; and when we take them to task they do not like it. But we are perfectly justified in putting forward our view; and when we do it we are charged with the crime of setting one community against another. We find certain liberty enjoyed by Anglo-Indians in India, whether officials or not; we are entitled to enjoy the same amount of liberty. Administration would be impossible but for this freedom of expression. We have every right to place our views before the Government and also the views of our community. Every Indian journalist tries to put forward his view before the Government both as regards the cause and the preventive measures to be adopted. I have given my view regarding the causes and will go on now to the preventive measures. The controversy is still going on and it is not yet ended. So these articles written from week to week have been written upon materials, as those materials were accummulated every week. For the first week we have a certain number of papers before us. A fortnight after we get English opinion; we answer it from our own point of view and it becomes another contribution to the controversy. For a week or two we discuss the Indian opinion, after that we discuss the English opinion; then a week after new newspapers come to hand with new materials for discussion, we have to express our opinion upon it; as a matter of fact every week something happens; somebody expresses his opinion either in the form of a letter addressed to the newspaper or in an editorial. All this occurs and it becomes a journalist's duty to represent the views of the community and to write whether he agrees with them or not. It is not a matter of choice, but of duty, and if a matter of duty, I ask you, gentlemen, what could you have done under the circumstances? Would you not have taken the current topic or would you have been content with thinking that as the times were disturbed, you should write on a religious subject or take up an antiquarian subject and write of the latest researches? I could not have done it. It is for the discussion of current subjects that newspapers are started and so long as I am independent and reply to the views of others I am perfectly justified in taking my views, from the standpoint which appears to me to be most efficatious. There is no question about it; and this is the point of view from which these articles have to be considered; and not only with the help of the maxim that every man intends the natural consequences of his acts. The Prosecution ought to have put all these matters before you and not left it for the defence to do that. All the facts, in fairness, ought to have been placed before you by the Prosecution; instead of that they have taken the article and charged me under 124 A; without looking whether it is covered by the first or second part of the section, they placed it before the Magistrate, and before you. They have read it to you, saying "here you are; if there are any exculpating circumstances allow the defence to point them out." Certainly I am not called here on the presumption that I am guilty. I want the Prosecution first to point out how I have erred, taking into consideration all the circumstances. The whole process is unfair as the burden has been erroneously placed upon the defence. That cannot be done; otherwise it becomes a simple matter. You have only to give an article to the Translator's Department. Get it translated; pin on section 124 A to a few sentences and in a few minutes the whole thing is done and the verdict obtained. Not only that but I want to put in the papers containing the controversy and objection is taken by the Prosecution. No witnesses have been called in this case, so we cannot cross-examine them. If they had been called to show intention we should have cross-examined them. It is allowed by law and therefore would have been allowed by his Lordship. I say the process followed here is not fair. Then about the translations you will see that there are certain distortions. There is a maxim in English "give a dog a bad name and then hang him." I don't say anything about deliberate intention. The process looks something like this. "Get the articles translated; you don't understand Marathi; don't worry; put in a few inuendoes from the distorted translations and the whole thing is done." I notice a very peculiar case, there is a sentence there (I did not put it) as to calling a rope a snake. It is a very common proverb in Marathi for expressing the idea of mistaking an innocent thing for an offensive one; for mistaking an innocent man for a thief and punishing him as such. It is the same as giving a dog a bad name and then haging him. But having been translated in the fashion in which it is translated here, the learned Counsel for the Crown hestened to draw the inference here that the writer by the word ' snake ', refers to the Government. I read the translation to you. "It is no use striking idly and continually a piece of rope after calling it a snake." This is an entirely distorted translation. I will read to you the original Marathi (Reads E) Now a translation like that is no translation at all. The Oriental Translator said that the Printer's Devil came to his help. A small ' k ' was turned into a capital ' K '. Probably the printers are very much afraid of sedition. They must have thought that if they set capital ' K ' they would be quite safe. One refers to ' the King ' and the other to ' kings ' in general. The other instance is राष्ट्रवध. The Translator thought that ' killing ' was a poor insignificant word, he wanted something grand. ' Assasssination ' is a grand word. He would appear, he thought, to have a greater command of the English language if he used such a grand word as ' assassination. '

Your Lordship asked me if I was going to question the translations. I said, Yes. In my own interest and in the interest of the cause I represent I was bound to question the translations which were completely distorted. Gentlemen, that is the material on which you have to judge whether the articles are seditious or not. That kind of translation will make anything seditious. I submit that it is simply intolerable that conviction for sedition should be based upon such translations. The errors may have been innocently made, but this is not the place where such errrors should be allowed. Many of you here may have visited the laughing gallery that was exhibited in the Exhibition held in Bombay a few years ago. There were displayed in it two mirrors, one containing concave and another convex glasses. On looking into those glasses, on the right and left, one found one's face distorted in various ways, sometimes like the face of a monkey and sometimes like that of some other hideous being; but it was the self-same face after all. So long as that laughing gallery was in the Exhibition one really enjoyed the fun of it; but when that laughing gallery, so to say, was placed in the Translator's department, it was a very serious thing indeed. I am bound to protest against it. That is not the place really where the laughing gallery should be placed; it is the last place in the world where it should find a locatiou. I think that after the discovery of such distortions the proper course is either to get new translations made or to acquit me altogether. Really speaking my articles are not the subject of the charge. It is these translations that are the subject of the charge. My articles are in Marathi. You distort them. I do not mean you, gentlemen of the Jury, but some one who is responsible for translation; and on the strength of such distorted translations two serious charges have been brought against me. If I succeed in showing that the wording of these translations is not correct, that in itself is enough to insure my acquittal. Nothing more is necessary. The words on which the Prosecution is likely to rely are found to be distorted images of the original words. If that fact is once proved, even in the case of ten words, how can you as reasonable men rely upon such translations? It is not my duty to cross-examine the translator and to see that every word was properly translated. If I were to do so it would take four or five days to examine the witness. I have pointed out that the principal words on which the Prosecution relies have not been correctly translated. For instance, in line 10th page first of the first article, in the phrase "perversity of the white official class" the word "perversity" is mistranslated, and the word "white" is wrongly used. We may say instead "stubbornness of the English bureaucracy." If we accept the phrase used in the translation it takes away the whole sense of it. Furthur on, in line 28, we have the phrase "the oppressive official class". Really it ought to be "the despotic bureaucracy." This is a perfectly legitimate expression, which, I say, has been used by every Indian writer on every political subject. "Despotic bureaucracy" or "arbitrary bureaucracy" are the phrases used for it both in Indian and English papers and they are never considered offensive. And because I had to represent in a few coined words in Marathi these constitutional ideas which the High Court translator does not understand, I am brought here before you to be tried on a charge of sedition. Then later on, there is the phrase "tyrannical and oppressive official class." I ask what the words are for "tyrannical", and "oppressive" in the origianal. There are no such words in the original. The phrase ought to have been rendered by "despotic and arbitrary official class" Now, when there are so many inaccuracies, would you say that it is my duty to find out every mistake? Certainly not. I am not called here to correct the translations of the High Court translator gratis. (Laughter).

The Judge:— If decorum is not preserved in this Court I will have the Court cleared.

The Accused:—I claim, therefore, that the charge is not maintainable. I never knew that the articles coud be so horridly distorted. Marathi langage is growing, and an attempt is here made to translate the Marathi language of 1908 with the aid of a dictionary published full fifty years ago. I knew that the High Court translator would take shelter in a dictionary; but old fortifications cannot stand before new guns. In this way not only these, but as I have explained in my statement, several words have been wrongly rendered. I do not attribute any motive to the translator. I have to say this in my self-defence, as the sword of Damocles is hanging over my head. I wish these translations had been substituted by new ones. And why was that course not taken? I asked the Advocate General whether he wished to put in a new witness to testify to the correctness of the translation? He said, No. Then, am I to be tried on these distorted translations? Why not acquit me? There is the rule of law that if a charge is shown to be faulty in any essential particular the defendant can claim an acquittal or a retrial. Why is that not done when the translations are shown to be faulty in material portions?

Now, look at some words in the second article, Ex. D. To begin with, there is a sample. (Reads. " The fiend of oppression has taken possession of the body of the Government of India " &c.) The insinuation is that we call the Government of India a fiend or Demon. There is a common expression " evil genius has taken possession of you, " and it applies here. I am thankful to the translator for not translating " demon of oppression." Then, again, the phrase " aberration of intellect." As I have shown in my cross-examination, it originally means nothing more than " error of judgement." Look at the difference between the two. This " error of judgement " is a common and inoffensive expression. " Aberration of intellect " ascribes lunay to Governmnet. The insinuation is that I call Government a fiend, I call Government tyrannical, that I chall Government oppressive; and it is on these mistranslations, gentlemen, that the Prosecution wishes to base this case. How for a moment it can stand I do not understand. I do not understand how any prosecution can be supported on these mis-translations. I do not know; the learned Advocate General may have some reply to give. Possibly he still thinks that the translations are correct. But if that be the view of the Prosecution I think more witnesses ought to have been called. The fact of correctness or otherwise of the translations can only be established by a witness. Had there been a Marathi-knowing Jury they could have judged of the articles for themselves. But here the only way in which the true meaning of the passages objected to can be brought to your notice is by producing a witness who will testify to the accuracy of those translations. Then and then alone, you can base your innuendoes or inferences upon them. It is a very serious inconvenience not only to me but also to you and I say that on translations like those it is impossible to condemn a man. Even if nothing more is proved by me than the words horribly distorted, I am entitled to an acquittal.

So the material placed before you by the Prosecution is nothing more than these translations. I am going to read all of them to you and explain the purport, the reasoning, the innuendoes that could be fairly drawn from them. As I have already said, I requested the Prosecution to mark out passages. No, they said, here is a bundle, you may take your chance. Why? Because the Prosecution has the right and is allowed by the law to do so. I do not question the legality of the procedure. But it is very hard. I have now to explain to you, though somebody will accuse me of waste of time, every sentence and be on my guard that none of them is perverted for making it the basis of an innuendo.

As regards surrounding circumstances the Prosecution is absolutely silent excepting that one card. If any gentleman of the Jury can read Marathi and can get himself satisfied I can give them copies of the original articles.

The Foreman :—We should like to see Ex. C. (Article of the 12th May).

The Judge :—Let all the original exhibits be shown to the Jury.

The Accused :—We have reprinted them in the form of a pamphlet and if your Lordship will permit me I will supply the jurors with the copies.

The Judge :—By all means do so.

This being done the Accused pointed out the lines and pages where the passages referred to by him occurred.

The Accused :—The first expression occurs in line 4. "English Ladies" In the translation the words are "two white ladies." The insinuation is that by referring to colour we mean a certain sense of disrespect. Again the word "gora" does not mean 'white.' It refers to complexion. Ordinarily it is so used in Marathi. It is not a term of reproach. In line 6 the word "titkara" has been rendered by "hatred." while it simply means "disgust." Then the words "gora Adhikari varga" "bureaucracy" appear in English. In order that the word might not be misunderstood I have put the word bureaucracy, and yet the translator misunderstands it. Then the two words that follow "bureaucracy" are "hatta" and "duragraha" and they are wrongly rendered. Then about five lines below is the word 'Nemanem'—That has been also wrongly rendered. Three lines still below occur the words " Badmash Mathephiru." I have called those that did the outrageous deed as "fanatics and felons" in the articles. I have called them "Atatai" felons and "Mathephiru" fanatics. But in the translation "Atatai" has been rendered as a "violent man" and what I call "fanatic" is according to the translator simply a 'madcap.' Where there is the question of blaming those that committed violence the words used in the translation are less strong than those in the original. But where it is a question of blaming the bureaucracy the English words used in the translation are stronger than those in the original. "Zoolmi adhikarivarga" which means a "despotic bureaucray" has been rendered by "oppressive or tyrannical bureaucracy " That entirely changes the meaning. Then comes the expression "Gora adhikarivarga." The expression is throughout rendered by " the white official class." I maintain that "white is a wrong translation altogether. Of course, "white" can be understood in a good sense. As for intance they speak of "the white man's burden." But it is likely that an innuendo may be based upon it to the effect that we call them "white" contemptuously. In a translation like this it is necessary not only to represent the original but also to see that no unnccessary element is introduced from which an adverse inference or innuendo may be drawn. In order to save time I will mark out lines of passages to whlch I wish yon to refer and I shall give them to you tomorrow; you have two days' leisure and you can for yourself ascertain whether the translations are correct or not.

The Judge: (To the aceused). Of course, whatever you may tell the Jury and whatever those among them who can read Marathi tell their colleagues is permissible. But I do not think it would be right for any gentleman of the Jury to have these articles read or translated by anybody else. You are at liberty to explain them to the Jury in whatever manner you like. You can tell them that this is the meaning given by the translator, that this is the Marathi word for it, and that that is your meaning, and those jurors who know Marathi will, I have no doubt, tell their colleagues whether your contentions are right or wrong. But they must not resort to any outside help. To the Jury) Gentlemen of the Jury, the Accused is entitled to point out to you what according to him are the correct translations, but you are not entitled to get those originals read to you by anybody else. You have before you the High Court official translations, which must be your guide; but the accused is entitled to point to you what he considers mistranslations in those translations, and those gentlemen of the Jury who can follow Marathi will be able to tell their colleagues, who do not know Marathi, whether the accused's contentions are correct or not. It is for you to judge, but you must not resort to outside help.

The Accused:—I must accept the ruling of his Lordship.

Continuing the Accused said: What observations I have to make on the translations I will reserve them for the present. I will now go over other points which are essential in this case. There is one point, however, which may occur to you, and it is, 'How can these translations be wrong'? I certainly do not attribute any motive to anybody. What has happened is this. We have to write upon current political topics; on political science, on political events, on historical events, and so on. The old Marathi language was not certainly capacious for the purpose. We have words, for instance, for "monarchy," but none for "democracy." The very idea of constitutional monarchy is to be expresssd in a round-about way. We cannot find words for it either in Molesworth's or in Candy's Dictionary. As to the words "Killing, murder, and assassination", there is a word for 'murder' and for 'killing' but not one word for assassination. That is the particularity of the language. The western ideas are new ideas and every writer in Marathi has a very peculiar duty to perform. He has not only to express his ideas in popular language but to coin words. Many such words are coming into use nowadays. You are probably not aware of the difficulty. The English is a highly cultivated language; every sentiment and shade of meaning can be very accurately expressed in it. But such is not the case with Marathi. So also on economic questions-protection, free trade, balance of trade are words and expsessions which it is very difficult to render in Marathi. All that you read in English papers—subjects of high politics, commerce, economics, is discussed in Marathi papers nowadays, and of course it is very difficult to render them in Marathi. The ideas occur to us in English, because we have received them through English books, while we have to write in Marathi. This has been going on for the last 20 or 25 years. Before the character of the language is changed, not only Englsh ideas but also English constructions are adopted. The present Marathi is a combination of English and Sanskrit styles with English ideas expressed by new coined words. It is impossible to find these words in any dictionary. The translations have not been intentionally wrcngly done. But the man, who did them could not have been acquainted with the literature of the present day. In order to properly render these Articles into English, the man must be up-to-date. The is the reason why these translations are not correct.

Then there is another point which the Jury will have to judge, and it is whether the innuendoes are correct or not. I do not know for the present what innuendoes the Prosecution are going to draw but I am anticipating them from some remarks which fell from the mouth of the learned Counsel for the Prosecution. There may be others but to those I have no opportunity of replying. Another point which I wish to bring to your notice is the difficulty of ascertaining the feelings of the Marathi community. I have said that in order to judge of the effect of an article on a particular community you have not to judge what the effect of that article will be on the English community or the Mahomedan community or on the Bengali community. They are all excluded. The articles were read by Marathi-knowing people, and the question is what the present state of Marathi-knowing people is. That is an important point. As I said yesterday you have to consider those points, the language of the article, the state of the society, and not merely the state of the society, but also the state of the society at a particular time. That is what you have to judge. It is, as I then said, an equation containing three unknown quantities, and unless and until these three things are ascertained, it is impossible to judge of the probable effect of those words upon the minds of the Marathi-speaking people. Do not thjnk that whatever impression those words in the translations have produced upon you, is also the the impression which is likely to be produced on the Marathi-speaking people. As I have alredy said the impression is different on different communities. For instance, as I have stated, an article on cow-killing would produce different impressions upon the two communities, namely, the Hindus and the Mahomedans. You have nothing to do as to what impression would be created in Bengal, N. W. P., or the Madras Presidency. My paper is not read in those parts of the country. I am not charged with exciting feelings of disaffection throughout India. But the charge is as to the effect that is likely to be produced on the minds of the readers of the *Kesari*. The proper course then was to put some readers of the *Kesari* into the witness box and ask them what effect those articles had produced upon them. That would have been the proper course. That is the chief point. If these articles are likely to produce an evil effect on those readers they are seditious, otherwise not.

The case was then adjourned till Friday.

FIFTH DAY.

Friday 17th July 1908.

Mr. Tilak resuming his address said:—

My Lord and Gentlemen of the Jury, yesterday evening when the Court rose I had only placed before you some of the points on which I wish to rely in my defence. I tried to show first that it was a controversy in which as a newspaper editor I was bound to take part; secondly in doing so I represented the opinion of my community, and did not invent any new argument, and thirdly that my arguments were in reply to the arguments advanced by the other side, and this was urged especially to show that when you have to judge of the arguments advanced by me you have to take into consideration the arguments to which they are replies. It is impossible to judge intelligently the effect of the arguments on the one side unless the arguments to which they are replies are also before you. Then I tried to show that you have to judge of the effects of the articles written in Marathi on a Marathi-speaking commmunity. The paper is not read all over India, but only by Marathi-knowing public. And I also adverted to the fact that the translations not being correct you were placed somewhat in an awkward position in judging of the effect of the words upon the minds of the Marathi-speaking people, as well in drawing your inference as in basing your inuendoes on the same. All these facts have to be considered as the surrounding incidents from which you have to draw your inference as to intention and motive. I mention this in contra-distinction to the legal fiction that a man must be presumed to intend the natural consequences of his acts. These circumstances will have to be taken into consideration in arriving at a proper conclusion as to my motive, considering the cause I had to represent at the time. Lawyers say, infer the conduct of a particular man from a particular act committed by him. The surrounding circumstances also are perfectly relevant. There are two or three points which are to be noticed. I wish to do it now, and then read some of the extracts from the papers to enable you to judge of the atmosphere surrounding me at the time the articles were written. As I have said I was making a suggestion to Government not merely giving a reply. Certain advice was tendered by the Anglo-Indian papers to Government which I thought was against the interest of my community. It was as a newspaper editor my duty to place my view before the Government in a different light from that in which the Anglo-Indian papers thought it fit to do. Gentlemen, here I must say one thing. Although I speak of the Anglo-Indian community, it is not a matter between Anglo-Indians and Indians as I observed yesterday. Political parties take the form of rival interests between communities in India. But that is not always the case; and in my controversy I should rather say instead of Anglo-Indian community and Native community we should say the pro-bureaucracy party and the anti-bureaucracy party; or if you do not want to use the word "anti-bureaucracy," let us say the pro-Congress party. These were the two parties, if properly defined. The object being to place both sides before Government I use the words pro-bureaucrat and 'pro-Congress' deliberately in order to show that their interests are not racial interests. It is a mistake to suppose that the controversy arose out of any racial differences. There was a real opposition ot interests, such opposition as we find in England between the Conservatives and Liberals. Of course an attempt will be made and has been made in the newspapers to represent this conflict of interest as racial, and as due to race animosity. Our view of the matter is that it is not racial; for you will find when I read some of the extracts from the newspapers that there are Indian gentlemen who have sided with the Anlo-Indian papers, and also that some Anglo-Indians side with the native papers. One of the articles put in by the Prosecution is put in to prove intention. It is dated 19th May and is headed 'A Double Hint.' (Ex. E.) That means a "hint" to the natives as subjects as well as to the Government. That discloses the object of an article which has been put in by the Prosecution to prove intention. "Double Hint" is a sugsestion made to Government and made to most of the native leaders who are siding with, or who are in favour of the views expressed by, Anglo-Indian papers. There is a double warning conveyed to both sides; and the warning conveyed to the people being not to go against their own interests in the hurry of the moment and not to forget what the real interests of the native community are. Because an outrage has taken place, let us not be confused but take a calm view of the situation. That is the purpose for which that article was penned; it was to convey a hint and warning to both sides and to Government. Another point to be considered is that proposals were then actually before Government, notice had been given that Government were going to pass a Press Act and an Explosives Act. (What they passed is not exactly a Press Act.) These two measures were known to be before the Government and my comments on these measures and the view of the community on these measures had to be communicated to Government and that has been done in the other two articles. Repressive measures were contemplated; and we had to give our views, just as it is perfectly legal for a man to give details of a bill, (in this case there was no publication as the time was too short) and to give his views on them either privately or publicly according to his position. So I had as a newspaper man to comment on the measures contemplated, and that is done with the purpose, with the object, of communicating my honest views to Government. Though Government may not agree with my views altogether I am perfectly within my right in communicating my views to Government. When I have notice of a certain measure being contemplated it is my duty to place my views before Government. So the situation is this. As against the legal maxim that a man intends the natural consequences of his acts, You have to take into consideration all these circumstances. I have summarised them shortly. (1) It is a reply to Anglo-Indian criticism. (2) It is a suggestion to Government and addressed to Government. (3) The articles are also addressed to the people. (4) It is a discussion of the situation. (5) It contains a warning to both parties which it is my duty as a journalist to convey and (6) It contains a criticism of the contemplated measures of Government. That is my defence, and it is on these grounds that I ask you not to rely solely upon the legal fiction but to take into consideration the other circumstances. If you find, as I have said, that perhaps writing on the spur of the moment, it was not possible for me to weigh my words in a balance, and if you find my motive has been good, I expect acquittal from you. Gentlemen, It is impossible in writing on the spur of the moment to make a choice of words. I asked Mr.

Joshi to give me a word for 'error of judgment,' He said he would give me one the next day. I must give the word at once and express my opinions. Week by week, we have to see what material gathers during the week and we have to give a summary of the public opinion; we have both to reply and to give our views on the same. That is what has to be done at short notice in a newspaper office. The pressure is greater in the case of a daily; it is not so great in the case of a weekly. But after all it is pressure under which we have to work. Now we work under that pressure, with the object of presenting our side before the people and the Government and replying to criticism in the press owned and controlled by the other party. That is really the situation. Place yourself in that situation and when you have done so say, if you had been an editor of a journal in these times, what you would have done? Possibly you are not aware of the volume of matter that comes before us. In my own office I get as many as two hundred newspapers a week. We have to sift, and summarise, and settle on lines of reply. In order to give you some idea of the pressure under which I have to work, I have put in those documents. I do not want to read them all to you. I do not wish to take up your time. In fact I can myself ill-bear the strain in the present state of my health. All I want to do is to give you some idea of the pressure under which we have to work and of the surrounding circumstances which influence our judgment for the week. That is done in every newspaper office. Now you will kindly give your attention to one of the comments which is to the effect that the arguments of the Anglo-Indian papers are "silly". Here are two notes, one relates to cause and the other to preventive measures. There are the two main points. Now on these two points the controversy was raised. One party diagnosed it in one way and the other in another way, and one party treated it in one way and another party in another way. You cannot form a judgment from one article taken singly isolated from the controversy. As I told you yesterday, the diagnosis of one party was political agitation. There is a party in this country which feels that the Administration is not all right. I am not asking you to agree with me. This is not a Political Club where we intend to argue with each other. This is a Court of Law where we have to see whether we have a right to put forth our views or not. It is impossible to make conversions here and I am not going to attempt it. I only say that every party has the right of expressing opinions in its own way and the same right must be conceded to the other party. Now that is the purpose for which these papers have been put in. If the other side had said that the arguments of this side are dangerous or preposterous I would have been perfectly justified in saying that they are talking nonsense. It is in that way you have to judge of the import of the words used by me in this controversy. It is a reply. It is as it were a tug of war and the tension on the rope can only be asertained by ascertaining the force on each side. It cannot be done otherwise. That is the reason why I want to read a few extracts to you to show what effect these words and arguments are likely to produce and had produced on the other side. It was the duty of the Prosecution to do that. The Prosecution is perfectly at liberty to take a different view. They have only placed before you one end of the rope in this tug of war. It is a rule in mathematics that no tension can be created by pulling a string at one end only.

When you want to find a tension you have to see what the forces are at both ends. And it is with that view, as I have said, that I have put in these papers. I wish to read some of the extracts from them to you. I am sorry it will take up your time but I cannot help that. It is not a question of who is right and who is wrong. If both parties are entitled to put forth their views, I request you to show the same consideration from the point of view of law and justice to both parties. If it were a controversy taking place in England between two parties one party would say that the other party had no right to be in power. Now the Liberals are in power, and the Conservatives say that they ought not to be in power. There is a controversy raised about the existence of the House of Lords itself. Do you mean to say that the controversy raised about the House of Lords is seditious? Then the late Prime Minister would have to be sent to jail for his speech against the House of Lords. He was not questioned at all as he was entitled to express his opinions. As I have said Government in the concrete should be distinguished from Government in the abstract. I am not here to advocate that my view is right. Some people think that the present state of things is all right, others think that it should be reformed. But in any case each party should have the liberty to place its view before Government. What is the advantage of a free Press? It has its disadvantages, but on the whole, advantages outweigh the disadvantages. India is fortunately ruled by a civilised nation. The liberty of a free Press is allowed to us. I know we have not had to fight for it, as the English people had to do in 1792; but after all it is a concession granted to us and so long as it is not withdrawn we are entitled to have the same liberty that is enjoyed in England. Now with these remarks I propose to read to you the first charge-article. It is the article which appeared in the *Kesari* dated 12th May. It deals with the events of the 29th and the 30th of April. Of course views on these events were published in the issue of 5th May 1908. When our views in the article were written we wanted to see what shape the controversy would take. In the meanwhile as an editor I had on my table a number of notes. What I do with these notes in this. I read them. I digest them and I give a summary of the news in my paper and at the same time if I think there is anything harmful to the interests of my community I try to reply. Now the reply must not be judged in the cool atmosphere of this room but taking into consideration the state to which my mind was brought on reading these notes. You must feel as I felt then, and it can only be done by placing before you the matters which were before me when I wrote these articles. This is the relevancy of the various papers that have been put in. Very likely you may be taking one or two of these papers, but you may have no idea of what the controversy is and it is to give you that idea that I put in these papers. You must be reading some of these newspapers but not all. What do the editors do? They do the work for you. But here you are brought to give a judgment, and I read these papers to you in order that you should arrive at a sound decision. Now the papers I have put in may be classified under three or four heads. You have the comments made by the English papers such as the *Pioneer*, the *Englishman*, the *Statesman*, the *Empire*, the *Times of India*, the *Advocate of India*. Then you have the reply of the Indian Press to the same in the *Bengali*, the *Hindu*, the *Madras Standard*, the *Patrika*, the *Punjabi*, etc. It is not only in the Marathi journals that the controversy is raised. It is raised all over India. The two views are represented by the exponents of the different parties in the press over which they had control or which represented them. That is the point to which I shall draw your attention. So you have first of all the opinion of the English papers in India and then the opinion of the native press in India. Then came after a fortnight home papers with the views on this incident of Englishmen. That becomes another chapter in this controversy. When I read to you the three or four articles which have been put in, you will find that they have not been written for nothing, but that there was an immediate cause which prompted the writing of these articles. This is the way we write from week to week. It was one of the arguments of the learned Counsel for the Crown that I had been going on from week to week issuing seditious articles. But the controversy went on from week to week. You have the English opinion, the Anglo-Indian opinion, and the Native Press opinion, and then we come to the view held in this Presidency and by the Marathi-speaking population. I am charged specifically with causing excitement not throughout India but among the Marathi-speaking population. I do not stand alone in my views. I put a question to Mr. Joshi as to how many parties there are among the Marathi speaking people as I wanted to show that the papers of all parties to which the writers belong and of all parties in the Marathi-speaking community took the same view as I did. That absolves me from any evil intention. If there is no personal prejudice against me, these articles will show that I was not prompted by any personal prejudices. They need not be looked at through coloured glasses. It was a natural outcome of the forces acting upon us at the time. In fact what I maintain is that, as they say in medicine, there are certain causes which are responsive to a reflex action. My intention is to show that these articles were written in answer to certain criticisms. The articles I have put in may be classed under these four heads. Then there are the proceedings of the Legislative Council as printed in the Gazette of India in connection with the passing of the Press Act. These proceedings form the subject of the comments in my article. It is in that way that these papers are relevant. Of course they are a great mass, but I do not want to read the whole lot but a few extracts only. But if you are not satisfied you can take them and read them and form your own judgment from them. It is not my wish to raise that controversy here.

Accused :—May I ask my Lord, if I may be allowed the use of certain papers that have been put in. I have already explained their relevancy.

His Lordship to Clerk of the Crown: —Give accused the whole bundle.

Now the first paper I have put in is the *Pioneer* of May 7th 1908. (page 2 Col. 1) The issue is only a week after the bomb incident and before I wrote my article of May 12th. What does the *Pioneer* say ? The heading is "The Cult of the Bomb" and that heading deserves to be compared with the heading of my article "The Secret of the Bomb" Now there is one sentence there. (Reads from "If" down to "for every life sacrificed". Vide Defence Ex. 1) That was the recommendation made ; an indiscriminate slaughter of the innocents.

Mr. Branson :—My Lord, do you think Mr. Tilak is entitled to read that passage and say it recommends the slaughter of the innocents ?

His Lordship :—Of course it is difficult to direct the use of language; we must leave him to exercise his discretion.

Accused :—Of course there is a qualification.

Continuing Accused said :—

There is another extract also which I want to read to you. (Reads "only class" to "striking for freedom".) Look at that ; If that is stated it is our bounden duty to state our side ; and that is how my article arises. (Reads down to "British Government may be tolerated temporarily.") Of course that is a somewhat perverted view of the aims of the Congress. (Reads down to "wicked".) And then the article goes on to say something about Keir Hardies and and Nevinsons. (Reads from " only force " down to "ignorant masses and to "bombs thrown in Calcutta. ")

So that this paper says that there is a logical connection between members of Council and Bomb-throwers in Bengal. When these serious comments are made in the Press is it not the bounden duty of the editors on the other side to place their side of the controversy before the people ? That is how the situation arises. Of course the article gives me more credit than I deserve here (Reads " By their bitterness " down to " it is wicked") We never denied that. (Reads "the nationalists may be" down to "by bomb.") Further on it says (Reads "It is impossible to judge" down to "not guilty") Indirectly charging that every one of us knew that bombs were going to be thrown. (Reads down to "astray".) Now these quotations are from this article, which extends to two columns. If any of the Gentlmen of the Jury wish to see the article your Lordship will direct that it should be handed over.

His Lordship :—If any one desires to see it I will allow it to be handed up to the Gentlemen of the Jury.

(The paper was handed up to the Clerk of the Crown).

Accused continuing :—

You will find that these are the comments of the *Pioneer;* I am specifically named both as editor of the vernacular paper of over thirty years standing and also by name. Now here is an extract from the *Aisan* which is coupled with an extract from the *Empire.* (vide Exhibit D 2.) Then comes (Reads "Mr. Kingsford is" down to "range".) He is recommended to shoot at short range; and then it goes on (Reads "we hope Mr. Kingsford will secure a big bag" down to "best of luck".) The next paper I wish to read is the *Gujrathi* of May 31st. page 773 Col. 2 which quotes from the *Englishman's* correspondent with the comment of the Editor upon it. (Reads "I submit that powers" down to "which they endeavoured to direct' (vide Exhibit D 3.) There was also the suggestion made that all these men should be whipped in public streets by public sweepers. I now put in the *Pioneer* of 11th may, page 2, Col. I to 3. (vide Exhibit D 4.) I have not been able to to procure all the articles of the *Pioneer* or I would have done so. The

Pioneer of 11th May 1908 speaking of the Seditious Publications Act, which was adopted in the Legislative Council, names Dr. Rash Behari Ghose and the Hon. Mr. Gokhale and goes on to say:-(Reads down to "liberty") Then it goes on to speak of the agitation in Madras and Bengal and other places and then goes on in this manner (Reads "The exhortation"down to "in effect"). This means that people should be prohibited from all public meetings Happily the PressAct was not passed then or the *Poineer* would have said that both meetings and the Vernacular Press should be suppressed (Reads down to "not prohibited".) In that way the article closes. Now I would like to read a few extracts from three or four articles from the Calcutta *Statesmau*. The feeling is not so strong on the Bombay side. It is particularly strong in Bengal. The *Statesman* from which I am going to quote is dated May 5 (vide D 5.) (Reads from "the people" down to "murderous outrage".) Further on it says:—(Reads from "it will be observed" down to " extremist agitators. ") And then there is a long tirade against the Extremists. We now next come to the *Statesman* of May 5th and 7th (Reads " so long as " down to " terrorists will remain. ") These two articles appear in the *Statesman* and you can satisfy yourselves that the extracts I am reading are correct. It is not a question of translations. Again the *Statesman* of May 15, page 6, Col. 2 and 3, says (Reads " Even in Russia" down to "many countries.") Then we have "the *Times of India*" of May 4, which says (Reads "The spirit" down to "motives may have been pure.") Of course that is one of the reservations made. Thus I say they contributed to the agitation. They attributed it of course to the extremists of the Congress. Again there is the *Advocate of India* dated May 4 page 6 Col. 2 and 3 (Reads " The one unnpalatable truth" down to " Hydra with the paper knife.") It advises Government to have recourse to the most repressive measures. Reads "It is no use" down to "now to deplore. ") Now these were the writings which were published between the date of my article and the date of the incident or outrage. They were all before the public. We honestly believed that these writings were mischievous, particularly the insinuations of those writers and they had to be counteracted. What were we to do ? Not put comments in our paper contradicting this ? If we had used equally strong terms should we have been allowed to do so quietly ? That is the point to be considered. In a controversy we have to counteract some other views. Of course this was done by the native papers and I have put in two or three issues of the *Bengali*. The editor of this paper is Surendranath Banarji and his name is mentioned by the *Pioneer* in the first article I read. Of course, the reply is that all these articles were written in the heat and excitement of the moment and that there is another side which must be placed before the Government. The Anglo-Indian papers are read by the officials. If they read the vernacular papers, it is from translations supplied by the Oriental Translator. Now the papers I wish to read from are the issues of the *Bengali* of May 5th, 6th, 8th, 9th, 10th, 13th, 28th, and 31st. All these papers are put in not with the object that the whole of them should be read here in Court, but with the object that any one of you Gentlemen of the jury, who wishes to see what the nature of the controversy was may be able to look at them. I will read only one or two sentences from each. I will take the Bengali of 5th May, page 5, Col. 1, 2, 3. First there is the reply to the *Englishman*. (Reads "The *Englishman* has gone mad" down to "machinations of the agitators.") Then there is a quotation from Burke. In the issue of May 6th page 5 Col. 2 and 5 there is another attack on the *Englishman*. (Reads " Now the *Englishman* has said this is a miserable " down to " police have at length unearthed. ") Then in the *Bengali* of May 8th, page 5, Col. 2 and 5 there is a comment on the *Pioneer* and *Englishman* combined and summary of the *Pioneer* article on the ' Cult of Bomb.' (Reads "as a result down to Congress moderates,—extremists and Co.") It then comments in the strain that all this is nonsense and what is required chiefly is a policy of coercion. We then come to the issue of May 9th, page 5 Column 2 of the same paper which quotes a passage from the *Englishman* (Reads "commenting on the Bengal" down to " unfair interpretation of that word.") Then the *Bengali* says " there is hardly " down to " dastardly outrages. ") Next we have the *Bengali* of 10th May. It is a comment on the *Pioneer* and *Englishman* together very much in the same strain stating (Reads "Nevertheless in theas days" down to "representive measures") I will refer now to the Bengali of the 13th May page 5 Col. 1 and 2; there is a quotation there from the Madras *Times* commenting upon this (Reads " The injuries " down to " qualities of the English") There is also a paragraph that refers to the news of Mr. R. C. Dutt (Reads "We learn from the writer" down to "quote".) You may say if he thought so why did he not warn the Government ? In fact a warning was given to Government in the council by Mr. Gokhale, but very little weight is attached to our opinion there. We might as well cry in the wilderness. It is not only the daily press and the weekly press but also the monthly press that does all this. I will refer to Modern Review for June 1908 page 547 published at Allahabad. There is a summary of the whole political situation. (Reads. 'The political situation and Western Sentiments ') That is the heading and that is the subject of the article. (Reads "we never expected" down to "such measures of Justice ".) It takes the view that such measures are imported here. Then there is a quotation from Mathew Arnold's description of murder. It also quotes the *Pioneer* and gives the genesis of the bomb in Bengal and controverts the *Pioneer's* view. This is written in the cool atmosphere of Allahabad. There are a number of other quotations, e. g. article signed A. K. C. whatever that may mean. Next I will read from the 'Indian World' for May, page 472. It is a monthly magazine and says much the same thing. It is an article on the progress of the Indian Empire and on the bomb-outrage. (Reads "Attempts have been made" down to "responsible for the party and then down to "members of the party are well-known".) It goes on to say (Reads from "battle of Plassey" to end of article.) It is written by a man who assumes a German name. Here is nother from Madras far away from the scene of the outrage. I put in the Hindu of May 9 page 4 Col. 1. The writer quotes Mr. Gokhale's speech at the Legislative Council with regard to the objection why the leaders did not warn Government of the coming evil. (Reads "Government Official Class" down to the end of para.) So the warning was conveyed a year ago. It is the same phrase as is used by me in the " *Kesari*. " Now we come to the Hindu of 21st May 1908. It gives Dr. Rash Behari Ghose's speech to the Congress delegates in 1906

(Reads down to "perhaps in Russia.") Mr. Gokhale, I believe, gave the same warning further on. I have here the Hindu of May 22nd, page 6, Col. 2 and 3. The article I want to read is a reply to the *Pioneer* by Nepal Chandra. It says; the *Pioneer* in commenting upon Russian Autocrats gave one view and commenting on Indian Autocrats gave another view. The letter was addressed to the *Pioneer* but was not published in the *Pioneer*. It appeared in some other papers. (Reads down to "such conditions do not last.") And yet the *Pioneer* thinks that they can last in India. Then we have the *Indian Patriot* of May 24th, page 4, Col. 1 and 2. It is a popular Madras daily paper. (Reads on "Anarchist in Calcutta" &c.). Of course the writer takes the Indian view. (Reads "Will the anarchists" down to "grievances.") There is also an article headed "The Danger to England." (Reads article down to "Official acts in Parliament.") I also have here the issue of the same paper for May 14, page 2, Col. 1 and 3. (Reads "Anglo-Indian" down to "animosity and hatred.") In the same paper for May 15th page 4, Col. 1 and 2 (Reads "of the people at large" down to "bureaucracy.") I will not read extracts from the *Madras Standard* but will pass on to the *Punjabi* and the *Tribune*. In the *Punjabi* of 9th May page 3, Col. 1. we find (Reads "Even the most depraved" down to "other races,") and there is a reference to Mr. Justice Amieer Ali.

Then we have *Tribune* of May 9 (page 4, Col. 1–2.) This paper belongs to another party (Reads "it must be admitted" down to "Anglo-Indian Journals.) Next we come to the *Indian Spectator* of May 9 page 362, Col. 2 and 3. This paper which is known to be the moderate of the moderates says (Reads "now what shall we say of" down to "class of punishment.") He then goes on to represent both sides. Then we have the *Gujarati* which is published in this Presidency. I have put in the *Indian Spectator* of May 16th, page 381, Col. 1. It is much in the same strain. It takes the same view as the other papers do. It is not only the Marathi-speaking community which takes this niew. In the issue of the *Gujarati* dated May 17, page 705–707, Col. 1-3 we find (Reads:—"who was to conceive that discontent was growing.") Then we have the *Gujarati* of May 31st page 777–79 Col. 1 to 3. Here is an eulogy on the Bomb. The writer sings to the Bomb, "you do not come to this Presidency." Next there is the "*Indu Prakash*" of May 5th page 7, Col. 1-3. It is a Bombay paper and the party to which it belongs is the party to which the "*Kesari*" does not belong. Mr. Joshi said so the other day. It takes the same view that it is the bureaucracy which must be reformed. Then it quotes Mr. Gokhale's Budget speech in the Viceregal Legislative Council which is the same thing done in the *Kesari*. (Reads "there is much in the present situation" down to "as the succeeding years continue"). Then comes the *Dnyan-Prakash* of Poona of 19th May page 2 col. 1-6. It is conducted by one who assists Mr. Gokhale with his services in the Servant of India Society since it was formed by him. (Reads "Representation will not eradicate the evil.") In the issue of 8th May page 2 col. 5-6 of the same paper (Reads down to "the sentences are nearly the same"). I have been reading from the translations but they can be referred to in the original. I have put in the original issues. The writer says that the authorities have been led to adopt these measures because public opinion is bound to be disregarded in India. Then there is the *Chikitsaka* of May 27th page 3 Col. 2. Here we have a paper completely hostile to the *Kesari* taking the same view as the latter. It admonishes the Anglo-Indian papers for siding with the Anarchists in Russia, and for coming down on all sorts of people in this country and holding them responsible for the Bomb outrage. Now there are also some open-minded Anglo-Indians and the Bishop of Lahore is one of them. In the *Advocate of India* of May 17 page 7 Col. 4 we find a speech in which this Bishop says (Reads "order can and may be preserved" down to "by persecution.") He takes the same view as we do. That is what I say. It is not a racial controversy. It is really a controversy between pro-Congress and pro-Bureaucratic parties. I now put in the *Maratha* of May 24 page 246 Col 1-2 giving the summary of the opinions in England. We had by that time received the Home papers. The Indian party there takes the view that the Bomb incident is the result of certain mistakes in the administration. Some one says we have to face the fact that the India of to-day is not the India of twenty years ago. We have Mr. Nevinson's opinion and also an extract from a French journal the Paris Times. Then we have the opinions of representative men such as Sir William Wedderburne and others and the remarks of the *Daily Chronicle*, *the Morning Leader* &c. (Read down to "served the purposes"). These are the notes and views on Indian matters in England. My own views before the Decentralisation Commission are also there. I have put them in my statement before this Court. They say in England that the situation cannot be improved except by having resort to self-Government. That is what I stated in March last. I will now quote you an extract from the *Times of India* dated May 12 page 7 col. 1. It gives the views of Lord Morley on the situation. Speaking at the Civial Service Club dinner he said (Reads "I think I can show" down to "aliens to rise in India") He admits this and as regards the remedy he says (Reads "our first duty" down to 'desirable.') It is the British Government that has taught us to ask for freedom of rights and for self-Government. Then comes a rather unpleasing observation (Reads "unless we somehow" down to "will not be theirs.) He plainly admits that it is the duty of the Government at this time to reconcile the maintenance of order with political progress. That is Lord Morley's view and that is the view I have taken in my article. The despotism of the bureaucracy can only be checked by the democratic following in England. That view of Lord Morley is very important when we come to consider Government in concrete and Government in abstract. When the highest head of the administration thinks in that way then it is not sedition for a mere writer like myself to say that pure representation is needed. There is another speech by Lord Morley on the subject that the partition of Bengal was a mistaken one. The controversy was raised in the House of Lords. Now what was Lord Morley's reply to Lord Curzon? (Reads "I accept Lord Curzon's views" down to "no damned nonsense.") Then there are certain other papers. This is, as I have said, about the cause of unrest. Diagnose the views and say if repressive measures would be a better remedy. Then there are two other papers I wish to read, extracts from the *Sudharak* of May 11th page 2 col. 2 and the *Subodha Patrika* dated May 10th page 2

Col. 2. and May 17th page 2 col. 2. These are the papers which represent different parties of the Marathas as Mr. Joshi stated in his cross-examination. I am not going to read any more extracts. What I have read will give you an idea of the kind of controversy which was raging when I wrote the articles. There was gross abuse of native aspirations in the Anglo-Indian papers. In Ex. E dated 12th May 1908 which is put in to prove intention, you see (Reads'' since the commencement of the bomb affair'' down to ''agitation.'') That is nothing but a fairsummary of other views. As I pointed out, abont the word missionaries, there is a wrong translation. (Reads from ''but this paper '' down to '' Swadeshi and Boycott agitation ''). Then comes a note about the cancelling the partition of Bengal (Reads down to''partition itself'') That is my comment. (Reads down to ''Swaraja.'') Now this passage was read to you and you were asked from it to infer that that was the opinion of the *Kesari* on Swaraj. (Reads down to '' vice '') I say it is no use waiting till the disease develops. (Reads down to ''Partition of Bengal'') This is put in to prove intention. It was really quite necessary to bring the import of this into articles read to you. You cannot understand the real import of this unless you know the circumstances under which the articles were written. This note has been put in by the prosecution. It was quite necessary to show what the *Pioneer*, *Statesman*, *Englishman*, *Times of India*. *Advocate of India* said and compare it with what I have said on the point. Now I will explain to you the position taken up in the first incriminating articles. You can understand it better now.

You know the right view to take. For every sentence here I can point out a parallel passage from the literature of our party. The arguments are not invented by me. I have of course represented them in a somewhat different form. The whole party is responsible for them. In charging me for sedition this will have to be borne in mind viz what impression will it produced on the Marathi-speaking public. The Marathi public is familiar wtih every one of the views I write. Then what effect can these articles have on their minds ? All they say is, well, the reply has been well given. What is the effect likely to be made on the minds of the Marathi-speaking public if there is nothing new ? I may be charged, in fact I am charged with attempting to excite their feelings. They are familiar with all already; so how would my writings prejudice their minds ? I have been writing nothing which I have not written for 28 years ; it is no new doctrine. It is from that point of view I draw your attention to the fact that the view expressed in my article has been already expressed previously by some leaders of our party.

Now I will commence to read the articles pointing out the errors in the translations. (Reads from Exhibit C, '*Kesari*' dated 12th May 1908.)

(Reads ''no one will fail to feel'' down to ''European Russia.'')

The Marathi words I have used are स्थितीस येऊं लागला हें पाहून (Reads furthermore'' to ''rebels.'') The word used by me is दुःख. दुःख means both physical sorrow and pain. The words I have used in connection with the painful incident at Muzufferpore were not what they are made in the translation The translator evidently thought it would be disrespectful to use the word women so he translated स्त्रिया by ladies and गोऱ्या by white. The word " hatred " there as I have explained should be "disgust". (Reads to " historical fact. ") That is rather too liberal. (Reads down to "white official class.") You will notice that the word Bureaucracy follows and you will see that the translator has put a marginal note to say that this is printed in parenthesis in the original in English. The English word is put there to qualify what is meant by white official class. We have often to use coined words and when we coin words which do not exist in Marathi, we print the word in English till the word becomes familiar. Bureaucracy is distinctly specified as distinct from the Government. Having expressed regret at the Muzufferpur outrage, I say that it cannot but inspire (fill) many with disgust and after writing a description of that outrage we state that such a crisis has occured in Russia. Proceeding further the article goes on to say that the political situation in India is reaching this stage. We say we never expected that the crisis was coming so soon. (Reads to "obstinacy and perversity") I have already stated that the word "perversity" should be "stubbornness" which is the word used in the original, and as the translator has rendered it in another place. It appears that matters have been brought to this stage by the obstinacy and stubbornness of the Indian Bureaucracy. It will be recollected that one of the points made by the Prosecution was that the word "perversity" showed intention. You can now infer what motive the writer could have had in his mind when he used the innocent word stubbornness which has been mistranslated by the translator. (Reads from "in such a short time" to "white official class.") These latter words mean nothing more than the Bureaucracy. The word "white" is introduced by the translator, it is not in the original. What is meant is that we never thought that the Indian people would so soon, on account of the acts of the arbitrary rule of the English Bureaucracy, be inspired with disappointment. (Reads to "the rebellious path.") The rebellious path is described further down as the path of the anarchist. (Reads "but the dispensations of God are extraordinary.") The original words are नेमानेम विलक्षण आहे.

Of course the English parallel "the dispensations of God are inscrutable would do but in translating we must be careful to use the phrase which cxactly represents the original (Reads from " bomb explosive at Mazufferpur" down to " mad-cap ") The words are stronger there than in the original (Reads " It does not appear from the statements of the persons arrested") When we search for the causes we have to examine the case and in connection with the bomb a long explanation is necessary. We must discover the reasons that prompted this fanatic to do this deed and then discuss his motives, much in the same way as I have read to you there are murders and murders ! (Reads "even Kudiram" down to "what then should be said of others.)" Now this does not convey the sense of the original. The other is an emphatic way declaring indignation and one can easily see that it is self-evident that others feel greater pain than the man Kudiram. (Reads to "such monstrous deeds") There is nothing remarkable about that. It is from the statements taken by the police officers. Again here the word " British rule " is a mistranslation for Bureaucracy, arbritary or despotic Bureaucracy. (Reads "to do away with the oppresive Official Class.) I have explained before that the word is despotic. The meaning of that is that the power is not shared with the Government. Unhappily the same word जुलमी stands for three or four words in different contexts as you have heard when Mr. Joshi was giving his evidence. I am not complaining of the tyranny of the Bureaucracy but of the unlimited selfish power which they possess and exercise without reference to public opinion. They may do it according to theory, but as a matter of fact they do not consult public opinion because the Bureaucracy is a despotic form of Government. Bureaucracy is a word used by a number of political writers. You will find it used by writers on political science and writers of constitutional history and by writers of ordinary history. I intend reading to you at the end a few passages from books in which the word Bureaucracy is used. And as I have said it is used in the English newspapers. What reason is there for supposing that the word "despotic". here is meant for tyrannical? I gave Mr. Joshi this sentence to translate. "A despotic government need not necessarily be tyrannical;" and the translator himself found it difficult to express two shades of meaning except by. using the same word जुलमी to make it clear. It is a difficulty which exists in the political vocabulary in Marathi and even the English vocabulary is deficient. Writers of political science use the word despotism in the sense of benevolent despotism. We have to write and we have to express the sense and express it in the best possible form and in the best words that the Marathi language supplies. In course of time we may have some new words by which we will be able to express ourselves more definitely and there will be two separate Marathi words to express " despotism " and " tyranny ". But at present we have to use such words as are in vogue already, which the people use and which appeal to their minds. If you read Trench on the use and abuse of words this is made clear. He says there is an evolution going on in the original meanings of English words. A similar process is taking place in Marathi. We have to use words in political matters and these notes in the *Kesari* have been responsible for adding several words to the Marathi language during the past 28 years. The burden of coining new words falls upon the *Kesari;* it is a fact which is well-known and our readers know the meanings of the words which we have used in these articles. Even other papers have adopted our words.

The Court then adjourned till Monday 20th July.

SIXTH DAY.

Monday the 20th July 1908.

At 11-30 A. M. Mr. Tilak continued his address. He said:—

My Lord and Gentlemen of the Jury:—

I think you are now fairly initiated into the controversy of which these articles form a part. The controversy is an old one. It is not raised on this present occasion by the bomb-outrage only. The Anglo-Indian view is well put by Lord Morley in the words " martial law and no damnned nonsense. " That is the attitude taken up by the pro-Bureaucratic Press. " Put down everything by means of martial law". Any sign of discontent, the least sign of agitation for political rights is to be put down by military force. That is the attitude of one party. The other party says that these crimes must be put down, but only by granting concessions and then only can permanent peace be restored. For myself I am glad to say that the present head of the Government is more inclined to the anti-Bureaucratic side than to the pro-Bureaucratic side. I want to point out that these parties are not of recent origin but are as old as 30 years or say from 1850. You must go back to that. I have said this article is a reply to certain charges brought against the popular party by the leading English journals like the *Pioneer*, *Englishman*, *Asian* &c. To save your time I will go on and read the articles as they are here translated and explain their relations to each other. As I have said in the beginning, the prosecution does not give me any ground for knowing what exactly the objectionable passages are. I have been able by reading Reuter's message sent home which appears in papers received here by last Mail to glean something, but it does not give me a full knowledge of what the passages are on which the Prosecution rely. (Reads article of 12th May " The Country's Misfortune. " commencing from " No one will find," down to "obstinacy and perversity of the white official class.") I have already explained that the word perversity (दुराग्रह) is mistranslated. It should be stubbornness. It may be translated stubbornness as the translator has himself translated it in another place. Perversity is not the right word. (Reads down to "Secret assassination of the authorities.") Assassination is not the word I used although it occurs here and also in Exhibit E. I would like to bring to your notice the original Marathi word which is (घात). You have in English the words killing, murder, and assassination. Killing simply means to act without intention, when there is intention it is murder, when there is treachery the act is assassination. How are we to translate these into Marathi? Killing is translated by (वध) murder by (खून) and assasaination by (गुप्तवध). (Reads down to "white official class.") "White official class" ought to be " English Bureaucracy. " Those are constitutional words which I have used in my statement. We manufacture some words because there are no words in Marathi to express the sense. (Reads down to "mutinies and revolts.") The original words here are (दंगे) and (बंडे)That being so the words should have been translated "revolts" and "disturbances" which would have been a more correct translation. (Reads down to "oppression"). This ought to be

(जुलमी) which means repressive. (Reads down to " their own countrymen.) The *Pioneer* writing in 1902 against the Russian atrocities said it was the direct result of the repressive policy. Why should it not be contended that unrest in India is from the same cause? It is in the nature of a reply to what the *Pioneer* says about the bomb-outrages. (Reads down to "patience of humanity.") The question is whether the spirit that marks a peace—loving nation still exists in India. Of course we have deteriorated but we have a claim still to some of that spirit of love (Reads down to " flat refusal to their request. ") The word पांडित in reference to Lord Morley means that he is a scholar. Now that word is used as indicating philosopher. I have used that word to show that he is more a scholar than a statesman. (Reads down to "inebriated with the insolence of authority.") the word is अधिकारमदानें in the original which means " blinded with power." The translator's phrase is not my phrase. I have used the word (धुंद) which means blinded. It is the word used by Burke when he is speaking of the official administration. It also occurs in the article which Sir. William Wedderburn contributed to the *Bombay Gazette* on the question of the Bureaucracy. So that it is not my phrase. Reads down to " inebriated with the insolence of authority ". Now the argument is it is impossible that not even a few amongst these thirty crores of people should become turnheaded, (fanatics). (Reads down to " excess " and the next sentence.) (Reads from " experience shows " down to " tries to kill him.") This is a more familiar simile than the usual one of a stag at bay; The simile of the stag is used further on. The simile of the cat is more easily understood by the Marathi-speaking public. (Reads down to " as occasion demands. ") Of course the Bengalis are better than cats and if a cat will turn to bay it is quite possible that Benglis will also turn to bay if pressed too hard. Lord Macaulay has called them a mild and effiminate race. This is a reply to that and Dr. Rash Bihari Ghose has spoken in the same way. The same idea has been expressed in a number of Bengali papers and also by the delegates who went to England to explain the situation. (Reads from article "It is true that India has been for many years " down to "spirit of vehemence. ") Vehemence is not the word in Marathi, it is आवेश. It denotes that you have the fire of spirit in you. It is a popular expression that foreign rule demands these qualities (Reads-"but under no circumstances" down to " perpetually in slavery "). That is in reply to the arguments which have been used that the people are peace-loving, and it is the agitators for political rights who roused them and that if we put them down, the people will be quiet. What we say is that it is a part of human nature; there is a limit to loving and honouring. Human nature can only stand it up to a certain point. I had to reply to this. I say abuse my party or abuse the idea, but I say you can not support the argument that the people are altogether completely devoid of sense and self-respect. Then the article says (Reads " it is not our rulers " down to " religious faith.") The whole policy of the Government of India is settled on the consideration of these points. I shall presently read an extract which will show you that this is a statement of fact. (Reads " English statesmen have " down to " by some English writers ") The writer here referred to is Mr. Thorburn who was Commissioner of the Punjab. (Reads "when one country," down to " self interest alone.") He goes on saying that one country does not acquire another for philanthrophy. It wants to get some profit out of it for itself as well as for the people of the country that is acquired. There are three views of the question, simple benevolence, simple self-interest and the two mixed together in a varying degree. I will read you what Mr. Thorburn says:—

"With a view to secure that good will, we gave India what was most likely to content her people—impartial justice internally between man and man; but externally we subordinated India's interests as a whole to our own. In furtherance of these principles, we strangled those of our Dependency's industries which clash with England's—India's silk, calico, muslin trades, for instance-and we rigorously excluded outsiders from sharing in the profits of our Indian estates. After the mutiny, when the nation collectively became directly responsible for the good Government of India, we opened the country to all comers, and gave Indians as full a measure of justice as was compatible with the superior claims of our own people. With these objects in view, we completed the destruction of the handloom cotton weaving manufactures of India, and insisted on the abolition of the duty on imported cotton goods, and not until the Treasury was empty and the whole press of India, English and Vernacular, united for once in history, condemned with one voice the selfishness of our proceedings, did we in 1896 sanction the reimposition for revenue purposes of very light cotton duties. It was the coersion of shame and fear, and not the pricks of conscience, which induced Parliament to accept what all India was demanding—shame at the "expose" of our selfishness, fear that persistence in refusal would alienate from us not only Indians but Anglo-Indians as well.—[*India page 33*, *1902*]

He says that we are governed by selfishness, (Reads " in my opinion " down to " on her administration.") As I have said there are three ways; (1) India should be governed for the benefit of the Indians, which has been expounded by Mill. There is another theory also that (2) India should be governed by enlightened self-interest. Thorburn is not alone in holding that theory; there are several English writers who hold the same theory. In any case it is not my phrase. The complaint at present is that Indians are not allowed any voice in the administration of the country. That was the evidence given by myself before the Decentralization Commission. I have not said it secretly in Marathi only, but I have stated it openly before the Royal Commission, specially brought out from England to find a means of removing the complaint. (Reads "The whole contract " down to "white official class in their own hands ") the word used by me is " सर्व मक्ता " "monopoly"; that is the ground of complaint that has been urged for the past fifty years. How can you say that this phrase will excite disaffection, when it has been used by Indian writers for the past fifty years and it has not yet excited disaffection ? (Reads down to " be uncomplainingly accepted "). Now I am explaining in all these passage what the bomb-outrages are due to. One party says it is due to the Indian Press, to the Extremists of the Congress party and to all kinds of agitators. I say it is due to failings in the administration, and if that administration is improved then this agitation will stop. As a matter of course, all this agitation by the Congress and by the Political leaders is the result of defects in the administrative system. That argument is taken up naturally for the purpose of writing against the Bureaucracy. The Pro-Bureaucratic Press says that it is these agitators who have brought about all these troubles. Let us put them down by a military and police regime. Our case is that it is not a true indictment and that it is the system of administration that has done this work already. We say that the Bureaucracy is becoming intolerable (not tyrannical), not because of actual tyranny but because of the absolute despotic exercise of the power held in their own hands. It is opposed to representation by the people. With the spread of education and the coming in contact with other foreign nations it will be impossible for these to continue. It is a controversy which has been going on for thirty years ever since Mr. Dadabhai Nowroji wrote his book 'Poverty and un-British Rule in India.' It is a goodly volume of five hundred pages propounding the same idea, and as far as I can see his arguments have remained unanswered upto this time. Major Evans Bell in his work ' Our Vassal Empire ' takes the same view of the situation. He says that some day the two parties are sure to come into conflict, one refusing to move an inch and the other knocking at the door for admission to the house of Bureaucracy. That is the way it has been put. It is not my own argument. It has been advanced for a large number of years and I have simply used it to show that the arguments of the pro-Bureaucratic Press are not logical and not sound. (Continues reading from article ' whatever things we might do ' down to ' our hands.') The learned Counsel said in his opening address ' they want power. ' Well, certainly I do not deny that; if that is seditious then I think all these works I am reading from must be confiscated and be destroyed. The Decentralization Commission asked me if I wanted this change at once. The word ' gradually ' in the original has been left out by the Translator and lost sight of and it is suggested here that I have stated that the whole power must come into the hands of the Indians at once. (Reads down to ' another Russia.') If the Bureaucracy had its own way, if it was not checked by democratic feeling in England, they will go to further lengths than this. There are checks even to a Bureaucracy, one of the checks being that the Bureaucracy is subject to Parliament. (Reads down to autocratic sway.) It is a clear warning clearly stated. It is one of the cases to which Lord Curzon refers. The word oppressive has been wrongly used here. The original word is जुलमी, which means repressive. The question here is—is the repressive administration likely to be popular in the time to come? And if not, should some change not be made? And as I have said bomb-outrages are a signal from which some warning may be taken by Government. (Reads down to ' horrible deeds.') I have pointed out what that means. That means that it cannot but be so. The original words I used here are प्रकट झाल्याखेरीज राहणार नाहींत; not that that was their will or their desire. Again to suggest that is not new, not of my own saying. The Hon'ble Mr. Gokhale himself in one of his speeches in the Legislative Council before the Viceroy said :—

'This then is the position. A few men in Bengal have now taken to preaching a new gospel, and here and there in the country one occasionally hears a faint echo of their teaching. But their power to influence the people—to the extent to which they are able to influence them—is derived mainly from the sense of helplessness and despair which has come to prevail widely in the country, both as regards the prospects of reform in the administration and as regards the removal of particular grievances. The remedy for such a state of things is therefore clearly not mere repression but a course of wise and steady conciliation on the part of the Govrnment.'

The warning was given by Mr. Gokhale and also by Dr. Rash Behari Ghose in his Budget speech of March last. That was the warning and Dr. Rash Behari Ghose said the same thing.

'The choice lies before you between a contented people proud to be the citizens of the greatest Empire the world has ever seen and another Ireland in the East. For I am uttering no idle threat, I am not speaking at random, for I know something of the present temper of the rising generation in Bengal, perhaps another Russia.'

He said this in his welcome address of the Congress of 1906. Why this was quoted by *The Englishman*. It is curious to note that *The Englishman* quoted this and stated that because Dr. Rash Behari Ghose gave this warning therefore he must have known something about the bomb-outrages beforehand. If he had not given that warning they would have said 'well, here you say you desire the welfare of the Government, why then did you not give the warning?' (Reads again from article of 12th May down to 'As you sow so shall you reap') The Translator has put in the English maxim which is practically the same. But I rely upon the original and I will only refer to differences in the translations which in my opinion are serious. (Reads down to 'human nature.') I am not the first to put such a soliloquy into the mouths of the Bureaucracy. Sir P. M. Metha said on one occasion:—

"In progress of time large numbers of Englishmen trained in the maxims of despotism and saturated with autocratic predilections, would return to their native home, where they could not but look with intolerance on free and constitutional forms. This is no visionary speculation. Careful English observers have already noticed traces of such tendency. In the course of a few generations, such a tendency, if not checked, would develope into a mighty influence and the free and constitutional Government of England which has been so long deprived of the world would be placed in the deadliest jeopardy. With a policy of force, as I have said before, the resources of India would be drained in the first instance in maintaining large costly armies and huge services; the country would be thus too much impoverished to admit of her developing the great material resources which nature has showered on her.

"In India, impoverished and emasculated, the English Merchant would only be an emaciated attendant in the rear of the English Soldier and the English Civilian, and English commercial enterprise, more glorious even than her military enterprise, would find no congenial field."

Sir Pherozshah Mehta in his speech welcoming the delegates to the 20th National Congress in Bombay in 1904 also said:—

"I wish to speak with all respect for these disinterested advisers; but I cannot help comparing them to that delightful "Poor Man's Friend," Sir John Bowley, so admirably depicted by Dickens:—"Your only business, my good fellow, is with me. You need not trouble yourself to think about anything. I will think for you; I know what is good for you; I am your perpetual parent. Such is the dispensation of an all-wise Providence, * * * What man can do, I do. I do my duty as the Poor Man's Friend and Father, and I endeavour to educate his mind, by inculcating on all occasions the one great lesson which that class requires, that is, entire dependence on myself. They have no business whatever with themselves." I venture to say that to accept this advice would be equally demoralizing to the rulers and the ruled. It ignores all the laws of human progress, it ignores the workings of human nature, it ignores environment and surroundings. We may be as well told to cease to breathe, to think, or to feel. Political agitation there will always be. The only question is whether we should suppress and bottle up our feelings and hopes and aspirations and our grievances in the innermost recesses of our own hearts, in the secret conclaves of our own brethren, or deal with them in the free light of open day.'

I have said the same thing. They ignore the awakening of human nature. Of course the instances introduced are recent ones, that have taken place since 1904. I simply wanted to show that the Bureaucracy ignored this aspect of human nature.

We have literature of our own and those books are held to be quite legal. They have never been suspected and when I was called upon for a reply I took my stand upon the principles of my side and I am here to answer for these charges. (Reads 'most of the Anglo-Indian papers' down to 'leaders.') You will again see that this reply to the Anglo-Indian press is written by myself on an occasion of provocation and not to excite disaffection. If you were in my position when such Repressive Acts were passed, if they were passed in your country, would you not come forward and say what I have said? Of course it may be unpleasant advice but a distinction must be drawn between unpleasantness and sedition. (Reads down to 'those leaders again'). That is the advice of the *Anglo-Indian Press* and in summing it up I have only omitted the abuse which they have cast upon us. I have tried to make my point clear by arguments and the only comment I have made is that the advice is most silly. Then I go on to give an illustration. (Reads down to 'unrestrained official class alone'). The dam begins to give way; but is it due to the rain or the flood? The rain represents the official class, and the flood the popular feeling. That is only an argument which I tried to use when endeavouring to show where the real causes of the present unrest lie. (Reads down to 'real state'). There is another illustration. We revolve round the world's axis and think the world is revolving and not ourselves. We do not perceive our own mind. The Bureaucracy makes mistakes but attributes those mistakes to others. Autocratic, irresponsible,-these are words that have been used for the past fifty years, and even stronger words in describing the situation. In fact 30 years ago people were quite satisfied with it. But with the spread of education new aspirations have arisen in the hearts of the people. I do not want to conceal this fact. The Bureaucracy may have done some good but it has also done harm, and the time is now ripe for a change. Are we to be charged with sedition for saying what has been said, in the Legislative Council, in the Congress and before public audiences in England and in India ? I don't think that this view could be objected to when put forth in a newspaper in reply to certain attacks. It remains for wise men to point out the real cause and lay the blame on proper shoulders (Reads down to 'subject people'). That is what the whole agitation in India is. There is one pro-Bureaucratic class, and in the Congress there are two parties–one calling themselves Moderates and the other calling themselves Nationalists, or, as they are called by others the Extremists ; and then again there is a class who are neutral. I have tried to give an explanation of this class here (reads down to ' the path of passive resistence'). I may tell you at once that I am appealing to this latter party. The aim and object of these parties is the same. They both want to have a share in the administration, but one of the parties wants to push it a little further. (Reads down to 'in all places'). For the words 'indignation ' and 'exasperation' the words should be 'fire of enthusiasm.' Of course the illustration is that the sun remains the same but his heat is less in Simla or Darjeeling than in Marwar. So the cause may be the same but the effect may be different in the case of different persons. I might point out that in the original the words are ' thousand-rayed sun. ' (Reads down to ' by an unpopular system '). This means despotic system; my words in the original are (जुलमी राज्यपद्धति) (Reads from ' If there is any lesson ' down to ' Muzzafarpore bomb-affair '.) The power of Government is not denied. They can put a stop to it at any time by a reign of terror or police regime. But is that what Government should do? It is not by resorting to repressive measures that anything can be done. As Lord Morley has said there is to be ' martial Law and no damned nonsence ' (Reads ' develope again in another part. ') The simile is taken from medical science. Some extraordinary medicine is necessary. The boil is not an extraordinary disease but this is an extraordinary boil. (Reads ' subject's great misfortune ' down to 'horrible calamities.') It is a misfortune to the country, a misfortune to the ruler and the ruled and to the whole country. The capital K in the sentence is a mistake. It is a common noun. The capital ' K ' has been attributed by the translator to the Printer's Devil. As translated by the Translator it means a ruler (Reads from ' it is plain ') It is not a military remedy; it is a civil remedy. I have said we rely upon getting this remedy. One diagnosis is that the cause is the agitators. We have said that we had been asking for certain rights for 50 years and that we must get some attention. No attempt is made to answer the *Pioneer* in the same strain although it has recommended that we should be whipped publicly by the sweepers. We have written in a calm and reasoning fashion. (Reads down to 'improper deeds'). This means that one man here and one man there may feel disposed to use this wrong means. (Reads down to 'instead of being stopped '). It is likely that Government may get excited over the matter; it would lead to more repressive measures; but at the same time advice is given to Government that it would not do to adopt a more repressive policy as suggested by the *Pioneer* and other papers. (Reads down to 'persistently and constitutionally '). All these words have to be coined anew. It is not denied that people who make efforts in a legal and constitutional manner need fear anything. In fact that is the principle upon which all political agitators go in India whether they be Moderates or Nationalists. The only thing is the degree to which we shall go in demanding these measures. (Reads down to ' out of control '). Because some people go mad or grow wicked you cannot say that all political agitators in India are seditious. That is a wrong way of reasoning, and is one that is adopted by the Bureaucratic Press. The whole matter is reasoned out in this article by means of arguments which we have found in the literature of our party. Here and there an illustration may be new but the arguments are familiar to the readers of the *Kesari* for the last 28 years. The arguments that are there, are familiar to the readers and to the leaders of the Indian parties for the last forty or fifty years. What can be the effect upon their minds? The same effect as ten or more years ago. They would only say that their arguments are marshalled very cleverly. I have marshalled my arguments without abuse or vilification leaving it to the readers to say if that is not more impressive (Reads down to ' Political rights are seditious'). It is a wrong inference which has been drawn. That is not the point; the point is to whom are the articles addressed, and what is their purpose? You have to take into consideration that they are addressed to the authorities and are not intended to stir up the people. All these arguments help in putting forward our views in a particular way. The Bureaucracy does not like power to pass from their hands; but it would be wise for them to do so and they should take a warning from this and know the state of the country. The article, however, says it is no use murdering an officer. If one is murdered another comes and succeeds. It is foolish to suppose that the British Government can be affected by the murder of any high officer, because another is sure to succeed him. (Reads down to ' exhausted '). The people may be as peaceful, as harmless, as poor as they can be; still just (as I have said) as the cat turns to bay, they may turn to bay. Advice is tendered to both sides, and I have given a double hint. I have said to people, ' your acts are wicked, you cannot affect Government in that way; ' and I have said to Government 'these acts are wicked and must be suppressed, but in order to prevent them in the future some rights should be given to the people;' (Reads down to 'despair'.) The capital 'K' there is wrong; it should only be a small letter. ' Traga ' is a word adopted into Marathi long ago; it means that a man inflicts some injury upon himself so as to throw the blame upon another. You injure yourself to bring your wishes before another. That kind of practice is always the result of persistent refusal of one's wishes. When you beseech and pray and beg, and you do not get you desire then 'traga' is committed. The word I used in original is (त्रागा) self-infliction. The advice given to Government is that their policy should be such that the public should not turn to bay, not even a few of them. This is the advice we are tendering to Government on this present occasion. We are giving that advice in place of bad advice—such as that which is given by the '*Pioneer*' and other Anglo-Indian papers. We say do every thing to punish outrage at Muzafarpore, to stop these fanatics, but give us some measure of political reform. The difference between Lord Morley and ourselves is the degree of reform which is to be granted. His is a modest measure of reform, we want something more. He said at the Civil Service dinner 'You can not govern by mere repression'. If that is the view of Government, if that is the view entertained by Lord Morely, then to state this view by suggestion before Lord Morley'speech was published in India is not sedition at all. (Reads down to 'Repudiated it'). Our duty is not only to point out faults but to suggest the remedy. What is the good of telling a man that he has phthisis, if you cannot tell him the remedy. (Reads down to "such extremities"). We do not want these crimes, these outrages; there is no question about it. But our whole duty as subjects is not done simply by expressing our abomination. Violence is repudiated and advice is given to Government and to the people not to become excited. Of course the advice may be unpleasant to the Bureaucrats, but unpleasantness and sedition are two different things. I would like you to notice that the tree of anarchism is called poisonous by me. (Reads down 'to misfortune to us all'). It is a misfortune to all around, as I have said, that this Muzafarpore affair should have occurred at this time, that the *Pioneer* should give such advice, and that Government should ignore our advice. All these things are a misfortune. Some times one has to say a disagreeable thing, but if the advice is beneficial no body can complain. You must take quinine occasionally although it any be unpleasnt to you. We do not want these wicked outrages. We advice people to stop them; if our advice is not followed what can we do? The matter is not in our hands. Providence has not left it to us. We merely deplore the wicked acts and at the same time we have a right to say that these acts can be stopped only by such and such means. This is a reply to the *Pioneer* who says that the people throughout the land should express their abhorrence for this outrage. I say do it by all means, but do not forget that it is necessary to give advice to Government for avoiding it in the future. Also *Anglo-Indians* want to mantain the Bureaucracy as it is at present; they only want to utilise these misfortunes. They are not in a temper to appreciate our efforts to obtain some concessions. I come down then to a review of political arguments by which the article is actuated. I say the duties are mutual. There is one duty for the subjects and a corresponding duty for the rulers. (Reads down to 'irresponsible'). I have said that, and the word irresponsible is used throughout to mean irresponsible to the people, not subject to the opinion of the people, as the Government in England is.

Irresponsible to themselves is not the meaning. It is used in the political sense meaning not subject to, and quite independent of, the people themselves (Reads down to ' is inevitable'). We say that in the case of Russia and Turkey. It was the state of England before the Revolution. (Reads down to 'with that object in view to-day's article has been writen').

Now in writing that article, I ask you what was the reason for writting it? I have read to you extracts from the *Pioneer* and *Englishman* and other papers to show how they utilize these incidents for their own purposes. This is a reply to that. We have as much right to put our views before Government. With those Papers before you now, judge of the wording in these articles by comparing them with the article of the *Pioneer*. If the Anglo-Indian papers are to have a monopoly of tendering advice to Government, then it would be better if we stop the Vernacular Press altogether. In return for the vilification and the abuse showered upon us by the English Press, this article with calm reasoning lays the popular view before the Government, with the arguments that have appeared in the literature of the party for the past generation. Perhaps some of them may be new to you, but you do not read the Vernacular papers. They are not new to the people or to the Government. We have been asking this all along, and on the present occasion it was necessary for some political party to put forth their views before Government, and I felt impelled to do so. The bomb-outrage is a peg on which these articles hang. That is the view that this article takes of the situation. I am not ashamed to own it. It has been written for that purpose, and I want to explain to you the purpose for which it is written. In the Dean of St. Assaph's case there is a small note saying that the pamphlet was written with such and such objects. I rely upon a similar ground. I have said why this article was written. I have referred to the *Pioneer*, *Englishman*, *Times of India*, &c., they have mentioned me by name. So what ground is there to suppose that this is not a reply to the *Pioneer*? That I am not entitled to convey the view of the Marathi-speaking population? I might say very truly the view of the whole of India? Of course there are some Indians on the side of the Bureaucratic Press just as there are Conservatives and Liberals in England. Would you hold anybody seditious under Section 124 A, for writing as I have done, in England? There are two parties in England and it is the duty of each party to represent its own views. There is nothing wrong in that. If the Vernacular Press should continue to exist it should exist only for this. I was bound to criticise the abuse of the *Pioneer* and to express my views couched in decisive terms. Is that sedition? What has been done? The outrages have been repudiated and condemned. I do not speak here with the object of making you converts to my view, but when one party goes on like that and abuses the other, they challange the other party. I know that some of you will say, ' yes the *Pioneer* has said so and so, why don't you file a suit? ' If we want to charge the *Pioneer*, we must file a complaint under Section 153 A. But to do so we must obtain the sanction of Government.

Government must sanction the Prosecution, and Government is not likely to give that sanction. A question was asked in Parliament as to whether the Government would peosecute the *Pioneer* for making certain statements, no reply was given. The papers arrived only here by last mail. It was Mr. O'Grady who asked why the Government would not prosecute the *Pioneer* and other papers. I do not want them to be prosecuted. I do not wish that any other Editor should be in the same predicament as I am today. I do not wish it even for my enemies. I do not want to be vindictive, but I think it is an instance to show. If it had been a personal matter I would certainly have filed a suit against the Editor of that paper. I might mention the case of Captain Hearsay who was libelled by the *Pioneer*. He did not waste any time in filing a suit. He went to the office and horsewhipped the Editor. That is how you, gentlemen of the Jury, would proceed if insulted like that and your name were concerned. The people of the Punjab once requested the Government to prosecute the '*Civil and Military Gazette*' for certain libellous statements made against them, but the Government refused to do so. If the Government believes that those papers are actuated by honest motives, though their language may be very strong, how can they believe that this article written in much milder language by me is seditious? It is only a reply to the advice tendered by the Anglo-Indian papers to Government. As a matter of fact we are entitled to greater latitude than the *Pioneer* since the Penal Code says that what is done in self-defence is not an offence. That referes to property and I maintain that property includes reputation. Are we not to be allowed the right of reply? We have referred to the article in the *Pioneer* in very mild terms; we have replied with arguments only. Are we to allow the *Pioneer* to go on abusing the mass of our readers and of the people in this country? In that case it would be much better to abolish the Vernacular Press, and leave the *Pioneer* in the field alone. It is my duty to reply to such vilification. Some say that political agitators are the cause of all this. They must be hunted down and whipped by sweepers. But our party says their argument is not sound, they heve gone mad. For the proper view is very different. These arguments are different. These arguments are set forth calmly and reasonably. I shall show you presently by reading a few quotations from important authorities that the description of the Bureaucracy I have given is not a new one. It has been given by eminent writers who are popular in England. You have further to remember that the Bureaucracy is not the Government. To criticise the Bureaucray is not bringing into contempt or hatred the Government established by law in this country. The Bureaucray call themselves the Services and for the purpose of 124 A the servant is at once turned into the Master or the King. They are the Services and no body pretends to say otherwise. I will read you a passage from Major Evans Bell's book "Our Great Vassal Empire" page 6. (Reads 'Government is not the administration'). Hence the administration is not the Government; the Bureaucracy represents the administration under Government; the Bureaucracy is not the mainstay of the British Empire. Are there not provinces of the British Empire which are not governed by the Bureaucracy? The Bureaucracy is not a synonym for 'British Rule in India'. Every writer in India has made a distinction between Government and the administration; and it is now recognised that to contend for the right of self-government, as ruled in I. L. R. 34 Calcutta, is not seditious. How can you demand a share in the administration unless you can show that the present administration has some defects ? If you cannot find any defects you have no claim for reformation. It may be unpleasant to the Bureaucracy, but there is nothing in it which brings contempt or hatred upon the Government—I mean Government in the abstract. It may not be agreeable. suppose I am the trustee of a certain estate; you may remove the trustee, but that does not destroy the estate. The Bureaucracy are thinking that they are Government established by law. It may be unpleasent, annoying and disagreeable for them to be told that they are not so; but that is not sedition. I will read to you a few more extracts. I will first read to you from "Problems of Greater Britain" by Sir Charles Dilke:—

'Foreign observers are, however, given to severely criticising our pretence that our Government of India is not a despotism; and, on the contrary they defend it as the perfection of an autocracy, a benevolent and intellegent rule which in their opinion suits the people governed, more closely than is the case with any other Government on the Earth's surface. It is indeed difficult to see upon what ground it can be contended that our Indian Government is not despotic. The people who pay the taxes have no control over the administration. The rulers of the country are nominated from abroad. The laws are made by them without the assent of representatives of the people. Moreover, that is the case which, as has been seen, was not the case under the despotism of Rome, or in India itself under the despotism of the Moghuls, namely, that the people of the country are excluded almost universally from high military rank, and generally from high rank in the civil service. The nomination of a few natives to positions upon the Councils is clearly in this matter but a blind, and it cannot be seriously contended that the Government of India ceases to be a despotism because it acknowledges a body of laws. On this principle the Russian Government is not a despotism, because the Emperor never takes a decision without some support for his views in the Imperial Senate.'

That is the argument of the pro-Bureaucratic party. Despotic is the term used in Political discussion and that is the word that I have used. I might remind you that Sir Charles Dilke was once a member of the Ministry and was a leader of this view. Sir W. Blunt has said the same thing:—

'The Government of the country was vested in a Board of Directors sitting at the India House, and delegating their executive powers to a Civil Service of which they themselves had in most instances been originally members, and whose traditions and instincts they preserved. It was a Bureaucracy pure and simple, the most absolute, and closest, and the freest of control that the world has ever seen; for, unlike the Bureaucracies of Europe, it was subject neither to the will of a Sovereign nor to public opinion in any form. Its selfishness was cheoked only by the individual good feeling of its members, and any good effected by it to others than those was due to a certain traditional largeness of idea as to the true interests of the company. '

Also Mr. Mill says in his ' Representative Government ' :—

' The Government of a people by itself has a meaning, and a reality; but such a thing as Government of one people by anothei does not and cannot exist. One people may keep another as a warren or preserve for its own use, a place to make money in, a human cattle farm to be worked for the profit of its own inhabitants. But if the good of the governed is the proper business of a Government, it is utterly impossible that a people should directly attend to it. The utmost they can do is to give some of their best men a commission to look after it ; to whom the opinion of their own country can neither be much of a guide in the performance of their duty, nor a competent judge of the mode in which it has been performed. '

These are English authors but there are also remarks of Mr. Bryan who is the Repulican Candidate for the Presidentship of the United States, who in his book ' India under Great Britain ' says the Government of India is arbitrary and despotic.

That is what we have been saying to audiences in England, that is what we have been asking from the platform and in the Press and books for the last fifty years. And now to drag me in 1908 before a Court because I have said the same thing after provocation from the pro-Bureaucratic Press is not, apart from the legality of it, even logical. I am not reading extracts from Sir Henry Cotton, Sir William Wedderburn and other members of the Congress party, because the Prosecution might say 'Oh they are just as seditious and we do not prosecute them because it is not good to do that just yet.' This is the creed of the party, and I have not gone beyond that or used words not previously used. There was a good occasion for my writing. There was provocation. A challenge was thrown out and I had a duty to discharge. And it was in the course of the discharge of that duty that this article was written. I think, I have quoted enough. I will not tire your patience by quoting any more. There are a number of other books here. Now I will read to you the two notes written on the same date 12th May 1908 and marked Exhibit E. (Reads from ' since the commencement of the bomb affair ' down to ' in future'). Again this is an article written upon the provocation received. It distinctly names the papers to which the reply is intended. (Reads down to ' stopped '). This means that the outrages are due to political agitation, and that all political movements in the country should be stopped. (Reads down to ' Tarkata Shastra.') Here I have used two marathi words meaning logic and sophistry, and they can only be understood in that language. In this article again the bomb outrges are deprecated but I have also pointed out that we might hope that these outrages will draw the attention of England to our grievaces as they did in Ireland at one time.

We now come to the Article of the 2nd June. (At this stage the Court adjourned for lunch.)

I have to read you the Article and the two paragraphs dated 12th May and marked Exhibits D and E. The incriminating Article is marked Exhibit D, and the two notes are marked Exhibit E, but the Prosecution have put in other Articles dated 19th May, 26th May, 2nd June 1908. Instead of reading the next incriminating article after this I think it will be better to read the Articles in their chronological order, so that I will be able to show you the various phases through which the matter passed, and you will be gradually led up to the Article of June 9. The three articles are put in to prove intention, but I want to read to you all the articles in the controversy. The first article was written on May 12th, and on May 19th &c., other articles were written in reply to articles that had appeared during the meanwhile. You can infer the intention of one article by reading the three. Certain things had been published on which criticisms were necessary. Those criticisms were made in the articles of the 19th May. On May 26th we received news from Home by the English Mail (fully a fortnight later) and we found the matter discussed in the English papers. Then we published our article of June 2nd which was a sort of review of the whole situation. Then two notes are based on this in the issue of the 9th June, and I put in the article in the issue of 16th June to complete the series. It was not put in by the Prosecution. These two articles of the 9th June, refer to the executive acts of Government. So from week to week the controvery was carried on as fresh arguments and fresh facts were urged by the other party. Then followed the two legislative Acts which were opposed. It is a continuation of the same subject. So how can it be that the articles were written with the intention of exciting the people? If you will read the articles you will find that I wrote every week, and touched upon a different situation, and met the arguments of the other parties in different ways. I do not think the controversy is yet over. In order to acquaint you with the details, I mean to read the articles in the order of their appearance. Of course I am not going into details as I did in the first article. These articles are put in to prove intention. You are not to rely on them like the incriminting articles. I am not going to deal so fully with them, as it would take up so much of your time. I shall have to read them fully, but I will only make a few remarks as I read to you. When the article of the 19th May was written you will find that during that week certain telegrams were received stating that meetings had been held in Bengal, presided over by the Maharaja of Durbhunga, expressing sorrow and regret at the bomb-outrage, at the same time condemning the outrage and attributing it to political agitators. Now these people belong to our party and it was necessary in the interests of the community to contradict the charges made, and to expose the charactar of those meetings. You will find there were no meetings all over India, but a few meetings which were managed by interested persons. We had to show that these were not representative meetings, and we had to issue a warning to Government. We did not disagree with them in expressing abhorrence and regret for the outrages, but regarding the other part we thought that they were playing into the hands of the other party. To prevent that this article was written, and consequently it is headed "A Double Hint" or a double warning. It was warning to the people themselves, and to the Government, that these meetings should not be taken as representative, with the corollary that at the present time it was necessary to make reforms in the administration. I have said in this article that bomb-throwing is not the method of obtaining Swarajya. It is not a logical method. It is not sanctioned by morality. (Reads to "suicidal in the extreme."). It means suicidal to the cause of a country. That is the meaning of the heading, 'a double hint.'

We may be right or wrong, but we place our view openly before Government, so that Government may not be misled by these resolutions. I have said that though Anglo-Indians may be glad of the few meetings they might mislead Government. It also gives a reply to the charge upon the political agitators in India, that they are trying to get power into their own hands for selfish ends, while the Bureaucracy is carrying on the Government for benevolent purposes. There is a point of differnece in the diagnosis. We say outrageous conduct is one of the effects of a bad system of administration. They say it is due to agitation. (Reads down to "in India".) By attributing it to agitation and the heated feeling as it is at present in India, they think that this trouble will cease by putting down agitation. It is a struggle between two parties, like the Liberals and Conservatives ; just the same as the Social Democrats in England and the Liberals. In this way the controversy goes on. The House of Lords is an old institution and has done much more good for England than the Bureaucracy for India, and yet it is a subject of controversy. (Reads down to 'in this manner'.) It is a way of party tactics, that each party should press forward its cause on every favourable occasion. This principle has been used by the bureaucratic Press, while on the other hand it has been contested and replied to by the Native Press.

I will not refer to the whole litereature of our party. But the evidence is so strong that it will convince anybody that this system of administration has been outgrown by the intelligence of the people. (Reads down to " in their minds. ") Here again we have a mistake in the translation. The word in the original is (संताप). (Reads down to 'human nature.') This is the same argument used in the previous reply but with a different phraseolgy. (Reads down to ' false report. ') 'Report' is not correct ; the original word used is (हुल) which means outcry or alarm. (Reads down to 'public opinion.') This is the History of the European countries in the 19th century. (Reads down to ' political agitators. ') It is something like this. Arsenic is a tonic if taken in certain quantities, but because a man commits suicide with arsenic that is no reason why arsenic must not be used at all. Because fire sometimes burns a city, must it be abolished? Because a turn-headed man takes to violence, should all political agitation be stopped ? That argument is false; it is not sound; and it is misleading. (Reads down to ' selfishness. ') That means that one party wants the Bureaucracy. It is not done from ignorance but from self-interest. (Reads down to 'would be considered foolish.') That is taken from history. It is an old story of the Peshwa, that Anandibai changed one letter in the order given by Ragunathrao to a Military Captain and in the place of ध in (धरावा) she substituted the letter मा and made it (मारावा) which made it ' murder ' instead of ' arrest. ' Would this justify a cry against female education? Similarly to stop all political agitation because one person has taken it into his head to murder an official, is a fallacy. (Reads down to ; in any country.') This is only another illustration. You know when the electric trams were started in Bombay there were a few accidents, but it would have been foolish to stop the trams because of those accidents. (Reads down to ' India alone.') It is a false process of reasoning to make the political agitators responsible for what has happend in Bengal. (Reads down to ' initiate it. ') When we have before our eyes what happend in Ireland, France, Germany, and Russia, we can see that it is not due to political agitators, not to what these young men read in the newspapers. (Reads down to 'our rulers. ') There again is the warning I offer to the Anglo-Indian Press and to Government (Reads down to ' Prescribed by Law. ') It is expressly stated here that the law ought to be put into action, though Government ought not to take repressive measures. (Reads down to ' we are helpless.') There is no excitement. This is an historical parallel taken from English history. There again is a mistranslation; the original word is (हितशत्रू) (Reads down to end of article.) This article again was written on the 19th of May. The view of the party is that we condemn bomb-outrages as strongly as any one in the country, and our claim is that matters have run such a course, it has now come to such a pass in this country that measures of reform must now be taken. That is the view of the Viceroy, that was the view of Lord Morley at the Civil Service Dinner. He said mere repressive measures will not do. That is the view that this article takes. Other people hold the same view. The purpose of this article was to warn Government against taking these resolutions as proper expressions of opinion. The object appears at the end. It appears from the different sentences of the article and if you do not go behind the article there is plenty of material from which the object of the article can be gathered. This article then forms one of the series, as I have stated, and it has just been ruled by His Lordship that they are all part of one transaction. These articles were written week by week as information came in. I contend that these articles cannot be used to infer the intention. Even if you did use them you cannot reckon them all as one transaction. We will now come to the article of 26th May which is headed 'The real meaning of the bomb.' (The Marathi originals were handed to the Jury with translations). By the side of the articles, you will notice, are published English opinions on the subject of the bomb-outrage. This article is written and a summary of new topics in connection with the controversy, given. Some of the English opinion is favourable to our party and some to the Anglo-Indian party. It is a divided opinion. Just as it was divided here it was divided there. But no one thought of prosecuting any one there as I have been here for writing these articles. The article is Ex. G. is dated 26th May and was based on English opinions received by the mail of the

23rd. These first appeared in the *Mahratta*, which is published on Sunday, and were then translated into the *Kesari* of the 26th. The article written embodies those views and also talks about the general commotion. It is a matter of satisfaction that the Government of India and Lord Morley take the same view. Lord Morley says that it is a modest reform that he is introducing, and the Viceroy said that he would not be daunted or turned away from his purpose of introducing the reform by reason of the recent occurrences. After all it is the Native Press that has won the battle to a certain extent. Even in England there were two parties and that you can see from the recent controversy between Lord Curzon and Lord Morley. Lord Curzon representing the school of 'Martial Law' and no damned nonsense about concessions',—and Lord Morley the other. Lord Morley said that such a policy could not be followed in view of the history and traditions of the English people. There is the same controversy here. (Reads.) 'The drowning man catches at the neck,' is not a proper rendering; it should be 'he is drawing his arms round his neck.' (Reads 'Swadeshi boycott' extracts.) I have read from the *Pioneer* and other Papers relating not only to political agitation, but also to Swadeshi, boycott, and other matters. The agitation is regarded with displeasure and condemned as seditious. (Reads;......letting loose the Mussalman gundas &c.) These are facts which have been proved and are not exaggerations. I may say here that I am not going to waste time by dwelling upon all the mistranslations of these articles as they are only put in for the purpose of showing intention. (Reads) 'Vetal' is one of the many kinds of fiends. He is accompanied by other 'pishachas'. Here what is meant to be conveyed is that when one gets mad he makes others mad; the way to stop that madness is not to get hold of the latter but to take possession of the source. (Reads 'reverberation of your tyrannical acts)' This means in other words that the bomb is a reaction. It may be due to madness or wickedness—that is not discussed—but it is reaction and not the original impulse. It is not as though Parliament or even the Liberal party don't contain 'turn-headed' people. I have said there are two sets of opinions in Parliament; the one which is represented by the Hon'ble Mr. Rees is in favour of the views expressed by the *Pioneer*, the *Times of India* and the *Englishman*. The other set of opinions is represented by the Indian Party. Mr. Rees said that the repressive measures were very mild upto now, but hereafter they should be far stronger. (Reads to 'when a man sees nothing hopeful'). It is the hope that keeps up man in the straight path, and Dr. Rash Behari Gosh says that 'despair, has caused these young men to go astray.' (Reads to 'called resolution.') This is a quotation from Spencer's 'Social Science' (concludes reading the article). This is what has been practically acknowledged by the Viceory, who said that he was quite assured of the new spirit that is engendered in the Indian Nation by the recent successes of Japan, and it was his desire to lead the people in the right path and to guide their movements rather than to suppress them. The same view was expressed by Dr. Rash Behari Ghosh and the Hon'ble Mr. Gokhale in the Viceroy's Council during the discussions on the Seditious Meetings Act or Bill. (Reads from Gazette of India page 186 from the Viceroy's speech on the same Bill beginning with the words 'I am well aware of the political hopes and ambitions of the people of this country &c.' You will see that these very arguments were used not only in newspapers, but also in the Legislative Council. There is no secrecy about them and their reasonableness has been acknowledged by the Viceroy himself. It is not a new thing. Here in this article they appear as criticism of Mr. Rees. These views, which have been published in the Government Gazette of the 2nd of November 1907, were authoritatively given by the gentlemen I have referred to at the meeting of the Legislative Council and have been finally approved. The only difference between the Government and the Indian political party is that the reforms are not thorough-going as explained by Lord Morley. He said that they are only modest. We say that they ought to be more thorough-going. The arguments used in the articles are the same as those which were put forward in the Legislative Council by the members representing popular feeling and finally when the Viceroy had to reply to them he spoke in the same strain in which the article concludes. (Reads: 'we may repress sedition, we may repress it with a strong hand &c.') There is no question whatever that if there is anything illegal the Government of India is prepared to repress it and it has the right to repress it. The controversy has been carried on in the Legislative Council, in Parliament and in the English and Anglo-Indian Press and I say it cannot be sedition if it is reproduced in the vernacular press in the manner in which it has been done here. It may be urged that in the vernacular press they might write anything they like as what they write is not translated. That is a mistake. It is translated every week. The Government has a special department for the purpose, and summary of every article is translated and sent to Government. What we write is not in the dark or behind the back of the Government.

There are two more articles before we come to the second incriminating article. One of these is that of the 2nd June. I am not going to criticise every line of the translation. I will read it so that you may have the whole controversy before you and judge in what spirit these articles have been written. The article of the 2nd June was written to answer an objection which has been raised against the popular party. It is asked do you condemn the bomb ? Yes. Then why don't you help Government in the repressive measures which Government is taking ? What is the position of the party ? What view do you take of the bomb ? There are certain thinkers who say if you condemn bombs you must go with Government as if there is no other alternative. Either condemn bomb and be with Government, or expose yourself to the charge of being considered seditious. That was the argument used and this article is a reply to it. What we say is that we condemn the bomb, but we also condemn repressive measures. We say use enough repression for the purpose of punishing this wickedness but beyond that no more repression is needed. That is the position we take, and the result is that we do not side with the Government and we do not approve of the action of those who committed the outrage. That is the clear position to which we were driven by our traditions, by our beliefs and by our opinions. That was the charge made against the Indian Political Party. It was 'Your position is not logical. How do you explain it ?' We say 'We condemn the outrage, but we also condemn the repressive measures.' The Press Act was passed afterwards but at the time of our writing Government's intention of passing it was known. It was to be passed at Simla and on the 8th of June it was actually passed. (I shall have to read a few extracts from the proceedings of the Legislative Council in order to explain to you the criticism which we passed upon it.) And explanation was therefore necessary, that if we condemn the bomb we should condemn the repressive measures also. Hence the article. It is translated. 'The secret of the bomb.' But the more proper rendering would be 'The Ethics of the Bomb'. There is an article on 'The Ethics of the dynamite' in the *Contemporary Review* of 1894 from which it appears that in 1893 a dynamiter was discovered with explosives in his possession. Immediately the Parliament met and passed the Act. At that time there was great sensation and excitement in England and the views expressed in the *Contemporary Review* are similar to those which are expressed in this article. In fact, an extract from the *Contemporary Review* was read by the Hon'ble Nawab Sayad Mahomed in the Viceroy's Legislative Council. The same view is taken more or less in this article. When a man walking in the street stumbles, he begins to consider what is his position. Bomb is wicked but it is a signal to pause and consider. Out of evil cometh good. It rivets our attention and makes us inquire searchingly into the present state of things. We have condemned the bomb-outrage. It is immoral, it is illegal, it is suicidal, it is a felonious deed. Now the last stage of the episode comes in when the Explosives Act is passed, and the Anglo-Indian Papers say 'You are hypocrites. You condemn the bomb but you do not side with Government in the represive measures.' We reply 'We are not hypocrites. We are sorry we cannot side with Government because Government has taken to a repressive policy.' Our position is a peculiar one. We condemn wickedness, but we cannot side with the Government in their repressive acts. This is explained and maintained in the articles of 2nd and 9th June, and the Act is criticised in details in the article of the 16th June. I believe it is the *Empire* which says "Your position is logical, but it is certainly not sympathy towards Government." (Reads article of 2nd June; 'From the murder of Mr. Rand &c.') Here is a comparison between the two. The Rand murder was more or less a personal affair, here is the outrage in Bengal which is a national affair. I also make a distinction not only in this article but also in other articles, between the anarchist as such—pure and simple who does not want any Government—and a man, misguided though he may be, who uses anarchist methods owing to his fanaticism. Modern science has made Government powerful in the use of the dynamite and other explosives for the purposes of war. It has also furnished a weapon powerful enough for the purpose of terrorism. Then follow in a philosophic train of thought the consequences or the effects of such acts, which you may call wicked or terrible, which arrest the man's attention and make him think of the course of life he has to pursue. (Reads 'Death is ordained at the very time of birth &c.,) This is an observation upon death taken from western philosophers showing that contemplation of death makes a man lead a holy life. (Reads down to ' Pride of Military strength. ') Here it is shown that the bomb will not cope with the military power. It is impossible. I will read to you a similar extract from Major Evans Bell. He says that as long as the administration goes on smoothly the officials think that everything is alright. They do not care to ascertain if anything is going on wrong until some disorder comes to light and then they begin to consider the situation, (Reads extract from Major Evans Bell at page 92 ' If the British people in their homes and in their Parliament &c. ') He says that the Bureaucracy is an unnatural form of Government. This book was written in 1875 by an officer, a former Resident of Mysore. (Reads the article down to ' wisdom. ') What is said here is that bomb outrage ought to be checked but it serves as the diagnosis (to use medical phrasology) of a disease or as a warning of a certain symptom from which Government should take a lesson or hint. The bomb does not destroy Government nor has it any power to do so. It only draws the attention of the Government to the desirability of certain reforms in the administration. (Reads ' the attention of the authorities was directed towards the disorder in the plague administration. ') Here it is pointed out that bureaucratic administration is carried on irrespective of the wishes of the people. At that time (that is 1897) various suggestions were made to Government to moderate the rigour of the plague administration. But not one of them was taken into consideration. We say the bomb serves the purpose at any rate of directing or rivetting the attention of the Government to the state of the administration. (Reads 'some things must be viewed from the people's stand-point &c.,') As I said Bureaucracy is intolerant of criticism. The Hon'ble Dr. Rash Behari Ghosh gave a warning at the Council Meeting and so he is now told that he must know something about the bomb.

His Lordship:—If you are not tired I should like to sit a little further.

Accused:—I am now tired as I have been on my legs the whole day.

The Court then adjourned to the 2Ist.

SEVENTH DAY.

Tuesday 21th July 1908.

Accused :—Among the papers I put in as Exhibits are Nos. 17, 21, 56, 58, 59, 62, 63 and 65. Will your Lordship kindly direct that they should be handed to me by the Clerk of the Crown ?

His Lordship :—Certainly.

The Papers were handed to Mr. Tilak.

My Lord and Gentlemen of the Jury :—I read to you yesterday the article dated 2nd June. It is followed by an article dated 9th June which forms the subject-matter of the 2nd and 3rd charges against me under 124 A and

153 A respectively. What I have to say in the beginning is that the matter dealt with in this article is somewhat different from the other articles read to you previously. There the subject-matter is the Explosives Act and Newspapers Act. These Acts were passed on the 8th of June at one sitting. As regards the Explosives Act certain objections were raised, not against the Act itself but it was held that certain sections of it were likely to prove oppressive in their administration, and it was also debatable whether a Press Act was necessary at this time. These were the two measures which formed the subject of criticisms in Exhibits E and D. So you will see that the two matters are entirely distinct and the papers to which I have to refer are different from those to which I have had to refer previously. I have here the proceedings of the Supreme Legislative Council. I wish to read to you certain portions from the proceedings and then read the articles to you, and after that I will comment on both the articles of the 2nd and 9th June 1908. I will complete the reading of the articles, and the criticisms can come afterwards. Now the Explosives Act was a new Act introduced here after the model of the English Act of 1883 and there is another Act passed with regard to incitement to murder. Both were hurriedly passed on the 8th of June 1908. This article was written soon after, without examining all the detailed sections of the Act because they were not available except such summary as was telegraphed on Saturday evening. That was on June 9th and the detailed comments and criticisms were put in on June 16th in the form of a leader. Now in the proceedings of Council it will be found that opposition was made by Native Members of the Viceroy's Council in the presence of H. E. the Viceroy. They did not vote against the Act but they expressed certain objections. Of course, Native members of the Council cannot expect to get a majority against any such measure. All that they have to do is to protest and to stop there. The act was passed at one sitting without previously publishing the draft of the Bill and all we got at the time was the expression of their dissent. No one ever objected to wicked persons, who commit outrages, being punished. But it was necessary that the Act should not invest the Police with powers which might be used to the serious annoyance of the people. The definition of 'Explosives' may include anything. It may include even saw-dust which is used for resisting or moderating the force of an explosive. It may even include kerosine oil. That was the objection taken in England in 1883. But the case in England is different from the case in India. There you have a Parliament to watch the administration of the Act, but here the whole power will be in the hands of the Police. So that, here to adopt a measure because it was adopted in England, was neither fair nor just.

The second objection was that the Act would not in any way put a stop to these outrages. That was the objection raised by the Hon: Syed Mahomed who is one of the Moderates. The Indian reform party throughout India took the same view. Both these Acts were objected to in the Indian Papers and the Hindus and Bengalis equally condemned the Acts. Now as I read these two articles to you it will be quite clear to you that these articles take the same view. They show that a measure like this will not carry out the object Government had in view. And it is the same argument again that unless concessions are granted to the people it will be impossible—even if you invest the Police with higher powers and improve the machinery, you cannot put a stop to these things. However the Act has been passed and we have nothing to do with it now, except for the pupose of explaining the meaning of this article. Now I will read to you the article. It is dated 9th June and is headed ' These Remedies are not lasting. ' I have not said that they are not remedies at all. The Marathi heading is (हे उपाय टिकाऊ नाहींत) meaning that they cannot be held to be permanently lasting. (Reads from ' this week ' to ' repression. ') I call it a new policy of repression because the Seditious Meetings Act was passed in November 1907 and these Acts were passed in June, 1908. (Reads ' the fiend of repression has possession. ') That is how it is translated, but I cleared up that in the cross-examination of Mr. Joshi. (Reads 'every five or ten years. ') This refers to the repressive policy carried out in 1897. (Reads ' the fact. ') There are all the facts. (Reads to ' ideals. ') These, Gentlemen, are again wrong translations. All that means that the fiends of repression still swarm when the Liberal party is in power. Then the simile is kept up there; some one there is, who controls the evil genius,and that man is calld a 'Mantrika.' The ' Mantrikas' carry out that control. They have to observe certain rules and observances for carrying out that control.. In plain words it means they ought to have been controlled by Lord Morley, but somehow they have not been controlled by him. 'Mantra' is a spell. One who exercises a spell is called ' Mantrika '; it means that the Government of India is not controlled by the Secretary of State, and that being so that check on the policy in India has not been used in this case. Then you have the policy of repression explained. (Reads upto ' repressive policy.') It is when those causes which produce the fire of enthusiasm in a nation are made to go back, that the policy is said to be retrograde, or repressive. (Reads from ' liberty of speech,' to 'nourish it.') This is an historicl truth put in to show that by passing the Press Act, you retard the growth of a nation. It is not my own phrase. It is quoted from English works. I will read to you one or two extracts to show you that that is the view taken by constitutional writers. The first of these is from " The Science of Politics ' by Amos. (Reads at page 210 down to ' out of love. ') And here is another quotation from Erskine's address in defence of Payne.

" The proposition which I mean to maintain as the basis of the Liberty of the Press, and without which it is an empty sound, is this:—That every man, and not intending to mislead, but seeking to enlighten others with what his own reason and conscience, however erroneously, have dictated to him as truth, may address himself to the universal reason of a whole nation either upon the subject of governments in general or upon that of our own particular country;—that he may analyse the principles of its constitution,—point out its errors and defects, examine and publish its corruptions, warn his fellow citizens against their ruinous consequences,—and exert his whole faculties in pointing the most advantageous changes in establishments which he considers to be radiclly defective or sliding from their object by abuse. All this, every subject of this country has a right to do, if he contemplates only what he thinks would be for its advantage, and but seeks to change the public mind by conviction which flows from reasonings dictated by conscience."

This is not a statement based on my imagination but based upon facts, and I will read to you a quotation from Malcolm's 'Government of India'.

"A very serious question arose regarding the Native Press over which so far as I can judge Government has little or no check. The editors of these papers are well acquainted with their freedom. I desired to prevent the continued publication in a Native paper of the disputes between Government and the Supreme Court and particularly translations into the Native language of some charges from the Bench which I thought were calculated to lower Government in the eyes of its Native subjects." (p. 137–38.)

Of course in certain matters he does not take a liberal view. He wants certain Native Papers not to publish a decision of the High Court, as it was considered that it would bring the Government into disgrace in the eyes of the people. In that case the Police were criticised in a judgment by the District Judge, and if the remarks were published the Police felt that it would bring them into contempt, and the administration would suffer thereby. That was also the view of Mr. Elphinstone in those days. I have here a book published in 1833, so that from that day there has been a complaint made by the bureaucratic powers that the Press in India should be controlled. You will find a similar recommendation by Lord Curzon in his recent speech, and Lord Morley has referred to it. (Reads from Lord Morley's Indian Budget speech) That view is repudiated in Mr. Norton's book '*Topics of Indian Statesmen.*' (Reads from page 338 down to 'in more need.') If a press is needed anywhere it is more needed in India than in England. Sir Harvey Adamson stated in his speech in introducing the Explosives and Press Bills that there are people who do not desire any Government of Law or anything of the kind. That is how these people have wrongly been described. You will find in Karl Joubert's 'Fall of Czardom' at page 65.

"Nihilism has no creed, for it believes in nothing—no God, no law, no Government, no virtue, no love, an eternal nothing. It is the apotheosis of negation. No doubt there are in the world fanatics of this description against whom society has to protect itself; but we should be cautious of libelling any persons or groups of people anarchists or nihilists, for if they are actuated by political motives, or even by vengeance for wrongs done to them, they cannot rightly be called either anarchists or nihilists, though they may be guilty of crimes deserving of punishment.

Thousands of such men I have met in chains and misery, yet I could not find one amongst them who did not love liberty, not one who was against law and order, not one who did not desire a well-regulated government. × × × ×.

Are these your Russians anarchists and nihilists? These men who love liberty and demanded an equal law and equal rights for all people; who only sought freedom to pursue their callings unmolested, to educate their childern at their own expense, to read the Bible to their families, to speak their mother-tongue, and to declare the truth as they understood it ?"

You will see that exactly the same distinction is made there that is made here. And further on he gives the definition of insurrection. Exactly the same statement which is made here is made in the recent work on the Russian Revolution. So you see that the words are not used by me for the first tirre. (Reads to 'weapon of the anarchists') This simply means that the Bengalis are not anarchists or murderers. (Reads to 'desire'.) This should be 'aspirations.' (Reads to 'resort to violence') The *Pioneer* has taken exactly the same view of the disturbances in Russia in an article dated 29th August 1906 an extract from which I will read to you. (Vide Defence Exhibit 21). That is the view which the *Pioneer* took and the London *Times* also, and this same view is reiterated here. It is not a new view of my own.

Advocate General:—What was the date of that article ?

Accused:—It is the *Pioneer* of the 29th August 1906.

(Reads article down to 'wings') This should be 'feathers' and not 'wings'. (Reads to 'out of the cage') This is exactly the language used by many authors to illustrate the poverty of India. I will read you such an extract from Torrens's 'Empire in Asia.'

' But communities denuded of native power, disspirited by disappointment and *drained* for generations of the accumulations of their industry cannot be expected to make such works for themselves. We have broken the limbs of enterprise, and we must find it splints and crutches. '

Then there is what Mr. Thorburn has said in the same strain. This simply refers to the industries of the country which are being killed in the interests of England, not to actually breaking legs or limbs. (Reads to 'savage'.) That should be 'stern'. (Reads to 'disarm their subjects'.) There are also English writers and English statesmen who have expressed the same views. One of these is Sir Thoms Munro. (Reads) That is a comparison between the British rule and the rule during the Mogul Empire. We have again the same view expressd by Mr. A. K. Connell in his book 'Discontent and Danger in India' (Reads) That is also an extract as you will see when I read to you from Major Evans Bell's work (Reads from page 92 down to 'no ideal of making a home there.') I am just reminded that I have omitted a pragraph and I will go back to it. It is this 'Then why do the English commit the great sin of castrating a nation.' That is an utterly wrong translation. You will recollect I put to the translator the sentence.

एकदा हिंदुस्थानचे लोकांचें मर्दानीपण नाहीसें झालें ह्मणजे पुनः त्यांचें पौरुष आणि तेज परत त्यांना प्राप्त करून देण्यास पुष्कळ वेळ लागेल.

The word I used was "manliness" but it has been translated into खशी करणें which means castrate. You will see from the extract that I read you that the words should have been 'emasculation' and not 'Castration' of the Nation (Read's from Sir Perozeshah Metha's speech at the 4th National Congress in 1888 at page 283. 'the reason why I support this resolution' to 'by emasculating the whole nation.') So you see that "manliness" was intended by me and that manhood is not the proper translation. Manhood refers to function; manliness refers to quality. Now

I do not mean to suggest to you the idea that I read these works at the time I was writing the article. I have been reading those books, I have been studying this literature and I have been working on these lines for the past 28 years. I know the arguments that are advanced on each subject. I do not say that when I wrote each passage of any article I referred to these works. No, I am familiar with the literature of our party and I use the same arguments but in different phraseology. [Reads down to 'correct'] Now correct is a mistranslation.

His Lordship :—The word is corrected in ink to 'covert'.

Accused :—I accept that; 'covert aim,' means that there is some principal object in view. Merely 'aim' would be quite enough. It means that Government should by decentralisation transfer some of the powers now in the hands of the Bureaucracy to the popular assembly or popular institutions by way of granting self-Government by the method of decentralisation. That was what I stated in my evidence before the Decentralisation Commission. (Reads Defence Exhibit 56 B.) Those were the views I expressed on the 9th of March before the Decentralisation Commission. Similar views are expressed all through this article of mine before you. What I mean to say is that some power should be transferred to the popular representatives. The date of the evidence is 9th March and the date of the article is 9th June 1908. (Reads from article again down to 'heedlessly.') (Reads down to 'up to time.') This is not an imaginaery case, it actually happened. The reference is to the case of 'Hayagrivacharya' whose house was entered by the Plague Inspector, who went into that part where gods were kept.

Advocate General:—Is this admissible ?

His Lordship:—It is irrelevent. Of course the accused is appearing in person, and I do not wish to hamper him.

Advocate General:—He is only wasting the time of the Court and the Jury. These are allegations which can be replied to.

His Lordship:—This is a statement which you are not entitled to make. The Jury have heard you with the greatest indulgence. You are entitled to address the Jury as you like. You may refer to any matters you like and to any books. But you cannot enter into any facts which may require to be contradicted.

Accused:—This is a case which appears in the Dharwar Plague Commission's Report. If necessary I will get the report.

His Lordship:—I do not think it will help you much.

Accused:—Then I will give it up.

Accused continues:—This says that the people were driven to exasperation. I will now read to you again from Major Evans Bell's book 'Our Great Vassal Empire (Reads from 'the political diagnosis of India' down to ' 'at present.') It is foreseen here what the consequences would be if this Bureaucracy were carried too far. Then further on there is a passage

(Reads from 'if the British people' down to 'be associated.') The question here is the same. It is not a question of contempt of Government, it is a question with regard to civil authorities. It is not a question of military authority. It does not mean that the bomb will redress the military authority. (Reads down to 'mitilary strength.') This is a sentence which the learned Connsel for the Prosecution said he could not understand. It refers to the intellectual, not to the material or visible thing, it is a knowledge, not a physical fabric. The words in the original are ज्ञानाचें स्वरूप अधिक आहे, दृश्य स्वरूप नाहीं. It is a thing to be known, and when a man knows it, then only a few materials are necessary, and a big manufactory is not required. The question is not one of materials but of knowledge. I am referring to the intellectual side. There are three words used, it is something like a spell, a charm, an amulet. (Reads down to 'big factory.') We extracted this statement from the evidence taken in Calcutta, and published in the *Times of India* on the 8th May, which quoted the expert opinion from the *Empire*. (Reads from '*Times of India*' of 8th May.) In that way several opinions were given in the Anglo-Indian Press, some holding that the Explosives Act as it was passed was not enough, but that something more was necessary to put a stop to the bomb, and bomb manufactures, and that strong measures should be taken to subjugate and contro their manufacturers. This was discussed in the Anglo-Indian papers and w have taken it from the Anglo-Indian papers as I have read to you. Counsel fo the Crown says it is incitement; that we are inciting the people by innuendoe to manufacture bombs. If I am responsible, why not the *Times of India* and the Anglo-Indian papers? It is not a statement I have made. It is taken from the Anglo-Indian papers. Of course it may be due te eagerness to give the first report. Can it be said that the papers, which gave the details of the Muzafferpore outrage, were guilty of the crime of murder? Every detail of the occurrence was published, was this an incitement to murder? There are instances given of poisoning and other cases published in the daily press. Thousands of such cases. Would you call these incitements to murder or to poisoning and would you prosecute the Editors of the papers? It is not that we are telling the people to make bombs. That inference is attributed to us by the Anglo-Indian papers. But it is they who have told the public how the bomb is manufactured by publishing the statement of the expert witnesses, who said that the materials were there for a very well equipped factory and the whole process has been described by every Calcutta Anglo-Indian paper.

Mr. Branson :—It is not true.

Accused :—Well, I have read to you the Anglo-Indian papers, and also the views of English Statesman, so that you may see that the views in the article are not my own. I have put in a copy of the *Oriental Review* marked Exhibit D 64, and you will find in the issue of July Ist 1908, an extract from the Calcutta correspondent of the *Morning Leader*. (Begins to read extract.)

Mr. Branson :—I am unwilling to interfere with the Accused exc when it is absolutely necessary. He now wants to read something wh is an extract from some English paper.

Accused :—The letter is dated Calcutta 7th May and was sent to England, and appeared in this paper on July 1st 1908.

His Lordship :—It could not have reached you before you wrote your article.

Accused:—That only shows the greater and independent corrorboration.

Advocate General :—It is absolutely irrelevent. Some person writes a letter which is uncorrorborated, and it appears in a paper which the Accused wishes to use as evidence.

Accused :—I hold it to be admissible as proving that some other Anglo-Indian resident in Calcutta takes a similar view to mine in this controversy.

His Lordship :—If the Accused thinks it is of importance to him I will let him use it.

Advocate-General :—As your Loidship pleases.

Accused :—(Reads article. (Vide D 64.)

Advocate-General :—Mr. Tilak ought to have been thankful to me for objecting to him relating that article. If he makes it a part of his defence I doan't mind. It is evident that his views are those of the writer. The dynimiter has come to stay !

[*The Advocate General* asks for the article and reads a portion of it to the Jury.]

His Lordship to Accused :—What did you read this article for?

Accused :—To show that the opinion is that the bomb has come to stay and that it cannot be stopped by these repressive measures.

His Lordship:-You have not read it to show that it reflects your views?

Accused:—No, my Lord, I have read it as corroborative of my views about repressive measures.

His Lordship to the Jury:— I do not think that you ought to be influenced bv that article. I take it the Accused merely reads it to show what the writings were with regard to this fact at the time.

Mr. Tilak continues:—Now, Gentlemen, these are the very views represented in the *Viceregal* Legislative Council. (*Gazette of India* dated June 13th 1908, Vide D 63.) And these remarks, Gentlemen, these remarks were made in the presence of the Viceroy himself. With this warning he supported the motion thinking it was useless to oppose and to give a different vote. The date of the discussion is 8th June, and it is printed in the proceedings of the Legislative Council of 15th June. Now the passage which he has quoted I have also put in. I have here the *Contemporary Review* (Vide D 65) which gives the whole article. It is headed the 'Ethics of Dynamite' and was published in 1894. It is the article to which reference was made in the speech I have just read you. There too the observations are to the same effect as the observations you find in my article, and also in the preceding article. The question is whether it will stop it, or are further measures necessary? In England and in India, the same views have been expressed, and the same thing has been said in my article of 9th June. Now it may be convenient for some people to draw the conclusion that in criticising the Explosives Act we were trying to incite the people to disaffection, hatred and contempt of the Government. The whole question to my mind is, do persons throw the bomb, or the community? Another question is whether the proposed repressive measures will be sufficient, or whether something more will have to be done. I have criticised this matter in the '*Kesari*' in the same way as it was done by the writers whom I have quoted to you on the same arguments, the same conclusions. Not only this, but the whole Indian press has expressed the same views. I can only guess at what the Prosecution intended. I have been rather inconvenienced by these articles being put together in the joint charge. These two acts have been objected to by all the organs of the Indian reform party. That is not my opinion alone, it is the opinion of every one of the papers. The object of the writer was to remark upon the Explosives Act. That Act has been passed, and has become law; but although the law has been passed there is no reason why one of us should not write to say that this Act will not do good, will not be beneficial to the people, its provisions should not have been what they are, and that it should have been framed on different lines and in a different spirit altogether. It is perfectly legitimate to do this in discussing the matter and to set forth these facts. I have supported my arguments from various authorities just as Mr. Syed Mahomed has taken the article from the '*Contemporary Review*' to put in his speech. I have shown you from the various extrcts that all arguments are the same, and it is for you to judge whether it was intended as suggested by the Prosecution, as a veiled attempt to excite people to throw bombs, or whether it was written in the interests of the people.

It will be for you to judge from the words of the article whether it was intended as a protest or as an attempt to sow the seeds of disaffection. The Prosecution says it is a veiled attempt to incite people to throw bombs. I say such an inference does not follow, and if you were to apply this maxim every account published in news—papers regarding a crime will be looked upon as an incitement to people to commit crimes. Crime is not the normal state of society; it is an unnatural tendency. People do not become criminals by reading accounts of crimes; and if it is held that they do, then journalists will have to give up their job. Suppose a man publishes accounts of the Mutiny of 1857, the Government will not suspect anything wrong if he is a member of the *Anglo-Indian press*; but if we do it should it be an act of incitement to sedition? The very day this was published at Poona the same thing was said in the Viceroy's Council. That shows the trend of public opinion as expressed in the public papers. This is not a veiled attempt. Had it been so there would have been only an isolated article. The whole thing is nothing else but a controversy from the beginning to the end. The Hon. Nawab

Syed Mahomed has taken the same view when speaking in the Viceregal Council, as also other newspapers. Then what reason is there to suppose that I alone am actuated by criminal motives, while the others wrote in good faith ?

I have put in Ex. 68, 69, 70, 48 B, 44, 45, 46 and 47 (The *Subodha Patrika*, the *Sudharak*, the *Dnyan Prakash*, the *Indu Prakash* 5th and 6th May, and the *Gujarati* 31st May and 14th June). These papers do not belong to the party of reform to which I belong though they are pro-Congress papers. Any one who doubts my statement may satisfy himself by reading them to see if the same thing has not been said by other papers, whether they are Marathi, or Gujrati or Anglo-Vernacular. It is the general view of all the parties not only in the Maharashtra but throughout the country that these repressive measures will be useless and that something more is necessary. I have also read to you the views of the Secretary of State. But even if my view was totally disapproved, I was entitled to bring it to the attention of Government. It was not totally disapproved by Government, and Lord Morley has considered it necessary to introduce some measures of reform far more advanced than he originally intended. The other day Lord Curzon spoke about the Amir of Cabul in the House of Lords, and Lord Morley deprecated the language used by him as he thought that it was likely to create irritation. But he never thought of prosecuting Lord Curzon for exciting the Amir against the Government of India. You cannot charge the Hon. Nawab Syed Mahomed with the intention of creating disaffection or exciting disaffection. It was his duty as a member of the Council to express his views. In the same manner it was my duty to give my opinion freely as a journalist. This is not my opinion only, but it is the opinion of the whole Indian Reform Party ; and if in expressing that opinion words are used which may be presumed to denote an attempt to excite disaffection according to a certain legal fiction, I ask you not to take that into your consideration. [Reads Ex. I. article of 9th June, 'English rule is admittedly alien.'] It has been shown that taxation in this country has affected the prosperity of British India, and it is out of all proportion to the taxation in Great Britain. I may be right or wrong. The question is whether I have a right to say it or not. The Anglo-Indian press has been openly saying that they do not want concessions to be given to the people. On the other hand we say that the agitation is due to the faulty system of administration and it can be stopped only by granting concessions to the people and not by repressive measures. It is a question of liberty of the press—it is not a question of an individual. The question is whether, when a repressive Act is passed, the people are entitled or not to express their views frankly and openly. If such language is open to misconstruction, I should like to know what is not likely to be misunderstood. I have quoted the case of Zenger on this point to show that judged from such a narrow stand-point, there is nothing in the world,—not even the words in the Bible—safe from misconstruction being put upon it. Therefore, what you have to look to is the spirit in which the controversy is carried on.

Now, I shall refer to the card, (K) which is put in by the Prosecution. That card has been found in the search. The Prosecution think it of such importance that they have photographed it and I shall be much surprised if it is not sent home for the inspection of Lord Morley. The history of that card is something like this.

His Lordship :—I have not seen the photograph ; it is not an exhibit.

Accused :—We have been supplied with a photograph. Of course, the insinuation to be drawn from the card is that I was engaged in manufacturing bombs or some explosives, and that is the reason why the names of these books appear in the card! It was found along with some other papers in the search in the drawer of my writing table—a drawer which was not locked up. It was found with other papers. I have put in those papers in order that you may judge of the character of the other papers that were found along with it and the purpose for which it was written and to show whether they were papers of ordinary daily business or whether it was kept in some other part of the drawer. That was the reason why I questioned the Police Officer and remarked that the card was found behind my back. This card was found among daily papers of business and not in some nook and corner where it could not be discovered by any one. I have told you that after I wrote this article we wanted to criticise in detail the provisions of the Explosives Act and especially the definition of an explosive, which according to the Act, includes even ordinary kerosine oil. It was necessary to collect materials to see whether the definition given in the Explosives Act tallies with the definition given in the works on explosives. The only reference book we had there was Encyclopedia Britannica and that was not enough and naturally the first impluse was to refer to the catalogue to see whether there was any work on explosives. If you will see the card you will find that there is one portion scratched and the names are rewritten with the prices. Here is the catalogue to to which I referred. It is a book which we can have anywhere. It is a yearly publication, but I do not purchase it every year. Now, in that card the name 'Modern Explosives' is an abbreviated name, and the other is found in the general index. My Lord, this may be inspected by the Jury. This is the general index. (Accused hands up Catalogue of Catalogues Vols: 1 & 2, 1902 Edition.) You will find these two names, first under the heading 'Explosives, Modern, by Eisler' and the name of the catalogue in which it is to be found. On page 34 the book in question is referred to, I have marked it with red pencil. If you will look at the card you will find there the title. Crosby is the name of the publisher. In the general index a particular catalogue is referred to and there you have the full name.

This was described as a folding card. But it was really an ordinary card and was folded subsequently. It was not intended to be sent to any body. I asked Mr. Sullivan if he went to my library and made a search there, as the catalogue was there. He said 'No,' he found the card in the drawer. He thought that enough and the card was carried away as a trophy of the search. Insinuations and innuendoes will be made before you in connection with this card, and I would, therefore, draw your attention to the order in which these two books appeared in the general catalogue. They are in the same order. 'Modern Explosives' is mentioned first and then follows 'Nitro-Explosive'; subjoined to these names are the prices, and the names of the authors and publishers.

Now, the papers found along with the card are the most ordinary papers. There is a letter from a gentleman asking as to how he should establish a school; then there is an abstract from an opinion on my book on the 'Arctic Home in the Vedas.' Also two long—hand reports of my speech at Surat. I ask you to judge of the card in connection with these papers. The scratched portion is taken from the general index and the other portion from the general catalogue. I do not know with what object the Prosecution have put in the card. It means nothing. If they mean to say that there is something hidden in it—something ulterior—there is nothing to support the suspicion, because the card was among other papers which were placed in an open drawer. If it is suggested that the card was purposely placed among these papers and the drawer purposely left open so as not to attract suspicion, then I say that if you are to suspect in that way there will be no end to suspicions. In that way, the fact that the catalogue was in the library might also be looked upon with suspicion. In short, I do not see what connection this card has with the whole case and how you can rely upon it. As I have already explained we were then engaged in commenting upon the Explosives Act and as a matter of fact the detailed provisions of the Act were criticised in the '*Kesari*' of the 16th June. (Vide D. 66) The heading of the article is 'A couple of New Acts' or the 'Twin Acts.' In that article the detailed provisions of the Explosives Act have been criticised and referred to. The definition of explosives is given at some length. The whole of the third column and fourth column criticises the definition of the Act, and the last column is devoted to comments on the Press Act. The definition of the Explosives Act has here been compared with the definition of the English Act of 1883.

[At this stage the court adjourned for lunch.]

His Lordship :—Can you give me any idea as to how long you will take?

Accused :—I think I will finish this evening. And I think if Your Lordship will give me 15 or 20 minutes to-morrow I can finish.

His Lordship :—Otherwise you have finished.

Accused :—Yes, My Lord.

[*AFTER TIFFIN.*]

I now come to the third charge. I do not know how the same article can legally be put in under two sections. I am not, just now, going to discuss the effect of having the same article placed under two sections.

Whether the charges are cumulative or alternative and whether a man can be punished cumulatively under the two sections, is another matter. I will read to you the sections and explain what they mean and you will then be able to say whether the writing comes under these two sections (Reads section 153 A.) Now the section provides ' whoever promotes or attempts to promote '. The wording of the section appears to me to be very faulty or defective. Promoting evidently does not mean a particular effect. It is inclusive and of course it comes too much into conformity with the words above. I think that ' promotes ' there is not intended as separate. The latter wording is 'attempts to promote.' It is the same kind of wording as in Section 124 A 'excites or attempts to excite'—"promotes or attempts to promote." As I have explained in the case of Section 124 A it seems to me that for the word "promotes" in the first part no intention is needed, while under the latter part of the section particular intention and object are included. As I explained then, no attempt can be an aimless attempt, the very word shows that something is aimed at. I throw a stone at random; it is not attempting anything. It is only throwing a stone and you may say my intention is to throw a stone. But when I throw a stone at the University Clock, I may miss it as it is too high to hit—but if it can be shown from other circumstances that I throw it with that object it is attempting it. My idea of attempt is that something must be aimed at. There cannot be as I have said an aimless attempt and here the attempt is to promote feelings of enmity. Like attempting to excite disaffection it requires intention and motive, both. You cannot conceive of an aimless attempt. There is no attempt without some end in view without a crime or action being kept in view. Well, if you have something else in view and something occurs which was not likely, that is not covered by this Section.

There is only one case I can find on that point. It is reported in the Punjab Weekly Reporter No. 14, April 1907. It is the case of the proprietor of the *Punjabi* in appeal. This was an appeal from the decision of the Magistrate to the Punjab High Court. It was not tried by a Jury. There the Judges were judges of Law and fact. That is the only case I find reported under Section 153 A. The Chief Justice there seems to interpret the word 'promote' to also mean intention, and takes it along with the word intention. I will read you his words. (Reads from Punjab Weekly Reporter No. 14 April 1907 from ' promotes' to 'effect.')

His Lordship:—May I see that case?

[Accused hands up the book and after His Lordship has read it he hands it back.]

And so the Punjab Judges have held that the phrase ' promotes or attempts to promote feelings of enmity or hatred ' here includes conscious intention as well as promotion. It is not to be inferred merely from the articles, it must be inferred from other circumstances. It is just like the word excite in section 124 A. Here it is between ' different classes of his Majesty's subjects.' What is to be inferred from this word ' classes.'? Can it mean two political classes ? I venture to say that it cannot mean two political parties, or classes which are based on different principles. It may mean Hindus and Mahomedans. It may mean as has been held between Europeans and Indians. But the distinction cannot be between two political parties. They are not called classes. They are called parties. It may mean Armenians and Catholics, Protestants and Jews but it cannot mean Conservatives and Liberals. As regards the question of His Majesty's subjects, it has been held to mean Europeans and Natives or Indians. Classes which have a prominent mark of distinction are to be regarded as different classes of His Majesty's subjects. But I contend that this cannot be taken to mean a distinction or division into political parties so far as the object of this section is concerned. Thus we have the explanation [Reads 'it does not amount' down to 'intention] That phrase again shows that malicious intention is intended by the word 'promotes or attempts to promote. '[Reads down to 'subjects.'] Again the word used is 'classes.' More or less in this section it is intended that feelings may not be roused between different classes or communities, that they may not act one against another. That seems to be the object of this section. Now in the one I pointed out it shows that some kind of criminal attempt is necessary to prove a case under this section and it is also held that without actual criminal intent something may be said, or written, anything of that kind may be done with the object of miminising differences or pointing out defects. Suppose I wrote a book pointing out the differences between the Hindus and Mahomedans saying who I think is in the right. That would not come under the section! As I have explained malicious intention does not come in here. As in the case of Section 124A. it is made clear in the explanation. So long as it is merely an explanation, merely intended to explain the words in the first paragraph, the burden is on the Prosecution to show that the case is not covered by this explanation.

His Lordship :—I have had the case to which you referred brought up. I see it is Punjab High Court Records Vol. 42, 23rd September.

Accused continuing said :—So in the first place what I want to show is that there are no classes mentioned in the article. A whole page of that article is full of criticisms on the Explosives Act and the Press Act. It could only be contended remotely by straining the words that in crticising the provisions of the Explosives Act it was intended to incite persons to throw bombs at the other community. I do not think that meaning could be put upon that article.

It is further doubtful whether Bureaucracy comes in the words of this section as a class of His Majesty's subjects. I am charged under section 153 A in regard to the second article. Which classes it does not say and I do not know whether it means between Europeans or Natives or between other classes.

His Lordship :—Let me see the charge.

Accused :—I do not think the classes are mentioned. They are not in the copy I received.

His Lordship :—I see that the words are as follows. 'By printed words promoted or attempted to promote feelings of enmity and hatred between classes of his Majesty's subjects.'

Accused :—That is all ; the classes are not specified.

His Lordship:—No, the classes are not specified.

Accused:—So, I am labouring under disadvantage. I cannot say whether it is between Europeans or whether it is between Hindus and Mahomedans or between Jains and Sikhs. Of course if I mention some particular class now the Prosecution may take up some other class afterwards. Some one is responsible for having made the charge defective. I presume Europeans and Natives are intended. But that defect in the charge, I would ask your Lordship to make a note of as it places me at great disadvantage in answering it and the charge must fail. The article was not intended to promote enmity or hatred between the classes, and it was a criticism upon the Press and Explosives Acts. The innuendo that is likely to be drawn from the words is; 'here it is; you promote or excite the people by saying that bombs can be easily made &c.. If you comment upon a particular thing you are bound to give not only your own views, but reasons in support of that view, and when you give those reasons you cannot be construed into meaning something else. The object is clear that I was commenting upon particular sections of these two acts. The aim and object is plainly before you, so there must be some evidence placed before the Jury to prove that my obiect was quite different. Many hypothetical cases might be put to you, likely or unlikely. Nothing is unlikely, just as in Napoleon's Dictionary, nothing was impossible. But we have to see what is the natural construction to be put upon it. Then again the same article has been made the basis of a charge under Section 124 A. Apart from the legal technicality it appears to me to be something like this A *guest comes to me and I present him with a dish of food, the empty dish I present to another guest* ! ! The same words are made to support two offences. We know that in Mathematics a stone can kill two birds at one time, if it has got sufficient velocity, but I did not know that one set of words could be charged under two Sections. That is why I wanted the prosecution to specify the words charged under 124 A and the words charged under 153 A.

This third charge is not only vague and defective, but Section 153A., I maintain, is not applicable to that article. The words are not mentioned, the classes are not mentioned, the bureaucracy cannot be a class under this section. On the point of law particularly, there is nothing to support the charge regarding this article.

Then, my Lord, I would like to refer to some sections of the C. P. C. I beg your Lordship's attention to sections 298, and 299, of the C. P. C. on the duties of the Judge and the duties of the Jury. I stated in the beginning in explaining section 124A. the English law on the subject. The jury may have the help of the legal maxim that "every man intends the consequences of his act,' but it is their duty also to examine all the surrounding circumstances. That has been the law since 1792. Now the practice in England ever since has been to leave the whole question to the Jury. In fact that was the reform effected, and that reform substantially effected the liberty of the press in England. The Judge has to give the law, and the Jury hae to take the surrounding circumstances into consideration and return a verdict on the facts. The Indian law is based on English law, and especially on the original side of the High Court. And the practice has been to leave the whole thing to the Jury. If your Lordship refers to section 298 and 299, you will find that the duties of Judge and Jury are clearly defined. Of course it is perfectly within the discretion of your Lordship to give any direction or not. The Judge may give his opinion or may not give his opinion. Now I will read the duties of the Jury.

(*a*) to decide which view of the facts is true and then to return the verdict which under such view ought, according to the direction of the Judge, to be returned.

(*b*) to determine the meaning of all teachnical terms (other than terms of law) and words used in an unusual sense which it may be necessary to determine, whether such words occur in documents or not;

(*c*) to decide all questions which according to law are to be deemed questions of fact;

(*d*) to decide whether general indefinite expressions do or do not apply to particular cases unless such expressions refer to legal procedure or unless their meaning is ascertained by law, in either of which cases it is the duty of the Judge to decide their meaning.

It is the same as in Fox's Libel Act. The second illustration I have read to you shows that the considerations include motive, and intention and mental state. These are matters for the Jury to consider. They are left entirely to them. The Jury is not to accept inference. They are to take all the surrounding circumstances into consideration. Of course so far as I can say there has not been a case where so many surrounding circumstances have influenced the case. The Jury is not to depend upon the words and the inference drawn from the legal fiction. Then there is the direction of the Chief Justice, Sir Lawrence Jenkins, in the case Empress-vs-Luxman, reported in Vol. II, Bombay Law Reporter 1900. I hope your Lordship will be pleased to direct them accordingly. Is it a question of pure law, or law and fact? The Jury must take into account all the surrounding circumstances the time, place &c. Now in cases which were decided in 1900 none of the surrounding circumstances was taken into account. It may have been due to the fact that they were not explained, that they were not considered by the Jury. I maintain that if those circumstances are explained the Jury is bound to take them into consideration. I maintain that the word 'intention' is more comprehensive than the word 'attempt.' The Chief Justice here says 'you have to say whether it is an attempt or not' After that you may use the legal maxim that every man intends the consequences of his acts, but if you wish to prove intention other circumstances must be taken into consideration. Then as regards the controversy I claim the right of private defence. Of course this does not come quite under the provisions of the I. P. C Has or has not a man any right of private defence in libel, or his only remedy is to go to a court of law, and if he cannot go to a court of law is there no other remedy ? In the present case going to a court of law depends upon the Government. Does it mean that the Anglo-Indian press has a licence to abuse the native press ? I don't think that it can be contended for a moment that is the state of the law at present. Speaking of the right of private defence against property I would only say that property includes reputation. It would be very strange to say that a man has no right to defend his reputation, and the reputation of his party ; to say that would mean that a man cannot prosecute another man for defamation. Reputation is considered a valuable property. Taking the case in that light, if certain newspapers charge me with bad motives, and they say that certain individuals ought to be whipped by sweepers in the public street there is surely some right, I maintain a legal right. There can be no question about it that a man must have some right to defend himself and his party. The matter may not go to the length of challenging another to a duel, but the right must extend to some length, and that length must extend to defending oneself and one's party in a newspaper. Anything said in self-defence does not come under the I. P. C. Then I would like to say a few words, My Lord, about the liberty of the press. It is said that it is given by the explanation of section 124A. But the word 'attempt' leaves a wide margin, and I don't think that the use of the word 'attempt' there is intended to show that there is only a legal inference, and if you do not go beyond that you are protected. English law is that the whole question is left to the Jury, and if the intention is to be inferred from the act alone then the right is very restricted. Any word you write may be interpreted in any way. You may have no criminal mind and you may be punished for it. Now I will read to you what is stated by Stephens in his work on Criminal Law (Reads from Page 348 Vol. 2)

'That the practical enforcement of this doctrine was wholly inconsistent with any serious public discussion of political affairs is obvious, and so long as it was recognised as the law of the land, all such discussion existed only on sufference.'

You could only beg, you could not claim as a right. Political discussion or conroversy could be carried on only on the sufference of Government.

So in all the three cases decided by this High Court the judges have given the direction to the Jury that a certain amount of liberty is allowed to the Press in this country. In England the question of inference and intention is left to the Jury. I contend that speaking from the legal point of view the only way in which the liberty of the press can be defended is by leaving the whole question entirely to the Jury as a safeguard to the liberty of the press. There is no definition except what we find in the explanation of the wording of Section 124 A. Even in these cases the question is left to the Jury; so we arrive at the same result as in England. I do not mean that English law is to be applied here. Indian law is codified but we can interpret it with the help of the English law which forms the basis of the Indian law. If the act is committed we can arrive at the intention of the act. The purpose for which these words were uttered cannot be inferred from the mere fact that these words were uttered or published. Now there is one more point we have to consider; whether any effect has been produced on the community. It is said that it does not matter whether any effect is produced upon the community, because an attempt must necessarily always be unsuccessful. I say that is not a correct view of the matter. You may take an article written in the *Kesari* two years ago. Is not the factor of time material there? The article has been before the public for two years; what effect has it produced? Time is an important matter in deciding whether it is an attempt or not. I do not say very great importance or value must be attached to it, but it would not be right to attach no value to it. I will read only one passage to show that it was not the intention of the writer to excite feelings of enmity and hatred. It may be said that I should have referred to the good work the Bureaucracy had been doing. I will refer to Erskine to show that that sort of argument was used in the case of Lambert and Perry in 1793. (Reads from Vol. 1 page 213 of Erskine's speeches from 'Mr. Attorney General' to 'the constitution.') Those are minor points but I answer them in explaining as there is no right of reply. I have not cited English law here with the wish that it should be used here instead of the Indian law. But the consideration of the English law is very important in the interpretation of the Indian law. In fact it has been very often said that Indian law is the same as English law and that we have in India the same liberty of the Press as is enjoyed in England and that Indian Editors may write with as much freedom as is enjoyed by English Editors. Stephens in his work says (Reads from 'now proposed' to 'hamper.') and again in Mr. Chowdhari's book in the Appendix page 8 the following occurs (Reads 'pale of law,' down to 'violent, personal or unfair.') The whole question is one of criminal intention. It may be violent or unfair but it must be written with criminal intention; some words may be stronger than the occasion demands, it may even be vehement but that does not matter. There can be no sedition without criminal intent and that intent is to be inferred from the surrounding circumstances. Then again it might be urged by the Prosecution that when it is alleged that it is a controversy as to a certain extent, I attempt to plead justification. That is not what is meant and I must clear myself on that point. We are not pleading justification but say that there is no seditious intention at all. Lastly it is likely that the old argument of lighting a cigar in a powder magazine may be urged. There is no evidence here that these articles were read in Bengal. I simply give expression to the view of the public; giving expression is a different thing from inciting unrest. I do not want to try your patience, Gentlemen of Jury, but if you like you may refer to those newpapers. I cannot be taken to task, for so may writers expressing the same thing in different words. There may be some differences of opinion. One man may agree in 10 points, another in 12 and still another in 45 points. It is a controversy. One section of the Public Press advocating the cause of the Bureaucracy and supporting them and their measures and another section of the Press supporting the Bureaucracy and at the same time condemning all these measures. The controversy has not been provoked or created by us. The bomb-outrages give rise to the controversy as being a topic of the day. Every newspaper writer was bound to express his opinion on it. Having allowed one section of the Press to express an opinion on the fact it was only fair that the other section of the press should have a similar liberty. The whole point in the case is this. Replies were necessary from week to week to the points raised in the controversy, which was due to the repressive policy of Government. By using innuendoes and insinuations this cannot be interpreted into meaning some thing different. I read one more passage which shows how intention is considered and how it is very delicate to infer a particular intention in a man from any particular act. I am going to read a case published in Hansard's Parliamentary Debates 1884. It is a case like that of Reg. V. Binns which was quoted previously. In this case Lord Salisbury took Mr. Chamberlain to task for having said that 100,000 men would march to London. His Lordship said that it was an incitement to violence and that Mr.Chamberlain ought to have been brought before a magistrate and tried (Reads from Hansard page 643). It is the same thing in the case Reg. V. Binus reported in 26 State Trials page 595. When a man is speaking or writing in view of the public it is impossible for him to weigh all his words with that calmness with which they are weighed by the lawyer or the judge. We have to write or speak on the spur of the moment. We cannot weigh our words; we use words, occasionally words which we too would not use upon deliberation. Gentlemen of the Jury, you ought to take into consideration this fact in coming to a conclusion as to the criminal intention in this case. It is due to the fact that sedition cases are left to the Jury that those cases are so rare now in England. They have a popular form of government in England, they know how to deal with Judges there. And so if intention is not proved by the incriminating articles the other articles cannot be used to prove or supplement the proof or supply the deficiency of proof in the incriminating articles. If what is in the articles is seditious it does not need the other articles to prove it. If the first article does not show intention, then the second cannot be used. If it is sedition it does not require extracts, to prove intention taken from here and there. That is why I objected to these articles going in at the beginning and I quoted a passage from Mr. Mayne where he takes the same view. It is on the last *Kesari* case that he makes these remarks. (Reads from Mayne's Criminal Law page 552, 3rd Edition up to 'into consideration.') He takes much the same view as I have placed before you here, namely, that if the articles are not seditious you cannot make them seditious by putting in other articles.

Then I wish to say something about the translations; and this is the last point I will refer to. I have pointed out the mistakes in these translations. There are minor errors here and there which I do not insist upon. When reliance is placed upon particular words such as 'tyrannical' or 'despotic' then the question really comes in. I will read here to you from Lewis on the use and abuse of political terms. (Reads from Chapter 3.) Oppression, tyranny and despotism are confounded there and have a distinctly different meaning in writings on political science. There has been that kind of confusion in the translations to which I object. I admit that the idioms of one language cannot be the same as those of another. I would like to point out that the translator was not placed in the witness box but someone else ; and he was asked to vouch for the correctness of the translation. Of course it is an official translation and therefore there is a certain presumption of correctness in that ; but where particular passages were pointed out as wrong the real translator ought to have been placed in the witness box. The charge is based not upon the original Marathi but upon the translation. It should have been based upon the original Marathi article and then the translations ought to have been put in. It may be said that the defence has not produced its own translation. That is a burden which the defence can not be made to bear. It is for the Proseution to prove that the translation is correct. Here the charge is based on the English translation and not on the original Marathi article. Supposing this was an English article and supposing an Englishman were charged with sedition the charge would fail if the prosecution proceeded on a document in which, it was proved, different words to those wrritten were inserted. Here there are differences between the original words in Marathi in the *Kesari* and the words used in the translations.

Advocate General :—If Mr. Tilak would be a little correct, I might have a few minutes. The charges are based upon the Marathi articles as translated. He may be a little correct even in small matters.

Accused :—The Marathi article in the original and the Marathi article as translated are two different things; the charge is based upon the English translation of these articles and if these translations are not correct the charge must fall through. The charges ought to have been based on the Marathi articles. I have shown that the translations are wrong in my cross-examination of Mr. Joshi. It may be the practice hitherto to base a charge on translations but I have never heard before that translations were so grossly incorrect. The effect is to be judged on the Marathi-speaking community. There is no evidence before your Lordship or the Jury as to what has been the effect on the Marathi-speaking community. It is very likely that Government has given sanction on the translations and not on the original articles. Therefore the Prosecution must stand or fall by the correctness or incorrectness of those translations. If the effect is to be judged on the Marathi-speaking people it must be of the original words. You cannot judge as to what stage of political education they have advanced. We have been in close touch with the Marathi community. We know what political views they hold and what their prejudices are and how these articles are likely to affect them. To convince the Jury of the effect, some evidence should be produced as to the state of that community. Of course in Bombay you say that the Marathi-speaking people are an ignorant community. Take these articles and you will see that it needs some intelligence to read and understand them. You must see the effect on the minds of the readers. That has been expressly admitted in the last *Kesari* case and also in the *Bhala* case. Poona is the centre of political activity. We have had the Sarvajanik Sabha there and from the time of Justice Ranade these doctrines have been preached. It has been so for the last 25 or 30 years. A community like that cannot be supposed to be an ignorant community ; and you must see what effect my words may produce upon an educated public. It is for you to judge what effect the articles are likely to have on the Marathi-speaking community. I hope your Lordship will devote your attention to this and take it into your Lordship's consideration. I have nearly finished but I would like to look at my notes to see if I have left any points.

[The Court was adjourned till Wednesday.]

EIGHTH DAY.

Wednesday 22nd July.

Mr. Tilak resumed his address at 11-30 A. M.

He said:—I have only, in support of what I said yesterday evening, to bring to your Lordship's notice Sections 294, 663 and 708 of Mayne's Criminal Law, 3rd Edition. I would like to read certain portions of them. Section 294 deals with the word intention in 124 A and it states. (Reads from ' but I add ' to 'circumstances').

That means in presuming intention from the words the Jury must take into account all the other circumstances. I am only referring you to the authorities. Of course I have dealt with this question myself before. Section 663 is about the charges; it reads (Reads from 663 down to 'no meaning'.) What I say, as I have brought it to your Lordship's notice, is that the charges are based on the translations; and even if they were based on the articles the Crown is bound by the interpretation they put on the originals. Section 708 says (Reads 708 from 'foregoing remarks' down to 'criminal intent.') These are the three sections which I say are in support of what I said last evening and which I wish to bring to your Lordship's notice. I have done now with my defence and my first duty is to thank you, Gentlemen of the Jury, for the indulgence you were kind enough to show me in listening to me for so many days. I was placed at a disadvantage by the vagueness of the charges. I did not wish to detain you so long but I was bound to do so in my own interest and in the interest of the cause which I represent. Of course I have taxed your patience. If I have done so, more than was necessary in your opinion, you will excuse me. The last word in such a prosecution is not with the Prosecution but with his Lordship; and, as I am confident, that word will be impartial. I have taken a course which has not formerly been taken. I must also express my thanks to the Prosecution. I knew that in undertaking to defend the case myself I would have to put up with interruptions as the law allows and I may have been interrupted on a number of occasions ; for as you know when a layman defends himself he is bound to make mistakes. I have to thank the Advocate General for the kindness and courtesy with which he has treated me. I do not possess his learning and ability and so I can only place my case before the Jury from a personal and common sense point of view. That is my only excuse for addressing you personally. But I ran some risks and one was that I might be interrupted and then it would have been difficult for me to go on. If the learned Advocate General had taken that course I should have been in a difficulty. I have had to make some remarks about the Prosecution; but that is a different question from the other question, that is the courtesy with which he has treated me. I should have liked to have availed myself of his learning; but I think I am expressing the opinion of everyone, not only here but outside the Court, that for the first time I find him in a wrong place. And now, Genlemen, once more I thank you for the patience with which you have heard me. The case is very clear and if I have put it to you rather bluntly it is because I am not used to forensic tactics. I have not delayed you intentionally. You have the articles before you and as I told you these articles have been written in the course of a controversy which is an old one—a struggle between the Bureaucracy and the people of this country. Here is a book in my hand. It gives proceedings of the Sarvajanik Sabha and the East India Association in the time of the late Rao Sahib Mandlik &c. From all these you will find that this controversy has been going on ever since the year 1860. It is an old controversy and I read to you a few extracts from the literature of the reform party to show that what I have said in my articles is not new and that there is nothing in them to excite feelings against the Government. If there is anything in it it is merely expressions of our views. I do not accept blindly all the opinions which are constantly placed before me. I do not mean to say that whenever I quote a book I feel every sentiment and accept every argument stated therein. In quoting them I wanted only to show that the controversy is not a new one and that it has been carried on for the past 30 or 40 years and that I am not entirely responsible for the views expressed in my articles. The Bureaucracy is not the Government. It is likely to be urged 'take away the Bureaucracy and what hope is left?' The correct way for a British Colony is not to be governed by a Bureaucracy; there are other ways. As Professor Amos says in his book on Politics—:

"Nevertheless the case is more clear in respect of countries like British India, in which, through a series of fortuitous circumstances, England has been called to govern a population of alien race, language, and customs out of all numerical proportion to the English residing in the country. In such a case, the duties of Government can neither be ignored nor resigned nor transferred. They are a trust for a coming generation and for a new age. Every opportunity must be taken, as it is being taken in practice more and more, to habituate the native population to the duties of self-government and to prepare them for a time when the imposed and alien rule can be first relaxed, then shared, and finally withdrawn."

It is not a question of the very existence of Government, but of the form of Government. I have already referred you to what Major Evans Bell says on the subject and that is exactly what Lord Morley says. The question does not touch the existence of Government. The bomb-outrages were quickly condemned in my paper as in the Anglo-Indian papers. We do not hold that bomb throwing is not a criminal act and is not reprehensible. We condemn it. But in condemning it we say that we must also condemn the repressive measures of Government. I also explain that it is a power which can be created without requiring much preparation. There are certain powers which can be created by means of a physical act. This is nothing of the kind; it is something like a spell and it deserves to be condemned; but in order to repress it and get rid of it certain reforms are necessary in the administration. Both parties are taking advantage of the presence of the bomb. The Bureaucratic party are taking advantage of it to suppress political agitation and the other party is taking advantage of it to claim some reforms. I can certainly ask at your hands the same privilege in this country as is enjoyed by the English Press at home. It is a very important question. It is the same question which was fought out by Erskine in the case of the Dean of St. Asaph. It is the question that was fought out in England as long ago as 1792. English people now enjoy the liberty of the Press which they demanded and got in the 18th Century. This is a similar case and all that I ask is to give it a patient hearing. I know you are placed at a certain disadvantage by not knowing Marathi; but you have another advantage which a Marathi-knowing Jury might not have possessed. You are proud of your traditions. You have got liberty of the Press after a long struggle and I believe that you attach more importance to that than even we do here. I can trace a great struggle between the people on the one hand and a mighty Burcaucracy on the other. And I ask you to help us, not me personally, but the whole of India in our endeavours to obtain a share in the Government of this country. The matter has come to a critical stage; we are in want of help ; you can give it to us. I am now on the wrong side of life according to the Indian standard of life. For me it can only be a matter of a few years, but future generations will look to your verdict and see whether you have judged wrong or right. The verdict is likely to be a memorable one in the history cf the struggle for the freedom of the Indian Press. You have a heavy responsibility upon you. It is, I state again and again, not a personal question. If at least one of you would come forward and say that I was right in what I did it will be a matter of satisfaction to me ; for I know that if the Jury are not unanimous in England another trial would take place. It is not so here but it would be a moral support upon which I would rely with great satisfaction. It is a question mainly of intention. You have all read the passages yourselves and you can determine the meaning cf thosc passages and can say what the intention was. Was it there an attempt to excite disaffection or enmity or hatred between any classes of his Majesty's subjects? And remember that an attempt includes intention and there cannot be an aimless attempt. When I was in school I was taught a small sentence. 'Caesar aimed at the crown but failed.' That clearly explains the word attempt. Now as I have put all the circumstances before you you must read the writings for yourselves and decide whether those passages do intend to excite disaffection or feelings of enmity. If you could come to a unanimous verdict, well and good. If not, then do not try to come to an artificial unanimity. Even one of you saying that I was right would be a source of satisfaction to me–a kind of moral support. If you cannot come to a unanimous conclusion you will state what you think, each of you, whether the articles in question are criminal or not. You might not agree with my views. Even if you do not agree, you are entitled to say that in your opinion the matter does not come under Section 124 A. You may agree or not with me, you may accept my views or not accept my views.

That is not the point at issue. The point is whether I was within my rights and whether a subject of his Majesty in India can or cannot enjoy the same freedom which is enjoyed by British subjects at Home, and the Anglo-Indians out here. That is the point at issue. It is not a matter of whether the views are correct. I may, who knows, alter my views, Gentlemen, and come to your views. You will presently hear what the Advocate General has to say and after him His Lordship will address you. The responsibility is yours; you will have to return a verdict of guilty or not guilty. Coming from the people and knowing their sentiments and thoughts you will have to say what you think would be the effect. I would ask you to forget all other circumstances outside this court. You must be reading the daily papers and finding in some of them, I wont say an attempt but a fact, to associate my name in connection with something which is going on in this city. I wanted to bring the matter to His Lordship's notice but I thought it was a small matter. Gentlemen of the Jury, you will have to leave all that out of your consideration. I know that there are certain prejudices against me. I request you to keep aside those prejudices. Judge me on facts. One reason I undertook to defend myself was that you would know the man. I have told you, perhaps bluntly, what I have done. I have concealed nothing from you. I have stated what my object is. If you find anything wrong therein you can return a verdict against me. But I believe, nay I am confident, you will find nothing in it against me. You will after taking all the circumstances into consideration return a verdict of not guilty. I am quite confident about it. I appeal to you not for myself but in the interest of the cause which I have the honour to represent. It is a cause that is sacred and I doubt not, Gentlemen, that He before whom all of us will have to stand one day and render an account of our actions will inspire you with the courage of your convictions and help you in arriving at a right decision on the issue involved in this case.

My Lord, I have done. I have already referred to the vagueness of the charges and if there is anything which I have not touched upon and is referred to by the lerned Advocate General and if he brings out anything new, I request that I may be given an opportunity of replying.

His Lordship:—Certainly, if there is any new point you have not touched upon, I will give you a chance of replying.

Accused:—My Lord and Gentlemen of the Jury, I have again to thank you for the great patience with which you have heard me.

The Advocate General's Reply.

Mr. Branson then addressed the Jury as follows :—

I think, gentlemen, you may safely leave future generations to look after themselves and in the interests of the present generation not to take up more of its time than is necessary. I must endeavour to confine myself in my reply to the sense of the word ' attempt ' and to be as brief in doing so as is consistent with my duty not only to the Crown but to the accused. I do not know why the accused should have anticipated that I would be inclined to treat him with any discourtesy. What would be gained by that? If it was only a question of motive of which we have heard so much; it would be to my advantage not to treat the accused with discourtesy but to do what I can for him consistent with my duty. I take it that it is the duty of Counsel appearing for the Crown not to overstate things or over-press the case, but put himself in the position of a person who is trying to help the tribunal to come to a right conclusion. I have tried to avoid saying anything about which it could be said that I had done something to induce you to come to a conclusion against the accused. But while doing that, I could not shorten your tortures in having to listen for five days to Mr. Tilak. I cannot guarantee abstaining from inflicting some torture on you, I can only say that as far as is consistent with my duties, I will endeavour to avoid all those faults which Mr. Tilak has been guilty of, the maddening reiteration, saying the same thing over and over again till you must have been as sick of it as he must have been himself. I decline to be drawn into any discussion whatsoever of politics. Neither you nor his Lordship, nor I have anything whatever to do with the politics which have been the source of discussion for the past three days. Kindly remember that. Put the whole of the discussion addressed to you on the question of politics and the position of the parties aside. You have nothing to do with that. I assure you I am not saying what I am saying to you of my own mind. I will refer you to what was said by the Chief Justice of Bengal in the sedition case mentioned at page 36 of No. 19 Indian Law Reports, Calcutta series and there is also another point at page 46 (Reads. 'His Lordship in pointing to the Jury their duty said' down to "the only question is the question of intention, you have nothing to do with the policy of Government"). If Mr. Tilak had extended his industries a little further he would have discovered the futility of putting before you speeches of Mr. Erskine finishing up with Evans Bell &c. You have to consider only the evidence in this case. You have to put aside the whole of this political discussion. It is not for you or for me to consider whether there exist or do not exist parties called the pro-Bureaucratic or anti-Bureaucratic. It does not matter whether there are or are not. What Mr. Tilak seems to have forgotten in his address is this. I will assume that he might be right and that there may be a number of reforms necessary. I will go further and assume the truth of the allegations which, we say, are made against the Government in these articles and assume that these articles show that the Government has been acting improperly and reforms are necessary. The whole of this is absolutely irrelevent to the trial of this case. I propose hereafter to lay before you certain propositions which I ventured to advance in the last sedition case and which met with the entire approval from the Bench as to the points to which you are to give your attention. But I must in this instance go over, to a certain extent, the address presented to you by the accused. You, as I have already said, have nothing to do with the question of whether reforms are necessary or desirable. You have nothing to do with that. It might be a startling proposition to you, and I intend to support it by the authority of the Chief Justice Mr. Strachey and the Full Bench of the High Court as well as the Privy Council. It makes no difference whether the complaints against Government are true or not, The question is, does the language used in the articles come within the provisions of Section I24A ? That is a point which evidently escaped the attention of Mr. Tilak and his advisers. I shall follow up later on with a more detailed discussion of the decisions of this High Court than has been entered upon by Mr. Tilak. I will draw your attention at once to what is said in Mayne, Para: 296 page 521 third edition 1904. Here he points out that the truth or othrwise of any charge under Section 124A need not be taken into consideration. Yet we have spent four days discussing whether the charges are true or untrue, whether well-founded, or ill-founded. This is the result of not carrying out the legal education with which Mr. Tilak started life. He is a pleader of 25 year's standing. If he had only carried out his education he would never have spent 4 days in stating what is absolutely inaccurate. It would have been better for him, for you and for me. Now it remains for me if I can correct the innumerable errors that characterised Mr. Tilak's address. It is for you on the basis of his own statement and the basis of the authorities which are cited to see which is correct. Here we have the authority of one of the best criminal lawyers in India (Reads paragraph 296 from Mayne's Criminal Law.) Now you will find that rule laid down by Mr. Justice Strachey in a case which it will be not necessary to identify.

Accused:—Your Lordship, as I find it difficult to hear I beg that I may be allowed to take a chair nearer to the Advocate-General.

His Lordship:—Yes, you may do so.

Advocate General:—I hope Mr. Tilak will acknowledge that I am continuing that courtesy that so much surprised him.

Advocate General continuing his address said:—I will go back to the question of the truth or falsity of the grievances alleged. You will find that it has been laid down in this case—I do not wish to identify it beyond stating that it is in reference to a former charge against somebody whom I do not at present name-but the law as laid down by Mayne, and as propounded not only by Mr. Justice Strachey, who tried the case at the Sessions, but by the Full Bench before whom it was afterwards taken because the accused was dissatisfied with Mr. Justice Strachey's summing up, and by the Privy Council, to whom it was taken. The Privy Council supported Mr. Justice Strachey's views, and you will find every point I am now stating to you with regard to the fact, the existence of any grievance real or supposed being no defence whatever to an offence under section 124 A. You will find that law laid down distinctly, and approved completely by the Privy Council in these terms, and therefore it is that I am directing your attention at the outset to the law which is completely subversive of all that Mr. Tilak has said. It will economise my time and yours, but it is sufficient for me to draw your attention now to what the Privy Council said and you will find that they approved of Mr. Justice Strachey's summing up as supported by a Full Bench on an application based upon a contention that the summing up was defective, and which was afterwards made the ground for an application to the Privy Council for leave to appeal. You cannot get leave from the Privy Council to appeal except with the permission of the Full Bench here. The Full Bench only grants permission on certain terms and under certain circumstances involving law-points, involving serious points of law, as for instance mis-direction. The application was refused by the Full Bench, but you will find that when the application was made to the Privy Council for special leave to appeal, two of the grounds which were put forward were (Reads 'the Judge has misdirected the jury ' down to 'readers') It is a curious commentary on the case that he himself put foward that there was a feeling of excitement outside this Presidency, as to which he says there can be no doubt. His readers, he says, have been familiar with his views for years, and his contention is that his readers know exactly what he means, and entertaining the views he entertains would not be likely to be affected by the article. Many writers besides himself stated that there was a feeling of excitement. I digress for a moment because of the peculiar appositeness of the point which was put forward in the appeal, by Mr. Tilak. (Reads from application from 'the Judge has not pointed out to the jury ' down to '*Kesari* of 15th June ') You will find that in the argument which was addressed to the Judicial Committee by Mr. Asquith, (Reads from Mayne down to 'that petition '). Lord Halsbury in delivering the Judgment of the Privy Council says this (Reads from 'taking into consideration' down to 'by the light of what he said on the other side '.) So that you have a most complete confirmation of Mr. Justice Strachey's summing up in the former case in which one of the chief points included against His Lordship's summing up is one of the most admirable on the question of the Section that I am aware of. Every point which can arise, and has arisen in this case, has been discussed by Mr. Justice Strachey in complete opposition to what has been the defence of Mr. Tilak. That is why I have pointed out to you the decision of the Privy Council, as supporting my contention that the truth of the language charged with sedition cannot be pleaded or proved. The absurdity of the proposition that you can plead or prove the truth of the allegation in reply to the complaint is shown by Mayne, para 296, page 523. (Reads paragraph.) This was a case where the same point was raised, and Lord Campbell for the first time urged that you can plead truth of allegation under the Civil Libel Act. This is an attempt to introduce the same effect in a Criminal prosecution. Now it has been tried to apply that in a criminal case, and Mr. Justice Lawrance said (Reads from 'the Court is gravely asked' down to 'exciting hostility.') That is the fatal absurdity which Mr. Tilak has been committing throughout the last four days.

Accused disclaimed having done so.

Advocate-General :—I have carefully avoided interfering with Mr. Tilak, and cannot I ask for the same consideration ? The only time when I interrupted him was on two occasions, one when he used an expression which seemed to me to be extremely offensive, and the other was on the occasion when he proposed to read an article (Exhibit 64,) as representing his views in the case. I objected, and as it turned out my objection was in his favour. His Lordship interposed and withdrew that Exhibit from you. I am going to refer to it again later on. These are the only two occasions when I interrupted, once rightly, and the other time in his favour, although I was not aware of it at the time, and I expect the same consideration, unless it can be said that I am misrepresenting something. But Mr. Tilak knows what a valuable asset it would be in the hands of a person who wished to divert attention from what the other person was laying before the Jury. I think I shall not be interrupted again; if I am I shall respond much more strongly than I have done. Now I shall come back to the law. Even assuming Mr. Tilak's contentions extending over many days, supposing that there are things which would be better for reformation, supposing everything alleged against Government in the articles is true, that is no defence whatever if you come to the conclusion that the article complained of comes within provisions of Section 124 A. As to Section 153 A I do not intend to occupy more of your time than five minutes at the end of my address. Section 124 A is the more important one. When you come to read the Section yourselves and study it you will find its applicability to this particular case. You will find that all the discussion put before you, and which I am not going to be led into the temptation of following—all that is irrelevent, and represents so much waste of time. I don't regret, you don't regret, listening to Mr. Tilak; otherwise there is no point in all he said. Suppose I had interrupted; he knew well what was irrelevent, because the law as laid down by him was contrary to the law laid down in the case of which he is himself personally aware. He ought to have known that it was improper, at all events fatal on his part to attempt to persuade you to take that view of the law which would be immoral and was corrected from the Bench, and which he must have known was an incorrect statement of the law. He suggests to you that he is entitled to discuss party questions between the pro-bureaucrats and anti-bureaucrats, and in doing so is entitled to say what he pleases, and if he does so from what he calls lofty motives and a pure mind he insists upon a verdict of not guitly. No greater mistake ever entered the mind of a legal practitioner. I shall directly call your attention to the real law of motive and intention, which has got so jumbled up in the mind of the accused that he could not present it in proper form before you. That is his misfortune. I do not desire to say anything regarding the time he occupied in his speech although it extended over five days, so that it would be impossible for him now to say that he has not said all that he had to say, and all that he desired to say. He has said all that he could say, and all that he wished to say, so far as this case is concerned. I do not look upon it as a case of any great importance. Of course it is of great importance to Mr. Tilak, and it has occupied a great length of time, and he has had a perfectly clear and impartial hearing; and if His Lordship or I wished to interrupt him as we were entitled to do, as Mr. Tilak acknowledges we had a right to do, you may be perfectly certain that in his own organs and in sympathetic organs published elsewhere, you would have heard the outcry " the man has not had a fair hearing &c." That cannot be suggested now. We may take it from that comment that he has had the opportunity of saying every thing he desired to say and that nothing remains, at least I hope not unless I introduce any new element into the case. This he will have a perfect right to do. But I do not intend to introduce anything new except by mere accident.

Well it is cooler here than where he was sitting before. I do not feel myself in present exasperation at his proximity or any prognostication as to what may happen from his proximity. I am acting as far I can to economise time. Perhaps you will think I have not done so so far. But I am telling you the reason why I declined to follow Mr. Tilak in that part of his address which refers to politics. I am doing so on the ground that it has been held that it is not discussable by this Court or by the Privy Council. I am able to say with confidence that your time will be very materially economised. You will find from what his Lordship will tell you that there are really and truly only three points which you have to consider in this case. In fact really and truly there are only two points. I will sub-divide one point. The first point is, did the accused print and publish the articles complained of and is he responsible ? The answer is yes. He himself said so. This is a matter of no interest to you because it is proved beyond a shadow of doubt. It was proved by the declarations under the Press Act. Those declarations were made in 1907 and declared Mr. Tilak to be the editor, printer and publisher of this paper. It is not necessary to pursue this matter, because I think he now admits that he is the editor, printer and publisher. If so, the law makes him liable, and he has done wisely to admit liability for everything that appeared in that paper, whether written by himself or not.

Then the second branch of the first question is answered by himself, in which he apparently glories and in which he somehow manages to see a glamour of humour. My recollection is that the humour consisted of a suggestion to murder, hatred &c. He admits that which the law imposes upon him. That admission to the first question is answered in both these questions. The next question that would arise would be, having got the fact that these articles were written, I won't say by himself–he does not say they were, but assumiug that they were not written by him, it matters not, the next question you have to consider is the thoughts, words and meaning of these articles. What he now says he meant by those articles, that is not the point. He has been trying his best to throw all the dust he could collect, even in the monsoon weather, into your eyes on this point. It is not what he now says he meant, but what he meant when he wrote them. Chapter and verse I will give you very shortly, when I discuss the words on which I am going to rely. And he cannot be allowed to say now ' of course I wrote sedition, and meant affection.' Words are not what you have to consider. You have to decide, Gentlemen, upon the language he used, and what he meant. You cannot take from him now a statement that what he wrote was not what he meant, but what he means now. You will find that that is the law.

Now it is for you, as solc judges of the facts, to draw your own conclusion from the words of the articles themselves as to what he meant. I have nothing I can say to you upon this point beyond what I shall presently have to say in referring to the articles themselves. That is a matter for you to decide. What do you think these articles meant when they were written? You cannot take his statement now that he meant something else, unless it is corroborated by the words of the articles themselves. Having got the meaning of the articles from the words of the articles, the next point to consider is what did he intend by these articles? Was his intention such as would bring him within the wording of the Section 124 A, or do the circumstances of the case bring him within the exceptions or explanations of Section 124 A? If you come to the conclusion that the articles complained of and charged come within the wording of the first clause of the Section there is an end of the case. On the other hand if you come to the conclusion that when he wrote these articles he knew they were capable of the interpretation that the Prosecution now puts on them there is an end of the case also. If you do this the next point to be considered is whether you can by any perversion of the language give him the benefit of the explanations 2 or 3. Now upon that point accused has made some remarks about the proof being wrongly put upon him. Presently when I am dealing more at length with individual remarks of the defence I will show you that he is completely wrong. The Judicial and Legislative authorities are absolutely against him. Once there is a *prima facie* case, to get out of a charge the burden of proof lies on the defence. And in this case he must bring himself under the explanation of the general law. Here again Mr. Tilak advances a proposition on an imperfect reading of Section 105. of the Evidence Act. Mr. Tilak complained yesterday that the case had been brought wrongly under Section 153 A. Now, in a few minutes I will call your attention to Section 105 of the Evidence Act, and you will see how fatal it is. The whole of his argument with regard to the extent of the circumstances pointing to the necessity of the advisability of reform of the Government is completely immaterial. (Reads Sec. 105.) There are one or two other points which I do not propose to follow Mr. Tilak in discussing. And I think that you will be charmed by my decision. We had to listen to a discussion of English law as it is supposed by Mr. Tilak, and what he called Jury-made law. I think that is a point I do not propose to follow. It may be interesting, no doubt, but anybody who has read that introduction to Fox's Libel Act, would have put the case before you in ten minutes. There was a time when Juries were inclined to take their stand in England, on Jury-made law but that does not apply to this country. But in this particular case of which Mr. Tilak must have an intimate knowledge Mr. Justice Strachey at the outset stated, I will read you his words so that I may not be said to be straining or misrepresenting what he said. He said (Reads ' I don't propose to discuss the English law ' down to ' Penal Code ') Now I have already told you that that summing up was approved by the Full Bench, and also approved by the Privy Council. Therefore I think I am entitled to say on the highest authority that the whole of the discussion with regard to the applicability or otherwise of the English law, in full or in part in a charge of seditious libel in India may be safely left out of the discussion. If you are curious to know the real law in England, or if you are curious to know what the circumstances were in regard to the introduction of Fox's Libel Act, you will find it in the introduction of Campbell's ' Life of Erskine.' You might have been spared all those books which have been wearily referred to in connection with Fox's Act of Seditious Libel and the possibility of its applying to this country. It is all stated in one and a half pages of the book I have referred to. I think, Gentlemen, that I may put it to you that unless you wish, or His Lordship wishes that I should say more upon the point than I have stated now, it will be safe for you to have it, as it stands, and so I do not intend to discuss the English law because it has been held that it does not apply to this country, and the Privy Council has upheld that decision. We have got the Penal Code, you cannot take away from it, and you cannot add to it. That brings one to the next point of these voluminous dicussions to which we have all had to listen, possibly with profit, I cannot say. You will say whether there has been any profit to your minds by the discussion on the liberty of the press. You have been told that you are guardians of the press Fiddlesticks ! You are guardians of the press no more than I am. Before God you are guardians of the Penal Code and the Penal Code protects the press. You have been told that you are guardians of the press over and over again, until one really felt inclined to rebel against the doctrine of the liberty of the subject. You are not the guardians of the press ; and I am not entitled to write what I please saying that I am writing in the interests of my party, or in the interests of the freedom of the press.' You will find that these are points which have all been dealt with first by Mr. Justice Strachey, then Sir Lawrence Jenkins, and lastly by Mr. Justice Batty. To all the three cases it will be my duty to draw your attention with a little more detail later on. I will take one instance now, a passage in which Mr. Justice Batty, in Indian Law Reports, 22 Bombay, page 137, says (Reads) He points out what is meant by this much-abused and misleading phrase liberty of the press. Mr. Tilak thinks it means that he is entitled to write what he likes no matter how seditious it may be, or how many suggestions it contains of murder or brings about a dastardly murder; he will justify himself by reference to his writings, which I cannot understand anybody with any human feelings sitting down to write and then saying " it is correct, my motives are pure so please return a verdict of not guilty against me." I will take a longer passage than what I intended to put at first and the passage which I am going to cite explains the law which is applicable, and which, your Lordship, I am perfectly certain, is actually the law. If you are of opinion that these articles come within Section 124 A, it matters not two straws whether as a matter of fact any disaffection was caused, or any hatred was caused. 'If you come to the conclusion that the meaning of the words published was an intention to excite hatred against the Government established by law, the effect of its failure or success is completely immaterial. It is equally immaterial that the excitement should not have been a disturbance to the point of mutiny. That is not a matter of any importance in judging of the criminal liability of any person charged with having written articles which come within Section 124 A. Now you will see that I have discussed a little upon this point for a few moments. I am now going to tell you what Mr. Justice Strachey says in his judgment when he deals not only with the Section, but with the word attempt. He lays down in the clearest possible terms in his summing up which has besn accepted by Sir Lawrence Jenkins and Mr. Justice Batty with regard to what a person may or may not write. Mr. Justice Strachey says this after discussing the examples of section 124 A as it existed before the year 1898. I shall have to draw your attention to the meaning of the Act for you will find that as it now stands it is due to the judgment of Mr. Justice Strachey as approved by the Privy Council and the Full-Bench following as it did rulings in Calcutta and Allahabad High Courts. In consequence of these series of rulings before 1898 and the fact that the Section was somewhat cumbrously worded it was amended. In discussing the Act as it originally stood his Lordship said (Reads from " You will observe that the section" to 'that he succeeds'). We have had a most extraordinary series of contentions extending over 3 days showing that Mr. Tilak had completely failed to understand the words used by the Chief Justice with regard to the word attempt. I must try to put the matter clearly before you,as the absurdity of Mr.Tilak's arguments may have raised a certain amount of uncertainty in your minds. He seems to think that you cannot have an attempt unless the attempt has been frustrated from some physical cause outside the control of the person making the attempt. That is to say that it must be a cause which independently of himself prevents success. Consider the absolute absurdity of such an observaion. If a man prevents himself in making an attempt he does not mean any attempt, or if he has started on the attempt and then stops himself he can claim *locus penitentie*, of which we have heard in one of the quotations in this case. Mr. Tilak has not understood the law laid down by Mr. Justice Batty, and the Chief Justice. They say with regard to attempt, (Reads down to " something over which the person has no control. ") I fail to follow Mr. Tilak's argument which never approaches the boundary mark of common sense. You will find Mr. Justice Batty's judgment in the case which has been the subject of affectionate reference on behalf of the accused. Mr. Tilak proceeds to say that the Jury can decide against the Judge, and he refers to Jury-made law. He quotes to you from a case which was cited by my learned friend Mr. Inverarity, and without misrepreseuting Mr. Tilak's own argument, I will refer you to the case in 1810 against Lambert and Perry cited by Mr. Inverarity. Mr. Tilak suggested to you that this was a case of Jury-made law, and that it is for the Jury to decide what is seditions, when he turned to the ruling cited by my learned friend as to the liberty and licence of speech I will read you what Mr. Justice Cave says with regard to intention. (Reads from page 365. 'a man cannot escape from the consequences' down to 'violence.') That is to say that Mr. Justice Cave was not aware of the existence of any rule of law or common sense, that you cannot have an attempt unless you show that there has been some physical interference between the attempt and the intended act. It is such abject nonsense that I can hardly believe that Mr. Tilak is not pulling the legs of the Jury in putting it forward. To suppose that Judges would use language which infers or suggests inuendoes, and use these particular words in summing up to juries, and in laying down what the law is, means audacious effrontery which I confess I never could regard the possibility of in my own mind. Now let us go back to what I was saying with regard to the freedom of the Press, a subject we heard of *ad nausium* till Mr. Tilak decided to sit down. This is what Mr. Justice Strachey says and I read it to you only to reinforce the judgments of the Chief Justice and Mr. Justice Batty (Reads from 'having discussed' down to 'excite feelings.') Let me pause for one moment to point out to you another fallacy which has some bearing upon this particular part of the case, put forward by Mr. Tilak. He seems to be under the impression that you must have something besides the article itself impeached as evidence, before you can convict. To show you that that is completely wrong, I will refer you again to Chief Justice Sir Comer Petheram's decision in Indian Law Reports 19, Calcutta, page 35. (Reads.) Here you find that if you have got the articles, from them you can draw your own inferences as to whether there was an attempt or not. Further evidence is unnecessary for the Prosecution, but the absence of it does not tell fatally against the accused. Perhaps I am travelling out of the course of the arguments upon which I first embarked, but you will allow me to go out of my way for a few minutes and follow Mr. Tilak's habit of jumping from subject to subject. Look at Mr. Tilak's position in this case. He says "from year to year I have been publishing the same views as appear in these articles; no one can be misled because they are exactly what their views and my views are; these views have been urged by the Congress for so long that there can be no possibility of my language being misunderstood by those who read it, and they are only old ideas clothed in new words. They convey to them no new ideas." That being so, how is it that of the hundreds of readers of the *Kesari* not a single soul has been produced to show that he took a different view of the language of those articles to what we place before the Jury.

Why, Gentlemen, he has been surrounded from the beginning of the trial. There are pleaders to right of him, pleaders to left of him, pleaders in front of him, while he did the thundering. He is quite right to do so; a man may defend himself in any way he likes. Many of them, indeed most of them know the accused's views and my own. And they will know that I am not contending anything with a view to annoying, but they well know that I am saying this to show that any of them might have come forward to say 'this construction on the articles is not correct.' Why does not somebody come forward to say 'you are wrong in your interpretation of the article.' I think that it was just as well perhaps that I was allowed to digress for a moment. I shall have to come back to it because it is a matter which will have to be dealt with more seriously later on. I think I was right to draw your attention to these questions of language and intention and that he had means of contradicting our evidence. Our evidence consists of the articles themselves, the words in which these articles are couchded and the evidence of the Oriental Translator. His evidence as testified, is to the effect that the translations are correct in every particular except in one case. I will come to that later. But otherwise the translations are correct. That is the evidence and there is no other evidence to contradict it. You cannot take Mr. Tilak's word that these translations are wrong. I have no objection to those of you who can read the original Marathi instructing their fellow jurymen and you will find that there is not a single point of any importance. If you decide on the evidence and nothing else, Mr. Tilak's arguments, his allegations as to wrong translations are of no effect. If you are satisfied that he is correct, give him the benefit by all means of the contentions he has put forward. The evidence uncontradicted is this, and the force of the terms uncontradicted is this: if Mr. Joshi's evidence was not true the accused had his host of readers in the mofussil and his host of pleaders to prove that the translations were wrong or distorted. But not a shred of evidence is produced to prove that the articles do not, as Mr. Joshi says they do, in English accurately represent the Marathi of the original to the ordinary Marathi reader. Inferred from the articles themselves this evidence as to the meaning of these articles and the translations of these articles is conclusive. It will only be necessary for me to say very little more when I come to deal with the individual words raised by Mr. Tilak including the alleged distortions.

Now I come back to Mr. Justice Strachey's views with regard not only to the extent and limitations of the rights of public speech and public writings and the manner in which you are entitled to get at the meaning of the articles which are impeached as going beyond the privileges conferred by the law. It must be obvious to you what I want to say, the only way, certainly almost the only way to discover what a man means is to read what he writes or hear what he says. If he says he did not mean what he said or wrote and does not produce any evidence, it may be, as the Chief Justice Sir Lawrence Jenkins says, the rough and ready means of arriving at a conclusion, but what other means have you got? Now Mr. Justice Strachey says this (Reads 'It is true that there is a charge before you' down to 'responsibility.') And then His Lordship went on to deal with one of the points made by Mr. Tilak the exact bearing of which I confess I did not at the time understand and have not yet understood. (Reads 'authority' down to 'of the Government.') And then, Gentlemen, His Lordship proceeds to deal with the examples of the section as they then stood. I should like to draw your attention to the wording of this section and examine the particulars of this section as it stood before 1898. The explanation is somewhat different in wording from the concluding part of the section. It was much the same as it is now. (Reads explanation of Section 124 A as it existed before 1898.) Practically it seems to my view very much the same, as the Section is now amended, although it is not concluded in language of such definite accuracy as the Section now is. His Lordship went on (Reads ' a man may point ' to ' intention. ') You will find that every word of this is applicable to the amended section as it stands now (Reads the revised explanations of Section 124 A.)

Now, his Lordship then went on to say (Reads 'If the writings can be reasonably' down to 'subvert or resist this authority.') Next his Lordship went on to discuss the question of what is the meaning of the words disaffection or disapprobation as intended in the Section as it then stood. He says (Reads 'a man may criticise' down to ' upon it. ') Whoever disputed this? Whoever disputed that there was this right of discussion either in speech or in the Press? The law says it must not be carried to the extent of license. The Section now reads (Reads Section 124 A as now constituted.) You may use language of the utmost violence provided you do not outstep the limit to the extent of exciting or attempting to excite hatred or contempt against the Government. Provided you do not do that you may comment upon the measures of Government, legislative or otherwise, proposed or carried into effect by the Government, in any language you please. Mr. Tilak must have known that this extensive liberty of the Press has been recognised not only by the legislature itself but by the judgments of judges one of which he must be personally familiar with. Look at the words of the Judge (Reads from 'he may discuss' down to 'unfairly'). What greater freedom of the Press can you want ? He follows on (Reads 'so long as' down to 'its motives') The imputations here are that the British Government with the idea of enriching England are robbing the people of India.(Reads to 'that will not save him'). That did not warrant Mr.Tilak in evading this statement of the law with which he must be familiar. It did not warrant his rushing off to a forest of books by means of which, if you read a sufficient number of them which you would not understand, he so hid the wood that you could not see the wood from the trees. Mr. Justice Strachey says (Reads ' not only to the Government ' down to ' to the people.') The Privy Council themselves say that this is the correct representation of the law. The Full Bench when applied to refused to accept that there was anything wrong in the summing-up. And now you will see the necessity and advantage of drawing your attention to the confirmation by the Judicial Committee of the whole of this summing-up in which they did not see reason to alter one single word. Now what comes of all this bunkum about the freedom of the Press? Freedom of the Press has been turned into an engine for the exercise of license which, so far as one can judge, has no limit, except the will of persons who claim to be exempt from all restraint upon what they call the liberty of the Press, including the right to abuse the Government and contend that liberty of the Press is inconsistent with the existence of the Government as it stands now. I put it to you that there is no escape from the contention put forward by the defence. So far as Mr. Tilak's contentions have gone that is what he says and nothing else. If you give Government any powers of restraint over the Press those powers must go. Government immediately becomes tyrannical, despotic, call it what you like, but Government with any power is inconsistent with the freedom of the Press, therefore do away with Government. That is the burden of his song. Can there be anything more dangerous? Anarchy would follow as sure as night following day. Once let it go to the public that, that contention is well-founded and that there is no harm in these articles and that there can be no limitations imposed by Government of the country upon what these people choose to call the liberty of the Press, and you will repent the day that you allowed this doctrine to be put forward. Anarchy will follow as sure as night follows day and with Anarchy will come naturally a reign of violence the sound of which Lord Morley said in anticipation he could hear roaring. Now I have very nearly exhausted this summing-up; but it is a summing-up of such vital importance to all concerned, among others to those who would first fall victims to the outbreak which would inevitably result upon Mr. Tilak's doctrines being accepted. When this summing-up is of such vital importance with regard to the discussion which you have had to listen to for the past five days, much against my will and I have no doubt much against yours, I have no option but to draw your attention to further passages. Mr. Justice Strachey says at page 138 (Reads 'for if a man comments' to 'explanation.') Then in discussing the more restricted view which had been put forward of the meaning of the Section, his Lordship went on to say (Reads from 'inclusive intention' down to 'forcible resistance'). Then he pointed out to the Jury what they were to do in directing their minds to the articles which were impeached (Reads from 'it was intended' down to 'Mahomedan general'). The articles in question consisted of a discussion with regard to Shivaji, and the alleged murder of Afzul Khan. It contained also something which is said to be in the vernacular, a poem. But when it is reduced to English it may be anything you like. It was supposed to be a poem about the hill-fort Pratabgarh. It was an article which concerned the death of Afzul Khan. His Lordship said (Reads 'there are questions' down to 'language of the articles') That follows the direction of all the English cases of which I am aware. Tha is more to the point, because English law is not applicable; it follows thetlines laid down in these Courts, and at Calcutta. You must infer intention from the articles, and you have to look at the surrounding circumstances. I quite admit that in order to arrive at the intention of the writer you have to take not only the language but all the surrounding circumstances of the case, as applying to the people to whom the articles are addressed, and of the writer himself. You have also to consider the probable effect on the minds of the readers. All this has to be taken into consideration in arriving at a conclusion whether or not he intended what the Prosecution say is the meaning of his words. You gather that intention first of all from the articles. You take into consideration certain conditions and from the articles put in you draw your conclusions.

Here we have articles between 12th May and 9th June published at weekly intervals, to the language of which I am going to ask your very serious attention, to what was in his mind at the time that he wrote them. And can you believe that what he indended to do, and what he says was that he disapprobated the bomb, and also the repressive measures? You will see for yourselves in a few moments that this was only a hypocritical plan. It is impossible to believe that the writer could have had in his mind anything but approving the hideous murders at

Muzzuferpur and Poona. As I said before, it seems impossible that any human person could praise the two acts of murder as he has done. I don't think, Gentlemen, you could have got the strength of these expressions when they were read to you at some speed. And when accused did not want to draw attention to particularly offensive passages, he gabbled them over as fast as he could as a safeguard and trusted to their escaping your attention. I come back to the summing-up because you have to look through a screen that is put up till you have pierced and obtained a view of the real figure behind that screen, which is intention, the screen being intended to obstruct the mind of the reader. So those who have to sit in judgment on the articles must, as Mr. Justice Strachey says—and he puts it in better language than I can frame—ask themselves what the intention of the writer is. (Reads 'You must ask yourselves' to 'of the writer.') And in the passage immediately preceding that frequent sentence his Lordships says. (Reads 'In judging of the intention' to 'criticism and comment.') Apply every one of those words to these articles before you and I venture to suggest, perhaps I ought not to use that expression, but I venture to submit that the case for the Prosecution is clear beyond doubt, by the evidence adduced in this case and produced by the accused himself, evidence which he cannot challenge. It comes from his own words. I am assuming of course that you agree in our contention that the articles themselves come within the provision of section 124 A. I have already said; if you come to the conclusion that the articles cannot by any means whatever be construed as falling within the provisions of that Section there is an end of the case. But I think it will give you pause to come to any such conclusion. You have had the articles read to you, but read in the spirit which I have described. The accused read them as fast as he could; he did not stop to consider the points against him; he tried to suggest wrong translations, and made grossly improper suggestions against the Translator's office. I maintain that the articles have been translated in the Translator's office by the interpretors sworn to do their duty. What reason therefore had Mr. Tilak to say that they deliberately distorted in this case to make a case for the Prosecution and ruin the accused? These were utterly groundless insinuations made by Mr. Tilak, who at the same time tried to wriggle out of them, but he had not the courage to state in so many words, and he had not the courage to attempt to contradict anything by evidence. " I suggest nothing against these people, but they are distorted translations." That may be a manly way of defending oneself, but I do not think it is a way that will recommend itself to your minds. So much for the contents of the documents, the manner in which the intention is to be derived from them, and the manner in which you must endeavour to form your own views as to the intention from the documents themselves, as to the meanings of the writings which can be adopted for the purpose of concealing the real meaning of the writer.

And now I shall draw your attention to expressions in favour of the accused, which I had proposed myself to say independent of the judgment. If you can consistently with the discharge of your duties, and with your conscience, having regard to your thoughts in the jury box and to what you have heard, come to the conclusion that these articles do not come within Section 124 A, then it is your duty to give the accused the benefit of any serious doubt. No one has disputed, or will dispute this proposition. You must, if you can, put an innocent interpretation consistent with your duty to the Government and the public, and to your conscience, and you must give the benefit of the doubt, and as nine honest men, stand up and say, 'we have read these articles and there is nothing in them which can be construed as coming within the meaning of the Section.' Give the words the most liberal consideration that you think they are entitled to, take into consideration what Mr. Justice Strachey says (Reads ' a journalist is not expected ' down to ' all this ') You must not take isolated words which strike you as being particularly offensive. That is not the right way to deal with this case. Take the writings as a whole. And in this case you have to take not only these two writings of 12th May and 9th June, but take the five intervening articles as throwing light upon the intention of the writer of the two incriminating articles. You will read them all as throwing a mild light upon each other, and from their rays you will be able to direct your own mental vision on the question of what the man means. You will read them all together, and as those writings shed light on these two bring your vision to bear on this question, and the only question to be considered in this case is, what is the intention of the writer. With regard to the question of the translations I might perhaps, as I am dealing with this summing-up, draw your attention to the sensible remarks which characterise the summing-up of Mr. Justice Strachey. In the course of his judgment he says (Reads from 'you have heard much discussion' to 'articles.') Then, his Lordship pointed out (Reads 'it is a mistake to suppose' to 'is called free'). Then he drew the attention of the Jury to the two sides of the translations, and gave his suggestions according as they came to the conclusion, whether one translation was correct, or the other was incorrect, as to what the Jury should do. Now gentlemen, before I leave this book I would like you to know that when the accused in this case proposed to take the case before the Full-Bench for the purpose of obtaining leave to appeal to the Privy Council, one of the grounds set forth in the petition for leave to appeal was that there had been mis-direction to the Jury on the following points. You need only concern yourself with one of them, ' That the word Government meant British Rule, or its representatives'. You see the same point was forced upon you by Mr. Tilak, as he maintained here. He seems to think Bureaucracy, which is his own favourite expression, does not represent the Government because the Bureaucracy is really the services. That is one part of the argument and the other part of the argument is that the Bureucracy represents the officers of Government at large. You see his view here was, that the Judge had misdirected the Jury, with regard to the word Government. This question of the Bureaucracy not representing the Government is all nonsense and sheer waste of time. Other points also made in the petition. ' A matter of great importance to the subjects of the Crown' that is Mr. Tilak's claim here ; he represents every one including himself except the Bureaucracy and the British

Government whom he claims to libel. He says "this case is one of the greatest importance.' Gentlemen, that contention was put forward in forwarding this petition, and is equally false. (Reads 'that your petitioner is also advised' down to 'in India') The objection was to the summing-up. The summing-up stated 'you can say what you like in language however offensive with regard to the legislative actions or any other actions of Government, provided you do not attack Government itself and provided you do not attack the British Government as constituted and as represented, and also provided you do not come within the words of section 124 A, and bring or attempt to bring into hatred or contempt the Government. You can say what you please in any foul and disgusting language you choose to adopt.' That was the summing-up of the Judge and it was afterwards contended that it was a wrong summing-up. It was so contended in the application to the Privy Council and the Full-Bench considered that there were no grounds whatever for interference, or for granting leave to appeal, and many other points which the Full-Bench dealt with. Sir Charles Farran, the Chief Justice, in delivering judgment said (Reads from ' the definition of the word Government ' to ' an illustration. ') Therefore, Gentlemen, that judgment shows in a most conclusive manner how the point has been dealt with. It is the same point that has been advanced in this case, and that discussion must be our guiding star in dealing with the facts and contentions on both sides, with regard to the articles impeached, and the articles put forward for the purpose of trying to guide you on the correct path to a decision on these two articles. You are to say what the intention was of the writer, and what inference you draw as a result of their perusal. You will find according to my contention when you come to look at the details of the case put forward by the accused, that the case has no merits, and no substance. It will be for you to say whether my contention is right or wrong. My contention is that there is really no defence which can be seriously considered, notwithstanding the length of time that the Accused took in elaborating the case, and which his advisers and admirers considered an admirable defence. And really it was a capable defence, in so far as it consisted in reading a large number of books and extracts and drawing wrong conclusions from them. You will find that there is nothing in his case. I propose to deal here very summarily and I hope to dispose equally summarily with the principal points which have been raised by Mr. Tilak. Besides this I have already mentioned to you that he might have saved himself the discussion and the expenditure of time and labour over the Marathi. I propose to make a very summary statement in disposing of Mr. Tilak's points, and I hope to avoid the necessity of going back to them more in detail, although it may be necessary at a later stage of the discussion. I don't think it will, and I hope by this summary disposal of his points to still further economise time which I feel I have been occupying. But I hope that there has been some justification having regard to the importance of the case to the public at large, including the interests which Mr. Tilak says he represents, namely the Liberty of the Press and his community. I think on four different occasions Mr.

Tilak found fault with the translations, the last occasion being this morning. Here again one can hardly believe Mr. Tilak was serious, but one can understand he is in a very dangerous, and I might say, a very desperate condition. Any straw that he can get hold of, to float on the tide of ruin on which he has swept himself, he must clutch at. And of course the first thing that he has to do is to impeach the translations, and he has the audacious effrontery to contend that he is being indicted upon articles, the translations of which are wrong and he must be acquitted. Do you really believe that he was serious in putting forward this defence? His contention is untrue; there is no proof whatever that there have been any mis-translations here. I do not know whether you have dictionaries, or would like them. I can give you chapter and verse for the words put forward by the translator. I can give you in each instance the pages where the expressions adopted by the Translator's office are to be found. What are Mr. Tilak's contentions? That king should not be capital K. Well, let him have a little k. Killing is just killing without any feeling. He objects to the word assassination. Can Mr. Tilak benefit if I will allow him the whole of his objections to the translations, eighteen words in all out of–I have,not counted the number of words in the articles impeached–eighteen words in all are disputed! And he has the effrontery to call them ' the distortions of the Translator's office '. It is a word that should never have been used unless he intended to carry the suggestion to its logical conclusions by proving by his own translations that the translations are wrong, otherwise he should not have used the words distorted. It is not a question of having revenge. That is to say that they were deliberately concocted for the purpose of ruining him and helping the Prosecution. Think of the absurdity of the thing! If there was a shade of truth in that it would result in the immediate detention of these misguided people in the Translator's office who were responsible for such a thing. It would mean their ruin for life and their dismissal from the office. And what for ? Does he contend that there was ill-feeling between Mr. Joshi of the Translator's office and himself? Does he suggest that there is any cause for ill-feeling between himself and Mr. Joshi to give a sardonic perversion of these articles ? Give him the benefit of the doubt with effect to these 18 words and just for one moment let us see what will happen.

His Lordship:—I was going to ask whether it would be any advantage if we retire earlier and return at 3 p. m.

Advocate General:—I am quite willing to go on now.

His Lordship:—I have no desire to hurry you, but I would just like to have some idea when you are likely to finish.

Advocate General:—Your Lordship is well aware that there is a great deal to explain but I hope I shall be able to close my remarks today.

His Lordship:—By this evening.?

Advocate General:—I earnestly pray so.

His Lordship:—We will rise now till 3 P. M. instead of 3. 30. P. M.

Advocate General, continuing his address after tiffin said: Gentlemen of the Jury, you have a list of the words upon which the accused relies, as having been merely mistranslated, and also of the words which he alleges are distorted. And I ask you to remember his affectation of indignation at what he calls distortions. I say with no hesitation or fear of contradiction that it was an expression for which there was no reason whatever. It was introduced for the purpose of finding fault with the Translator's office, to which Mr.Joshi belongs.It failed because Mr.Joshi was not the Translator of these two articles. Mr. Joshi's evidence was not contradicted, and it was shown that not a single point could be made by Mr. Tilak. I am content for the sake of peace and the saving of time to give him the benefit of those eighteen words which he says ought to appear in the translations. I don't care one atom where they appear. If you have the industry to go through the two articles, in which it is alleged the mistakes have occured, I venture to predict that at the end of a long and toilsome task you will find that there is not one single material syllable in the translstions which require amendation. If that be so what does it matter whether, as Mr. Justice Strachey says (Reads). Whether there is some palpable alteration or amendation necessary or advisable, it does not affect the question of the general tenor of and character of these articles. I pass on then to what seems to me to be the next point put forward by the Accused which we know his Lordship will tell you, there is absolutely nothing in; and that is the point that there is no proof that anything followed as the effect of these articles. If it be necessary, I will go through again and quote other cases which have been decided in this Court. I will give his Lordship references to them. They appear in 2. Bombay Law Reporter page 294, and 304. and 8 Bombay Law Reporter page 421. You will find from these reports and the one which I have referred to at considerable length, namely 22. Bom. That this proposition can be adduced and I will state them at once in order that I may be able, if possible, to redeem my promise or conditional promise of sitting down at 5. p. m. I will state my proposion now, and I think these authorities will support me. I am perfectly confident, that his Lordship will tell you there is nothing faulty with the proposition which I am going to put before you, and you will see that nine-tenths of Mr. Tilak's points are swept away. My first point is this that the accused being Editor, Publisher and Proprietor of this paper is responsible for everything that appears in it. I have already told you that there can be no dispute upon the facts at issue in this case. They are all now admitted, but you must not suppose that because they are admitted by the Accused, that they are to be adjudged to him for righteousness. There was no use denying it. It was proved and the law makes him responsible. That is my first point. You have his responsibility from every point of view. My next point is that he is liable for all that appears, and has appeared in that paper, and for what he meant to write, or for what he now says he meant to write. It is for you to judge his style, and to judge of the effect that the meaning of the writing has; not for him to say 'oh, I meant this, that, or the other thing.' We say it means what he meant when he wrote those articles. From those articles you have to adduce the meaning which it is your duty to adduce as jurymen, and it is idle waste of time for the Accused to say that you must not judge of intention from what he has written. I will not refer more in detail, as I do not want to waste time, as his Lordship will tell you that my proposition is beyond dispute, and that the authorities from the earliest times, up to the decision in the last case show that that is what you have to do. It may be a short and ready means of doing so, but there are no other means. You have already had the decision of Sir Comer Petheram, and you will find that this proposition supported by Mr. Justic Strachey in the case reported on page 272, and 520, of Mayne's Criminal Law. Again I say, and in favour of the Accused, you judge his intention not by any single word or sentence. but you take both articles and the articles put in to prove intention, and from them and the mutual light they throw upon each other you draw your own conclusions. My next point is this that in considering the law applicable to this particular case, and the charges against the Accused, you need not trouble yourselves to find out what the English law is but I may tell you that the Accused, though I do not know whether he did it intentionally, mixed the law in England as to the relations of the Judge and Jury. Yesterday he had the effrontery to tell you that it was the universal pratice in England, and in these Courts to leave the Jury the whole question of law and fact ; he went on to say that the law in England was Jury-made law, and you can deal with this case as you please. Well, the only excuse that I can think of for such a proposition being put before the Court is that a somewhat similar proposition seems to have been put forward in Calcutta, I will not mention any name as he may be alive and regret the position he took up. Well Gentlemen, the Chief Justice Sir Comer Petheram, promptly disposed of this by saying ' it is my duty to instruct the Jury on the construction of this Section.' It may be that Mr. Tilak has some slight recollection of this case, and only that could have justified him in telling the Jury what he did. It is absolute nonsense, it is a contradiction in terms, and Mr. Tilak, as a pleader of 28 years' standing, knows that you have to take the law from the judge, while you judge of facts. I think Mr. Tilak began to realize about the end of his address, that he had been a little wild in his proposition. There can be no doubt if you look at these Sections what is intended. According to the terms of the Section, (Reads Sections) it is the duty of the judge to direct the jury upon all points of law, and it is the duty of the Jury to return a verdict upon all points of fact. Then to say that it has been the practice in the English Courts to leave all questions of law and facts to the Jury, is a misrepresentation of facts. One begins to doubt the purity and loftiness of people who will try to miselad a Jury in this way. Mr. Tilak is an old and experienced lawyer, surrounded by a heavy battery of Pleaders and Attorneys, and it is impossible that the suggestions could have been made *bona fide*. Believe me there is no foundation in law for that proposition, but I will tell you, as a matter of fact and as a matter of law, that you have to take his Lordship's direction. But I admit that you are the sole judges of fact, I do not dispute that for one moment. The other point, as far as I have been able to gather, was one which I have already admitted. I regret my inability to follow Mr. Tilak's subject in full, but I think I have the main points of it. The next point which he tried to make was that you ought to draw no presumption against him because there was no evidence as to any effect having been produced by these articles. Again his Lordship will tell you that I am right in the point I am going to submit that the question of success or failure of the attempt, supposing you find that there was an attemtpt, is entirely immaterial. Having succeeded, his conviction would be the more certain and his sentence would be adequate ; if he failed, so much the luckier for him, but to say that he must be shown to have failed from physical or some other obstruction not emanating from himself is a misunderstanding of the English language and the decisions of the judges of law. I will not repeat this again, having stated it clearly and his Lordship will tell you that success or failure is immaterial. You have only to look at the articles to see if they come within the words of section 124A. One other point is this, the question of free speech, free writing. Well I have said what I have to say on this point as representing the Prosecution. I can summarise all that I have said and desire to say on this point. What the freedom of the Press and freedom of speech is quite clear by the very words of the Section. I have read you the summing-up of Mr. Justice Strachey which shows that in the exercise of that freedom of speech and writing you may write what you like about the legislative or administrative actions of Government in whatever language you like, make it as offensive as you like, but you step outside that, you step outside the explanation under 124A. Again it will be necessary for me to deal further on with this aspect of the case. I am convinced that I am right and his Lordship will tell you that I am right and by itself all Mr. Tilak's address may well be wiped from your minds. This I have already told you but I will mention it again that the existence of a real or fanciful grievance is no defence whatever. You will find that laid down in the summing-up of the Chief Justice, now at home, and here again I do not expect, I am not in the least degree apprehensive, that I shall be told by his Lordship that I am telling you something not correct in law; and there I submit is the whole discussion of the grievances and necessity for reform, are past the mark and are simply part and parcel of an address, directed to vilification of Government and stirring of unrest in the cause of self-defence. There is also another part of Mr. Tilak's defence that may also be swept away being absolutely irrelevant. He says these articles did not mean what they contained but we assume is that they did mean what he wrote. He says they were in reply to a controversy. We assume that though of course this is a very violent assumption. He says these were replies to articles criticising himself and the Marathas whom in a loyal sort of way he claims to represent and these articles were a contradiction or reply to the Anglo-Indian newspapers. If the language comes within section 124A he can defend himself by saying 'these articles were written because A B & C. wrote other articles. This is a controversy. I am going to resent it. My brain has got into such a state of confusion and imbecility, because from day to day I have got information and at the end of the week I accumulate this information and I reply to the attack of the Anglo-Indian papers.' That is no defence and though I considered it unnecessary for him to go into details of the newspapers produced, I did not object. As a matter of fact you will find that there is no justification for the allegation that the Anglo-Indian Press attacked him or his brother journalists, or the Natives, or the Congress, in any terms which called for violent anger, and I do not care if they did. That is no justification. If it is true that there was any such suggestion made about whipping by public sweepers, of course it was most disgraceful. But if you turn to the real point, you will find that he did not produce some of the articles in the original but read extracts from other papers, which were alleged to be extracts from the *Asian* and *Empire*. Neither of these papers is produced in the original. I did not know this at the time, and of course it was not my business to go into each of the newspapers without knowing whether they were going to be used. As a matter of fact the *Asian* and *Empire* which are supposed to be the most offensive are not produced in original. but are quoted by some paper, called, I think, The *Gujarati*. That is not the way to prove articles. (Having received from the Clerk of the Crown, the *Pioneer* of 7th May) I think I am a little inconsistent in saying that these matters have not been appearing, and I find that there was an attack made on the Indian Press by the Anglo-Indian Press, but they do not justify the writing of the incriminating article. The *Pioneer* of 7th May is referred to in the article which appeared in the *Kesari* on May 9. Now look at the words of this article (Reads 'if the moral disease' down to 'heroic measures.') Now, what has he got there? It is a comment directed to the state of things in the world at large. It is not directed to Mr. Tilak in any shape or form whatever. It refers to the Native Press as a body and generally contends that if this moral disease is to spread as it did in Spain then (Reads down to 'bombs.') Now take the next passage. Of course, if Mr. Tilak likes to fit on the cap, I have no objection. This is the cap (Reads down to 'let us only' to 'situation') At present Mr. Tilak is not in sympathy with the Council but if he wishes to assume the Counciller's cap let him, if he likes. We have had Burke and Mill quoted at each hearing. I do not think we had Milton. (Reads again down to 'Congress moderate.') Well, Mr. Tilak is not a Congress Moderate and the evidence in the case shows that he is an Extremist. I do not know if he is a Congress Extremist. The last Congress disappeared under Mr. Tilak's moderation. (Reads down to 'that its revenue.') There is one other part. (Reads down to 'feeble minds astray.') Now what is there that any sensible man can object to. Is there a word there that can justify the allegation that there were disgraceful attacks in the *Pioneer* which caused the great souls of the *Kesari* to swell in anger and show themselves in the words of the article complained of? I put it to you that the excuse is a falsity on its face so far as the facts are concerned, and even if it were true his Lordship will tell you that I am right in saying that it would be no defence. I think I have put nine points before you and that exhausts all that I have to advance in this case as to the proper way in which you as the Jury should approach the consideration of the facts of these points because almost all of them were made by Mr. Tilak and there is one which remains which I will deal with at once. Mr. Tilak suggests that the onus has been laid wrongly upon him in bringing him within the exemption terms of section 124 (A) and 153 (A). That again, Gentlemen, is due to a faulty misapprehension of the law Statutory original law. We are concerned only with the Indian Statute. The Statutary law is to be found in section 105 of the Evidence Act. That section says that when a person is accused of any offence the burden of proof falls or him, (Reads section). You have only to accuse; here Mr. Tilak is committed on a charge. Therefore it is quite clear according to the terms of the Evidence Act that there has been no wrong placing of the onus on Mr. Tilak's shoulder in this case. He is charged with this offence and he says he is not guilty because he comes under explanation 2 of section 124A. On him lies the burden of proving that he comes in some way under that protection. Then we have the doctrine advanced, in a number of different ways, Protean in their form but all meaning what I stated to you a short time ago, that the Accused was entitled to write these writings because some one else had written articles attacking him and his party and his paper and that by reading these articles in the heat of the discussion, or controversy as he called it, between the pro-Bureaucrats and the anti-Bureaucrats; as if he wrote it by way of advice to Government or by way of intimation of the existence of defects in the Government, calling for reformation, or by way of a declaration on his part to those who agree with him in a preference for a particular form of Government which is entertained either by the writer or his community to which the writtings are addressed. Would that justify any language which he chose to use ? There is no sense in the article unless you carry it to that extent. It amounts to this, that in the heat of the controversy or because he wanted to obtain reforms of abuses, or because he wanted to give Government, intimation that if they did not give some reforms, "We will give you bombs" that he is entitled to use language whether it comes under the Section or not. That is the meaning of his argument. That you will find when you call back to your mind the general tenor of his defence and you will find that this is his real defence except that extraordinary incident which took place yesterday or today–the idea of self-defence ! Here again can you conceive anybody with the faintest knowledge of law putting forward such a suggestion seriously that he was entitled to write these articles, no matter what was their language, no matter whether they were included or excluded from the exceptions in 124 A, as he did it in self-defence. Would you like to know what the right of self-defence is. It appears in Section 96 and following sections of the Penal Code. These are the rights (Reads section 96). This is the right that Mr. Tilak put forward in his defence yesterday as justifying his action. I think the accused must have laughed when he left the Court after having put forward that defence to think that it was received in silence instead of Homeric laughter. He says the articles were written in the heat of controversy or as giving advice or expressing a preference for certain forms of Government, entertained by the Accused and his community or people to whom the article was addressed. That was his opening part, when he went into a description of the manner he collects his information for discussing affairs in his newspaper which occur from week to week. It is a repetition of the same point over and over again to the point of exasperation. Of course the answer is that it is too preposterous a claim to be just by any law; opposed to common sense and opposed to public interest and the safety of order at large. It would result in this ludicrous absurdity that you can have such a thing as patriotic sedition. "I am an editor; I want reforms, if you don't give them I will bomb you and that is not sedition because of my motive. My motive is high". Just turn back your memory to what he said on motive and intention. The two things are totally different. But he jumbles them together and you will find that he says something to the effect that, if his motives and his intentions are pure, he can commit any kind of crime he likes and it cannot affect him. If he goes through life much longer with those views in his mind and acts upon them, he will find himself in a very much worse predicament than he is now. You see the Indian Penal Code does not say anything about motive, it does not enter into it. You may enter into a crime with a very high motive but you will be punished all the same. The question of motive may come into consideration and help in reducing the sentence. It is one of those propositions that one may hardly suppose he was serious in putting it forward. Of course one can give any number of instances to show the fallacy of that argument that because your motive may be good or not criminal, you must be excused. Why, Gentlemen, if this were so you would be putting the greatest temptation that humanity could be subjected to. The taking of life for the purpose of preserving your own; what will be the result? You will be brought up in Court, I don't think you will be hanged, although you may deserve to, but you will certainly be transported for life. It is no excuse that you have commited an offence from motives of self-preservation. And I think one of the most horrible illustrations of that doctrine is to be found in a case which, I have no doubt, some of you remember. It is a case where some men were ship-wrecked, and to preserve the lives of some the rest were sacrificed to provide food. The motive might have been in the minds of these, of their own self-preservation. I need not labour the point any more; his Lordship will tell you that it is no defence whatever, from the fact that you might have had good motives for committing the crime. Of course I am assuming every thing in favour of the Prosecution, that these articles do absolutely come within the Section. I will just revive your memory that Mayne points out that it is a point outside the law that you may commit the offence of libel and libel a man from the highest possible motives. That will not help you, if you have commited the offence of libel; motive or no motive, you will be punished, And otherwise the whole of Mr. Tilak's arguments on the points of motive and intention involves the absurdity that a man may commit the offence of patriotic sedition. You may show the circumstances in which you have written the article, which *prima-facie* comes within the section 124A. You may show circumstances which might go to reduce or modify the sentence. That is totally different to proposing that it is in defence of the substantive charge. He refers us to Mayne, and you will find at page

244, (Reads from 'intention must not be confounded' to 'for spite') That disposes of the lengthy argument involving much confusion of ideas between motive and intention.

We come back now, Gentlemen, to a very short consideration of Mr. Tilak's contentions with regard to intention, whether it can be inferred by what he calls fictitious means. He suggests that it is an exploded doctrine, and that it is a very fragile means of arriving at a conclusion. Now what he calls an exploded doctrine is the doctrine that you infer a man's intentions from what he has said, or done, or written. Well, I don't know whether the explanation itselt is to be found in the Bengali Bombs. It is a doctrine which stands to this day supported by all authorities except Mr. Tilak. Some of the more prominent judicial authorities I have given, and his Lordship will tell you that it forms a safe guide. There are cases in which it would be unsafe to infer a man's intentions from words written or spoken. Mr. Tilak says that the circumstances in this case point to the conclusion that he receives information from week to week, and bases his remarks on information received from India and England which led him to indite these articles for the particular purpose which I have mentioned. That is his idea of there being in this case surrounding circumstances in existence, which entitle him, no matter what his language may be, to say what he likes. This is his chorus from beginning to end. "No matter what my language is, the Penal Code does not apply to me, and you must return a verdict of not quilty.' This is a fallacy which runs through the whole of his argument. You are bound, as you are entitled, to look into all the circumstances surrounding him; the time at which the articles were written and the persons to whom they were addressed. All these things have to be taken into consideration. Then you have to exercise these powers of common-sense which Mr. Tilak says you must not exercise in this case, When you arrive at that step you must apply the law, and say whether in your opinion the provisions of section 124A are applicable to the case or not. Mr. Tilak's argument is nothing but going round in a circle, a process which has no end, and will not enable you to reach any conclusion at all. You will find, I am right when I tell you, that his argument goes back to this. He says 'it does not matter what I say or do under Sections 153 A and 124 A, if you find that my intentions are lawful.' That is not the law, as I am confident you will be directed by the Judge. There is one more point. Mr. Tilak says there is no evidence beyond of course what you can draw from the wording of the Section, there is no evidence from which you can infer intention except the card. Well, so far as he is concerned, I cannot carry that matter any further. What I rely upon for the Crown is this that the card was found in Mr. Tilak's house in a drawer. Look at the circumstances connected with it, and his connection with the articles. It is entirely a matter for your consideration. I am unwilling to unduly press the matter, if you think or if his Lordship thinks that it is a matter that should not be pressed, but unduly press it I will not. But that it is a matter of relevance to the charge I think nobody can dispute. You see that it is certain in the circumstances in which the search was made that it was impossible for anybody to have put that card there for the purpose of implicating Mr. Tilak. It is not suggested that there was anybody who did put the card there. In fact so far as I can understand Mr. Tilak practically admits the card is in his own handwriting. That being so there is no effect in saying that the card was initialled by Mr. Tilak's manager and was in the custody of the police ever since it was found. Now I ask you to recall Mr. Tilak's attempt to cross-examine the Police Officer. Did it not strike you as a suggestion that the card was found behind his back? Does it not suggest that somebody put it there behind his back? I put it to you that he had not made up his mind at first what course to pursue with regard to that card, and when he found it was absolutely futile to attempt to avoid the fact that the card was found in his premises and in his drawer and amongst his other papers. He knew it was impossible to accept any defence. And what was his explanation ? That he thought it necessary to procure books on explosives for the purpose of considering the definition of explosives in the Explosives Act. It is for you to say what reliance you can place on this statement having regard to the manner in which he has apparently approached this grave question. But, Gentlemen, the man who can write as Mr. Tilak has written, passages from which I am going to refer to again on behalf of the Prosecution, this incident of the finding of the card is looked upon with sufficient suspicion to suppose that it is particular evidence to come to the conclusion as to the intention of the writer of these articles which have been impeached or as throwing light upn them. Our suggestion is that the whole object of Mr. Tilak's articles was to threaten the administration and to threaten Government, that if they did not grant the demands as a price of peace, then bombs would follow. If necessary I shall go through the chief points of the main articles and prove that those contentions are correct. If the general contents of the articles are sufficient to prove that there was an attempt to terrorise the Government, by threats open or concealed, to the effect that bombs will be thrown, I put it to you whether the effect of the existence of this card is not a fact to be taken into consideration in considering the action of the Accused. As I say if this is not a threat what is it ? You find this man by his words and articles repudiating the bomb; but while repudiating the bomb and its use he tells Government that unless they guarantee reforms bombs will continue. He says Government has had a salutary warning and when you find a card about explosives in that man's own handwriting I must leave you to come to the conclusion. Now I will refer to one passage in the article of June 9th. It may be necessary to go into this article in a little more detail, but I am going to show you a passage upon which I rely as showing how much truth there is in the suggestion when he repudiates bombs. Turn to page 3 and you will see (Reads "The bomb is some form of knowledge" down to "a charm and an amulet.") This is the gentleman who repudiates bombs. You will see throughout the whole of the rest of the article and the other articles to which I am going to refer there is not only a veiled but a distinct threat to Government that to use the words of Exhibit 64 (Reads from "temporary" to 'bomb has come to stay.') Here again I am subject to his Lordship's directions. If his Lordship thinks I ought not to make any lengthy reference to that article I will not do so. But mind you it is his exhibit and I understand him to say that it represents his views. But that is for you to decide. You will have to consider whether you will make use of it or not. But remember the accused puts it in as part of his defence. If he disapproves of bombs why write of them as of "more the form of knowledge, a kind of witchcraft a charm and an amulet." Then there is another article which you will find of 2nd June. You will be asked to sap this is prohibitory of bombs. This is the man who is desirous of supporting Government and objects to the taking of life at all. Look at the 4th line of the article headed "Secret of the Bomb" (Reads from "the murder of Mr.Rand" down to "of Bengal.") It is curious how that Rand murder fascinates the Poona writers. Now read those following sentences and if you can give credence to Mr. Tilak's protestation that he abhors murders give him the benefit. (Reads down to "intention.") That is the passage, I say, I cannot conceive any person actuated by feelings of humanity, and claiming to be a humane being, could have written. He is praising two dastardly murders and the murderers are submitted to promotion or distinction according as he thinks superiority in point of skill and daring. Where was the skill and daring in connection with the Poona murders. Two midnight assassins, creeping in the darkness to kill their unsuspecting victims. Where was the skill, where was the daring in these wicked murders? I had intended to avoid language of passion altogether because I was satisfied that Mr. Tilak's own language carried with it its own damning conviction. But having the misfortune to sit through these ravings from morning to morning, from day to day, it is impossible to cast from one's mind the effect which such doctrines produce in the minds of any who have to deal with him. These are two of perhaps the choicest quotations from the articles which go to show what was working in his mind. I am not touching the point. I promise only to show that the Prosecution cannot be charged with being unreasonable, when they say that when a person is capable of formulating and putting into print such things you cannot wonder if suspicion is directed to him when you find such enthusiasm for the bomb and when you find in his house, in his own hand writing, a card by the means of an address on which he will be able to procure bombs. There are many other paragraphs that go to show that he revelled in the thought of the cheapness and economy with which bombs can be manufactured. (Reads from "the very system of administration" down to "beneficient act.") So you may be a beneficent murderer in the opinion of Mr. Tilak, though I hope not in the opinion of those who follow him. (Reads "in the case of the Poonaites" down to 'terrorists.') He slurred over the fact when he was reading the articles, but now when I have read the whole of that passage, and the enormity of it occurs to you, can you wonder that this is ground for the Prosecution that the discovery of the card is significant, and that you must take it into solemn consideration before you part? So much, Gentlemen, for the intention to be drawn from the card, the circumstances and from the arguments about the presumptions which are to be drawn from the writings. I have nothing further to say in reference to these discussions of motive and intention. As to the question of the relative rights of Judge aud Jury, you have my views and the authorities I have mentioned. It is quite untrue to suggest that you are the judges of the law in this country. I have nothing further to add on that point to what I have already stated. I think that I have dealt, shortly perhaps, but none the less I hope effectually with all the other arguments addressed to you up to the last day but one.

Now on the 17th of July there was a fresh opening of precisely the same points as had been commented upon before and I have about twenty pages of notes all referring to the same subject, in different words, one portion of the reference being what struck me as being a somewhat unfortnnate one. He referred to Lord Morley, speaking of him as Pundit Morley, to show that Lord Morley and Mr. Tilak were of one mind.—great minds arriving at the same conclusion. But unfortunately for Mr. Tilak who says it is not sedition for him to say, "You cannot have repressive measures," that is not Lord Morley's view. I only allude to this incident of the Civil Service dinner, which seems to have had some great attraction for Mr. Tilak, to point out whatever views Lord Morley may have expressed about the desirability of extending liberal reforms to India. He had to approve of the repressive action of Government, "repressive" or "oppressive" I don't care which. He quotes from Lord Morley praying that Lord Morley may not approve of the repressive action which constitutes the burden of Mr. Tilak's song. Just look at the ludicrous absurdity of Mr. Tilak's argument. Bombs are to be thrown, any amount of disturbances of the peace may take place, bnt Government must not take any action. What is Government here for except to maintain order? And then he says if you maintain order you are entering upon a course of repression, brought upon you by a number of fiends, or evil geniuses who come upon you every ten years! This means a proof of repression. 'And if you do not stop it, we warn you, bombs will continue.' Put it into plain language and still you are asked to say that that is not sedition. Well if it is not, the sooner the law is altered to reach the person who has these convictions the better for all parties concerned, and the longer will the anarchy be deferred which will certainly come upon us. Well I will put it in this way. If the conduct and policy of Mr. Tilak and his party meets with the approval of any Court of Justice then the flood-gates of anarchy will be opened and disaster must follow as night follows day. Well I will pass over Mill, and Blunt, and Amos, and other authors quoted by Mr. Tilak on Representative Government in the various extracts he has read to you, as having no concern with the question that you have to consider, and now I can faithfully say that I have come to the last part of Mr. Tilak's address, which was based upon Section 153 A. With regard to Section 153 A. I do not propose to take up the time of the Court. It has never been the subject of any authoritative decision that I am aware of; but it really does not matter, because the wording of the Section is perfectly clear, and it is fiction, pure and simple, for him to say that he does not understand the charge. He is charged with creating ill-will between two different classes of his Majesty's subjects. The whole of the arguments have been to show that there are two hostile camps pro-Bureaucrats and anti-Bureaucrats, and then for him to pretend he does not know what the charge means! I leave him to you to dispose of. To say that you cannot charge a man under Section 153 A, and also 124 A is again to completely misunderstand the law. There may be two completely different offences, or joint-offences under 153 A and 124 A. The charges are practically well-framed, and practically plain, and it is contended wilfully to show otherwise. Personally, Gentlemen, I do not care very much what happens to the charge under 153A. For this reason, that if there is a conviction under 124A. well, it would not be worth while bothering much about Section 153 A. It would not affect the case one way or another, and therefore I feel the less anxiety in dealing with the charge under that section. I hope, I have put before the Court with sufficient intelligence as to be clear as to my meaning of the different points of the case as presented by the Prosecution and the Accused, and nothing remains for me but a word or two about the implicated sections as throwing light upon the situation. I accept the whole of what my learned friend Mr. Inverarity stated in his opening and I will submit to you and to the Court that it is obvious from the wording of the article "The Country's misfortune," that the whole political situation in India which it is said has resulted from (Reads "the obstinacy and perversity" down to "rebellious path.") Gentlemen, I do not propose to follow the offensive attitude taken up by Mr. Tilak in his numerous references to Russian history, the reasons of the introduction of the bomb into Russia &c. I am not certain what the facts which would be necessary to be placed before you, are. Fortunately Russia does not require to be defended by Mr. Tilak, but the truth is exactly the opposite of what Mr. Tilak represented it to be. May I just say that the real history is opposed to Mr. Tilak? It was not the bomb which forced the granting of reforms, and the establishment of the Duma; the bomb reduced a number of privileges which were granted. Any body who knows anything about Russia's modern history will tell you so. But Mr. Tilak's party uses this as showing that bombs forced the granting of reforms in Russia, and you must follow the example here. Whether he is right or wrong there can be no question that his doctrine is subversive to the Government, but the whole object of all these articles is to show first of all that it is due to the action of the white Bureaucracy in India that certain young gentlemen in Bengal–gentlemen is the gentle euphemism for bomb throwers–have become "turned headed" and taken to bomb–throwing. That is held up for the public, who have the misfortune to read these papers, as being the course to be adopted. This is the way that reforms are to be obtained from Government, the obstinate white Bureaucracy. Now read down a few sentences lower, and you will find all these horrible sentiments being announced broad–cast throughout the country, and he says that the only mistake you can make in throwing bombs is to throw them at the wrong people. Throw bombs by all means, but throw them straight. (Reads to "in place of Mr. Kingsford.") If it had hit Mr. Kingsford it would have been all right. Don't make any mistake, and you will win the approval of Mr. Tilak and his followers. (Reads down to "official class.") If this is not language of the most violently seditious character, and calculated to bring Government into hatred and contempt, tell me what is. (Reads down to "officials.") Try and exercise a little common sense when considering languge like this. Here you have it suggested that the Russian people practise the throwing of bombs on account of the exasperation produced by unrestrained power. How much worse is the case of India, where the oppression is practised by alien officers? Throughout, the whole burden of the song in these articles runs in this strain. You have an alien Government; get rid of it as soon as you can. In other countries bombs are thrown, well select bombs. Don't throw them more often than you can help unless you can throw straight. Now we come to that much discussed question of the partition of Bengal. Do you know, does any one know, what the real greivance is as to the partition of Bengal? It was only a redistribution of boundaries. It was only a redistribution of governing bodies. (Reads from 'since the partition of Bengal' down to 'execsses'). Well, you have had these views before you, for your proper consideration. Was he justified in saying this, as also the illustration about the cat? I do not wish to repeat what has already been said on this. Then we have the next sentence. (Reads down to "the country is alien, or white Bureaueracy") (Reads down to 'cooled down.') Well that is a distinct libel on the Indian troops who have been so lately distinguishing themselves, and always will continue to distinguish themselves in spite of this allegation that the alien rule of the white Bureacracy has destroyed the manhood of the Indians. But so long as no abuse can be directed against the Government or the white Bureaucracy they do not care how many insults they heap on their own countrymen. I read this to show you how utterly reckless they are in their abuse. Go three or four lines further down, and you have the alien introduced again (Reads down to "exasperated.") Let the experienced leaders each devise to keep disaffecticn within bounds as far as possible and conceal it as far as possible (Reads 'but it is impossible' down to "bounds") But people will (Reads 'remain perpetually in slavery.") This is represented to be the cause of unrest (Reads down to "white official class".) Then comes the passage (Reads down to "in their own hands") Is not that attempting to bring Government into hatred and contempt? (Reads down to "self-interest.") By the self-interest of Government India will be the poorer (Reads down to "that impression.") That is an untruth to begin with, and directed to the suggestion that every Englishman in India is posessed of the right of free speech over the Hindus, and then is the suggestion at the bottom of the page (Reads down to "horrible deeds.") The next passage is one in which it is said in reference to Mr. Gokhale (Reads down to "in the presence of the Viceroy".) That is the hint about bombs. Then again you have a passage with regard to the effect it would have on the minds of the Maratha-speaking people (Reads "as you sow, so you reap,") Then (Reads down to "sedition.") This suggests that this is the action which Government is persuing (Reads to "common human nature".) So you have a further illustration of what Government is doing and the oppression practised by it, and the effect of that oppression. Then I pass over some of the sentences that follow as they do not appear to me to call for very serious attention and we come to this (Reads "the rule of the autocratic" down to "unbearable to the people"); and then as to the remedies (Reads down to "accomplished"). That is what you are to do. Put the spoke in the wheel of the administrative car, then you will get your desires accomplished (Reads down to "certain degree.") Then you have that curious illustration of a man wanting to go somewhere and going in the opposite direction. (Reads down to "places") Now take the rest of the article, Gentlemen, which is a very long rigmarole and I put it to you that the general effect of the rest of the article is an allegation that the outrages were the result of an unpopular Government, and that the oppression of Government will increase in consequence of such outrages, and that the crisis has been caused by the (Reads from unrestricted authority" down to "certain occasions.") Again you have a suggestion that the Government (Reads "have driven people to the climax.") Then the article while pretending disapproval of the outrages imputes them to Government and says (Reads from " reform is" down to " responsibility ".) I have given a fair construction of the whole article. Now then take shortly the second article of 9th June. I have already referred to the article of 2nd June 1908. This is headed " These Remedies are not Lasting " and is the second incriminating article. There you have the Government described as entering upon a campaign of 'restriction' and 'repression' or of 'opression', I don't care what the term is, and Government is liable to these demoniacal attacks every five or ten years. It is sufferring from one of these attacks now, and is entering upon a series which is supported by Lord Morley himself as shown by the Mantrikas (Reads from "Seeing that these " down to " bomb in Bengal. ") What is the meaning of this, Gentlemen? That because of the cases of violence and murder that have taken place throughout the country,the Government, which is responsible for the saftey and welfare of the country and its citizens, takes steps to put a stop as far as possible to these acts of violence, Government is represented as entering upon a fiendish scheme of repression in consequence of a damnable decision. There can be no question that the Government is accused of a policy of repression which suggested coming destruction. Of course that may mean nothing. It reads as a covert threat of mutiny. Whether it was intended so or not, I cannot say. But read the words and put what construction you can upon them. (Reads from "seeing that Government" down to "authorities.") If that is not a veiled threat of coming mutiny I confess I cannot understand what is. Now you have these differences in the mind of the man who objects to bombs but who thinks that between the Bengali bombs and the bombs known to Europe there is all the difference between heaven and earth. The Bengali bombs are the heavenly ones and deserve to be sung of, and the Russian bombs are earthly bombs and deserve to be consigned to another place. The Bengali bomb is due to a crisis of patriotism. This is in an article which Mr. Tilak told us the other evening has a spice of humour. Perhaps I shall come across the humour directly. This class of article shows the humour of which Mr. Tilak is capable. (Reads from "the Bengalis are not anarchists" down to "but to the second.") Well you have a cause of patriotism, and approach the Government with it in the shape of a bomb, and you will get your desires. The Bengalis are not anarchists, they have brought into use the weapons of the anarchists, that is all and then we have those curious distinctions between the classes of bomb-throwers (Reades down to "the King of Portugal") How can any man in his senses write this article without showing what he is meaning to do from beginning to end (Reads to "resort to violence.") Heavenly bombs, and earthly bombs ! One or the other must fail or succeed in their object. Let us carry out the sam principle in India ! Then, Gentlemen, you have a long passage which I think I can put into shorter language than his. There is a remark made with regard to the dis-armament policy of the British Government and the dis-armament policy followed by the tyrannical Governments of Europe. (Reads from "even a savage race" down to "castrating a nation.") Call it emasculation if you like, (Reads down to "Moguls") That is one way of expressing the deficiencies of Government. (Reads down to "military strength.") Is not this a direct incitement to the thirty crores of people of India that they should rise in their might and destroy the English troops who cannot possibly withstand them any more than the Mahomedans did for more than twenty five years at the outside? This is a suggestion that the English troops can no more resist the might of India for more than twenty five years at the outside, than the Mogul troops did (Reads from " as compared " down to " military strength. ") Then follows a part of the article the real meaning of which is easily drawn from the language itself, namely (Reads " the English Rule will not last in India even a quarter of a century after that.") Then we have (Reads from " Imperial sway" down to "permanent.") But owing to the bomb all this is altered now, and yet this is the gentleman who disapproves of the bomb (Reads to " to this time.") That is what would have happened before the advent of the bomb. We could have grumbled but we would have got nothing. If the Mahomadens had ruled the country like the British they would have had to resort to repressive measures, as the British Government has done, to which the tyrannical Rulers of Europe do not resort, and to which the savage Mohamedans did not resort, namely, the disarmament of the people. That is all put a stop to by the coming of the bomb, and as a Government, you know that the tyranny is beginning to be felt. (Reads from "unless a beginning" down to "detective Police.") Then you have this eulogy of the bomb (Reads 'the bomb is more' down to 'an amulet.') Then follows a description of the use which can be made of it, the possibility almost of the fact of its being manufactured being discovered, and the fact of its being able to bring pressure upon the Government to grant the reforms required. (Reads from 'Government has passed the Newspapers Act, with a view to stop the process of awakening' down to "disposition.") And then we have, (Reads down to "Swarajya.") That is what I said, "Swarajya or bombs." If you don't give Swarajya or if you don't make a beginning to give it, we won't stop the bombs.

Advocate General:—May I ask whether your Lordship proposes to go on and finish this case to-night?

His Lordship:—I propose to do that. The Jury will find refreshments downstairs; we will have an interval of twenty minutes.

The Advocate General (Continuing after tea) said:–I do not propose to occupy your time with any remarks on the articles of the 12th May Exhibit E. or of the 19th May. It is not worthwhile wasting time. The only point it is desirable to keep in mind is that the writer while showing the greatest sympathy with the Government, and feeling of the people in regard to this dreadful case, advocates the bomb. There are only a few lines in the article of the 19th May that I want to draw your attention to particularly. They are at page 2 (Reads "the evidence required for proving" down to "administrative system.") And you have again a reference made to the uncontrolled system of the administration. The whole article teems with expressions that go to show the feelings animating the writer and at page 4 you will find (Reads from "there is no wonder" down to "day by day.") And in the article of 26th May, the next article, where the opinions of Sir William Wedderburn, and Sir Henry Cotton are alluded to, you have this statement attributed to Sir Henry Cotton. There it is, lie or truth. If it is true no evidence has been produced; the presumption therefore is that it is a lie, and if so it must have been a lie within the knowledge of the writer of the articles. (Reads 'Sir Henry Cotton says' down to 'the King.') Sir Henry Cotton said that, or he did not. If he said it I think we should have had his discourse put before us in the shape of telegrams and articles now that so many articles have appeared. But having regard to the character of the words, the presumption is that it is absolute fiction. I hope that it is so. If it is only fiction and not fact it has a very strong bearing on the state of mind that actuated the writer of this article, and I have done with them all. I think I have referred to the more pungent parts of the article on "The secret of the Bomb." Now turn to page 2 of the article (Reads 'that would improve' down to 'equally guilty.') And now, Gentlemen, there has not been a word said in support, or any evidence adduced to justify these two infamous statements. What conclusion can you draw except that they are absolutely without foundation, and if so then they show the spirit of intention that runs through these two articles, one after another, as they all form part of a series of weekly articles commencing from 12th May and going on to 9th June 1908. And if these extracts which I have given you are not sufficient to show you what the spirit is that has been actuating the writer of these articles, well I am afraid there is nothing else we can put before you. I contend that if you look at all these articles yon will find that they are all influenced by the same desire, the desire to bring the Government of India into hatred and contempt on the grounds of its acting with obstinacy and oppression. That is, obstinate in that they refuse, as they say, to grant reforms, and oppressive in that they pass repressive measures, as they say, such as the Press Act and the Explosives Act and that the Government of India is at once repressive and opressive over attempting to maintain order which it is its highest duty to maintain.

I did not intend at one time to indulge in the language of offence at all, because I was satisfied of the effect that the language of the Accused would have on all right-minded people. If I have been led into saying anything considered by you or his Lordship not justified by the language that I have been criticising, I am prepared to stand by any rebuke that may be offered to me. But I cannot in my own mind think that I have said one word which is not justified by the language which I have quoted to you. I do not propose to speak further and must leave it in your hands, agreeing for once with the suggestion of the Accused and asking you to let nothing bear upon your minds except what you have heard in this Court. Let no outside talk, or preconceived opinion affect your verdict in this case which should be based entirely upon the articles, and by giving the best possible consideration to the statements and arguments advanced by the Accused.

His Lordship then Summed up the case.

THE JUDGE'S SUMMING UP

AND

CHARGE TO THE JURY.

Gentlemen of the Jury,—I am afraid your patience has been sorely taxed during the eight days which this trial has taken; and I do not propose to tax your patience to any extent as the case for both sides has been adequately put before you. Before saying anything else I think that it would be the merest and idlest of pretences to say that you had not heard of this case before or heard of the accused before. I have no doubt that the case has been discussed by your friends in your houses or in your hearing. I feel that I need not tell you that it is your duty to confine your consideration entirely in this case to what you have heard or read within the four corners of this court. I have no doubt you will not allow any passion or prejudice or outside information to influence you in the least in coming to a decision in this case. I hear with great satisfaction that the accused trusts you and your verdict. I ask you, gentlemen, to regard him as standing before you as one of your fellow subjects merely. You shall give sympathetic consideration to all that he has urged and then come to a decision, and coming to that decision return a verdict without fear or favour. One thing I would like to guard you against, and that is against giving any undue weight to the fact that the Crown prosecutes. There is nothing in that to prejudice you against the accused or against the prosecution. The Crown is the legitimate prosecutor in all cases before the Sessions. There is nothing which ought to weigh with you or influence you in the fact that the Crown prosecutes in this case. It is the duty of the Crown to prosecute when it considers, on its responsible legal officers consider that the law has been transgressed. It leaves the Judge and Jury to decide whether the law has been transgressed, whether there has been a breach of the law or not. The offences charged against the accused are themselves of a public or political nature and in order to guard against frivolous or factious prosecutions started under those sections, the law guards and protects journalists, publicsits and public speakers by providing that no such prosecution shall be started without the sanction of Government. That fact is the only reason why this sanction is required for the prosecution to be started under these two Sections we have heard the accused state that lower officers consider that a sanction is a mandate. I do not think that the accused really intended the words to be a suggestion to this court. It would be most improper for any one anywhere to send a mandate to you or to me which we are bound to obey. We are here to perform our duties. The only mandate that I obey and that you are bound to obey is the mandate of our conscience. My one desire has been to give the accused a perfectly free and fair trial. He has entered into every kind of discussion from every point of view; and it is possible that there were some things which were not relevant to the case. But we lost nothing by giving the accused the opportunity to unburden his mind before you and to tell you his point of view, his explanation of his conduct, of his writings and the sentiments to which he has given expression. Gentlemen, before I proceed further I think it would be as well if you had a perfectly clear idea of what your duties are and what my duties are. The duties of a Judge are defined in the Criminal Procedure Code and I will not take you through all those duties; but one thing a Judge has to do is to decide on all questions of law, to decide the admissibility of everything tendered as evidence and to decide what is for his own decision and what is for that of the Jury. And the judge's dicision on that point is binding on the jury. A judge might in the course of his summing up express his opinion on any question of fact or any question of mixed law and fact. Then comes the duty of the Jury which is defined in the next section. (Here his Lordship read from the Code the words of the section 299 Cr. Pr. Code.) You have heard the view of the prosecution and you have heard the view of the accused. Both have addressed you fully. I am entitled to express my own opinion. I am entitled to give you directions. But the accused has expressed his confidence in you and I am going to add to that responsibility by leaving the consideration of the whole case entirely in your hands. From my point of view the case presents no difficulty. The law is there. It is well settled law now. During the past ten years cases have come before the Court and every case has been most carefully considered and has been the subject of important legal decisions. I do not propose to give you any law that has not been settled before. I do not propse to give you my own view of the law. But I will give you the view of eminent judges who have had these cases before them and you will be bound to follow those views. The learned Advocate General has directed you largely from the summing up of Mr. Justice Strachey. With the exception of a small slip which did not matter in the least that summing up has received the approbation of a full Bench which was in that case presided over by Chief Justice Sir Charles Farran. It has received the approbation of the Privy Council. That judgment has been followed in other cases in other High Courts and has been referred to with approval. Quotations from that judgment have been largely read to you and therefore I will not traverse the same ground again. But before we proceed you must have a clear idea of the three charges on which you are trying the accused. He is charged in the first instance under Section 124 A of the Indian Penal Code with regard to an article published on May 12 (Exhibit C.) That is the first charge of sedition. And that is the only charge with regard to the first article. The next charge is again one of sedition under the same section with respect to an article dated June 9. The last charge is under section 153 A and is one of exciting feelings of hostility between different classes of His Majesty's subjects. That refers to the same article. So you will remember that there are three charges based on articles which are before you and which are marked Exhibit C and D. If you will read the words of the section which I believe are before you, you will find that a great many of the supposed difficulties and a great many of the considerations which have been urged will disappear. All you have to see is that these Sections are supposed to be a safe-guard or a check against any one who by speech or writing or visible means does or attempts to do certain things.

And what is more, he must not bring or attempt to bring into hatred or contempt the Government established by law. There is no question now that the Government established by law and referred to here is the British Government, or the English Government, whichever you like to call it, that rules over this country; and no one must excite or attempt to excite feelings of disaffection, against that Government. Does the word contempt require definition and does hatred require definition? We have all of us our feelings; we have all of us our passions, and I dare say there has been a time in the life of each one of you, when you have felt hatred or contempt for some one else. Disaffection has been much discussed, it is a peculiar word it is not used as between two persons, it is always used more in the sense as being applied between subject and ruler. The explanation leaves you in no difficulty. The explanations to the sections you must always bear in mind. They are intended to protect criticism of Government measures and administrative acts. Journalists have perfect freedom to discuss measures of Government, to disapprove of them and to use forcible language if necessary and to do every thing which is legitimately honest in bringing before the public and the Government the fact that their measures or actions are disapproved by a section of the public or by a particular speaker or by a particular journalist. He is entitled to urge every reason that he can in forcible langnage to show his views with regard to the administrative or executive acts of Government. Gentlemen, you must remember that no journalist or speaker has any right to attribute dishonest or immoral motives to Government. The freedom of the press is, I have no doubt, a most valuable right, you will be anxious to protect that freedom as I myself would be. You will consider all that accused has urged with regard to the freedom of the press. The law says however that that freedom should not be used to bring into hatred or contempt the Government established by law or to excite feelings of enmity. Barring that the liberty of the press must be protected. The press or publicists are entitled to protection against any prosecution that savours of persecution, and is entitled to come to the Jury and say "I have not transgressed the legitimate rights of a Journalist." Section 153 A is a simple section. You find that whoever promotes or attempts to promote feelings of hostility between different classes of his Majesty's subjects come under that Section (reads section 153 A. I. P. Code.) It only means that no subject of the crown is entitled to write or say or do anything whereby the feelings of one class should be inflamed against another class of his Majesty's subjects. I take it that this is generally a salutary provision of the law for the purpose of preserving peace between different classes of subjects of the Crown in this country.

Leaving the sections under which the accused is charged I will now draw your attention to two or three cases and to various judgments that have been delivered in the Bombay High Court and other High Courts in connection with similar cases. The first of the cases I am referring to is a case which has already been referred to by the learned Advocate General and is known as the Bangobasi case. I will read you from 19 Calcutta the summing up of Sir Comer Petheram in that case. He says disaffection means a feelings contrary to affection. In other words, dislike (reads from the Judgment down to the words " by them "). The last sentence of the summing up is the most important because that is the settled law. (Reads from " It is sufficient" down to "calculated"). The evidence of intention can only be gathered form the articles themselves. (Reads) Then he goes on directing the Jury as follows (reads from " directions which " down to " enmity against the Government "). That was I think in 1897 and I believe it was followed by a case in the Allahabad High Court in 1898. That is the Judgment delivered by Sir John Edge and two other justices of the Allahabad High Court. Sir John Edge in that case after referring to Justice Stratchey's summing up goes on to say (Reads " it is reasonably obvious " down to " the intention of the speaker or writer ") and then (again reads " it is immaterial whether the words were true or false.") Then, Gentlemen of the jury, there are two cases which came before Sir Lawrence Jenkins when he was presiding over the sixth Criminal Sessions in the the year 1900 and I will tax your patience by reading one or two extracts from his summing up which clears the position most completely and gives you an idea of what the law of sedition is. (Reads from the " main position of the section " down to " which have been considered ") Then you have the definition of the word attempt (reads " attempt is a preparatory " down to " accomplishment "). With reference to the word 'attempt' gentlemen, you have to take it in the ordinary meaning which attaches to the word 'attempt'. A man is supposed to attempt something which would be the natural and reasonable consequence of his act; if he fails he does not fail because he did not attempt but from other causes. Whether he fails or whether he succeeds the Law says no attempt should be made to excite feelings of hatred and disaffecfion. As to whether any particular action is an attempt it is for you to judge. There are the articles placed by the prosecution before you. The prosecution says those articles are calculated to excite feelings of disloyalty and enmity against the Government. I leave you to judge entirely the effects of those articles and it is for you to say whether the accused is right or the prosecution is right. In doing so there are several considerations which must be before your minds and to which I will refer later. Sir Lawrence Jenkins says ·(Reads " for the purpose of determining " down to " to produce mischief "). While judging the articles, from the articles themselves you will remember that the accused has pressed you to take, into consideration the circumstances under which these articles were written. By all means do so. Give the fullest effect to the surrounding circumstances, to the explanations he has given of them, which accused has urged and then say whether the articles are seditious and within the purview of the law or whether the circumstances urged by the accused form any justification for his saying that it does not come within the purview of the law. There are two other cases. I think it is as well to refer to one of these cases. In the Punjab Law Reports reference to which has been made by the accused (reads) so far it was read to you. but the conclusion was not read to you. In that case it comes to this that a man ran after another with an axe raised over his shoulder. When about four paces from his intended victim he was stopped by some other person. He was charged with attempting murder and it is quite true as accused had claimed that he was found not guilty. I have looked into this case however and found that while discharged on this account he had been convicted of attempting to cause gevious bodily harm under Sec. 511. The Court said the accused might have intended to give a lighter blow and therefore we will not convict him of murder but we will convict him of attempt to cause grevious bodily harm. If a man runs after another man with an axe he does not do it for fun and must be guilty of some offence. Then, gentlemen, a great many English cases have been referred to, cases centuries old, cases that took place in other countries in other circumstances where the surrounding circumstances were very different. You have had numerous readings from Counsel's speeches of those times. You have had numerous cases cited between the years 1700 and 1800. A hundred years ago; take them, I say, take them all (I find that they are all collected in a book on the law of sedition by a Bengali gentleman.) Take all those cases. Take all you were told about the liberty of the Press. I go further and say as to the accused, stand between himself and any persecution of the native press. Judge the native press with greater consideration than you do the English Press. It is a younger institution and probably more enthusiastic; take the articles read them and say what effect it produces on your minds and if you think these articles do not trangress the provisions of Section 124 A then you must return a verdict of not guilt.

What do these English cases lay down ? They lay down this. Lord Ellenborough says:—(Reads from "I am not prepared" down to "liable") Then in another case another judge says:—(Reads from "I am of opinion", down to "liberty of the press") And in another case again (Reads from "you should recollect" down to "it is not sedition".) Test the articles by the principles laid down by great English Judges. Let this be before you and let the address of Lord Fitzgerald "You are the guardians of the liberty of the press" before you. If you think the liberty of the press is not abused, and you can only think so if you think that the articles do not transgress the law: if you think that the articles which are before you are articles which are not calculated to give rise to feelings of hatred and contempt and disloyalty to and not likely to create enmity against the Government, then the accused is entitled to the benefit of that conclusion at your hands. If on the other hand you think that the articles imputed baseness and immoral motives to Government: if you think they incite to violence and disorder: and if you think these articles are calculated to convey to the minds of readers that political murders are approved of by the writer, then you will have to consider the effect that they have on the minds of the readers. I join with the accused in asking you not to be led by stray words, stray expression and stray items in his writings. Give all the weight that he asks you to give to the fact that the Marathi language is a language in which certain expressions are wanting and that the articles are written in high flown Marathi; judge them as a whole and on the impression created on your minds in reading them as a whole. Having read the articles, ask yourselves what is the effect produced on your minds. If the two articles

Exhibits D and C which are called the incriminating articles, if these two articles in themselves contain sufficient materials for you to decide whether what is written there amounts to an attempt to excite feelings of hatred and contempt against the Government established by law in India, then you need not go further. If you have any doubts you are entitled to look at the other articles to enable you to judge of the intention of the accused. What was the intention of the accused ? You must go to the articles, expressions and the sentiments in their ordinary natural meanings. The ordinary meaning which is attributed to that particular form of language.

The accused had made complaints about the translations. Mr. Joshi was submitted to a long cross-examination in the box on this point. It is for you to judge of the impression produced on your minds. It seems to me that Mr. Joshi was a man who gave his evidence without any bias or animus whatsoever against the accused and he went through the examination with a knowledge of Marathi which was a credit to himself as a Marathi scholar. He was prepared to give translations of the words and had his dictionary at his elbow. He seemed to have given much time to these articles. You have been told that they were not Mr. Joshi's translations. They were translations of the responsible translator to the High Court, who would not be the Translator and Interpreter to the Court unless he were an efficient man capable of translating correctly. The ordinary rule of this Court is that where a document is officially translated by the High Court Interpreter it is accepted as a correct translation. The accused has not attributed to the High Court Translator any animus against him, then why does he call these translations distortions ? It might be that the spirit of the articles might be lost in translations but you have heard the accused take Mr. Joshi through a long cross-examination. He has explained to you where the mistranslations came in as alleged. I think that the fairest thing to do is to accept the accused's tranalations in every particular. As I have stated the authorities are bound by the official translations in this Court. Still man is liable to err and it is possible that the translators some times err. It is quite open to the accused to bring other translations before the Court. He could do so in a number of ways. He could do so by submitting witnesses for the prosecution to cross-examination. This the accused did to Mr. Joshi. The prosecution asked one question which I thought was not necessary. He was asked to say whether the translations, which were not his, were correct. The accused taking advantage of Mr. Joshi being in the box to cross-examine him, Mr. Joshi has given you what he considers right and what he considers to be wrong. Accused has told you all. Well, for the purpose of this case accept all his corrections. I have taken down a great many of them:–Sorrow for pain, disgust for hatred, perverse for obstinate; violence for indignation; oppressive for repressive; manliness for manhood; obstinacy for stubbornness; despotic for autocratic; fanatic for turnheaded; despotic for tyranical &c. Well, gentlemen, I say accept those corrections. It may be that in reading the articles with them they may affect your minds differently. If they do this, by all means give the benefit to the accused. When we read a book or an article are we guided by the expressions in the writings or are we guided by the sentiments? If you think the translation is, as the accused says, distorted and unfair, substitute his translations and then consider whether the sentiments that are expressed in these articles are sentiments that are diffrent from the sentiments that are conveyed to your minds by the translator. Then again, gentlemen, in judging these articles you have to take into consideraton, as accused has pointed out, all the surrounding circumstances. The accused has told us that he has a very large circulation, the largest circulation, he said, so far as Indian or Anglo-Indian papers are concerned. All that he has written would be rea d by many of his thousands of subscribers and I suppose by learned men, by Marathi scholars and also by people who are not learned and not intelligent and by people who are not sensible or able to weigh matters for themselves. It may possibly be read by people who have no conception of political parties. You have to consider what effect these writings would have on those people and then say whether if those articles read by a large and promiscuous body of readers, what would be the effect on their minds. For you must remember that those readers have not had the adantage of 21 hours and 10 minutes explanation which the accused has offered on those articles. However you may assume, if you like, that these people knew the purpose for which these articles were written as explained by the accused. A great deal has been said by both sides as to intention and motive. The law with reference to intention and with reference to the fact whether it is true or not is crystalised here (reads from Mayne's-" Since the crime" down to " the truth of the argument. ") Well gentlemen, we are here as Judge and Jury to decide wether the writings of the accused have excited or were likely to excite feelings of harted and contempt and disloyalty against the Government. Now is it possible to prove that by evidnece? If we call one hundred men belonging to one side, for instace that of the accused, they will say that the articles do not produce any feelings against Government, indeed they promoted love to the Govrnment. One hundred men on the other side would say the opposite. It would be impossible for the prosecution to bring any evidence on this point. The true test you have to apply is to look at the various articles and judge of them as a whole, judge of the effect that they would have on your own minds in the first instance, judge whether they are calculated to produce feelings of disloyalty and hatred against the Government, judge whether languge like this is not calculated to excite Hiudus against Englishmen or Englishmen against Hindus. You judge it by your own common sense. One thing you must keep before your mind; violence disorder and murder can not take place by the hand that does not entertain feelings of hatred, contempt and violent enmity twoards those who are responsible for the good Government of the country. If we have violence and murder they are the acts of people who bear hatred towards the ruling classes. It must be so. If these people have proper feeling for the Government and for the people who are most responsible for the safety of property and safety of the subjects, there would be no trouble and no bomb-throwing. I have told you I thaink that the law does not require that the attempt should be successful. The law does not require that the attempt should be to excite rebellion or mutiny or violence. The law is much stricter than that. The accused says "law may be harsh and hard; stand between me and the law and protect the liberty of the press." You have to judge the accused according to the law as it stands. It was not for you or for me to judge whether the law is strict or harsh. I am here to administer it. You are here to tell me whether he has transgressed it. We are not judges of the law. We are not here to say whether the law is hard or not hard. It is the law of the land and it is the bounden duty of every subject to obey that law in every particular. No motive, no honest intention can justify a breaeh of that law. Of course a man, if he is a human being, is always actuated by some motive in doing an act; that motive may be proper or improper; there may be some cases where these motives before you are in doubt and where there may be protestations of honest motives. It may be interesting to read the articles and then say whether these articles are consistent with the protestations of the accused. That may be interesting but we are not concerned with motives, but only with what has been written. We are not concerned with the truth or untruth of the writings. The truth may sometimes be perverted. True or not it is not for you to judge. You may look at the articles and say for yourself how far they are true but what you have to do for the purpose of this case is to read the articles and say whether they amount to an attempt to excite hatred or contempt towards the Government, whether they are attempts to excite disaffection. If you think that these articles raed by you are calculated to give rise in the minds of readers to feelings of hatred or contempt against Government if you feel that these articles are calculated to engender feelings of hatred and disloyalty against Government, if you feel that these articles are likely to give rise to disorder or violence, then it will be your duty to consider whether that is not a transgression of the law. In reading the articles you must make all allowances for oriental modes of thought or oriental modes of exporession and language. Your first duty ought to be, in fairness to the accused, to try and put an innocent constructive on these articles. If you can consicienciously say that these articles are articles which are capable of innocent construction and that they do not transgress the law that will be your first duty if you that they are not transgressions of the law as it is if you feel any reasonable doubt as to whether the accused has transgressed the law, give him the benefit of that doubt. It is his right to have the construction placed upon his articles that is most favourable to him. It is only when you are constrained to say that these are articles which we cannot conscientiously say, come within the purview of the law then you must come to that decision. You must remember that expressions of crimes of violence may be made for the purpose of emphasising the real object of the article. You must not therefore be guided by a stray sentence which you might think is an incitement to violence or by any sentence which might be taken to mean disapprobation of the crimes under discussion. Gentlemen, the Crown prosecutes and the Crown has as much right as a private individual to say "protect the Government from attacks or libels which are likely to lead people to entertain feelings af enmity and disloyalty against it. The Government as we have heard lately are fair game and by all means let Government measures legislative and executive be subjected to as harsh and uncompromising criticism as you like. There the liberty of the press must be protected. They may complain but we shall listen to their complaints, but that criticisms must be free from imputations of dishonest motives and suggestions of immorality and must be free from the taint of language which would be likely to engender feelings of disloyalty, enmity and hatred against the Government.

You must again bear in mind in favour of the accused that Government has no right to say our subjects shall love us or shall regard us with affection. A man is not bound to feel any affection for Government. They have no right to ask it. A man may feel the utmost hatred and entire disloyalty towards the Government but he must not express them or write them or speak them in a manner which would be calculated to give a rise in the minds of others to similar feelings. A man, if he likes might write manuscripts and carry them about in his pocket or keep them at his home, but he must not publish them. He must give no expression to those feelings of enmity and disloyalty by writing or speeeh. Of course you must remember that the accused owes no duty to any body but himself. He is entitled io defend himself in any manner he pleases. He is not under any obligation to prove anything. It is for the prosecution to prove the case. The prosecution has placed before you certain articles and those articles are complained of. Accused says " I am a journalist, I have two hundred papers lying on my table every week, I have to read, digest and write on the spur of the moment! " That is argument which you have to take into consideration. If you think he has written those articles on the spur of the moment you must take that into consideration. If a man on the spur of the moment and in haste writes a paragraph which may be construed as a paragrah that would come within the section you must make allowance for that. Give the amplest consideration to the argument that is urged by the accused. If you think he has written these articles on the spur of the moment take that into consideratiou. The spar of the moment here commenced on May 12 and the bomb outrages took place at the end of April. If you think that these articles which were written nearly a fortnight after the occurrence could be considered to be writings on the spur of the moment yor are entitled to take that into consideration. Then you are told " I did this in self-defence. " I could understrnd self-defence if some one pulled a man's nose and he boxed his ears. I could make allowances. But if some one pulls your nose and you box the ears of another man how is that self-defence? According to the accused the 'Pioneer' attacked the native agitators and may have said some things which might be quite improper. What is there to show that the 'Pioneer' is a Government paper? I am only expressing views which strike me as features in the case. I am leaving you free. Anything which am saying to you which does not meet with your commendation, reject it. I am simply saying that these are aspects of the case which present themselves to me. You are the judges of facts. It is on your verdict that I rely. It is for you to say whether the accused is guilty or innocent. I beg of you not to be iufluenced. If your views are views that coincide with anything that I have said, well and good. If not, give prominence to your own views in the matter. As the case has been so long and as so many points of view have been placed before you

I think it is only fair that some of them should be discussed. You must also remember that great number of matters were argued before you and quoted to you and many extracts from books read, you must not allow yourselves to be prejudiced against the accused by this. It may be that appearing for himself he identified himself with those writings. It is not any excuse for the accused to say "I have written seditious articles because somebody else has been wrting seditious articles for some time." That is no excuse. I do not say that the accused said this. He simply said that he wrote in a similar strain to other people. It is not for us to say why these other people were not prosecuted. Your duty lies in reading the articles and telling the judge whether in your opinion accused has transgressed the law as it stands. Accused has told you that he was carrying on an open constitutional fight. He has said that he has a God-sent mission, that his cause is the cause of righteousness. If you think that these articles are written in furtherance of an open constitutional fight, if you think that these articles are written in furtherance of a God sent mission in the great cause of righteousness, you are entitled to give the whole benefit of that to the accused. Gentlemen! what is the theme? What is the subject of these articles—the advent of the Bomb. One needs no telling that in the case of a bomb the atrocity of the crime can only be equalled by its cowardice. That is the subject that is being discussed. The murderer kills one man, a bomb may kill a dozen. It is asubject which every right-minded man ought to regard with horror. That subject is under discussion before you in the five or six articles. If you regard that subject as being argued in a proper manner, by all means acquit the accused. Is the accused prepared to argue that the bomb is a legitimate means of political agitation, and do these articles convey to you that meaning? In that case you will have to adjudge what the effects would be on the minds of the readers. Accused has said that agitators are falsely charged as being responsible for bomb-throwing, and therefore he has provocation. It is not for you to judge whether agitators were or were not responsible for that. But one thing was certain. It was only when feelings of hatred and contempt and disloyalty and enmity against the Government are engendered in the minds of men—it is only when those feelings reach a most acute stage that they find vent in those deeds of violence. The matter has been discusssed before you. "The cult of the Bomb" and the "Secret of the Bomb" and "The Double Hint" are before you. And it is for you to judge whether those articles contain expressions of approval at the advent of the bomb.

You have the bomb party just as you have the Liberal party and the Conservative Party and the National party. Mr. Joshi told us of certain parties existing but he did not mention the bomb party. It is only when we come to the articles that this party is heard of. It is for you to say whether that reference and the manner in which it is made, are calculated to bring Government into hatred and contempt. It is for you to say whether these articles before you are compatible with a man who merely discussses political problems and resents attack. You were again told gentlemen, a great deal about "I shall be charged with inuendoes and veiled attacks". Looking at the articles, gentlemen, is there much room for inuendoes or veiling ? One thing you can say about the articles is that there is a great deal of plain speaking. Whether that plain speaking is justifiable it is your duty to judge. Whether the effect of these articles is to make you believe that bomb throwing is a proper means for obtaining greater rights and privilege it is for you to say.

I would like to say that you must not judge of the articles, merely because some of it may be written in what may be considered bad taste, every journalist may write as he likes.He is not bound to write in good taste. All he has to consider is that he must keep within the law. Now the article of the 12 th May 1908 which forms the subject-matter of the first charge has only recently been read to you by the learned Advocate General and I do not propose to read much from any of the articles at this hour. Take for instance the first article (Reads: bottom of page 2 of translation from " However " down to "indignation or exasperation" and then to " recklessly ".) Now just judge of the effect produced on the minds of Marathi readers by this sentence. We want Swarajya and if we don't get it some people will be so horribly annoyed that they will embark on the commission of horrible deeds. " The horrible deeds " referred to is the incident of Muzafferpur where a boy threw a bomb and killed two innocent ladies. We are told Swarajya must be given and if we don't get it some turn-headed men will become violent. (Reads: from middle of page 3 " some people think " down to " accomplished ".) What is the spoke that is going to be put into the wheel of the car of the administration ? The bomb or what else is it? Then again(Reads from middle of the page 4 from " But while certain efforts " down to " are seditious".) I am bound to point out on page 5 some sentiments that appear to be perfectly proper on the same day. If you wish to know what the intention of the accused was and what he was writing you have to turn to Exhibit " D " which are editorial notes or " Stray Thoughts of the Editor " in the paper published on the 12th May. Take the first Stray Thought, look at the latter part of it. (Reads from " Some people" down to "Bengal") "Murders are useful sometimes in order to direct the attention of the authorities to grievances." Here we have the murder of two ladies and we are told that it is useful in directing the attention of Government to the grievances of the Bengalis. Take the second Stray Thought (Reads:—" It is only " down to " national assassination ".) The suggestion here is that the rulers wish in their minds to wipe out some people or institutions. This is capable of explanation, I dare say such an explanation has been made and it is for you to say whether it is adequate.

Then we come to the consideration of the second article dated 9th June 1908. It is very difficult to comment on this article. It has been read to you. I would rather leave you to judge for yourselves what the effect of that article is. What is the article ? What does it contemplate ? What does it preach under the heading of " These Remedies are not lasting"? He says repressive measures are not effective and goes on discussing the bomb. He makes comparisons between the various people who use bombs and in doing so says. (Reads:—" The authorities have spread" down to " the policy of repression".) Do you talk of patriotism in the case of bombs–bombs that effect murders? You are judges of whether such a discussion does or does not tend to bring the Government as established by Law in India into hatred and contempt. Take the top of the second page. (Reads:- " The most mighty Czar " down to "as a matter of course".) Bow down to the bomb! Then there is a simile of the parrot with its wing plucked and its leg broken. I suppose it is intended for the Indian, Nation. Then there is the comparison between the sway of the Mogal Emperor Aurunzebe with the sway of the English Nation and then you have some sentences which may or may not effect your minds with regard to the subject matter of these three charges. (Reads:—" The residence of the English" down to "aftar making a seperate division".) You have then a whole page which I have no doubt you have read and which it is unnecessary to discuss with you. In the similies you have the effects of the bombs explained is various ways. Its usefulness (Reads:- "The bomb has more the form" down to "it is a charm, an amulet".) Those of you who can read Marathi will be able to read the original articles. The accused has read the article to you and given an explanation, of his meaning. (reads:" The bomb has more the form of knowledge it is a kind of witchcraft, it is a charm, an amulet.") I have had portions of the original article written out for me in readable caligraphy and the words are.

ही एक जादू आहे.

हा एक मंत्र तोडगा आहे.

(Hi Ek Jadu ahe)

(Ha Ek Mantra Todga ahe)

When an accused person is charged with attempting to excite feelings against the Government and other articles are put in for the purpose of showing intention and the individual is desirous of refuting this contention then articles which tend to confirm the subject-matter of the charge may be considered as there may be other things which throw light on the question whether they are calculatd to raise feelings of disaffection. For instance in Exhibit G page 2 you will find (Reads "The Bengalis continually agitated " down to " national regeneration. ") It is a perfectly proper sentence, you cannot find fault with it. But look what follows. (Reads:—down to " honour of their women. ") He says that when the Bengalis were resorting to perfectly proper and legitimate meaus for their national regeneration Government become irretated by this patriotism of the Bengalis and letting loose some Musalman bud-mashes caused damage to their property and the honour of their women. Is it fair ? Is it or is it not a charge against the Government of inciting Mahomedans for the most improper purposes to attack the Bengalis loot their property and violate their women ? It is for you to say. Would anybody after reading that have any respect for Government or would their feelings be those of hatred and contempt and disloyalty ? As I have said before these articles have been before you a long time and it would take me a great deal of time to discuss the effect of all those articles, I repeat again judge of these articles for yourselves do not allow what I have said to influence you beyond drawing your attention to the articles. If anything that I have said commends itself to you, accept it, if not reject it without hesitation. There is one other small subject to be discussed and that is the Post Card (Ex. K.) you are the best judge of what effect to give to it. To my mind it is not a piece of evidence which ought to affect your minds. It contains the names of two books on explosives. The production of catalogues to show that the books were mentioned in those catalogues is of course of no importance. The accused has given his explanation that it was his intention to study the books with a view to criticising the Explosives Act. That may be true. We did not know whether these books are books which deal the manufacture of explosives. Because I should have thought that if they refer to the manufacture of explosives the Card might have some meaning. Now it is not a piece of evidence which ough to weigh in your minds against the accused. The accused discussed bombs and may have been anxious to discuss the explosives Act in some form or another. Well Gentlemen, I am afraid I have detained you longer than I intended. The case is one which as I have stated it will be entirely for you to decide. The accused has applied to you or to some of you to differ, at least one or two, and he says it would be a great consolation if you differ, I do not konw what he means or what his object is in asking you to differ. I shall ask you to make every effort if necessary to be unanimous. If you think that the accused is not guilty by all means without fear or favour acquit him. If you think he is guilty you must find him guilty. But if any of you, gentlemen, feel you cannot conscientiously agree with the others you are entitled to differ.

If after giving the fullest consideration to what accused has stated after giving your sympathatic consideration to everything accused has urged in his defence, you feel you have reasonable doubts of the guilt of the accused by all means say so. On the other hand if you find that he has transgressed the law and that his writing amounts to an attempt to bring the Government into contempt and hatred it will be your duty to return a verdict accordingly, I do not think I can usefully say anything more.

I ask you again to judge of the accused by what is before you. On what you have heard in this room and what you have read of his writings. Put out of your minds everything you may have heard before you became members of this jury and all that you have heard and read outside since. Apply your minds entirely to the articles before you and tell me, gentlemen, what is your verdict upon the charges. There are three charges ouy are at liberty to acquit or convict on all three or acquit or convict on any two of the charges. There are two charges under Section 124 A and one charge under Section 153 A. Consider each charge seperately and return a verdict on each one of the charges separately and I shall ask you to return a verdict that is unanimous, if posssible. I shall have to administer the law in accordance with your verdict. The case is a very important one to the accused. The charges are very serious. If you feel that he is guilty you must say so. But if you have any doubt give him the benefit if there is any reasonable and substantial doubt in your minds.

The Jury retired at 8-3 P. M.

The Jury returned at 9-20 P.M.

Verdict and Sentence.

The Jury returned at 9-20 P. M.

Clerk of the Crown : Gentlemen, are you unanimous ?

Foreman of the Jury : No !

Clerk of the Crown : I do not want you to tell me the Verdict, simply give me the number you are divided by.

Foreman : 7 to 2.

Clerk of the Crown: On all the charges?

Foreman: Yes. on all the charges.

Clerk of the Crown: On the first charge under Section 124A of sedition with respect to the article of 12th May 1908, what is the verdict of the majority?

Foreman: Guilty.

Clerk of the Crown: 7 to 2 ?

Foreman: Yes.

Clerk of the Crown: On the second charge under Section 124 A of sedition in respect of the article of 9th June 1908, what is your verdict?

Foreman: Guilty!

Clerk of the Crown: 7to2.?

Foreman: yes.

Clerk of the Crown: On the third charge under Section 153A of raising ill-feeling amongst classes in respect to the article of 9th June 1908 what is your verdict?

Foreman: Guilty !

Clerk of the Crown: 7 to 2 ?

Foreman: Yes.

His Lordship: Mr. Foreman, is there any chance of your being unanimous ?

Foreman: I am sorry to say my Lord, that I am afraid there is none.

His Lordship: No chance of becoming unanimous ?

Foreman: No chance.

His Lordship: Under Section 305 of the Criminal Procedure Code if the Jury is divided by more than 6 to 3 the Judge is bound to state whether he agrees with the majority or not and the law lays down that if the Judge agrees with them he shall give judgment in accordance with the verdict and I have no option but to pass sentence.

Advocate General: There is another charge I wish to prefer before your Lordship passes judgment.

Accused: I apply for certain points of law to be reserved under Section 434 Criminal Procedure Code.

His Lordship: What are the points?

Accused: I will read them.

(Reads the following application for law points to be reserved).

POINTS which Defence prays may be reserved and referred to Full Bench under Sec. 434 of the Criminal Procedure Code.

1. Whether the whole trial is not vitiated owing to three offences-two of them under Section 124 A and the third under Section 153 A forming subjects of two distinct commitments having been tried together in opposition to defence objections and whereby accused has been prejudiced.

2. Whether Exhibit D could be made the subject, simultaneously of two charges one under Section 124 A and the other under Section 153 A without in either case specifying the portions coming thereunder.

3. Whether having regard to Sec. 222 Criminal Pro. Code the charges were legally defective in as much as none of them gave the accused notice of the particular objectionable portions, and if so whether the whole trial is not vitiated thereby.

4. Whether the charge under Sec. 153 A is not legally deficient in not indicating the classes between whom the accused is alleged to have promoted or attempted to promote feelings of hatred &c, and if so whether the trial on that charge is not wholly vitiated thereby.

5. Whether the prosecution for the offences under Sec. 124 A or 153 A is proved to have been properly initiated without putting in the complaints and examining the complainants.

6. Whether the provisions of Sec. 196 Criminal Procedure Code have been satisfied in this case and if not whether the trial is sustainable.

7. Whether Exhibit B. is legally sufficient to support the prosecution under Sec. 153 A.

8. Whethr Exhibit E–J are admissible and if so for what purposes.

9. Whethr the accused in this case loses his right of reply by the mere filing of the several papers forming Exhibit No. 1 with which Exhibit A was recovered by the Police.

10. Whether Exhibit A is admissible and relevant in this case.

11. Whether the accused is entitled to rely on the papers accompanying his statement.

12. Whether the accused had not in this case a right of reply.

13. Whether charges based on translations that have been shown to be untenable are sufficient in law to sustain a trial thereon.

14. Whether in the face of the objections by the defence challenging the correctness of the translations of Exhibits C & D it was not illegal to have admitted the same without having been proved by the Translator who translated them aud submitting the Translator for cross-examination.

His Lordship: With reference to this application every one of the points had arisen and been discussed and there is not one single point, I assure the accused, in this application which I have not most anxiously considered. I would be most anxious, if I had the smallest doubt in my mind, if any one of these points were worth discussing or reserving, I should be most willing to reserve any one of these points for consideration by the Full Bench. But I have most anxiously considered every argument and contention of the accused. Most of these points are covered by authorities and the other points are so elementary that they hardly admit of any argument. If I feel there was the least use or that it could do the least possible good to the accused to reserve these points or any one of them, I should have been most willing to do so. I do not think that any of these points have any substance in them and I decline to accede to the application.

Advocate General: I propose to put up the accused on another charge of previous conviction. He will have to plead to the charge, yes or no. And the jury will have to decide. If he denies it we will prove it.

Clerk of the crown: Reads further charge (Reads "Prisoner at the bar! On the 14th September 1897 you were convicted at the 4th Criminal Sessions of this High Court under section 124 A I. P. C, to 18 months simple (?) imprisonment.") Do you plead guitly or claim to be tried?

Accused: I do not know how the question arises. Under Section 75 I. P. C. I do not think such a question can arise; besides it is not in the charge.

His Lordship: I suppose Mr. Advocate General you apply under Section 221 and 310.

Advocate General: Yes, my Lord, under Section 221 and 310; and if he denies I will prove it under Section 511.

His Lordship: This is not a proceeding under 75 I. P. C. It is a proceeding under the C. P. C. and you have to plead to the charge.

Accused: It is not in the charge. It arises out of Section 75 I. P. C. and is not admissible for enhancement of punishment for this class of offences. So how can it be inserted?

His Lordship: This is a charge which, if the verdict of the Jury is properly made against you, you must plead to.

Accused : It does not become relevant for the purpose of enhancement of punishment.

His Lordship : Whatever the reason is you must plead whether the charge is correct or not.

Accused : I take it that Your Lordship thinks that at the present stage it is rightly put in here ?

His Lordship : Yes, at the present stage it is rightly put in here.

Accused : In that case I admit it.

Advocate General : That means he pleads "Guilty" my Lord.

His Lordship : Yes, I have taken down "admits previous conviction."

His Lordship to the accused : Do you wish to say any thing more before I pass sentence ?

Accused :—All I wish to say is that in spite of the verdict of the Jury I maintain that I am innocnt. There are higher Powers that rule the destiny of things and it may be the will of the Providence that the cause which I represent may prosper more by my suffering than by my remaining free.

His Lordship :—It is my painful duty now to pass sentence upon you. I cannot tell you how painful it is to me to see you in this position. You are a man of undoubted talents and great power and influence. Those talents and that influence, if used for the good of your country, would have been instrumental in bringing about a great deal of happiness for those very people whose cause you espouse. Ten years ago you were convicted and the Court dealt most leniently with you then, and the Crown dealt still more kindly with you. After you had undergone your (simple ?) imprisonment for one year, six months of the sentence was remitted upon conditions which you accepted. The condition which you signed then was this. (Reads from document.—"I hereby accept and agree to the above conditions, understanding the meaning to be such act or writing as is considered as an offence." It seems to me that it must be a diseased mind, a most perverted mind that could say that the articles which you have written are legitimate weapons in political agitations. They are seething with sedition ; they preach violence ; they speak of murders with approval and the cowardly and atrocious act of committing murders with bombs not only seems to meet with your approval but you hail the advent of the bomb in India as if something has to come to India for its good. As I said, it can only be a diseased and perverted mind that can think that bombs are legitimate instruments in political agitations. And it would be a diseased mind that could ever have thought that the articles you wrote were articles that could have been legitimately written. Your hatred of the ruling class has not disappeared during these ten years. And these articles deliberately and defiantly written week by week, not, as you say, on the spur of the moment but a fortnight after that cruel and cowardly outrage had been committed upon two innocent English women. You wrote about bombs as if they were legitimate instruments in political agitations. Such journalism is a curse to the country. I feel much sorrow in sentencing you. I have considered mos-

anxiously in the case of a verdict of guilty being returned against you what sentence I should pass upon you. And I decided to pass a sentence which I considered will be stigmatised as what is called "misplaced leniency". I do not think I can pass, consistently with my duty and consistently with the offence of which you have been found guilty, a lighter sentence than I am going to give you. And I think for a man in your position and circumstances that sentence will vindicate the law and meet the ends of justice. You are liable to be transported for life under the first two charges. I have considered whether to sentence you to transportation or imprisonment. Having regard to your age and other circumstances I think it is most desirable in the interest of peace and order, and in the interest of the country which you profess to love, that you should be out of it for sometime. Under Section 124 A I am entitled to pass sentence of transportation for life or any shorter period, and I pass a sentence of three years' transportation under each of the first two charges, the sentences to run consecutively. You will thus have six years, transportation. On the third charge which is punishable not by transportation but by fine or imprisonment I do not think I will add to your troubles any additional period of imprisonment. I therefore fine you Rs. 1000.

Advocate General: I now apply for the withdrawal of the fourth charge against the accused under Section 333.

His Lordship: I grant such withdrawal. Such withdrawal to be tantamount to an acquittal. So far as the accused is concerned this is a discharge.

The Jury on the application of the Foreman were exempted from service for three years.

The Sessions were then adjourned.

Judge's Notes in the case.

Monday 13th July 1908.

Bal Gangadhar Tilak.

The Advocate General with Mr. Inverarity and Mr. Binning for the prosecution.

Accused defends himself.

The Advocate General applies for one trial in respect of three out of four charges.

26 All. 195.

16 Bom. 414.

10 Bom. 254,

25 Madras P. C,

Sec. 333 Cr. Pr. C.

Accused in person. :—

Sec, 227 applies and not the sections referred to by the Advocate General.

P. C. Order that the Accused be tried at one trial on three out of the four charges on which the Accused is committed.

Note. The Advocate General says he will apply under Sec. 333 of the Criminal Procedure Code with reference to the fourth charge. He says he will not prosecute the charge under 153 A. in connection with the article of 12 May 1908.

I intimate that I will order the discharge to be acquittal.

The Advocate General intimates that he will make the application under Sec. 333 Criminal Procedure Code, after the present trial has ended, so as to avoid any possible question of law as to being *already acquitted*. All charges read to the accused.

Accused pleads not guilty to all the charges and says that the words should be set forth in the charges showing what portions of the articles are charged as seditious.

Mr. Inverarity says the prosecution charge that the whole of both aritcles are seditious and applies that the charges may be amended by incorporating in them the whole articles.

P. C. Charges ordered to be amended by incorporating the articles and the articles are read as part of the charges (after the first article is read accused says the other may be taken as read.)

I explain to the accused that the prosecution charge him with three charges at this trial; under 124 A in respect of article of 12 may 1908, and charges under 124 A and 153 A in respect of the article of the 9th of June 1908.

Mr. Inverarity for the prosecution opens:—

Reads article 12th May 1908 and comments.

2 Campbell 399. 402. 403.

With decency and respect & without attributing motives.

Words to be taken in the sense which they are intended to convey.

Bhaskar Vishnu Joshi. S. Xd. by Mr. Binning.

I am first assistant to the Oriental Translator to Government. I am a Bachelor of Arts. I recognise the signature of Mr. H. O. Quin, Acting Secretary to Government Judicial Department. This Document is signed by him. It is sanction to prosecute with reference to article in the Kesari of the 12th May 1908.

Ex. A. Sanction dated 23rd June 1908. Ex. A.

This is another sanction signed by Mr. Quin also. It is dated 26th June 1908. It gives sanction to prosecute in respect of the article in the Kesari of the 9th of June 1908.

Ex. B. Sanction dated 26 June 1908. Ex. B.

Both the documents are signed at the foot by Mr. H. G. Gell, the Commissioner of Police.

I produce a copy of the " Kesari " newspaper of the 12th of May 1908. at pages 4 and 5 is an article which I translated. This is the High Court Official Translation. In the usual course of my business I received this copy of the 12th of May 1908 of the Kesari in my Office. The article I translated is headed " The Country's Misfortune."

Ex. C. Article with translation put in Ex. C. (12th May 1908).

I produce another copy of the Kesari of the 9th of June 1908. It came to me in the same way in the usual course to my office. At page 4 columns 2 to 4 of this issue there is an article headed "These remedies are not lasting" This is the High Court official translation.

Article with translation put in & marked Ex. D. (9th June 1908). EX. D.

In Ex. C the Kesari of the 12th of May 1908 there is an article at page 5 column 3. It comes under the "Editor's Stray Thoughts" Notes 3 & 4 These are translations of these notes.

Mr. Binning tenders.

Accused objects.

Accused cites Mayne p. 522.

P. C. Admitted.

Notes in Kesari of the 12th May 1908 EX. E. EX. E.

I produce an issue of the Kesari of the 19th of May. At page 4 columns 4 & 5 and col., 1 of page 5, I find an article headed "A Double Hint." This issue came to me in the same way as the others. This is the official translation.

Article with translations put in & marked EX. F — EX. F

(19th May 1908.)

I produce the issue of the Kesari of the 26th May 1908. At page 4 Columns 3, 4 & 5 there is a Marathi leader headed "The Real Meaning of the Bomb." This issue came in the same way as the others. This is the translation.

Article with translations put in & marked Ex. G — EX. G.

(26th May 1908)

After lunch.

I produce a copy of the issue of the Kesari of the 2nd of June 1908 on page 4 columns 3, 4, 5 there is a leader entitled "Secret of the Bomb" This paper came to me in the usual course of my business.

Ex. H. Article with translation put in & marked Ex. H. (2nd June 1908).

In Ex. D, (Kesari 9 June 1908) at page 5 columns 2 & 3 there are stray thoughts of the editor. Note No. 11 begins with "English Rule is openly an alien rule" this is the translation of that note.

Ex. I. Note 11 with translation put in and marked — Ex, I.

Xd by the Accused—

The translations produced are High Court translations. I can vouch for the accuracy. I have compared all except Ex. G. I have before this translated all of them. In minor matters they differ with my translations; where they differ in most cases the High Court translations should be preferred. I have not got my translations here. The official translation of Ex. C. is 2nd July 1908. I don't remember when I translated this. I produce the translation in the Magistrate's Court. It must have been prepared before the 25 of June 1908. This is my translation. This is the original article. ગોરા means white or fair. White is more comprehensive than Gora ગોરા. European and white will convey same meaning. I translated ગોરા as European with a marginal note saying it literally meant white.

In my official capacity I am a regular reader of Marathi papers. Many new words have to be coined in Marathi in expressing modern current political ideas and writers occasionally insert the English word after the Marathi word to clear up his meaning. "Bureaucracy" is in in English in Ex. C. It stands for official class. Not white official class. અધીકારી means official class. સરકારી અધીકારી વર્ગ will do to express "Ruling Classes." ગોરે અધીકારી વર્ગ will also mean the same thing. "ગોરા" "ઇંગરેજ" સરકારી and રાજ્ય કરતા વર્ગ will mean the same thing. "Ruling Class" "White Official Class" "English Official Class" "Official Class in power." Bureaucracy has been translated by me as અધીકારી વર્ગ means a "class of officials." Bureaucracy does not mean the Ruling Official Class. The word does not convey the idea of Rule. Aristocracy does not convey the idea of Ruling. I cannot give you the exact meaning of Plutocracy. અધીકારી is official, and the વર્ગ means class. The expression અધીકારી વર્ગ would include both Europeans and Natives. If you have to confine it to one of the two classes these words must be qualified by an adjective.

I translate Despotism as જુલમી રાજ્ય Tyrannical is જુલમી Oppressive is જુલમી I would translate coercive as જુલમી also. Repressive દડપશાહચા it is so used by you. It is a coined word. Meaning must be according to context. Despotic Rule is the Rule of a Despot or Despotic officials. I don't know the difference between despotic and tyrannical. Despotic Rule is the same as tyrannical Rule. I have not come across the expression that a despotic Rule need not necessarily be a tyrannical Rule. I don't remember જુલમી રાજ્યપદ્ધતી જુલમાચી અસલી પાએજે અસા નાહી would be the meaning of that expression.

The words Autocratic, absolute, arbitrary are translated thus :—

Absolute is અનિયંત્રિત.

Arbitrary is આળા નાહીં અસા.

Autocratic is અનિયંત્રિત.

Uncontrolled is alo અનિયંત્રિત.

Irresponsible is બેજબાબદાર.

Imperialistic is બાદશાહી બાણ્યાચા.

"Government of India is a despotism tampered by public opinion in England" would be translated thus હિંદુસ્થાન સરકાર હે ઇંગ્લંડાંતીલ લોકમતાને સામ્ય આલેલે જુલમી રાજ્ય હૂએ.

માથેફીરૂ is translated as "turnheaded".

Fanatic is Marathi the same as in Hindi ગાઝી.

Devoid of religions meaning the translation would be વેડા or માથે ફિરલેલા.

આતતાયી is violent, heady or furious man.

I have not come accross its use for a felon. I don't know who were called આતતાયી in Sanskrit. In the Sanskrit Dictionary six classes of people are called આતતાયી. I have said Molesworth is an antiquated dictionary. માથેફિરૂ cnoveys stronger idea આતતાયી is a sanskrit word and very few would understand it. I am not aware if આતતાયી is generally quoted in Marathi. In the Dictionary (Apte's) આતતાયી is rendered as a felon. I can't say if felon is a stronger word than fanatic. Writing in Marathi words have to be coined or borrowed from Sanskrit to give expression to modern English Political phrases.

State, Government, administration, rule and sway. Of these words I can give Marathi equivalents. I don't know subtle distinctions.

State is રાજ્ય or સરકાર

Government is સરકાર, શાસનપદ્ધતિ

Administration is રાજ્યપદ્ધતી.

Rule is રાજ

Sway isઅંમલ orરાજ્ય.

Manliness, vigour, sense of honour as qualities of a ruling nation or a living nation would be translated thus:

Manliness મરદાનીપણા or પૌરૂષ.

Vigour સામર્થ્ય.

Sense of honour અભિમાન બુદ્ધિor માનબુદ્ધિ.

તેજ I have not used for sense of honour.

તેજસ્વી does not mean a man having sense of honour

I would say a man with fiery energy or spirit. I can't say if it would be applied to a man who cannot brook an insult.

The sentence you read is in Sanskrit. I have an idea as to what it means, but I cannot translate offhand.

The word સંતાપ means indignation

દુઃખાને સંતપ્ત means afflicted with sorrow.

ક્ષોભ is passionate anger.

આવેશ is vehemence, agitation, Rage. The translations I am giving are studied by me from the Dictionary. I have used three Dictionaries. Molesworth's Candy's and Apte's, and I have sometimes referred to Monier William's Dictionary. In translating I select such articles as I think best. I can't tell what new meaning a writer may wish to attach to these expressions. I know that good many words have to be coined in Marathi to express new ideas.

" Evil genius haunting a man " is translated as દુષ્ટબુદ્ધિ માણસાચ્યા પાઠીમાગે ભુતાસારખી લાગલેલી.

I translate સાક્રેતીસાચ્યા માગે ભુત લાગલે હોતે.

as a Fiend pursued Socrates. It may be translated as Evil genius haunted Socrates.

The second sentence can be translated as the " Evil genius of repression seizes the Government of India every five or ten years. " Seizes is a free translation of what expression is used in Marathi.

માંત્રિક in Ex. D is not meant in its literary sense.

માંત્રિક is a man who recites charms or is well versed in incantations.

ધ્રભ્રષ્ટ is one who has failed from his vows or practices or observances.

In Ex. D. " Abjured their ideals " is a correct translation. I think the translation correctly represents the context.

સુળસુળાટ is translated 'swarming everywhere'. The word refers both to action and number. I can't say if it refers more to one than to another. The expression "Evident activity" is a very far fetched translation.

બુદ્ધિભ્રંશ is infatuation or aberration of intellect.

" Error of Judgment " I can't translate this off hand.

I will try and give you the translation to-morrow.

બુદ્ધિ કશી ચળલી "How is intellect become fatuated."

ચળલી literally means dislodged. The expression cannot mean "Erred in Judgment."

Decentralization of Power is અધિકાર વિભાગણી.

Ex. D. Page 2 . 7 lines from bottom. This passage does not refer to Decentralization of Power. Such a translation does not fit the context. વાટણી is not a word that could be used in connection with the idea of Decentralization. અધિકાર વિભાગણી is a coined expression in Marathi. Decentralization could be rendered by the expression અધિકારાચી વાતની.

5–30 P. M.

TUESDAY 14TH JULY 1908.

Bal Gangadhar Tilak.

Continued from yesterday.

Bhaskar Vishnu Joshi further cross–examination by the Accused.

Shown Kesari of 17th March 1908.

In the article the expressions અધિકારાચી વાતની are used as meaning apportionment of power, and not Decentralisation of Power. In the sentence you put to me the meaning would still be apportionment of power between the Provincial Government and the Government of India.

In C તીટકારા is the word for "hatred" દ્વેષ is "hatred or enmity." I am not aware of any difference in the meaning. The first is Marathi the second is Sanskrit. If તીટકારા means disgust or not I cannot say without looking in the dictionary. I do not remember to have referred to the dictionary. Referring to Molesworth I find the meaning is given as "feelings of disdain or disgust." It is not translated as "hatred."

In Ex. C the word for "perversity" is દુરાગ્રહ and for "obstinacy" is હટ The two words are not synonymous and used to make the idea stronger.

There is the conjunction "and" between the two words. દુરાધર may be translated as "stubborness" but that word would not suit the context. I can't say what would be necessary to make the word દુરાધર stubborness. હઠ કિંવા દુરાધર would mean "obstinacy or perversity," but it would not mean stubborness in my opinion. Shown Ex. F. (19th May 1908), at page 3 the original words for obstinacy or stubborness are હઠાને કિંવા દુરાધરાને. The words are used for Rulers.

In Ex. C these are the words "But the dispensations of God are extraordinary." The word used is નેમાનેમ for dispensation. The dictionary meaning is apportionment or dispensation. નેમાનેમ is a reduplication of નેમ and મેમ is derived from નીઅમ meaning rule or regulation. It may be rendered " the ways of God are strange " ઉરમત means "overbearing or violent." It may mean "rude."

Insolently may or may not be translated as impertinently or rudely. I can't say off hand. Patience of humanity can equally be rendered as human patience, but it would not be a literal translation. The meaning of ક્ષુબ્ધ is " excited. " The translation in Ex. C is exasperated. In Ex. C page 2 the original word for insolence is મદ and the word for inebriated is ધુંદ. I can't say whether ધુંદ means blinded. The dictionary meaning is "of dulled vision through sickness." The meaning of મદ in the dictionary is arrogance " haughtiness " also " intoxication. " " Blinded by the intoxication of power" may be a right rendering of that sentence.

The words for "monopoly" would be મક્તા ઘેતલેલા, સર્વ મક્તા would be a free rendering of the word monopoly. Monopoly would not be a correct substitute for the words "whole contract" in Ex. C.

અસા ઝાલા ખેરીજ રાહુનાર નાહીં would be translated as " this cannot fail to take place. " It cannot be translated as " this cannot but be so. "

In Ex. C bottom of page 2 " will not fail to embark " may be translated as " they cannot but " the words for " nbark " in the original are પ્રવૃત હોને, "Embark" is not high flown rendering.

In Ex. C at page 3 the original for "as you sow so you reap " is " જસા પેરાવે તસા ઉગવતો." ઉગવતો literally means germinate. It is the same as the Sanskrit saying યથાબીજં તથા અંકુર: " As the seeds so the sprout. "
સીરજોરપના is recklessness.

એ બાયકો સીરજોર ઝાલી હુએ would mean this woman has become a shrew or termagant. In that context the word does not mean reckless. સીરજોર in dictionary means head-strong etc. અધીકારી સીરજોર ઝાલા હુએ, Authorities have become *reckless*, not *domineering*. અરેરાવી અને સીરજોર would mean blustering and reckless. અરેરાવં is translated in Ex. C as high-handed and સીરજોર has not an allied meaning there. Domineering is rendered in Marathi હુકમત

ચાલવનારા not અંમલ ગાજ્વનારા. સીરજોરપના does not mean lording it over. Lording over would be અંમલ ચાલવનારા

In સાપ સાપં મનુન ભડવને the meaning of મનુન is "saying" not "mistaking" તેઓએ સાકર મનુન મીઠ ખાલી would be "he ate salt thinking it to be sugar."

ચેાર મનુન માલા મારૂ નકેા is "don't beat me thinking I am a thief." In Ex. C page 3, 8th line from the bottom the word સહઅરશમી is omitted. It means one who has thousand rays. It seems intensity of heat.

At page 4 Ex. C the word King begins with a Capital K. It may be a printer's Devil. The original words mean Ruler & Ruled.

At the bottom there is another captil K. That also is the printer's Devil. The word રાજા in the original is used as a common noun.

રાજા & પ્રજા would be king and subjects. Ruler & Ruled. રાજા does not mean many rulers.

At page 4 at the bottom the original for "means of protection" cannot be correctly translated as "means of escape or resource".

"Political science" in Marathi is રાજનીતીચે શાસ્ત્ર. It may be રાજધરમાચે શાસ્ત્ર

At page 5 in Ex. C the words " the scripture laying down the duties of kings in original are the રાજ્યધરમ શાસત્ર કંઠ રવાને સાંગત હએ. The words" It is settled conclusion of the science of politics,' can't be rightly used for the original words.

Ex. C.

In Ex. E the translation "controlled by the missionary policy" one of the meanings of the words used in the dictionary is a line of conduct.

In Ex. E રાસત્રવધ is translated as " national assassination ". રાસત્ર is nation and વધ means assassination. The word may mean "killing the nation." હુલ ઉઠવને is to raise a false report not alarm.

Dictionary gives the meaning of હુલ as alarm, out-cry.
In Ex. H. 15 lines from the bottom the word 'world' is a mistranslation. The word "world" ought to be "man" and "none" should be "he." I think the translator has misread the original.

EX. D

The original of the word "Savage" in the second para at page 2 of Ex. D is કડવા You may substitute *Harsh* for savage.

For manhood the original word is પેારૂસ manliness may be used for manhood. Apte's Dictionary gives "Manliness" as one of the meanings of પેારૂસ. Molesworth gives the correct meaning as manhood. In the sentence given to me I have translated manliness for પેારૂસ in the sentence.

I have translated the word emasculation as ખચી કરના. In the original article Ex. D the marathi words used are ખચી કરના and પૈારૂષ. They are correctly translated in the official translation as castration and manhood.

At page 2 of Ex. D the word wobbbling cannot be substituted by the word lingering.

At page 2 in the last line the word "heedlessly" is translation of બેગુમાન-પનાને in Marathi. The expression cannot be translated as "irresponsible". For ગુમાન other Marathi words are ખાતર or પરવા. It may mean heed or regard.

In બે ગુમાન I can't say whose ગુમાન is referred to.

"Migratory bureaucracy" I would translate as ઊપરી અધીકારી વરગ. The phrase occurs in Ex. D. Migratory is not the literal meaning of ઊપરી. The word migratory may do for the expression "officers having *temporary* interest in the country". The original word for *nose-string* is વેસન. The corresponding English idea is "bridle." I would translate નાહક as gratuitous. It may mean "unnecessary."

The literal meaning is *causelessly*. ખાહુન ચાહુન પરકા is devoutly or openly. It also means "goes without saying."

Ex. G.

હીતસતરૂ is one adverse to the weal of others.

તેા માઝા હીતસતરૂ હએ means, he is opposed to my weal. Indirectly it conveys a meaning that a man professing to be good does harm. The words do not convey the meaning of "a false friend." Literally rendered it is not "an enemy in the garb of a friend."

I do not know if હીત is used for a friend. It means welfare.

વકરૂદૃષ્ટી is evil glance, literally cross-glance. Its remote meaning is disfavour.

તેનચી અમચાવર વક દીરૂષ્ટી આલી હએ I would translate this as "He is looking at me with an evil glance," meaning I have incurred his displeasure. (See. Ex. G page 2 line 3.) Disfavour is a remote meaning for the word.

ગલાલા મીઠી મારણે means :—Throw arms round another man's neck. It is translated at page 2 of Ex. G line 23 as "catch by the neck." This is uncouth though correct.

After Lunch.

એક દૃષ્ટી in dictionary is translated as "of one side." This word in Ex. C is translated as autocratic. The translation is according to the context. I know how the word સનદસીર is used in the article Ex. C It means constitutionally. It is a coined word.

અડવણુક is a word with a new meaning. It meant obstruction, resistance etc. It is now used by Journalists to denote passive resistance. બહીષ્કાર is used in the sense of boycott. This is the use of this word in a new sense. These meanings can be got from the dictionaries of Candy, Molesworth or Apte. The use of these words in these meanings has come into use during recent times. Marathi is a growing language. Dictionaries would be no guides in the case of the new meanings now attaching to some of the words. Some of the old dictionaries in English would be useless in respect of words that have come into vogue in modern times. " Error of Judgment " may be translated as વીવેક વીભ્રહમ. I have not come across the word before. I coined it yesterday. Error of Judgement is an idea which so far as I know has not been expressed in one word hitherto. Some one may have expressed the idea. I don't know. બુધી is used in the sense of વીવેક in Sanskrit. According to my idea મન is different from બુધી. There is a passage in the Gita where, these two are distinguished. In the words વીવેક વીભ્રહમ instead of વીવેક-બુધી may be used. I would translate વીવેક વિભ્રહમ as " one whose Judgment is destroyed. It does not mean who has erred in his judgment. It means one whose judgment has wandered away. બુધી ભરમત refers to one whose mind has suffered aberration.

In my official capacity I have to read Marathi newspapers. I am acquainted with the general trend of Marathi newspapers. There are Marathi newspapers which are divided into parties. There are three or four parties. The Kesari is the leading exponent of one party. The Indu Prakash is the leading exponent of another party. The Sudharak is a leading paper of another party. Subodh Patrika leads a fourth party.

Re-examined by the Advocate General

The articles would be read by the ordinary readers in the way I have explained. I am satisfied that the official translations are correct except that in one place the word "world" ought to be "men". I was asked about the word stubbornness. The Marathi word is દુરાધર, This is not sufficiently strongly expressed in English. It means "obstinate extension of a wrong opinion."

"Embark" is translation for પ્રવૃત. The translation is correct. This occurs at bottom of page 2.

The word in vernacular for assassination is વધ. The translation of that word by " assassination" is quite correct. વધ is translated as killing, slaughter or assassination according to the context. The Kesari is a leading paper. It belongs to the Extremist party.

Note. The Accused at this stage volunteers a statement that he is the Editor, Proprietor and publisher of the newspaper called the Kesari and that he is responsible for all the articles put in the case Viz: Exhibits C to I.

Certified copies.

Two Declarations dated 1st July 1907 put in and marked J. colletively.

Narayan Jagannath Datar Xd. by Mr. Binning.:

I am a clerk in the Customs Reporter General's Department. On the 12 th of May and on the 19th of June last I was agent of the newspapers of the Kesari and the Maratha. I was the agent in Bombay. Off and on I was connected with the Kesari for the last 25 years. I became agent about 1900 and gave up the agency on the 4th of July this year. In May 1908 I used to get about 2800 and in June 1908 I got 3000 copies in Bombay. There are 1250 subscribers in Bombay. I read the paper myself. I read both the issues of the 12th of June last. I also read copies of the issues of the 19th of May last, 26th of May last and 2nd of June last. Copies of all these issues were sent up to the office in Bombay. Every week I supplied copies to subscribers. The subscription is Re. 1 : 12 annas per annum. The price for each copy to a non-subscriber was 3/4 of an anna. I was paid agent and got 30 Rs. a month. After supplying subscribers the other copies were sold in Bombay through newsboys.

No Cross-Examination.

Peter Sullivan: Xd.

I am Inspector of the Bombay Police. I got a warrant for execution in the case. It was for the search of the houses, press and office of the Accused. The warrant was from the Chief Presidency Magistrate. I took the warrant to Poona and it was executed by Mr. Davies, District Superintendent of Police, Poona. I was present when the warrant was executed. I was present when the Accused's house, Press and Office were searched. The search was conducted by Mr. Power, Deputy Superintendent, Mr. Daniel, Assistant Superintendent, Mr. King, the City Inspector, myself and other Native officers. Mr. Davies was there. Mr. Kelkar (this gentleman) was present. I found in the course of the search this Post card. I found this on the right hand top drawer of a writing table in a room in Mr. Tilak's residence which was apparently used as Office. When I found the card I showed it to Mr. Power and Mr. Davies. I also showed it to Mr. Kelkar. I kept the card myself. I produced it before the Magistrate in Bombay. I had it in my custody all the time. Mr. Kelkar initialled the Post card.

The Advocate General tenders the Post card.

Rex. Vs. Bernard

1 Foster & Fulayson 240,

3rd Volume Russell on Crimes. P. 386,367.

The Accused says the card was discovered behind his back.

He disputes the relevancy of its contents.

Ex. K. P. C. Admittted, Ex. K.

XXd by the Accused.

I fonud other papers in the search. I brought them to Bombay and gave them to the Magistrate. I have not brought them here. We went into several rooms. I don't know if I went into the library or not. Other papers were found in the same place where Ex. K was found. Some papers were in the same drawer as Ex. K. The drawer was not locked. It was open. I don't know if any one searched your library. The card was amongst other papers. I came to it after I had looked at some papers. The papers were taken one by one from the drawer and examined. I can't tell you how many papers were in the drawers. The drawer was practically full of papers. I have a list of all the papers I brought to Bombay. The list is included in the Panchnama. Some cuttings from American papers were found. I think they are with the Magistrate. In all there are 63 items of what was taken in the Panchnama.

WEDNESDAY 15TH JULY 1908.

Bal Gangadhar Tilak.

Continued from yesterday.

Peter Sullivan further cross-examined by the Accused. All the papers seized in the search are now here. (Accused allowed to examine all the papers received from the Chief Presidency Magistrate.)

I had been to Singhgad to search your house under the Chief Presidency Magistrate's warrant endorsed by the District Magistrate of Poona searched the residence at Singhgad. The Poona and Singhgad houses were searched under the same warrant. Singhgad was specifically mentioned by the District Magistrate. I only assisted in the execution of the warrant. I have seen the warrant. I believe the warrant was endorsed by the District Magistrate of Poona authorising search at Singhgad. The warrant is returned to the Chief Presidency Magistrate Bombay. We did not take any of your men to Singhgad. There was your watchman there. The watchman opened the house at Singhgad. The men had no keys and we broke the cupboards open. There were two cupboards in the hall. I did not inform your men at Poona that we were going to Singhgad. We got nothing at Singhgad. We left the locks as they were. The locks were not broken. We removed the hinges. We did not put things in proper order again.

(Note 1. Witness to be recalled after some of the papers which are not here are received from the Magistrate's court).

No re-examination.

The Advocate-General closes the case for the Prosecution.

Accused's statement before the Magistrate in both cases read to the Jury.

I ask the Accused if he wishes to make any statement to explain the evidence given in the case.

(Ss. 289 & 342) Cr. Pr. Code.

Accused says he will make a statement after the papers, that were taken in the search and which are not here, are produced.

(Note 2.) Papers sent by the Chief Presidency Magistate in conformity with the directions given yesterday evening, compared with the list of papers taken possession of by the Police as mentioned in the Panchnama. Papers Nos. 19 to 52 except No. 46 are not before this Court.

Peter Sullivan recalled, further xd. by the Advocate General.

I produce the original Panchnama made when the search warrants were executed. There are two search warrants that I took to Poona for execution.

Panchnama of 25th June 1908 Ex. L.

Search warrants collectively put in and marked Ex. N. (Accused desired their production and on production were inspected by him.)

Accused says all the papers are now here.

Peter Sullivan, Cross-examined by the Accused.

Some of the papers were found on the top of the writing desk and some in the drawers. Large manuscripts were on the top. Smaller papers including newspaper cuttings were found in the drawers. I can't tell as to which paper or as to where it was found. (Search warrants shown.) The search warrant for residence was endorsed by the City Magistrate at first. When I went to Poona, the District Magistrate was not at home so I took the warrants to the City Magistrate. The City Magistrate endorsed them on the 24th of June last in the evening. I went to your residence the following morning after daybreak. I did not execute the warrant. The warrant for searching residence was returned as executed on 25th of June. The Poona residence search was finished between 9 and 10 A. M. We started for Singhgad about 12 noon. Mr. Davies and Mr. Power went with me. I don't know how the endorsement of the District Magistrate came to be made. The warrant was with Mr. Davies when we went to Singhgad I saw it with him. What we took at Poona was in conformity with what was ordered by the warrant.

This bundle of papers was found either on the desk or in the drawers.

All the papers in the bundle put in and marked collectively by the Accused Ex: No I.

(Note. The Accused puts in these papers after it was explained to him by me both to-day and yesterday that he would lose his right of addressing the Jury last).

The Advocate General closes the case for the Prosecution.

Statement made by the Accused to the Committing Magistrate in both cases read to the Jury again.

Accused is asked if he wishes to make a statement.

He reads a statement in writing.

The Accused says he does not wish to adduce any evidence.

The Advocate General objects to the list annexed to the Accused's statement, says those documents mentioned are irrelevant.

Accused before addressing the Jury says he is entitled to address after the Advocate General.

Refers to a Calcutta case.

Timol's case.

Cal. W. Notes Aug. 1906.

P. C. I feel bound by the judgment of Batty J. in Emperor vs. Bhaskar.

8 Bom. Law. Rpr. 421.

Accused addresses the Jury:– 3. 35.

Attempt 8. B. L. R. p. 438.

Stephen's History of the Criminal Law Vol.II p. 221. Mayne's Criminal Law.

3 B. L. R. Ap. C. p. 55

Lord Cockburn's Law of Sedition.

Law is strict but Juries have stood between the strictness of the law and liberty of the press.

Every dictionary contains seditious words therefore the author of a dictionary would have to go to Jail.

It is necessary to direct the Jury to all the surrounding circumstances to *inculpate* the accused.

Excite, To inflame, call out. To increase or add to exciting feeling.

If twelve of his countrymen think a man has written something that is blamable then he may be convicted of sedition.

Government is defined in the Indian Penal Code and includes a Police Constable.

If a man says the Government should no longer exist he does not necessarily harbour feelings of enmity against the Government.

You are not bound to return a verdict of guilty. It is open for you to say that the evidence is insufficient and we cannot make up our minds.

Sedition does not consist in the mere act of writing. It consists of evil intention—evil mind.

You must consider that malicious intention does exist before you convict.

Mere character of writing may be some evidence of intention but is not sufficient evidence.

Inferior officers have taken a sanction to be a mandate. Juries have differed from a Judge.

A man may be an intemperate man. The language used by me may not be used by another man. There must be a distinct wicked intention.

THURSDAY 16TH JULY 1908.

Bal Gangadhar Tilak.

From yesterday.

The accused continues his address.:—

Attempt includes both intention and motive.

Jivan Dass. 39 Panjab Reports Cr. Cases P. 83 Attempting to kill.

Russell's law of Crimes P. 725.

Motive may be good but the act may be bad. Man commits theft to give the proceeds in charity.

R. Vs. Lambert 22 State Trials 985

" " State Trials 325

After lunch.

If you want to put down the bomb you must also put down the bureaucracy.

Perversity=stubborness.

Oppressive official class=Despotic bureaucracy.

FRIDAY 17TH JULY 1908.

Bal Gangddhar Tilak

Resumed from yesterday.

The accused continues his address to the Jury:-

Pioneer 7th May 1908 Cult of the Bomb.

Ex. C. alleged mistranslation.

Sorrow=Pain.

White=English.

Hatred=Disgust.

Perversity=Stubbornness, haughtiness, obstinacy.

Obstinacy=Haughtiness.

Extraordinary=Strange.

Madcap=Fanatic.

Badmash=Criminal.

Identical=Those very.

જુલમી=Oppressive official class=Arbitrary or despotic bureaucracy.
Oppressive official class=જુલમી અધીકારીવર્ગ.

2 : 30 P. M.

Both sides not objecting adjourned to Monday to enable the Jury to attend to their Mail work.

MONDAY 20TH JULY 1908.

Bal Gangadhar Tilak.

From Friday 17th instant.

Accused continues to address the Jury.

add (Treachery) add (Intention)

Assassination=Killing or murder.

ગુપ્ત ખુન વધ વધ

Mutiny—Revolt—Disturbances.

Exasperated=Excited.

Inebriated=Blinded.

Insolence of authority=Intoxication of authority.

Uncomplainingly=Ungrrudgingly.

Oppressive enactments=Repressive enactments.

Reckless =Domineering.
Movement=Agitation.
Improper=Imprudent.
Vehemence=Keenness.
Who are adverse to Government=Who are false friends of Government.

5-50 P. M,

TUESDAY 21ST JULY 1908.

Bal Gangadhar Tilak.

From yesterday.

Accused continues to address :—

Ex. D. Fiend of repression=Evil genius of repression.
False report=False cry.
Madcap patriot=Fanatic patriot.
Needlessly=Irresponsibly.

After lunch.

Punjab weekly Reporter 14. 1897.
Jeshwantrai & Athavale.

Punjab Records.
Vol. 42 No, 9 p. 23.
Sep. 1907.

Fiend=Demon.

Accused commenced addressing on Wednesday at 3 : 35

	2 hrs.
Thursday	5 hrs.
Friday	3 hrs.
Monday	5 hrs.
Tuesday	5 hrs.
Wednesday	1 hr.
	21 hours.

WEDNESDAY 22ND JULY 1906.

Bal Gangadhar Tilak.

From yesterday.

Accused continues to address the Jury :—

Section 294, 663, 708 Mayne's Criminal Law.

The Advocate General sums up for the Prosecution.

12 noon.

(1) Printing, Publication and Responsibility.

(2) What is the meaning of those articles.

(3) What was the writer's intention.

Resumed at 3 P. M.

Section 105 Evidence Act.

Advocate General concludes his address:

I sum up.

Verdict 7 to 2 on all the charges.

Majority for guilty, on all the charges.

No chance of being unanimous. *I agree with the verdict of the* majority. 1st Charge 124A Article 12th May 1908.

2nd Charge 124A Article 9 June 1908.

3rd Charge 153A Article 9 June 1908.

The Accused asks that certain points may be reserved for the consideration of the Full Bench.

Hands in a written paper stating the points he wishes to have reserved.

Application refused. Points covered by authority & too elementary to need further discussion. Most of the points were considered and discussed as the case progressed.

Accused charged with a previous conviction.

He admits the charge of previous conviction.

Sentence on the first charge Transportation for 3 years.

Sentence on the second charge Transportation for 3 years.

Sentences to run consecutively.

Sentence on the third charge 1000 Rs. Fine.

Charge under Section 153A Article 12 May 1908.

Further charge withdrawn under Section 333 Cr. Pr. Code by the Advocate General.

I discharge the Accused and direct that this discharge be tantamount to an acquittal on this charge.

Sessions dissolved.

Petition to the Full Bench.

In the High Court of Judicature at Bombay.

CROWN SIDE.

In the matter of criminal case

Emperor.

V/s.

Bal Gangadhar Tilak.

To,

The Honourable the Chief Justice and the Judges of the High Court of Judicature, Bombay.

The Petition of the above named

Bal Gangadhar Tilak

sentenced to transporation but now incarcerated in the Sabarmati Central Jail at Ahmedabad.

SHOWETH :—

1. (*a*). That on the 24th day of June 1908, your petitioner was arrested in Bombay in pursuance of a Warrant issued by the Chief Presidency Magistrate of Bombay and committed to prison.

(*b*). That on the 25th day of June 1908 your petitioner was placed before the said Magistrate upon a complaint of having committed offences punishable under Sections 124 A and 153 A, of the Indian Penal Code, in respect of an article entitled, " The Country's Misforune " printed in the issue of a weekly Marathi Journal styled the " Kesari " for the 12th day of May, 1908.

(*c*). That on the said 25th day of June 1908 the learned Magistrate recorded some evidence against your petitioner and remanded him to prison, bail being objected to by the Prosecution and refused by the Magistrate.

(*d*). That on the 29th day of June 1908 certain further evidence was recorded by the Magistrate against your petitioner and he was thereafter charged by the Magistrate with offences under Sections 124A and 153A of the Indian Penal Code and committed to the Criminal Sessions of this Honourable Court to be tried on the said charges. A copy of the said charges is hereto annexed and marked **A.**

(*e*). That this case eventually appeared as case No. 16 in the list of cases put up for trial before the third Criminal Sessions of this Honourable Court.

2 (*a*). That on the 27th day of June 1908 your petitioner, while still in custody, was served with another warrant issued by the Chief Presidency Magistrate, Bombay.

(*b*). That on the 29th day of June 1908 your petitioner was placed betore the said Magistrate upon a second complaint of having committed other offences punishable under Sections 124A and 153A of the Indian Penal Code in respect of an article entitled, "These remedies are not lasting" printed in the issue of the "Kesari" of the 9th day of June 1908.

(*c*). That on the said 29th day of June 1908 the learned Magistrate instituted a separate inquiry into the complaint, recorded certain evidence against your petitioner and thereupon charged the prisoner with the offences under Sections 124A and 153A of the Indian Penal Code and made a separate commitment to the Criminal Sessions of this Honourable Court to be tried on the said charges. A copy of the said charges is hereto annexed and marked **B.**

(*d*). That the case eventually appeared as case No. 17 in the list of cases put up for trial before the 3rd Criminal Sessions of this Honourable Court.

3. That on the 2nd day of July 1908 your petitioner applied for bail through Counsel, to enable him to prepare for his defence, to the Honourable Mr. Justice Davar who presided at the 3rd Criminal Sessions of this Hanourable Court, but the application was opposed by the Prosecution and refused by the learned Judge for reasons, which he said, he did not desire to disclose as they might prejudice your petitioner; but thereby the learned Judge prejudiced your petitioner much more seriously than could be possible by any disclosure of the reasons.

4. That on the 3rd day of July 1908 the Crown applied for a Special Jury in each of the cases Nos. 16 and 17 but your petitioner opposed it on the ground *inter alia* that a Special Jury would under existing circumstances be composed of a majority of Europeans, not conversant with the Marathi language, and thereby deprive him of the benefit of a Jury of his countrymen who know the language in which the articles were written; but the objection was overruled and a Special Jury was granted to the prejudice of the Defence.

5. That your petitioner through Counsel in open Court offered to waive his objection and accept a Special Jury instead of a Common Jury provided it was composed of Jurymen acquainted with the Marathi language, but the said offer was rejected by the Prosecution.

6. That the above two cases Nos. 16 and 17 came on for trial before the Honourable Mr. Justice Davar, one of the Judges of this Honourable Court, on the 13th day of July 1908 at the 3rd Criminal Sessions of the High Court, when your petitioner appeared in person and was undefended.

7. That on the said 13th day of July 1908 the Honourable the Acting Advocate General proposed that your petitioner be tried at one and the same trial upon all charges contained in the two committals under Sections 234 and 235 of the Criminal Procedure Code, but upon His Lordship observing that the two cases could not be consolidated as there were four charges, the learned Advocate General declared that he proposed not to put the Accused up upon the second charge with reference to the article in case No. 16 i. e. charge under Section 153 A. of the Indian Penal Code.

8. That your petitioner objected to the amalgamation of the two cases and the trial at one trial of the three charges, charging him with distinct offences as the procedure was prohibited by the express provisions of Sec. 233 of the Criminal Procedure Code and also objected that such a joinder of charges was calculated to embarrass and prejudice him in his defence and cause confusion; and he even went to the length of expressing his inability to conduct the defence of all the three charges together, but his objection was over-ruled.

9. That His Lordship doubted the applicability of Section 235 but expressed his willingness to order one trial under Section 234 provided one of the four charges was omitted, intimating at the same time that he would direct that the discharge upon that charge should amouut to an acquittal and, leaving it to the Advocate-General to make his choice.

10. That thereupon the learned Advocate-General expressed his apprehension that such an order "might lead to a serious question whether it does not amount to "*autrefois acquit*" and asked his Lordship "not to pass such order till the case is over."

11. That thereupon the following dialogue ensued between the learned Judge and the learned Advocate-General.

His Lordship :—"That could not affect the other charges on the other articles. It will apply to this article on which you propose to hold over the charge. That would not affect the other charges."

Advocate General :—"I can see perfectly well how it may be ingeniously argued that it can. That is why I ask your Lordship not to pass such order till the case is over."

His Lordship :—" Have you to make the application before the case is over or after ? "

Advocate General :—" I have made the application, so far as it is an application now I am not applying. I am stating that it is my proposal to put the Accused upon three separate charges. "

His Lordship :—" So long as there are only three charges I order that the charges be tried at one trial. You will undertake, Mr. Advocate-General, to apply for the stay and that such stay shall be final. "

Advocate-General :—" I simply undertake that I will not further prosecute. I am entitled to do that.

His Lordship :—" That will be the application.

Advocate-General :—" Yes, when the three charges are over I shall tell the Court as I have already adumbrated before the Court that I do not intend to proceed further. "

His Lordship :—" My present order then will be that the Accused will be tried on three charges, that is, one charge in case No. 16 and two charges in case No. 17. "

12. That after the above order was passed by His Lordship the Clerk of the Crown read to your petitioner all the four charges against him in both the cases Nos. 16 and 17.

13. That upon the said charges being read your petitioner complained that the charges did not give sufficient notice of the matter with which he was charged in not specifying the alleged seditious passages for the purposes of Section 124 A. of the Indian Penal Code and the particulars of the manner in which he committed the offence under Section 153 A. of the I. P. Code.

14. That the Counsel for Prosecution thereupon proposed that the whole article be inserted in the charge, but your petitioner objected to the course as insufficient to cure the defect and supply omission complained of.

15. That His Lordship thereupon observed as follows:- "If you think you have not sufficient notice of what you are charged with, Mr. Inverarity will put in the whole article. He is entitled to do that. I cannot judge at this moment which are the seditious passages."

16. That His Lordship finally ordered that the whole of the articles be set forth in the charges themselves.

17. That accordingly the indictments were amended by inserting therein English translations of the Marathi articles made by the

High Court Translator. A copy of the said charges as amended is hereto annexed and marked C collectively.

18. That thereafter the Clerk of the Crown read to your petitioner all the four amended charges and was asked wether he pleaded guilty to these four charges or claimed to be tried.

19. That your petitioner claimed to be tried whereupon a Special Jury was empanelled, composed of seven Europeans and two Parsees.

20 That your petitioner was thereafter and on the 14th, 15th, 16th, 17th, 20th, 21st and 22nd day of July tried by the Honourable Mr. Justice Davar and the Special Jury.

21. That your petitioner believes that only three charges were read to the Jury, namely the first charge under Section 124A I. P. Code in case No 16, and two charges under sections 124 A and 153 A of the I. P. Code. in case No. 17.

22. That in the course of the said trial certain other articles appearing in the issues of the " Kesari" for the 19th and 26th May 1908 and 2nd June and 9th June 1908, being Exhibits E. to J. and a post card Exhibit K. found on the said Prisoner's premises during the Police search were tendered in evidence by the prosecution for the purposes of showing the animus and intention of the said prisoner in publishing the articles forming the subject matter of the charges.

23. That your petitioner objected to the admissibility of these Exhibits for the purposes for which they were tendered but the said objection was overruled. Your petitioner submits that the reception of the said articles in evidence practically formed fresh subject matter of the charges and greatly prejudiced him in his trial.

24. That on the 22nd day of June 1908 His Lordship summed up the evidence in the case. A copy of the said summing up is hereto appended and marked with the letter D.

25. That on the 22nd day of July 1908 at 9-30 P. M. your petitioner was found guilty by a majority of seven to two on each of the said three charges and the learned Judge agreed with the opinion of the majority.

26. That thereupon the learned Advocate-General informed the Court that he would not further prosecute your petitioner upon the charge held over under Section 153 A. of the I. P. Code with reference to case No. 16

27. That thereupon the learned Advocate-General proposed to prove tha previous conviction under Section 124 A. I. P. Code for the purpose of enhancing the sentence.

28. That your petitioner objected to the course upon the ground that the previous conviction was not specified and did not form part of the charge, and that such conviction did not come within the scope of Section 75 of the Indian Penal Code but the said objection was overruled.

29. That your petitioner was thereupon questioned by the Clerk of the Crown whether he admitted the previous conviction under Section 124A. of the Indian Penal Code and the said prisoner answered in the affirmative.

30. That thereupon the learned Judge sentenced your petitioner to three years' transportation upon the first charge under Section 124 A. I. P. Code to three years' transportation upon the second charge under Section 124 A. I. P. Code, and to a fine of Rs. 1000/—upon the charge under Section 153 A. I. P. Code, the sentences to run consecutively and directed that the discharge with reference to the charge under Section 153 A. I. P. Code in case No. 16 should amonnt to an acquittal.

31. That before the sentence was pronounced your petitioner applied to the said learned Judge under section 434 of the Criminal Procedure Code to reserve the points enumerated in the annexture E. for the decision of this Honourable Court consisting of two or more Judges of this Honourable Court, but his Lordship refused to reserve any point whatever.

32. That your petitioner submits as follows :—

(*a*). That the learned Judge erred in refusing bail to the prejudice of your petitioner.

(*b*). That the learned Judge erred in granting a Special Jury to the prejudice of your petitioner or at least in not ordering that it should consist of Marathi knowing persons.

(*c*). That the learned Judge erred in consolidating the two Cases Nos. 16 and 17 founded on separate commitments to the prejudice of your petitioner.

(*d*). That the Court acted ultra vires in taking cognizance of offences punishable under Sections 124A. and 153 A. without having in evidence any complaint made by order of the Local Government and without examining the complainant.

(*e*). That the terms of Exhibit B, being the order of the Local Government are insufficient in Law to authorise a complaint under Section 153 A. I. P. C. so as to enable the Court to take cognizance of the same.

(*f*). That the charges as framed were bad being founded not upon the words used by your petitioner but upon inaccurate and misleading English translations of those words thereby prejudicing your petitioner.

(*g*). That the charges as framed were bad as they did not contain particulars of the manner in which the alleged offences were committed, and did not give sufficient and express notice of the matter with which your petitioner was charged and did not specify the persons or classes against whom the offence under Section 153 A. was comitted, thereby prejudicing him in his defence. That each of the charges as framed is illegal being contrary to the provisions of Section 233 of Cri. Pr. Code.

(*h*). That the learned Judge acted illegally in trying your petitioner at one and the same trial for at least three offences, not of the same kind and not committed in the same transaction, contrary to the express provisions of Section 233 of the Cr. Pro. Code and in opposition to your petitioner's objection thereby vitiating the whole trial and rendering it illegal null and void—ab initio.

(*i*). That the learned Judge acted ultra vires in passing an order before the commencement of the trial staying proceedings upon one of the four charges without acting under Section 273 of the Cr. Pro. Code.

(*j*). That the trial and conviction upon the English words charged but not proved and not used by your petitioner renders the trial null and void and the conviction illegal.

(*k*). That the words charged were not proved and that your petitioner did not use the English words charged and he ought therefore to have been acquitted.

(*l*). That the learned Judge erred in admitting as evidence Exhibits E. to I. and Exhibit K. to the prejudice of your petitioner.

(*m*). That the learned Judge erred in admitting in evidence the official translations of th3 incriminating articles, Exhibits C. and D, without being proved by the translator and without submitting him for cross-examination, though your petitioner asked that he should be called as witness by the Prosecution.

(*n*). That the learned Judge erred in ruling that your Petitioner lost his right of reply merely for filing Exhibit I. containing papers found by the Police during search with the exception of exhibit K. which the Prosecution tendered in evidence.

(*o*). That your petitioner had a right to rely on the papers accompanying his statement made on the close of the case for the Prosecution.

(p.) that the learned Judge acted illegally in permitting the Crown to prove previous cnviction under Section 124 A. I. P. C. for the purposes of enhancing the sentence.

(q.) That the learned Judge erred in taking the previous conviction into consideration for the purposes of enhancing the sentence, as is evident from his remarks in passing sentence, copy of which is hereto annexed and marked with the letter F.

(r.) That the learned Judge acted illegally in passing two sentences under Section 124 A. I. P. C. and one under section 153 A. I. P. C if it be held by the Court that the transaction is one and the same; but your petitioner submits that the transaction is not the same as ruled by the learned Judge.

(s.) That the learned Judge acted illegally in passing two sentences, one under section 124 A I. P. C. and the other under Section 153 A. I. P. C. in case No. 17 upon one article and the one and the same act.

(t.) That the learned Judge erred in construing the explanations to Section 124 A. I. P. C. as equivalent to exceptions, thereby seriously restricting the scope of the Freedom of speech and Liberty of the Press, and erroneously placing the onus of proof on your petitioner to the prejudice of his defence.

(u.) That the learned Judge erred in construing the word 'attempt' in Section 124 A. I. P. C. as equivalent to its ordinary meaning and not the legal meaning.

(v.) That the learned Judge erred in accepting the verdict of the Jury which does not specify to what part of the charge under Section 124 A. the verdict relates.

(w.) That the learned Judge erred in not explaining the law properly and correctly to the Jury especially the words "attempt" and "government as established by law in British India".

(x.) That the sentences are too severe.

33. That in the course of his charge to the Jury the learned Judge inter alia directed, and as your Petitioner is advised misdirected, the Jury as follows:—

34. (a) That the learned Judge did not direct the Jury that a specific intention to bring the Government established by Law in British India into hatred or contempt, or to excite disaffection against the said Government, was necessary to constitute an attempt within the meaning of the words as used in Sec. 124 A.

(b) That the learned Judge practically directed to the effect that a specific intention was immaterial e. g. " However you may assume, if you like, that these people knew the *purpose* for which these articles were written as explained by the accused. " " No motive, no honest intention can justify a breach of that Law. "

(c) that the learned Judge directed the Jury to the effect that the mere use of language calculated to excite feelings of disloyalty, contempt or hatred against the Government established by Law in British India was sufficient to constitute the offence of Sedition under Section 124 A. e. g. :—" A. great deal has been said on both sides as to intention and motive. The Law with reference to intention and with reference to the fact whether it is true or not is crystalised; (here Reads from Mayne " since the crime " down to " the truth of the argument. ") Well, Gentleman, we are here as Judge and Jury to decide whether the writings of the accused have excited or were likely to excite feelings of hatred and contempt and disloyalty against the Government. Now it is impossible to prove that by evidence. If we call one hundred men belonging to one side, for instance, that of the accused, they will say that the articles do not produce any feelings against Government; indeed that they promote love to Government. One hundred men on the other side would say the opposite. It would be impossible for the Prosecution to bring any evidence on this point. *The test you have to apply* is to look at the various articles and Judge of them as a whole, to Judge of the effect it would produce on your own minds in the first instance, to judge whether they are calculated to produce feelings of disloyalty and hatred against Government, to judge whether language like this is not calculated to excite Hindus against Englishmen or Englishmen against Hindus. You Judge it by your own common sense. One thing you must keep before your mind. Violence and disorder and murder cannot take place without feelings of hatred, contempt and violence and enmity towards those who are responsible for the good Government of the country. If we have violence and murder they are the acts of people who bear hatred towards the ruling classes. It must be so. If these people have proper feelings for the Government and for the people who are responsible for the safety of property, and safety of the subjects, there would be no trouble, no bomb-throwing. (2.) " No motive, no honest intention can justify a breach of that Law ....we are not concerned with motives, but only with what has been written......If you think that these are calculated to give rise in the minds of readers to the feelings of hatred or contempt against Government......then it will be your duty to consider whether that is no transgression of the Law. "

(*d.*) That the learned Judge directed the Jury that a man must be taken to intend the natural and reasonable consequences of his act. It is submitted that this rule or maxim has no application where no consequences have as a matter of fact ensued as in the present case.

(*e.*) That the learned Judge directed—" A man is supposed to attempt something which would be the natural and reasonable consequence of his act. "

(*f.*) That the learned Judge directed that —"With reference to the word attempt, Gentleman, you have to take it in the ordinary meaning which attaches to the word attempt. " It is submitted that the legal meaning should be taken and not the ordinary meaning.

(*g.*) That the learned Judge directed—" No motive, no honest intention can justify a breach of the Law......we are not concerned with motives......we are not concerned with the truth or untruth of the writings. The truth may sometimes be perverted. True or not it is not for you to Judge. ". It is submitted that truth or honest motives should not have been entirely excluded from consideration and are useful means to enable Juries to determine whether the intention is criminal or innocent.

(*h.*) That the learned Judge drew no distinction between intention and motive and in consequence the Jury must have been misled, and confused intention with motive by the learned Judge's direction regarding motives.

(*i.*) The learned Judge directed that-" Section 153 A. is a simple section.........It only means that no subject of the Crown is entitled to write or say or do anything whereby the feelings of one class would be influenced against another class of His Majety's Subjects." It is submitted that malice is essential.

(*j.*) That the learned Judge ought to have directed that political parties are not classes within the meaning of Section 153 A. I. P. C. nor can Bureaucracy form a class under Section 153 A. 1. P. C. or be deemed Government under section 124 A. I. P. C.

(*k.*) That the learned Judge directed that " When an accused person is charged with attempting to excite feelings against the Government and other articles are put in for the purpose of showing intention and the individual is desirous of refuting this contention, the articles which tend to confirm the subjuct matter of the charge may be considered as there may be other things which throw light on the question whether they are calculated to raise feelings of disaffection. For instance in Exhibit 9 page 2, you will find (reads the

"Bengales continued agitation"........... down to "National Regeneration"). It is a perfectly proper sentence; you can find no fault with it. But look what follows—(Reads down to "honour of their women")......... ......Is it fair? Is it not a charge against

Government of inciting Mahomedans for the most improper purposes to attack the Bengalees, loot their property and violate their women ....Would anybody after reading that have any respect for Government or would not the feelings be those of hatred and contempt and disloyalty?"

35. That the learned Judge exceeded all reasonable limits and misdirected the Jury in charging them as follows:—

(*a*). "Accused has told you that he was carrying on an open constitutional fight," down to "whether the effect of these articles is to make you believe that bomb-throwing is a proper means of obtaining greater rights and privileges it is for you you to say." (See p—of summing up.)

(*b*). "The Accused had made complaints about the translations. Mr. Joshi was submitted to a long cross-examination.................... They were the translations of the responsible Translator of the High Court who would not be the Translator and Interpreter to the Court unless he were an efficient man capable of translating correctly"...... etc, etc., down to "You have to consider what effect these writings would have on those people...articles read by a large and promiscuous body of readers, and then say what would be the effect on their minds. You have to remember that those readers have not had the advantage of 21 hours and 10 minutes explanation which the Accused has offered on those articles". It is submitted that the majority of the Jury being Europeans it was necessary to explain the articles at length, but it is not correct to say that 21 hours and 10 minutes were devoted to this explanation.

36. That your petitioner ought to have called the attention of the Jury to the said Petitioner's contention that his articles were intended as an answer to the outrageous charges prefered against the Indian people and their leaders by the Auglo—Indian Press and to press upon Government the futility of mere repressive measures unaccompanied by substantial political concessions.

37. That your petitionsr is advised and verily believes that in addition to the specific instances above mentioned the learned Judge also misdirected the Jury upon other points, and that if the learned Judge had not so misdirected the Jury, the majority of the Jury would not have found a verdict against your petitioner.

38. That the learned Judge erred in practically directing the Jury that " the spoke in the wheel of the administration " could be nothing else than the Bomb.

39. That your petitioner thereafter through his Solicitor, Mr. B. Raghavaya, applied on the 1st day of August 1908 to the Honourable the Advocate General for a certificate under Section 26 of the Letters Patent, but the Honourable the Acting Advocate General declined on the same date to grant it.

40. Your petitioner therefore humbly prays that your Lordship will be pleased to declare under clause 41 of the Letters Patent that this case is a fit one for appeal in His Majesty's Council.

And your petitioner, as in duty bound, will for ever pray.

(Sd.) Raghavaya Bhimji and Nagindas
Petitioner's Attorneys.

I Bal Gangadhar Tilak, the petitioner, above named do solemnly declare and say that what is stated in the foregoing petition is true to the best of my information and belief.

Solemnly declared at Sabarmati Central Prison, this 7th day of August 1908.

(Sd.) Bal Gangadhar Tilak.

Before me

Court fee Stamp one Rupee

(Sd.) Nanavati
City Magistrate
Ahmedabad
7-8-08.

First Class Magistrate Seal. Ahmedabad.

7-8-08
Superintendent
Ahmedabad Central Prison.

It may be mentioned here that soon after the end of the sessions trial an application was made by Mr. Raghavaya, Solicitor for Mr. Tilak, to Mr. Branson, Advocate General, substantially in the same terms as the above application to the Chief Justice, praying for a certificate that owing to certain law points in the case being wrongly decided by the Judge and owing to misdirections given by him to the Jury the present was a fit case for appeal to the Full Bench of the Bombay High Court. But Mr. Branson refused the application nearly in the terms of the prayer itself without giving any reasons.

The High Court Appeal.

Application for a *Rule Nisi.*

On Tuesday 18th August Mr. Joseph Baptista made an application in the first Division Court, on the Appellate side of the High Court, before the Hon'ble Mr. Justice Scott, Chief Justice, and the Hon'ble Mr. Justice Batchelor.

Mr. Joseph Baptista, instructed by Messrs. Raghawaya Bhimji and Nagindas and Mr. R. P. Karandikar High Court Pleader stated that he appeard on behalf of Mr. Bal Gangadhar Tilak, who was sentenced at the last Criminal Sessions of the High Court to six years' transportation and a fine of Rs. 1000 for sedition by the Hon'ble Mr. Justice Dinshah Davar, the presiding Judge. He applied for further directions in the matter of the petition presented on behalf of the accused to the Judges of the High Court throuth the Clerk of the Crown.

Mr. Baptista said that he had applied to their Lordships for a declaration under the Letters Patent that this was a fit case for appeal to the Privy Council. They had applied for the certificate, and they were told by the Clerk of the Crown to make the application to the First Division Bench. Mr. Baptista then read the letter received from the Clerk of the Crown and said that on the last occasion when the accused was tried for sedition and convicted, a Full Bench was constituted, notice was issued by the Clerk of the Crown and the matter was argued. In the present case they were directed to go to the First Division Court.

The Chief Justice said that on the Criminal Side of the Court of Appeal when an application was made, if the Court thought fit, a rule or notice was issued and that rule or notice was served through the Court.

Mr. Baptista :—Then I shall have to make an application to your Lordships.

Chief Justice :—You can make it by this petition.

Mr. Baptista :—Would I be in order if I present it now ?

Chief Justice :—Yes.

Chief Justice :—On what points do you require the rule?

Mr. Baptista :—The points on which I rely can be devided into two parts. The first relates to the points of law mentioned in paragraph 32 of the petition and the second relates to misdirections mentioned in paras. 33, 34 35 and 36.

Chief Justice :—But you must show us some cause why the rule should be granted.

Mr. Baptista said that he was not prepared to argue the points and he would like to have some time to consider. He had really come for further directions in the matter of the petition. He might, however, mention one point. The Accused was tried and convicted on the two articles of the 12th May and 9th June which were two distinct transactions, and the learned Sessions Judge had also held that they were two distinct transactions. In the trial there was a combination of the three charges, two under section 124 A of the Indian Penal Code and one under section 153 A. Thus there was a combination of three offences not of the same kind and under the provisions of sections 233 and 234 of the Criminal procedure Code those charges could not be tried together at one and the same time.

Chief Justice :—Is that the only point you wish to urge?

Mr. Baptista said that was only one of his points.

The Hon'ble Mr. Branson, Advocate General, here rose up and said that that very point was argued at full length in another Division Court and it was but fair that his learned friend ought to have mentioned it to the Court.

Mr. Baptista said that he had not yet finished his arguments.

Chief Justice :—We can't issue a rule as a matter of course; if you want time to consider you can have the time.

Mr. Baptista :—I would ask your Lordships to give me some time.

Chief Justice :—You might again mention it on Thursday next.

Mr. Baptista said that Thusday was too short a time.

Chief Justice :—Would you be ready on Monday?

Mr. Baptista said that he would like to have e week.

Chief Justice :—Would you be ready then ?

Mr. Baptista replied in the affirmative, and their Lordships fixed Tuesday 25th August for the hearing of the arguments.

Preliminary Hearing of the Argument for a *Rule Nisi.*

In the Bombay High Court, on Tuesday 25th August before the Hon. Mr. Basil Scott, Chief Justice, and the Hon. Mr. Justice Batchelor, application was made by Mr. Joseph Baptista, Barrister at Law (Cantab) instructed by Mr. Raghavaya, Solicitor, and Mr. K. P. Karandikar, High Court Pleader for the granting of a Rule directed to the Crown to show cause why a certificate should not be issued to Bal Gangadhar Tilak, (who had been tried and convicted in the last Criminal Sessions, under Sections 124 A and 153 A of the Penal Code, by the Hon. Mr. Justice Davar and a Special Jury,) that his was a fit case to go in appeal before His Majesty's Privy Council in England. The application was made ' ex parte ' on Tuesday 18th August and postponed to 25th to allow Mr. Baptista opportunity to prepare his arguments.

On the Court assembling the Chief Justice addressing Mr. Baptista asked:—

Do you apply for the rule now?

Mr. Baptista—: Yes, My Lord. I apply now for a rule by which your Lordship will declare that this is a fit case to go to His Majesty's Privy Council under chapter XIV of the Letters Patent.

Chief Justice:—On what grounds do you apply for the rule?

Mr. Baptista:—The points divide themselves into two parts, the first part relates to points of misdirection to the Jury. The points of law are enumerated in para 32 of the petition at page 5.

Chief Justice:—Have you selected any points ? The other side may want to argue them.

Mr. Baptista:—We are anxious to argue all the points, but I may mention what our chief points are.

Chief Justice:—You had better mention the chief points.

Mr. Baptista:— The first of my chief points is that the consolidation of the two different commitals into one is illegal. By the consolidation of the four different charges four distinct charges for four offences were tried at one trial. The dropping of one of the four charges, I argue, is also illegal.

Chief Justice:—Where is that point in the petition?

Mr. Baptista:—It arises from the consolidation of the charges and is mentioned in para 32 (I) at page 6.

Chief Justice:—What is your next point ?

Mr. Baptista:—That the adding of a fresh charge, that of previous conviction under Section 75, was illegal.

Chief Justice:—What point is that ?

Mr. Baptista:—Legally a fresh charge cannot be added.

Chief Justice:—What are the facts of the fresh charge; are they set out in the petition?

Mr. Baptista:—Para 27, my Lord, sets it out and para 28 refers to the grounds of objection that were raised on the occasion.

Chief Justice:—What really happened ?

Mr. Baptista:—After the verdict was returned by the Jury the learned Advocate-General asked that the accused be put up on a fresh charge under section 310 of the C. P. C. for the purpose of enhancement of punishment. In the report of the proceedings which accompanies this petition the detailed facts are mentioned at page 13. We will give your Lordship the detailed report of the proceedings which took place at the Sessions Court. (Reports handed up.)

Chief Justice:—Has this been checked by the Judge ? Is it the official record?

Mr. Baptista:—No, My Lord, they are the reports of the proceedings taken down by the shorthand writer for the defence where they can be found.

Chief Justice:—The Judge's notes are the only notes that we can accept. There is, I believe, a ruling to that effect; that where a Judge's notes differ from other notes, the Judge's notes were to be preferred to the others.

Mr. Baptista:—I am aware of the ruling, My Lord; we do not think we were entitled to ask the Judge to revise the report; we shall do so now.

Chief Justice:—I understand you to say that after the verdict of the Jury was returned the learned Advocate-General proposed to put him up on a fresh charge?

Mr. Baptista:—Yes, the charge was made under Section 310 and was reduced to writing on the application of the Advocate-General and I contend that it forms a fourth charge. The charge is dated 22nd July whereas the trial commenced on the 13th July. The charge was read to the accused after the return of the verdict by the Jury and he was asked to plead to it. He objected to the addition of the fresh charge; he was over-ruled and he was told that he must plead or the previous conviction would be proved. He ultimately pleaded to the effect that he was guilty.

Chief Justice:—He pleaded that he was guilty ?

Mr. Baptista:—What he said, My Lord, was, (Reads from report) "I take it that Your Lordship thinks that at the present stage it is rightly put in here ?" and his Lordship affirming, accused said "In that case I admit it."

Chief Justice:—He admitted the previous conviction ?

Mr. Baptista:—Yes, My Lord.

Chief Justice:—Do you say that is illegal ?

Mr. Baptista:—I contend it is illegal under Section 75 in this case.

Chief Justice:—Was it under Section 75 ?

Mr. Baptista:—It could only be under Section 75 for the purpose of enhancement of sentence.

Chief Justice:—Was it said to be under Section 75 by the Advocate-General?

Mr. Baptista:—No, My Lord, the Advocate-General applied under Section 310 C. P. C.

Chief Justice:—We have two points now; what is your next point. ?

Mr. Baptista:—The joinder of charges. The point of joinder of charges is divided into two parts; one, the consideration at the same trial of more than three offences not of the same kind, as under Sections 233, 235 and 236. Section 233 explains the clauses; and 2nd misjoinder of charges in this sense that two charges of the same kind are charged as two different offences. What I contend is that the misjoinder exists in that the substantive offence and the attempt to commit the offence are wrongly joined. This is illegal and bad law under the code.

Chief Justice:—Under what section do you say this is bad ?

Mr. Baptista:—Under Section 233.

Chief Justice:—What is your next point?

Mr. Baptista:—That the sanction of Government is insufficient in as much as it does not comply with the requirements of section 196 C. P. C. That is referred to in para 32 (*e.*) (*f.*) (*g.*)

Chief Justice:—What is your point on the subject of Government sanction to prosecute?

Mr. Baptista:—What happend in this case was that Government ordered Mr. Gell, Police Commissioner of Bombay, to make the complaint under Section 124 A and left it to the Commissioner to make the charge under section 153 A or not according to his discretion. I shall read the order to your Lordship (reads order). I submit that the sanction of Government is insufficient as the terms of Section 196 do not authorise anyone to lay a complaint under Section 153 A, unless specifically set out in the sanction to prosecute as applied to the terms of Section 196. Even the ' classes ' was left to the Commissioner to decide under S. 153 A.

Chief Justice:—Let me see the sanction.

Mr. Baptista:—Your Lordship will see that there is no sanction to prosecute under Section 153 A., I. P. C. inside the terms of Section 196 of the Criminal Procedure Code.

Chief Justice:—How does that arise ?

Mr. Baptista:—I submit that the terms of order do not authorise anyone to complain under Section 153 A. specifically. No one was authorised or bound to make a complaint under the inadequate directions contained in the sanction.

Chief Justice:—I do not understand your point.

Mr. Baptista:—I contend that the sanction itself does not run in the terms of the Section 196 C. P. C. to prosecute under Section 153 A or not. It is Government that ought to determine the Section on which the sanction is given to prosecute.

Chief Justice:—But the Act does not say so.

Mr. Baptista:—It means that the Government should give authority to sanction under a certain Section just as they gave sanction to prosecute under Section 124 A. but the sanction leaves it open to the discretion of the Commissioner of Police to prosecute under Section 153 A. or not. Again the condition does not specify the classes to the Commissioner of Police who delegates it no doubt to Mr. Sloane who made the complaint.

Chief Justice:—Have you any authority on the point?

Mr. Baptista:—I shall argue on the words of the Section. There is no complaint in Case No. 17.

Chief Justice:—Was the complaint made by Government?

Mr. Baptista:—It was not in evidence during the trial.

Chief Justice:—You have to show that it was not made!

Mr. Baptista:— There is no evidence; there was no complaint before the Sessions Court and there was no complaint in evidence in the Magistrate's Court.

Chief Justice:—In that case how could the Magistrate have taken any cognisance without a complaint? Surely you do not suppose the Magistrate would take cognisance without sanction?

Mr. Baptista:—I presume there must have been sanction before the Police officer could file an information and the warrant be issued.

Chief Justice:—What is your next point?

Mr. Baptista:—My next point, My Lord,is the meaning of the term "Government, as established by law in British India."

Chief Justice:—What part of your petition are you now on?

Mr. Baptista:—So far all this is on the point of law and not on the point of direction.

Chief Justic:—Where is it referred to in the petition?

Mr. Bptista:— In para 32(W)

Chief Justice:—What is your point about the meaning of the words "Government established by law in British india?"

Mr. Baptista:—The Limited Monarchy of England. Not necessarily the Government of India. It means, I contend it is, the Limited Monarchy of England as comprised by the King and the Parliament and the Lords and the Commons, not the executive Government.

Chief Justice:—Where do you say there is misdirection on that to the Jury?

Mr. Baptista:—The Judge did not explain the term to the Jury; he said that there was no question but that Government referred to was the Government established by law in British India, or the Britsh Government whichever you like to call it.

Chief Justice:—Do you take exception to that?

Mr. Baptista:—Yes, it would amount to misdirection. He maintains that the Government established by Law is the Monarchy of England as represented by the King, Lords and Commons. The learned Judge omitted to signify the specification of Government established by Law in British India.

Chief Justice:—Your next point?

Mr. Bapsista:—Under Section 124 A there are three explanations; these have been treated by the learned Judge as if they were exceptions instead of explanations defining the scope of the Section. Section 124 A has two explanations for the purpose of explaining what is meant by the Section. His Lordship said they were not exceptions under which a party could derive benefit by bringing himself within any of the explanations.

Chief Justice:—How is it shown? I want you to show me whether there is any thing the Judge has said which bears that out.

Mr. Baptista:—The Advocate General said the onus of proof rests with us.

Chief Justice:—You said that the learned Judge treated the explanations as if they were exceptions; where is that stated in the petition ?

Mr. Baptista:—No; it is in the statement of objections.

Chief Justice:—We have the corrected shorthand notes of the Judge's summing-up before us. I will read you the portion on the points. (Reads portion of summing-up relating to privilege of publicists to criticise the acts of Government.) As yours are shorthand notes also, I take it that they are the same.

Mr. Baptista:—The learned Judge charges the Jury there, as if it comes within the explanation. What we contend is that you can go beyond that and you may attack the constitution of Government itself so long as you do not bring it into contempt or hatred. That would be permissible although it did not come within the explanation. We say we are at liberty to go beyond the explanation and attack not only the measures of Government but the constitution of Government itself provided we do not go beyond the Section itself and that the motive was good.

Chief Justice:—Is there anything in the Charge which shows what you say?

Mr. Baptista:—The learned Judge said that the explanation provided for the liberty of the Press, on condition that one remained within the exception itself. On the contrary the Advocate General urged that under Section 105 of the Evidence Act the burden of proving the innocence of the Accused was thrown upon the defence. This was not proper and his Lordship failed to correct this statement of the learned Advocate-General.

Chief Justice:—What is your next point?

Mr. Baptista:—With regard to the inadmissibility of the post card (Exhibit 'K') referred to in Para 22 and 23 of page 4 of the petition. I may mention that Exhibit 'K' is not in reference to any of the charges. It contained the names of books required to study in order to properly criticise the provisions of the Explosives Act.

Chief Justice:—What did the Judge say about it?

Mr. Baptista:—This is what the Judge says:—(Reads from summing-up of the Judge) He gives his opinion to the Jury but he is constantly telling the Jury that they must not be influenced by what he says but that they must judge for themselves. This inadmissibility relates to Exhibits E to J as well as to 'K'.

Chief Justice:—Were they used in the trial?

Mr. Baptista:—Yes, My Lord, very much used. There were other articles which appeared in the *Kesari* which were used to show criminal intention.

Chief Justice:—Do you say that is inadmissible?

Mr. Baptista:—They are used as substantive charges. The learned Judge asked the Jury to look at these articles and say what would be the effect of these articles on the minds of the readers.

Chief Justice:—I think it has been very often held that other articles may be used to prove intention.

Mr. Baptista:—I shall not labour the point, My Lord, I simply want to call attention to it. The learned Judge went beyond that and told the Jury to consider what would be the effect of these articles on the minds of the readers. This is what he says:—(Reads from Judge's Charge to the Jury).

Chief Justice:—Is he referring to other articles than those in the substantive charges.

Mr. Baptista:—Yes, My Lord!

Chief Justice:—How do you make that out?

Mr. Baptista:—Because there is only one article charged under section 153 A. There are two articles charged under Section 124 A and only one under Section 153 A.

Chief Justice:—Will you show me where that point is raised in the petition?

Mr. Baptista:—On page 9 para 34. Here is a distinct charge of bringing Government into hatred and contempt. He should not have said that to the Jury at all.

Chief Justice:—What is your next point?

Mr. Baptista:—My next point relates to the verdict. In the verdict the attempt and the substantive charge are taken as distinct charges It is not clear whether the Jury found the verdict on the substantive charge or the attempt.

Chief Justice:—Was there a general verdict on each charge framed?

Mr Baptista:—Yes, my Lord.

Chief Justice:—Why do you say this is bad?

Mr. Baptista:—There are two views of that article which the Prosecution placed before the Jury the substantive charge and the attempt. It was the duty of the Jury to find which view is the true one. In the Section which defines the duties of jurors we find (reads Section 299).

Chief Justice:—Do you say that the accused was prejudiced by this?

Mr. Baptista:—Yes, My Lord, upon the prejudice depends the punishment. If the substantive charge failed and he was convicted of the attempt his punishment would be smaller.

Chief Justice:—But under Section 124 A the substantive charge and the attempt are combined and complete, so the punishment is complete. The offence and the attempt are identical under the section.

Mr. Baptista:—But I contend that in awarding sentence the gravity of the substantive charge must carry more weight than the attempt.

Chief Justice:—Under Section 124 A it is the same offence.

Mr. Baptista:—I submit that there is all the difference in awarding the punishment.

Chief Justice:—If both constitute the same offence the punishment must be the same.

Mr. Baptisa:—I do not dispute that under Section 124 A. the offences are the same, My Lord. I should however, like to call your attention to the Calcutta Judgment.

Chief Justice:—Is that on a charge under Section 124 A ?

Mr. Baptista:—No, My Lord. It is on an alternative charge of perjury and says when law charge itself is doubtful the Jury must define in the verdict; the law says that the Jury must determine which view is correct.

Chief Justice:—Here we have two offences in which the punishment is the same. What is your next point?

Mr. Baptista:—The next point is mentioned in para 32 *(d)* at page 5 of the petition, and refers to the Court having taken cognisance of offences punishable under Section 124 A. and 153 A without having in evidence any complaint made by order of the local Government and without examining the complanant.

Chief Justice:—Was not any Government official examined?

Mr. Baptista:—Only Mr. Joshi, the Oriental Translator was examined as to the signature of Mr. Quinn, Secretary to Government.

Chief Justice:—Was there any cross-examination on that point?

Mr. Baptista:—No, My Lord. I would next like to say with regard to the enhancement of the sentences.

Chief Justice:—Where is there anything to show that the sentences were enhanced ?

Mr. Baptista:—In the sentence, My Lord, where the learned Judge says:— (Reads from page 13 of petition from 'Ten years ago' to 'which you accepted'.) I submit also that Sections 124 A. and 153 A. are merely alternative charges and that there cannot be two different Sections.

Chief Justice:—Have you made a point of that in the petition?

Mr. Baptista:—Yes, My Lord, at page 7 para 32 (s.) We contend that these different sentences are illegal.

Chief Justice:—Do both these points relate to Case No. 17 ?

Mr. Baptista:—One relates to Case 16 and other to Case 17. There were two charges under Case No. 17, one under 124 A and the other under 153 A and one charge under 124 A in Case No. 16.

Chief Justice:—You submit that the transactions are not the same ?

Mr. Baptista:—Yes, My Lord, I submit that the transactions and the offences are not the same.

Chief Justice:—How do you say it is illegal to pass two sentences under Section 124 A and Section 153 A on one article?

Mr. Baptista:—Because it is doubtful which offence the verdict is on under Section 236 of the C. P. C.

Chief Justice:—What about Section 235 ?

Mr. Baptista:—If it comes under Section 235 even then under explanations 2 and 3 of that section it would be bad.

Chief Justice:—These are provided for by Section 71 of I. P. C.

Mr. Baptista:—I submit, My Lord, that Section 71 provides for those cases which fall within part of the sub-sections 2 and 3.

Chief Justice:—Why do you say that ?

Mr. Baptista:—The illustration says so. There are numerous decisions on the point.

Chief Justice:—Decisions on the construction of the Section?

Mr. Baptista:—I contend that the decisions explain the Section.

Chief Justice:—Why not part 2 of Section 71 ? (reads Section.)

Mr. Baptista:—What I submit is this. We have one prosecution under Sections 124A and 153A, one against the State, the other against classes. It seems to me that it does not constitute two offences in that light.

Chief Justice:—What is your next point ?

Mr. Baptista:—I would mention that so far as the Post-Card is concerned we had to put in certain exhibits to counter-act this evidence and so we lost the right of reply. We had to show whether the Prosecution had put a proper construction on it or not.

Chief Justice:—Where is that mentioned in the petition?

Mr. Baptista:—In Para 32 (o)

Chief Justice:—Under what section do you say that is illegal?

Mr. Baptista:—Under Section 292 because you sacrifice the right of reply if you adduce any evidence.

Chief Justice:—Is it not true that you put in evidence?

Mr. Baptista:—It has been ruled by Mr. Justice Batty and in English cases that if any documents are put in the defence the right of reply is lost. The whole of the matter hinges on the post-card. If the post-card was not put in we need not have put in articles to rebutt it. Therefore if the post-card is held to he inadmissible it has a very serious bearing on the case as but for its admission we would have had the right of reply.

Chief Justice:—And now you wish to deal with the question of misdirection?

Mr. Baptista:—The points of misdirection are divided into two parts the first part referring to Section 153 A.

Chief Justice:—That is para 34.

Mr. Baptista:—Yes, My Lord, I submit that for a proper construction of 153 A. malicious intention is essentially necessary to properly construe the Section. We have set out the words of the lerned Judge and our contention is that malicious intention is necessary in para 34 (I). "Here is what the Judge said- (reads from bottom of page 2 from "Section 153A. is a simple section" to His Majesty's subjects.")

Chief Justice:—What is the misdirection there?

Mr. Baptista :—(Reads from page 5, ' You have to consider ' to ' for the good Government of the country. ') What does the learned Judge say here? He says use these articles; both these articles. Now the charge under Section 153 A relates only to the 2nd article.

Chief Justice :—Have you taken the point in the petition?

Mr. Baptista :—Yes my Lord in 34 I and J. generally. We have not quoted the words specifically ; we have taken it generally in para 37. The learned Judge used all the articles and confined himself to the effect of these articles without any reference to intention. Of course it was complicated by the fact that so far as the first article was concerned Mr. Tilak was acquitted under section 153 A. But the Jury had nothing to do with that acquittal.

Chief Justice :—What is your next point ?

Mr. Baptista:—Misdirection under Section 124 A, my Lord. The general point here is misdirection regarding intention. This is set out in the petition in para 34 A, B, C, D, E, F, G, H, all of which relate to intention.

Chief Justice:—Do you say it is misdirection to say what the Judge says?

Mr. Baptista :—I submit for example, my Lord, the learned Judge says you may assume that it is for the purpose of exciting disaffection that he wrote the article. Even if the article is written with a good object in view you must see the effect it has and convict. What we say is that a specific criminal intention is necessary and must be shown. But the Judge says, never mind the purpose ; if the article raises feelings of disaffection, you must convict even if the intention is not bad. But I submit that purpose and intention are the fundamental principles of the Sedition Section 124 A.

Chief Justice :—Can you quote any authority ?

Mr. Baptista:—Ample authorities, my Lord, to show that the Section requires that there should be specific intention. Specific intention is always behind and is required when considering what effect is calculated to be created by the article. You have to prove that the accused had that intention. There is the decision of Sir Comer Petheram C. J. printed in 19 Calcutta page 44 in what is known as the Bangabasi case where it is laid down that intention is necessary to the charge. The same view was held in the Bombay High Court by Sir Lawrence Jenkins C. J. and Messrs. Justice Strachey and Justice Batty. It has never been disputed that specific intention is necessary for the success of a charge under Section 124 A. Of course it is included in the definition of the word attempt.

Chief Justice :—Show me the passage referred to in para 34 c.

Mr. Baptista:—The first passage is at page 5 of the summing-up where the Judge says ' these readers have not had the advantage of 21 hours and 10 minutes explanation which the Accused has offerred. ' Perhaps the readers may not have known the Accused's views. The moment the Court admits that the purpose for which he wrote the articles was to bring about a reform in the administration of the country the effect has nothing to do with the matter ; he is entitled to an acquittal.

Chief Justice:—What authorities have you to show for that ?

Mr. Baptista:—The line of argument which I shall adopt will be to trace the old law to the new law. Stephens will give us the old law; then we will come to Fox's Act when special specific intention became necessary; then to the passing of the Libel Act enlarging the liberty of the press. I will give the English decisions and then I will come to the Indian decisions which follow the same line. In 19 Calcutta page 44 in the Bangabasi Case the Judge says (Reads) It will be seen from this that intention is necessary.

Chief Justice:—(Reads from Daver J's summing up from ' You must apply your mind to the intention ') Where is the misdirection in that ?

Mr. Baptista:—Yes, but he destroys the effect of it by saying ' no honest intention justifies an infringement of the law.

Chief Justice:—He was reading that from the judgement of Sir Lawrence Jenkins C. J. (Reads from page 5 of Davar J's summing-up.) I do not see how you can ask us to say that there is misdirection in passages like that.

Mr. Baptista:—But the learned Judge says there that the people knew the purpose for which these articles were written.

Chief Justice:—(Continues reading of summing up ' the law × × × is crystalised here ' and then reads Mayne as quoted by Davar J.) Where is the misdirection there ?

Mr. Baptista:—He says intention is unnecessary. Even if the intention was innocent ; what he says is even if you find that the writer wrote this with honest purpose, no honest intention can justify an infringement of the law. He distinctly gives the Jury to understand that if these articles are likely to excite feelings that are a transgression of the law, the intention should be inferred from the maxim that every man intends the consequences of his acts. What the learned Judge has centered the mind of the Jury upon—He says even if the intention is honest, if they created feelings of hatred and contempt or disorder or violence the accused was guilty. That is what I submit is wrong. Then the meaning of word attempt; so far as the word attempt is concerned we have the definition given by Sir Lawrence Jenkins who said ' we must take the ordinary meaning of the word attempt (Reads) Having explained that he says you must take the ordinary meaning of the word attempt.'

Chief Justice:—Do you say that nothing more than the ordinary meaning should be taken ?

Mr. Baptista:— Yes, my Lord, the ordinary meaning; there can be no other meaning to the word attempt.

Chief Justice:—Does Sir Lawrence Jenkins say there is nothing more than the ordinary meaning?

Mr. Baptista:—What his Lordship says is the ordinary meaning of the word attempt must be taken to mean intention.

Chief Justice:—If you mean to try to do a thing do you not try to do it ?

Mr. Baptista:—I submit that intention is necessary for the attempt.

Chief Justice:—How does that come in?

Mr Baptista:—The substantive offence and the attempt. With attempt you require intention.

Mr. Baptista:—With reference to the question of motive we say in the petition (Reads para 34 *g*). The learned Judge told the Jury they were not concerned with motives. He could not have intended that. According to Lord Cockburn motive was taken into consideration for the purpose of showing and arriving at an estimate of intention. This was not given due consideration to by the learned Judge.

Coming to the question of the translations of the articles the learned Judge says that because the High Court translator had made the translations they must be authorised and correct; that was not a correct view to put to the Jury. There is something said about putting 'a spoke in wheel of the administration'. The learned Judge says that nothing else could have been meant by the spoke but the bomb. That direction implied that the Accused advocated the bomb and that must have produced a tremendous effect on the Jury.

As regards Section 153 A, the classes are not specified in the charge itself. As a matter of fact so far as the charge is concerned it is based on the translation and not the original article. The words of the original article should have been stated and the English translations should have been handed over to the Jury in order to enable them to see whether the translations were correct. It was for the Prosecution to establish the fact that the translations were correct.

Chief Justice—The language of the Court is English and the charge must be made in words comprehensive to the Court. I suppose the original marathi article was put in and the translations were set out with the charge.

Mr. Baptista—But the spirit of an article may be lost in translation. That has a good deal to do with the articles in this case. Even the learned Judge admitted that the spirit of the articles might have been somewhat lost in the translations.

Chief Justice—I suppose the spirit of the writings was explained by the Accused in his defence.

Mr. Baptista—Yes, my Lord, he explained it in person and the Judge left it to the Jruy to take that view or not.

Chief Justice—He had the right to do that I suppose.

Mr. Baptista—If the original spirit were there, there would be no discretion left to them. The articles should have been translated in the form brought out by Mr. Joshi's cross-examination.

Chief Justice—Does the Judge say the spirit is actually lost?

Mr. Baptista—No, my Lord, he says the spirit may have been lost (reads from Judge's summing up.)

Chief Justice—Now have you mentioned all your points?

Mr. Baptista—Yes, my Lord.

Chief Justice—We will decide at 3 30 p. m. whether we will grant you a rule or not.

Mr. Baptista—These are only the points, my Lord. I desire to elaborate those points by arguments.

Chief Justice—If the rule is granted you will argue them before the Court.

Mr. Baptista—But I desire to support the points mentioned by arguments before your Lordship.

Bachelor Justice—Then what have you been doing since 11-30 ?

Chief Justice--I thought you had been arguing the points

Mr. Baptista :—No, my Lord, You asked me questions and I answered them; so far I have only enumerated the twelve points that I wish to argue.

Chief Justice :—Will you then begin your arguments now ?

Mr. Baptista :—Before I come to that, I want to point out that the consolidation of the cases is illegal.

Chief Justice :—You had better take the points one by one. The first is the consolidation of the two committals.

Mr. Baptista:—I submit that the law does not provide for such consolidation and quote Sections 194, 213, 215, 226 and 227 C. P. C. None of them provide for the consolidation of two cases. Sections 218, 226 and 227 provide that no alteration can be made in a charge.

What happened here, my Lord, was that the accused was first committed in two cases in each of which he was charged with two offences, so that he was indicted on four charges. The Crown combined or consolidated the two cases and the two committals and dropping one charge proceeded on one trial with three charges. The Crown had no right to combine the charges of two committals into one trial by dropping one charge and proceeding on three. The Crown had no right to drop or combine charges in this way, as it was not intended for the purpose of making the trial good.

Chief Justice :—I do not see what the High Court had to do with the Magistrate's committals; the question is, how many charges were there before the Judge at the High Court trial.

Mr. Baptista :—The lower Court framed four charges in two committals. The question is when does a trial commence ? Does it begin when the accused is asked to plead or when the Jury is empanelled ? What happened here was that the charges were read to the prisoner and objection was taken before the Jury was empanelled. The learned Advocate-General said that he wanted to put the Accused up on three charges at one trial, one charge under Section 124 A, in case No. 16, and two charges i. e., 124 A and 153 A, in case No. 17 and stated that he would not ask for a discharge on the fourth charge till the trial ended in case the point of *atrefois acquit* was raised. The Judge then intended that such discharge would amount to an acquittal. The charges were then reversed and read to the accused who claimed to be tried and made certain objections to this procedure and after that the Jury was empanelled so that so far as the Jury was concerned they had only 3 charges before them.

Chief Justice:—You say the consolidation of the three charges is illegal ?

Mr. Baptista:—How could there be three charges when there are two committals ?

Chief Justice:—If an accused person is committed by the Magistrate on a number of charges he is not asked to plead to all of them, he is usually charged on three of them selected by the Crown.

Mr. Baptista:—In that case, my Lord, there would be only one committal; here we have two.

Chief Justice:—It is only a question of how many charges will be tried.

Mr. Baptista:—Do you not hold, my Lord, that the trial begins when the accused is asked to plead. The words used in section 234 C P C are as follows (Reads).

Chief Justice;—The trial does not begin till the accused claims to be tried.

Mr. Baptista—The moment the accused pleads not guilty the trial begins.

I submit it does not begin after the Jury is empanelled but before, as, should he plead guilty, no Jury is empanelled. Under Section 271A the moment the accused pleads, the trial begins. In this case the accused is asked to plead to 4 charges before the Jury was empanelled. There is a case in 5 Calcutta Weekly Reports which shows when a trial commences. Assuming the trial commences when the accused is asked to plead then there were four charges and the Court had no power to drop any one of the charges. There is no provision of law which gives the High Court power to strike out a charge. There is a case also in 25 Madras and your Lordship will find the argument at page 94. Assuming this the 3 charges framed were bad and in contravention of Sections 233 and 234. Mayne refers to the question at page 239 and argues that the Court has no power to drop a charge. In 29 Madras at 572 your Lordship will find a case in which it was also held that the High Court had no power to drop a charge.

So far as the additional charge under Section 75 is concerned the accused is not charged originally with that. Such a charge is inconsistent with Section 271 clause 7 of the Criminal Procedure Code.

Chief Justice:—I do not think it comes under Section 271 (Reads Section). The Court is competent to award punishment; previous conviction does not affect the case.

Mr. Baptista:—But the Court awarded the maximum punishment. Under Section 75 the Court may enhance the punishment.

Bachelor Justice:—The question is one of the Court being competent. It was competent to the Court to award transportation for life or three years.

Mr. Baptista:—The Judge awarded the punishment of three years.

Bachelor Justice:—It is a question of competency of power, not of sentence.

Chief Justice:—It is not altered in any way by the fact of previous conviction. How do you say that previous conviction alters the competency of the Court?

Mr. Baptista:—The sentence could be enhanced under Section 75.

Bachelor Justice:—But it does not apply!

Chief Justice:—It is no use proceeding on a Section that does not apply.

Mr. Baptista:—The objection was taken as to enhancement of sentence.

Chief Justice:—The previous conviction was not used as an additional charge. The Crown was entitled to show that there had been a previous conviction. You have been arguing under Sections 271 and 75, and neither of them have anything to do with the case.

Mr. Baptista:—According to the section 310 the Code lays out the procedure to be adopted in the case of previous conviction (Reads section) In this case the charge was not ready till five days after the trial commenced. The trial commenced on 13th of July whereas this charge was dated 22nd July 1908.

Chief Justice:—Do you say the Court could not add the charge ?

Mr. Baptista:—Section 221 provides for that.

Chief Justice:—Do you say that the Court could not add the charge during the course of the trial ?

Mr. Baptista:—The Court could only add such charges as were before the Court. In this case it was added after the return of the verdict. If your Lordships will refer to 2 Bombay Law Reports page 321 you will find that the Chief Justice refused to add a charge after the trial had commenced.

Chief Justice:—That case does not seem to be in your favour. I remember that discussion very well and my suggestion was that under section 221 it was not necessary to frame a charge.

Mr. Baptista:—In this case the charge was read after the verdict was given. Your Lordship held (reads from page 137 of the report.) This matter was considered in Allahabad report at page 321. It was originally thought that a previous conviction added to the competence of a court to enhance punishment; but 11 Allahabad corrected this impression. It is said that the charge must be laid before enhanced pnnishment could be awarded.

Chief Justice:—You are again referring to the competency of the Court. [The Court then adjourned for lunch.]

Mr. Baptista:—I have here 5 Calcutta Weekly Reports to show when a trial begins (Reads from pages 169-70). So far as previous conviction is concerned it may be used in two ways either under section 75 or under section 221 which affects the punishment the Court is competent to award.

Chief Justice:—Sections 221 and 75 are identical.

Mr. Baptista :—The charge is under Section 310, Section 271 requires that the charge shall be read in Court. Intimation must be given to the accused that the charge existed.

Chief Justice :—What is the substance of this point ?

Mr. Baptista :—That the punishment was enhanced by the Judge.

Chief Justice :—Why do you say that ?

Mr. Baptista :—Because that is the only purpose for which it can be used.

Chief Justice :—What substance is there in your argument ?

Mr. Baptista :—Without that the ordinary punishment would have been less, probably 2 years or 18 months.

Chief Justice :—The learned Judge according to the sentence (Reads sentence) does not award any punishment on that, so that your point has no substance whatever. I do not see how it affects the case.

Mr. Baptista :—There cannot be a separate charge and conviction.

Chief Justice :—I am only answering your arguments. You say that the punishment must have been enhanced by reason of the charge of previous conviction.

Mr. Baptista:—The learned Judge passed sentence of three years on each charge and referred to the previous conviction so that it indicates that he gave a higher sentence by reason of the previous conviction.

Chief Justice:—It does not appear anywhere that the previous conviction resulted in a higher punishment.

Mr. Baptista:—It must be assumed that it had that effect, otherwise it is a meaningless charge.

Chief Justice:—It is quite possible that the learned Judge had this before him when he took into consideration the undertaking of the accused which was set out in the bail application. The previous conviction is set out in the bail application and this must have at all events brought it to the mind of the Judge who is entitled to take into consideration everything he knows.

Mr. Baptista:—The application was ex-parte and the Judge would not hear the other side and refused bail.

Chief Justice:—He must have read the affidavits. A Judge is entitled in sentencing to take into consideration what he knows about the prisoner. Strictly speaking so long as the Judge does not exceed the punishment laid down by the law for the offences he is within his rights.

Mr. Baptista:—The point is that he took the fourth charge into consideration though he did not say so. In regard to the application for bail he said he would not give bail and would not state his reasons for refusing as it might prejudice the accused.

Chief Justice :—Do you say that the Judge is not entitled to take into consideration the fact of previous conviction as to the sentence he will inflict ? It seems to me that he is entitled to do so.

Mr. Baptista :—If it were a point of evidence the Judge would be competent to use it.

Chief Justice :—These matters are left to the discretion of the Judge.

Mr. Baptista :—I feel it my duty to say that this additional charge must have weighed with His Lordship in passing the sentence that he passed.

Mr. Baptista :—Now, I come to the point of the joinder of the charges; they are referred to in para 32 (*h*.)

Chief Justice :—We have decided to give you a rule on that point. I say that at once in order not to trouble you to any length into the matter.

Mr. Baptista :—Then, there is the point of the substantive charge and the 'attempt' being put in one and the same charge.

Chief Justice :—We are against you on that point. But you may if you like argue it.

Mr. Baptista :—On that point I rely on Indian Law Reports 26 Allahabad, page 195–196 (Reads.)

Chief Justice :—I do not see how that is relevant to the point you are now arguing.

Mr. Baptista :—He refers to offences in one charge and defines the substantive charge and the attempt.

Chief Justice :—Under Section 124 A. the charge in the Code includes both the substantive charge and the attempt. The more correct form of pleading would be that there are two seperate heads to the charge.

Mr. Baptista :—Then the Jury would have to bring in a verdict under the two different heads. That was laid down by Mr. Justice Starling.

Chief Justice:—Mr. Justice Starling had a wide experience in the Criminal Courts of England where double pleading is regarded as not good pleading. The substantive charge and the attempt was then not taken into one count. Mr. Justice Starling used to plead in that way. Why should we follow a peculiar pleading ?

Mr. Baptista:—Here we have two distinct offences.

Bachelor Justice:—The Section says ' whoever brings or attempts to bring.'

Mr. Baptista:—That is just what we say.

Bachelor Justice:—There are several Sections in which the attempt goes with the substantive charge. I think that it means that it makes no difference under the Section.

Mr. Baptista: It might affect the evidence, then their might be some difference.

Chief Justice:—Now we come to the question of the sanction of Government to prosecute.

Mr. Baptista:—Section 196 C. P. C. requires that the complaint should be ordered by Government; no complaint could be otherwise made to a Magistrate under Section 153 A.

Chief Justice:—You said that there was a complaint laid by the Police Commissoner ?

Mr. Baptista:—Yes, but the Sanction is not in evidence.

Chief Justice:—The Magistrate would not take cognisance of the information and issue a warrant without satisfying himself as to sanction being granted.

Mr. Baptista:—We had no evidence of it either in the Police Court or the High Court.

Chief Justice:—You do not suggest that the Magistrate took cognisance without sanction ? There is I am afraid no substance in that point.

Mr. Baptista—Was it right for Government to authorise the Police Commissoner to charge or not under Section 153 A? This is a power which should be exercised with the greatest caution.

Chief Justice:—The Government sanction the prosecution and instruct the Police Commissioner to proceed.

Mr. Baptista:—There is specific sanction to proceed under Section 124 A but only discretion to act under 153 A. This brings 153 A to the level of other offences. The sanction is a very important provision of the Act and has to be cautiously carried out. Government itself must resolve to prosecute and specify the Sections.

Chief Justice:—The prosecution was conducted by Government.

Mr. Baptista :—Government has not expressed its view about 153 A; it is left to the Police Commissioner's discretion. That is my point.

Chief Justice :—You have Mr. Quin's opinion in the sanction.

Mr. Baptista :—I submit that Government should not have delegated the power to other hands. The intention of the Legislature was that Government should give the sanction and decide on the Sections; they can not be left to the Police Commissioner to select. The Section says (Reads 196.) It is a matter which must be resolved upon with the exercise of the greatest care and deliberation. Again the order does not mention the classes between whom enmity is raised. In the charge itself also no classes are mentioned.

Chief Justice:—What does it say in the charge?

Mr. Baptista:—There is the charge framed by the Magistrate and the revised charge as framed by the Clerk of the Crown.

We now come to the meaning of the word Government and I submit that it is the Limited Monarchy—the King, the Lords and the Commons. It means the temporary Government and not the State. India is only a part of the British Empire established by law.

Chief Justice:—Do you say that the Government established by Law in England is the same as the Government established by law in India?

Mr. Baptista:—It is explained at page 551 (reads). Erskine says the Government means the Limited Monarchy of England as represented by the King, the Lords and the Commons. The executive power is in the Crown. In India the whole executive power has been vested in the Crown since 1858. The Government of India is the instrument of the Crown with executive and legislative power. I submit therefore that the Government established by law in India is the executive Government.

Chief Justice:—Is the Indian Government established by law in India ?

Mr. Baptista :—I do not find any power was given to it till 1858. As a matter of fact the Ilbert Bill says the Government of India is the Executive Government and then we have the General Clauses Act where the Government is defined. Under Section 124 A the words are the Government established by law in India, and it was necessary for the learned Judge to explain what the meaning of that definition is.

My next point is with regard to the explanation being taken as exception. The learned Judge erred in construing the explanations of Section 124 A I. P. C. as eqivalent to exceptions. If that is so you have committed the offence of sedition unless you can show that you come within the exception. The explanation gives an idea what is permissible under this Section itself. But it is not an exhaustive explanation.

Bachelor Justice:—I do not see here the error you impute to the Judge.

Mr. Baptista:—We are entitled to criticise and to point out defects of the existing administration. The explanation says you must not criticise the Government; you can only criticise the measures of Government. The learned Advocate-General said the whole onus of proof lay on the accused to show that he came within the explanation, or the exception, call it what you like.

Chief Justice :—That would be the case where a *prima facie* case has been established. The onus rests with the accused to prove that he does not come within the Section. In this case the Prosecution relies on the main Section and the accused on the explanation.

Mr. Baptista :—The explanation only gives leave to criticise the measures of Government; if you go beyond that you fall within section 124 A.

Chief Justice:—In fact it was stated that explanation is the exception.

Mr. Baptista:—That is the point, My Lord. We are entitled to criticise the administrative acts of Government so long as we do not bring the Government into contempt. I am entitled to do this under Section 124 A but according to explanation we cannot do more than criticise the measures of Government; if we do more than that we come within the Section.

Bachelor Justice:—Where has the Judge said that the explanation and exception are the same ? The Judge is not expected to correct all the mistakes of law as propounded by the Advocate-General.

Mr. Baptista:—It is a question of putting the law wrongly before the Jury.

Bachelor Justice:—There is no sign that the Jury were affected by it.

Mr. Baptista:—I submit we cannot attack the constitution of Government but that we can ask for a change in the constitution. This is a privilege which the Accused elaborated very carefully.

Chief Justice:—You say you can attack the constitution of Government and ask for a change although you thereby bring the Government into contempt.

Mr. Baptista:—I say we do not bring it into contempt. I can, if the explanation and exception are held to be the same, only attack the measures of Government, that is the effect of that.

Chief Justice:—I do not follow your argument.

Mr. Bnptista:—If it is held that the explanation and the exception are equivalent, then we can only attack the legislative measures of Government and not the Government or the constitution, not even to point out defects in the administration. I contend that under the Section we are entitled to do this so long as we do not bring the Government into contempt or hatred. If we did that, of course, we would come within the Section. According to the Advocate-General the explanation is the limit of the exception.

Chief Judge:—Let us take what the learned Judge says (Reads from summing-up of Davar J.)

Mr. Baptista:—It was what the Advocate-General said that must have influenced the Jury.

Chief Judge:— The Jury found that accused tried to bring the Government into contempt and to excite enmity between classes.

Mr. Baptista:—They said it was an attack on the Government.

Bachelor Justice:—Say what you impute to him. Confine yourself to that argument.

Mr. Baptista:—So far as that goes I can only say that there has been non-direction. I would refer your Lordships to Bombay Law reports page 528 where Mr. Asquith explains what explanation and exception is.

Chief Judge:—Was that 'explanation' under the same section ?

Mr. Baptista:—No, my Lord it was different. I cannot point out any words in the summing-up to support my argument; I can only say that there was non-direction. As to the admissibility of the post card Exhibit K and the articles Exhibits E. to J. I submit that the post card was inadmissible. It was put in for the purpose of showing intention but there was no charge with which to connect it.

Chief Judge:—It added to the weight of evidence.

Mr. Baptista:—Apart from its admissibility it had a very great effect on our defence. We had to put in articles to meet it and so lost the right of reply.

Chief Judge:—You need not have done that.

Mr Baptista:—We were bound to do so; otherwise it might have had a serious effect on the Jury.

Chief Judge:—If it had no weight, you need not have done so.

Mr. Baptista:—If it was not admitted we would not have been compelled to put in articles to meet it. If it is inadmissible we complain that its admission cost us the right of reply.

Chief Judge:—I have not read the articles charged but I understand that the second article has something to say about bombs and as the post card has something to do with explosives. I understand that the Prosecution suggested that there was some connection between the two. The inference of the article was that bombs should be used.

Mr. Baptista:—Can that possibly have any connection with the post card ?

Chief Justice:—It is a question of weight of evidence.

Mr. Baptista:—I go further and say that the admission of the post card cost us the right of reply. Under Section 11 the post card is not admissible.

Chief Justice:—It was tendered under section 14.

Mr. Baptista:—So far as the Card was concerned it was found in the accused's drawing room among a large number of other papers.

Chief Justice:—I do not see how it cannot be admissible. The Judge in his summing-up has dealt with the post card in a manner most favourable to the accused. He tells the Jury to take very little notice of it.

Mr. Baptista:—If it is admissible I cannot complain although we lost the right of reply. Of course, my Lord, so far as that is concerned the learned Judge had to note the effect of this post card on the minds of the Jury. In that connection I would take leave to quote " Bombay Law Reports 1896, where at page 19, the Judge deals with Section 14. " (Reads).

Chief Justice:—You also say the other articles appearing in the *Kesari* should not have been admitted. There is a direct rule on that point (Reads from summing up of Mr. Justice Strachey.) And in the case before Justice Batty also other articles were put in.

Mr. Baptista:—The question of admissibility is a very important one and I submit that it is a question which should go before the Privy Council which is the highest Judicial Tribunal. Therefore I ask your Lordships to certify it. The learned Judge told the Jury that they were to look at the incriminating article and if thay could not find the accused guilty on that they were to look at the other articles to see what the intention of the accused was and say what effect they would have on their minds.

Chief Justice:—That does not affect the question of admissibility.

Mr. Baptista:—I shall come next to the charges as framed, and I submit that they are bad. I will read you Section 299 as to the duties of Jurors (Reads.) And I should also like to call your attention to 13 Bengal Law Reports page 324 where several views of one criminal offence have been placed before the Jury. Here we have the substantive charge as well as the attempt and this does not apply to the requirements of Section 299. The Chief Justice did not agree with the other Judges. The observations of Juslice Jackson appear on page 350.

Bachelor Justice:—You are quoting the minority of the bench.

Mr. Baptista :—Then as to the subject of previous conviction.

Chief Justice :—That has been already argued.

Mr. Baptista :–I need not elaborate that point. Now the next point is with regard to two sentences in a transaction which is the same. That is para 32 (S.)

Chief Justice :—You may argue that on the rule.

Mr. Baptista:—I should like to point out about section 153A that the learned Judge referred to more than one article (Reads from summing—up).

Chief Justice:— You can argue that. We are prepared to grant you a rule on two points, namely 32 (*h*) and 32 (*S*)

Mr. Baptista:—Will your Lordships also add 32 (T.) ?

Chief Justice:—Yes we will grant a rule on that also.

Mr. Baptista:—With regard to misdirection?

Cheaf Justice:—We will decide about that and pass orders tomorrow or on Thursday.

THE DECISION.

On Wednesday 26th August the Chief Justice gave his decision in the matter of the application made by Mr. Tilak and which was argued upon the previous day. In passing orders on the application for a Rule For leave to appeal to the Privy Council, the Chief Justice said:—

As we stated yesterday we issue a Rule calling upon the Crown to show cause why the Court should not grant a certificate that this is a fit case for Appeal to the Privy Council on the points mentioned in paras 32(H) 32(S) and 32(T) in the petition of the Accused. We have taken time to consider whether we should issue a Rule upon any other points, and we have come to the conclusion that there is no substance in any of the other points which have been taken. We think it right here to mention with regard to point 32(R) as to the addition of a fresh charge at the close of the case with reference to the previous conviction, that it appears to us that the procedure adopted is not contemplated by the C. P. C. It was evidently adopted in order to bring to the mind of the Judge in passing sentence the fact that the prisoner had been previously convicted, but that fact was obviously already present to the mind of the Judge because he had cited copiously from the summing—up of Mr. Justice Strachey in the previous Tilak Trial in 1897 and he had before him and present to his mind the affidavit that had been made in the bail application which mentioned the previous conviction and the undertaking which had been given by the prisoner upon his release. We, therefore, think there is no substance whatever in the objection that had been taken and that it would not be right to needlessly occupy the time of the Court in arguing a point which has no substance whatever.

The Chief Justice said—"We make the rule returnable next Wednesday."

Mr. Baptista:—As to misdirection I understand your Lordships do not grant a rule.

Chief Justice:—No.

That ended the proceedings for the day.

Final hearing of the *Rule Nisi*.

On wednesday, the 2nd September the *Rule Nisi* came on for final hearing before Mr. Justice Scott. C. J. and Mr. Justice Bachelor. Mr. Baptista, Bar-at-law, instructed by Mr. Raghavaya, Solicitor, and Mr. R. P. Karandikar, High Court Pleder, appeared for Mr. Tilak, the Crown being represented by Mr. Robertson, acting Advocate-General. The following is a summary of the argument of Mr. Baptista who appeared to support the Rule.

In this matter, my Lords, the accused complains that in spite of his objection, the trial has been conducted illegally. That constitutes one of the gravest complaints that can be made against the administration of Law and Justice. If it be well-founded, it should be remedied regardless of all other considerations. I submit the complaint is well-founded. I shall endeavour to codense my arguments in the briefest possible compass consistent with my duty. I believe it will save time if I deal with the Rule in the following order :—

I.—What is a distinct offence ?

II.—How many distinct offences are charged ?

III.—Is the trial illegel ?

I—Distinct Offences.

The object of this inquiry is to show (1) That the offences under Sections 124A and 153A are quite distinct offences falling within Sections 35, 235 I. and 403II. of the Criminal Procedure Code, and not within Section 236 of the Criminal Procedure Code.

The expression " Distinct Offence" is nowhere defined in the Code, but for the purpose of this Rule distinct offences may be divided into two classes *viz*., (1) Non-Separable and (2) Separable.

1. *Non-Separable.*—Non-Separable offences are those falling within Section 35 Criminal Procedure code. Their charactristic is that they can be *punished* separately within the limitations imposed by Section 35 Criminal Procedure Code. A conviction or acquittal on any one of them is no bar to a subsequent trial on the remaining ones under Section 403, Clause (2) of the Criminal Procedure Code. This Clause reveals what offences are contemplated by Section 235, Clause (1.) They are the chief offences chargeable upon the acts alleged, *e. g.* lurking house trespass by night (Section 454 I. P. Code) and not minor offences which are only the costituent elements of the major offence, *e. g.*, trespass, (Section 447) or house-trespass (Section 448) or lurking house trespass (Section 453).

Section 35 Criminal Procedure Code is therefore the severest test of distinctiveness that can be applied.

Now Sections 124A and 153A are distinct in the sense of Section 35 Criminal Procedure Code.

Section 124 A is no part of 153 A and *vice versa*.

Section 124 A relates to offence against the State under Chapter VI, whereas Section 153A relates to offence against classes under Chapter VIII. Indeed Sec. 153A did not even exist in 1897 and was invicted only in 1808.

There is absolutely no connection whatever between the two. These two offences suggest wholly distinct facts and need different evidence to meet them. To promote hatred between Hindoos and Moslems has nothing in common with creating the ill-feelings against Government contemplated by Section 124 A. To do so against Europeans has similarly nothing to do with 124 A, but as Europeans belong to the ruling class they are easily identified with Government in point of fact, but this is not so in point of Law. Nobody ever said these two offences were not distinct offences. Indeed in the *Hind Swaraj* case Mr. Justice Chandavarkar admits that " the offence under Section 124A of the Penal Code is not an offence of the same kind as an offence under Section 153A of the Code. "

These offences could be separately charged under Section 235 Clause (1) and separately punished under section 35, Criminal Procedure Code and under Section 403 Clause (2), Criminal Procedure Code, there could even be a second trial on one of them after acquittal or conviction on the other, if no charge were framed on that offence in the first trial. As a matter of fact they are separately charged under 235 Clause (1) in this case, and separately punished under Section 35, as distinct punishments have been inflicted on 124 A and 153 A of the second article. As a matter of fact also, there has practically been a subsequent trial and acquittal on Section 153 A of the first article. Therefore Section 124 A and 153 A satisfy the severest test of distinctiveness in this case.

2. *Separable offences.*—These all come within Section 71 of the Penal Code. They cannot be punished separately, though they can be charged separately. All these separable offences may be further subdivided into two heads, *viz.*, (i) convictable and (ii) non-convictable.

(*i*) *Convictable.*—If Section 71 Penal Code be read with Section 235 Clause (2) and (3) of the Criminal Procedure Code, it will be seen that the separable offence of Section 71 of the Penal Code are thoes contemplated by Section 235 (2) and (3). It will be perceived that Clauses 2 and 3 of Section 71 of the Penal Code are to the same effect as Clauses 2 and 3 of Section 235 of the Cr. P. Code. The illustrations tell that these can be charged separately or *convicted* separately though not *punished* separately. (Weir 895 and 899).

Weir 895:—" When a prisoner is tried on several heads of charge in the same transaction, the principal legal offence involved should be the first head of charge; the object of adding others is not the accumulation of punishments, but to provide against the event of the evidence failing to establish the principal charges. "

Weir 897 *at* 899:—" Read together, paras II and III of Secton 235 come to this:—You may join them but if when joined, several meke-up one compound offence, you shall only punish for one. They shall be considered to make up such a compound when one of them is the criminal result at which the other has arrived. "

Empress vs. *Ram Partab*, *I. L. R.* 6 *Allahabad* 121 *at p.* 124:—" Now I presume, it never could be seriously contended that a Court might sentence a convicted person to separate punishments upon the same facts, for the offence of being a member of an unlawful assembly and for riot, for a necessary component part of riot is an unlawful assembly and it is only when force or violence are super added, that the offence of rioting is completed. In short riot is no more than an aggravated form of unlawful assembly. "

These minor offences which can be separately charged all graduate to some one major offence, *e.g.*, lurking house-trespass by night (Section 456) which is composed or compounded of the separate offences of Criminal trespass (Section 447), house-trespass (Section 448) and lurking house-trespass (Section 453).

(2). *Non-Convictable.*—The second head of separable offneces are those falling within Section 236 of the Criminal Procedure Code. In this case several separable offences may be charged but there can be a conviction on *only one* of them. This Section provides for a state of facts which render the application of Law doubtful. There is no doubt, *only one* offence is committed, but which particular offence is committed cannot be determined definitely. The facts are clear, but the Law is doubtful. This then comes within the provisions of Sectino 72 of the Penal Code, and the directions in Section 367 Clause (3) must be complied with. It is incumbent on the Court to express that it is doubtful which offence is committed and then pass judgment in the alternative. But then under Section 72 of the Penal Code " *The offenders shall be punished for the offence for which the lowest punishment is provided.*"

The cases on the point are *22 Punjab Recorder No. 43, p. 105 ; I. L. R. 23 Calcutta 174 ; 31 Calcutta 955 and 33 Calcutta 1256*, *and 22 Bombay 377*.

22 Punjab Recorder 105 :—Section 236 relates not to distinct acts, but to a *single act* or *series of acts*, where the *facts* being ascertained it is *doubtful*, *which* of the *several* sections is applicable."

I. L. R. 23 Calcutta 174 and 177 :—It appears to us that Sections 236 of the Criminal Procedure Code contemplate a state of facts constituting a *single* offence, but where it is doubtful, whether the act or acts involved may amount to one or another of several *cognate* offences. Where that is the case, the accused may be simultaneously charged with or tried for the Commission of all or any of such offences, and after acquittal or conviction cannot again be tried on the *same facts* either for the specific offence or offences for which he was already been tried or for any other offence for which he might have been tried under the provisions of that Section.

I. L. R. 31 Calcutta 955 :—See head note. Section 236 only authorises a charge in the alternative when it is doubtful which of the several offences the fact which can be proved will constitute and not where there may be a *doubt as to facts* which constitute one of the elements of the offence.

Weir 897 :—"It can scarcely be meant that the element of doubt is the governing point."

I. L. R. 33 Calcutta 1256 at 1263 ;—"I know of no authority for saying that a conviction for theft can take place on a charge of receiving or retaining stolen property. Section 237 allows an accused who has been charged with one offence, to be convicted of another, *but by reference to Section 236*, *the operation* of that Section is *confined* to cases, where it is *doubtful*, *which of several* offences will be constituted by the facts which can be proved; which is not at all the case here."

I. L. R. 22 Bombay 377 and 382;—We wish it to be distinctly understood that what we have said above is intended to apply only to those Cases which are contemplated by Section 236 of the Code of Criminal Procedure, and in which the accused is charged with distinct offences arising out of a single act or series of acts, it being doubtful *which* of these offences the act or acts constitute, and the accused is convicted by the first Court of one of these and acquitted of others."

Nota Bene.

In the present case there is no question of doubt to import the operation of Section 236 or Section 237. Not only is there no doubt but there are actual separate convictions and separate sentences and even separate trials. To make out a case of doubt would be to make out a case that was never dreamt of even by the prosecution—certainly not by the Court. No such new case can no be made for the sole purpose of curing an illegality.

TABLE.

Distinct offences.

- **I Non-Separable.**
  1. Chargeable = SS. 233, 234, or 235 Cl. (1) of = Cr. P. Code.
  2. Convictable separately.
  3. Punishable separately = S.35 Cr. P. Code.
  4. Triable after acquittal or conviction = S. 403, Cl. (3) = Cr. P. Code.
- **II. Non-Convictable.**
  - **A. Convictable.**
    1. Chargeable = S. 235 Cl. (2) and (3) Cr. P. Code.
    2. Convictable separately. See Illustrations S. 235 Cl. (2) and (3).
    3. Non-Punishable separately. See Sec. 71 I. P. Code. Explanation to S. 35 Cr. P. Code.

       and

       Illustration to S. 35 Cr. P. Code.

       Cases:—

       Weir's Criminal Rulings pp. 895 and 899.

       I. L. R. 6 All. 121.
    4. Non-triable = S. 403 Cr. P. Code.
  - **B. Non-Convictable.**
    1. Chargeable = S. 236 of Cr. P. Code.
    2. Non-Convictable separately. Illustrations to S.236 do not speak of convictions as they do in S. 235 Cl. (1) (2) and (3).

       Cases:—

       I. L. R. 23 Cal. 174 at 177. *cognate.*

       " 31 Cal. 955

       " 33 Cal. 1256 at 1263

       " 22 Bom. 377 at 382

       " 22 Punjab Recorder No. 43 p. 105.
    3. Non-Punishable separately S. 72 I. P. Code and S. 367 Cl. (3) Cr. P. C.
    4. Non-Triable = S. 403 Cr. P. Code.

II—The Number of Distinct Offences.

There are three charges by the Clerk of the Crown excluding the charge of previous conviction, and the fourth charge under Section 153A on the first article of the 12th of May 1908, " the country's misfortune. "

The first charge alternatively charges the accused with "exciting" or " attempting to excite " feelings of disaffection against the Government established by Law in British India. This is rather an informal made of charging. There ought at least to have been a separate head of charge for the substantive offence and for the attempt as per Form II on Section 241 in schedule V prescribed by or at least recommended under Section 555 Criminal Procedure Code.

The substantive offence and the attempt are no doubt offences of the *same kind*, but they are distinct offences of the same kind. This is recognised by Section 511 Criminal Procedure Code which places attempts in a separate section of the Code. *But under Section 511 the punishment being one-half they would not be offences of the same kind.* The *attempt* is on level with *abetments* of offences in so far as they are distinct offences. S. 237 cl. 2 shows they are distinct. It makes no difference that the attempt is inserted with the substantive offence in the same Section 124 A. But the frame of 124A is disjunctive. Even if it had not been placed under Section 124 A, it would come under Section 511 ordinarily.

The attempt can be charged without the substantive offence and *vice versa*. If the attempt only is charged there can be no conviction on the substantive offence showing they are very distinct. Of course if the substantive offence is charged, there can be a conviction on the attempt under S. 237 cl. 2 Cr. P. Code. (See also 8 Bom. 200 and 22 Cal. 1906. See abetment 3 C. W. N. 367.) But though convictions are possible they are distinct offences otherwise an acquittal on one would necessarily mean an acquittal on the other. In the first Tilak trial Mr. Starling charged them separately in separate Counts (*See I. L. R. 22 Bombay* 112 *at p.* 115.) In the Cases of *Luxman* and *Vinayek*, 2 *Bombay L. R.* 286 *and* 304 only the " attempt " was charged. In *Vinayek's* Case Sir Lawrence Jenkins, C. J. observed :—"As the case is formulated by the Advocate-General it is not suggested that the publication has in fact created ill-feelings " (2 Bom. L. R. at 296.) In the present case though the charge is made no evidence whatever was tendered to establish that the ill-feelings were in fact created. Mr. Justice Davar charged the jury that it would be a fruitless inquiry to embark upon. The accused on the other hand, demanded that he should be acquitted on that part of the charge. The verdict, however, does not acquit the prisoner of that part of the charge. Such a verdict is perhaps good, but the sentence is bad as it does not comply with the provisions of Section 367 Clause (3), Criminal Procedure Code, and they do not come with Section 236, Criminal Procedure Code. But assuming they do the offences are never the less distinct offences, and even the terms of Section 236 show they are distinct offences even under the Section.

Nota Bene.

If this view be accepted it follows that each count really charged two distinct offences. There would therefore be four offences under 124 A and two under 153 A in the three counts, *i. e.*, SIX IN ALL. This is exclusive of the fourth charge, and the charge on previous conviction under Section 221 Clause 7 of the Criminal Procedure Code and Section 75 of the Penal Code.

If Section 75 be charged, there must be a separate charge framed and recorded (Dorasami 9 Madras 284 and Weir 886. See also I. L. R. 29 Bombay 449 and 453 per Rusell J., who regards a previous conviction as a 'distinct transaction.') I. L. R. 11 Allabad 393 directs committals under Sections 411-75 to the Court of Sessions.

Further Analysis.

A further examination of schedule V *re* charges, prescribes 3 heads of charge for one single section 382 Penal Code. Each head takes one or the other of the ingredients of that offence, *viz.* 'Death', 'Restraint' or 'fear of Death.'

Similarly Section 124 A comtemplates 3 sets of ill-feelings. This was clearly pointed out by Sir L. Jenkins C. J. in 2 B. L. R. 304 at page 307:- 'You have three sets of feeling against which it is considered that Government should be protected, *viz.*, hatred, contempt or disaffection.'

This careful specification under separate heads of charge is common in the English indictments. In *Reeve's Case* 26 St. Trials 530 the Courts varied the *criminal intent* in 4 diffrent ways in 4 different counts (See *ibid* the charges at page 530 and explanation of the Attorney General at page 536). If the form were carefully adhered to in Bombay there would really be 6 distinct offences charged in the first count, 6 in the second and 4 in the third charge. This would make in all 12 offences under 124 A and 4 under 153 A.

Conclusion.

There are certainly 4 offences under 124A and 2 under 153 A charged if we exclude from consideration the three ill-fellings and regard them merely as one.

III.—Illegality.

MISJOINDER.

I now come to the question of illegality occasioned by the misjoinder of offences at one trial. The line of argument I propose to pursue is this:--The trial contravenes the provision of Section 233 of the Criminal Procedure Code. This constitutes an illegality which vitiates the whole trial *ab initio*, unless it be sanctioned by the exceptional cases specified in Sections 234, 235 and 236. But none of these cases apply.

Section 233.

Section 233 says:—For every distinct offence of which any person is accused, there shall be a *Separate charge* and every such charge shall be *tried separately* except in the cases mentioned in Section 234, 235 236 and 239.'

The fundamental rule, therefore, is that there should be a separate trial for each offence subject to the exceptional cases. Any contravention of this rule constitutes an illegality incurable by Section 537. So held in *Subramania Aiyar's-Case. I, L. R. 25 Madras 61.* It is true that in Subramania's case there was in reality, though not in the frame of the charge, a large number of offences charged. But the decision of their Lordships in the Privy Council did not depend upon that and would have been the same if the number had exceeded the statutory limits of three by the smallest figure. The *Lord Chancellor* observed :— 'This was plainly in contravention of the Code of Criminal Procedure, Section 234, which provided that a person may *only* be tried for 3 *offences* of the *same kind*, if committed within a period of 12 months. 'The number therefore beyond that prescribed by Section 234 or 235 or 236 does not affect the *ratio decidendi*. This decision has been loyally accepted by all the Courts in India and has been followed in numerous cases. In this Court it has been followed in several cases reported in 4 Bombay L. R. 53, 433 and 440; 6 Bombay L. R. 725, and I. L. R. 29 Bombay 449.

In *6 Bombay L. R.* 725 there were only two offences charged under Sections 380 and 414, but the Court quashed the conviction. In *I. L. R. Bombay* 449 Mr. Justice Batty quashed the conviction, for a similar misjoinder and emphatically declared:—

There has been no legal trial. Therefore there can be no legal acquittal. . . . No such order for re-trial seems even possible . . . ." (See *Ibid* p. 467.)

In *Nawab Khayal Solemullah Bahadur* 9. C. W. N. 908 the Calcutta Court went the length of holding that the trial was illegal under the rule of 25 Madras simply for omitting to serve the notice prescribed in Section 145 Clause 3 of the Penal Code. (9. C. W. N. 908.)

And so long ago as in 1875 Sir William Wedderburn quashed the conviction upon an *alternative* charge under Section 192 of the Penal Code on the ground that it was forbidden by Section 234 in I. L. R. 10 *Bombay* 124. (See also Shamrao Vithal's argument.)

Other Cases:—26 Bombay 533, 22 Bombay 449; 26 Madrass 125, 127 and 592; 28 Madras 437, 29 Madras 558 and 569; 30 Madras 328; 29 Calcutta 385; 31 Calcutta 928, 32 Calcutta 1015, 33 Calcutta 68 and 1256; 1 C. L. J. 475, 5 C. L. J. 231, 6 C. L. J. 320 and 757; 8 C. W. N. 344, 9 C. W. N. 909, 11 C. W. N. 789; 24 Allahabad 254, 26 Allahabad 195; (1904) W. N. 165 and 223.

Nota Bene.

The law is therefore thoroughly settled. According to 6 Bombay L. R. 725, a joinder of two offences not of the same kind would vitiate the trial. Therefore the joinder of 124 A with 153 A vitiates the whole trial. Mr. Justice Chandavarkar held in the *Hind Swaraj* case 'that the offence under Section 124A of the Penal Code is not an offence of the same kind as an offence under Section 153A of the Code. And the Criminal Procedure Code no doubt to provide that these offences cannot be tried together.' Furthermore if the attempt be a distinct offence then there are 4 offences under 124 A alone charged and two under 153A. This would make the trial all the worse.

I shall however, proceed to consider whether the exceptions sanction such a trial.

EXCEPTIONS.

Section 234:—The first exception to Section 233 is Section 234.

Section 234 says—"When a person is accused of more offences than one of the *same kind*, committed within the space of 12 *months*, from the first to the last of such offences he may be charged with and tried at *one trial*, for any number of them *not exceeding three*"

"Offences are of the *same kind* when they are punishable with *the same amount* of punishment under the *same section* of the Indian Penal Code or any special or local law."

Comment:—(i) The first requisite of joinder in 234 is that they must be offences of the same kind. But here they are not of the same kind as already explained, *viz.*, 124A and 153A. They do not fall within the *same* section. Moreover, Section 124 A is punishable with transportation for life or 3 *years* rigorous imprisonment, whereas 153 A is *not* punishable with transportation at all but with only 2 *years* rigorous imprisonment. The *amount* is not the same.

(ii) The second requisite is that the number shall not exceed *three*. But here there are 16 offences exclusive of the fourth charge on 153 A, and the fifth charge about previous conviction. But even if the three sets of feeling do not consitute three distinct offences, at least the attempt is distinct from the substantive offence. If so there would be at least six offences, *viz.*, 4 under 124 A and 2 under 153 A. This too would contravene Section 234. It is only when the attempt and the substantive offence is regarded as one and the same offence and not distinct offences, that the offences are reduced to three. But the reduction can only be achieved by ignoring and obliterating the essential distinction between the substantive offence and the attempt. In mathematical language attempt *plus* success constitutes the principal or substantive offence. The want of success reduces the substantive offence into an attempt. The facts required to establish either are obviously not co-extensive. Under the circumstances it is impossible to regard the two as one offence only. *Therefore Section 234 does not Sanction the joinder and trial thereon of* six offences, much less of six offences not of the same kind. But even the minimum 3, not of the same kind, vitiates the trial; and Section 234 alone does not help.

Section 235.

This Section 235 does not apply because there are two transactions here, *viz*, the publication of the article of 12th May 1908 entitled "*The country's misfortune* " and the publication of the article of 9th June 1908 entitled " *The remedies are not lasting.*"

It is submitted that this Section 235 applies only to the offence committed in the *same* translation. This is clearly so, so far as Section 235 Clause 1 is concerned, The very terms say so.

Sub-section 2 is equally confined to the same transaction. The words " the acts alleged " in Sub-section 2, refer manifestly to the " series of acts " in sub-section 1.

The illustrations to clause (2) indicate that the transaction is the same. Moreover, it has been so held in *Gopol ani Narasaya*, Weir 892.

Weir 892 *says* :—" Section 235 seems to apply to a case in which the different offences are parts of *one* transaction and *not* a series of similar offences committed on different dates."

Again in Empress vs. Bogi Ram:—(1897) 22 Punjab Recorder, No. 43 p. 105 it was held that " Neither Section 235 nor *Section* 236 relates to *two* acts which form *two* distinct transactions. Section 236 relates not to distinct acts but to a *single act* or *series of acts*, "where the *facts* being *ascertained* it is *doubtful which* of *several* Sections is applicable."

Reductio ad absurdum.

Section 235 must be wholly confined to acts in the same transactions. If not, it would suffice to allege A stole a watch from B, robbed C the next day, burnt D's house the third, committed dacoity on the fourth, forged E's signature on the fifth, murdered F on the sixth, and so on to bring the offences under Section 235 Clause 2. These could never be tried together. If they could, it would render that protection designed by Section 233 Criminal Procedure Code entirely nugatory. Practically it would repeal Section 233, even 234 and 235 Clause 1. Section 235 must therefore be confined to the same transaction. If not, there can never be any misjoinder of offences. The ruling in 25 Madree 61 must be cast into oblivion. So must the numerous cases on the misjoinder of offences. This is impossible.

Nota Bene.

It follows then that Section 235 cannot apply because, here, there are *two* transactions. The offence under Section 124 A was committed on the 12th of May in an act which cannot be said to form part of the same transaction in which the offence of 153 A was committed on the 9th of June 1908.

Section 236.

This section must likewise be confined to the *same* transaction. The remarks made and cases quoted on the question of section 235 apply with equal force to Section 236.

Section 236 can have no application for two reasons, *viz.* (i). The transactions are not the same and (ii) there is *no case of doubt* as contemplated in Section 236. Here the offences are so distinctly plain upon the acts alleged that there are separate convictions on 153 A and 124 A and separate punishments as well. There has even been an acquittal on the fourth charge on 153 A.

Conclusion.

Conclusion:—It is therefore quite clear that the exceptions in Sections 234, 235 and 236 taken individually and disjunctively do not sanction the adopted mode of trial or in the language of the Judgment of the Privy Council in 25 Madras 61 "these trials are prohibited in the mode they were conducted." The trials were conducted jointly in spite of the objection cf the accused whereas they ought to have been conducted separately.

Prejudice.

The question ot *prejudice* has nothing to do with a trial illegally conducted. That cannot convert an illegal into a legal trial. If prejudice is required, it must be presumed from the very mode of trial. But there was great prejudice in admitting to Exhibits D, E, F, G, H and I. These could not possibly be given in evidence against the first article of the 12th of May as they are all of a latter date. But they were given and were actually utilised to establish criminal intent for both articles. Exhibit D is moreover the subject of a second charge on 124 A. The trial on that would be pending but for the joinder. While it was pending it could not be given in evidence against the accused to the first trial. Its admission must thefore have intensified the prejudice. Had these trials been separated there can be but little doubt that no Jury would ever convict the accused on the first article. The Crown must have realised that, for they hastened with lightening speed to institute a second prosecution on the article of the 9th of June 1908. There was no need for this haste but the sound fear of an acquittal. The second sanction is dated 26th June 1908 i. e. after arrest and inquiry on 24th June. The first order is dated 3rd June 1908.

This view that no prejudice is required is borne out by the observation in *Abdul Majid*, I. L. R. Calcutta 1256 at 1264 :—There is no question of whether the accused have actually been prejudiced by being tried together. The question is whether the rule that has been broken is such, that its breach *in other cases* is likely to prejudice the accused and to produce evils such as those referred to in the Judgment of the Privy Council." That is the ground on which the decision is based, and that is the safest principle.

IV—CONSTRUCTION.

It has been suggested and contended that though this mode of trial is not covered by the excepted case taken *singly*, it is so covered if two exceptions be taken *cumulatively*. The question then arises can these exceptions be taken cumulatively? This naturally depends upon the proper construction of Section 233.

Maxwell.

Now, my Lord, the policy of Section 233 is plainly designed for the protection of the accused for the purpose of preventing confusion, embarrassment or prejudice to him by the very multiplicity of the charges. This is the mischief aimed at. It is denominated a "humane rule" by Lord Blackburn. Therefore that construction would be the true one which would 'suppress the mischief and advance the remedy' in the words of Lord Coke. There are some pertinent observations on this point in *Maxwell* on the *Interpretation of Statutes* Chapter X, Section I—Construction of Penal Laws, page 367. (Third Edition by A. B. Kempe.) I shall quote only two passages.

First:—'The rule which requires that penal and some other statutes shall be construed *strictly* was more rigorously applied in former times. But it has lost much of its force and importance in recent times, since it has become more and more generally *recognised* that the *paramount duty of the Judicil Interpreter* is to put upon the language of the Legislature, honestly and faithfully, its plain and rational meaning and *to promote its object*. It is founded, however on the *tenderness* of the law for the *rights of individuals* . . . It is unquestionably a reasonable expectation that, when the former intends ......an encroachment on natural liberty or rights . . . it will not leave its intention to be gathered by mere doubtful inferences, or convey it in 'cloudy and dark words' only, but will manifest it with reasonable clearness. The rule of strict construction does not, indeed, require or sanction that suspicious scrutiny of the words, or those hostile conclusions from their ambiguity or from what is left unexpressed, which characterise the judicial interpretation of affidavits in support of *ex-parte* applications, or of *convictions*, where the ambiguity goes to the Jurisdiction . . . This would be to defeat, not to promote the object of the Legislature; to misread the statute and misunderstand its purpose.(*See* Maxwell pp.367-369.)

Page 385 :—"The rule of strict construction, however, whenever invoked, comes attended with qualifications, and other rules no less important; and it is by the light which each contributes that the meaning must be determined. Among them is the rule that, that sense of the words is to be adopted which best harmonises with the context and promotes in the fullest manner the policy and object of the Legislature. The paramount object, in construing *penal* as well as *other statutes*, is to ascertain the legislative intent: and the rule of strict construction is not violated by permitting the words to have their full meaning, or the more extensive of two meanings, when best effectuating the intention. They are, indeed, frequently taken in the widest sense, sometimes even in a sense more wide than etymologically belongs or is popularly attached to them, in order to carry out effectually the legislative intent, or, to use Lord Cok's words, to suppress the mischief and advance the remedy." (*see* Maxwell, p. 385.)

Now, my Lords, applying this rule of interpretation a combination of the exceptions is impossible. The natural meaning of the words in Section 233 appears to be that the general rule shall prevail unless the departure is authorised by any one of the *limited* exceptions taken *singly* and not *cumulatively*. The Courts are not justified in adding to the limited number of exceptions to the process of permutation and combination thereby setting at naught the limitation in Section 233 and the elaborate provision intended to cover the whole ground of exceptions. To so construe these Sections would be to hold that the word offences in Section 204 means not only the three offences of the same kind mentioned therein but also every other offence of *any other* kind which is committed in any act so connected with any one of these three offences as to form parts of the same transaction. But this clearly cannot be intended by the legislature for in Section 235 it provides for the trial of offences, *not* of the same kind. In this connection the addition of Clause (2) in Section 222 makes it clear that the offence as used in Section 234 was not intended to include every act so connected with that offence as to form part of the same transaction. (See 40 P. R. C. R. P. 4 also I. L. R. 25 Madras 61 at p. 73.)

Similarly the elimination of the explanation to Section 453 of the Old Code (Act X of 1872) points to the same conclusion. Section 453 of the Old Code is now Section 234. The old explanation extended the meaning of the expression *offences of the same kind* so as to incorporate Section 455 of the Old Code which corresponds with Section 236 of the New Code. (*See I. L. R. 9* Cal *371*.) In the old Code such separable offences could be deemed offences of the same kind within the meaning of the term in Section 453 old and 234 new. But the explanation from the new Code excludes Section 455 old (now 236) formerly incorporated in old Section 453, now 234 by the explanation. There is now no room for doubt under the new definition. Clearly therefore no combinations are intended.

On the other hand, if the legislature had contemplated a combination of exceptions it would have used appropriate words sanctioning such a combination. Moreover, this limited interpretation would prevent the law from being circumvented by the addition of fictitious charges. For example it is admitted that the offence of 124A, on the first article could not be joined with the offence of 153A of the second article, but if 124A be added in the second article either under 235 or 236 of the criminal procudure Code then it would be tried. Therefore all that is necessary is to add a fictitious charge under Section 124A, although the offence cannot be proved. As a matter of fact in the *Hind Swaraj* case, I submit with all respect that Mr. Justice Chandavarkar did make use of a fictitious excuse to legalize the trial. He said:—It is admitted by Mr. Baptista that the charge for the offence under Section 124 A of the Penal Code in respect of one of the two articles in question could be legally joined to the charge for the offence under the same section in respect of the other article. And in such a case it is equally clear from Sections 236 and 237 of the Code of Criminal Procedure that, if in respect of each of the articles the evidence recorded substantiated the offence under Section 153 A, instead of the offence under Section 124 A, the accused could be legally convicted of the former offence, even though it did not form the subject matter of the charge. That being the case the addition of the offence under that section in the charage sheet cannot be held to be illegal. "

Now this is bringing Section 153 A within the doubtful case of law provided for by Section 236. But in the *Hind Swaraj* case nobody even suggested a doubt either in the Magistrate's Court or in the Appellate Court. There was no doubt in the Magistrate's mind as he charged and convicted the accused on both the offences, though only one joint punishment was awarded.

He had no recourse to Section 367 Clause (3) Criminal Procedure Code or Section 72 of the Penal Code. In other cases on the very same article I believe he has inflicted seperate punishments for 124A and 153A. So that was absolutely no case of doubt, but it was so treated by Mr. Justice Chandavarkar.

But worse things will happen if once the door for fictitious charges be opened. For this reason in *Abdul Majid* I. L. R. 33 Calcutta 1256 the Court firmly refused to listen to the arguments which insidiously sought to introduce a fictitious charge with much more plausibility.

Mr. Justice Harrington observed as follows:--It has been pressed in argument that because the prisoners might have been justly indicted for dishonestly retaining the whole proceeds, they cannot have been prejudiced by being jointly tried on separate charges for separate offences and therefore Section 537 applies. As to this the Privy Council have held that Section 537 does not apply in a case where a man is tried on several charges together in breach of Section 233, although such a trial under the practice obtaining in England of joining several misdemeanours in one indictment, need not be necessarily unfair to the prisoner. " (33 Calcutta at 1267—68).

But apart from the danger of fictitious charges the addition does not meet with the approbation of reason. For it is conceded that the offence under Section 124A of one transaction could not be joined with 153A of another. How then can the addition of a third offence, whether under 235 or 236 Criminal Procedure Code improve matters. If the joinder of two offences is embarrassing and prejudicial, surely the interpolation of a third one must intensify the embarrassment and prejudice. This constitutes the strength of the argument against such joinder and this exposes the weakness of the case for such joinder.

Extension.

But if such joinder be toleretad, it logically leads to further extension. And such extension is the basis decision of the Appellate Court in the *Hind Swaraj* case. Mr. Justice Chandavarkar said:—It is true that, as urged by Mr. Baptista, the offence under Section 124 A of the Penal Code and is not an offence of the same kind as an offence under Section 153A of the Code And the Criminal Procedure Code no doubt provides that these two offences cannot be tried together. But there is nothing in the Code which directs that where an accused person is alleged to have done two or more acts, each of which may fall within the definition of an offence under one or another of the Section of the Penal Code, the section or sections in either case, being the same, the joinder of the charges under these sections is illegal. Substantially the acts amount in such a case, to offence *punishable* under the same section of the Penal Code and therefore they are offences of the same kind." It is difficult to follow the reasoning in this case but this view is supported by Mr. Justice Heaton. He says:— "The offences in this case were two in number, namely, the publication of the 4th April, and the publication of the 11th April. These two offences were, as charged, punishable under the same *sections* of the Indian Penal Code and were, therefore, it seems to me offences of the same kind. If the word "Section" in the second clasue of section 234 be read as incapable of meaning "Sections" that is if it be read invariably singular, then Mr. Baptista's argument is good, not otherwise. But I do not think it is the intention of the Code, either expressed or implied, to exclude from the operation of section 234 an offence because it is made the subject of more than one charge. Charging one act or a series of acts under more than one section of the Indian penal Code is a proceeding provided for in section 235 Clause (5) and in section 236 of the Criminal Procedure Code."

Comment.

Mr. Justice Chandavarkar apparently does not invoke the aid of Section 235 but reads the word "Section" in 234 as capable of reading "Sections." So does Mr. Justice Heaton. But this reading is unwarranted. By this process the number of offences is made to exceed the limit of three. The very object of Section 234 is thereby frustrated. Such a reading means this. If in one transaction a man commits the offences of murder, arson and theft and in the other transaction the same three offences, and in the third transaction the same three offences, all of them may be joined together. In principle it makes no difference if ten offences instead of of three are committed in each transaction. Thus thirty offences may be tried together. Yet it is conceded that no more than three offences of the same kind can be tried together under 234. For example in one transaction A hurts B and C and in another A hurts D and E. Here in two transactions there are committed four offences of the same kind, *i.e*, hurt. These four of the same kind cannot be tried together yet an assortment of forty offences of different kinds may be if "Section" be read as "Sections" in Section 234. This is not reason. and Law is the perfection of reason.

If the aid of Section 235 or Section 236 be invoked for purposes of combination then the offeces in each transaction *need not even be of the same kinds* as the offences in the other transactions, provided only that *one offence* in each transaction is of the same kind, *e. g.*, A. commits house-breaking with arson, theft and forgery in one transtction; he commits house-breaking with hurt, and rape in another, and house-breaking with murder and dacoity in a third. The connecting link, the judicial cement, is the single offence of house breaking. All these could be tried together.

The very statement of such a combination renders the construction impossible. It is certainly unreasonable. It renders the protection given by Section 233 practically nugatory. "It is difficult to understand how there could ever be a misjoinder if such a procedure were authorized" (Lord Herschell in (1894) A. C. 494 at 501). It would virtually abrogate Section 233. *Moreover* it really means the combination of sections which are mutually destructive.

Mutually Destructive.

Section 234.—The basal characteristic in Section 234 is the similitude of the offences. It looks exclusively to *number*, *time*, *and sameness* of the offences without regard to the number of transactions, except in so far as they would be limited by the number of offices of the name kind triable under Section 234.

Section 235.—On the other hand Section 235 is the converse of Section 234. In 235 the transaction must be the same, but it is utterly indifferent to time and the kind or number of offences. The time may extend over 12 months and the offences may be unlimited in number and of different kinds. These Sections are therefore practically antagonistic and mutually detsructive. How can they be combined? How can a construction charged with such results be the true construction? Plainly this does not repress the mischief in view nor effectuate the intention of the Legislature. There is therefore no reason to construe the singular into plural or convert the disjunctive into conjunctive.

"The essence of the Code" says the Judgment in I. L. R. 29 *Madras at* 560-1 is to be exhaustive on the matters in respect of which it declares the law, and it is not the province of a Judge to disregard or go outside the letter of the enactment according to its true construction. See L. R. 29, I. A. 196 as to the Code being exhaustive or not."

Sections 234, 235, 236 *and* 239.

But if Sections 234 and 235 can be taken jointly, why not Sections 234 and 239, and, indeed, why not all the Sections 234, 235, 236 and 239. The very hypothesis demonstrates such a construction of the Sections an unreasonable and impossible one. The Legistature would have used plainer language instead of this circumlocution. Under these circumstances I submit the exceptions must be taken singly and not cumulatively. The view is also borne out by authority.

V.—Cases

1. The first case to which I would ask your Lordship's attention is *Queen-Empress* vs. *Moulna I. L. R. 14 Allahabad* 502. In this case the joinder was disapproved, but it was not condemned as an illegality. But this was before the Privy Council decision in 25 Madras 61. Before the Privy Council judgment there was much difference of opinion as to what constituted a mere irregularity curable by Section 537. But my point is that 14 Allahabad regards it as irregular at least.

2. The next case is *Bhagwat Dial vs. The King-Emperor 40 Panjab Recorder (1905) Cr. Ruling page* 4. This case completely answers the

case for combination and also deals with the view which apparently forms the *ratio decidendi* in the *Hind Swaraj* case. According to this case there can be no combination of offences even if they fall within the same sections, supposing the word Section in 234 can be read as Sections in the plural.

This case also adverts to the argument based upon the addition of Clause 2 to Section 222 of the Criminal Procedure Code.

3. This very argument based on Section 222 Clause 2 was also used by the Chief Justice in I. L. R. 25 Madras 61 at p. 73. It says " Moreover the provision of Section 222 Clause (2) shows the intention of the Legislature that no further departure from the law as laid down in Sections 233, 234 and 235 should be made than was necessary for the purposes of that particular enactment. " (See p. 73.)

4. The Punjab Case (40 P. R. 4 (1905)) was followed in *Emperor* vs. *Kasi Viswanath I. L. R. 30 Madras 328.* In this case there were three distinct transactions in each of which the same offences under Sections 409 and 477A of the Penal Code were committed. The joinder was held to be illegal. This case refers to 4 Bombay L. R. 433. The Bombay case inferentially supports the decision in 30 Madras according to the view taken by the Madras Court.

5. In an earlier case the Madras High Court held such a combination "irregular," but this also was prior to the Privy Council decision. (See I. L. R. 12 Madras 273). There were two offences under Sections 372 and 373 committed in *two* transactions. It could be sanctioned under the simultaneous operation of Sections 234, 235 and 239.

6. The next case is *Nga Lun Maung vs. King Emperor 2, Lower Burma* Rulings (1903) 10. This was a case decided in 1902 in which the Chief Court of Lower Burma took the same view. This case is not quoted in the Panjab and Madras Cases but it is a case so well reasoned out that it ought to dispel all doubts upon this point. It was a reference made by the Chief Justice. In the reference he deals with Section 236 which he holds cannot apply except in the case of doubt. The words of the reference are:—'The question seems to be one of very considerable difficulty and I think it is desirable to obtain a final decision on it.'

The full Bench consisted of three Judges. T. White, C. J. Fox and Trevin, J. J. The Chief Justice concurred with the proposed answer which fully meets the arguments in support of the contention that Section 234, 235 and 236 can operate cumulatively. The Court holds it can operate singly only, and not cumulatively. It refers to the possible circumvention of the Law by the addition of fictitious charges opening the order to the very mischiefs and abuses intended to be suppressed and the virtual abrogation of Section 233 Cr. P. Code.

The next case is that of *Badhai Sheik* Vs. Tarap sheik *10 C. W. N. 32*. In this case the members of an unlawful assembly looted certain persons on the 22nd of February, thereby committing offences under Sections 143 and 379, Indian Pennal Code. The same persons committed the same offence the next day in another place. The transactions were diffrent. Held the Joinder was illegal, although it came within the joint operation of Sections 234 and 239. In this case the Court consider whether singular could be read as plural under the General Clauses Act and whether such reading was repugnant to the context. The last para in the judgment deals with the combination of Section 239 into Section 234. If this Section 234 cannot be combined with Section 239 the word 'and' in Section 233 has no force of combination and if 234 cannot be combined with 239, there is no reason upon the same words to hold that 234, 235 and 236 or any two of them can be combined. This case also shows the singular 'transaction' in 239 cannot be read as plural, why then should 'Section' or 'kind' in 234 be read as plural.

8. So long ago as 1866 a *Queen* vs. *Itworce Dome*, *6 W. R.* 83, the Court held a joinder under Section 234 and Section 239 was illegal. Held that when persons are charged for three separate and distinct robberies, committed on the same night in three different houses, they must be tried separately on each of these three charges. (*6 W. R. 83.*)

Other cases. See Weir, Criminal ruling, pp. 900 and 901 and 35 Cal. 161 *re* Bipin Chandra Pal.

9. There is thus a concensus of opinion against any combination of the exceptions in Section 233. They must be taken singly and not cumulatively. There is also authority against extension of Section 234 by reading Section as Sections and thus opening the door for a budget of offences sufficient to crush a man by its very weight. The solitary exception is the decision in the *Hind Swardj* case, but that is erroneous, and even if correct it is distinguishable from the present case as I shall presently explain.

VI.—"Hind Swaraj" Case.

Distinguishable.—The "Hind Swaraj" case is distinguishable from the present case in several respects.

1. The Court regarded the charges of 124 A and 153 A as alternate charges for the purposes of Section 236 only as a case of doubt, but there is no case of doubt in this case. The Court had power to deal with punishment in appeal if the trial was legal.

2. In the case of doubt there can be a conviction on one offence only although several are charged and the Appellate Court confirmed the conviction on 124A only, but not on 153 A. The Court ought thereupon to have reduced the punishment, but it did not do so. However the punishment imposed did not exceed the punishment imposable on the less grave offence according to Section 72 of the Penal Code. But in this case the punishments are imposed both under 124 A and 153 A. Besides three years, transportation is awarded, which could not be done under Section 72.

3. The facts are not the same upon the view of the case taken by the Appellate Court.

Ratio Decidendi.

1—SECTION.

1. The word Section cannot be read as plural, but most invariably be read as singular.

2. But the definition refers not only to the same Section but the *same amount*.

Even offences falling under the same section may not be of the same kind within the meaning of Section 234. for example, if the amount of punishment differed as in the offences under Section 454 and 457 of the Penal Code, they would not be of the same kind.

3. Section 234 does not speak of charges, it is true, but only of offences. But as under Section 233 each distinct offence is to be chaged separately, it follows there can be only three charges tried together under Section 234.

II.—ACT.

1. The words " Act " and " Offence, " are not synonymous terms. They cannot be equated. Offence is not equal to act but only *means* an act punishable under the Code and any Local Law. (Section 4 clause (o). Act and offence cannot be substituted for each other. If we substitute the word " Acts " for " offences " in Section 234 we get this meaning :— "Acts are of the same kind when they are punishable with the same amount of punishment. " But the Offence of 124A may be committed by words, signs, ar representations. Surely these acts could not be of the same kind though the offence is identical and the amount of punishment the same.

2. Mr. Justice Heaten holds that the one act of publication can constitute only one offence though punishable under several sections, but not punishable cumulatively. This is obviously erroneous.

(i) Here the publication is an act no doubt, but publication itself is no offence. The publication of the article is an offence. But the article is a series of acts so connected together as to form one transaction together with the publication. Each word written is an act. The acts requisite for 124A are not the same as the acts required for 153A. Appropriate acts must be extracted from the article for each offence. Even when the words are the same, the meaning cannot be the same to constitute both the offences.

(ii) But even if the act of publication be taken as constituting the offence, then one act does not mean only one offence. Each act may constitute several distinct offences seperately chargeable and even separately triable and punishable. *For example*, A fixes a gun whereby he hurts B, disables C, kills D and sets a house on fire. Surely this is not one offence punishable under various Sections. They are distinct offences punishable seperately, cumulatively and triable seperately under Section 403.

Simialrly, A, publishes an article whereby he defames B, C, D and E. Each can complain under the Penal Code and A is liable to punishment seperately for each offence. The character of C, D and E will not be vindicated by the exclusive complaint of B.

Therefore this publication constitutes two offences, under two Sections against two distinct persons.

(iii) Sections 235, 236, 237 and 238 all recognise that the same act may constitute separable and distinct offences. This is more forcibly brought out in Sections 403 Clause 3 which allows second and third trials upon the same acts.

Submission.—I therefore sumbit an act is not an offence and one act may give rise to several offences all distinct.

Applicability of Section 236.

1. Section 237 is limited in its operation to the case mentioned in Section 236 (See I. L. R. 33 Calcutta 1256 at 1263.)

2. Therefore conviction under Section 237 is possible only if a charge under Section 236 is frameable. This is assumed in the judgment in the *Hind Swaraj* case by Mr. Justice Chandavarkar. But Section 236 cannot operate with Section 234 cumulatively. Therefore no conviction is possible under Section 237. The reasoning therefore does not apply.

3. Weir 897:—"It can scarcely be meant that the element of doubt is the governing point." This means doubt cannot convert dissimilar offence into offences of the same kind.

VII.—Sentences

1. If the trial is illegal there can be no conviction and no sentence. If it is legal, then the case must be considered from two aspects depending upon whether the transaction is the *same* or *different*.

2. There is one acquittal and three convictions, and there are three sentences ; one on each conviction.

3. Now if the transactions are the *same*, there cannot be two sentences on 124 A, but one sentence only according to Section 7 of the Penal Code. See illustrations also. Furthermore if the charge on 124A and 153 A are alternative under Section 236 there could be only *one* conviction and one sentence and that too for the offence of 153 A only under Section 72 of the Penal Code. There cannot be 3 sentences, not even two, but only one sentence and only one punishment not exceeding two years' imprisonment.

4. If the transactions are not the same but distinct then.

(*i*) The acquittal on 153 A on fist article is a bar to the trial on 124 A of the first article under Section 403 Clause 2; if Sections 124 A and 153A are alternative under Section 236 as the Prosecution contends.

True the order was passed after the end of the trial on 124 A, but this is only formal. In substance that was decided before the trial on 124 A commenced.

(*ii*) There can be no punishment on 124 A, for, if the article taken as a whole constitutes the offence of 153A as found by the Jury nothing is left for 124A, and therefore there can be no conviction or sentence on 124 A or *vice versa*. It is contended by the Prosecution that the article taken as a whole constitutes the offence of 124 A and and it is simultaneously contended that taken as a whole it constitutes the offence of 153 A. This is incomprehensible, but be it as it may, if the whole is thus absorbed by 124A, how can there be any conviction on 153 A and *vice versa*. But if there be a conviction there should be one punishment only and that only on the charge of 153 A according to Section 72 I. P. Code.

5. Again if the contention be upheld that Section 153A is charged alternatively under Section 236 then the punishment must be regulated by Section 72 of the Penal Code. Therefore the minimum punishment only could be given. Transportation for 3 years is illegal under Section 72. Much more so is both transportation and fine separately.

Rule Absolute.

Illegal sentence would be good ground for a declaration that the case is a fit one for appeal upon the principle laid down ,for appeal to the Privy Council. (See I. L. R. 22 Bombay 112 at page 150 and also at page 535):—"His Majesty will not review criminal proceedings unless it be shown that by a disregard of the form of legal process or by some violation of the principles of natural justice or *otherwise* substantial and grave injustice was done. (See L. R. 12 App. Cas. 459). According to Sir Charles Farran C. J. an important question of Law or want of jurisdiction would be a fit case for appeal. This is unquestionably an important question of law. Unless corrected the illegal joinder would create a precedent that would divert the law into new channels and prove prejudicial to the accused in other cases and open the door to grave mischiefs and serious miscarriage of justice. The form of legal process is disregarded by the mode of trial adopted. If the trial is illegal the convictions and sentences are illegal. To enforce them is to violate the principles of natural justice. A day's detention in jail is unjust. But there is no means of remedying it except by an appeal to the Privy Council. This also comes within the rule of jurisdiction. Such a trial goes to the very root of the jurisdiction of the Court. The Court has no power to try a man on such a misjoinder of charges. There is no conviction. The Court is not even competent to pass any order in a trial void *ab-initio*. It is also desirable to obtain the decision of the highest tribunal in the Empire. With the establishment of an Appeal Court in England appeals to the Privy Council should be easier now. There is therefore substantial and grave injustice and other good reasons for a declaration that this is a fit case for appeal in order to enable the Privy Council to determine whether grave and substantial injustice has been done to the petitioner.

VIII.—Same Transaction.

This term is nowhere defined in the Code.

Stephens defines it thus:—"A group of facts so connected together as to be referred to by a single name, as a crime, a contract, a wrong, or any other subject of inquiry which may be in issue." (See Cuningham on Evidence p. 92.)

No principle is stated on authority to determine whether the alleged acts constitute the same transaction or not. The expresstion is vague but the decisions are sufficiently indicative. The question was fully considered and discussed in 15 Bombay 491.

Jardine J:—" In cases cited in Section 309 of Taylor on the Doctrine of Election, the existence of concurrence or proximity of time appears to have been the general criterion as to whether several felonies could be tried at the same trial." The passage referred to will be found at p. 260-1 of the 10 Edition. It runs as follows:—" In cases of felony however, this rule from motives of humanity have been considerably modified as . . . several counts calculated to embarrass a prisoner in his defence. It is now the practice for the Judge to call upon the prosecutor to elect one felony. and to confine himself to that unless the offences *though distinct in law*, seem to constitute in fact but parts of one continuous transaction, in which latter event an election will be enforced."

The general criterion is continuity and Proximity of time, but there may be a break in time. When that occurs the acts must be connected by a specific pre-conceived criminal intent. This is the link connecting the acts. This was the view taken by Mr. Justice Birdwood in the case (see remarks at page 495 of 15 Bombay.)

Rule in 16 Bombay 424 :—The matter was further considered in 16 Bombay 424. The Court held :—We think that the proximity of time combined with the case as to intention and similarity of action and result . . . bring it within the words same transaction." This was then the final rule extracted from the cases in 15 and 16 Bombay.

4 Bombay L. R. 789 :—The same point came up for consideration in *4 Bombay L. R. 789*. The principle of continuity and common pre-conceived criminal intent was applied. In another case reported at 4 Bombay L. R. 920, the Court affirmed the principle of continuity and held that this was not necessarily broken by a mere interval of time. The Court held that " Their inter-relation and inter-dependence must be considered. " Are they so related to one another in point of purpose or as cause and effects, or as principal, and subsidiary, as to constitute one continuous action. "

These are the criteria. Upon these criteria the publications of 12th May and 9th June do not form the same transaction. The subjects are not the same. The authors are not the same. This we would prove but for the ruling of Justice Davar that the two publications did not constitute the same transaction. There is an interval of nearly a month. They were regarded as distinct transactions or acts. The Government sanction is not the same. There were two complaints, two warrants of arrest, two inquiries by the Magistrate and two committals. Then in the High Court there were two applications for Special Juries and two were ordered. The Judge did not regard it as the same transaction. The Jury convicted on each offence under 124A and the Judge passed two sentences on 124A and a third on 153A. In the face of two sanctions, two complaints, two warrents, two inquiries, two committals, two orders as to special Juries, two convictions and two sentences in 124 A alone, a third on 153 A and acquittal on the other 153 A, it is impossible for the Prosecution to contend now, with any fairness, that the transactions are the same.

The Advocate General's Reply.

Mr. Robertson, the acting Advocate General, then opposed the rule on behalf of the Crown. The following is a summary of his argument.

He said that mere irregularity was not sufficient to allow appeal. The question was whether there was substantial injustice done. The question was what was the meaning of the words in section 234 C. P. C.

What is punished is really the "act;" the word "offence" really meant the act, which was made criminal by law. In Section 233 the word offence meant act or omission made punishable by one or more laws. To lay a charge meant that the accused was charged with doing an act or omission, not with "the offence." In murder the accused is charged with a certain act that caused death and then it is said that the act is punishable under such and such section.

Mr. J. Batchelor—But when once you name the Section and give to the act the name of the offence given in that section, then how can you refer to the act?

Mr. Robertson—The charge is always for the act and offence is defined to be act or omission punishable under one law or another.

Turning to S. 234 C. P. C. Mr. Robertson said that two offences under S. 124A could surely be joined under it. But it does not prohibit another offence being joined to any one thereof. In the case of different charges joined in one trial, really there are separate trials for each separate charge. And therefore 124A and 153 A could be joined.

J. Batchelor—You cannot join grievous hurt and theft. How do you say you can join them if you add a third charge to either. You have not met Mr. Baptista's position that charges under 124A and 153A cannot be joined under S. 234.

Mr. Robertson:—It is clear that the two articles could very well be charged together under Section 124 A and discussed together. By joining a charge under section 153 A no injustice was done. The two articles formed part of a series as the Judge said. It was fortunate for the Accused to be charged only with two of them. Mr. Robertson here read passages from the various articles and urged that the whole was really one transaction in which offences under Sections 124 A and 153 were committed. Where was the injustice done then? He said that his purpose was only to show that though there might have been irregularity still there was no injustice to the Accused. If the words under Sec. 234 were to be given artificially the restricted meaning urged by Mr. Baptista, many criminals would be able to evade justice. In the present case the point was really this. The case was to be sent to the Privy Council because the Crown omitted in regard to the first Article a charge under S. 153A.

C. J.:—This assumes that offences of the same kind means acts falling under more than one Section.

Mr. R.—There can be no doubt about it. S. 234 allows charges under three acts to be joined. It does not matter what offences the different acts give rise to, so long as all the acts give rise exactly to the same offences. If two acts come under one section, they can be joined. It does not matter if one of these comes also under another section. And there Section 235 comes to the help in regard to each of these two acts and the offences they give rise to.

Counsel argued that the language of 235 and 236 showed that one act could give rise to several offences. The charges made could, therefore, be validly joined and the Code provided that the Jury must give a verdict on each of the charges. Counsel quoted passages from the article showing that they may come within 124 A. or under 153 A. There Section 236 C. P. Code providing for alternate charges applied.

J. Batchelor—S. 235 contemplates more than one offence arising out of one act. S. 236 contemplates only one out of two offences, which precisely being a matter of doubt. It seems to me that the charges fall under both S. 124A. and 153 A and I would proceed under S. 235 and not S. 236 at all.

Counsel then referred to S. 237 and said that this section also could apply. The Accused could have been convicted of 153 A even though he had not been charged thereunder. So then really he was not prejudiced. There was no substantial violation of law. Ingenuity had been exercised to show irregularities. But that was not enough to justify leave for appeal. There was no damage done to the prisoner, no injustice. Counsel said that his suggestion was that the joinder of 153 A and 124 A was really valid under section 235, second part. The decision of Mr. J. Candavarkar in the *Hind Swarajya* case supported the view he, Mr. Robortson, had taken. It was really unnecessary to have convicted under S. 153 A after convicting under S. 124 A. But it was not illegal. Counsel also quoted from Mr. J. Heaton's Judgment in the case in support of his contention that what had occurred in the case of Mr. Tilak was only an irregularity. Counsel quoted cases to show that the Privy Council had declined to allow appeals merely for violation of formal rules etc. As to sentences, Mr. Robertson argued that they were immaterial unless the whole trial was to be held to be vitiated and therefore null and void. The Judge, J. Davar, had given reasons for the sentence awarded. The Privy Council would not interfere merely to lessen the sentence.

Mr. Baptista having briefly replied to the argument of Mr. Robertson the Chief Justice intimated that their Lordships would give a written judgment in the case.

The High Court Judgment.

On Tuesday the 8th September the Chief Justice delivered the Judgment of the Court at 11-30 A. M. by which the *rule nisi* was discharged, and Mr. Tilak's application for a certificate for leave to appeal to the Privy Council was rejected. The following is the text of the Judgment.

Emperor
V/s } High Court Crown Side.
Bal Gangadhar Tilak.

Coram :—Scott C. J. and Batchelor J.

(Judgment delivered by Scott C. J.) 8th September 1908.

This is a rule granted by us on a petition for a certificate that the decision of the Judge and Jury in the case of Emperor v/s B. G. Tilak is a fit subject for appeal to His Majesty in Council.

Before granting the rule we required Counsel for the Petitioner to specify the grounds upon which he was prepared to support his application. He then argued that a certificate should be granted as prayed for each of the reasons specified in para 32 to 35 of the Petition. After hearing his arguments we decided that it was unnecessary to call on the Crown to show cause upon any points except points (h), (s) & (t) of para 32 of the Petition and we accordingly granted a rule upon those points.

The rule has now been argued. We can only grant the required certificate if in our opinion the case is a fit one for appeal. The test of fitness is furnished by various decisions of the Judicial Committee which show the circumstances under which they will entertain appeals in Criminal Cases. It is sufficient to refer to *In re Carew* 1897, A. C. page 719 and *Dinizulu* v/s *Attorney-General of Zululand*, 61 C. J. page 740 in both of which the Judgment was delivered by Lord Halsbury. In the former case the rule was stated thus:—'It is only necessary to say that, save in very exceptional cases, leave to appeal in respect of a Criminal investigation is not granted by this Board.' The rule is accurately stated in the course of the argument: *In re Dillet* 12 A. C. page 459. 'Her Majesty will not review or interfere with the course of Criminal proceedings unless it is shown that by a disregard of the forms of legal process or by some violation of the principles of natural justice or otherwise substantial and grave injustice has been done.' In the latter case the Lord Chancellor said:—" It appears to them that nothing could be more destructive to the administration of Criminal Justice than a sort of notion that any criminal case which was tried in any Colony from which an appeal lay to this Committee can be brought here on appeal, not upon the broad grounds of some departure from the principles of natural justice but because some form or technicality has not been sufficiently observed. That is a principle which they believe never has been permitted and never, they trust, will be permitted." Therefore before granting the certificate asked for we must be satisfied that there is reasonable ground for thinking that grave and substantial injustice may have been done by reason of some departure from the principles of natural justice.

We are not sitting as Court of error. It is not for us to decide whether such injustice has in fact been done. We have to be satisfied that a reasonable case has been made out.

The Petitioner was tried before Davar J. and a Special Jury on a Charge framed under Section 124A, Indian Penal Code, in respect of an article published in the *Kesari* of which he was *Editor* and Proprietor on the 12th of May 1908 and on another charge under Section 124A and one under Section 153A in respect of an article in the *Kesari* of the 9th June 1908. He was found guilty and sentenced on each of the first and second charges to 3 years' transportation and on the third charge to a fine of Rs. 1000.

It is now argued tnat the trial was illegal as being in contravention of the provisions of Section 233 Criminal Procedure Code, which lays down that every distinct offence shall be a separate charge and every such charge shall be tried separately except in the cases mentioned in the Sections 234, 235, 236 and 239.

The Accused was originally charged separately before the Chief Presidency Magistrate on the 29th June under Sections 124 A and 153 A in respect of the article of the 12th May and under the same Sections in respect of the article of the 9th June.

He was committed to the High Court Sessions for the trial on both sets of charges.

In the Sessions Court (as appears from the notes of the official shorthand writer corrected by the learned Judge) the Advocate General appearing for the prosecution asked that the Accused should be tried on the four charges at one trial, contending that the article forming the subject of the charge and certain other articles intermidiate in point of time formed one transaction in which the offences charged had all been committed and that therefore the joinder was permissible under Section 235 (1) Criminal Procedure Code. The learned Judge objected that if the charges were consolidated there would be four charges. The Advocate General then said he would not put the Accused up on the charge under Section 153 A in respect of the first article.

The Accused who conducted his own case with the assistance of several well-known lawyers objected, first that there was no provision of the Code by which different charges could be amalgamated as proposed; and secondly that though the articles were in the course of the same transaction yet they formed different subjects altogether and it would be more convenient to have them tried separately, and confusing if they were taken together; that Sections 234 and 235 were permissive while section 233 was imperative; that the articles were separate articles dealing with seperate aspects of the question and did not form part of one transaction. Eventually the learnedf Judge said he thought it would be extremely desirable and in the interest of the Accused himself that there should be one trial and that the whole question should be before one Jury. The Accused under Section 233 was entitled to be tried seperately unless the provisions of Sections 234, 235 and 236 come into operation. He had grave doubts as to the applicability of Section 235 as there would be some difficulty in holding that seperate newspaper articles written week after week would come under the same transaction, but he had no difficulty in ordering the trial under Section 234 provided the charges did not exceed three.

The trial then commenced on three charges, one under Section 124A on the article of the 12th May and one under Section124 A and another under Section 153A on the article of the 9 th June with the result above stated.

After the verdict and before sentence the Accused applied that certain points should be reserved and referred under Section 484 Criminal Procedure Code, for the decision of the Full Bench. The points mentioned are included in the points raised in the present Petition. The judge however declined to reserve any points.

Dealing now with the legal arguments addressed to us that the trial was altogether unlawful as having been in contravention of the terms of Section 233 it is apparent that the argument involves two assumptions (1) that the offences charged were not committed by the same person in a series of acts so connected together as to form the same transaction and therfore did not fall within the scope of Section 235(1); (2) that the exceptions mentioned in Section 233 are mutually exclusive. The justification for the first assumption is by no means apparent. Besides the preliminary discussion upon the points to which we have already referred we note that at the trial in addition to the article of the 12 th May and the 9th June other articles and notes published by the accused in the *Kesari* from the 12th May to the 9th June inclusive were put in (Ex. E to I). the Judge in his Charge to the Jury pointed out that the subject of all the articles including those of the charge was and the advent of the bomb. The Accused himself when opening his defence read to the Court a written statement in which he stated that the charged articles were part of a controversy in which he had endeavoured to maintain and defend his views in regard to the political reforms required in India at the present day. In this connection we may also refer to paragraph 26 of the Petition now before us. we think, therefore, that there are good resons for the contention placed before us by the Advocate-General that the charges all fall within the scope of Section 235 (1).

Assuming, however, that the Advocate General's contention just referred to is unsustainable, the Petitioner has still to make good the second assumption viz. that the exceptions mentioned in section 233 are mutually exclusive. The words of the Section do not favour this view. If it has been intended that section 235 (2) or 236 should not be made use of in co-operation with section 234 this intention could have been easily expressed. If the exceptions are mutually exclusive the provisions of the section 236 or 237 could never be invoked to prevent a miscarriage of justice arising from a failure to make good all the details of a charge joined with two other charges under Section 234.

For example, if A were charged with three thefts in a building within the year and the evidence established that in one case the theft was committed on the roof and not in the building the Accused could not be convicted of simple theft under the powers conferred by Section 237 because the application of Section 236 would be negativeed by the mere fact of the joint trial under Section 234.

We find it difficult to believe that the legislature intended that a joint trial of three offences under Section 234 should prevent the Prosecution from establishing at the same trial the minor or alternative degrees of criminality involved in the acts complained of. For these reasons we think that the exceptions are not necessarily exclusive and that sections 235 (2) and 236 may be resorted to in framing additional charges where trial is of three offences of the same kind committed within the year.

It is of course possible for ingenuity to suggest cases in which the full exercise by the Court of the permissive powers conferred by the Section which we have been dicussing may produce embarrassment. In such cases the discretionary power of the Court still remains to decline to avail itself of its full powers.

The view which commends itself to us was also taken by another Bench of the Court in the recent case of *Imperator* v/s Tribhowandas Purshotamdas. In our opinion the learned Judge at the trial (though he appears to have overlooked Section 234 (2)) might have allowed the trial to proceed on all four charges without violating the provisions of the law.

If we now for the purpose of argument assume that the Petitioner has established the second assumption also, we have still to be satisfied that resonable grounds exist for thinking that grave and substantial injustice may have been done at the trial before we can grant the certificate. As we understood the argument on the rule, it is not contended that injustice has been done except in so far as the alleged disregard of the provisions of the Criminal Procedure Code in itself constitutes an injustice but we were urged to grant the certificate as the case would be important as a precedent.

We do not think the Accused was in any way prejudiced by what took place at the trial. An Accused person may, it is clear, be properly tried and convicted in one trial under Section 124 A or Sec. 153 A on charges framed on three disconnected articles. How then can it be said that grave and substantial injustice has been done by the arraignment and conviction of the Accused on three cognate charges in respect of only two (and those not disconnected) articles?

As regards the question raised by para 33 (s) and (t) of the Petition with respect to the number of separate sentences imposed, the Jury found Accused guilty of three distinct offences and the Judge awarded a punishment for them which in the aggregate is much below the maximum punishment allowed for one of the offences under Section 124 A. There has, therefore, been no violation of the provisions of Section 71 of the Indian Penal Code.

For the above reasons we discharge the Rule. Before leaving the case, however, we think it right to point out that the Advocate-General according to the note of the official shorthand writer stated that the charges under Section 124A and 153A would be treated as being alternative charges, or charges framed in order to meet the possibility of one other set of facts being proved, in which case each offence might or might not be proved. This may mean either that the second and third charges fell under Section 235 (2) or that they fell under Section 236. The charges as framed were not expressed to be in the alternative and the verdict of guilty was given in respect of each charge separately. There was, we think, nothing illegal in this; but it was the intention of the Crown that the second and third charges should only operate alternatively. The result intended can now be arrived at by the excerise by the Government of its powers under Chapter 29 of the Criminal Procedure Code in respect of the sentence imposed under Section 153 A upon the third charge.

(Sd) B. Scott.

(Sd) S. J. Batchelor.

Certified to be a true copy.

This 10th day of September 1908.

(Sd) M. R. Jardine

Clerk of the Crown.

Ex. A.

SANCTION TO PROSECUTE.

A. H. S.
24-6-08.

Under section 196 of the Code of Criminal Procedure 1898 His Excellency the Governor in Council is pleased to order Herbert George Gell, Commissioner of Police Bombay or such Police officer as may be deputed by him for this purpose to make a complaint against Bal Gangadhar Tilak, editor and proprietor of the *Kesari*, a weekly Vernacular newspaper of Poona in respect of an article, headed the "*Country's Misfortune*" printed at columns 4 and 5 page 4, and columns, and 2 page 5 of the issue of the said newspaper dated the 12th May 1908 under section 124 A of the Indian Penal Code and any other Section of the said Code (including Section 153 A.) which may be found to be applicable to the case.

By order of His Excellency.
the Governor in Council.

Dated Bombay }
the 23rd June 1908. }

(Sd.) H. QUINN,
Acting Secretary to Government,
Judicial Department.

P. T. O.

Pursuant to the within written order, I hereby depute Superintendent Sloane of the K. division, Bombay City Police, to make the complaint therein referred.

(Sd.) H. G. GELL.
Commissioner of Police,
Bombay.

Head Police Office,
Bombay, 24th June 1908.

Ex. B.

SANCTION TO PROSECUTE.

A. H. S.
27-6-08.

Under section 196 of the Code of Criminal Procedure 1898 His Excellency the Governor in Council is pleased to order Herbert George Gell, Commissioner of Police Bombay, or such Police officer as may be deputed by him for this purpose to make a complaint against Bal Gangadhar Tilak, editor and proprietor of the *Kesari*, a weekly Vernacular newspaper of Poona in respect of an article, headed "These remedies are not lasting" printed at columns 2, 3 and 4 of page 4 of the issue of the said newspaper dated the 9th June 1908 under section 124 A of India Penal Code and any other Section of the said Code (including Section 153 A.) which may be found to be applicable to the case.

Dated Bombay the 26th June 1908.

By order of His Excellency the Governor in Council.

(Sd.) H. QUINN.
Acting Secretary to Government,
Judicial Department.

P. T. O.

Pursuant to the within written order, I hereby depute Superintendent Sloan of the K. Divison, Bombay City Police. to make the complaint therein referred.

(Sd.) H. G. GELL.
Commissioner of Police,
Bombay.

Head Police office,
Bombay, 27 June 1908.

Ex. C.

Stamp Rs. 25.

" Re. 1.

(Translation of the Marathi leader printed in columns 4 and 5 of page 4 and columns 1 and 2 of page 5 of the issue of the Kesari *newspaper, dated 12th May 1908, and having a footnote, as translated, "This newspaper, was printed and published at the* 'Kesari' *Printing Press, No. 486, Narayan Peth, Poona, by Bal Gangadhar Tilak.")*

THE COUNTRY'S MISFORTUNE ! !

No one will fail to feel uneasiness and sorrow on seeing that India, a country which by its very nature is mild and peace-loving, has begun to be in the condition of European Russia. Furthermore, it is indisputable that (the fact of) two innocent white ladies having fallen victims to a bomb at Muzzafferpore will specially inspire many with hatred against the poople belonging to the party of rebels. That many occurrences of this kind have taken place in European Russia and are taking place even now, is a generally known historical fact. But we did no think that the political situation in India would, in such a short time, reach its present stage, at least that the obstinacy and perversity of the white official class (*a*) (bureaucracy) (*a*) of our country would (so soon) inspire with utter disappointment the young generation solicitous for the advancement of their country and impel them so soon to (follow) the rebellious path. But the dispensations of God are extraordinary (*b*). It does not appear from the statements of the persons arrested in connection with the bomb explosion case at Muzzafferpore, that the bomb was thrown through the hatred (felt) for some individual or simply owing to the action of some badmash (*c*) madcap. Even Khudiram, the bomb-thrower, himself feels sorry that two innocent ladies of Mr. Kennedy's family fell victims (to it) in place of Mr. Kingsford; what, then, should be said of others ? It is plain from the statements of those identical young gentlemen, who took this work in hand by founding a secret society, that they were fully aware that it was not possible to cause British rule to disappear from this country, by such monstrous deeds. None of the arrested persons have stated that the mere establishment of a secret society at the present time would do away with the oppressive official class. Some of the Anglo—Indian journalists have cast ridicule on these young men by insolently asking the question " Will the English rule disappear by the manufacture of a hundred muskets or

[*a*]—[*a*] [Printed in English within parenthesis.]

[*b*] [Meaning, presumably, inscrutable].

[*c*] [Bad, wicked ; a person leading a bad life.]

ten or five bombs ?" But we have to suggest to the said editors that this is not a subject for ridicule. The young Bengali gentlemen, who perpetrated those terrible things, do not belong to the class of thieves or badmashes (*c*); had that been so, they would not also have made statements frankly to the Police, as (they have done) now. Though the secret society of the young generation of Bengal may have been formed like (that of) the Russian rebels for the secrect assassination of the authorities, it plainly appears from their statements that it has been formed not for the sake of self-interest but owing to the exasperation produced by the autocratic exercise of power by the unrestrained and powerful white official class. It is known to all that the mutinies and revolts of the nihilists, that frequently occur even in Russia, take place for this very reason; and, looking (at the matter) from this point of view, (one) is compelled to say that the same state of things, which has been brought about in Russia by the oppression of the official class composed of their own countrymen, has now been inaugurated in India in consequence of the oppression practised by alien officers. There is none who is not awere that the might of the British Government is as vast and unlimited as that of the Russian Government. But rulers who exercise unrestricted power must always remember that there is also a limit to the patience of humanity. Since the partition of Bengal, the minds of the Bengalis have become most exasperated, and all their efforts to get the said partition cancelled by lawful means (have) proved fruitless; and it is known to the world that even Pandit Morley, or now Lord Morley, has given a flat refusal to their (request). Under these circumstances, no one in the world, except the white officials, inebriated with the insolence of authority, will think that not even a very few of the people of Bengal should become turn-headed and (*d*) feel inclined (*d*) to commit excesses. Experience shows that even a cat shut up in a house rushes with vehemence upon the person who confines (it there) and tries to kill him. That being the case, the Bengalis, no matter however powerless they might be thought to be, are human beings; and should not the official class have remembered that, exactly like those of other men, the feelings of the Bengalis, (too), are liable to become fierce or mild as occasion demands ? It is true that India having now been for many years under the sway of alien rulers the fire, spirit or vehemence natural to the Indian people have to a great extent cooled down; but under no circumstances can this vehemence or indignation descend to zero degree and freeze altogether. Old or experienced leaders can, so far as they themselves are concerned, keep this indignation permanently within certain prescribed limits with the help of (their) experience or (mature) thought; but it is impossible for all the people of the country thus to keep their spirit, indignation or irritability always within such bounds; nay, it may even be said without hesitation that the inhabitants of that country in which it is possible for this feeling of indignation to always remain thus within prescribed bounds, are destined to remain perpetually in slavery. It is not that our rulers are not aware of this principle. English statesmen have settled the lines of British policy, fully bearing in mind that British

(*c*) [Bad, wicked; a person leading a bad life.]

[*d*]—[*d*] [or proceed to commit excesses.]

rule in this country is alien and of the people of a different religious faith. When one country rules over another, the principal aim of the rulers is self-interest alone; but the extent of such self-interest is bounded in such a way that the subjects might not get exasperated. What is called statesmanship consists only in this; and this very thing has been designated (*a*) enlightened self-interest (*a*) by some English authors. British rule in India has been carried on on this very principle, but the great mistake that is being committed in that (connection) is that the English official class does not at all take the advice or opinion of the subjects or their leaders in the matter of our administration. The whole contract of settling in what the welfare of the subjects consists and in what their loss consists has been taken by the white official class in their own hands. And they are vain enough to think in this wise.—'Whatever thing we might do or whatever policy we might decide upon in (the light of) our wisdom or enlightened self-interest, must alone be uncomplainingly accepted as beneficial to themselves by the people of India and they must invoke a blessing upon us (for the same).' But owing to the spread of Western education, it is not now possible for this condition to last (any longer). However enlightened the self-interest of the rulers might be, India must still be a loser thereby; and in order to prevent this loss the power in the hands of the white official class must gradually come into our hands; there is no other alternative; such is now the view of many people in India and it is gaining ground. Such an impression being ultimately injurious to the ruling official class, the white official class here has become eager to suppress completely the writings, speeches or other means which produce that impression; and if they had been able to drive the car of the entire administration solely according to their own views, many oppressive enactments like the Prevention of (Seditious) Meetings Act would by this time have been passed, and India would fully have become another Russia. But the experienc gained from history, democratic public opinion in England and the awakening caused throughout the whole continent of Asia by the rise of an oriental nation like that of Japan have come in the way of the oppressive policy of our white official class and have imposed some restrictions on their imperial (autocratic) sway. However, the desire of the people gradually to obtain the rights of *Swarajya* (*e*) is growing stronger and stronger, and if they do not get rights by degrees, as desired by them, then some people at least out of the subject population, being filled with indignation or exasperation, will not fail to embark upon the commission of improper or horrible deeds recklessly. The Honourable Mr. Gokhale himself had, in the course of one of his speches in the Supreme Legislative Council, given a hint of this very kind to our Government in the presence of the Viceroy; and when Lala Lajpatrai was deported without trial and the proclamation (? ordinance) about the prevention of meetings promulgated, other native editors of newspapers also had, like ourselves, plainly given the Government to understand that if they resorted in that manner to oppressive Russian methods (of administration), then the Indian subjects, too, would be compelled

[*a*]–[*a*] [Printed in English within parenthesis.]

[*e*.] (Lit. one's own rule or government; selfgovernment.)

to imitate, partially at least, (the methods of) the Russian subjects! 'As you sow, so you reap' is a well-known maxim. For rulers to tell their subjects "We shall practise whatever oppression we like, deport any one we choose without trial, partition any province we like, stop any meeting we choose, or prosecute any one we like for sedition and send him to jail; (but) you, on your part should silently endure all those things and should not allow your indignation, exasperation or vehemence to go beyond certain limits," is to show to the world that they do not know common human nature. Most of the Anglo-Indian newspaper editors have committed this very mistake when writing on the Muzzaferpore affair. They have brought a charge against the Indian leaders that it was by the very writings or speeches of the said leaders who passed severe comments on the high-handed or contumacious conduct of the English official class, that the present terrible situation was brought about; and they have next made a recommendation that Government should henceforth place greater restrictions upon the speeches, writings or movements of these leaders. In our opinion, this suggestion is most silly. Just as when a dam built across a river begins to give way owing to the flood caused by excessive rain, the blame for the (mishap) should be thrown on the rain and not on the flood, even so, if in society there is any transgression of legal bounds in a few cases owing to the discontent or exasperation engendered by the oppressive acts of an irresponsible and unrestrained official class, the blame or the responsibility for it must be placed on the policy of the unrestricted official class alone. Take any man you like; it is true that he does not see his real state. The crores of people, revolving round the earth's axis along with the earth itself, think that (it is) the world (that) is revolving and not they themselves. But wise men should, instead of falling into such a delusion, find out the true reason of any particular thing and direct their attention to it. It is no use striking idly and continually a (piece of) rope after calling it a snake. The rule of the autocratic, unrestricted and irresponsible white official class in India is becoming more and more unbearable to the people. All thoughtful men in India are putting forth efforts in order that this rule or authority, instead of remaining with the said official class, should come into the hands of the representatives of the subject people. Some think that this thing can be accomplished by supplicating this intoxicated official class itself, or by petitioning the Government in England who exercise supervision over it. Some others think this improbable, and they have persuaded themselves into the notion that, in accordance with the maxim, 'the mouth does not open unless the nose is stopped', unless a spoke is put somewhere into (the wheels of) the car (of the administration) of the present rulers, their desired object will not be accomplished. The opinion of this party is that whatever may be wanted (by them) should be plainly stated and it should be obtained by (following) the path of (passive) resistance. But to say that not even a single man out of the thirty crores (of people) in the country should go beyond these two paths in the paroxysm of the indignation or exasperation produced by this oppressive system of Government, is like saying that the indignation or exasperation of the thirty crores of the inhabitants of India must always necessarily remain below a certain degree

And it is impossible to fix such a limit for the whole country. Just as a man who cherishes a desire or makes an effort that when the sun in summer reaches the meridian the arid country in Márwàr should remain as cool as Darjiling or Simla, must fail (to secure his object), similarly it is vain to entertain a desire or to make an effort that the indignation, exasperation or vehemence produced in the minds of the subjects by an unpopular system of administration should remain necessarily within a certain limit at all times and in all places. If there is any lesson to be learnt by our rulers from the Muzzafferpore bomb affair and from the statements of the young gentlmen implicated in it, it is this alone; and we humbly take permission to bring this very thing again and again to their notice. We are aware that our Government will, by assuming a stern aspect (and) by the adoption of harsh measures, be able to stop immediately outrages like the one that occurred at Muzzafferpore. But even if such means be necessary at the present time to maintain peace, still that will not completely remove the root of the disease, and so long as the disease in the body has not been rooted out, no one will be able to guarantee that if a boil in one part (of the body) is cut away, another will not develop again in some other part. It is the King's and the subjects' great misfortune that such times should befall a mild country like India which is naturally loyal and averse to horrible deeds. There is no difference of opinion that those who are responsible for the maintenance of peace in the country should immediately stop outrages of this kind on their coming to light, but the remedies that are to be adopted with a view to prevent the repetition of such horrible calamities should only be adopted with foresight and consideration. It is now plain that not only has the system of Government in India become unpopular but also that the prayer made many times by the people for the reform of that system having been refused, even some educated people forgetting themselves in the heat of indignation have begun to embark upon the perpetration of improper deeds. Men of equable temperament and of reason in the nation will not approve of such violence; nay, there is even a possibility that in consequence of such violence increased oppression will be practised upon the people for some time (to come) instead of its being stopped. But a glance at the recent history of Russia will show that such excesses or acts of violence are not at all stopped by subjecting the people to increased oppression. It is true that in order to acquire political rights efforts are required to be made for several successive generations and those efforts, too, are required to be made peacefully, steadily, persistently and constitutionally! But while such efforts are being made who will guarantee that no person whatever in society will go out of control? And as such guarantee cannot be given, how would it be reasonable to say that all persons who put forth efforts for acquiring political rights are seditious? This is what we do not understand. Just as it is difficult to lay down a restriction that not even a tear or two must fall from the eyes of a man while his heart has become sorely afflicted by sorrow in the same manner it is vain to expect that the unrestricted method of administration, under which India is being ruled over in a high-handed and reckless manner, should become only so far unbearable to the people that no one should become unduly exasperated and resort to excesses on that account. It may be said that, with the exception of some few individuals, the educated and uneducated classes in the country are not as yet prepared to transgress lawful or constitutional limits: nay, even such a desire has not risen in their minds. Under such circumstances to throw the responsibility of the horrible Muzzafferpore affair on that class is adding insult to injury. It cannot be that these things are not understood by a wise Government of the twentieth century, but the intoxication of unrestricted authority and the earnest desire to benefit one'a own countrymen is so extraordinary that even wise men become blind thereby on certain occasions. The calamitous occasion which has befallen India at the present time is of this very kind. There is no possibility of the structure of British rule giving way in consequence of the murder of high white officers. If one passes away a second will come in his place, if the second passes away a third will succeed, there is no one whatever so foolish as not to understand this. But Government should take this lesson from the Muzzafferpore affair that the minds of some (persons) out of the young generation have begun to turn towards violence on seeing that all peaceful agitation for the acquisition of political rights has failed, just as a deer attacks a hunter, totally regardless of its own life, after all means of protection have been exhausted. No sensible man will approve of this excess or sinful deed. But it is impossible not only for the subjects but even for the King to avoid or to totally stop this traga (*f*) of desperation, and traga (*f*) really speaking is at all times the result only of a climax of exasperation and despair. True statemanship, it may be said, consists, indeed in not allowing these things to reach such an extreme or (critical) stage, and this is the very policy we are candidly and plainly suggesting to Government on the present occasion. We do not think that we have done the whole of our duty as subjects by humbly informing Government that the affair that occurred at Muzzafferpore was horrible and that we vehemently condemn or repudiate it. All heartily desire that such improper things should not take place and that none from amongst the subjects should have an occasion to resort to such extremes. But at such a time it must also be necessarily considered how far the ruling official class should, by utterly disregarding this desire of the subjects, try their patience to the uttermost; otherwise it will not be possible to maintain cordial relations between the rulers and the subjects and to carry on smoothly the business of either. We have already said above that the Muzafferpore affair was not proper (and) that it was regrettable. But if the causes which give rise to it remain permanent in future exactly as they are at present, then in our opinion it is not possible that such terrible occurrences will stop altogether; and it is for this very reason that we have on this very occasion suggested to Government the measures which should be adopted in order to put a stop altogether to such undesirable occurrences. The time has, through our misfortune, arrived when the party of 'Nihilists,' like that which has arisen in Russia, Germany, France and other countries, will now rise here. To avoid this contingency, to prevent the growth of this poisonous tree is altogether in the hands of Government. These abscesses affecting the country will never be permanently cured by oppression or by harsh measures. Reform of the administration is the only

[*f*.] (Inflicting upon one's own person some injury in order to bring evil or blame upon another.)

medicine to be administered internally for this disease; and if the official class does not make use of that medicine at this time then it must be considered a great misfortune of all of us. The Government official class may perhaps dislike this writing of ours, but we cannot help it; for, as a poet has said, words both sweet and beneficial or hard to obtain. What we have said above is, in our opinion, true and reasonable and beneficial also to both the rulers and the subjects in the end.If in spite of this, our writing proves to be of no use, it must be considered a great misfortune of the country. What else? And when once a misfortune overtakes (one) who can tell what calamities will befall (him) in future? No one desires calamities or difficulties; but sometimes God does not leave it in our hands to avoid them. The present affair is becoming one of this sort; and if the Government official class do not recognize this fact, what can we do? Our duty extends to the giving of a hint; and we are discharging that duty, remembering God and Truth. It is our desire also that the state of the country should not become distressful; but at the same time, we must also exercise the right which we have of insisting that the present intolerable system of administration should be reformed as soon as possible. It is no use being bewildered for nothing. We are aware that the white official class or the Anglo-Indian journalists will most astutely utilize Muzzafferpore affair to lessen the vehemence of our efforts; nay, their self-interest also lies in this. But it is our duty to strongly condemn also this perversion of the true state of things by Anglo-Indians, while condemning the desperate and suicidal deed perpetrated at Muzzafferpore. Just as it is the duty of the subjects to assist in preventing the murder of ruling officials, so also it is the duty of the rulers to admit (the voice of) public opinion into the administration (of the country) according to the present times, instead of keeping it (*i. e.*, the administration) irresponsible. The scripture laying down the duties of kings is declaring at the top of its voice that it is not possible for the ruling individuals to forget this duty or to deliberately disregard it and to make the subjects only discharge their duties punctiliously; nay, (it further says that this) will be beneficial to neither party. Where this duty is disregarded, there the occurrence of calamities, some time or other, like that at Muzzafferpore is inevitable. Therefore, if the rulers wish that these undesirable incidents should not come to pass, our suggestion to them is that they should in the first instance impose restrictions upon their own system of administration itself, and it is only with that object in view that to-day's article has been written.

[His Imperial Majesty's High Court, Bombay,

Translator's Office, 2nd July 1908.] A true Translation.

N. L. MANKER,

Third Translator.

Ex. C.

[*The following is the original Marathi text of the article of which Ex. C. is a translation.*]

देशाचें दुर्दैव !!

(केसरी, तारीख १२ मे १९०८).

स्वभावतःच गरीब आणि शांतताप्रिय हिंदुस्थान देश युरोपांतील रशियाच्या स्थितीस येऊं लागला हें पाहून कोणासही अस्वस्थता व दुःख वाटल्याखेरीज राहणार नाहीं. त्यांतून मुझफरपूर येथें दोन निरपराधी गोऱ्या स्त्रिया बाँब गोळ्यास बळी पडल्या, यानें तर पुष्कळांस बंडखोर पक्षाच्या लोकांबद्दल तिटकारा उत्पन्न होईल हें निर्विवाद आहे. अशा तऱ्हेचे अनेक प्रकार युरोपांतील रशियांत घडलेले आहेत व अद्याप घडत आहेत, ही गोष्ट इतिहासप्रसिद्ध आहे. पण हिंदुस्थानांतील राजकीय प्रकरण इतक्यांतच अशा थरावर येऊन ठेपेल–निदान आमच्या येथील गोऱ्या अधिकारीवर्गाचा (bureaucracy) हट्ट व दुराग्रह स्वदेशोत्कर्षाबद्दल आस्था बाळगणाऱ्या तरुण पिढीस पूर्ण नाउमेद करून बंडखोर मार्गास इतक्या लवकर प्रवृत्त करील–असें आह्मांस वाटत नव्हतें. पण ईश्वराच्या घरचा नेमानेम कांहीं विलक्षण आहे. मुझफरपूर येथें जो बाँब गोळा उडविण्यांत आला तो कांहीं व्यक्तिविषयक द्वेषानें अगर निव्वळ एखाद दुसऱ्या बदमाष माथेफिरूच्या कृत्यानें उडाला, असें सदर प्रकरणांत पकडलेल्या लोकांच्या जबान्यांवरून दिसून येत नाहीं. मि. किंग्स्फर्डच्या ऐवजीं मि. केनडीच्या घरच्या दोन निरपराधी स्त्रिया बळी पडल्या याबद्दल बाँब गोळा फेकणारा खुद्द खुदीराम यासही वाईट वाटत आहे; मग इतरांची कथा काय ? ज्या तरुण गृहस्थांनीं एक गुप्तमंडळी स्थापून हें काम हातीं घेतलें, त्यांस असल्या अघोर कृत्यांनीं इंग्रज सरकारचें राज्य या देशांतून नाहींसें करतां येणें शक्य नाहीं, हें पूर्णपणें माहीत होतें, असें त्यांच्याच जबान्यांवरून उघड होतें. आज एखादी गुप्तमंडळी निघाली कीं, तेवढ्यानेंच जुलमी अधिकारीवर्गाचा नायनाट होईल असें पकडलेल्या इसमांपैकीं कोणींही ह्मटलेलें नाहीं. कित्येक अँग्लोइंडियन वर्तमानपत्रकारांनीं " शंभर बंदुका किंवा दहा पांच बाँब गोळे केल्यानें इंग्रजी राज्य जातें कीं काय ? " असा उर्मटपणानें प्रश्न विचारून या तरुण मंडळीचा उपहास केलेला आहे. पण सदर पत्रकारांस आमची अशी सूचना आहे कीं, हा उपहासाचा विषय नव्हे. ज्या तरुण बंगाली गृहस्थांनीं या भयंकर गोष्टी केल्या ते कांहीं चोराच्या किंवा बदमाषाच्या वर्गांतले नव्हेत; तसें असतें तर त्यांनीं हल्लींच्याप्रमाणें पोलिसांपुढें मोकळेपणानें जबाबही दिले नसते. बंगाल्यांतील तरुण पिढीचा गुप्त कट हा जरी रशियांतील बंडखोर लोकांप्रमाणें अधिकाऱ्यांचा गुप्त खून करण्याकरितां झाला असला तरी तो स्वार्थाकरितां नसून अनियंत्रित आणि बलाढ्य अशा गोऱ्या अधिकारीवर्गाच्या एकमुखी सत्तेनें उत्पन्न झालेल्या संतापामुळें झालेला आहे, हें त्यांनीं दिलेल्या जबान्यांवरून स्पष्ट दिसत आहे. रशियांतही ' निहिलिस्ट ' लोकांचे वारंवार जे दंगे व बंडें होतात तीं याच कारणाकरितां होतात, हें सर्वांस माहीत आहे; आणि अशा दृष्टीनें पाहिलें ह्मणजे स्वदेशी अधिकारीवर्गाच्या जुलमानें रशियांत जी स्थिति झाली आहे तशीच परकीय अधिकाऱ्यांच्या जुलमामुळें हिंदुस्थानांत होण्यास आतां सुरुवात झाली, असें ह्मणणें भाग पडतें. इंग्रजसरकाराचें सामर्थ्य रशियन सरकाराप्रमाणेंच फार मोठें आणि अमर्यादित आहे ही गोष्ट कोणासही माहीत नाहीं असें नाहीं. पण मनुष्य-

मात्राच्या सहनशीलतेसही कांहीं मर्यादा आहे, ही गोष्ट अनियंत्रित सत्ता चालविणाऱ्या राज्यकर्त्यांनीं नेहमीं लक्षांत ठेविली पाहिजे. बंगालची फाळणी झाल्यापासून बंगाली लोकांचीं मनें अत्यंत क्षुब्ध झालीं असून सदर फाळणी कायदेशीर रीतीनें रद्द करून घेण्याबद्दलचे त्यांचे सर्व प्रयत्न निष्फळ झाले; आणि पंडित मोर्ले, किंवा आतां लार्ड मोर्ले, यांनींही त्यांस वाटाण्याच्या अक्षता दिल्या हें जगजाहीर आहे. अशा स्थितींत बंगाल्यांतील कांहीं अत्यंत थोड्या लोकांचीं देखील डोकीं फिरून जाऊन त्यांनीं अत्याचारास प्रवृत्त होऊं नये, असें अधिकारमदानें धुंद झालेल्या गोऱ्या अधिकाऱ्यांखेरीज जगांत दुसऱ्या कोणासही वाटणार नाहीं. घरांत कोंडलेलें मांजर देखील त्वेषानें कोंडणाऱ्याच्या अंगावर धांवून जाऊन त्यास मारण्याचा प्रयत्न करतें, असा अनुभव आहे. मग बंगाली लोक कितीही निर्बल मानले गेले असले तरी तीं माणसें आहेत; आणि इतर मनुष्यांप्रमाणेंच त्यांचे मनोविकार प्रसंगानुसार तीव्र किंवा सौम्य होऊं शकतात, हें अधिकारीवर्गाच्या लक्षांत रहावयास नको होतें काय? हिंदुस्थान देश आज पुष्कळ वर्षें परकी राजांच्या अमलाखालीं असल्यामुळें हिंदी लोकांच्या आंगचें तेज, आवेश किंवा त्वेष पुष्कळ कमी झालेला आहे खरा; पण कांहीं झालें तरी या त्वेषाचें अगर संतापाचें मान शून्य डिग्रीवर येऊन तो अजीबात गोठून जाणें शक्य नाहीं. वयोवृद्ध किंवा पोक्त पुढाऱ्यांस अनुभवानें किंवा विचारानें हा संताप स्वतःपुरता कांहीं विवक्षित मर्यादेच्या आंत कायमचा ठेवतां येईल; पण देशांतील यच्चयावत् लोकांस आपला आवेश, संताप किंवा चीड अशा रीतीनें सदर मर्यादेच्या आंत नेहमींच ठेवतां येणें अशक्य आहे; किंबहुना अशा रीतीनें हा संताप ज्या देशांत सदैव विवक्षित मर्यादेच्या आंतच राहूं शकतो, त्या देशांतील लोकांच्या कपाळीं ब्रह्मदेवानें कायमची गुलामगिरी लिहिलेली आहे, असें ह्मण-ण्यासही हरकत नाहीं. आमच्या राजकर्त्यांस हें तत्व माहीत नाहीं असें नाहीं. इंग्रजी राज्य या देशांत परकी आणि परधर्मी आहे हें ध्यानांत ठेवूनच इंग्रजी राज्यपद्धतीचें धोरण इंग्रजी मुत्सद्यांनीं ठर-विलेलें आहे. एका देशानें दुसऱ्या देशावर राज्य करण्यांत स्वार्थ हाच राज्यकर्त्यांचा प्रधान हेतू असतो; पण त्या स्वार्थाची धांव प्रजाक्षोभ न पावेल अशा बेतानें मर्यादित केलेली असते. मुत्सद्दीपणा ह्मणतात तो हाच. आणि यालाच कांहीं इंग्रजी ग्रंथकारांनीं उदात्त स्वार्थ (enlightened selfinterest) असें नांव दिलें आहे. हिंदुस्थान देशांतील इंग्रजी राज्य याच तत्वावर चाललेलें आहे, पण त्यांत जी मोठी चूक घडत आहे ती ही कीं प्रजेची किंवा प्रजेच्या पुढाऱ्यांची सल्ला किंवा मत इंग्रजी अधिकारीवर्ग आमच्या राज्यकारभारांत बिलकूल घेत नाहीं. प्रजेचें हित कशांत आहे आणि नुकसान कशांत आहे हें ठरविण्याचा सर्व मक्ता गोऱ्या अधिकारीवर्गानें आपल्या हातांत घेतलेला आहे. आणि त्यांस अशी घमेंड आहे कीं आह्मी आपल्या शहाणपणानें किंवा उदात्त स्वार्थबुद्धीनें जी जी गोष्ट करूं, किंवा जें जें धोरण ठरवूं तेंच हिंदुस्थानांतील लोकांनीं आपल्या हिताचें म्हणून बिनतक्रार अंगीकारून आम्हांस दुवा दिला पाहिजे. परंतु पाश्चिमात्य शिक्षणाच्या प्रसारामुळें ही स्थिति आतां राहणें शक्य नाहीं. राज्यकर्त्यांचा स्वार्थ कितीही उदात्त असला तरी हिंदुस्थान देशाचें त्यामुळें नुक-सानच आहे; आणि हें नुकसान बंद करण्यास गोऱ्या अधिकारीवर्गाच्या हातांतील सत्ता हळूहळू आमच्या हातांत आली पाहिजे, एरव्हीं गत्यंतर नाहीं, असा हिंदुस्थानांतील पुष्कळ लोकांचा आतां समज झाला आहे; व होत चालला आहे. अशा प्रकारचा समज राजकर्त्या अधिकारीवर्गास परिणामीं अपायकारक असल्यामुळें सदर समज उत्पन्न करणारे लेख, व्याख्यानें, किंवा इतर साधनें अजिबात खुंटवून टाकण्यास येथील गोरा अधिकारीवर्ग उत्सुक झालेला आहे; व राज्यकारभाराचा गाडा केवळ त्यांच्याच मतानें त्यांस हाकतां आला असता, तर सभाप्रतिबंधक कायद्याप्रमाणें आजमितीस अनेक जुलमी कायदे होऊन हिंदुस्थान पूर्ण प्रतिरशिया बनून गेलें असतें. परंतु इतिहासाचा अनुभव, विलायतेंतील प्रजापक्षीय लोकमत आणि जपानसारख्या पौर्वात्य राष्ट्राच्या अभ्युदयानें सर्व एशिया खंडांत झालेली जागृति, हीं आमच्या गोऱ्या अधिकारीवर्गाच्या जुलमी धोरणाच्या आड येऊन त्यांनीं सदर अधि-

कारीवर्गाच्या बादशाही अमलास कांहीं आळा घातलेला आहे. तथापि उत्तरोत्तर स्वराज्याचे हक्क मिळविण्याची लोकांची इच्छा अधिकाधिक प्रबळ होत असून लोकांच्या इच्छेप्रमाणें जर त्यांस हळूहळू हक्क मिळत गेले नाहींत, तर प्रजेपैकीं कांहीं लोक तरी संतापानें किंवा त्वेषानें भरून जाऊन सारासार विचार न करितां अनन्वित किंवा घोर कृत्यें करण्याकडे प्रवृत्त झाल्याखेरीज राहणार नाहींत. खुद्द ना० गोखले यांनीं वरिष्ठ कायदे कौन्सिलपुढें केलेल्या आपल्या एका भाषणांत अशाच प्रकारची इशारत व्हॉइसरॉय साहेबांच्या समक्ष आमच्या सरकारास दिलेली होती; आणि लाला लजपतराय यांस बिगरचौकशीनें काळें पाण्यावर पाठवून सभाबंदीचा जाहिरनामा जेव्हां बाहेर पडला, तेव्हां आमच्याप्रमाणें इतर देशी वर्तमानपत्रकारांनींही सरकारास असें स्पष्ट कळविलें होतें कीं सरकार जर याप्रमाणें जुलमी रशियनपद्धतीचा अंगिकार करूं लागलें तर हिंदुस्थानांतील प्रजेसही रशियन प्रजेचें कांहीं अंशीं तरी अनुकरण करणें भाग पडेल ! जसें पेरावें तसें उगवतें, हा न्याय सुप्रसिद्ध आहे. आम्ही काय वाटेल तो जुलूम करूं; वाटेल त्यास बिनचौकशीनें काळ्या पाण्यावर पाठवूं, वाटेल तो प्रांत विभागूं, वाटेल ती सभा बंद करूं, किंवा वाटेल त्यावर राजद्रोहाचे खटले करून त्यास तुरुंगांत पाठवूं; तुम्हीं मात्र या सर्व गोष्टी मुकाट्यानें सहन करून आपला संताप, त्वेष किंवा आवेश विवक्षित मर्यादेच्या बाहेर जाऊं देऊं नये, असें राजकर्त्यांनीं आपले प्रजेस सांगणें ह्मणजे सामान्य मनुष्य-स्वभावाची आपणास ओळख नाहीं, असें जगास प्रदर्शित करणें होय. मुझफरपूर प्रकरणावर लिहितांना बहुतेक अँग्लो–इंडियन पत्रकारांनीं हीच चूक केलेली आहे. इंग्रजी अधिकारीवर्गाच्या अरेरावी वर्तनावर किंवा शिरजोरपणावर कडक टीका करणाऱ्या हिंदी पुढाऱ्यांच्या लेखांमुळें किंवा भाषणामुळेंच हल्लींची भयंकर स्थिति आलेली आहे, असा त्यांनीं सदर पुढाऱ्यांवर आरोप ठेविला आहे; आणि नंतर अशी शिफारस केली आहे कीं, सदर पुढाऱ्यांच्या भाषणांस, लेखांस किंवा चळवळीस इतउत्तर सरकारानें अधिक आळा घातला पाहिजे. आमच्या मतें ही सूचना अत्यंत वेडेपणाची आहे. अतिशय पाऊस पडून नदीस आलेल्या पुरानें जर नदीस बांधलेलें धरण ढांसळूं लागलें, तर त्याचा दोष पुराकडे न देतां ज्याप्रमाणें पावसाकडे दिला पाहिजे, तद्वतच बेजबाबदार आणि अनियंत्रित अधिकारीवर्गाच्या जुलमी कृत्यानें जो असंतोष किंवा संताप उत्पन्न होतो त्यानें समाजांत क्वचित स्थलीं कायद्याच्या मर्यादेचें उल्लंघन झाल्यास त्याचा दोष किंवा जबाबदारी अनियंत्रित अधिकारीवर्गाच्या राज्यपद्धतीच्या माथ्यावरच ठेविली पाहिजे. कोणींही मनुष्य घेतला तरी ज्याला त्याला आपली खरी स्थिति दिसत नसते, हें खरें आहे. पृथ्वीबरोबर तिच्या आसाभोंवती फिरणाऱ्या कोट्यावधी लोकांस स्वतः आपण न फिरतां जग फिरत आहे असें वाटत असतें. पण ज्ञात्यांनीं अशा भ्रमांत न पडतां कोणत्याही गोष्टीचें खरें कारण शोधून काढून तिकडे आपलें लक्ष पुरविलें पाहिजे. उगीच साप साप ह्मणून दोरीवर ताडण करीत बसण्यांत कांहीं हांशील नाहीं. हिंदुस्थानांतील एकमुखी अनियंत्रित आणि बेजबाबदार गोऱ्या अधिकारीवर्गाची सत्ता उत्तरोत्तर लोकांस असह्य होत चालली आहे. ही सत्ता किंवा अधिकार सदर अधिकारी–वर्गाकडे न राहतां प्रजेच्या प्रतिनिधींच्या हातांत यावा ह्मणून हिंदुस्थानांतील सर्व विचारी पुरुष प्रयत्न करीत आहेत. कित्येकांना असें वाटतें कीं, ही गोष्ट या मदांध अधिकारीवर्गाचीच विनवणी करून किंवा त्यांच्यावर देखरेख करणारे विलायतेस जें सरकार आहे त्यांस अर्ज करून प्राप्त करून घेतां येईल. दुसऱ्या कित्येकांस ही गोष्ट असंभवनीय वाटत असून नाक धरल्याखेरीज तोंड उघडत नाहीं, या न्यायानें हल्लींच्या राज्यकर्त्यांच्या गाड्यास कोठें तरी खीळ घातल्याखेरीज आपला इष्ट हेतु तडीस जाणार नाहीं, असें त्यांच्या मनानें घेतलें आहे. काय पाहिजे असेल तें स्पष्ट सांगावें आणि अडवणूकीच्या मार्गानें तें प्राप्त करून घ्यावें, असें या पक्षाचें ह्मणणें आहे. पण देशांतील तीस कोटीपैकीं एकाही पुरुषानें या जुलमी राज्यपद्धतीमुळें उत्पन्न झालेल्या संतापाच्या किंवा त्वेषाच्या भरांत वरील दोन मार्गांच्या पलीकडे जाऊं नये, असें ह्मणणें ह्मणजे हिंदुस्थानांतील तीस कोट लोकांचा संताप किंवा त्वेष सदैव अमुक डिग्रीच्या आंतच राहिला पाहिजे,

असें ह्मणण्यासारखें आहे. आणि सर्व देशास अशी मर्यादा घालणें अशक्य होय. उन्हाळ्यांतील सहस्त्ररश्मी सूर्यनारायण मध्यान्हीं आला असतां मारवाडांतील रुक्ष प्रदेश दार्जिलिंग किंवा सिमला येथील प्रदेशाइतकाच थंड रहावा, अशी जर कोणी इच्छा धरील किंवा प्रयत्न करील तर तो जसा व्यर्थ होईल, तद्वतच लोकांना अप्रिय झालेल्या राज्यपद्धतीमुळें प्रजेच्या मनांत उत्पन्न झालेला संताप, त्वेष अगर आवेश अमुक एक मर्यादेच्या आंतच सर्व काळीं सर्व स्थळीं राहिला पाहिजे, अशी इच्छा धरणें किंवा प्रयत्न करणें व्यर्थ होय. मुझफरपूर येथील बॉंब गोळ्याच्या प्रकरणावरून आणि त्यांत सांपडलेल्या तरुण गृहस्थांच्या जबान्यांवरून जर आमच्या राज्यकर्त्यांनीं कांहीं बोध घ्यावयाचा असेल तर तो हाच होय; आणि आह्मी पुन: पुन: हीच गोष्ट त्यांच्या कानीं घालण्याची नम्रपणें परवानगी घेतों. आह्मांस माहीत आहे कीं, मुझफरपूर येथें घडून आलेल्या प्रकारचे अनर्थ आमच्या सरकारास उग्र स्वरूप धारण करून सक्तीनें तावडतोब बंद करितां येतील. पण शांतता राखण्यास अशा उपायांची सध्यां जरी जरूर असली तरी यानें रोगाचें मूळ कांहीं नाहींसें व्हावयाचें नाहीं, आणि शरीरांतील रोग जोंपर्यंत निर्मूल झाला नाहीं, तोंपर्यंत एका ठिकाणचें गळूं कापून काढलें तर इतर ठिकाणीं तें पुन: उद्भवणार नाहीं, अशी कोणासही हमी घेतां यावयाची नाहीं. हिंदुस्थानसारख्या गरीब आणि निसर्गत:च राजनिष्ठ व घोरकर्मापासून पराङ्मुख असलेल्या देशास असे दिवस यावे हें राजा व प्रजा यांचें मोठें दुर्दैव होय. देशांत शांतता राखण्याची ज्यांचेवर जबाबदारी आहे, त्यांनीं असल्या प्रकारचे अनर्थ उघडकीस आल्यावर ते तावडतोब बंद केले पाहिजेत, याबद्दल कोणाचाही मतभेद नाहीं; पण असल्या भयंकर अनर्थांची पुनरावृत्ति न व्हावी ह्मणून जे इलाज करावयाचे ते मात्र दूरदर्शीपणानें आणि विचारानें केले पाहिजेत. हिंदुस्थानांतील राज्यपद्धति लोकांस अप्रिय झाली आहे, इतकेंच नव्हे तर सदर राज्यपद्धतींत सुधारणा व्हावी अशाबद्दल लोकांनीं अनेक वेळां केलेली विनंती अमान्य झाल्यामुळें कित्येक सुशिक्षित लोकही संतापाच्या भरांत देहभान विसरून जाऊन अनन्वित कृत्यें करण्यास प्रवृत्त होऊं लागले हें आतां उघड आहे. राष्ट्रांतील समधात किंवा विचारी पुरुषांस अशा प्रकारचा आततायीपणा संमत होणार नाहीं; किंबहुना अशा प्रकारच्या आततायीपणानें जुलमाचा प्रतिकार न होतां कांहीं काळपर्यंत लोकांवर अधिक जुलूम होण्याचाही संभव आहे. पण रशियाच्या अलीकडील इतिहासाकडे पाहिलें तर असें आढळून येईल कीं, अशा प्रकारचा अत्याचार किंवा आततायीपणा लोकांवर अधिकाधिक जुलूम करून कांहीं बंद होत नाहीं. राजकीय हक्क संपादन करण्याकरितां पिढ्यानपिढ्या खटपट करावी लागते, आणि ती खटपटही शांतपणें, धिमेपणानें, नेटानें आणि सदनशीर रीतीनें करावी लागते, हें खरें ! पण अशी खटपट चालली असतां समाजांतील कोणताही मनुष्य उच्छृंखल होणार नाहीं अशी हमी कोण घेणार ? आणि अशी हमी देतां आली नाहीं ह्मणून राजकीय हक्कांकरितां खटपट करणारे सर्व लोक राजद्रोही आहेत असें ह्मणणें सयुक्तिक तरी कसें होणार ? हें आह्मांस समजत नाहीं. शोकानें अंत:करण अतिशय संतप्त झालें असतां मनुष्याच्या डोळ्यांवाटे एखाद दुसरा तरी अश्रू बाहेर पडूं नये असा निर्बंध घालणें ज्याप्रमाणें दुर्घट होय, त्याप्रमाणें हिंदुस्थानावर अरेरावीपणानें आणि शिरजोरपणानें राज्य करणारी अनियंत्रित राज्यपद्धति लोकांस इतकीच असह्य व्हावी कीं, त्यामुळें कोणीही फाजील संतापून अत्याचारास प्रवृत्त होऊं नये, अशी आशा बाळगणें व्यर्थ होय. कांहीं थोड्या व्यक्ती खेरीज करून देशांतील सुशिक्षित आणि अशिक्षित वर्ग अद्याप कायदेशीर किंवा सनदशीर मर्यादेचें उल्लंघन करण्यास प्रवृत्त झालेला नाहीं; किंबहुना तशी इच्छाही त्यांच्या मनांत उद्भवली नाहीं, असें ह्मटलें तरी चालेल. अशा स्थितींत मुझफरपूरच्या भयंकर प्रकरणाची जबाबदारी या वर्गावर टाकणें ह्मणजे त्यांच्या दु:खावर पुन: डागण्या देण्यासारखें आहे. विसाव्या शतकांतील शहाण्यासुरत्या सरकारास या गोष्टी समजूं नयेत असें नाहीं. पण अनियंत्रित सत्तेचा मद आणि स्वजातीयांचा फायदा करण्याची हांव इतकी कांहीं विलक्षण असते कीं, तिनें शहाणे लोक देखील प्रसंगविशेषीं आंधळे बनून जातात. हल्लींचा हिंदुस्थानावरील प्रसंग अशाच प्रकारचा आहे. मोठमोठे गोरे अधि-

कारी यांचा खून केल्यानें इंग्रजी राज्याची इमारत ढांसळणें शक्य नाहीं. एक गेला तर त्याच्या जागीं दुसरा येईल, दुसरा गेला तर तिसरा येईल; हें न कळण्याइतका कोणीही मूर्ख नाहीं. पण राजकीय हक्क मिळण्याकरितां केलेली शांततेची सर्व चळवळ निष्फळ होते असें दृष्टोत्पत्तीस आल्यानंतर, बचावाचे सर्व मार्ग नाहींसे झाल्यावर एखादा हरीण ज्याप्रमाणें पारध्यावर आपल्या प्राणाची मुळींच पर्वा न ठेवितां तुटून पडतो, त्याप्रमाणें तरुण पिढींतील कांहींकांचीं मनें आततायीपणाकडे वळूं लागली आहेत, ही गोष्ट मुझफरपूरच्या प्रकरणावरून सरकारानें लक्षांत घेतली पाहिजे. ह्या अत्याचारास किंवा पापास कोणीही समंजस मनुष्य संमति देणार नाहीं. पण हा निरुपायाचा त्रागा—आणि त्रागा ह्मटला ह्मणजे तो केव्हांही संतापाच्या आणि निराशेचा पराकाष्ठेनेंच उत्पन्न होतो–टाळणें किंवा अजिबात बंद करणें प्रजेसच नव्हे तर राजासही अशक्य आहे. खरी राजनीति ह्मटली ह्मणजे अशा निकरावर किंवा थरावर या गोष्टी न येऊं देणें हीच होय; आणि हीच नीति सरकारास मोकळ्या मनानें आणि स्पष्टपणानें आह्मीं या प्रसंगीं सुचवीत आहों. मुझफरपूर येथें घडलेला प्रकार भयंकर असून त्याचा आह्मीं तीव्र निषेध किंवा अव्हेर करतों, असें सरकारास नम्रपणें कळविल्यानें प्रजा या नात्यानें आमचें सर्व कर्तव्य आह्मी केलें, असें आह्मांस वाटत नाहीं. असे अनन्वित प्रकार घडूं नयेत अगर तितक्या निकरावर येण्याचा प्रजेपैकीं कोणासही प्रसंग येऊं नये अशी सर्वांची मनापासून इच्छा आहे. पण राज्यकर्त्या अधिकारीवर्गानें प्रजेची ही इच्छा धाब्यावर बसवून प्रजेचा कोठपर्यंत अंत पहावयाचा याचाही अशा वेळीं अवश्य विचार झाला पाहिजे; एरव्ही राज्यकर्ते आणि प्रजा यांच्यामध्यें सलोखा राहून दोघांचेही व्यवहार सुरळीत चालणें शक्य नाहीं. मुझफरपूर येथें घडलेला प्रकार योग्य नाहीं, खेदजनक आहे, हें आम्हीं वर सांगितलेंच आहे. पण तो ज्या कारणांमुळें घडून आला तीं कारणें जर जशींच्या तशींच यापुढें कायम राहतील तर असले भयंकर प्रसंग अजिबात बंद होणें आमच्या मतें शक्य नाहीं; आणि ह्मणूनच असले अनिष्ट प्रकार अजिबात बंद करण्यास ज्या तजविजी केल्या पाहिजेत त्या आम्हीं याचवेळीं सरकारास सुचविल्या आहेत. रशिया, जर्मनी, फ्रान्स वगैरे देशांत 'निहिलिस्टां'चा जो पक्ष उत्पन्न झाला आहे, तसाच तो आतां इकडे उत्पन्न होण्याची आमच्या दुर्दैवानें वेळ आली आहे. ही वेळ टाळणें, हा विषवृक्ष वाढूं न देणें, सर्वस्वीं सरकारच्या हातांतील गोष्ट आहे. जुलमानें किंवा सक्तीनें देशाला होत असलेलीं हीं गळवें कधींही कायमचीं बरीं व्हावयाचीं नाहींत. राज्यपद्धतींत सुधारणा करणें हाच काय तो या रोगावर पोटांत देण्याचा दवा आहे; व सदर दव्याचा अधिकारीवर्ग जर यावेळीं उपयोग करणार नाहीं तर तें आह्मां सर्वांचें मोठें दुर्दैव समजलें पाहिजे. आमचें हें लिहिणें सरकारी अधिकारीवर्गास कदाचित अप्रिय वाटेल, पण त्यास आमचा इलाज नाहीं; कारण एका कवीनें ह्मटल्याप्रमाणें गोड आणि हितकारक असें भाषण दुर्लभ होय. आह्मीं जें कांहीं वर सांगितलें आहे तें आमच्या मतानें खरें आणि वाजवी असून परिणामीं राज्यकर्ते आणि प्रजा ह्या दोघांसही हितकारक आहे. इतक्या उपर जर आमच्या लिहिण्याचा कांहींच उपयोग होणार नाहीं, तर हें एक मोठें देशाचें दुर्दैवच समजलें पाहिजे; दुसरें काय ? आणि एकदां दुर्दैव ओढवलें ह्मणजे पुढें काय काय अनर्थ होतील हें तरी कोणीं सांगावें ? अनर्थ किंवा संकटें कोणासही इष्ट नसतात; पण तीं टाळणें परमेश्वर कधीं कधीं आमच्या हातांत ठेवीत नाहीं. हल्लींचा प्रकार अशांतलाच होत चालला आहे; आणि सरकारी अधिकारीवर्गास या गोष्टीची जर उमज पटली नाहीं, तर त्यास आह्मी तरी काय करणार ? इशारा देणें एवढें आमचें काम आहे; आणि परमेश्वरास आणि सत्यास स्मरून तें कर्तव्य आह्मी बजावीत आहों. देशाची स्थिति कष्टमय होऊं नये, हें आह्मांसही इष्ट आहे; पण त्याचबरोबर हल्लींची दुःसह राज्यपद्धती होईल तितक्या लवकर सुधारली पाहिजे, असा आग्रह धरण्याचा जो आमचा हक्क आहे तोही आह्मी बजाविला पाहिजे. विनाकारण गांगरून जाण्यांत कांहीं अर्थ नाहीं. गोरा अधिकारीवर्ग किंवा अँग्लोइंडियन पत्रकार मुझफरपूर येथील प्रकरणाचा मोठ्या

धूर्ततेनें आमच्या प्रयत्नाची तीव्रता कमी करण्याचे कामीं उपयोग करून घेतील हें आह्मी जाणून आहों; किंबहुना यांत त्यांचा स्वार्थही आहे. पण मुझफरपूर येथील त्रागयाचा निषेध करतांना वस्तुस्थितीचा अँग्लो-इंडियन लोकांकडून जो हा विपर्यास होत आहे त्याचाही जोरानें निषेध करणें, हें आमचें कर्तव्य होय. राज्यकर्त्या अधिकाऱ्यांचा खून न होण्यास प्रजेनें साह्य करावें, हा प्रजेचा ज्याप्रमाणें धर्म आहे त्याप्रमाणेंच राज्यपद्धति बेजबाबदार न ठेवितां सध्यांच्या कालमानाप्रमाणें लोकमताचा त्यांस समावेश करणें, हें राज्यकर्त्यांचेंही कर्तव्य होय. हें कर्तव्य विसरून जाऊन किंवा त्याजकडे जाणून बुजून दुर्लक्ष करून राज्यकर्त्या पुरुषांनीं प्रजेचा धर्म मात्र त्यांजकडून असिधाराव्रताप्रमाणें पाळविणें शक्य नाहीं; इतकेंच नव्हे, तर दोघांपैकीं कोणासहीं फायदेशीर व्हावयाचें नाहीं, असें राजधर्मशास्त्र कंठरवानें सांगत आहे. हा धर्म जेथें सुटला तेथें कधींना कधीं तरी मुझफरपूरप्रमाणें अनर्थ घडणें अपरिहार्य होय. करितां हे अनिष्ट प्रकार घडूं नयेत अशी जर राज्यकर्त्यांची इच्छा असेल तर स्वतःच्या राज्यपद्धतीसच त्यांनीं पहिल्यानें आळा घालावा, अशी त्यांस आमची सूचना आहे; व तेवढ्याच हेतूनें आजचा लेख लिहिला आहे.

Ex. D.

(Translation of the Marathi leader printed in column 2, 3 and 4 of page 4 of the the issue of the " Kesari *" newspaper, dated 9th June 1908, and having a foot-note, as translated, 'This newspaper was printed and published at the "*Kesari*" printing press, Narayen Peth, No. 486, Poona, by Bal Gangadher Tilak'.)*

These remedies are not lasting.

From this week the Government of India have again entered upon a new policy of repression. The fiend of repression has possession of the body of the Government of India after (every) five or ten years. The present occasion, too, is of this very kind. The Prevention of Meetings Act was passed, certainly after Lord Morley had become Secretary of State for India, and now an Act relating to newspapers has been passed. (The fact) that the fiends of repression should swarm everywhere while the Liberal party is in power and while a philosopher (and) an expounder of the principles of Liberalism like (Mr.) Morley is holding the reins of administration, will make it evident to (our) readers how the Mantrikas (*a*) themselves have (*b*) abjured their ideals (*b*). What does a policy of repression mean? Repression means not only stopping future growth but nipping off past growth also To stop the future progress of those causes which have given birth to the nation in India, which have developed the nation and which have created the national fire for the rise of the nation, and to drag those (causes) backwards by pulling them by the leg is called a retrograde or repressive policy. Liberty of speech and liberty of the press give birth to a nation and nourish it. Seeing that these had begun to turn India into a nation, the official class had for many days entertained the desire to smash (*c*) both of them; and they have gratified their ardent desire by taking advantage of the bomb in Bengal. Now the question arises, will this repressive policy bring about that which is in the mind of the official? The first desire of the official class is that bombs should be stopped in India, and that the mind of no one should feel inclined towards the manufacture or the throwing of bombs. That the authorities should entertain such a desire is natural and also laudable. But just as he who has to go towards the North goes to the South, or, he who is bound for the East takes the way to the West, in the same manner the authorities have taken a path leading to the very opposite direction (of their goal). This is exactly what is called infatuation. This aberration of the intellect

(*a*) (A Mantrika is a reciter of Vedic texts; judging from the context it presumably refers to Lord Morley as a philosopher expounding the principles of the art of government.)

(*b*)........(*b*) (*Lit.* fallen off from their vows, practices, principles or ideals)

(*c*) (*Lit.* bring a cudgel against.)

suggests coming destruction; and seeing that Government has adopted a repressive policy, (we) feel extremely grieved (to think) that more sorrowful days are henceforward (d) in store (d) for the subjects and the authorities

(d)......(d) (Lit., to come.)

See how the understanding of the Government has become fatuous. The authorities have spread the false report that bombs of the Bengalis are subversive of sosiety. There is as wide a difference between the bombs in Europe desiring to destroy society and the bombs in Bengal as between the earth and heaven. There is an excess of patriotism at the root of the bombs in Bengal, while the bombs in Europe are the product of the hatred felt for selfish millionaires (e). The Bengalis are not anarchists but they have brought into use the weapon of the anarchists; that is all. The anarchist murdering the President in Paris simply because he is the President, is one man; while the madcap patriot of Portugal throwing a bomb at the King of Portugal because he suppresses the Parliament is a different (person). The anarchist who murders a millionaire in America for the only reason that he is a millionaire is one man, while the exasperated Russian patriot who throws a bomb in despair because the Czar's officers do not grant the rights of the Duma in Russia, is different. No one should forget that the bombs in Bengal do not belong to the first category but to the second. The bomb in Portugal effected a change in the system of government in Portugal and the ministry of the new boy-monarch had to abandon the previous repressive policy. The most mighty Czar of Russia, too, had perforce to bow down before the bomb, and, while making repeated attempts to break up the Duma, was at last obliged to establish it as a matter of course. That the bombs came to a stop in Portugal, or, that the series of bombs in Russia did not lengthen will not be set down by any one to the credit of the policy of repression. New desires and new ambitions have risen amongst the people and are gathering strength every day; such was the interpretation put upon bombs by the statesmen of both the aforesaid countries; and accordingly they changed the character of the administration in such a way that the desires and the ambitions of the people should at least be partially gratified and that they should not become utterly desperate and resort to violence.

(e) (Lit., rich men.)

The present repressive policy of Government is of two sorts. First, the very manufacture of bombs is to be made impossible, and, secondly, such measures are to be taken that the people should not feel inclined at all to manufacture and throw bombs. After the parrot is first put into the cage, the door is closed. Accordingly, Government first disarmed the people. In order that the caged parrot should feel delight only in remaining within the cage, people who are fond of pleasure and sport, make arrangements for (providing it there with) sweet fruits and grain and water. But the Indian Government has not only closed the door of the cage, but it has also commenced to pluck the wings and break the leg (of the parrot) in order that it should not go out (of the cage)! Even the tyrannical rulers of Europe did not disarm their subjects; even a savage race like the Musalmans did not disarm the Hindus while exercising their imperial sway over India. Then, why did the English do so? If common muskets and coommon swords be in the hands of the subjects, they can never equal the military strength (of Government). If there is nothing detrimental to the military strength (of Government) even in allowing the people to be with arms, then why did the English commit the great sin of castrating a nation ? The answer to this question is that the manhood of the nation was slain by the Arms Act in order that the authority exercised even by petty officials from day to day should be unopposed and that the selfish administration might be carried on all right without any hitch (and) without granting the subjects any of the rights of *swarajya* ! The English have not got even as much generosity as the Moghuls and they have not even as much military strength as the Moghuls. As compared with the imperial sway of the Moghuls, the English Empire in India is extremely weak and wanting in vigour from the point of view of military strength. The Emperor Aurungzebe exercised tyranny of various kinds over the Hindus from the point of view of religion though not from the point of view of the distribution of wealth ; and his ten or twenty láksh of troops also perished completely during his Deccan campaigns of ten or twenty years. Still the Empire of Delhi lasted for a hundred and fifty years, albert in a hobbling manner, after his death. If the English army in India were to be confronted by difficulties similar to those which Aurungzebe's forces encountered, then the English rule will not last in India even for quarter of a centuy after (that). The principal reason of this is that the English remain in India like temporary (*f*) tenants or mere (*g*) birds of passage (*g*). The residence of the English in India not being permanent, and the English authorities as well as the English merchants having a covert aim at enriching England, they are, quite naturally, not ready to give into the hands of the natives any portion of the ruling power after making a separate division (of the same). Had the Moghuls exercised (their) imperial sway over India, for the sake of the prosperity of the land of their original residence, by sending out officers like temporary tenants, then the Moghuls, too would have been obliged to be illiberal in dealing with Princes and Chiefs or village institutions, like the English themselves, and there would have been no other alternative but to disarm the subjects. Owing to the power given by Western science and the helplessness produced amongst the subjects in consequence of their being disarmed, the administration can be heedlessly carried on without any hitch (and) without even a consideration of the desires or the aspirations of the people. Owing to the bomb this state (of things) has not remained permanent. The subjects, armless; and the Government, admittedly powerful owing to the modern science of arms. Up to this time there was no means at all for Government to know (*h*) that the people, becoming disappointed owing to some acts of Government, get exasperated and become even turn-headed. How was Government at all to know that the tyranny of its acts has become unbearable to the subjects ? What happened usually up to this time when Government did any act and the subjects disapproved of it? The people used to submit petitions, to prefer requests; the authorities used to say that it was temporary froth, that it would subside, in a short time, of itself. The people

(*f*) (*Lit*., a tenant or farmer having no rights of occupancy.)

(*g*)......(*g*) (*Lit*. Passengers upon the road, wayfarers,)

(*h*) (*Lit*, estimate.)

become despondent, the impatient fretted and fumed within themselves in exasperation, and the turn-headed, in their own violent emotion, burnt their bodies and in a fit of passion made an offering of themselves alone,-without even any report of ony kind reaching the ears of Government; such was the state (of things) up to this time. The turn-headed men destitute of arms became provided with arms in consequence of the bomb, and the bomb reduced the importance (*i*) of military strength. Unless a beginning be made to divide wealth and authority with the subject, with greater liberality than was shown by the Moghuls, England will not henceforward be able to carry on the administration, without any hitch, through officers having (only) a temporary (interest in the country). The bomb is not a thing like muskets or guns. Muskets and guns may be taken away from the subjects by means of the Arms Act; and the manufacture, too, of guns and muskets without the permission of Government, may be stopped; but is it possible to stop or to do away with the bomb by means of laws or the supervision of officials or the busy swarming of the detective police? The bomb has more the form of knowledge, it is a (kind of) witchcraft, it is a charm, an amulet. It has not much the features of a visible object manufactured in a big factory. Big factories are necessary for the bombs required by the millitary forces of Government, but not much (in the way of) materials is necessary to prepare five or ten bombs required by violent, turn-headed persons. Virendra's big factory of bombs consisted (*j*) of one or two jars and five or ten bottles; and Government chemical experts are at present deposing that the factory was, from a scientific point of view, faultleess like a Government bomb-factory. Should not Government pay attention to the true meaning of the accounts published in (the course of) the case of Virendra's conspiracy? Judging from the accounts published of this case, the formula of the bomb does not at all appear to be a lengthy one and (its) process also is very short indeed. The power of keeping the knowledge of this formula a secret from one who is turn-headed, has not now been left in the laws of Government. This knowledge is not a secret in Europe, America, Japan and other countries. In India it is still a secret knowledge. But when the number of turn-headed (persons) increases owing to the stringent enforcement of the policy of repression, what time will it take for the magical practices, the magical lore of Bengal to spread throughout in India? The labour of acquiring this lore will not be as hard to those who are turn-headed as the labour of bringing their brains again to a normal condition; and even in putting this lore to a practical use there is very little possibility of the exasperation being even calmed down through a Magistrate, owing (to the plot) being frustrated by the skill and vigilance of the detective police. To speak in (the language of) hyperbole, this factory can be brought into existence in a trice and (also) broken up in a trice! Therefore, how can the nose-string of the law be put on these turn-headed wizards of the bomb? When the Explosives (k) Act was passed in England (about) ten or fifteen years ago, the

(*i*) (*Lit.*, awe.)

(*j*) (*Lit.*, was stored in.)

(*k*) (*Lit.*, Act about bombs.)

bomb had not attained such a form of knowledge (as at present). The bomb had not (then) become a (*l*) mere toy (*l*) of the Western sciences. At that time elaborate(*m*) appliances, too, were required; also special materials were required and the factory also used to be a big one. Such tings can be prevented by law; but when science begins to exhibit wonders like the bomb in mere sport (and even) while walking, talking (and) sleeping, how can these simple sports of science be put a stop to? The Westerners propitiated the goddess of science for (securing) commercial progress and military stregth. How will it do to accept only the gift of the blessing of the propitiated goddess and to refuse only those things which that very goddess may be doing in mere sport in order that no one may become intoxicated with the bestowal of the blessings? While the knowledge of the science of the Westerners is being thus easily obtained (by people) every day, and while new discoveries are being daily made that produce terrific powers in no time with a simple process from common chemicals themselves which are constantly required for trade and industries, how long will Government stop, by legal restraints, the current of the sport of scientific experts? In our opinion, Government are going to put themselves aad the subjects to loss for nothing, by pursuing impossible things. If the perfect state to which scientific knowledge has attained in Europe and America be considered, (one) has to say that Government has been engaged in the vain attempt of making an impossibility a possibility. At such (a) time (as) this, chemists, persons engaged in industries and petty manufacturers cannot fail to be subjected to unjust compulsion for nothing. The object desired by Government cannot be accomplished by the Explosives Act, but, on the other hand, it will serve as an instrument in the hands of the police and the petty officials to persecute good men. This effort to impose (*n*) a Prohibition (*n*) upon the scientific knowledge about bombs and the materials (for making bombs) is vain. If bombs are to be stopped this is not the proper means (for it); Govrrnment should act in such a way that no turn-headed man should feel any necessity at all for (throwing) bombs. When do people who are engaged in political agitation become turn-headed? It is when young (political) agitators feel keen disappointment (by being convinced) that their faculties, their strength and their self-srcrifice cannot be of any use in bringing about the welfare of their country in any other way than by acts of turn-headedness, that they become turn-headed. Government should never allow keen disappointment (to take hold) of (the minds of) those intelligent persons who have been awakened (to the necessity of) securing the rights of *swarajya*. Government should not forget that when the desires and aspirations of the awakened intelligent people spread throughout the nation and begin rudely to awaken the whole nation, the disappointment instead of decreasing becomes all the more keen, if this process of awakening is stopped at such a time. Government has passed the new 'Newspapers' Act with a view to put a stop to the process of awakening; and, therefore, there is a possibility of the disappointment assuming a more terrible form and of turnheadedness being produced even amongst people of

(*l*)....(*l*) (*Lit*, the dirt of the body, as it were.)

(*m*) *Lit*., many.)

(*n*)....(*n*) (*Lit*., do away with.)

thoughtful and quiet disposition. The real and lasting means of stopping bombs consists in making a beginning to grant the important rights of *swarajya* (to the people). It is not possible for measures of repression to have a lasting (effect) in the present condition of the Western sciences and that of the people of India.

[H. I. M.'s High Court, Bombay,

Translator's Office, 7th July 1908.]

A true translation.

N. L. MANKAR,

Third Translator.

M. 579.

Ex. D.

[The following is the original Marathi text of the article of which Ex. D. is a translation.]

हे उपाय टिकाऊ नाहींत.

(**केसरी**, तारीख ९ जून १९०८).

ह्या आठवड्यापासून हिंदुस्थानसरकारनें दडपशाहीच्या नवीन धोरणास पुन्हा प्रारंभ केला आहे. दडपशाहीचें भूत पांच दहा वर्षांनीं हिंदुस्थानसरकारच्या अंगांत संचार करीत असतें. अशांतलाच सांप्रतचाही प्रसंग आहे. लॉर्ड मोर्ले हिंदुस्थानचे स्टेटसेक्रेटरी झाल्यावरच सभाबंदीचा कायदा पास झाला व आतां वर्तमानपत्रांसंबंधाचा कायदा पास झाला आहे. लिबरलपक्षाचे कारकीर्दींत व मोर्लेसारखा उदारमतवादी तत्ववेत्ता राज्यकारभाराचीं सूत्रें हालवीत असतांना दडपशाहीच्या पिशाचांचा चोहोंकडे सुळसुळाट व्हावा ह्यावरून खुद्द मांत्रिकच व्रतभ्रष्ट कसे झाले आहेत, हें वाचकांचे ध्यानांत येईल. दडपशाहीचें धोरण ह्मणजे काय? दडपून टाकणें ह्मणजे पुढील वाढ खुंटविणें इतकेंच नव्हे, तर पूर्वीचीही वाढ कुरतडून टाकणें होय. हिंदुस्थानांत राष्ट्रास जन्म देणारीं, राष्ट्राचा विकास करणारीं व राष्ट्राच्या अभ्युदयासाठीं राष्ट्रीय तेज उत्पन्न करणारीं जीं कारणें आहेत त्यांची पुढील गति बंद पाडून त्यांची तंगडी ओढून त्यांना फरफटत मागें ओढणें, ह्याला पिछेहाटीचें किंवा दडपशाहीचें धोरण असें ह्मणतात. भाषणस्वातंत्र्य व मुद्रणस्वातंत्र्य हीं राष्ट्रास जन्म देतात व पोसतात. ह्यांनीं हिंदुस्थानचें राष्ट्र बनविण्याचा उपक्रम केलेला पाहून ह्या दोहोंवर गदा आणावी, अशी अधिकारीवर्गाची फार दिवसांची इच्छा होती; आणि बंगाल्यांतील बाँबगोळ्यांचा फायदा घेऊन त्यांनीं आपली हौस भागवून घेतली आहे. आतां असा प्रश्न उद्भवतो कीं, ह्या दडपशाहीच्या धोरणानें अधिकारीवर्गाच्या मनांत आहे तें घडून येईल काय? अधिकारीवर्गाची पहिली इच्छा अशी आहे कीं, बाँबगोळे हिंदुस्थानांत बंद झाले पाहिजेत; आणि बाँबगोळे करण्याकडे किंवा बाँबगोळे फेंकण्याकडे कोणाचेही मनाची प्रवृत्ति होतां कामा नये. अधिकाऱ्यांची अशी इच्छा असणें साहजिक आहे व स्तुत्यही आहे. पण ज्याला उत्तरेस जावयाचें आहे त्यानें दक्षिणेला जावें किंवा पूर्वेस जाणारानें पश्चिमेचा मार्ग धरावा, ह्याप्रमाणें अधिकाऱ्यांनीं रस्ता मात्र अगदीं उलट दिशेचा धरला आहे. बुद्धिभ्रंश ह्मणतात तो हाच. हा मतिभ्रंश पुढील विनाश सुचवितो, आणि सरकारनें दडपशाहीचें धोरण अंगिकारलेलें पाहून प्रजाजनांना व अधिकाऱ्यांना ह्यापुढें अधिक दुःखाचे दिवस येणार ह्मणून अत्यंत वाईट वाटतें. सरकारची बुद्धि कशी चळली आहे तें पहा. बंगाल्यांचे बाँबगोळे समाजाची उलथापालथ करणारे आहेत, अशी खोटी अफवा अधिकाऱ्यांनीं पिकविलेली आहे. समाजाचा विध्वंस करूं इच्छिणारे युरोपांतील बाँबगोळे व बंगाल्यांतील बाँबगोळे, ह्यांमध्यें जमीनअस्मानाचें अंतर आहे. बंगालच्या बाँबगोळ्यांच्या बुडाशीं देशभक्तीचा अतिरेक आहे, व युरोपांतील बाँबगोळे आप्पलपोट्या श्रीमंताच्या द्वेषामुळें उत्पन्न होतात. बंगाली अनार्किस्ट नाहींत, तर अनार्किस्टांचें हत्यार त्यांनीं उपयोगांत आणलें आहे, इतकेंच. पारिस शहरांत प्रेसिडेंटाचा खून तो प्रेसिडंट आहे एवढ्याच करितां करणारा अनार्किस्ट निराळा; आणि पोर्तुगालचा राजा पार्लमेंटसभा बुडवितो ह्मणून त्यावर बाँबगोळा टाकणारा पोर्तुगालचा एखादा स्वदेशभक्त माथेफिरू निराळा. अमेरिकेंत एखाद्या कोट्याधीशाचा खून तो कोट्याधिश आहे, एवढ्याच कारणाकरितां करणारा अनार्किस्ट निराळा आणि रशियांत झारचे अधिकारी ड्यूमा सभेचे हक्क

देत नाहींत ह्यामुळें हताश होऊन बाँबगोळा फेकणारा रशियांतील वैतागलेला देशभक्त निराळा. बंगाल्यांतील बाँबगोळे पहिल्या कोटींतील नसून दुसऱ्या कोटींतले आहेत, हें कोणीही विसरतां कामा नये. पोर्तुगालमधील बाँबगोळ्यानें पोर्तुगालमधील राजपद्धत पालटली, व नवीन बालराजाचे प्रधानमंडळास पूर्वीचें दडपशाहीचें धोरण सोडून द्यावें लागलें. रशियांतील अत्यंत बलाढ्य झारलाही बाँबगोळ्यांपुढें नमावेंच लागलें व ड्यूमा सभा मोडून टाकण्याचा प्रयत्न करतां करतां अखेरीस ड्यूमा सभा स्थापनच करावी लागली. पोर्तुगालमधील बाँबगोळे बंद झाले किंवा रशियांतील गोळ्यांची मालिका लांबली नाहीं, ह्याचें श्रेय दडपशाहीच्या धोरणाला कोणीही देणार नाहीं. - लोकांत नवीन इच्छा व नवीन महत्वाकांक्षा उद्भवल्या असून त्या रोज जोरावतात, असा बाँबगोळ्यांचा अर्थ सदर दोन्हीही देशांतील मुत्सद्यांनीं केला, व त्याप्रमाणें लोकांच्या इच्छा व महत्वाकांक्षा अंशतः तरी भागतील आणि ते अगदींच निराश होऊन आततायी होणार नाहींत, अशा रीतीनें त्यांनीं राज्यकारभाराचें स्वरूप पालटलें.

सरकारचें सांप्रतचें दडपशाहीचें धोरण दोन प्रकारचें आहे. एक बाँबगोळे तयार करणेंच अशक्य करावयाचें व दुसरें बाँबगोळे करण्याकडे व फेंकण्याकडे लोकांची प्रवृत्तिच होऊं नये, असा बंदोबस्त करावयाचा. पोपटाला प्रथम पिंजऱ्यांत घातल्यानंतर दार बंद करून घेतात, त्याप्रमाणें सरकारनें प्रथम प्रजेला निःशस्त्र करून सोडलें. कोंडलेल्या पोपटाला पिंजऱ्यांत राहण्यांतच गोडी लागावी म्हणून हौशी लोक मधुर फळांची व दाण्यापाण्याची व्यवस्था करून ठेवतात. पण हिंदुस्थान सरकारनें पिंजऱ्याचें दारं बंद केलें इतकेंच नव्हे तर पोपटानें बाहेर जाऊं नये म्हणून पंख उपटण्याचा व तंगडी मोडण्याचा उपक्रम चालविला आहे ! युरोपांतील जुलमी राजांनींही आपल्या प्रजेला निःशस्त्र केलें नाहीं, मुसलमानांसारख्या कडव्या जातीनेंही हिंदुस्थानांत बादशाही गाजवितांना हिंदूंना निःशस्त्र केलें नाहीं. मग इंग्रजांनींच कां केलें? प्रजाजनांच्या हातांत साधारण बंदुकी व साधारण तरवारी असल्यानें लष्करच्या सामर्थ्याची बरोबरी प्रजेच्या हातून केव्हांही होऊं शकत नाहीं. प्रजा सशस्त्र राहूं दिल्यानेंही जर लष्करी सत्तेस कमीपणा येत नाहीं तर एखाद्या राष्ट्रास खच्ची करण्याचें महत्पाप तरी इंग्रजांनीं कां केलें ? ह्या प्रश्नाचें असें उत्तर आहे कीं, रोजचेरोज किरकोळ अधिकाऱ्यांनींही गाजवावयाची सत्ता अबाधित असावी व स्वराज्याचे कोणच्याही प्रकारचे हक्क प्रजेला न देतां बिनखटका आप्पलपोटेपणाचा कारभार यथास्थित चालावा, म्हणून राष्ट्राच्या पौरुषाचा वध हत्याराचे कायद्यानें करण्यांत आला ! मोंगलांच्या इतका उदारपणाही इंग्रजांत नाहीं व मोंगलांच्या इतकें लष्करी सामर्थ्यही इंग्रजांत नाहीं. मोंगली बादशाहीच्या मानानें पाहिलें असतां हिंदुस्थानांतील इंग्रजी साम्राज्य लष्करी सामर्थ्याच्या दृष्टीनें फार निर्बल व निःसत्व आहे. औरंगजेब बादशहानें—संपत्तीच्या वांटणीच्या दृष्टीनें जरी नाहीं तरी—धर्मदृष्ट्या हिंदूंवर नानाप्रकारचे जुलूम केले, व त्याचें दहावीस लाख सैन्य दहावीस वर्षांच्या दक्षिणेच्या मोहिमेंत गारदही झालें. तरी त्याच्या मरणानंतर दीडशें वर्षेंपर्यंत—रडत कढत कां होईना—दिल्लीची बादशाही टिकली होती. औरंगजेबाच्या सेनेवर जसले प्रसंग आले तसले प्रसंग जर हिंदुस्थानांतील इंग्रजी सेनेवर आले तर पुढें पांचपंचवीस वर्षेंही इंग्रजी सत्ता हिंदुस्थानांत टिकणार नाहीं. ह्याचें मुख्य कारण इंग्रज हिंदुस्थानांत उपरी कुळासारखे किंवा वाटसरूसारखे राहतात हें होय. हिंदुस्थानांत इंग्रजांची वस्ती कायमची नसल्यामुळें व इंग्लंडची भर करण्याकडे इंग्रजी अधिकाऱ्यांचा व इंग्रजी व्यापाऱ्यांचा कटाक्ष असल्यामुळें राजकीय सत्तेचा कोणताही भाग पृथक् वांटणी करून नेटिवांच्या हातांत देण्यास बे साहजिकपणेंच तयार नाहींत; उपरी कुळाप्रमाणें अधिकारी पाठवून मूळवस्तीच्या ठिकाणचे भरभराटीकरितां जर मोंगलांनीं हिंदुस्थानची बादशाही चालविली असती तर मोंगलांनाही राजेरजवाड्यांशीं किंवा ग्रामसंस्थांशीं वागतांना इंग्रजांप्रमाणेंच अनुदार व्हावें लागलें असतें व प्रजाजनांना निःशस्त्र केल्याशिवाय गत्यंतर नसतें. पाश्चिमात्य शास्त्रानें दिलेलें सामर्थ्य, व प्रजा निःशस्त्र केल्यामुळें प्रजेच्या अंगीं आलेला दुबळेपणा, ह्यांमुळें लोकांच्या इच्छेचा किंवा महत्वाकांक्षेचा विचारही न करतां बेगुमानपणानें बिनखटका राज्यकारभार हांकला जातो. बाँबगोळ्यामुळें ही स्थिति कायम राहिली

नाहीं. प्रजा निःशस्त्र व सरकार आधुनिक अस्त्रविद्येनें बलाढ्य ठरलेलें. सरकारच्या कांहीं कृत्यांनीं लोक निराश होऊन संतापी बनून माथेफिरूही होतात, हें सरकारला अजमावण्याला आजपर्यंत मार्गच नव्हता. सरकारच्या कृत्यांचा जुलूम प्रजेला असह्य झाला आहे, हें सरकाराला समजावें तरी कसें ? सरकारनें कोणचीही गोष्ट केली व प्रजेला ती नापसंत असली, तर आजपर्यंत काय होत असे ? लोक अर्ज करीत, विनंति करीत; अधिकारी म्हणत हा क्षणैक फेस आहे, थोड्या वेळानें आपोआप खालीं बसेल. लोकांनीं निराश व्हावें, उतावीळ झालेल्यांनीं संतापून जाऊन मनचे मनांत जळफळावें व माथेफिरूंनीं स्वतःच्या आततायीपणानें स्वतःचें शरीर पिचवून स्वतःच्या क्रोधांत आपली एकट्याचीच आहुती–सरकारच्या कानीं कोणच्याही प्रकारची वार्ताही न जातां–द्यावी, अशांतला आजपर्यंतचा प्रकार होता. बाँबगोळ्यानें निःशस्त्र माथेफिरू सशस्त्र झाले, व बाँबगोळ्यानें लष्करी सामर्थ्याचा दर्प कमी केला. मोंगलांनीं दाखविलेल्या उदारपणाहून अधिक उदारपणानें संपत्तीची व अधिकाराची वांटणी प्रजेशीं करण्यास आरंभ केल्याशिवाय उपरी अधिकाऱ्यांच्या मार्फत बिनखटका राज्यकारभार इंग्लंडास ह्यापुढें चालवितां येणार नाहीं. बाँबगोळा हा बंदुकी किंवा तोफा ह्यांच्यासारखी वस्तु नाहीं. हत्याराचे कायद्यानें बंदुकी व तोफा प्रजेपासून काढून घेतां येतील, आणि बंदुकी व तोफा सरकारी परवानगीशिवाय तयार करण्याचेंही बंद पाडतां येईल; पण बांबगोळा कायद्यांनीं किंवा अधिकाऱ्यांच्या देखरेखीनें, अथवा गुप्त पोलीसाच्या सुळसुळाटानें बंद पडतां किंवा नाहींसा करतां येणें शक्य आहे काय ? बांब गोळ्याला ज्ञानाचें स्वरूप अधिक आहे, ही एक जादू आहे, हा एक मंत्र, तोडगा आहे. मोठ्या कारखान्यांत तयार होणाऱ्या दृश्यवस्तूचें स्वरूप ह्याला फारसें नाहीं. सरकारी लष्करला लागणाऱ्या बांब गोळ्याचे मोठमोठे कारखाने असावे लागतात, पण आततायी माथेफिरूंना लागणारे दहापांच बांब गोळे तयार करण्यास विशेषसी सामुग्री लागत नाहीं. विरेंद्रचा बांब गोळ्याचा मोठा कारखाना एक दोन बरण्यांत, व दहापांच बाटल्यांत सांठविला होता, आणि हा कारखाना सरकारी बांब गोळ्याचे कारखान्याप्रमाणें शास्त्रीयदृष्ट्या बिनचूक होता, अशा साक्षी सरकारी रसायनशास्त्रवेत्त्यांच्या सांप्रत होत आहेत. विरेंद्राच्या कटाचे खटल्यांत प्रसिद्ध झालेल्या हकीकतींच्या खऱ्या अर्थाकडे सरकारनें लक्ष पोंचवावयास नको काय ? ह्या खटल्याची जी हकीकत प्रसिद्ध झाली आहे, त्यावरून पाहतां बाँब गोळ्याचा मंत्र कांहीं लांबलचक दिसत नाहीं, व तंत्रही फारच अल्प आहे. जो माथेफिरू आहे त्याच्यापासून ह्या मंत्राचें ज्ञान लपवून ठेवण्याचें सामर्थ्य आतां सरकारी कायद्याचे अंगीं उरलें नाहीं. युरोप, अमेरिका, जपान, वगैरे देशांत हें ज्ञान गुप्त नाहीं. हिंदुस्थानांत अद्याप हें गुप्त ज्ञान आहे, पण दडपशाहीचें धोरण जोरानें अंमलांत येऊन त्यामुळें माथेफिरूंची संख्या वाढल्यावर जादूगिरी बंगालची मंत्रविद्या हिंदुस्थानांत चोहोंकडे पसरण्यास कितीसा वेळ लागणार ? जे माथेफिरू आहेत त्यांना ही विद्या संपादन करण्याचे आयास त्यांचें डोकें पुनः ताळ्यावर आणण्याइतके कठीण नाहींत; व ह्या विद्येला व्यावहारिक स्वरूप देतांनाही गुप्त पोलीसच्या चातुर्यामुळें व दक्षतेमुळें ऑफेंस होऊन मॅजिस्ट्रेटमार्फत संताप उतरण्याचाही संभव फार कमी आहे. अतिशयोक्तीनें बोलावयाचें असल्यास हा कारखाना चुटकीसरसा अस्तित्वांत आणतां येतो व चुटकीसरशी मोडतां येतो ! तेव्हां बाँबगोळ्यांच्या ह्या माथेफिरू चेटक्यांना कायद्याची वेसण कशी घालतां येईल ? दहा पंधरा वर्षांपूर्वी इंग्लंडांत जेव्हां बाँबगोळ्यांचा कायदा झाला त्यावेळीं बाँबगोळ्यांना इतकें ज्ञानमय स्वरूप आलें नव्हतें. पाश्चिमात्य शास्त्रांच्या अंगचा मळ बाँबगोळा होऊन बसला नव्हता. त्यावेळीं उपकरणेंही फार लागत, सामुग्रीही विशेष लागे व कारखानाही मोठा असे. असल्या गोष्टींचा प्रतिबंध कायद्यानें होण्यासारखा आहे. पण ज्यावेळीं शास्त्र चालतां चालतां, बोलतां बोलतां, निजतां निजतां, सहज लीलेनें बाँबगोळ्यासारखे चमत्कार करून दाखवूं लागतें, त्यावेळीं शास्त्राच्या ह्या सहज लीला कशा बंद पाडावयाच्या ? व्यापारविषयक उन्नत्तीकरितां व लष्करी सामर्थ्याकरितां शास्त्रदेवता पाश्चिमात्यांनीं प्रसन्न करून घेतली. देवतेला प्रसन्न करून घेऊन वरप्रदान घ्यावयाला तेवढें पाहिजे, पण तीच देवता वरप्रदानानें कोणी उन्मत्त होऊं नये ह्मणून ज्या सहज लीला करित असते तेवढ्या मात्र नकोत, असें कसें होईल ? पाश्चिमा-

त्यांच्या शास्त्राचें ज्ञान रोजचेरोज अशा रीतीनें सहज प्राप्त होत चाललें असतांना, आणि व्यवहाराला व उद्योगधंद्याला हरहमेष लागणाऱ्या रासायनिक साध्या वस्तूंपासूनच हां हां म्हणतां भयंकर शक्ति लहानशा तंत्रानेंच निर्माण करणारे शोध रोजचेरोज नवीन लागत चालले असतांना, शास्त्रीय मांत्रिकांच्या लीलांचा प्रवाह कायद्याच्या बंधनानें सरकार किती दिवस थोपवून धरणार ? आमच्या मतें सरकार अशक्य गोष्टीच्या नादीं लागून स्वतःचें व प्रजाजनांचें व्यर्थ नुकसान करूं पाहत आहे. शास्त्रीयज्ञानाची युरोपांत व अमेरिकेंत जी परिणत स्थिति आहे, त्या स्थितीचा विचार केला असतां अशक्य गोष्ट शक्य करण्याचा वृथा खटाटोप सरकार करूं लागलें आहे, असें म्हणावें लागतें. ह्या वेळीं रसायनशास्त्रवेत्त्यांवर, उद्योगधंदेवाल्यांवर व लहानसहान कारखानदारांवर नाहक जुलूम झाल्यावांचून राहणार नाहीं. बाँबगोळ्याचे कायद्यानें सरकारचा इष्ट हेतु सिद्धीस जाणार नाहीं, तर उलट पोलीसच्या व लहान अधिकाऱ्यांच्या हातांत हें सज्जनांना छळण्याचें एक हत्यार होऊन बसेल. बाँबगोळ्यासंबंधाचें शास्त्रीयज्ञान व सामुग्री नाहींशीं करण्याचा हा खटाटोप व्यर्थ आहे. बाँबगोळे नाहींसे करावयाचे असल्यास हा उपाय योग्य नव्हे; बाँबगोळ्यांची जरूरीच कोणच्याही माथेफिरूला वाटूं नये, असें सरकारनें केलें पाहिजे. राजकीय चळवळींत पडलेले लोक माथेफिरू होतात केव्हां ? आपल्या बुद्धीचा, आपल्या शरीराचा व आपल्या स्वार्थत्यागाचा उपयोग आपल्या देशाचें कल्याण करण्याचे कामीं माथेफिरूपणाशिवाय इतर दुसऱ्या कोणच्याही मार्गानें होणारा नाहीं; अशी तीव्र निराशा झाल्यानंतर चळवळ करणारे तरुण माथेफिरू होतात. स्वराज्याचे हक्क संपादन करण्यासंबंधानें जागृत झालेल्या बुद्धिमंतांची तीव्र निराशा सरकारनें केव्हांही होऊं देतां कामा नये. ज्यावेळीं जागृत झालेल्या बुद्धिमंतांच्या इच्छा व महत्वाकांक्षा सर्व राष्ट्रभर पसरतात व सर्व राष्ट्राला खडबडून जागे करूं लागतात; त्या वेळीं हीं जागृतीची क्रिया बंद पाडल्यानें ही निराशा कमी न होतां अधिकच तीव्र होते, हें सरकारनें विसरतां कामा नये. जागृतीची क्रिया बंद पाडण्याकरितां वर्तमानपत्रांचा नवा कायदा सरकारनें पास केला आहे, व त्यामुळें निराशेचें स्वरूप अधिक भयंकर होऊन विचारी व शांत स्वभावाच्या लोकांतही माथेफिरू निर्माण होण्याचा संभव आहे. बाँबगोळे नाहींसे करण्यास खरा व टिकाऊ उपाय म्हणजे स्वराज्याचे महत्वाचे हक्क देण्यास आरंभ करणें हा होय. दडपशाहीचे उपाय पाश्चिमात्य शास्त्रांच्या व हिंदुस्थानांतील लोकांच्या सांप्रतच्या स्थितींत टिकाऊ होणें शक्य नाहीं.

Ex. E.

(*Translation of a Maráthi article printed in column* 3 *of page* 5 *of the issue of the* ' Kesari ' *newspaper, dated 12th May 1908, and having a foot-note, as translated,* " *This newspaper was printed and published at the* ' Kesari ' *Printing Press, No. 486, Narayan Peth, Poona, by Bal Gangadhar Tilak.* ")

Since the commencement of the bomb-affair all the Anglo-Indian newspapers have been incessanty advising Government as to what should be done, if such calamities are to be averted in future. The *Engalishman* of Calcutta and the Bombay *Times* and other newspapers have imputed the whole blame to political agitation. The *Statesman* newspaper of Calcutta being controlled by the missionaries was not, so long, much opposed to political agitation. But this paper has now given out its opinion that since terrible occurrences of bomb (outrages) spring from the *Swadeshi* and boycott agitation, this agitation should be stopped. The *Swadeshi* agitation gives rise to bomb-outrages and the Bengal partition gives rise to the *Swadeshi* agitation; then why not first cancel the Bengal partition itself ? The *Tarka-shastra* (*a*) of Anglo-Indian newspaper(editors) has, owing to (their) heads being turned, now become *Markata-shastra.* (*b*) When secret plots of a very similar kind were discovered in Ireland, the statesman Mr. Gladstone, instead of making use of the *Tarkata-shastra*, (*c*) made use of the genuine *Tarka-shastra*,(*a*) and made efforts to grant " Home Rule," (*i. e.*), " *Swarajya*," to that country. Some people pay attention to the evil effects of a vice firmly established in the body, only when (that) vice begins to inflict trouble upon the body in the shape of a terrible abscess; and an effort is then made to remove the vice. The terrible murders that took place in Ireland spontaneously rivetted England's attention to the grievances of that country and then " Home Rule " or *Swarajya* for Ireland began to be discussed. Such usefulness, of one sort, of these murders has been indirectly described by Lord Morley in one place. Will the terrible occurrence at Muzzaffarpur rivet Lord Morley's attention to the grievance about the partition of Bengal ?

(*a*) (The science of logic,)

(*b*) (The science of monkeys,)

(*c*) (The science of falsehood,)

The opinion of the Allahabad *Pioneer* about the bomb-outrage is that if Government wants completely to prevent these terrible occurrenecs, it should keep ready a list of the " suspected leaders " of bomb (-throwers) for each province, district or tàluka and notify that if there was any bomb-outrage within such and such limits, ten, twenty (or) twenty-five persons out of that list would be hanged ! It cannot be denied that this is one way of striking terror (into the public mind) ; but it is a truth established by history that outrages like those of bombs increase instead of diminishing by (the adoption of) such remedies. The Conservative party passed the "Coercion Act," that is to say, a law to put down the people, with a view to bring the Irish people to reason. (*d*) The present Parliament is engaged in the business of passing a bill to repeal this very measure. Were those who passed (*e*)repressive laws(*e*) terrorizing the Irish people, wise, or, is the present Ministry that repeals those very laws wise? The history of Ireland bears witness (to the fact) that repressive (*f*) laws prove useless in the end. It is only when rulers wish in their minds to wipe out of existence any society, any group of people or any nation, that in the first instance repressive laws and afterwards laws that (would) partially wipe them out of existence are brought into force. But mankind has never benefitted through such national assassination. If, owing to the bomb-outrage, the nation's assassination is begun in India, then we can plainly say that its consequence would never prove beneficial to the Anglo-Indians. As the Anglo-Indians have not sufficient strength in their wrists to accomplish this work of national assassination, it is certainly desirable that they should not listen to the advice of those like the *Pioneer* who are hostile to their interests. It is possible (for England) to make Ireland remain only in name, by coaxing it, swallowing it, putting it into the stomach and digesting it. England may possibly(*g*) be able to accomplish the national assassination of Ireland but it is not possible to do (this)—in the case of India. Another statement of the *Pioneer* is that there does not exist at present any cause sufficient to produce so much excitement among the people as would manifest itself in the shape of bomb (outrages). The Bengal partition, the agitation consequent on such partition, the riots, *zulum* and prosecutions resulting from this agitation—are not all these facts indicative of the excited condition of the people? At one time such oppression gave rise to small insurrections in England; and it was only when the people of that country rose in rebellion, and, after dethroning the King, introduced constitutional rule that no occasion was left for them to resort to violent means for effecting administrative reforms. To disregard facts that increase the exasperation of the people, and then to ask the question as to why the Bengalis should have gone off their heads so much, this high-handed chicanery becomes only a newspaper like the *Pioneer* enjoying the protection and patronage of Government.

(*d*) (Lit., agreement.)

(*e*)—(*e*) (Lit., laws having the character of the voracious demon Bakasur.)

(*f*) (Lit., terrorizing.)

(*g*) (Lit, at one time.)

[*H. I. M.'s High Court, Bombay,*

Translator's Office, 7th July 1908.]

A true translation.

N. L. MANKAR,

Third Translator.

Ex. E.

[The following is the original Marathi text of the editorial notes of which Ex. E. is a translation.]

पत्रकर्त्यांच्या स्फुट सूचना.

(केसरी, तारीख १२ मे १९०८).

बाँबगोळ्याचे प्रकरणास सुरवात झाल्यापासून सर्व अँग्लोइंडियन पत्रांनीं असेल अनर्थ पुढें टाळावयाचे असल्यास काय केलें पाहिजे, त्यासंबंधानें सरकारास उपदेश करण्याचा एकसारखा सपाटा चालविला आहे. कलकत्त्याचें 'इंग्लिशमन' व मुंबईचें 'टाईम्स' वगैरे पत्रांनीं सर्व दोष राजकीय चळवळींच्या माथीं मारला आहे. कलकत्त्याचें स्टेट्स्मन पत्र मिशनऱ्यांच्या तंत्राचें असून इतक्या दिवस राजकीय चळवळीच्या फारसें विरुद्ध नव्हतें. पण ह्या पत्रानें आतां आपलें असें मत जाहीर केलें आहे कीं, स्वदेशी व बहिष्कार ह्या चळवळींमुळें बाँबगोळ्यांचे अनर्थ उद्भवतात, तेव्हां ही चळवळ बंद करावी. स्वदेशी चळवळीपासून बाँबगोळ्यांचे अनर्थ उद्भवतात, आणि बंगालच्या फाळणीपासून स्वदेशी चळवळ उत्पन्न होते; मग बंगालची फाळणीच प्रथम कां रद्द करूं नये ? डोकें फिरून गेल्यामुळें अँग्लो-इंडियन पत्रांचें तर्कशास्त्र सांप्रत मर्कटशास्त्र झालें आहे. आयर्लंडांत अशाच प्रकारचे गुप्त कट जेव्हां उघडकीस आले, त्या वेळीं मुत्सद्दी मि. ग्लॅडस्टन ह्यांनीं तर्कटशास्त्राचा उपयोग न करतां खऱ्या तर्कशास्त्राचा उपयोग केला व आयर्लंडला 'होमरूल' 'स्वराज्य' देण्याची खटपट केली. शरीराला जडलेलें एखादें दुर्व्यसन जेव्हां एखाद्या भयंकर गळवाच्या रूपानें शरीरास त्रास देऊं लागतें, तेव्हांच कांहीं कांहीं लोक दुर्व्यसनाच्या दुष्परिणामाकडे लक्ष पोंचवितात; व मग तें दुर्व्यसन नाहींसें करण्याचा प्रयत्न करण्यांत येतो. आयर्लंडांत जे भयंकर खून झाले त्यामुळें आयर्लंडाच्या दुःखाकडे इंग्लंडचें मन आपोआप वेधलें गेलें व नंतर आयर्लंडच्या 'होमरूला' ची ऊर्फ स्वराज्याची वाटाघाट होऊं लागली. अशी या खुनाची एक प्रकारची उपयुक्तता लॉर्ड मोर्ले यांनीं एके ठिकाणीं पर्यायानें वर्णन केली आहे. मुझफरपूरच्या अनर्थामुळें लॉर्ड मोर्ले यांचें लक्ष बंगालच्या फाळणीच्या दुःखाकडे वेधलें जाईल काय ?

बाँबगोळ्यांचे अनर्थासंबंधानें अलाहाबादच्या 'पायोनियर' चें असें मत आहे कीं, ह्या अनर्थांचा पक्का बंदोबस्त जर सरकाराला करावयाचा असला तर सरकारानें बाँबगोळ्याच्या 'वहिमी पुढाऱ्यां' ची याद प्रत्येक प्रांताची, जिल्ह्याची किंवा तालुक्याची तयार ठेवावी; व ह्या यादींपैकीं दहा, वीस, पंचवीस इसम अमक्या तमक्या हद्दींत बाँबगोळ्याचा अनर्थ झाल्यास फांशीं चढवूं, असें जाहीर करावें! दहशत बसविण्याचा हा एक उपाय आहे; नाहीं असें नाहीं. पण असल्या उपायांनीं बाँबगोळ्यासारखे अनर्थ कमी न होतां अधिक वाढतात, असा इतिहासाचा सिद्धांत आहे. आयर्लंडच्या लोकांना ताळ्यावर आणण्याकरितां कान्सरव्हेटिव पक्षानें 'कोएर्शन अक्ट' ह्मणजे लोकांना दाबून टाकण्याचा कायदा पास केला. हाच कायदा रद्द करण्याचें बिल पास करण्याचे उद्योगांत सांप्रतचें पार्लमेंट गुंतलें आहे. आयर्लंडच्या लोकांना दहशत बसविणारे बकासुरी कायदे पास करणारे शहाणे, कां तेच कायदे रद्द करणारें आजचें प्रधान मंडळ शहाणें ? दहशतीचे कायदे अखेरीस निरुपयोगी ठरतात, अशी साक्ष आयर्लंडचा इतिहास देत आहे.

एखादा समाज, एखादा लोकसमूह किंवा एखादें राष्ट्र जेव्हां राज्यकर्त्यांच्या मनांतून नामशेष करावयाचं असतें, त्यावेळीं मात्र प्रथम दहशतीचे व मागाहून अंशतः नामशेष करून टाकणारे कायदे अंमलांत आणण्यांत येत असतात. पण असल्या राष्ट्रवधापासून मानवजातीचें केव्हांही हित झालेलें नाहीं. बाँबगोळ्यांच्या अनर्थामुळें राष्ट्रवधास जर हिंदुस्थानांत प्रारंभ करण्यांत आला, तर त्याचा परिणाम अँग्लोइंडियनांना केव्हांही हितकर होणार नाहीं, असें आम्ही स्पष्ट सांगूं शकतों. हें राष्ट्रवधाचें काम तडीस नेण्याइतकी ताकद अँग्लोइंडियनांच्या मनगटांत नसल्यामुळें 'पायोनियर'सारख्या हितशत्रूंचा उपदेश त्यांनीं ऐकूं नये, हेंच चांगलें. आयर्लंडला चुचकारून, गिळून, पोटांत घालून, पचवून नामशेष करतां येणें शक्य आहे. आयर्लंडचा राष्ट्रवध इंग्लंडला एक वेळ करतां येईल; पण हिंदुस्थानचा करतां येणें शक्य नाहीं. 'पायोनियर'चें दुसरें एक असें ह्मणणें आहे कीं, बाँबगोळ्यांच्या रूपानें दिसून येणारा प्रजासंक्षोभ उत्पन्न होण्यास पुरेसें कारण सांप्रत नाहीं. बंगालची फाळणी, ह्या फाळणीमुळें झालेली चळवळ, ह्या चळवळीमुळें झालेले दंगेधोपे, जुलूम व खटले, ह्या सर्व गोष्टी प्रजासंक्षोभ दाखविणाऱ्या नाहींत काय ? इंग्लंडांत एकेकाळीं असल्या जुलुमामुळें लहान सहान बंडें होत असत, व इंग्लंडच्या लोकांनीं मोठें बंड करून राजाला पदच्युत करून जेव्हां सनदशीर राज्यव्यवस्था सुरू केली तेव्हांच राज्यकारभारांत फेरफार घडवून आणण्याकरितां दंग्याधोप्यांचे मार्ग आक्रमण्याचें कारण इंग्लंडांतील लोकांना उरलें नाहीं. प्रजेचा संताप वाढविणाऱ्या गोष्टींकडे दुर्लक्ष करावयाचें, आणि फिरून बंगाल्यांना इतके माथेफिरू होण्याचें काय कारण होतें, ह्मणून प्रश्न विचारावयाचा. हा अरेरावी मानभावीपणा सरकारच्या पंखाखालीं असणाऱ्या 'पायोनियर'सारख्याच पत्राला शोभतो.

Ex. F.

(Translation of the Marathi leader printed in columns 4 and 5 of page 4 and column 1 of page 5 of the issue of the "Kesari" newspaper dated 19th May 1908, and having a foot-note, as translated, 'This newspaper was printed and published at the "Kesari" printing Press, No. 486, Narayan Peth, Poona by Bal Gangadhar Tilak.)

A double hint.

There is certainly no doubt that the heads of those young gentlemen who manufactured bombs or brought them into use at Calcutta were turned. But the disease of turnheadedness is so contagious that, though the heads of the young persons of Calcutta (may) have become cool in consequence of their having vomited the poison in their heads, the heads of some other gentlemen have already been turned or have now begun to be turned by the poison vomited by them. These people are of two sorts. The first (sort consists of) Anglo-Indian gentlemen or journalists, and the other (of) some cowardly and (*x*) self-conceited (*x*) men amongst us. The only difference is that the wiliness of the Anglo-Indian journalists has helped them in the turning of their heads; while cowardice has inspired those amongst us whose heads are in a disordered condition. The only fact that some boys of Calcutta prepared bombs and tried to blow off a European Magistrate, and that two innocent white women fell victims in that (attempt), has sufficed to distract some cowards amongst us, who call themselves alone lovers of peace. It is not the case that these people may not have read in newspapers the news of such terrible things always occurring in Russia. But their mind is persuaded not only that it was most dreadful that such a thing should have happened in India, and that, too, against white officers, but also that it (has) caused immense loss to India; and, in order to show their burning (sentiments of) loyalty, these gentlemen are now most vigorously forwarding to Government suggestions or resolutions of the following sort:—" We protest most strongly against such a thing ; bomb-throwers are, in no way, connected with us ; and we have no concern with their shocking deeds; nay, Government should at once stop the writings or speeches which are the cause of these shocking deeds, we have no objection to it; nay, such is also our desire ! " This, in our opinion, is the height not only of cowardice but also of folly. And though Government officers may be aware of this fact, they indirectly consent to it in as much as it is only to their advantage to obtain such an admission at present. We, too, consider it reprehensible that any one, for any reason, should take the life of another by bombs or by (any) other means. Not only has it no sanction of the code of morality, but also no one else, just like ourselves, considers that if some white officers were

(*x*)............(*x*) (Literally, one who has gained fame and celebrity : used with reproach of a person who sits down satisfied with his present acquisition and strives for glory no further; or used with irony generally.)

murdered in this manner, we would thereby at once obtain *swarajya*. We have already stated in our last issue that such is not the belief even of the young persons themselves who threw the bombs. In short, no one will fail to disapprove of taking the life of any one belonging to the official class by means of a bomb; and if any one were to express his disapproval to that extent, there is also nothing improper in it. But the admission that these horrible deeds are caused by the writings or lectures of some political agitators, which some people from amongst us, while expressing such disapproval, have now begun to make, is wrong and suicidal in the extreme ; (and) it is our duty to tell this not only to these (persons) but also to the rulers themselves. Anglo-Indian people or journalists are, at this time, absolutely in need of such an admission from us. Though it may be a fact that the people's heads are turned by the vexation (caused) by the unrestrained and irresponsible official class in India, it is desirable for the Anglo-Indians to distort it, for their own interest; and therefore, they have spread a false report that it is not owing to the bad acts of white officers but owing to the writings and speeches of those who without any reason make severe comments on the said officers, that the exasperation of the people has reached the stage of bomb-throwing. This allegation of the Anglo-Indian journlists is utterly false. But, under the present circumstances, they have no alternative but to say so. If they admit that the system of administration in India is bad, they would be utterly ruined. They will always say this (and this) only, that the political agitation against white officers, which exists in India is carried on by a few mischievous people for a selfish purpose; and that it is not owing to the sin of white officers at all that the stage of bomb-throwing has been reached; but that this is solely (and wholly) the result of the very agitation of the mischievous people aforesaid. Nay, they consider the bomb-affair to be a very good opportunity that has easily offered itself to the Anglo-Indian journalists or officers for suppressing the political agitation now carried on in India. And some shrewd people among them have already begun even to make use of the said opportunity in this manner. The only thing to be regretted is that some cowardly and selfish people among us, by voluntarily rushing (*a*) into this their net have set about ensnaring their countrymen ! The (present) juncture is, indeed, very difficult or trying, but it is for this very reason that we say that our people should exercise particular vigilance at such a time. We have nothing to say about those who wish to always pass their time in slavery under the irresponsible and uncontrolled sway of the white officers in India. But all those, who, finding the present system of administration in India to be intolerable, think that the said system of administration should be reformed some time or other, should take care that they do not, while expressing their disapproval of the fact that some innocent persons lost their lives by means of bombs, give to Government, either knowingly or through cowardice, any absurd admission from them (an admission which, if given, would be) just the thing desired (by Government and obtained by them) without any effort (on their part). Express (your) disapproval of, or protest against, murder once, or if you like, ten times ; no one is against it. But, in the interests of the country, we only beg of these people that they should not, of their own accord, convey the utterly false information to Government

(*a*) Literally, leaping.

officials that such acts of turn-headedness are the result of the atrong writings or speeches of political agitators. The evidence required for proving the loss which India is sustaining from the political, industrial, moral and material points of view, owing to the entire administration of India being carried on solely under the sole guidance of the white official class only (and) in utter disregard of public opinion, is so very strong that none but the friends of the said official class will have any doubt of the iniquitous character of the present administrative syetem. That such an administrative system should come to bo disliked by the people is the effect of Western education itself; and seeing that, in spite of many years' exertions, the said system of administration is not reformed and that real rights of *Swarajya* are not yet granted to the deople owing to the obstinacy of the rulers, the political leaders in the country cannot fail to have violent anger produced in their minds. It is true that the said leaders will always be able to keep this anger within lawful limits; but to think that not even a single person should arise in the country, whose rage would overstep the lawful limit is, as it were, to proclaim to the world that one does not know human nature. Of course, we think that it is an extremely mean act to cannect ths turn-headedness of bomb-throwers with the writing or speeches of the peoples' leaders who give expression to the unrest or discontent which has arisen in the minds of the people on account of the uncontrolled system of administration. It is only in accordance with the selfish aim of the Anglo-Indian journalists that they spread such false report; there is no wonder in it. The only thing which is really regrettable or surprising, is that we are decived by it. It is a matter well-known in history and assented to by the politicians everywhere that if the administrative system in any country be bad, discontent arises among the subjects of that country, that the leaders of the people set about removing the defects in the administrative system, and that, having roused public opinion for that purpose, they promote the cause of their country on tha strength of the said public opinion. If, however, owing to the movement originating in such a cause, any turn-headed person in the country—and in every country turn-headed persons are sure to be (found)—had his head turned by violent anger and if he became engaged in a dreadful deed, it would never be proper, as stated above, to lay the blame of it upon the political agitator. If the present attempt of the Anglo-Indian journalists to establish a far-fetched connection had been merely foolish, we would not have felt sorry for it; but we cannot help saying that it is mean, since it arises not from ignorance but from selfishness. The person, who says that all political agitation should be stopped because one gentlemen had, through rage, caused the explosion of a bomb, will be considered as unreasonable or foolish as he, who argues (*b*) that female education should be entirely stopped because under the Peishwa's regime Anandibai had changed (the letter) ध (dha) to मा (ma), would be considered foolish. There is no such thing (to be found) of which there is not the least likelihood of being carried to an extreme at any time. If tomorrow Government attempted to stop all (practice of) surgery in medicine because some person had died in consequence of his boil having been opened by a doctor, would any one allow it in any country? Just as the English themselves have not given up sea-

(*b*) (*Literally* proves).

voyage because of some person (occasionally) meeting with death by the sinking of a ship so also is the case of political agitation. As declared by Dadabhai Naoroji at the National Congress held at Calcutta, whatever be the disappointment in the work of effecting political reform, true leaders of the people never lose (c) their composure (c) through anger or rage; but how is it possible that this quality of the leaders should be possessed by every man in the country ? In particular, when several attempts at improving the political condition have proved fruitless owing to the obstinacy or stubbornness of the rulers, is it in any degree unnatural if one or two persons in the country had their heads turned by rage and proceeded to commit (some) excess ? Such spirits exist and are found in all countries (and) in all places. Why, then, should there be such a clamour if such a thing takes place in India alone ? And what, forsooth, is the reason of scattering calumnies against political agitators on that account ? We do not understand this. It is true that this is the first time that this method of Russian excesses had come into India, but inasmuch as the history of political revolutions in Russia, Germany, France, Ireland and other places is daily coming before our eyes, how is it possible that not even one or two persons in this country should not have a mind to imitate it ? In short, history bears open witness to the fact that in any country where an irresponsible and unrestrained official class—be it native or alien,—exercises authority over the subjects without any control, the subjects of that country are sure to be always discontented ; and that if the prayer or demand of the said subjects be overbearingly rejected many times, one or two of them at least are sure to become heedless and feel inclined occasionally at any rate to commit excesses. We need hardly say that the occurrences in India are not a deviation from this course of history. If Government were to put a wrong construction upon them just as the Anglo-Indian journalists do, then it would be not only our misfortune but also that of our rulers ! Just as if a son committed some excess owing to his having been kept unmarried for many years, it is the duty of wise parents to take a warning from the said excess and get the son married as soon as possible, even so it is the duty of a wise and statesman like Government to realise that political discontent has reached the stage of some officer being murdered by means of a bomb and to soon remove the primary causes that might (be found to) exist of the said political discontent. We do not at all say that the person committing the excess should not be punished or that his excess should not be repudiated. Whether the matter be social or political, an excess is only an excess ; and whatever be the primary cause making (men) to feel inclined to commit the said excess, the said excess must certainly be punished with the sentence prescribed by law. But to bear in mind that such excesses are unavoidable in some cases and to take a proper lesson from them is itself a mark of true statesmanship and we hope that our Government will consider the dreadful bomb affair of Calcutta only from such a point of view. No leader whatever, who is engaged in political agitation, need be told afresh that *swarajya* cannot be secured by means of a bomb. The bomb-affair of Calcutta is a disquieting but acute symptom showing how intolerable the defects in the existing political system are becoming or have become to the people; and as a physician, in case a fever patient begins to talk incoherently through delirium, without getting frightened by that symptom, takes a warning

(c)..................(c) (*Literally*, ran off wildly).

from it and coolly prescribes a more efficacious medicine for the disease, so the Indian Government should act quietly on the present occasion. It is of no use at all to get frightened by the selfish wrath or reasoning of the Anglo-Indian journalists. The political agitation among the subjects is never groundless. The said agitation is, indeed, produced generally in consequence of the defects that might (be found to) exist in the administration of the country; and we need not tell our Government that to stop (all) political agitation in the country by means of an oppressive law, because somebody has, in a paroxysm of rage, committed the murder of some official is to produce greater irritation among the people. Just as an engineer is required to take a hint when the steam in the steam-boiler escapes for the first time in disregard of the weight of the safty-valve and is called upon to take measures for lessening the force of the steam thereafter, similarly it behoves our Government, without bringing into their head the wicked thought of taking revenge, to make provision in future for reforming their administration in order that the violent anger of the subjects might not reach the stage of throwing bombs. It is not the case that anyone does not want (the reign of) peace and law; but to strike, under the pretext of (maintaining) tranquillity, at the root of the agitation that has sprung up among the people in consequence of the real defects in the administration, while denouncing such terrible deeds as bomb-outrages, is to adopt the path of taking revenge, not of wisdom or statesmanship. It is the experience of history that in consequence of such a mistake, even constitutional agitation eventually acquires the form of a revolution; if this experience or this suggestion of taking a warning which can be learnt from this experience is not acceptable to our Government, we are helpless. We are humbly telling Government only that which appears true to us; and it is our belief that in it alone lies our good and the good of our rulers. To tell Government that the writings and speeches of the political agitators in the country were the cause which led to the perpetration of the atrocious crime of murder by means of the bomb is like deliberately driving Government into a ditch. There is no wonder if those white gentlemen who wish to espouse the cause of the white official class and who wish that their oppressive sway should continue uninterrupted in this country, give such advice to Government. But that our people should be ready, while denouncing the bomb (outrage), to give such advice under (the influence of) the one-sided or delusive encouragement of Anglo-Indian journalists, or that Government should commit the unstatesmanlike (act) of taking such suggestions into consideration,—neither of these two things, is, in our opinion, (a sign of) calmness (or) statesmanship or conducive to the welfare of the country. The minds of those who make these suggestions are, in one case, stricken with cowardice and with craftiness in the other case. Therefore, both and especially Government, should consider this thing by keeping their heads cool : such is our request to them. There is an old adage (which says) 'One(*d*) should avoid an excess in all cases.'(*d*) How much longer do Government mean to wait for the anger produced in the minds of the people by the defective system of administration, reaching an extreme degree? It is not at all desirable for a civilised and wise Government to sorely try the patience of the subjects. Tranquillity

(*d*)........(*d*) (This text is in Sanskrit.)

must of course be maintained and do maintain it ; but, under the pretext of (maintaining) tranquillity, do not spread thorns on the paths by which subjects (usually) acquire (their) natural rights, on the excuse of the suggestions made by flatterers who are adverse to the weal (of Government). This kind of administrative policy has not hitherto proved beneficial to any one, and, if the experience of history be true, will not prove so in future also; this is certain. We say once more that hard times are coming day by day. If, at such a time, both Government and the subjects do not keep their heads cool and do not take a proper lesson from undesirable but inevitable incidents, they should both bear in mind that in consequence of it permanent harm will be inflicted on the country. The present difficulty can be (temporarily) warded off by (spreading) a false report ; but it cannot be a permanent solution. For that, finding out the truth and regulating one's conduct in future in accordance with it is the sole (and) single remedy; and it is our prayer to God that Government may be inspired with the thought of enforcing that remedy alone.

[H. I. M.'s High Court, Bombay,

Translator's Office, 9th July 1908.]

A true translation.

N. L. MANKAR,

Third Translator

Ex. F.

[*The following is the original Marathi text of the article of which Ex. F. is a translation.*]

दुहेरी इषारा!

(केसरी, तारीख १९ मे १९०८).

कलकत्त्यास ज्या तरुण गृहस्थांनीं बाँब गोळे तयार केले किंवा उपयोगांत आणिले त्यांचीं डोकीं फिरलीं होतीं, यांत शंका नाहींच. परंतु माथेफिरूपणाचा रोग इतका संसर्गजन्य आहे कीं कलकत्त्याच्या तरुण गृहस्थांनीं आपल्या डोक्यांतील वीष ओकून टाकिल्यामुळें त्यांचीं डोकीं जरी थंड झालीं, तरी त्यांनीं ओकून टाकिलेल्या विषानें दुसऱ्या कांहीं गृहस्थांचीं डोकीं आतां भणाणून गेलीं आहेत, किंवा जाऊं लागलीं आहेत. हे लोक दोन प्रकारचे होत. पहिले अँग्लो-इंडिअन गृहस्थ किंवा पत्रकार, आणि दुसरे आमच्यापैकीं कांहीं लब्धप्रतिष्ठित भेकड. भेद एवढाच कीं, अँग्लो-इंडिअन पत्रकारांचीं डोकीं फिरून जाण्यास त्यांच्या कावेबाजपणानें त्यांस मदत केली आहे आणि आमच्यांतील ज्यांचीं डोकीं शुद्धीवर नाहींत त्यांच्या बुद्धींत भेकडपणाचा संचार झाला आहे. कलकत्त्यांतील कांहीं पोरांनीं बाँब गोळे तयार करून एका युरोपियन मॅजिस्ट्रेटास उडवून देण्याचा प्रयत्न केला, आणि त्यांत दोन निरपराधी गोऱ्या स्त्रिया सांपडल्या एवढीच गोष्ट आमच्यांतील कांहीं आपणांसच शांतताप्रिय म्हणवून घेणाऱ्या भ्याड गृहस्थांची तारंबळ उडून जाण्यास बस्स झाली आहे. रशियांत नेहमीं होत असलेल्या असल्या भयंकर प्रकाराची बातमी या लोकांनीं वर्तमानपत्रांतून वाचली नसेल असें नाहीं. पण हिंदुस्थानांत अशा प्रकारची गोष्ट आणि तीही गोऱ्या अधिकाऱ्यांच्या विरुद्ध घडावी, यांत भयंकरपणाची कमाल झाली, इतकेंच नव्हे, तर हिंदुस्थानचें परमावधी नुकसान झालें, असें यांच्या मनानें घेतलें आहे; आणि आपली ज्वलत् राजनिष्ठा व्यक्त करण्याकरितां "आम्ही या गोष्टीचा तीव्रातितीव्र निषेध करीत आहों; बाँब उडविणारे आमचे कोणी नव्हत; आणि त्यांच्या अघोर कृत्यांशीं आमचा संबंध नाहीं; इतकेंच नव्हे, तर हीं अघोर कृत्यें ज्या लेखामुळें किंवा भाषणामुळें होतात ते लेख व तीं भाषणें सरकारनें ताबडतोब बंद करावीं, आमची त्यांस हरकत नाहीं; किंबहुना तशी आमची इच्छाही आहे." अशा प्रकारच्या सूचना किंवा ठराव हे गृहस्थ सरकारकडे हल्लीं मोठ्या जारीनें पाठवीत आहेत! आमच्यामतें ही भ्याडपणाचीच नव्हे तर मूर्खपणाचीही कमाल होय. आणि सरकारी अधिकाऱ्यांस जरी ही गोष्ट कळत असली तरी सध्यां अशा प्रकारची कबुली घेण्यांतच त्यांचा फायदा असल्यामुळें त्यांची यास पर्यायानें संमति आहे. बाँब गोळ्यांनीं किंवा अन्य साधनांनीं कोणत्याही कारणाकरितां कोणी कोणाचा जीव घेणें हें आम्हीही गर्ह्य समजतों. नीतिशास्त्राचा त्यास आधार नाहीं, इतकेंच नव्हे, तर अशा रीतीनें कांहीं गोऱ्या अधिकाऱ्यांचा खून झाला तर तेवढ्यानें स्वराज्य आपणास ताबडतोब मिळेल असेंही आमच्या प्रमाणें दुसऱ्या कोणासही वाटत नाहीं. गेल्या अंकीं आम्हीं लिहिलेंच होतें कीं, खुद्द ज्या तरुण गृहस्थांनीं बांब टाकले त्यांचीही अशी समजूत नाहीं. सारांश, बांबगोळ्यानें अधिकारीवर्गापैकीं कोणाचा जीव घेणें कोणासही नापसंत झाल्याखेरीज राहणार नाहीं; व तेवढ्यापुरती जर आपली नापसंती कोणी व्यक्त करील तर त्यांत कांहीं वावगेंही नाहीं. परंतु अशी नापसंती व्यक्त करतांना हीं घोर कृत्यें कांहीं राजकीय चळवळ करणाऱ्या लोकांच्या लेखांनीं किंवा व्याख्यानांनीं घडून येतात, अशी आमच्यांतील कांहीं लोक जी या प्रसंगीं कबुली

देऊं लागले आहेत, ती मात्र अत्यंत चुकीची आणि आत्मघातकीपणाची होय, हें त्यासच नव्हे, तर खुद्द राज्यकर्त्यांसही कळविणें आमचें काम आहे. अँग्लो-इंडियन लोकांस किंवा पत्रकारांस आमच्याकडून यावेळीं अशा प्रकारची कबुली जरूर पाहिजे आहे. हिंदुस्थानांतील अनियंत्रित आणि बेजबाबदार अधिकारीवर्गाच्या त्रासानें लोकांचीं डोकीं भणाणून जातात, अशी जरी वस्तुस्थिति असली तरी अँग्लो-इंडियन लोकांस आपल्या स्वार्थासाठीं तिचा विपर्यास करणें इष्ट असल्यामुळें त्यांनीं अशी हूल उठविली आहे कीं, बांब गोळे उडविण्यापर्यंत लोकांच्या संतापाची जी मजल आली ती गोऱ्या अधिकाऱ्यांच्या दुष्कृत्यामुळें नव्हे तर सदर अधिकाऱ्यांवर विनाकारण कडक टीका करणाऱ्यांच्या लेखांमुळें आणि भाषणामुळें आली आहे. अँग्लो-इंडियन पत्रकारांचें हें ह्मणणें सर्वथैव खोटें आहे. परंतु हल्लींच्या स्थितींत असें बोलल्याखेरीज त्यांस गत्यंतर नाहीं. हिंदुस्थानांतील राज्यपद्धति वाईट आहे, असें त्यांनीं कबूल केलें, ह्मणजे त्यांचें सर्व घर बुडालें. ते नेहमीं असेंच ह्मणणार कीं, हिंदुस्थांत गोऱ्या अधिकाऱ्याविरुद्ध जी राजकीय चळवळ आहे ती कांहीं थोड्या उपद्व्यापी लोकांनीं आपमतलबाकरितां चालविली आहे; आणि बांबगोळ्यापर्यंत जी मजल आली ती कांहीं गोऱ्या अधिकाऱ्यांच्या पापामुळें नसून केवळ वर सांगितलेल्या उपद्व्यापी मंडळीच्या चळवळीचाच परिणाम आहे. किंबहुना बांबगोळा प्रकरण ह्मणजे अँग्लो-इंडियन पत्रकारांस किंवा अधिकाऱ्यांस हिंदुस्थानांत सध्यां चालू असलेली राजकीय चळवळ हाणून पाडण्यास अनायासें प्राप्त झालेली एक उत्तम संधी होय असें ते समजतात. आणि त्यांच्यातील कांहीं धूर्त लोक याप्रमाणें सदर संधीचा उपयोगही करून घेऊं लागले आहेत. खेदाची गोष्ट एवढीच कीं, या त्यांच्या जाळ्यांत आमच्यांतील कांहीं भेकड आणि स्वार्थपरायण लोक आपण होऊन उड्या घालून आपल्या देशबांधवांस फशीं पाडण्याच्या उद्योगास लागले आहेत! वेळ मोठी कठीण किंवा परीक्षेची आहे, हें खरें; पण ह्मणूनच अशा वेळीं आमच्या लोकांनीं विशेष सावधगिरी ठेविली पाहिजे असें आह्मी ह्मणतों. ज्यांना हिंदुस्थानांतील गोऱ्या अधिकाऱ्यांच्या बेजबाबदार व अनियंत्रित सत्तेखालीं सदैव गुलामगिरींत दिवस काढावयाचे असतील त्यांच्याबद्दल आमचें कांहीं ह्मणणें नाहीं. पण ज्यांना हिंदुस्थानांतील सध्यांची राजपद्धति दुःसह होऊन सदर राज्यपद्धतींत केव्हांना केव्हां तरी सुधारणा व्हावी असें वाटत आहे त्या सर्वांनीं बाँबगोळ्यानें कांहीं निरपराधी मनुष्यें प्राणास मुकलीं ह्मणून, त्याबद्दल आपली नापसंती प्रदर्शित करितांना, जाणूनबुजून किंवा भ्याडपणानें आपल्या हातून भलतीसलतीच कबुली आयती सरकारास मिळूं नये, अशी खबरदारी घेतली पाहिजे. खुनाबद्दल नापसंती किंवा निषेध एकदां सोडून दहादां व्यक्त करा; त्याबद्दल कोणाची ना नाहीं. पण असलीं माथेफिरूपणाचीं कृत्यें राजकीय चळवळ करणाऱ्यांच्या तीव्र लेखांमुळें किंवा भाषणांमुळें होतात, असें निव्वळ खोटें आपण होऊन सरकारी अधिकाऱ्यांस कळवूं नका, एवढेंच देशाच्या हिताकरितां या लोकांजवळ आमचें मागणें आहे. हिंदुस्थानचा सर्व राज्यकारभार लोकमताची यत्किंचितही पर्वा न धरतां केवळ गोऱ्या अधिकारीवर्गाच्याच एकमुखी तंत्रानें चालत असल्यामुळें राजकीय, औद्योगिक, नैतिक आणि सांपत्तिक दृष्ट्या हिंदुस्थानचें जें नुकसान होत आहे तें सिद्ध करण्यास लागणारा पुरावा इतका भरभक्कम आहे कीं, सदर अधिकारीवर्गाच्या कैवाऱ्यांखेरीज कोणासही हल्लींच्या राज्यपद्धतीच्या अन्यायीपणाबद्दल शंका राहणार नाहीं. अशी राज्यद्धती लोकांस नकोशी व्हावी, हें पाश्चिमात्य शिक्षणाचेंच फळ होय; आणि पुष्कळ वर्षें प्रयत्न करीत असतांही सदर राज्यपद्धतींत सुधारणा होऊन लोकांस खरे स्वराज्याचे हक्क राज्यकर्त्यांच्या दुराग्रहानें अद्याप मिळत नाहींत, हें पाहून देशांतील राजकीय पुढाऱ्यांचा मनांत संताप उत्पन्न झाल्याखेरीज राहणार नाहीं. हा संताप सदर पुढाऱ्यांस कायदेशीर मर्यादेच्या आंत नेहमीं ठेवतां येईल खरा; पण ज्याचा संताप कायदेशीर मर्यादेचें अतिक्रमण करील, असा देशांत एकही पुरुष निघूं नये असें मानणें ह्मणजे मनुष्यस्वभावाची आपणास ओळख नाहीं, असें जगास कळविण्यासारखें आहे. अर्थात अनियंत्रित राजपद्धतीमुळें लोकांच्या मनांत जी अस्वस्थता किंवा असमाधान उत्पन्न झालेलें आहे, तें व्यक्त करणाऱ्या प्रजेच्या पुढाऱ्यांच्या लेखांशीं किंवा भाषणांशीं बाँबगोळे फेकणाऱ्या लोकांच्या माथेफिरूपणाचा संबंध

जोडणें हें अत्यंत नीचपणाचें कृत्य होय, असें आह्मीं समजतों. अँग्लो-इंडियनपत्रकारांनीं अशा तऱ्हेची हूल उठविली हें त्यांच्या आपमतलबी धोरणास अनुसरूनच आहे; त्यांत कांहीं नवल नाहीं. आह्मी त्यानें फसून जातों, हीच कायती खरी खेदाची किंवा आश्चर्याची गोष्ट होय. कोणत्याही देशांतील राज्यपद्धती वाईट असेल तर तेथील प्रजेंत असंतोष उत्पन्न होऊन प्रजेचे पुढारी राज्यपद्धतींल दोष काढून टाकण्याच्या उद्योगास लागतात आणि त्याकरितां लोकमत जागृत करून सदर लोकमताच्या जोरावर आपल्या देशाचें कार्य साधून घेतात, ही गोष्ट इतिहासप्रसिद्ध असून राजधर्मशास्त्रज्ञांस सर्वत्र संमत झालेली आहे. पण अशा कारणानें उद्भवलेल्या चळवळीमुळें देशांतील एखाद्या माथेफिरूनें—आणि देश आहे तेथें माथेफिरू आहेतच—संतापानें डोकें फिरून तो जर एखाद्या अघोर कृत्यास प्रवृत्त झाला, तर त्याचा दोष वर सांगितल्याप्रमाणें राजकीय चळवळ करणाऱ्याकडे लावणें कधींही योग्य होणार नाहीं. अँग्लो-इंडियन वर्तमानपत्रकारांनीं हल्लीं जो बादरायण संबंध जोडण्याचा प्रयत्न चालविला आहे तो जर केवळ मूर्खपणाचा असता तर त्याबद्दल आह्मांस वाईट वाटलें नसतें; पण तो अज्ञानाचा नसून आपमतलबीपणाचा असल्यामुळें नीच आहे, असें ह्मटल्यावांचून आमच्यानें राहवत नाहीं. पेशवाईंत आनंदीबाईनें 'ध' चा 'मा' केला एवढ्यावरून स्त्रियांस शिक्षण देणें अजिबात बंद केलें पाहिजे, असें जर कोणी प्रतिपादन करूं लागला तर तो जितका शहाणा ठरेल तितकाच एका गृहस्थानें संतापानें बॉंबगोळा उडविला ह्मणून सर्व राजकीय चळवळ बंद केली पाहिजे, असें म्हणणारा इसम असमंजस किंवा मूर्ख समजला जाईल. अशी कोणतीही गोष्ट नाहीं कीं, जिचा केव्हांही विकोप होण्याचा यत्किंचितही संभव नाहीं. एखाद्या डाक्तरानें एखाद्याचें गळूं फोडून तो गृहस्थ मेला ह्मणून वैद्यकीची सर्व शस्त्रक्रिया उद्यां बंद करण्याचा जर सरकारनें प्रयत्न केला, तर कोणत्याही देशांत कोणी तरी तो चालूं देईल काय ? समुद्रांत तारूं बुडून एखादा मनुष्य मरतो ह्मणून खुद्द इंग्रज लोकांनीं ज्याप्रमाणें समुद्रयान सोडून दिलें नाहीं तद्वतच राजकीय चळवळींची स्थिति आहे. दादाभाई नौरोजी यांनीं कलकत्त्याच्या राष्ट्रीयसभेंत सांगितल्याप्रमाणें राजकीय सुधारणा करण्याच्या कामीं कितीही निराशा झाली तरी प्रजेचे खरे पुढारी कधींही संतापानें किंवा त्वेषानें बिथरून जात नाहींत; पण पुढाऱ्यांच्या अंगचा हा गुण देशांतील प्रत्येक मनुष्याच्या अंगीं कोठून असणार ? विशेषेंकरून ज्यावेळीं राजकीय स्थिति सुधारण्याकरितां केलेले अनेक प्रयत्न राज्यकर्त्यांच्या हट्टामुळें किंवा दुराग्रहानें निष्फळ झालेले असतात, तेव्हां देशांतील एखाद दुसऱ्या इसमाचें संतापानें डोकें फिरून जाऊन तो अत्याचारास प्रवृत्त झाल्यास त्यांत कांहीं अस्वाभाविक आहे काय ? सर्व देशांत सर्व ठिकाणीं अशा प्रकारचे अत्याचारी पुरुष असतात व आढळण्यांत येतात. मग हिंदुस्थानांतच असा प्रकार झाल्यास त्याचा एवढा बोभाट कां ? आणि त्याबद्दल राजकीय चळवळ करणाऱ्या लोकांवर आग पाखडण्याचें कारण तरी काय ? हें आम्हांस समजत नाहीं. हिंदुस्थानांत रशियन अत्याचाराची ही पद्धत पहिल्यानेंच आली हें खरें; पण रशिया, जर्मनी, फ्रान्स, आयर्लंड वगैरे ठिकाणचा राज्यक्रांतीचा इतिहास जर आमच्या नजरेपुढें प्रत्यहीं येत आहे तर त्याचें अनुकरण करण्याची इकडे एखाद दुसऱ्यासही बुद्धि होऊं नये हें व्हावें तरी कसें ? तात्पर्य, ज्या ज्या देशांत बेजबाबदार आणि अनियंत्रित अधिकारीवर्ग—मग तो स्वदेशी असो वा परदेशी असो—आपली सत्ता प्रजेवर निरंकुशपणानें गाजवीत आहे त्या त्या देशांत प्रजा नेहमीं असंतुष्ट रहावयाचीच, आणि सदर प्रजाजनांची विनंती किंवा मागणी अनेक वेळां दांडगाईनें अमान्य झाली तर त्यांच्यापैकीं एखाद दुसरा तरी बेफाम होऊन त्याची प्रवृत्ति कधींकधीं तरी अत्याचाराकडे व्हावयाचीच, अशी इतिहास उघड साक्ष देत आहे. हिंदुस्थानांत घडलेला प्रकार या इतिहासाच्या सरणीस सोडून नाहीं, हें आम्ही सांगावयास नकोच. अँग्लोइंडियन पत्रकार म्हणतात त्याप्रमाणें सरकार जर त्याचा अर्थ विपरीत समजूं लागलें तर तें आमचेंच नव्हे तर आमच्या राजकर्त्यांचेंही दुर्दैव होय. मुलाला पुष्कळ वर्षे अविवाहित ठेविल्यानें त्याच्या हातून जर कांहीं अत्याचार घडला तर सदर अत्याचारापासून इषारा घेऊन होईल तितक्या

लवकर त्या मुलाचा विवाह करून टाकणें हें जसें शहाण्या आईबापांचें कर्तव्य, तद्वतच बॉंवगोळ्यानें ए-खाद्या अधिकाऱ्याचा खून होण्यापर्यंत राजकीय असंतोषाची मजल आली हें लक्षांत आणून सदर राजकीय असंतोषाचीं जीं मूळ कारणें असतील तीं लवकर काढून टाकणें हें शहाण्या व मुत्सद्दी सरकाराचें कर्तव्य आहे. अत्याचार करणाऱ्यास शिक्षा होऊं नये किंवा त्याच्या अत्याचाराचा निषेध होऊं नये असें आम्ही बिलकूल ह्मणत नाहीं. बाबत सामाजिक असो किंवा राजकीय असो अत्याचार तो अत्याचारच; आणि सदर अत्याचार करण्याकडे प्रवृत्ति होण्यास मूळ कारण कांहीं असलें तरी सदर अत्याचारास कायद्यानें जें शासन व्हावयाचें तें झालेंच पाहिजे. परंतु असले अत्याचार कांहीं प्रसंगीं अपरिहार्य असतात हें लक्षांत आणून त्यापासून योग्य बोध घेणें हेंच खऱ्या मुत्सदीपणाचें लक्षण होय; आणि कलकत्यास झालेल्या भयंकर बॉंब गोळा प्रकरणाचा अशाच दृष्टीनें आमच्या सरकाराकडून विचार होईल अशी आह्मांस उमेद आहे. बॉंबगोळ्यानें स्वराज्य मिळत नाहीं, हें कांहीं कोणाही राजकीय चळवळींत पडलेल्या पुढाऱ्यास नव्यानें सांगावयास नको. प्रचलित राजकीय पद्धतींतील दोष लोकांस किती दुःसह होत चालले आहेत किंवा झाले आहेत, याचें कलकत्त्यांतील बॉंबगोळाप्रकरण हें उद्वेगजनक पण तीव्र लक्षण आहे; आणि एखादा वैद्य ज्याप्रमाणें एखादा तापकरी रोगी वायूनें बडबड करूं लागल्यास त्या लक्षणानें भांबावून न जातां त्यापासून इशारा घेऊन शांतपणानें रोगावर अधिक उत्तम औषधाची योजना करतो, तद्वत हिंदुस्थान सरकारानें हल्लींच्या प्रसंगीं आपलें वर्तन शांतपणाचें ठेवलें पाहिजे. अँग्लोइंडियन पत्रकारांच्या आपमतलबी त्वेषानें किंवा कोटिक्रमानें भांबावून जाण्यांत कांहीं अर्थ नाहीं. प्रजेमधील राजकीय चळवळ कधींही विनाकारण असत नाहीं. देशांतील राज्यपद्धतींत जे कांहीं दोष असतात त्यामुळेंच सदर चळवळ उत्पन्न झालेली असते; आणि एखाद्यानें संतापातिरेकांत एखाद्या अधिकाऱ्याचा खून केला ह्मणून देशांतील राजकीय चळवळ जुलमी कायद्यानें बंद करणें ह्मणजे लोकांत अधिक चीड उत्पन्न करणें होय, हें आह्मी आमच्या सरकारास सांगावयास पाहिजे असें नाहीं. वाफेच्या बॉयलरांतील वाफ सेफ्टी व्हॉल्व्हच्या वजनास न जुमानतां एक वेळ बाहेर पडली ह्मणजे इंजीनियरनें त्यापासून इशारा घेऊन वाफेचा जोर पुढें कमी करण्याची ज्याप्रमाणें तजवीज करावी लागते, त्याप्रमाणें इतउत्तर बॉंबगोळा टाकण्याइतकी प्रजेच्या संतापाची मजल न येऊं देण्याबद्दल आमच्या सरकारानें सूड उगविण्याची दुष्टबुद्धि मनांत न आणितां आपली राज्यपद्धती सुधारून तजवीज केली पाहिजे. शांतता व कायदेशीरपणा कोणासही नको आहेत असें नाहीं; पण शांततेच्या सबबीवर बॉंब गोळ्यासारख्या घोर कृत्यांचा निषेध करतांना राज्यपद्धतींतील खऱ्या दोषांमुळें लोकांमध्यें जी चळवळ उत्पन्न झालेली आहे ती हाणून पाडणें हा सूड घेण्याचा मार्ग आहे, शहाणपणाची किंवा मुत्सद्दीपणाची गोष्ट नव्हे. अशा चुकीमुळें पद्धतशीर चळवळीसही परिणामीं राज्यक्रांतीचें स्वरूप येतें, असा इतिहासाचा अनुभव आहे; हा अनुभव किंवा सदर अनुभवावरून शिकण्यासारखी ही सावधगिरीची सूचना आमच्या सरकारास जर मान्य होत नसेल तर आमचा नाइलाज आहे. आम्हांस जें खरें दिसतें तेंच आम्ही सरकारास नम्रपणें कळवीत आहों; व आमची अशी समजूत आहे कीं, त्यांतच आमचें व आमच्या राज्यकर्त्यांचें हित आहे. बॉंबगोळ्यानें खून करण्याचें अघोर कृत्य करण्यास देशांतील राजकीय चळवळ करणाऱ्या लोकांचे लेख व भाषणें कारण झालीं असें सरकारास कळविणें म्हणजे सरकारास जाणून बुजून खड्यांत ढकलण्यासारखें आहे. ज्या गोऱ्या गृहस्थांस गोऱ्या अधिकारी वर्गाचा कैवार घ्यावयाचा आहे व ज्यांची जुलमी सत्ता या देशावर अबाधित चालावी अशी इच्छा आहे, त्यांनीं सरकारास अशा प्रकारची सल्ला दिल्यास त्यांत कांहीं नवल नाहीं. पण आमच्या लोकांनीं बॉंबगोळ्याचा निषेध करतांना अशा प्रकारची सल्ला देण्यास अँग्लो-इंडिअन पत्रकारांच्या एकतर्फी किंवा मायावी प्रोत्साहनानें तयार व्हावें किंवा सरकारानें अशा सूचना विचारांत घेण्याचा गैरमुत्सद्दीपणा करावा, या दोन्हीही गोष्टी शांत वृत्तीच्या मुत्सद्दीपणाच्या अगर देशाच्या हिताच्या आहेत असें आह्मांस वाटत नाहीं. एकपक्षीं भ्याडपणानें तर दुसऱ्या पक्षीं कावेबाजपणानें या सूचना करणाऱ्यांचीं मनें ग्रस्त झालेलीं आहेत. करितां दोघांनीं आणि

विशेषतः करून सरकारानें आपलें डोकें शांत ठेऊन या गोष्टीचा विचार करावा, अशी त्यांस आमची विनंती आहे. 'अति सर्वत्र वर्जयेत्' अशी एक जुनी म्हण आहे. सदोष राज्यपद्धतिमुळें उत्पन्न झालेल्या लोकांच्या मनांतील संतापाचा अतिरेक होण्याची सरकार आणखी किती वेळ वाट पहाणार? प्रजेचा अंत पाहणें हें कांहीं सुधारलेल्या व शहाण्या सरकारास इष्ट नाहीं. शांतता अवश्य राखली पाहिजे व राखा; पण शांततेच्या सबबीवर प्रजेचे नैसर्गिक हक्क प्रजेस मिळण्याचे जे मार्ग आहेत त्यांत हितशत्रू खुषमस्कऱ्यांनीं केलेल्या सूचनांच्या सबबीवर कांटे पसरूं नका. असली राजनीति आजपर्यंत कोणासही श्रेयस्कर झालेली नाहीं व इतिहासाचा अनुभव खरा असेल तर पुढेंही व्हावयाची नाहीं, हें निश्चित होय. आह्मीं पुनः सांगतों कीं, उत्तरोत्तर दिवस कठीण येत चालले आहेत. अशा वेळीं सरकार व प्रजा या दोघांनींही जर आपलीं डोकीं शांत ठेऊन अनिष्ट पण अपरिहार्य गोष्टीपासून योग्य बोध घेतला नाहीं, तर त्यामुळें देशाचें कायमचें नुकसान होईल, हें उभयतांनीं लक्षांत ठेविलें पाहिजे. खोट्या हुलीनें आजची वेळ मारून नेतां येईल; पण त्यानें कायमचा निर्वाह होणें शक्य नाहीं. त्यास सत्य शोधून काढून त्याप्रमाणें पुढें वर्तन ठेवणें हा एकच उपाय आहे; आणि तोच उपाय अमलांत आणण्यास सरकारास बुद्धि होवो अशी परमेश्वराजवळ आमची प्रार्थना आहे.

Ex. G.

(Translation of the Marâthi leader printed in column 3, 4 and 5 of page 4 of the issue of the " Kesari " *newspaper, dated 26th May 1908, and having a foot-note, as translated, 'This newspaper was printed and published at the* "Kesari" *printing press, No. 486, Narayen Peth, Poona, by Bal Gangadhar Tilak'.*)

The real meaning of the bomb.

Great commotion was caused not only in India but also in England by the secret bomb society discovered in Calcutta and by the bomb which exploded at Muzzaffarpur. At this juncture two kinds of news were simultaneously flashed to England! One (was) that the bomb had taken birth amongst the Bengalis and the other (was) that ten or twenty thousand Afghan troops having attacked the fort of Landi Kotal, an indication began to appear that war would break out with the Amir. Not only was there no special commotion in the public opinion of England owing to the news of the fighting on the frontier, but even the news of the war with the Amir paled before the news of the bomb. For some days the bomb in India had become the sole subject of talk and writing in England. This news produced an extraordinary effect upon the people who are always eager to hear sensational news, upon the writers in newspapers and upon Members of Parliament; nay, it bewildered even the wealthy bankers of London, who carry on financial operations, holding in their hands the strings of the wealth of the whole of the continent of Europe; and they refused to lock up (their) capital in India on merely the old terms! The East India Railway Company was trying (about) this time to raise a pretty large loan in the City of London; but the bomb having thrown a little discredit in England on the Indian administration and on the huge concerns dependent upon that administration, the money-lenders and the banks in London did not agree to subscribe to the loan without demanding a considerable premium above the stipulated interest. So much commotion did not take place in England even at the time when Mr. Rand was murdered on the Jubilee day in the year 1897. The minds of the people of England were not so much attracted towards India even when Lala Lajpatrai was deported and Government declared that an attempt was made to tamper with (the loyalty of) the Sikh Regiments; even the Tinnevelly riots did not create so much stir in the public opinion of England. The public opinion in England is distinctly seen to be inclined towards the view that if any extraordinary event has occurred in India since the year 1857, it is the birth of the bomb.

To understand the real meaning of the bomb, all the following three things (a) should be calmly considered, (namely), what (is the) cause (that) led to the birth of the bomb party in India, how will this party fare in India, and what effect will this party

(a) Lit., conditions.

produce on the administration and the people? All thoughtful people seem now to have formed one opinion as to the cause that gave birth to the bomb party. This bomb party has come into existence in consequence of the oppression practised by the official class, the harassment inflicted by them and their obstinacy in treating public opinion with recklessness. The bomb exploded owing to the official class having tried the patience of the Bengalis to such a degree that the heads of the Bengali youths became turned. The responsibility of this calamity must, therefore, be thrown not on political agitation, writings or speeches, but on the thoughtlessness and the obstinacy of the official class. In the last two issues we had published it as our opinion that doing away with the rights of the subject (and) passing new oppressive laws was no remedy against the bombs, and that the bombs would cease only with the grant of important rights to the subjects and by increasing their prosperity. It is a matter for satisfaction that in England, too, opinions quite similar to those published in the *Kesari* have been publicly expressed by even high Government pensioners like Sir Henry Cotton (and) Sir William Wedderburn. Covernment have taken to disregarding the advice of good people by placing reliance upon the false reports of the wicked detctive Police who are adverse to the weal of Government; and owing to this, the obstinacy of Government to view the people with a malignant eye and to exercise a harsh sway over them does not lessen. It is the opinion of Sir William Wedderburn that this obstinacy gives birth to the bomb. Sir Henry Cotton says that Bengali youths, having been subjected to the punishment of flogging, became naturally exasperated in consequence of the affliction of disgrace and joined the bomb party. The (sentence of) flogging (inflicted) by the Magistrate drove the youths towards the bomb party; was this the fault of the youths or that of the whip in the hands of the official class? (The officials) flog the backs of the youths over and over again and drive them to the mouth of a ditch; and (then) if any one of them, despairing that (his) suffering does not cease no matter what he does, thinks in a paroxysm of discomposure why he alone should fall into the ditch, and jumps into the ditch after catching hold of the leg of the person flogging him, who is (to be held) responsible for this mishap? Why do you, in the first place, drive the youths to the ditch of despair by repeatedly flogging their backs? It is human nature that one should try to drag down the precipice along with oneself the man who has flogged him to the ditch of despair, sorrow and exasperation. At such a time, will it be reasonable to say, 'You should perish alone, falling down (the edge of) the cliff, why do you drag me also'? If a man be drowning in water and some one approaches him with the good desire to save him, even then the drowing man does not fail to catch him by the neck. A man bewildered by difficulties becomes ready to do harm even to (his) benefactor. Then, if one, while drowning in water, gets within reach of the person who has thrown him into a sea (*b*) of trouble, where shall we find among worldly persons (a man of) such generous and cool temperament that he will not drag the other (person) along with

(*b*) Lit., deep part in a river.

himself towards the path of death? The Bengalis persistently agitated against the partition of Bengal in a constitutional (c) mannar; but they did not get redress. Well, it did not matter if there was no redress. Thinking (d) that they would improve their condition by resorting to *swadeshi*, boycott, national education and other approved methods of self-reliance, they betook themselves to the path of national regeneration: thereupon some of the authorities caused their (own) heads to be turned by this patriotism of Bengal, and letting loose some Musalman gundas (e) upon the Bengalis, caused damage to their property and to the honour of their women. This lesson of taking indirect revenge for going against the inclination of the official class was set by some turn-headed officials to the Bengali youths. As you sow, so you reap. The officials become turn-headed; the Bengali youths also became turn-headed. On the occasion of the Comilla and other riots, some of the authorities resorted to a path of violence partaking of the nature (of gratification) of private grudge, *viz.*, thrashing the Bengalis indirectly by secretly taking advantage of private or religious feuds and overawing them by means of terrorizing; (and) the Bengali youths also adopted that very path of violence. The action of both is of the same nature and both are equally guilty. Calm and thoughtful philosophers will weigh both in the same scale and put the same value upon both. When (f) Agya Vetal (f) moves abroad, bombs are bound to explode in rear and in front; this is the settled course of nature. At such a time, the deities, regulating the creation, do not pray to the god Brahma for putting a stop to bombs, but they pray to Him (as follows):—" Please stop the wanderings of Agya Vetal and make him sit calmly with the four boundaries of the temple assigned to, and prescribed for, the demon". The bomb is the reverberation of the terrific roar of Vetal when he leaves his place and wanders according to (his) whim. The Creator of the world has not so constructed the earth that the echo of shrill and terrible shouting should be sweet to the ear. Like sound, like echo; the only difference being that the waves of the echo continue to become more and more minute and disappear. The echo of a sweet sound is called an *alap* (g) and as these *alaps* become more and more minute and indistinct, the minds of the hearers become the more pleased; but when an echo is heard that a network of minute and secret societies has been spread in the surrounding hills and caves owing to (the inauguration of) a terribee and fearful policy, then all persons become anxious to see when the harsh, asinine voice of the official class will stop.

(c) Lit. proper.

(d) Lit, saying.

(e) A sharper, knave.

(f)....(f) (A demon. In his name there is a *mantra* at the recitation of which fire is kindled in the person or property of the man to be injured.

[g] [Humming of a tune.]

It is not that the Parliament and even the Liberal party does not contain turn-headed men who support the views of the *Pioneer*, the *Englishman*, and the Bombay *Times*. The Honourable Mr. Rees is a Member of Parliament belonging to the Liberal party, and his view about the bomb-affair is that the bombs have come into existence owing to the official class not having been able to strike sufficient terror (into the minds of the people) by repressing the natives and exercising stringent sway (over them)! The people should have been well ground down; how would they, then, have ventured to make bombs? For making bombs, some knowledge, the power of a little money and some assistance of men are required. Why has the official class given even such facilities to the people as would leave them sufficient knowledge (and) sufficient amount of wealth to prepare bombs and as would produce even one or two irritable men (among them)? It seems to be the opinion of (the Honourable) Mr. Rees that the people have not been so sternly oppressed as they should have been. If any man is to be slapped in the face, then the slap that is to be given should be so severe that no strength either to cry or even to murmur should be left to him. The blow was mildly given and, therefore, the loud crying (in the shape) of the bomb is heard. Mr. Rees, therefore, advises Government—"If repression is to be practised, then press down forcibly without love or mercy, crush down the heads of all in one and the same fashion, let a level plain be made all round, and then the reverberation of your tyrannical acts will be heard nowhere. If Government leave all bounds, as suggested by the Honourable Mr. Rees, then the consequence thereof shall never be beneficial to Government and to India. Even bombs can be prepared with a little knowledge, at a small cost and with small effort, still there is not much danger from them at present to the official class. The bomb is not as dreadful in India as it is in Europe; the reason of this is stated by the *Bombay Advocate* to be that even though some turn-headed people (ready to) prepare bombs are found, still, there being the Police and other people anxious to give information about such turn-headed persons to the authorities, secret bomb societies cannot fail to be immediately brought to light in India like the one of Calcutta. A few turn-headed persons have been produced by the policy of repression at present in force. If, as the Honourable Mr. Rees advises, (h) all the authorities in all places begin to intimidate one and all in one and the same fashion, and (if all people) (i) becoming of the same sort are converted (i) equally into turn-headed persons throughout their lives, then the number of the backbiting gentry will (fast) dwindle down; and who can say that turn-headed men will not begin to appear even amongst the Police? The spread of English education in India, the pride of nationality which is being born amongst the people and the sun of Japan's rise which is mounting to the meridian, if all these facts be taken into consideration, (it appears that) if Government act upon Mr. Rees' advice, (j) they will not possibly be benefited thereby to the smallest degree. It is a mistaken idea in itself that the people prepare bombs owing to their having been puffed up. He who tells Government at this juncture that the intoxication of the people culminates in bombs, should be regarded by Government as their enemy. Government allowed the natives and some of the Members of Parliament to write without restraint, (and) to speak without restraint and allowed unrestricted agitation to go on; (and) thereby the minds of the people, too, lost all restraint and some of the youths became turn-headed: this argument itself is indicative of the aberration of the intellect. (Suppose) a son comes of age, (and) the father refuse to get him married at his (proper) stage

(h) (Lit., says)

(i)—(i) (Lit. beads woven on the same string.)

(j) (Lit., saying.)

of life and if the strength (sufficient) to withstand the influence of that stage of life is not found in him, then who has exceeded the due limit ? The father or the son ? By whom have the bounds of the stage of life been transgressed ? By the father or the son ? A son in the form of a nation was born in India in consequence of English education, (and) in the ordinary course of nature he came of age in accordance with the tendency of the times which brought about the rise of Eastern nations like Japan, etc.; now it is proper in view of his stage of life to associate him only witn institutions (carrying with them) the rights of *swarajya*. As Government are neglecting to take care of (*i. e.*, to maintain) this congruity (befitting) the stage of life (of the nation), the conduct of some of the youths has transgressed (due) bounds. Before this unrestrained conduct becomes the rule of every day life, Government should, by recognizing (the meaning of) the (present) stage of life, take measures first of all to bring turn-headed persons to their senses by associating the youths (of the country) with institutions (carrying with them) the rights of *swarajya*. The father who is himself adulterous, whose predilection is to spend the whole of the family property upon his own indulgence and unrestrained conduct, and who does not fail even to throw the burden of debt on the next generation for the sake of his own pleasures and sports, that father alone conducts himself in a turn-headed manner with a turn-headed son and (thus) sets about committing the heinous sin of making the son conduct himself without restraint every day (of his life). To interpret the bomb as meaning that the the people are puffed up and are beginning to defy Government, is like asking Government to imitate (the doing of) a self-willed, unrestrained and licentious father. The meaning of the bomb is not well explained by the theory of the arrogance of the people. The bomb is an instrument showing how exasperation is growing amongst the people by the acts of Govenment, and how the policy of the Government has departed from (all) correspondence with the proper wishes of the people. If there be any means of measuring the extreme degree of the people's disappointment and of the exasperation engendered by such disappointment, these are (to be found in) the excesses like bombs. If there is any (influence) that keeps (a man) from violence when (he) is separated from things dear (to him), it is the (slender) thread of hope, and when even this thread of hope is cruelly snapped, then those who are scorched by separation (from their beloved objects) become turn-headed. When a man sees nothing hopeful at all in his surroundings, then his mind naturally becomes disgusted with those surroundings. When the surrounding circumstances are such that they connot be agreeable to the condition of a society, or when a society becomes despondent and finds it impossible to bring itself into conformity with its surroundings, then terrible occurrences like bomb-outrages, transgressing all bounds, begin to take place. It is the opinion of Spencer that when a Government begins obstinately to practise oppression and persistently refuses to give proper respect to public opinion, then such a state of things is positively produced that changes in the administration are not brought by means other than terrible means ; the nature of the people and such surrounding circumstances no longer harmonise with each other ; and the terrible things that are required to be done at such a time to maintain harmony are called a revolution. Government should, at the present juncture, keep this philosophy of Spencer constantly before their eyes; owing to Western education, the spread of the idea of nationality and the rise of an Eastern nation, the old national character of natives is at present undergoing a change. An opposition has arisen between the national character of India and the institutions of Government, and the time is approaching for action being taken to bring about a harmony—an action of revolution. The means of recognizing this are, according to the philosophy of Spencer, acts of violence and recklessness like the bomb (outrages). This time of revolution has not yet begun in India (but) it is to begin hereafter. Therefore, like a wise person, Government should, from the very first, seize with their hands this coming time by the forelock; and, instead of leaving to the people the work af bringing about the revolution, they should of their own accord begin to effect proper reforms in th e system of administration; this will prove more beneficial both to the people and to Government.

[H. I. M.'s High Court, Bombay, A true translation.

Translator's Office, 11th July 1908]. L. N, MANKAR,

Third Translator.

M. 587.
F. 35.

Ex. G.

[*The following is the original Marathi text of the article of which Ex. G. is a translation.*]

बाँब गोळ्याचा खरा अर्थ.

(केसरी, ता. २६ मे १९०८.)

कलकत्त्यास सांपडलेल्या बांबगोळ्याच्या गुप्त मंडळीमुळें व मुझफरपूर येथें उडालेल्या बाँबमुळें हिंदुस्थानांतच नव्हे तर विलायतेसही मोठी गडबड उडाली. ह्या प्रसंगीं दोन प्रकारच्या बातम्या विलायतेस एकदम जाऊन धडकल्या ! एक बंगाली लोकांत बाँब गोळ्याचा अवतार झाला, व दुसरी दहा वीस हजार आफगाण लष्कर लँडी कोटाल किल्यावर चाल करून आल्यामुळें अमीराशीं लढाई उपस्थित होण्याचा रंग दिसूं लागला. सरहद्दीवरील लढाईच्या बातमीमुळें विलायतेच्या लोकमतांत विशेष गडबड उडाली नाहीं इतकेंच नव्हे, तर बाँबगोळ्याच्या बातमीपुढें अमीराच्या लढाईची बातमीही फिकी पडली. हिंदुस्थानांतील बाँबगोळा हा एकच विषय बोलण्याचा व लिहिण्याचा कांहीं दिवस विलायतेस होऊन बसला होता. चमत्कारिक बातम्या ऐकण्याकरितां नेहमींच उत्सुक असलेल्या लोकांवर, वर्तमानपत्रांतील लेखकांवर व पार्लमेंटांतील सभासदांवर ह्या बातमीचा विलक्षण परिणाम झाला; इतकेंच नव्हे, तर सर्व युरोपखंडांतील द्रव्याच्या दोऱ्या हातांत धरून पैशाची हालचाल करणाऱ्या लंडनच्या धनाढ्य सावकारांनांही ह्या बातमीनें चकित करून सोडलें व हिंदुस्थानांत पैसे पूर्वींच्याच शर्तीवर अडकवून ठेवण्याचें त्यांनीं नाकारलें ! ईस्ट इंडियन रेल्वे कंपनी ह्या वेळीं लंडन शहरांत बरेंच मोठें कर्ज काढण्याच्या खटपटींत होती; पण हिंदुस्थानच्या राज्यकारभाराची व ह्या राजव्यवस्थेवर अवलंबून असलेल्या प्रचंड कारखान्यांची विलायतेस बाँबगोळ्यामुळें थोडीशी नापत होऊन बरीचशी मनोती मागितल्याशिवाय कर्ज देण्याचें लंडनच्या सावकारांनीं व बँकांनीं कबूल केलें नाहीं. १८९७ सालीं ज्युबिलिच्या दिवशीं रँडसाहेबांचा खून झाला, त्याप्रसंगींही विलायतेस इतकी गडबड उडाली नव्हती. लाला लजपतराय ह्यांना हद्दपार केलें, व शिखांच्या पलटणींत फितूरी करण्याचा प्रयत्न झाला असें सरकारनें जाहीर केलें, तरीं हिंदुस्थानांकडे विलायतेच्या लोकांचीं मनें इतकीं वेधलीं नाहींत; तिनेवेल्लीच्या दंग्यामुळेंही विलायतेच्या लोकमतांत इतकी हालचाल झाली नाहीं. १८५७ सालानंतर हिंदुस्थानांत जर कोणची विलक्षण गोष्ट घडली असेल तर ती बाँबगोळ्याचा अवतार ही होय, असें ह्मणण्याकडे विलायतच्या लोकमताचा कल स्पष्टपणें दृष्टीस पडत आहे.

बाँबगोळ्याचा खरा अर्थ समजण्यास बाँबपक्ष कोणच्या कारणामुळें हिंदुस्थानांत जन्मास आला, हिंदुस्थानांत ह्या पक्षाचें कसें काय चालण्यासारखें आहे, आणि ह्या पक्षाचा परिणाम राज्यकारभारावर व लोकांवर काय होईल, ह्या तीनही स्थितींचा शांतपणें विचार केला पाहिजे. बाँब-पक्षाचा जन्म कोणच्या कारणामुळें झाला, ह्याविषयीं सर्व विचारी लोकांत आतां एकमत झाल्यासारखें दिसत आहे. अधिकारीवर्गाच्या जुलुमामुळें, जाचामुळें व लोकमताशीं बेपर्वाईनें वागण्याच्या हट्टामुळें हा बाँब-पक्ष जन्मास आला. बंगाली तरुणांचीं डोकीं फिरून जाईपर्यंत अधिकारी वर्गानें बंगाल्यांचा अंत पाहिल्यामुळें बाँबगोळा उडाला. तेव्हां या अनर्थाची जबाबदारी राजकीय चळवळीवर, लेखांवर किंवा भाषणांवर न टाकतां अधिकारी-

वर्गाच्या अविचारावर व हट्टावर टाकली पाहिजे. प्रजाजनांचे हक्क नाहींसे करून नवीन जुलुमी कायदे अमलांत आणणें हें बॉंबगोळ्यांवर औषध नसून प्रजेला महत्त्वाचे हक्क दिल्यानें व प्रजेची सुखसंपत्ति वाढविल्यानेंच हे बॉंबगोळे बंद पडणारे आहेत, अशा तऱ्हेचा आम्ही आपला अभिप्राय गेल्या दोन अंकांत प्रसिद्ध केला होता. केसरींत प्रसिद्ध झालेल्या मतांसारखीच मतें विलायतेसही सर हेनरी कॉटन, सर विल्यम वेडरबर्न सारख्या सरकारी बड्या पेनशनरांनींही प्रसिद्ध केलीं आहेत, ही समाधानाची गोष्ट होय. सरकारचे हितशत्रू जे खोडसाळ गुप्त पोलिस त्यांच्या खोट्या रिपोर्टांवर भिस्त ठेऊन भल्या लोकांच्या सल्लयाचा अनादर करण्याची सरकारास चटक लागली आहे आणि त्यामुळें लोकांवर वक्रदृष्टि करून करडा अंमल गाजविण्याचा सरकारचा हट्ट कमी होत नाहीं. हा हट्ट बॉंबगोळ्यास जन्म देतो, असें सर विल्यम वेडरबर्न यांचें मत आहे. सर हेनरी कॉटन ह्मणतात कीं, बंगाली तरुणांना फटके मारण्याची शिक्षा करण्यांत आली; त्यामुळें अपमानाच्या दुःखांत साहजिकपणें चवताळून जाऊन त्यांनीं बॉंबपक्षाची कांस धरली. मॅजिस्ट्रेट साहेबांच्या फटक्यांनीं तरुणांना बॉंबपक्षाकडे हांकलून दिलें; हा अपराध तरुणांचा कां अधिकारीवर्गाच्या हातांतील चाबुकाचा? तरुणांच्या पाठीवर कोरडे ओढओढून त्यांना खड्याच्या तोंडापर्यंत पिटाळावयाचें आणि त्यांपैकीं एकाद्यानें, असेंही करून दुःख नाहींसें होत नाहीं तसेंही करून भोग सुटत नाहीं, अशी निराशा झाल्यावर आपण एकटेच खड्यांत कां पडा? असा उद्वेगाच्या भरांत विचार करून, चाबुक मारणाराचा पाय धरून जर खड्यांत उडी घेतली, तर ह्या अनर्थाबद्दल जबाबदार कोण? पाठीवर कोरडे ओढीत ओढीत निराशेच्या खड्यापर्यंत तुह्मी तरुणांना अगोदर पिटाळतां कां? ज्यानें आपणाला उद्वेगाच्या, निराशेच्या व संतापाच्या खड्यापर्यंत चोपीत आणलें त्याला आपणाबरोबर कड्यावरून खालीं ओढण्याचा प्रयत्न करणें हा मनुष्यस्वभाव आहे. अशा वेळीं तूं एकटाच कड्यावरून खालीं पडून मर, मलाही खालीं कां खेंचतोस, असें म्हणणें सयुक्तिक होईल काय? पाण्यांत मनुष्य बुडत असला आणि त्याला वाचविण्याच्या सदिच्छेनें एकादा त्याच्या जवळ गेला तरी त्याच्या गळ्याला मिठी मारण्यास बुडणारा चुकत नाहीं. संकटामुळें भांबावून जाऊन उपकार करणारासही अपकार करण्यास मनुष्य उद्युक्त होतो. मग पाण्यांत बुडत असतांना संकटाचे डोहांत सोडणारा जर आटोक्यांत आला, तर त्याला स्वतःबरोबर मृत्यु–पंथाकडे न ओढण्याइतकें उदार व शांत मन संसारी लोकांत कोठून दृष्टीस पडणार? बंगाली लोकांनीं योग्य रीतीनें वंगभंगाविरुद्ध एकसारखी चळवळ केली; पण त्यांची दाद लागली नाहीं. बरें दाद लागली नाहींतर नाहीं; स्वदेशी, बहिष्कार, राष्ट्रीय शिक्षण वगैरे शिष्टसंमत व स्वावलंबनाच्या मार्गानें आपण आपली सुधारणा करून घेऊं ह्मणून ते राष्ट्रीय उन्नतीच्या मार्गाला लागले; तेव्हां बंगाल्याच्या ह्या स्वदेशाभिमानामुळें कांहीं अधिकाऱ्यांनीं आपलें डोकें फिरवून घेतलें, आणि बंगाल्यांवर कांहीं मुसलमान गुंडे सोडून बंगाल्यांच्या मालमत्तेची व बायकांच्या अब्रूची खराबी करविली. अधिकारीवर्गाच्या कलाचे विरुद्ध गेलें ह्मणजे पर्यायानें सूड उगविण्याचा हा धडा कांहीं माथेफिरू अधिकाऱ्यांनीं बंगाली तरुणांना घालून दिला. जसें पेरावें तसें उगवतें. अधिकारी माथेफिरू झाले; बंगाली तरुणही माथेफिरू झाले. लपून छपून, खासगी किंवा धार्मिक भांडणांचा फायदा घेऊन, पर्यायानें बंगाल्यांना झोडपून काढण्याचा, व भीतीनें गांगरून सोडून दरारा वसविण्याचा, खासगी द्वेषाच्या स्वरूपाचा आततायीपणाचा मार्ग कांहीं अधिकाऱ्यांनीं कोमिल्लाचे वगैरे दंग्याचे वेळीं आक्रमिला; बंगाली तरुणांनींही तोच आततायीपणाचा मार्ग धरला. दोघांचीही कृति एकच स्वरूपाची व दोघेही सारखेच अपराधी. शांत व विचारी तत्त्ववेत्ते दोघानांही एकाच तराजूनें जोखणार आणि दोघांचीही एकच किंमत ठरविणार. आग्यावेताळाचे संचाराचे वेळीं मागेंपुढें बॉंबगोळे उडावयाचेच, हा सृष्टिचा क्रम ठरलेला आहे. अशा वेळीं सृष्टीचें नियमन करणाऱ्या देवता बॉंबगोळे बंद कर ह्मणून ब्रह्मदेवाची आराधना करीत नाहींत, तर आग्यावेताळाचा संचार बंद पाडून वेताळाला ठरवून दिलेल्या व नियमित केलेल्या देवळाचे चतुःसीमेंत थंडपणें बशीव ह्मणून

ब्रह्मदेवाची आराधना करीत असतात. लहरीमुळें जागा सोडून भटकणाऱ्या वेताळाच्या भयानक बुभुःकाराचा प्रतिध्वनि बाँबगोळा होय. कर्कश व भेसूर ओरडण्याचा प्रतिध्वनि कर्णमधुर निघावा अशी पृथ्वीची रचना जगत्स्रष्ट्यानें केलेली नाहीं. जसला पहिला ध्वनि, तसलाच प्रतिध्वनि; प्रतिध्वनीच्या लाटा सूक्ष्म व गुप्त होत जातात एवढाच फरक. मधुर ध्वनीच्या प्रतिध्वनीला आलाप ह्मणतात, व हे आलाप जसजसे सूक्ष्म व अव्यक्त होत जातात तसतसें श्रोत्यांचें मन अधिक प्रसन्न होतें; पण भेसूर व भयानक राजनीतीमुळें सूक्ष्म व गुप्त मंडळ्यांचें जाळें सभोंवारच्या गिरिकंदरांत पसरलेलें आहे, असा प्रतिध्वनि जेव्हां उमटूं लागतो, तेव्हां अधिकारिवर्गाचा कर्कश गर्दभी सूर केव्हां बंद पडेल असें सर्वांना होऊन जातें.

'पायोनियर' 'इंग्लिशमन', व मुंबईचा 'टाईम्स' ह्यांच्या मताला पुष्टि देणारे माथेफिरू पार्लमेंट सभेंत व लिबरल पक्षांतही नाहींत असें नाहीं. ना. रीस साहेब हे एक लिबरल पक्षातर्फेचे पार्लमेंटचे सभासद असून बाँबगोळाप्रकरणासंबंधानें त्यांचा अभिप्राय असा आहे कीं, नेटिवांना दावून टाकून जितका करडा अंमल गाजवावयास पाहिजे होता तितका सक्त दरारा अधिकारीवर्गाला बसवितां आला नाहीं, ह्मणून बाँब-गोळे उद्भवले ! लोकांना चांगलें भरडून काढावयाचें होतें, मग काय बाँबगोळे करण्याची लोकांची छाती होती? बाँबगोळे करावयाला थोडीशी अक्कल लागते, किंचित द्रव्यबल लागतें जरासें मनुष्यबल लागतें, बाँबगोळे करण्याइतकी अक्कल लोकांच्यापाशीं शिल्लक राहील, इतकें द्रव्यबल दिसून येईल, व एखाददुसरा तरी संतापी निपजेल, इतक्या सवलती तरी अधिकारी वर्गानें लोकांना कां दिल्या? रीस साहेबांचें असें ह्मणणें दिसतें कीं, लोकांवर जितका करडा जुलूम व्हावयाला पाहिजे तितका झालेला नाहीं. दुसऱ्याच्या थोबाडींत जर लगावयाची तर त्याला रडण्याचें व हूं का चूं करण्याचेंही सामर्थ्य राहूं नये अशी जालीम चपराक लगावली पाहिजे. मिळमिळीत ठोसा मारला ह्मणून बांब गोळ्याचा आक्रोश ऐकूं येत आहे. तेव्हां रीससाहेब सरकारास सल्ला देतात कीं दडपशाही करावयाची तर दया माया न करतां सपाटून दडपून टाका, सर्वांचीं डोकीं सारखीं ठेंचून चोहोंकडे सपाट मैदान बनवा, ह्मणजे तुमच्या जुलमी कृत्यांचा प्रतिध्वनि कोठेंच उमटावयाचा नाहीं. ना. रीस सुचवितात त्याप्रमाणें सरकारनें जर सर्व मर्यादा सोडून दिल्या तर त्याचा परिणाम सरकारास व हिंदुस्थानास केव्हांही चांगला होणार नाहीं. बांबगोळा अल्प ज्ञानानें, अल्पकिंमतीनें व थोड्याशा खटपटीनें जरी होत असला तरी सांप्रत त्यापासून अधिकारीवर्गास विशेष भीति नाहीं. बांबगोळा युरोपांत जितका भयानक आहे तितका हिंदुस्थानांत नाहीं; त्याचें कारण मुंबईच्या 'अॅडव्होकेट'नें असें दिलें आहे कीं बाँबगोळा करणारे माथेफिरू जरी कांहीं उत्पन्न झाले तरी अधिकाऱ्यांना असल्या माथेफिरूंची माहिती देण्यास पोलीस व इतर लोक उत्सुक असल्यामुळें बाँबगोळ्याच्या गुप्त मंडळ्या कलकत्त्याच्या बाँबगोळ्याप्रमाणें हिंदुस्थानांत ताबडतोब उघडकीस आल्यावांचून राहणार नाहींत. हल्लीं अंमलांत असलेल्या दडपशाहीच्या धोरणानें कांहीं माथेफिरू निर्माण झाले. ना. रीस ह्मणतात त्याप्रमाणें सर्व ठिकाणचे सर्वच अधिकारी सरसकट सर्वांना सारखेच दटावूं लागले, व एका माळेचे मणी होऊन सारखे माथेफिरू तहाहयात बनले, तर चुगल्या सांगणाऱ्या प्रतिष्ठितांची संख्या संपुष्टांत येऊन पोलिसांतही माथेफिरू दिसूं लागणार नाहींत कशावरून? इंग्रजी शिक्षणाचा हिंदुस्थानांत झालेला फैलाव, लोकांत उत्पन्न होऊं लागलेला राष्ट्रीयत्वाचा अभिमान, व माध्यान्हीं चढत चाललेला जपानच्या भाग्याचा सूर्य, ह्या सर्व गोष्टींचा विचार करतां रीससाहेबांचें ह्मणणें सरकारनें जर जमेस धरलें तर त्याच्यापासून सरकारचें काडीचेंही हित होणें शक्य नाहीं. लोक शेफारून गेले आहेत ह्मणून बाँबगोळे तयार करितात, ही कल्पनाच चुकीची होय. लोकांच्या उन्मत्तपणाचें पर्यवसान बाँबगोळ्यांत होतें, असें सरकारास ह्या वेळीं सांगणारा मनुष्य सरकारनें आपला शत्रू समजला पाहिजे. सरकारनें नेटिवांना व पार्लमेंटांच्या कांहीं सभासदांना बेताल लिहूं दिलें, बेताल बोलूं दिलें व बेताल चळवळी चालू दिल्या, ह्मणून लोकांच्या बुद्धीही बेताल होऊन कांहीं तरुण माथेफिरू निपजले, हा कोटिक्रमच बुद्धिभ्रंशाचा निदर्शक होय. मुलगा वयांत आला, बापानें त्याच्या अवस्थेच्या स्थितीप्रमाणें लग्न करून देण्याचें

नाकारलें, आणि अवस्थेचा अंमल झुगारण्याची ताकद जर त्याच्या अंगीं दिसली नाहीं तर ताळ कोणी सोडला ? बापानें कां मुलानें ? अवस्थेची मर्यादा कोणी उल्लंघिली ? बापानें कां मुलानें ? इंग्रजी शिक्षणानें राष्ट्रस्वरूपी मुलगा हिंदुस्थानांत जन्मास आला, जपान आदीकरून पौर्वात्य राष्ट्रांच्या अभ्युदयाच्या कालाच्या ओघानें आपोआप तो वयांत आला; आतां त्याला त्याच्या अवस्थेनुरूप स्वराज्याच्या हक्कांच्या संस्थांशींच संलग्न करणें योग्य होय. हा अवस्थेचा ताल संभाळण्यांत सरकार हयगय करीत असल्या- मुळें कांहीं तरुणांचें वर्तन बेतालपणाचें झालें आहे. हें बेतालपणाचें वर्तन नेहमींचीच दिनचर्या होऊन बसण्यापूर्वी अवस्थेचा ताल ओळखून स्वराज्याच्या हक्काच्या संस्थांशीं तरुणांना संलग्न करून माथेफिरूंना ताळ्यावर आणण्याचा उद्योग सरकारानें प्रथम केला पाहिजे. जो बाप स्वतः बाहेरख्याली असतो, स्वतः- च्याच चैनीकडे व बेताल वर्तनाकडे कुटुंबाची सर्व मिळकत खर्च करण्याची ज्याची प्रवृत्ति असते, आणि स्वतःच्या ख्यालीखुषालीकरितां पुढच्या पिढीवर केवळ ऋणाचा बोजा ठेवण्यास जो चुकत नाहीं, तो बोजा मात्र माथेफिरू मुलाशीं माथेफिरूपणानें वागून मुलाचे हातून रोज बेतालपणाचें वर्तन होईल, असलें घोर पाप करण्यास प्रवृत्त होतो. बांबगोळ्याचा अर्थ लोक शेफारून सरकारच्या डोक्यावर मिरें वाटूं लागले आहेत, असा करणें ह्मणजे स्वछंदी, बेताल व दुर्व्यसनी बापानें अनुकरण करण्यास सरकारास सांगण्यासा- रखें आहे. लोकांच्या उन्मत्तपणाच्या कल्पनेनें बांबगोळ्याची पंची नीट लागत नाहीं. सरकारच्या कृत्या- मुळें प्रजाजनांत संताप किती वाढत चालला आहे, व प्रजाजनांच्या योग्य इच्छेचा ताल सरकारच्या धोरणानें कसा सोडला आहे, हें दाखविणारें यंत्र बांब–गोळा होय. प्रजेची निराशा व ह्या निराशेमुळें उत्पन्न होणारा संताप ह्यांची पराकाष्ठा मापण्याचें जर कोणचें साधन असेल तर तें बाँबगोळ्यासारखें अत्याचार होत. प्रिय गोष्टीचा विरह झाला असतांना आततायीपणापासून जर कोण पराङ्मुख करीत असेल, तर तो आशातंतु होय, व हा आशातंतुही ज्या वेळीं निर्दयपणानें तोडला जातो तेव्हां विरहानें पोळले जाणारे लोक माथेफिरू बनतात. सभोंवारच्या स्थितींत जेव्हां मनुष्याला कांहींच आशा दिसत नाहीं, तेव्हां त्याची बुद्धि आपोआप त्या स्थितीला विटून जाते. सभोंवारच्या स्थितीला ज्यावेळीं एकाद्या समाजाचा ताल संभाळतां येत नाहीं, किंवा एकादा समाज निराश होऊन ज्यावेळीं सभोंवारच्या स्थितीचा ताल त्याला संभाळतां येणें अशक्य होण्यास आरंभ होतो, तेव्हां बाँबगोळ्यासारखीं बेतालपणाचीं भेसूर कृत्यें घडून येऊं लागतात. स्पेन्सरचें असें मत आहे कीं, सरकार ज्यावेळीं हट्टानें जुलूम करूं लागतें व लोकमताला योग्य मान देण्याचें एकसारखें नाकारतें, तेव्हां भयंकर मार्गांशिवाय इतर मार्गांनें राज्यकारभारांत फेरफार घडून न येण्यासारखीच परिस्थिति उत्पन्न होते; लोकस्वभाव व ही परिस्थिति हीं एकमेकांचा ताल संभाळीतनाशीं होतात; आणि अशा वेळीं समतोलपणा राखण्याकरितां कराव्या लागणाऱ्या भयंकर गोष्टींना क्रांति असें म्हणतात. स्पेन्सरचें हें तत्वज्ञान सरकारनें, ह्यावेळीं आपल्या डोळ्यांपुढें सतत ठेविलें पाहिजे; पाश्चिमात्य शिक्षणानें, राष्ट्रीयत्वाच्या कल्पनेच्या फैलावानें, व पौर्वात्य राष्ट्राच्या अभ्युदयानें, नेटिव लोकांचें पूर्वीचें राष्ट्रीय शील आतां पालटत चाललें आहे. हिंदुस्थानचें राष्ट्रीय शील व सरकारी संस्था ह्यांमध्यें विरोध उत्पन्न होऊन समतोलपणानें राखण्याची क्रिया–क्रांतीची क्रिया–सुरू होण्याची वेळ जवळ येऊन ठेपत आहे. हें ओळ- खण्याचें साधन ह्मटलें म्हणजे स्पेन्सरच्या तत्वज्ञानाप्रमाणें बाँबगोळ्यासारखीं आततायीपणाचीं व बेतालपणाचीं कृत्यें हीं होत. ह्या क्रांतीच्या वेळेला हिंदुस्थानांत सुरवात अद्याप झाली नसून पुढें व्हावयाची आहे. तेव्हां शहाण्या माणसाप्रमाणें ह्या पुढील वेळेची शेंडी सरकारनें अगाऊच आपल्या हातांत धेऊन क्रांति घडवून आणण्याचें काम लोकांवर सोंपविण्यापेक्षां स्वतःच राज्यपद्धतींत योग्य फेरफार करण्यास सुरवात करावी, हें प्रजाजनांना व सरकारला दोघांनाही अधिक हितावह होय.

Ex. H.

(Translation of the Marathi leader printed in columns 3, 4 and 5 of page 4 of the issue of the "Kesari" newspaper dated 2nd June 1908, and having a foot-note, as translated, " This newspaper was printed and published at the " Kesari " printing press No. 486 Narayan Peth, Poona, by Bal Gangadhar Tilak ")

THE SECRET OF THE BOMB.

From the murder of Mr. Rand on the night of the Jubilee in the year 1897 till the explosion of the bomb at Muzzaffarpur,no act worth naming (and) fixing closely the attention of the official class took place at the hands of the subjects.There is considerable difference between the murders of 1897 and the bomb (outrage) of Bengal. Considering (the matter) from the point of view of daring and skill in execution, the Chaphekar brothers take a higher rank than (the members of) the bomb-party in Bengal. Considering the end and the means, the Bengalis must be given the greater commendation. Neither the Chaphekars nor the Bengali bomb-throwers committed murders for retaliating the oppression practised upon themselves; hatred between individuals or private quarrels and disputes were not the cause of these murders. These murders have assumed a different aspect from ordinary murders owing to the supposition (on the part of the perpetrators) that they were doing a sort of beneficient act. Even though the causes inspiring (the commission of) these murders be out of the common, the causes of the Bengali bomb are particularly subtle. In the year 1897 the Poonaites were subjected to great oppression at the time of the Plague, and the exasperation produced by that oppression had not exclusively a political aspect. That the very system of administration is bad, and that, unless the authorities are singled out and individually terrorized, they would not consent to change the system—this sort of important question was not before the eyes of the Chaphekar brothers. Their aim was (specially directed) towards the oppression consequent upon the plague, that is to say, towards a particular act. The Bengali bombs have of course their eye on the Partition of Bengel; but the glance of the bomb is (also) playing upon a more extensive plains brought into view by the Partition of Bengal. Moreover a pistol or a musket is an old weapon, (while) the bomb is the latest discovery of the Western sciences. The Western sciences have strengthened the power of the official class in every country. One ruler is able to fight with another ruler, but it has become difficult for the subjects in any country to fight with the army of that very country. The power of the army has terribly increased in consequence of new scientific discoveries; and the bravery of the people most celebrated for their valour proves useless in an instant before new guns new muskets and ammunition of the new sort. It was owing to this reason alone that the revolutionary plans of the Russian subjects failed in the year 1905-06; and if tomorrow the army of England becomes completely subservient to (the will of) the Emperor Edward VII, and if His Majesty be so inclined, (he) will be able to reduce to dust, without taking much time, the institutions of *Swarajya* like the Parliament in England, whatever fitness for (exercising the rights of) *Swarajya* the people of England may possess. The Western sciences have made the might of armies so terrible. But in that identical minute seed which contains the power to produce a mighty tree, is also born, along with the birth of that tree itself, the (principle of) death, which is destined to destroy the tree. Death is ordained at the very time of birth. Birth is first seen; the veil over death subsequently begins to be gradually removed God Himself creates the Universe (and) God Himself is the Governor of the Universe; it was the Westerners' science itself that created new guns, new muskets and new ammunition; and it was the Westerners' science itself that created the bomb. (Fearing) that the people would uselessly continue to live on (indefinitely) and that (thus) there would be an excessive (number of) living (people in the world), God created the sovereign remedy of death. This daily death does not possess the ability to put a stop altogether to life in (this) world; even though the operations of death be going on without a hitch, the force of mundane life is not lessened. Death does not change the current of worldly life nor does it do away with worldly life. The duty of taking away the pride of worldly life is assigned to death (and) therefore, death takes care not to allow life to become impure. The military strength of no Government is destroyed by the bomb; the bomb has not the power of crippling (the power of) an army; nor does the bomb possess the strength to change the current of military strength; but owing to the bomb the attention of Government is riveted to (*a*) the disorder which prevails owing to the pride of military strength.

(*a*)......(*a*) (Or, attracted towards.)

Owing to the murders of 1897, the attention of the authorities was directed towards the disorder (in) plague (administration); and since that time the aspect of the Plague administration began to change and complete tarnsformation took place in the plague administration very soon after. It is at present being asserted that Government care two straws for the bombs of the Bengalis. What do the words "care two straws" mean? The Bengali bomb-makers have themselves admitted that the English Government cannot be overthrown by the bomb. There is no cause for Government to feel any fear of the bomb too; but the pride of military strength must necessarily be afraid of the bomb and it is not derogatory to any mighty power to frankly admit this fear. The plague administration in the beginning was (such that it was) disliked by the people, was extremely vexatious and exasperating; this fact was not at first known to Government. Mr. Rand's murder brought this mistake to the notice of Government: and after plague-riots occurred everywhere subsequently, Government did not also hesitate to openly admit the mistake. It (*b*) is not to be understood (*b*) that because Mr. Rand's murder took place, the plague administration was (proved to be) mistaken; the administration was a mistaken one from the very first, was wrong from the very start; but it did not appear to be mistaken to the authorities owing to (their) conceit about

[*b*]......(*b*) [Lit., it is not the gist that.]

(their own) wisdom. Some things must be viewed from the people's stand-point; it is by no means enough to look at them only from one's own point of view; this light had not dawned (c) upon the minds (d) of the authorities. This light dawned (upon their minds) owing to the murder of Mr. Rand, and the conceit of wisdom having produced knowledge (within itself), the conceit left the authorities so far at least as plague administration was concerned. What was there amiss in this? Where was (any) stigma cast upon the might of the English Government in this? That (one) should not forget to make use of the eyes while walking, when is this (lesson) to be learnt if not when one has (actually) stumbled? The man who says 'Though I may stumble any number of times. I will remain blind like an intoxicated (person), despite (my) having eyes,' is his own enemy. The Indian Government have had a stumbling (in the shape) of the bomb; and if Government do not make use of this stumbling in reforming the administration (of the country), they will prove their own enemies. Such stumbles are (e) necessary in life whether in the case of a king or a pauper; nay, God has so arranged the very constitution of the world that such stumbles should be experienced by all spontaneously at the proper time and at the proper place. When the world goes on without a hitch for a considerable time, none begins to forget his duty and the intoxication of remaining alive without restraint begins to come over his eyes. The machine of the universe is moving automatically (f) in such a way that he should suffer the stumble (in the shape) of his father's death for the removal of this intoxication. It is not the case thast Death does not know that even if the father be dead, (his) son succeeds him in his place, that even if the son be dead, the grandson carries on worldly affairs (and that further) even if the grandson dies, the great-grandson comes forward (to take his place). Death is not able to root out mundance existence; but the father's death imparts wisdom to the son, the son's death keeps the grandson in a wakeful condition and the grandson's death makes the great-grandson a man of wisdom. When a man refuses to learn wisdom from the stumble of death, he becomes the cause of his real ruin. Newspapers like the *Bombay Times* that are making a suggestion to Government that they should, without paying any regard to the bomb, go on conducting themselves with even greater intoxication, are, it seems to us, taking their revenge now upon Government (for acts done) in a past life. When a son is wild and licentious, he does not learn the lesson to be learnt from his father's death, but on the contrary becomes still more blind from intoxication in consequence of such stumbles; such has been the condition of some Anglo-Indians. Just as the liqor-shop keepers and the prostitutes in a village are over) joyed to hear the news of the death of the father of a licentious son, so the Bombay "Times" (which is) stupidly intoxicated by nature, and some native (news) papers of Poona (and) Bombay included amongst journals indirectly supported by Government, seeing that the troublous time of the bomb has overtaken Government, are beginning to think that they would (now) fare sumptuously. This (over) joyed band of blackguards are

[c] [Lit., illumined.]

[d] [Lit, heads.]

(e) (Lit, required to be suffered.)

(f) Lit, under self-inspiration.)

saying to Government that Government have had the stumble (in the shape) of the bomb owing to the writings in newspapers and the speeches of the National party; (and) that, therefore, without paying any heed to the bomb, Government should muzzle these papers and speakers. In 1897 this set of blackguards had bought very similar imputations (against newspapers) ; and Government have tasted, (g) in the shape of of the bombs, the bitter fruits of that policy of repression that has been continuonsly maintained by them for the last ten years on account of their being half-influenced by these imputations. If Government do not change this policy at this time, its consequence will not fail to be even more terrible than at present to the rulers and the subjects.

[g] Lit., the bitter fruits have fallen into the end of their upper garment].

The answer given by the newpapers enjoying the favour of the official class to (the question) as to why the bombs should be utterly disregarded, is that this is an attempt to intimidate Government and that if the people once come to know that Government are afraid, they will not fail to harass Government by showing them the bugbear of bombs even in every trifling matter. This is a trick of begging for alms by intimidating Government ; it is not desirable to throw a piece of bread to those who intimidate (Government) in this manner, but the only path of wisdom is to give (them) two slaps in the face ; the master of the house should never allow beggars to form an idea that alms can be secured by the (h) inflication of injuries upon their own bodies. The host and the moderate mendicants should, by combining together, drive away these beggars whe gave trouble by raising a clamour. The beggars should, taking into consideration both the wishes of the host and their own poverty, beg alms in a low tone and in soft words ; they should not emit a harsh sound like that of a bomb by overtaxing their (vocal) strength. The Bombay Times and other Anglo-Indian journals have, in the above fashion, given (their) reason why the policy of represaiou should be stringently enforced. Sophistrical reasoning of the above kind has been made use of owing to the nature, power and true meaning of the bomb not having been understood. To start with, the very idea that bombs are thrown from a desire to beg alms by seeking to intimidate Government, is a mistaken one ; for, terrible and deplorable occurrences like bomb (outrages) are considered by none to be pleasant and convenient. Bombs explode when the repressive policy of Government becomes unbearable. Oppression is required to be practised by Government first, while oppression (in the shape) of bombs at the hands of the people follows next. The above is a dishonest attempt to make it appear that Government are not at all at fault, and that bombs are thrown in a hateful or overbearing spirit. If a system of rule, under which the pressure of public opinion is brought to bear on the administration, be not in vogue, if the situation be such that, while public opinion is on one side, those who hold (the reins of) authority are on the opposite side, then such a state of things does not fail to become unfavourable to the rise of the nation. It is not

(h) (Lit. [following the] methods of a class of beggars who extort alms by gashing their arms breasts, &c.

looked upon as a sign of cowardice in England that the authorities should consider that public opinion is (entitled) to hold them answerable and that they themselves are responsible to public opinion. In India, the official class is irresponsible, and the efforts of the National party are (directed) towards making it responsible, or, in other words, towards securing the rights of *Swarajya* to the people. To give the rights of *Swarajya* at least partially to the people, what are the authorities required to do? The authorities have to conduct themselves in subservience to public opinion, in proportion to the rights of *Swarajya* acquired by the people. That power should remain in the hands of such authorities as may be approved by the people and that it should be taken away from the hands of such authorities as may not be liked by the people, this itself is called (the exercise of) the rights of *Swarajya*. If the rights of *Swarajya* are granted to the people as they become fitted for the same, then, disquieting calamities like bomb (outrages) do not befall anyone at all. When a struggle ensues between the fitness of the people for the rights of *Swarajya* and the miserliness of the authorities in granting those rights, and when the authorities begin to act wildly, being intoxicated with the pride of military power, then the deplorable bombs are naturally constrained to intervene in order that the attention of the authorities may be attracted to the intoxication which obstructs real progress. When obstruction is caused to the progress of a nation through cupidity or temptations, by taking undue advantage of the terrible power which the Western sciences have produced in the army of the Government, then bombs spontaneously spring into existence in order to remove that obstruction; no one manufactures them with tha object of terrorizing the authorities by means of intimidation. Calamities like bomb (outrages) have never been interpreted in the history of any country (to mean) that the people are not fitted for the rights of *Swarajya*, or that the people have begun to mock the rulers with bombs owing to the latter having indulged the people more than they deserved. When the official class begins to overawe the people without any reason, (and) when an endeavour is made to produce despondency among the people by unduly frightening them, then the sound of the bombs is spontaneously produced to impart to the authorities the true knowledge that the people have reached a higher stage than the vapid one in which they pay (implicit) regard to such an illiberal (policy of) repression. The authorities have got this opportunity to see calmly what the real state of things is. A powerful desire has arisen amongst the people that they should have some sort of control over the acts of the authorities; if Government do not bring into force simple and universally acknowledged measures to meet this desire, that is to say, if Government do not make a beginning to grant the rights of *Swarajya*, then some impatient or turn-headed persons will not fail to attempt to bring about secretly, deviously and improperly that very thing which should be brought about with the consent of Government (and) in conformity with the condition of the people. If (Government) have a desire that the people should not betake themselves to a secret and terrible path in impatience and violence, they should, understanding the real secret of the bomb, give up hurting the subjects for nothing, and should make a beginning to grant liberally the rights of *swarajya* (to the people); and the official class should not allow themselves to be carried away by the false notion that such a step is derogatory to the might of Government; this is at present beneficial to all.

[H. I. M.'s High Court, Bombay
Translotar's Office, 8th July 1908.]

A true translation.
N. L. Mankar,
Third Translator.

M. 583.
F. 33.

Ex. H.

[*The following is the original Marathi text of the article of which Ex. H. is a translation.*]

बाँबगोळ्यांचें रहस्य.

(**केसरी**, तारीख २६ मे १९०८).

१८९७ सालीं ज्युबिलीच्या रात्रीं रँडसाहेबांचा खून झाल्यानंतर मुझफरपुरास बाँबगोळा उडेपर्यंत अधिकारीवर्गाचें मन वेधणारें नांव घेण्यासारखें कृत्य प्रजाजनांच्या हातून झालेलें नाहीं. १८९७ सालचे खुनांत व बंगालचे बाँबगोळ्यांत बरेंच अंतर आहे. धाडस व काम करण्याची शिताफी ह्या दृष्टीनें विचार केला असतां चाफेकर-बंधूंचा नंबर बंगाली बाँब-पक्षाचे वर लागतो. उद्देश व साधनें ह्यांचा विचार केला असतां बंगाल्यांची तारीफ अधिक केली पाहिजे. चाफेकरांनीं किंवा बंगाली बाँबवाल्यांनीं त्यांच्या स्वतःवर झालेल्या जुलुमाचे प्रतिकारार्थ खून केले नाहींत; व्यक्तिव्यक्तींचा द्वेष किंवा खासगी भांडणतंटे ह्या खुनांना कारणीभूत झालेले नाहींत. आपण एक प्रकारचा परोपकार करीत आहों, ह्या भावनेमुळें सामान्य खुनांहून ह्या खुनांचें स्वरूप निराळें झालें आहे. ह्या खुनांची प्रेरणा करणारीं कारणें असामान्य असलीं तरी बंगाली बाँबांचीं कारणें विशेष सूक्ष्म आहेत. १८९७ सालीं प्लेगच्या वेळीं पुणेंकरांवर विशेष जुलूम झाला होता, व त्या जुलमामुळें उत्पन्न झालेली चीड केवळ राजकीय स्वरूपाची नव्हती. राज्यकारभाराची पद्धतच खराब आहे व अधिकाऱ्यांना निवडून काढून व्यक्तिशः भय दाखविल्याशिवाय ही पद्धत बदलण्यास ते संमति देणार नाहींत अशा तऱ्हेचा मोठा प्रश्न चाफेकरबंधूंच्या नजरेपुढें नव्हता. प्लेगच्या जुलुमावर म्हणजे एका विशिष्ट कृत्यावर त्यांचा कटाक्ष होता. वंगभंगावर बंगाली बाँबांचा तर कटाक्ष आहेच, पण वंगभंगामुळें दृष्टीस पडूं लागलेल्या अधिक विस्तृत मैदानावर बाँबगोळ्याची नजर खेळत आहे. शिवाय पिस्तूल किंवा गोळीबार हें जुनें हत्यार आहे; बाँब-गोळा हा पाश्चिमात्य शास्त्रांचा अगदीं अलिकडील शोध आहे. पाश्चिमात्य शास्त्रांनीं कोणत्याही देशांतील अधिकारी-वर्गाची सत्ता दृढ केली आहे. एक राजा दुसऱ्या राजाशीं भांडूं शकतो, पण कोणच्याही देशांतील प्रजेला त्याच देशांतील लष्कराशीं भांडणें दुरापास्त झालें आहे. नवीन नवीन शास्त्रीय शोधांमुळें लष्करची सत्ता भयंकर वाढली असून नवीन तोफा, नवीन बंदुका व नवीन तऱ्हेचा दारूगोळा, ह्यापुढें अत्यंत शूर म्हणून नांवाजलेल्या लोकांचें शौर्य हां हां म्हणतां निरुपयोगी ठरतें. १९०५-०६ सालीं रशियन प्रजाजनांचे राजक्रांतीचे बेत ह्याच कारणामुळें फसले; आणि उद्यां जर इंग्लंडचें लष्कर बादशहा सप्तम एडवर्ड यांच्या मुठींत गेलें व त्यांना तशीच बुद्धि झाली, तर इंग्लंडांतील पार्लमेंटसारख्या स्वराज्याच्या संस्था, इंग्लंडांतील लोकांच्या अंगीं स्वराज्याची पात्रता कितीही असली तरी, फारसा वेळ न लागतां धुळीस मिळवितां येतील. पाश्चिमात्य शास्त्रांनीं लष्करचें सामर्थ्य इतकें भयंकर केलें आहे. पण ज्या सूक्ष्म बीजांमध्यें प्रचंड वृक्ष उत्पन्न करण्याचें सामर्थ्य असतें त्याच बीजांत त्या वृक्षाचा नाश करणारा मृत्यूही वृक्षाच्या उत्पत्तीबरोबरच उत्पन्न झालेला असतो. जन्माच्या वेळींच मरणाची सिद्धता झालेली असते. जन्म प्रथम दिसतो; मृत्यूवरील पडदा मागाहून हळूहळू दूर होऊं लागतो. परमेश्वरच विश्व उत्पन्न करतो, परमेश्वरच विश्वाचा नियंता आहे; पाश्चिमात्यांच्या शास्त्रानेंच नवीन तोफा, नवीन बंदुका व नवीन दारूगोळा उत्पन्न केला; व पाश्चिमात्यांच्या शास्त्रानेंच बाँब-गोळा तयार केला. लोक उगीच एकसारखे जगत राहून, जगण्याचा फाजीलपणा चोहोंकडे माजून राहील म्हणून मरणाची मात्रा परमेश्वरानें उत्पन्न

केली. जगांतील जगणें अजीबात बंद पाडण्याचें सामर्थ्य ह्या रोजच्या मृत्यूच्या अंगीं नाहीं; मृत्यूचा कारभार अव्याहत चाललेला असला तरी, जगण्याच्या संसाराचा जोर कमी होत नाहीं. मृत्यु संसाराचा ओघ बदलीत नाहीं किंवा संसार नाहींसाही करीत नाहीं. संसाराचा दर्प हरण करण्याचें काम मृत्युकडे आहे; ह्मणून जगणें अशुद्ध होऊं न देण्याची खबरदारी मृत्यु घेत असतो. बांबगोळ्यामुळें कोणत्याही सरकारचें लष्करी सामर्थ्य नाहींसें होत नाहीं, लष्कर पंगू करण्याची ताकद बांबगोळ्याचे अंगीं नाहीं; व लष्करी सामर्थ्याचा ओघ बदलण्याचीही शक्ति बांबगोळ्याचे अंगीं नाहीं; पण लष्करी सामर्थ्याच्या दर्पामुळें जी अव्यवस्था माजते तिजकडे बांबगोळ्यांमुळें सरकाराचें लक्ष वेधलें जातें.

१८९७ सालच्या खुनांमुळें प्लेगच्या अव्यवस्थेकडे अधिकाऱ्यांचें लक्ष गेलें व तेव्हांपासून प्लेगच्या कारभाराचें स्वरूप बदलण्यास प्रारंभ होऊन लवकरच प्लेगची व्यवस्था अजीबात पालटली. सांप्रत असें सांगण्यांत येत आहे कीं, बंगाल्यांच्या बांब–गोळ्यांना आह्मी भीक घालीत नाहीं; ह्या शब्दांचा अर्थ काय? बांबगोळ्यानें इंग्रज सरकार उलथून पडत नाहीं, हें बंगाली बांबवाल्यांनींच कबूल केलें आहे. बांबगोळ्यांचें भयही सरकाराला वाटण्याचें कारण नाहीं; पण लष्करी सामर्थ्याच्या दर्पाला बांबगोळ्याचें भय वाटलेंच पाहिजे, व हें भय प्रांजल बुद्धीनें कबूल करण्यांत कोणत्याही प्रचंड शक्तीला कमीपणा नाहीं. प्लेगची प्रारंभींची व्यवस्था लोकांना न आवडणारी, अत्यंत त्रासदायक व संतप्त करून सोडणारी होती; ही गोष्ट प्रथम सरकारास समजली नाहीं. रँडसाहेबांच्या खुनानें ही चूक सरकारचे ध्यानांत आली; व पुढें प्लेगचे चोहोंकडे दंगेधोपे झाल्यावर सरकारनें चूक उघडपणें कबूल करण्यास कांकूही केलें नाहीं. रँडसाहेबाचा खून ह्मणून प्लेगची व्यवस्था चुकीची झाली, अशांतला भाग नाहीं; ती व्यवस्था प्रथमपासूनच चुकीची होती, मूळचीच चुकीची होती; पण शहाणपणाच्या घमेंडीमुळें अधिकाऱ्यांना चुकीची दिसली नाहीं. कांहीं गोष्टींकडे लोकांच्या दृष्टीनें पाहिलें पाहिजे, केवळ स्वतःच्याच तेवढ्या डोळ्यांनीं पाहून भागत नाहीं, हा प्रकाश अधिकाऱ्यांच्या डोक्यांत पडला नव्हता. हा प्रकाश रँडसाहेबांच्या खुनामुळें पडला व शहाणपणाच्या घमेंडीला ज्ञान उत्पन्न होऊन तिनें अधिकाऱ्यांना निदान प्लेगच्या व्यवस्थेपुरतें सोडून दिलें. ह्यांत काय वावगें झालें? इंग्रज सरकारच्या सामर्थ्यास ह्यांत कोठें बट्टा लागला? चालतांना डोळ्यांचा उपयोग करण्याचें विसरूं नये, हें ठेंच लागली असतां शिकावयाचें नाहीं, तर केव्हां शिकावयाचें? कितीही ठेंचा लागोत, मी उन्मत्ताप्रमाणें डोळे असून आंधळाच राहणार, असें ह्मणणारा मनुष्य स्वतःचा शत्रू होय. बाँबगोळ्याची ठेंच हिंदुस्थान सरकारास लागली आहे, व ह्या ठेंचीचा उपयोग राज्यकारभार सुधारण्याकडे जर सरकारानें केला नाहीं, तर सरकार स्वतःचे शत्रू ठरेल. अशा ठेंचा संसारांत राजास काय, रंकास काय लागाव्या लागतात; किंबहुना अशा ठेंचा योग्य वेळीं व योग्य स्थळीं सर्वांना आपोआप लागतील, अशी ईश्वरानें सृष्टीची रचनाच करून ठेविलेली आहे. बरेच दिवस बिनखटका जगत गेलें ह्मणजे मनुष्य कर्तव्याला विसरूं लागतो व अप्रतिबंध जगण्याचा मद त्याच्या डोळ्यावर येऊं लागतो. हा मद नाहींसा करण्याकरितां बाप मेल्याची ठेंच त्याला लागावी, अशा धोरणानें सृष्टीचें यंत्र स्वयंप्रेरणेनें फिरत असतें. बापाला मरण आलें तरी मुलगा त्याच्या जागीं येतो, मुलगा मेला तरी नातू संसार चालवितो, नातू चचला तरी पणतू पुढें येतो, हें मृत्यूला माहीत नसतें असें नाहीं. मृत्यु संसाराचा उच्छेद करूं शकत नाहीं; पण बापाचें मरण मुलग्याला शहाणपण देतें; मुलग्याचा मृत्यु नातवाला जागृतावस्थेंत ठेवतो, व नातवाचा काल पणतूला ज्ञानी बनवितो. ज्यावेळीं मृत्यूचा ठेंचेपासून शहाणपणा शिकण्याचें मनुष्य नाकारतो, त्यावेळीं मनुष्य स्वतःच्या नाशास कारणीभूत होतो. बाँबगोळ्यास सरकारानें भीक न घालतां अधिक उन्मत्तपणानेंच वागत सुटावें. अशी सरकारास सूचना करणारीं मुंबईच्या टाईम्ससारखीं पत्रें सरकारचा पूर्वजन्मींचा दावा ह्यावेळीं उगवींत आहेतसें आह्मांस वाटतें. मुलगा उच्छृंखल व बदफैली असला ह्मणजे बाप मेल्यापासून शिकावयाचा धडा तो शिकत नाहीं, तर उलट असल्या ठेंचांमुळें

अधिकच मदांध होतो, अशांतली स्थिति कांहीं अँग्लो-इंडियनांची झाली आहे. बदफैली मुलांचा बाप मेल्याची बातमी ऐकून गांवांतील कलालांना व विश्वयोषितांना जसा आनंद होतो, त्याप्रमाणें बाँबगोळ्याचा प्रसंग सरकारवर आलेला पाहून स्वभावतः तारवटलेला मुंबईचा 'टाईम्स' व सरकारनें पर्यायानें पोसलेल्या पत्रांत मोडणारीं पुण्यामुंबईचीं कांहीं नेटिव पत्रें, ह्यांना स्वतःची पोळी पिकणार असें वाटूं लागलें आहे. ह्या आनंदित झालेल्या चांडाळचौकडीचें सरकारास असें सांगणें आहे कीं, वर्तमानपत्रांतलि लेखांमुळें व राष्ट्रीय पक्षांच्या भाषणामुळें बाँबगोळ्याची ठेंच सरकारास लागली; तेव्हां बाँबगोळ्यास भीक न घालतां सरकारनें ह्या पत्रांच्या व वक्त्यांच्या मुस्क्या बांधून टाकाव्या. १८९७ सालीं त्या चांडाळचौकडीनें असेंच काहूर माजविलें होतें, व त्या काहूराच्या अर्धवट नादीं लागून गेलीं दहा वर्षें जें दडपशाहीचें धोरण सरकारानें चालू ठेवलें त्याचीं कडू फळें बाँबगोळ्याच्या रूपानें सरकारच्या पदरांत पडलीं आहेत. यावेळीं सरकारनें जर हें धोरण बदललें नाहीं तर त्याचा परिणाम राज्यकर्त्यांना व प्रजाजनांना याहुनही अधिक भयंकर झाल्यावांचून राहणार नाहीं.

बाँबगोळ्यांना भीक कां घालूं नये, ह्याचें उत्तर अधिकारीवर्गाच्या खाकेंतील पत्रांनीं असें दिलें आहे कीं, हा सरकारला दरडावण्याचा प्रयत्न आहे व सरकार भितें असें जर का एकदां लोकांच्या ध्यानांत आलें म्हणजे हरएक क्षुल्लक बाबींतही बांबगोळ्यांचा बाऊ दाखवून हे लोक सरकारास सळो का पळो केल्यावांचून राहणार नाहींत. सरकारला भय दाखवून भीक मागण्याची ही युक्ति आहे; अशा रीतीनें दरडावणाऱ्यांच्या तोंडावर भाकरीचा तुकडा टाकणें इष्ट नसून तोंडांत दोन लगावणें हाच शहाणपणाचा मार्ग आहे; खरखरमुंडेपणाला भिक्षा मिळते अशी समजूत यजमानानें भिक्षेकऱ्यांची केव्हांही होऊं देतां कामा नये. ह्या यजमानानें व मवाळ भिक्षेकऱ्यांनीं दोघांनीं मिळून ओरडाओरड करून त्रास देणाऱ्या खरखरमुंड्यांना पिटाळून लावलें पाहिजे. यजमानाची इच्छा, व आपली गरीबी हीं दोन्हीं लक्षांत घेऊन भिक्षेकऱ्यांनीं मवाळ शब्दांनीं हळूच भीक मागावी, शक्तीबाहेर बांबगोळ्यासारखा कर्कश आवाज काढूं नये. मुंबईचा 'टाइम्स' आदिकरून अँग्लो-इंडियन पत्रांतून, दडपशाहीचें धोरण कां जाज्वल्य केलें पाहिजे, ह्याचीं कारणें वरील तऱ्हेनें दिलीं आहेत. बांबगोळ्याचें स्वरूप काय, बांबगोळ्याची ताकद काय व बांबगोळ्याचा खरा अर्थ काय हें न समजल्यामुळें वरील तऱ्हेचा भ्रामक कोटिक्रम करण्यांत आला आहे. सरकारला दरडावून पाहून भीक मागण्याच्या इच्छेनें बांबगोळे उडतात, ही कल्पनाच मुळीं चुकीची आहे; कारण बांबगोळ्यांसारखे भयंकर व शोचनीय प्रकार कोणालाच सुखाचे व सोईचे वाटत नाहींत. सरकारच्या दडपशाहीचें धोरण लोकांना असह्य होऊं लागलें म्हणजे बांबगोळे उडतात. सरकाराकडून प्रथम जुलूम व्हावा लागतो व बाँबगोळ्यांचा जुलूम लोकांकडून मागाहून होतो. सरकाराकडे कांहीं दोष नाहीं, आणि मुरदाडपणानें किंवा उर्मटपणानें बांब उडत आहेत, असें भासविण्याचा खोडसाळपणाचा वरील प्रयत्न आहे. लोकमताचा दाब राज्यकारभारावर बसविणारी राज्यपद्धति जर सुरू नसेल, एका बाजूला लोकमत तर सत्ताधारी विरुद्ध बाजूला अशी जर स्थिति असेल, तर ती स्थिति राष्ट्राच्या अभ्युदयाला प्रतिकूल झाल्यावांचून राहत नाहीं. लोकमत आह्मांला जाब विचारणारें आहे व लोकमताला आह्मीं जबाबदार आहों असें अधिकाऱ्यांनीं समजणें, हें इंग्लंडांत भित्रेपणाचें लक्षण समजलें जात नाहीं. हिंदुस्थानांत अधिकारीवर्ग बेजबाबदार आहे, तो जबाबदार व्हावा, अर्थात् स्वराज्याचे हक्क लोकांना मिळावेत, अशी राष्ट्रीयपक्षाची खटपट आहे. स्वराज्याचे हक्क अंशतः तरी लोकांना देणें ह्मणजे अधिकाऱ्यांनीं काय करावयाचें असतें? ज्याप्रमाणानें स्वराज्याचे हक्क लोकांना मिळालेले असतात त्याप्रमाणानें अधिकाऱ्यांनीं लोकमताच्या तंत्रानें वागावें लागतें. लोकांना पसंत असतील अशा अधिकाऱ्यांच्या हातांत सत्ता राहणें व लोकांना नापसंत अशा अधिकाऱ्यांच्या हातांतील सत्ता नाहींशी होणें, ह्यालाच स्वराज्याचे हक्क असें ह्मणत असतात. स्वराज्याच्या हक्कांना लोक जसजसे पात्र होतात, तसतसे जर

त्यांना स्वराज्याचे हक्क मिळत गेले तर बांबगोळ्यासारखे उद्वेगजनक प्रसंग कोणावरही गुदरत नाहींत. स्वराज्याचे हक्कांविषयींची लोकांची पात्रता व हे हक्क देण्याचे कामांत अधिकाऱ्यांचा कंजुषपणा ह्यांचा जेव्हां झगडा सुरू होतो व लष्करी सामर्थ्याच्या मदानें धुंद होऊन फाजिलपणानें जेव्हां अधिकारी वागूं लागतात तेव्हां खऱ्या प्रगतीला अडथळा करणाऱ्या धुंदीकडे अधिकाऱ्यांचें लक्ष वेधण्याकरितां शोचनीय बांबगोळ्यांना निसर्गतः मध्यें पडावें लागतें. पाश्चिमात्य शास्त्रांनीं सरकारच्या अंगीं जी भयंकर शक्ती उत्पन्न केली आहे तिचा बाजवीहून फाजिल फायदा घेऊन लोभानें किंवा मोहानें जेव्हां राष्ट्रोन्नतींत अडथळा करण्यांत येतो तेव्हां हा अडथळा दूर करण्याकरितां बांबगोळे आपोआप उद्भवतात; अधिकाऱ्यांना दरडावून भीति दाखविण्याचे हेतूनें हे कोणी उत्पन्न करींत नाहींत. लोकांच्या अंगीं स्वराज्याच्या हक्कासंबंधानें पात्रता नाहीं, लोकांचे लाड तुह्मीं त्यांच्या योग्यतेहून अधिक केल्यानें लोक तुह्माला बांबच्या वाकुल्या दाखवूं लागले आहेत, असा बांबगोळ्यासारख्या अनर्थांचा अर्थ इतिहासांत कोणत्याही देशांत केव्हांही करण्यांत आलेला नाहीं. लोकांना अधिकारीवर्ग जेव्हां निष्कारण दरडावूं लागतो, बाजवीहून फाजील भीति दाखवून लोकांत निराशा उत्पन्न करण्याचा जेव्हां प्रयत्न करण्यांत येतो, तेव्हां असल्या अनुदार दडपादडपीला भीक घालण्याच्या निस्सत्व स्थितीहून अधिक वरच्या दर्जास लोक पोंचले आहेत, हें खरें ज्ञान अधिकाऱ्यांना करून देण्याकरितां बाँबगोळ्याचा शब्द स्वयंस्फूर्तीनें होत असतो. खरी वस्तुस्थिति काय आहे, हें शांतपणानें पाहण्याची ही संधि अधिकाऱ्यांना प्राप्त झालेली आहे. अधिकाऱ्यांच्या कृत्यांवर कांहींना कांहीं आपला दाब असावा, अशी प्रबल इच्छा लोकांत उत्पन्न झाली आहे; ही इच्छा भासविण्याचे सरळ व राजमान्य उपाय जर सरकारनें अमलांत आणलें नाहींत, ह्मणजे स्वराज्याचे हक्क देण्यास जर सरकारनें सुरवात केली नाहीं, तर जी गोष्ट लोकांच्या अवस्थेला अनुसरून सरकारच्या संमतीनें व्हावयाची तीच गोष्ट लपूनछपून आडमार्गानें व अयोग्य रीतीनें करण्यास कांहीं उतावळे किंवा माथेफिरू लोक प्रवृत्त झाल्यावांचून रहावयाचे नाहींत. उतावळीपणानें व आततायीपणानें चोरट्या व भयंकर मार्गास लोकांनीं लागूं नये, अशी इच्छा असल्यास, बाँबगोळ्याचें खरें रहस्य जाणून प्रजेला नाहक दुखविण्याचें सरकारनें सोडावें, स्वराज्याचे मुबलक हक्क देण्यास प्रारंभ करावा आणि ह्यामुळें सरकारचे सामर्थ्यास कमीपणा येतो, अशा खोडसाळपणाच्या कल्पनांचे नादीं अधिकारीवर्गानें लागूं नये, हें सांप्रत सर्वांस हितावह आहे.

Ex. I.

(Translation of the Marathi article printed in columns 2 and 3 of page 5 of the issue of the Kesari *newspaper, dated 9th June 1908, and having a footnote, as translated, " This newspaper, was printed and published at the "* Kesari *" Printing Press, No. 486, Narayan Peth, Poona, by Bal Gangadhar Tilak.")*

English rule is openly an alien rule. Well; (and) that, too, has not been carried on like Moghul rule, by the rulers mixing with Indian society; and they are going to carry it on always as strangers indeed. Moreover, they are not satisfied even with keeping only the ruling power in their hands; but they want also to seize possession of the trade and industries of this country forcibly and unjustly or to ruin them. Well, even after doing so much, they should (at least have) kept the burden of taxation on the people light; but the very reverse of it is seen to be the case! In short, *Swarajya*, (*a*) albeit of the old type, is gone, trade has been ruined, industries have collapsed, glory has come to an end, wealth has departed, ability has disappeared and courage has failed. There is no education according to the new system, no rights, no respect for public opinion, no prosperity, no contenment; (but only) there is the violent pressure of the three " d " s of *daridrya*-(*b*) *dushkal* (*c*) and *dravyashosha* (*d*) constantly troubling (*e*) us. The moment an attempt is sought to be made according to (one's) strength to raise up the head of the nation out of this, the head is sure to be bruised by the stone-roller of the system of British rule ? In such a state (of things,) the fact that the bomb party and secret socities have now arisen in India is not at all to be wondered at, although it may be deplorable. On the contrary, if such a state of things had arisen in any country in Europe, then the people of that country would never have shown as much patience and forgiveness, (*f*) as the Indians have done. The adage that life is the dearest of all things to all is generally true. But when an individual begins to think that the value of exalted sentiments like religion, morality, benevolence, self-respect, the honour of (one's) family or country patriotism, etc., is greater than that of life itself, it is an evidence of his spiritual elevation. No sooner do these sentiments begin to take (their) rise in a nation, than it (becomes) the duty of true rulers to provide an outlet for their flow. Whenever, instead of doing that, an attempt is made to obliterate, under the pressure of tyranny and high handedness, these sentiments wherever they might rise, or to check them on the spot by means of big embankments, it should be understood that misfortune is sure to overtake that country (including both) the subjects and the ruler. The result of the rulers, having so (*g*) long disregarded this truth established by the history of the world, is visible in the shape of the Bangali bomb.

[*a*] [Lit, one's own government or true; self-government,]
[*b*.] [Poverty,]
[*c*] [Famine,]
[*d*] [Sucking up of wealth]
[*e*] [Lit pursuing.]
[*f*] [Lit, forgiving nature,]
(Lit., uptill today).
(Lit., has come out);

H. I. M.'s High Court, Bombay,
Translator's Office, 7th July 1908.]

A true translation.
N. L. MANKAR,
Third Translotar.

No. 580

Ex. I.

[*The following is the original Marathi text of the article of which Ex. I. is a translation.*]

पत्रकर्त्यांच्या स्फुट सूचना.

(केसरी, तारीख ९ जून सन १९०८).

बोलून चालून इंग्रजांचें राज्य परकीय राज्य आहे. बरें तेंही मोंगली राज्याप्रमाणें राजकर्त्यांनीं हिंदी समाजांत मिसळून जाऊन चालविलेलें नसून ते नेहमीं परकीपणानेंच चालविणार. शिवाय नुसती राज्यसत्ता हातीं ठेवूनही त्यांचें समाधान नाहीं तर या देशाचा व्यापार व उद्योगधंदेही त्यांस बळकावयास किंवा बुडवावयास हवेत. बरें इतकें करूनही रयतेवरील करांचें ओझें हलकें ठेवावें, तर त्याच्या उलटच प्रकार दिसून येतो! सारांश जुन्या पद्धतीचें कां होईना, स्वराज्य गेलें, व्यापार बुडाला, उद्योगधंदे ठार झाले, वैभव संपलें, संपत्ती गेली, कर्तृत्व लोपलें व हिंमत खचली. नव्या पद्धतीचें शिक्षण नाहीं, हक्क नाहींत, लोकमतास मान नाहीं, सुबत्ता नाहीं, समाधान नाहीं, दारिद्र्य, दुष्काळ व द्रव्यशोष या तीन 'द' कारांचा दपटशा सारखा मागें लागलेला. यांतून राष्ट्राचें डोकें वर उचलण्याचा यथाशक्ति प्रयत्न करूं लागलें कीं इंग्रजी राज्यपद्धतीच्या वरवंट्यानें डोकें ठेंचलेंच! अशा स्थितींत हिंदुस्थानांत आतां बांब पक्ष व गुप्त मंडळ्या उद्भवल्या, ही गोष्ट शोचनीय असली तरी बिलकुल आश्चर्याची नाहीं. उलट युरोपांतील कोणत्याही देशांत अशी स्थिती झाली असती तर तेथील लोकांनीं हिंदी लोकांइतकी सहनशीलता व क्षमावृत्ति केव्हांही दाखविली नसती. सर्वांस सर्व गोष्टीपेक्षां जीव प्यारा असतो, हा न्याय सामान्यतः खरा आहे. पण धर्म, नीति, परोपकार, स्वाभिमान, कुटुंबाची व राष्ट्राची अब्रू, देशभक्ति, इ. उच्च कल्पनांची किंमत प्राणाहूनही अधिक आहे, असें व्यक्तीस वाटावयास लागणें, ही त्यांच्या आत्मिक उन्नतीची साक्ष आहे. या मनोवृत्तींचा उदय राष्ट्रांत होऊं लागला कीं त्याबरोबरच या मनोवृत्तीच्या ओघासाठीं वाट करून देणें खऱ्या राज्यकर्त्यांचें कर्तव्य आहे. तें न करतां या मनोवृत्ति जेथें जेथें उद्भवतील तेथें तेथें त्या जुलमाच्या व जबरीच्या भारानें बुजवून टाकण्याचा अगर मोठमोठे बांध घालून जेथल्या तेथें अडवून टाकण्याचा प्रयत्न झाला कीं, त्या देशाचें–प्रजेचें व राजकर्त्यांचें–दुर्दैव ओढवलें म्हणून समजावें. जगाच्या इतिहासानें प्रस्थापित केलेल्या या सिद्धांताकडे राज्यकर्त्यांनीं आजपर्यंत दुर्लक्ष केल्याचें फळ बंगाली बांबचे रूपानें बाहेर पडलें आहे.

Ex. J. 1.

(Mr. Tilak's declaration as a Press—owner.)

I, Bal Gangadhar Tilak, do hereby declare that I have a printing Press called the Kasari Press at 486 Narayan Peth, Poona City.

Poona City.

1st July 1908. (Sd). Bal Gangadhar Tilak.

Declared before me at Poona this 1st day of July 1907.

(Sd.) H. F. Carvalho,
City Magistrate F. G..
Poona.

25—6—08 True copy.

(Sd). City Magistrate F. C. Poona.

Sela of the
City Magistrate Poona.

Ex. J. 2.

(Mr.) Tilak's declaration as Printer and Publisher.)

I, Bal Gangadhar Tilak do hereby declare that I am the Printer and Publisher of a weekly vernacular paper called the Kesari which is printed and published every Tuesday at House No. 486 Narayan Peth Poona City.

Poona Ctry.

1st July 1907. (Sd). Bal Gangadhar Tilak.

Declared befor me at Poona this 1st day of July 1907.

(Sd). H. F. Cravalho.
City Magistrate F. C. Poona.

25-6-08 True copy

Ed, (Sd.) City Migistrate F.C.
Poona.

Seal of the
City Magistrate of Poona.

Ex. K.

Handbook on
Modern Explosives
by M. Eissler
Publ. Crosby Lockwood and sons

12/6

Nitro=Explosives
By P. Gerad Sanford

9/-

Modern Explosives
by Eissler
Nitro=Explosives
by Sanford

A fancy card.

Ex. L.

[PANCHNAMA OF THE SEARCH AT POONA.]

PANCHNAMA, DATED 25-6-08.

(1) Sivram Pachandas Marwadi, having his shop in Ravivar Peth Kapadganj, Poona.

(2) Laxman Balkrishna Katrajkar, Budhwar, Poona.

(3) Raoji Lalji Takkar, inhabitant of Kasba Peth, Poona. House No. 335.

We the members of the Panch were called by the District Superintendent of Police, Poona at 7 a. m., on the 26th June 1908, on Thursday, in Gaikwad's wada in Narayen Peth, and in our presence the District Superintendent of Police broke the seals of the Kesari's Manager's office, and other rooms in connection with this paper, and on searching the same took possession of the papers &c. as stated below :—

(1) Current file of the Kesari Nos. 1 to 25 i. e. from 7-1-08 to 23-6-08

(2) Loose numbers of the Kesari as above, 1-25.

(3) Do. Do. Do.

(4) Receipt Books Nos. 1-5 of the Kesari for the current year, dated 1st Jsnuary 1908 to 25th June 1908, i. e. serial numbers 1-1252.

(5) One Ticket Book of the Kesari, with a brown paper cover.

(6) Day-Books for 1908 from 1st January 1908, to 24th June 1908 (one rough and one fair all two.)

(7) One Bill book of the Kesari for the current year.

(8) Seven Registers of the Kesari's subscribers (List Books).

(9) Line direction Books.

(10) One copy of the Marathi Sarojini play.

(11) One copy of Shri Maha Sadhu Shri Dnyaneshwar Maharaja's Life.

(12) One copy of the book called Prince William Orange or a history of the rebellion in the Netherlands.

(13) Four rough memoranda of the Postage Stamp Account.

(14) One money order Book for the current year.

(15) Kesari's three printed Sample Post cards.

(16) One letter in English dated 15-10-07 addressed to the Editor Marhatta, Poona from Carnel Boot Dyer Advertising Company from America.

(17) One photo of Shriyuta Bipin Chandra Pal.

(18) One Note Book of the sale of the *Kesari* from Godbole.

(19) Three letters printed in English regarding the Dhulia Conference. (The address given by Rao Bahadur Joshi.)

(20) One copy of the book called " What it cost to be vaccinated "

(21) One issue of the Dharma Masik Pustak including 5–7 numbers.

(22) Full text of the Presidential Address, Pubna Provincial Conference 1908–manuscript copy.

(23) Rules of the Deccan Vernacular Translation Society.

(24) One copy of a leaflet–'Hear the other side.'

(25) Surat Congress Papers.

(26) National Memorandum.

(27) A letter in English dated 28–12–7 written by B. G. Tilak to Bijaya Chandra Chatterji, Bar-at-law.

(28) One copy of the India House Magazine.

(29) One paper giving the astrological results of Tilak.

(30) One printed copy in English of the proceedings of the 23rd Indian National Congress.

(31) One manuscript letter sent by V. Vaijanathum from Kumbbhakonam adressed to Tilak signed "Vande Mataram" headed 'An Ardent Appeal.'

(32) Some portions of the Amrita Bazar Patrika issues dated –28–11–07 and 1-12-07.

(33) One letter in English from Woodhouse.

(34) Notes from Sections of the Indian Penal Code.

(35) One paper regarding a complaint against Paradkar Shimpi.

(36) Tilak's speech at Surat on 28-12-07.

(37) Notes on the proceedings of the Surat Conference.

(38) Cutting from the *Panjabi* dated 10–8–07

(39) A cutting from the 'Public Leisure' of Philadelphia dated 15–9–07.

(40) A cutting from the Mysore *Standard* dated 19–8–07.

(41) Three pieces of cuttings.

(42) Five miscellaneous letters.

(43) Account of the Shivaji Fund.

(44) A letter dated 4-9-05 from C. R. Gupta and Company to Tilak.

(45) A letter dated 6-1-05 from Tilak to Lala Lajpatrai.

(46) One card with names of Hand-book on Modern Explosives.

(47) One letter dated 6-5-05 from Madhava Raghunath of Kolhapur.

(48) A telegram dated 16-8-05 from Station Master Dhamangaon.

(49) Speech of Babu Arvinda Gosh dated 24-12-07.

(50) The Aretic Home in the Vedas.

(51) A telegram dated 18-10-5 from Bipin Chandra Pal to Tilak about delivering lecture.

(52) One letter addressed to Tilak regarding the establishment of religion.

(53) Address of Southern Mahratta Country subscribers of the *Kesari*- numbers 1 to 83.

(54)	Do.	Ratnagiri	page	1	to	52.
(55)	Do.	Bombay	page	1	to	40.
(56)	Do.	Dharwad	page	1	to	40.
(57)	Do.	Poona	page	I	to	21.
(58)	Do.	Guzrat	page	1	to	19.
(59)	Do,	Ahmednagar	page	1	to	22.
(60)	Do.	Sholapur	page	1	to	52.
(61)	Do.	Indore State	page	I	to	41,
(62)	Do.	Nasik	page	1	to	22:
(63)	Do.	Khandesh	page	I	to	101.

Papers as mentioned above are taken possession of by the Police in our presence-dated 25-6-08.

(Sd.) Raoji Lalji Takkar.

(Sd.) Shriram Pachandas Marvadi.

(Sd.) Laxman Balkrishna Katrajkar.

Before me

(Sd.) Digby Davies.

D. S. P. Poona.

(Sd.) A. C. Danniel.

Ex M. 1.

Case No. 421 of 1908

Complainant's Name—Supt. Sloane

Address-Bombay.

Fee nil.

No. of 190

To.

The District or City Magistrate

Poona

The Superintendent of Police Division

And all constabales and others of His Majesty's Officers of the peace for the town of Bombay.

WHEREAS information has been laid before me of the commission of the offence of sedition and promoting enmity between classes and it has been made to appear to me that the production of files of the newspaper *Kesari*, register of subscribers, draft proofs, manuscripts, correspondence, books of account and other documents relating to the said *Kesari* newspaper is essential to the inquiry about to be made into the said offence.

This is to authorise and require you to *search* for the said books, documents, writings and newspapers *in the press of the Kesari* situated at 486 Narayan Peth Poona and, if found, to produce the same forthwith before this Court returning this warrant, with an endorsement certifying what you have done under it immediately upon its execution.

Given under my hand and the seal of the Court.

This 24th day of June 1908.

Seal of the Presidency Magistrate's Court, Bombay.

(sd). A. H. S. Aston

Chief Presidency Magistrate,

Bombay.

Forwarded.

Forwarded to the District Superintendent of Police Poona for execution.

24-6-08.

(Sd). City Magistrate

Poona.

Returned duly executed

(Sd). J. Davies

D. S. Police, Poona.

Returned to the Presidency Magistrate, Bombay

Sd. District Magistrate Poona.

25-6-08.

Complainant's name and Address.

Ex. M. 2.

Case No. 421 of 1908.

Complainant's Name—Supt. Sloane

Address—Bombay.

No. of 190

To,

The Ditsrict or City Magistrate Poona,

The Superintendent of Police Diviosin

And all constables and other His Majesty's

officers of the peace for the town of Bombay.

WHEREAS information has been laid before me of the commission of the offence of sedition and promoting enmity between classes and it has been made to appear to me that the production of the Files of the newspaper *Kesari*, register of subscribers, drafts proofs, manuscripts, correspondence, books of account and other documents relating to the said *Kesari* newspaper is essential to the inquiry about to be made into the said offence.

This is to authorize and require you to search for the said books, documents, writings and newspapers in the *residence* of Bal Gangadhar Tilak *situate at Poona*, and if found, to produce the same forthwith before this Court returning this warrant with an endorsement certifying what you have done under it immediately upon its execution.

Given under my hand and the seal of the Court.

This 24th day of June 1908.

Seal of the Presidency Magistrate's Court, Bombay

(Sd). A. H. S. Aston

Chief Presidency Magistrate,

Bombay.

Forwarded to the District Superintendent of Police, Poona for execution.

24-6-08.

(Sd.) City Magistrate, Poona.

Returned duly executed.

(Sd). J. Davies

25-6-08. D. S. Police, Poona.

Returned to the Dis. S. Police, Poona.

This warrant cannot be considered to be fully executed until the residence of Bal Gangadhar Tilak at Singhgad has been searched. This search should now be made.

(Sd). G. Carmichael

25-6-08. District magistrate, Poona.

Executed. Nothing found at Singhgad.

(Sd). J. Davies.

D. S. Police, Poona.

Returned to the Presidency Magistrate.

Bombay.

(Sd). D. M.

25-6-08.

LIST OF NEWS PAPERS PUT IN BY MR. TILAK ALONG WITH HIS WRITTEN STATEMENT.

D 1 *Pioneer*, May 7, p. 2, Col. I.—Cult of the Bomb. 'Pioneer' recommends use of indiscriminating penalties and shooting ten suspected terrorists for one life taken.

D 2. *Gujrathi*, (quoting 'Asian'), May 31, p. 773, col. 2-3.—'Asian' recommends governing with utmost harshness and rigour under the heel, and shooting the Babus point blank.

D 3 *Gujrathi*, May, 31, p. 773, col. 2-3.—'*Englishman's* correspondent advices flogging of Indian agitators in public by town-sweepers and confiscating presses.

D. 4. *Pioneer*, May 11,p, 2, col. 1-2-3.—Acknowledges joy at the forging of the engine of destruction of popular liberty viz. the Press and the Explosives Act.

D. 5. *Statesman*, May 5, p. 6, col, 2-3.—Charges nationalist speakers with bomb-outrages as a consequence of their speeches.

D. 5A. *Statesman*, May 6, p. 6, col. 2-3.—Charges respectable people with internally sympathising with crackbrained authors of outrages.

D. 6 *Statesman*, May 7, p. 6, 1-2.—Charges nationalist speakers with porducing gang of terrorists.

D. 6A. *Statesman*, May 15, p. 6, 2-3.—Says that under-rating danger is folly but exaggerating it is greater folly.

D. 7, *Times of India*, May 4, p. 6, col. 4-5.—Charges native press and well-known nationalist speakers with the responsibility of working ferment in the yeasty brains.

D. 7. A. *Advocate of India*, May 4, p. 6. 2-3.—Alleges that authors of inflamatory literature are responsible for crimes. Says repression not successful only because not thorough enough.

D. 8. *Bengalee*. May 5, p. 5. Col. 1, 2, 3.—Asserts that anarchism is a reaction against unhealthy political conditions.

D. 9. *Bengalee*, May 6, p. 5, col. 2.—Quotes Burke-"Coercion is a feeble instrument of Government, conciliation the sovereign remedy."

D. 10. *Bengalee*, May 8, p. 5, col. 2, 5.—Quotes Indian *Daily News* which says—"Unrest is a passing phase but permanent problem of administration remains."

D. 11. *Bengalee*. May 9, p. 5, col. 2.—Criticises Anglo-Indian press for attacking boycott as leading to crime.

D. 12. *Bengalee*, May 10, p. 5, col. 1.—Asserts that controversy is raging between Anglo-Indian and Indian press.

D. 13. *Bengalee*, May 17, p. 5, col 1, 2.—Contends that Government policy is largely responsible for prevailing discontent. So-called agitators had already given warning.

D. 14. *Bengalee*, May 13, p. 5. col. 1, 2.—Criticises *Madras Times* for speaking of the Tiger qualities of the race in this connection.

D. 15. *Bengalee*, May 28, p. 5, col. 6.—Quotes *Englishman's* correspondent who calls the native press 'Reptile 'press.

D. 16. *Bengalee*, May 31, p. 5, col. 1.—Discusses question of responsibility for unrest and quotes Mr. Macnicol of Poona who recommends generous and prompt measures to satisfy reasonable demands.

D. 17. *Modern Review*, June, p. 547.—Writers about the philosophy of political crime; condemning the outrages at the same time. Quotes Mathew Arnold. Also says outrages are due to despair and disappointment.

D. 18. *Indian World.* May 19, 1908, p. 472 & onwards—Deals with the Psychology of Bombs. Says outrages are natural results of all that precedes it and calls Anglo-Indian Press 'blood hounds.'

D. 19. *Hindu*, May 9, p. 4, col. 1, 2.—Charges Government with disregarding popular advice and warning Government. Says Government should have expected to reap the whirl-wind.

D. 20. *Hindu*, May 21, p. 4, col. 3.—Quotes Rash Behari Ghosh who in 1906 said that Young Generation in Bengal would make India another Russia.

D. 21. *Hindu*, May 22, p. 6, col. 2, 3.—Gives Nepal Chandra Roy's answer to the 'Cult of the Bomb,' who fastens responsibility on both Anglo-Indian Press and Bureaucracy.

D. 22. *Indian Patriot*, May 4, p. 4, col 1, 2.—Says repressive *regime* is more responsible for troubles.

D. 23. *Indian Patriot*, May 5, p. 2, col. 2.—Says that national movement is democratic and derives its strength from the character of alien Bureaucracy.

D. 24. *Indian Patriot*, May 6. p. 4, col. 2.—Says Bureaucracy in India is reared in the atmosphere of despotism. The only hindrance to them is notice taken by Parliament.

D. 25. *Indian Patriot*, May 14, p. 2, col. 1, 3,—Repression will kindle the flame of animosity and hatred rather than soothe the feelings.

D. 26. *Indian Patriot*, May 15, p. 4. col. 1, 2.—Without freedom of speech and Press it is impossible to keep alien Bureaucracy straight and says the present system of autocratic Government free from constitutional restraints has enslaved people.

D. 27. *Madras Standard*, May 4, p. 4, col. 3—Expresses sympathy for Bengal and blames Anglo-Indian Press for inciting Government to sternest repressive measures.

D. 28. *Madras Standard*, May 6. p. 4, col. 2. Says—Lord Curzon is the real author of all the present unrest in India and blames Anglo-Indian Press for campaign of villification.

D. 29 *Punjabee*. May, 9. p. 3, col. 1.—Regrets that there are Anarchists or Sycophants only and no advisers.

D. 30. *Tribune*, May 19. p. 4, col. 1, 2.—Denies responsibility of Varnacular press and says that every red hot extremist paper is natural counter-part of fire-eating Anglo-Indian Journal.

D. 31. *Patrika*, May 5. p. 6, col. 1, 2.—Says, measures like partition and Kingsford's severities are the cause of unhinging the minds of Bengalee youths and impelling them to commit crimes.

D. 32. *Patrika*, May 6, p. 6, col. 1, 2.—Quotes "Hindu Patriot" and says that the best pest policy is to govern in such a way as not to create conspirators.

D. 33. *Patrika*, May 7, p. 6, col. 1.—Dwells upon the easy and small means of the bomb campaign.

D. 34. *Bengalee*, June 13, p. 6, col. 1,—Explains how timid Bengalees are turned into fanatical gazis.

D. 35. *Bengalee*, May 20, p. 5, col. 1. 2 and 3.—Blames Government for not punishing Anglo-Indian papers who preach violence against people.

D. 36. *Patrika*, May 31, p. 3, col. 2, 4.—Attacks bureaucracy and says that they are all Kings in India.

D. 37. *Indian Spectator*, May 9, p. 361, and 362, col. 2. 3.—Distinguishes between crimes which are offsprings of pure selfishness and crimes done in larger interests. It says western literature and political agitation favour development of aspirations and of independence into seditious conspiracies.

D. 38. *Indian Spectator*, May 16, p. 381, col. I—Playfully deals with the situation.

D. 39. *Gujrathi*, May 17, p. 707, col. 1. 2. 3 ; p. 705, col. 2, 3 : p. 706, col. 1, 2, 3.—Investigates into causes of unrest and holds Government responsible for the same.

D. 40. *Gujrathi* May 31, p. 779 col 1 ; p. 777, col. 1. 2 ; p. 778, col I, 2, 3.—Charges Government and Anglo-Indian Papers with sowing seeds of discontent.

D. 41. *Gujrathi*, June 14, p. 858, col. 2.—Has a humorous skit on God Bomb, says Bomb will make his name permanent if he will bring reforms.

D. 42. *Indu-Prakash*, May 5, p. 7. col. 1, 2, 3.—Says there is a connection between anarchism and surrounding political conditions.

D. 43, *Indu-Prakash* May 8, p. 2, col. 5. 6.—Connects outrages not so much with newspaper articles as with repressive measures and Police high-handedness.

D. 44 *Dnyan-Prakash* May 19, p. 2, col. 1, 2, 3, 4. 5, 6.—Dwells on despotic policy of Government and says repression will not root out discontent.

D. 45. *Dnyan-Prakash*, May 26, p. 2, col. 5.—Says outrages are the venomous fruits of the poison tree planted by Lord Curzon.

D. 46. *Dnyan-Prakash*, May 30, p. 2 col. 3, 4, 5.—Says Anglo-Indian Press hates native Press because it hints that political discontent has led to anarchims.

D. 47. *Dnyan-Prakash* June 7, p. 2, col, 3, 4, 5.—Dwells on Irish Crime's Act in this connection.

D. 48. *Chikitsaka*, May 27, p. 3 col. 2, 3. 4, 5.—Says—failure in political agitation will lead to anarchism and this was foretold.

D. 48. A. *Chikitsaka*, May 13, p. 2. cols. 1, 2, 3, 4.—Holds Curzon responsible who trampled public opinion under the feet like a Sultan and extremism is due to unjust and domineering policy ; attacks Anglo-Indian Press as lap-dogs of Government barking at people.

D. 48. B. *Chikitsaka*, May 20, p. 2, col. 1,—Attacks Anglo-Indian Press as idiotic relations on the wife's side (शालक) of Government who are cruel, deceitful silly, vain, worthless hiding behind the tail of Imperial Lion.

D. 49. *India*, May 8, p. 231, col. 2; p. 232, col. 1, 2; p. 533, col. 1.—Expresses English opinion on the situation.

D. 50. *India*, May 15, p. 243, col. 2: p 244, col. 2; p. 245, col. 2.—Expresses English opinion on the situation.

D. 51. *India*, May 22, p. 258, col. 1 & 2—Expresses English opinion on the Bomb-outrages and the situation and gives Mr. Dutt's interview.

D. 52. *India*, May 29, p. 269 col. 2; p. 270, col. 1. 2.—Expresses English opinion on the Bomb-outrage and the situation and Mr. Dutt's interview.

D. 53. *India*, June 5, p. 279, col. 2; p. 281, col. 1; p. 282, col. 1.—Expresses English opinion on the Bomb-outrage and the situation.

D. 54. *India*, June 12, p. 593, col. 2; p. 295, col. 1.—Expresses English opinion on the Bomb outrage.

D. 55. *Advocate of India*, June 19 p. 7, col. 4.—Quotes Bishop of Lahore who said that order could not be preserved only by repression and by smiting on the head any who takes up a prominent position in the new birth of India.

D. 56. *Mahratta* May 24, p. 246, col. 1, 2.—Summarising English opinion on the situation in Bengal.

D. 56 A. *Mahratta*, June 28, p. 304, col. 1.—Giving Gladstone's opinion obout incitement to violence.

D. 56 B. *Mahratta*, March 15, p. 126, col. 2; p. 127, col. 1, 2.—Gives Tilak's statement before the Decentralisation Commission.

D. 57. *Times of India*, May 12, p. 7, col. 1.—Contains telegrams about Mr. Dutt's and Gokhole's first words about Bomb-outrages.

D. 58. *Oriental Review*, May 6, p. 131, col. 1, 2.—Holds Curzon responsible and says anarchism is the child of despair.

D. 59. *Times of India* June 25, p. 7; col. 7. p. 8. col 1.—Gives *Morley's speech* at the I. C. S. dinner,

D. 60. *Bombay Gazette*, July 2, p. 7: col. 1, 2.—Morley and Curzon debate in the Lords.

D. 61. *Gazette of India*, Nov. 2 (1907), p. 164 and 165.—Rash Behari on Seditious Meetings Bill.

D. 62. *Gazette of India*, June 8, p. 1, 2, 3, 4.—Explosives and Press Acts.

D. 63. *Gazette of India*, June 13, p. 142.—Syed Mahomad's speech on Explosives Act quoting "Ethics of Dynamite" from "Contemporary Review."

D. 64. *Oriental Review*, July 1, p. 239, col, 1, 2.—Letter to the Morning Leader of its Calcutta correspondent saying "Bomb has come to stay."

D. 65. *Contemporary Review* May 1894, p. 978 and onwards.—Article on Ethics of Dynamite.

D. 66. *Kesari*, June 16, p. 4, col. 3.—Commenting upon Definition of 'Explosives' in 'Explosives Act.'

D. 67. *Mahratta*, September 1 (1907), p. 411, col. 2 - Containing account ot Zenger's case of seditious libel from Phelp's letter from New York.

D. 68. *Sudharak*, May 11, p. 2, col. 2.—Saying Bomb was foretold by Gokhale in 1905.

D. 69. *Subodha Patrika*, May 10, p; 2, col. 2—Says Anarchism was foretold.

D. 70. *Subodha Patrika*, May 17, p. 2, col. 2—Policy of repression was sure to end in anarchism.

D. 71. *Sudharak*.

DEFENCE EXHIBITS.

Ex. D 1.

PIONEER—May 7, P. 2, Col. 1.

" If the moral disease were to spread elsewhere as it has done in Spain, the non-criminal portion of mankind would eventually be forced to meet the Nihilist by penalties indiscriminating as the bomb. A wholesale arrest of the acknowledged terrorists in a city or district coupled with an intimation that on the next repetition of the offence ten of them would be shot for every life sacrificed, would soon put down the practice, if it should become necessary. "

\+ \+ \+ \+ \+

" Let us only glance over the smooth Legislative Councillor with his quotations from Burke, Mill and Milton complaining of rights wrested from the people, of the drainage of the country's wealth to England, of unredressed grievances, oppression and want of sympathy, language which no doubt means no more than Mr. Churchill's appeal to the electors of Dundee."..... " Then comes the Congress moderate who believes that the British Government may be tolerated temporarily, as a choice of evils as long as it does not cross " the will of the people, " who deprecates strong measures against it, because they are not likely to succeed, but approves of minor ones, and by principle of all. Next, the more candid Extremist who would openly have the Government out if he could and to that end is ready to experiment with different weapons of boycott, strikes, abstention, and so forth, which the ingenuity of the party suggests until a better may be forth coming. Below the Extremist come the lecturer and the vernacular editor, the latter of whom has been steadily at his work for the last thirty years and more, the former a new development, and both having for their aim the direct inflamation of the minds of the people."..... ..." Who can wonder that in the last grade come the bomb-maker and the wretched, infatuated student whom he gets to do the work? They are the logical outcome of the whole movement as it stands. The nexus from top to bottom is complete." " No one will suppose that in saying this it is implied that the average leading men of the different sections of the Indian " Nationalist " agitation actively approve of the use of the infernal machine as an instrument of politics. Be their bitterness what it may, men as intelligent as Mr. Tilak and Mr. Gokhale, not to speak of those of the school of Messrs Rashbehari Ghose ahd Surendernath Banerjee, must be well aware that the bomb is as stupid as it is wicked. The Nationalist may be assured in spite of anything the Keir Hardies and Nevinsons may tell him, that the British people have not the remotest intention of retiring from India and still less of being driven out of it by bombs. The Revolution that is to make head must have behind it real forces and real wrongs : not the insufficient separation of Judicial and Executive functions or a Bill (which is only remarkable as a dead letter) of precautions against seditious public meeting. The only force that is apparent behind the present agitation is the sentiment of race-hatred. That indeed had been steadily fanned by the educated community until it has at last taken hold in various quarters of the ignorant masses."

Ex. D 2.

GUJARATHI—(*Quoting 'Asian'*) *May 31, P. 773, Col. 2–3.*

" Bengal should be treated and governed with the utmost harshness and vigour by a ruler who is not afraid to put his heel down and—keep it there."....." During Mr. Keir Hardie's tour in India, he sowed more seeds of sedition than any man who has ever gone before him, or who is likely to come after him. "....." Mr. Kingsford has a great opportunity and we hope he is a fairly decent shot at short range. We recommend to his notice a Mauser pistol with the nick filed off the nose of the bullets or a Colt's Automatic which carries a heavy soft bullet and is a hard hitting and punishing weapon. We hope Mr. Kingsford will manage to secure a big 'bag' and we envy him his opportunity. He will be more than justified in letting day-light into every strange native approaching his house or his person, and for his own sake we trust he will learn to shoot fairly straight without taking his weapon out of his coat pocket......We wish the one man who has shown that he has a correct view of the necessities of the situation the very best of luck ! "

Ex. D 3.

GUJARATHI—May 31, P. 773, col. 2-3—Quotation from a Correspondent of the *Englishman* :—

" I submit, " says the writer of the letter, " that powers should be given to the authorities to suppress these agitators by the most ready and simple methods ; and were a few of these worthy agitators flogged in public by the town sweepers and their presses confiscated, much of the glamour of the righteousness of their agitation for the people would be destroyed and their dupes would see them as they are, and not in the kaleidoscopic light which they endeavour to attract to themselves. "

Ex. D 4.

PIONEER—*May 11, p. 2, col. 1–2–3.*—Acknowledges joy at the forging of the engine of destruction of popular liberty viz. the Press and the Explosives Act.

Ex. D 5.

STATESMAN—*May 5, P. 6, Col. 2–3.*

But since the Partition of Bengal, the crowning folly of Lord CURZON's régime, a different spirit has manifested itself, whose weapons are apparently to be bombs and dynamite. The Moderate Nationalists have found themselves ousted in the favour of the student world by a new school preaching a doctrine of unreasoning hatred of England and hinting as clearly as a regard for their own safety would permit at the necessity of doing deeds which were only possible if the perpetrator was willing to die for his country. These apostles of violence scoffed at the "mendicant policy", as they called constitutional agitation, and advocated a vague and undefined but obviously mischievous gospel of "self-help." In the discoveries made by the Calcutta police yesterday, in the mangled bodies of an unoffending lady and her daughter, we see the results of this ineffably silly but, unhappily, dangerous propaganda. How far Bepin Chandra Pal and others of the same extremist views intended that their wild talk should be taken seriously, or how far they had the capacity to see what would be its probable consequences, we do not know. But there can be little doubt that their teaching has had the effect of turning the heads of a number of enthusiasts. These fanatics have become imbued with a morbid notion that in some way which they cannot explain their conntry has suffered a grievous wrong, of which they are to be the avengers. Being, many of them, without any useful employment they brooded over their fancied grievances until they were ripe for murder.

Ex. D 5A.

STATESMAN—May 6, P. 6, col. 2-3.

If the confessions of some of the prisoners are to be believed, they received money to assist their machinations from people who were not in the plot but who were anxious that blood should be shed to avenge the Partition of Bengal and the sedition trials. "Respectable people," says the *Amrita Bazar Patrika*, "can, have no sympathy with such dark deeds." Respectability is a matter of definition, but it would appear that men who were at least well-to-do have subscribed funds to enable the Terrorists to send one of their number to Europe to study explosives and to maintain missionaries who went about India sowing the seeds of revolt. Without money revolvers cannot be purchased, dynamite cartridges cannot be procured, and materials for the manufacture of bombs accumulated. The prisoners do not appear to be men who could out of their own means carry on an expensive campaign, and we are, therefore, driven to the inference that people who would ordinarily be called respectable have given their support to the wicked folly of the Terrorists. But the fact remains that the crack-brained enthusiasts who entered the conspiracy of bomb-throwing apparently had sympathisers among the respectable classes, which have generally been regarded as loyal and moderate.

Ex. D 6.

STATESMAN—May 7, P. 6, Col. 1-2.

That the Extremist propaganda is violent and bitter needs no demonstration. The newspapers by which it is carried on are engaged in a constant vilification of England. Its orators teach the doctrine that the regeneration of India must be secured without the help of a foreign Government, and the general character of the aims of its leaders is shown by their determination to wreck the Congress rather than subscribe to a creed which is suggestive of loyalty to English rule. No argument is needed to show that the general effect of this hostile and bitter agitation upon ill-informed youths must be to turn them into potential rebels. The significant confession of the Mozafferpore bomb-thrower, that he derived his inspiration from the seditious vernacular press and the speeches of Extremist leaders, is conclusive on this point. Speaking and writing of the Extremist type have actually produced a gang of Terrorists in Bengal......But as long as the boycott inculcates social hatred, as long as the schools are political seminaries, and as long as a veiled disloyalty to England is no disqualification in a political leader, the forces which tend to produce Terrorists will remain.

Ex. D 6A.

STATESMAN—May 15, P. 6, Col. 2–3.

No one denies that a grave and critical situation has arisen in this country. A new and hideous peril has manifested itself, constituting a fresh problem which will tax all the resources of statesmanship. But these are conditions which call for a cool head and wisely considered action. To underrate the danger would be folly, but to exaggerate it is still more foolish. What is gained by drawing an indictment against a whole nation? If it were true, it would be a truth to be dissembled; while if false it tends to create the very evil that it imagines and prompts the Government to unjust and needless severities.

Ex. D 7.

TIMES OF INDIA—May 4, P. 6, Col. 4–5.—Charges native press and well-known nationalist speakers with the responsibility of "working ferments in the yeasty brains."

Ex. D 7A.

ADVOCATE OF INDIA—May 4, P. 6, Col. 2–3.

But, apart from anarchist organiztaions, a more persistent and open factor in the spread of political crime has to be taken into account. The dissemination of seditious literature goes on in spite of the severity of the penalties imposed on responsible and guilty parties, and that the poison often does its work is only too clearly proved in the case of the infatuated youth who with an accomplice carried out the murder of the two ladies. That he was a mere tool and that he was incited to the crime probably by the Calcutta "agency" is evident; but the fact is that his mind has been carefully educated for the work by reading the inflammatory literature which in one form or another is scattered broadcast over the country. We advocate no measure of undue repression when we hold that something more must be done to limit the criminal output of the printing press. The plain impalatable truth is that repression so far has failed, not because it is repression but because it has not been thorough enough. It is foolishness to attempt to cut off the heads of the hydra with a paper knife and it is the spectacle of that attempt which we are now learning to deplore.

Ex. D 8.

BENGALEE—May, 5, P. 5, Col. 1, 2, 3.

Anarchism and nihilism are undoubtedly very bad things, but more often than not they represent a reaction against a state of things which is by no means either healthy or normal. Not even the *Englishman* will contend in his saner hours that India is in a sound state politically or that the present abnormal condition of things can last for ever. It was inevitable that there should be a reaction. The reaction has naturally taken a healthy form in properly constituted minds and to-day the forces of nationalism in India are, by universal admission, forces to reckon with. But diseased minds there shall always be, as there have always been. And it is quite possible that a great awakening like that we have in this country should not only arouse enthusiasm among the bulk of sane people but excitement of the dangerous kind among people of a different temperament and of a differnt mental constitution.

Ex. D 9.

BENGALEE—May 6, *P. 5, Col. 2.*—Quotes Burke—"Coercion is a feeble instrument of Government, conciliation the sovereign remedy."

Ex. D 10.

BENGALEE—May 8, P. 5, Col. 2-5.

After all, there is, as there must be, a logical connection between all the different movements which owe their existence to the operation of the same great forces and which have assumed different characters merely by reason of the different materials and the different mental constitutions on which those forces have worked. But from this point of view there is a close connection not only between the Congress and the bomb-outrage, but between the bureaucracy and its advisers on one side and the bomb-thrower on the other. Would such an outrage as we have recently had have been possible in modern England ?......It is difficult to avoid the conclusion that it is only in countries despotically governed and where no means exist for making the voice of the people effective in their own government, that anarchism and similar *isms* can expect to grow. No more convincing proof of the truth of this general statement can possibly be found than is afforded by the discovery of an anarchist organization in Calcutta, the capital city of India. If ever there was a country which might be expected, from its traditions, its culture, its peculiar race-characteristics, to be averse to such a crime as the one recently committed at Muzafferpur, it is India. The bomb-thrower, let it be distinctly understood, is a very different person from one who is resolved, even determined, to have political wrongs righted.......The bureaucratic form of government and its advocates and champions, therefore, must share with the Nationalist and his movements the responsibility for having brought the bomb-thower into existence. Indeed the responsibility of the former is much greater than that of the latter. The latter have only this in common with the bomb-thrower that they are the products of the same forces, the effects of the same cause. Can the same thing be said of the former ? ...“ After all, the Unrest is but a passing phase, the permanent problems of the adminstration remain ; ” so writes the *I. D News*, which is not now unsympathetic to Indian aspirations. The *Statesman* speaks of the Partition as “ the crowning folly of the Curzon regime. ”

Ex. D 11.

BENGALEE—May 9. P. 5, Col. 2.

There is hardly a single sentence in this paragraph which does not contain a misleading statement or a still more misleading suggestion. In the very first sentence there is the insinuation—as false as it is wicked—that a connection exists or has been established between Swadeshi cum-boycott-cum-Swaraj propaganda and the recent outrage. Yet the whole controversy between the Anglo-Indian and a section of the Indian Press rages round the question whether such a connection does really exist. We have shown again and again that on the same grounds on which a connection may be established between the outrages and the Nationalist movement, the same if not a more intimate, connection, must be admitted to exist between the bomb-thrower and the bureaucracy.......But we are more concerned with the *Englishman's* paragaraph. Our contemporary seeks to controvert the statement that “ the boycott is a movement based entirely upon love ” by reference to a number of alleged occurrences for not one of which can the boycott as a movement be held responsible. If a boycotter here and there went to excesses, there were the courts of law to take cognizance of his doings. They could not discredit the movement unless either of two things were shown. Is there anything in the fundamental ideas of the movement—is there anything in the professed methods—which shows that the movement is based upon hatred of the foreigner ? And has the movement in practice been carried on by the bulk of those who owe allegiance to it in a manner which proves that, if not based upon hatred, it must, at any rate, be fostered by it ? On both these points only one answer is conceivable and that answer has long been recorded by the impartial historian. It has never been contended by those who urged that the movement was based upon love and not hatred that the boycott of foreign goods could be effected without creating any bitterness in any quarter. Certain interests were bound to be affected and it was inevitable that those whose interests were affected would take up a hostile attitude towards it. Is the movement to be blamed because it excited hostility in that sense ? That would be another way of saying that India's economic servitude must contnue for all time. Surely if “ love ” only means acquiescence in an abnormal and certainly ruinous state of things, we have yet to understand the meaning of that word.

Ex. D 12.

BENGALEE—May 10, P. 5, Col. 1.

There are two sets of opinion which have gathered round the bomb-outrage incident, contending for the mastery. There is the body of Anglo-Indian opinion, of which the *Pioneer* and the *Englishman* are the exponents. In better days the *Statesman* assumed an attitude of healthy neutrality, taking up no sides, but declaring for justice and truth. Unfortunately those days are past and gone; and the *Statesman* to-day is as keen in its support of Anglo-Indian opinion as the most rabid of Anglo-Indian newspapers. Opposed to the Anglo-Indian journals are the organs of the educated community throughout India. The Anglo-Indian newspapers will not be satisfied with the punishment of the offenders. They want repressive measures—they want a modification of the existing law, so that the hands of the Executive Government may be further strengthened. The Indian section of the Press, on the other hand, is of opinion that the present law is amply sufficient for all purposes.

Ex. D 13.

BENGALEE—May 17, P. 5, Col. 1.

There is a tendency in some quarters to denounce the so-called agitators for the present unrest and the consequences that have followed in its train. Nothing could be more irrational or short-sighted. The agitators are in no way responsible for the present unrest. What they have done is to give voice to the public sentiment and here and there to organize the public impulses for definite expression. It is the policy of the Government that is largely responsible for the prevailing discontent. The agitators would not have been listened to if their appeal did not find a response in the deepest feelings of the nation. The policy of the last sixteen years is responsible for the present deplorable state of affairs. It is a policy which has been marked by re-action and repression and by a total disregard of public opinion. This reactionary policy reached its climax during the days of Lord Curzon. And the partition of Bengal was the crowning folly of that *regime* ...... The open sore of the partition still remains. It is the root-cause of the prevailing discontent and the partition was followed by a policy of repression unheard of in the annals of British rule in India. Here have we not the explanation of the whole situation? It is no use denouncing the agitators. They are not the authors of the crisis with which the country stands confronted to-day. On the contrary more than once did they raise their warning voice. The historian will lay the blame upon the heads of the bureaucracy, which rejected their counsels of prudence, and those of their supporters in the Press.

Ex. D 14.

BENGALEE—May 13, P. 5, Col. 1-2.

Of the same type as the *Asian* and its backers in Calcutta is the *Madras Times*, whose Calcutta correspondent had the goodness to telegraph a few days after the

Mozefferpore outrage :—"The injuries received in the outrage are too ghastly and painful to describe. If detailed, the narration would produce a feeling of universal horror and angry clamour for lynch law, and would stir every European to some emphatic and active protest. as the feeling of revulsion would be too strong to suppress." Thereupon the *Madras Times* discoursed editorilly on the " tiger qualities " of the race, and amiable things of that sort ! Our only object in referring to these silly effusions is to warn the Government that they should not hesitate to let it be known how they view conduct, so unworthy of Englishmen in a situation of some gravity. It is no answer to say that there are writers in the " native " press who write undiluted nonsense similar to that in the *Asian* and the *Madras Times.* The difference is this; the writers in the " native " press get punished, whereas the superior gentlemen who spout venom in the Anglo-Indian press are unscathed. The leaders of the " native " community are expected and, indeed, peremptorily called upon to express their abhorrence of undesirable writings in the " native " press; but apparently there is no corresponding obligation upon the leaders of the European community to do likewise as regards simillar writings in the Anglo-Indian Press. There is another important difference. These spouters of venom—these inciters to racial feeling—expressly declare that they are voicing the feelings of the entire non-official European community when they say that Indians should be lynched or shot indiscriminately. Their confreres in the " native " press do not profess to speak on behalf of their community......... We think it is time that Government taught a lesson to these gentlemen, who prostitute their position for the purpose of stirring up civil strife by deliberately fomenting racial hatred. It would be a reproach to Government if they fail to mark their disapproval of these incitements to racial passion habitually indulged in by Anglo-Indian papers of the gutter press variety.

Ex. D 15.

BENGALEE—May 28, P. 5, col. 6. (Quotes Englishman's correspondent).

Meanwhile what many of us now see is a reptile press day after day delivering itself of statements of opinions which can only be interpreted as seditious, disloyal and thoroughly harmful to the country at large. Experience has shown that the present enactments are not sufficiently strong to check the mischief which is being done and most people in Simla hope that the home Government and the Government of India will quickly come to a conclusion that measures which may be called more Russian in their method are becoming absolutely necessary for the safety of the country.

Ex. D 16.

BENGALEE—May 31, P. 5, col. 1.

Who is responsible for the present state of things with their many unhappy developments ? The Anglo-Indian Press, the mouthpiece of the bureaucracy, throws the responsibility upon the political agitators. The Indian Press, voicing the public feeling of the country, lays the blame upon the bureaucracy. It says that the Govevrnment has, for the last fifteen years and more, followed a policy of reaction in utter contempt of public opinion, that the efforts of the constitutional party for reforms have been a series of failures and in consequence a section of the community have lost faith in such methods. The result has been the birth of wide-spread unrest and discontent, in which it was only natural that some people should lose their heads. Therefore, if contentment and happiness are to be restored and things are to be brought back to their normal condition, a policy of conciliation and reform should be adopted without the least possible delay. Repression will not touch the heart of the evil. It can at best deal with only the outward symtoms. Mr. Macnicol, writing to the London *Spectator* from Poona, says :—"No one can doubt that slow-moving as India has hitherto been, of recent years she has been advancing politically with remarkable rapidity, and the advance has been unmistakably towards ideals that are becoming increasingly difficult to reconcile with British domination. If she is to be persuaded to halt on her way to that goal it will only be, in the opinion of many, if generous and prompt measures are taken to satisfy resonable demands of the moderate leaders, and associate her people in the government of the country, both at the top in the Executive Councils and at the bottom in Village and District Councils." Sir George Birdwood is an official of officials, and one would expect that he would be the last person to say anything which would imply a reflection upon the present methods of administration. But this is what he writes :—

"Our rule is strong and just, but it is not sympathetic; and the more impregnable in a material sense our position in India becomes the more likely are we to be confirmed in the egotistical methods of scholastic, literary and artistic education and of religious proselytism, we have so strenously enforced on its many-languaged and its many-religioned peoples. We are destroying their faith and their literature and their arts, and whole continuity of the spontaneous development of their civilisation, and their great historical personality : in a word, we are destroying the very soul of the nation. This is the cause of the restlessness that by those who have eyes to see and ears to hear is to be found everywhere fretting into the very hearts of English educated peoples in India."

Ex. D 17.

MODERN REVIEW—June 1908, P. 547—551.

POLITICAL ASSASSINATION AND WESTERN SENTIMENT.

We never suspected the existence of any secret society in India with aims and objects like those of the Fenians, Nihilists, Anarchists or Terrorists. Secret societies with political assassination as their object or method of work, are a product of Western civilization. The Russian exile Prince Peter Kropotkin is said to be a great advocate of such methods and societies. But the soil of India is not favourable to the taking root or growing and thriving of such an institution. It is foreign to the genius of our race. The truth of our assertion is borne out by the miserable failure of the plot of the terrorists (they are not anarchists) of Calcutta. In Western countries political assassinations are not condemned by even thoughtful and respectable people as they ought to be. Their perpetrators are looked upon as heroes, and, if caught and executed as martyrs. They are not branded as murderers. This is evident from what Matthew Arnold says in one of his poems from which we extract the following lines :—

" Murder !—but what is murder ? When a wretch
For private gain or hatred takes a life,
We call it murder, crush him, brand his name.

But when, for some great public cause, an arm
Is, without love or hate, austerely raised
Against a power exempt from common checks,
Dangerous to all, to be thus annull'd—
Ranks any man with murder such an act ?
With grievous deeds, perhaps; with murder, not. "

Such approval of political murders cannot be found in Indian literature. Nor is the justification of political assassination rare in English ephemeral literature. For instance, when in 1906 certain persons were assassinated in the villa of M. Stolypin, the Russian premier, the *Pioneer* wrote in its issue of the 29th August, 1906 :—" The horror of such crimes is too great for words, and yet it has to be acknowledged, almost, that they are the only method of fighting left to a people who are at war with despotic rulers able to command great military forces against which it is impossible for the unarmed populace to make a stand. When the Czar dissolved the Duma, he destroyed all hope of reform being gained without violence. Against bombs his armies are powerless, and for that reason he cannot rule, as his forefathers did, by the sword. It becomes impossible for even the stoutest-hearted men to govern fairly or strongly when every moment of their lives is spent in terror of a revolting death, and they grow into craven shirkers, or stustain themselves by a frenzy of retaliation which increases the conflagration they are striving to check. Such conditions cannot last. "* Again, in the year 1900, the *Pioneer* published in one of its issues what it no doubt considered a very humorous poem, but what every right-thinking man will consider an almost open justification of or incitement to the political murder of " Babus " by Englishmen. We quote the last stanza :—

" And he travelled by train to that Babu Bhagwan,
And slew him with Handle-Broom wood,
And lessened the number of Babus by one.
Don't blame him. He did what he could. "†

Thus it will be seen that even Anglo-Indian papers approve of or justify the conduct of political assassins or murderers when such crimes are committed by Europeans in India or in the Christian countries of the West ; though they cannot be expected to take the same attitude when the scene is India, the assassins are coloured men and the victims are colourless. But we condemn such crimes, wherever or by whomsoever they may be committed. Righteousness uplifteth a nation and a good cause has never been advanced by crimes. The well-known Persian poet Shaikh Saadi has said :—

" *Rahi rast baroh agar cha dur ast.*"
"Always walk in the path of righteousness, even if the goal be distant."
This is also our advice to our countrymen.

The Calcutta bomb-makers have presented Viscount Morley with an unquestionably new fact, which he wanted for the reconsideration of the Bengal Partition question though even such a fact will not, we are sure, unsettle his " settled fact. " Our most radical Secretary of State must get the credit of having produced the bomb-thrower,—a unique performance. The ultimate cause of terrorism in Bengal must be sought in the utterly selfish, highhanded and tyrannical policy of the Government, and in the contemptuous and insulting manner in which most official

---

* This passage is taken from the *Prabasi* for the month of *Fyaishtha*, in which it was first extracted.

†Quoted by Babu Nepal Chandra Roy in a letter which he addressed to the *Pioneer*, which the latter had neither the fairness nor the courage to print.

and non-official Anglo-Indians have spoken of and treated Bengalies. They have ridden rough-shod over the feelings of the Bengalis and turned a deaf ear to their strongest and most reasonable respresentation, supported by facts and figures. The Russianization of the administration in spirit and methods has led to the conversion of a small section of the people to the methods of Russian terrorism. It is simply a question of action and reaction, " stimulus " and "response," Persistently unrighteous administration has an inevitable tendency to make men seek desperate remedies. Finding no remedy in constitutional agitation, burning to wreak what they considered "national vengeance," impatient and eager to wipe off the cowardly libel that Bengalis are cowards, some desperate young men have had recourse to desperate and unrighteous methods. The result has been a mistake, horrible in its consequences. Instead of the man they wanted to kill, they have murdered two innocent women whose death is deeply deplored. That is almost invariably a feature of assassination by bomb-throwing. More often than not, it is innocent persons who die, not those whom the bomb-throwers consider guilty. Even when the latter are killed, some innocent persons are killed along with them. So that the method is essentially reckless and wicked, and we may add, cowardly. For there is no heroism in killing an unarmed person, whom, moreover, the assailant has not the courage to face. It appears from the confession of one of the terrorists that they were clear-headed enough to understand that they could not make their country free by political murders : and they were right. Political liberty is gained as the result of a trial of strength, which may take either the form of a blood-less struggle including passive resistance and industrial competition, or that of an armed rebellion, which latter is out of the question in India. In either case, though the preparation may be made in secret, the fight must necessarily be open. The weak cannot win, the victory rests with the strong ; and righteousness adds strength to a cause. But, leaving aside the question of righteousness, what element of strength is there in assassination ? If you are strong, why not come out in the open and fight ? If you are not strong, you will be crushed. If you are not strong, bomb-throwing is not the way to develop or acquire strength. The very fact that from start to finish terrorism must have recourse to secrecy and craft, shows its inherent weakness. It is imaginable that bomb-throwing may be practised on a very extensive scale, on the scale of a regular war. But though imaginable, it has never yet been found practicable even in European countries, where, unlike India, *ahimsa* (abstention from killing) is not considered a supreme virtue. Even if it were practicable, it would be none the less wicked, as involving the reckless sacrifice of innocent lives. Moreover, terrorism even on an extensive scale has not secured freedom to any country. Besides, terrorism may be put down by the use of still greater brutal violence ; but when a nation takes its stand on righteousness nothing can crush it,—all the forces of the universe are on its side.

" HOW TO DARE AND DIE. "

But the bomb-thrower may reply, as in fact their alleged leader Barindrakumar Ghosh has to all intents and purposes done, " your sermon is lost labour. We did not mean or expect to liberate our country by killing a few Englishmen. We wanted to show people how to dare and die." We admit that they have shown great daring, strength of nerve and coolness, and have proved that they are not afraid of death ; their truthfulness (with the exception of one) and their unbroken resolve not to betray their supporters and purvayors of arms and ammunition, as they had evidently given their word not to do so, are also exemplary. Great, too, is their devotion to the country's cause, as they understood it. They recognise, too, that God's curse is upon their work. Would that there were in our country careers open to our young men where they could in legitimate and honourable ways show how to dare and die ! Would that all offices in the army and navy were open to indigenous worth ! For military virtues still exist even in Bengal. Would that the Government could understand that when the avenues of honorabl ambition are closed, the aspiring spirit is not crushed, but only led astray into wrong paths ! Would that these young men were not misled into crime ! Would that all our young men could serve the Motherland with equal devotion, daring, truthfulness, steadfast loyalty and skill, in the righteous path of the loving service of every son and daugter of India! What a great pity it is that such qualities of head and heart should not only not be available for the uplifting of India, but on the contrary should earn their possessors the condemnation of all right-thinking men. Both Government and the people are in the presence of a most difficult problem. To Government we have nothing to say. For, the bureaucracy may not understand that the highest courage and statesmanship consist in recognising one's mistake and retracing one's steps from the path of selfish tyranny, and that any further Russianization of the administration is sure to be confronted with a fiercer Russian response on the part of at least a section of the people. To our countrymen our humble advice is that they should steadily follow the path of righteousness in the midst of all temptations, trials and provocations. Let them not give way to panic. Let them not weakly believe that the mistake, however criminal and terrible, of a few young men, can obstruct their progress, if they are true to their country's cause. Let them do all that will make the nation physically, intellectually, and spiritually strong. Let them dare, but dare righteously, and die, if need be, in the country's cause. Let them not indulge in cowardly and insincere exaggeration in condemning the misguided young men under trial. It is not for us to judge. God will judge. It may be easy for arm-chair critics who are incapable of risking or sacrificing anything for humanity to inveigh in unmeasured terms against persons who have made a terrible mistake, but who, nevertheless, were prepared to lose all that men hold dear, for their race and country ;—persons whose fall has been great, because, perhaps, equally great was their capacity for rising to the heights of being : but, for ourselves, we pause awe-struck in the presence of this mysterious tragedy of mingled crime and stern devotion. Deplore as we do the death of the two European women, and strongly condemn the murderous deed, we scorn to associate ourselves, even in our condolence and condemnation, with those Anglo Indian editors and others who have not even a word of regret to express when brutal Anglo-Indians kill inoffensive and defenceless Indians or assault helpless Indian women. What ever feelings we express, we must do independently and in measured terms.

Ex. D 18.

INDIAN WORLD—May 1908, P. 472—76.

The Bomb Outrage.

The bomb has come at last. All through its long and anxious period of travail signs were not wanting to show that the cult of violence was daily gaining ground. Leaders of public movements looked with the greatest concern and anxiety upon the new developments, which were every day growing in the public life of the country. They felt that a tone of almost brutal anger, so far foreign to Indian politics, was fast showing itself among the ranks of the younger patriots. They found that the tight grip that they had over the public movements of the country was fast loosening and that they could no longer be sure of the almost mechanical discipline which guaranteed the peacefulness of all public movements in the past. The principles upon which they pinned their faith would no longer appeal to the people and they were ever and anon breaking loose from the strait lace of discipline and constitutional agitation. Leaders of the people who knew their temper and had the interest of the country at heart were not slow to appreciate the gravity of these developments and felt with the greatest concern that each step forward in the game of represssion that the Government took only fanned the smouldering anger of the people ; and it might any day burst into flame : Dr. Rash Behari Ghose with all the flower of his rhetoric and Mr. Gohkale with passionate earnestness appealed to the Government from their seats in the Supreme Legislative Council to stop the game yet and save the country from a great disaster.

The Government met these appeals with almost amused contempt. Mr. Baker on one occasion, referring to the apprehension that sedition might be driven underground by repression said that he had no such apprehension. Notoriety, he said, was as the breth of the nostrils of the sedition-monger and if only opportunities for that notoriety were taken away his occupation would be gone. So the Government sat tight in its settled conviction that the only thing to do was to govern "thoroughly;" neither the age and wisdom of Dr. Ghose nor the passionate anxiety of Mr. Gokhale caused them the least flutter. The Bomb only shows that, here as ever before in History, the representatives of the people were right and the Government was wrong.

The Psychology of the Bomb.

Laboured attempts have been made to father upon all and sundry the responsibility for the outrage at Mozaffarpore and it has been suggested that the leaders of public movements in India are in a way responsible for the outrage; for it was they who set the ball rolling by ventilating the political grievances of the people. If you go at that rate, you may have to land in the long run on the battle of Plasey or perhaps on the first advent of the English in India. That sort of argument will never do. You have to take account of the natural impulses of mankind and then look for the proximate causes. Taking Indians to be endowed with the common gifts and failings of all mankind you have to consider the natural effect of things. In the most disciplined societies there must be desperate characters, and because the utterance of an honest truth about a person might rouse such men to acts of violence, no canon of legal or moral responsibility will saddle the honest truth-speaker with the burden of the desperate act. In the Indian national party there has recently been an accession of a large number of men of all sorts. The aims and objects of the party as well as their actions have all been above board—They have only sought to see that right be done to India and the wants of the people be properly attended to, that steps be taken with a view to the ultimate self-Government in India. They got stolid indifference, studied establishment of neglect, open persecution and undeserved contempt and contumely for all their troubles. Of late their patience has been sorely tried. The leaders of the movement have kept their heads wonderfully cool, cool to such a degree as to have themselves been branded by their more ardent compatriots as infamous cowards. But the more excitable amongst the people have broken off from their leaders. They would not brook this insult upon the people at large but would retaliate. They became Sinn Feiners and acute disaffection was ringing in their breasts. But the government had made up its minds to be foolish and heaped on all sorts of acts on the heads of these people and displayed an attitude which would rouse up the temper of people in any country. It is a matter for wonder that some at least amongst these ardent patriots driven to desperation should be taken up with thoughts of taking revenge by means which, to the sober minded man, may seem to be ridiculously out of proporation to the end in view, but was in fact all that they had at their disposal. It was silly and unwise from all points of view whether you look upon peace and order as too sacred to be lightly touched or whether you look upon any revolution as justified at any time and by any means and for what ends soever, you cannot but look upon the bomb-outrage as indiscreet, injudicious and harmful to the last degree to any cause you wanted to be furthered. All the same, this outburst on the part of some warm young men cannot but be regarded as the natural results of all that preceeded it. It is certainly the result in the long run of constitutional agitation and the consequent waking up of the people to a sense of their right; but that perfectly legitimate function would never come to these excesses if the government had not by a series of wonderful acts sought to insult public opinion and its leaders and if it had not sedulously cultivated in the minds of these young men morbid unreasonable suspicion that all that government did or said was inspired by nefurious motives. It is a notorious maxim when it is done by a wrongful act or with a wrongful intention that provoking crime is only wrong.

The Lesson of the Bomb.

That these young men were inspired by a very lofty desire is quite clear. Their mischief lay in a certain intellectual aberation which led them to magnify the quality of oppression of the British Rule and to minimise the desirability and utility of peace and order. It is certainly true that revolutions are sometimes justified and more than once in history have secret secieties been the cradle of legitimate revolutions. In themselves than, their actions are not villainous or immoral. What makes them most to be deprecated is the failure to take a proper measure of things and in their convincing themselves that British Rule *per se* was such an intolerable nuisance that it has to be got rid of by immediate violence. It is the loss of a sense of proportion in things that has led these young men to hold the violent views that they have held and do the acts that they have done. The culpability of these acts lies in their running counter to the best interests of the people and the matter for congratulation is that their attempts have so signally failed. A larger amount of success would have made the situation disastrous if not impossible. The proper thing for us now therefore is to dispel the false notions that have got hold of the people of the magnitude of the evil of British Rule *per se* and is to develop a correct opinion about our political position with a view not to seek anybody's favour or good opinion but in the best interests of the people themselves. Indignation meetings therefore made to order or otherwise will not do. What we want is an honest endeavour at a proper education of public opinion.

The Government Attitude.

The Government would seem so far to have approached the question with the proper amount of calmness and discretion and I take this opportunity to congratulate it for the first time within a good number of years for having taken a correct position. The elements of disorder have to be put down with a strong hand but in such a manner as not to encourage the growth of a great deal more While on the one hand the arrest and trial of offenders must be made, the people should be conciliated by proper regard to their feelings. They must no more be given any excuse for being driven to desperation. For desperate spirits are not counted by those who actually do these acts, but there is always a large reserve of such men in every society. And if they take to the sort of thing to which their eyes have been opened by the bomb-makers—well, the Government cannot surely be upset, but if bombs become anything like the order of the day, the government would become impossible, and then adieu to the peace and order of British Rule in India. That would be precisely the result of the sort of policy the bloodhounds of the Anglo-Indian Press advocate, the policy, for instance, of the *Asian* and the *Englishman*.. My readers would be edified to hear that the first named paper has suggested that if the Government fail to behave properly (by killing all Bangalees outright, I suppose) the Anglo-Indian in India would be doing the proper thing to shoot down every stray Indian that he comes across without waste of any words. Were it not that I prize peace above a great many things else, I should like to see the game tried for a month.

Ex D 19

HINDU—May 9, P. 4, col. 1, 2.

It is, however, a deplorable fact that a deadly engine of human destruction has been successfully introduced into the hitherto calm and placid atmosphere of Indian national life and we fear that once an evil seed has been planted and borne fruit, it is not in human agency to uproot it from the soil entirely. We note that the Anglo-Indian Press, which is always on the prowl to bespatter with mud the people of the country, is frantic in its efforts to connect all and sundry with participation, express or implied, in the organization of the anarchists. Many of the Anglo-Indian organs seem or affect to think that a nest of anarchists in the country is a deadly menace to the safety and lives of the Europeans in the country, and that the rest of the population must stand security for them against the intended attacks of the gang. It is conveniently forgotten that an anarchist is a foe to be dreaded as occasion arises, as much by his Indian neighbour as a European resident.........No healthy and well-ordered commonwealth can lead to the springing up of so noxious an organization, whose hand may turn against any man, and against whom every man's hand will be turned. Instead, therefore, of turning its misguided and unholy wrath against the other sections of the Indian population, the Anglo-Indian Press would do well to probe to the bottom the causes which have led to this unhealthy phenomenon in the Indian body politic, and try to find out practical remedies. The manner, however, in which the question is dealt with by a section of the more prominent among the Anglo-Indian papers, shows that they have little regard for fairness, considerations of fair play or truth. They want to make use of the occasion to smite Indians of all grades, classes and views, and tosmother all attempts at political reformation in the country.........The *Pioneer* has also the sagacity to suggest a heroic remedy for outbreaks of this kind in the following form : " A wholesale arrest of the acknowledged terrorists in a city or distict, coupled with an intimation that on the next repetition of the offence ten of them would be shot for every life sacrificed, would soon put down the practice." It is counsels such as these that have guided the policy of the Government in the past towards the people of India, and if one sows the wind, one must expect to reap the whirlwind.

Ex. D 20.

HINDU—May 21, P. 4, Col. 3. (Quotes Dr. Rash Behari Ghose).

Dr. Rash Behari Ghose in his welcome address to the delegates of the Calcutta Congress in 1906 said : ' Do not misread the signs of the time ; do not be deluded by theories of racial inferiority ; the choice lies before you between a contented people proud to be the citizens of the greatest empire the world has ever seen and another Ireland in the East ; for I am uttering no idle threat.—I am not speaking at random for I know something of the present temper of the rising generation in Bengal,—perhaps another Russia. '

Ex. D 21.

HINDU—May 22, P. 6, Col. 2-3 (Quotes Nepal Chandra Roy's letter to Pioneer).

Sir,—In your issue of the 29th August 1906 refering to the assassination of certain persons at the Russian Premier Mr. Stolphine's villa you wrote :—

" The horror of such crimes is too great for words, and yet it has to be acknowledged, almost, that they are the only method of fighting left to a people who are at war with despotic rulers able to command great military force against which it is impossible for the unarmed populace to make a stand. When the Czar dissolved the Duma he destroyed all hope of reform being gained without violence. Against bombs his armies are powerless and for that reason be can not rule as his forefathers did by the sword. It becomes impossible for even the stoutest—hearted men to govern fairly or strongly when every moment of their lives is spent in terror of revolting death, and they grow into craven shirkers, and sustain themselves by a frenzy of retaliation which increases the conflagration they are striving to check. Such conditions cannot last." But now that such an outrage has been perpetrated in this country, and not the Russiaan autocrates but the British bureacrates are concerned, you just ask the

Government to " sustain themselves by a frenzy of retaliation " forgetting that it only " increases the conflagration, they are striving to check. " Evidently what in Russia you acknowledge to be " the only method of fighting left to a people who are at war with despotic rulers able to cammand great military forces against which it is impossible for the unarmed populace to make a stand, " you consider in India an " abominable and callous outrage, " " a ghastly and useless barbarity, " and in your " frenzy of retaliation " ask the Government to adopt repressive measures and even suggest resort to lynch laws. You possibly flatter yourself with the idea, as you have hitherto done, that human nature in India is not what it is in Europe, and therefore in India such measures will not " increase the conflagration " and that " such conditions may last, "

Ex. D 22.

INDIAN PATRIOT—May 4, P. 4, Col 2-3.

While the authorities may count upon the complete sympathy and support of the country at large in regard to the measures that they may take to suppress dangerous developments of this sort, the statesmen at the head of affairs have also to be reminded of the importance of insight and sympathy at this juncture. There is no use of blinking over the fact that thers is widespread discontent in the counry, discontent which is the result at once of unsatisfied aspirations and unredressed grievances. The aspirations are perhaps confined to the educated classes ; but the sense of grievance extends over a wider area. Mere suppression of the symptoms of discontent without applying the remedy at the root will have no permanent effect. It is in Bengal that repression on a large scale has been tried ; and it is in Bengal precisely that the most unexpected developments have occurred. With each successive repression there has been a new development..........We have had prosecutions for sedition, and severe punishment of boys and grown up men in connection with a variety of cases. We have also had prohibition of public meetings and speeches. None of these things have in the least improved the situation, but on the other hand have brought into existence a number of desparadoes bent on obtaining the crown of the anarchist and the assassin. The far-seeing statesman will surely read in all this a meaning which may not be very apparent to shallow minds. Nor are the signs of discontent confined to one porticular province. All over the country, for one reason or another, there have been similar indications. The question is whether it is easier to suppress them all by vigorous measures, or, while trying to suppress them, to take also such measures as may tend gradually to diminish the force of discontent, and thus to weaken the hands of those who are for not removing the grievances, but for revolutionising the entire system of order and peace.

Ex. D 23.

INDIAN PATRIOT—May 5, P. 2, Col. 2.

Says that national movement is democratic and derives its strength from the character of an alien Bureaucracy.

Ex. D 24.

INDIAN PATRIOT—May 6, P. 4, Col. 2.

We do not doubt for a moment that, if the principle of non-interference were upheld, if both parties agreed that India should be above party, the only certain result would be that India would remain separte in principles and methods of Government; and England, encouraged to acquiesce in injustice and unrighteousness, would lose her sense of both righteousness and justice. She would become incapable of acting towards her dependency in accordance with her traditions and her instincts, and in course of time she would lose her title as a righteous and freedom-loving nation, and finally she would begin to cherish at home those very principles and methods which she permits abroad. Despotism is always demoralising to those who practise it; it must be as much demoralising to an organised body as it is to a nation. The English nation can no more escape the demoralisation than an English official. The bureaucracy in India has been reared in the atmosphere of despotism, and the only hindrance to its continuous development is the change of the Viceroy every five years and the notice that is taken of official acts in Parliament. But for the constant fear of English public opinion, we should have had the worst form of despotism. It is the force of English public opinion that enforces adherence to forms of law, and to the general principles of freedom and justice. When Lord Curzon asked the English people to "trust the man on the spot," he did not surely mean that the man on the spot should be left to modify the principles and traditions of British rule just as he likes. No servant of the Crown has the right to retard or subvert those principles and traditions which are the distinguishing features of British rule. It is possible and necessary to leave certain latitude to authorities on the spot. But it is not this kind of latitude alone that the bureaucracy wants. It will be satisfied with nothing less than complete power to pervert the English principles of freedom and justice to an oriental polity which they have come to prefer.

Ex. D 25.

INDIAN PATRIOT—May 14, P. 2, Col. 1-3.

Repression will kindle the flame of animosity and hatred rather than soothe the feelings.

Ex. D 26.

INDIAN PATRIOT—May 15, P. 4, col. 1, 2.

Their chief concern is to see the country governed in the way they like; and it is not always possible to have the country so governed when there is the persistent voice of criticism both from the Indian Press and the platform. The Anglo-Indian Press is perfectly satisfied with the existing administrative arrangements; and it does not want any change to be effected except with regard to the freedom which is now allowed to the people, while Indians attach very high value to the only means they have of neutralising the evil of autocracy. Those who look a little beneath the surface will easily see the meaning of these two different and mutually antagonistic attitudes. The meaning, so far as the Anglo-Indian is concerned, we have indicated ; and we will explain it as bearing on the attitude of the Indians. The latter is not satisfied with the administration as it exists ; he wants changes to be introduced suited to his needs and conditions. And he knows that agitation is the essence of progressive reform under the British Government. No great reform has anywhere been effected within the British Empire except with the help of agitation carried on persistently for a long period ; and the press and the platform constitute the main machinery of agitation. They are at once a safeguard against injustice and oppression, and the means of influencing opinion in favour of reform and progress. Most Indians think that the Government in India must be reformed according to the changing needs of the times, and that it is only when it is reformed according to the enlightened sense and the intelligent desire of the people that it will be productive of the best benefit. The one thing to be ever borne in mind is that the average Britisher never believes in grievances unless there is something to evidence its existence. If there is no agitation, he takes it that the people accept everything that is proposed for them. Measure after measure has been passed by the Government on this assumption regardless of protests made by the representatives of the people. The necessity for deferring to public opinion being admitted as a matter of public policy, the next step is to evade doing so by denying the existence of any opinion opposed to a particular course. When there is no criticism and no agitation, the inference is very satisfactory ; but when there is agitation and noise, then the idea is that it is all the work of mischief-makers. There is a cetain impossibility in reconciling honesty with hypocrisy ; and it is this impossibility that necessitates so much inconsistency in the profession of even responsible men. The people have been long taught that unless they make the masses move with them, they would not be seriously listened to, bnt when the masses are moved, those who move them are charged with creating "disaffection." To the people at large, the freedom of speech and the freedom of the press are invaluable boons, in return for which they would give up many other things. They know that without such freedom it is impossible to keep an alien bureaucracy straight. Imagine the result if the District official is supported by the local Government, the local Government by the government of India, and both by the Secretary of state, in the honest belief, no doubt, that all of them are right, and the people, injured or affected have not even the means of making a noise, and we can easily imagine the result. What can be more conducive to the development of the worst form of despotic government in India ? What can be better calculated to enslave a people than a system of autocratic Government free from constitutional restraints of all kinds, and absolutely protected against exposure and criticism ?

Ex. D 27.

MADRAS STANDARD—May 4, P. 4, Col. 3.

We hope that the authorities in Bengal will keep their heads cool and will not "govern in anger." But unhappy Bengal must also come in for sympathy. For over two years it has known no rest, has had no freedom from the worries consequent on the feeling against the partition. We can well imagine that what has now been brought to light has deepened the confusion. In the face of all that has happened it is not improbable that measures for the improvement of the Province will not for a time at any rate be vigorously prosecuted. In the state of panic in which it finds itself and with the Anglo-Indian press inciting the authorities to the sternest repressive action, it is likely that the energies of the Government will be devoted to the adoption of the severest measures in the name of peace and order. The authors of the disorder are comparatively few in number. But their delinquency and dark deeds are likely to bring troubles innumerable to the entire population whose loyalty and law-abiding nature are proverbial. What Bengal wants is rest. How is rest to come from a situation so grave is the question that will be asked. If, however, the Bengal Government and the Government of India see through the whole affair and declare that the law-breakers are a small minority for whom no sympathy whatever is felt and that if the law is left to take its own course without having recourse to any stringent executive or legislative action, the excitement will abate itself.

Ex. D 28.

MADRAS STANDARD—May 6, P. 4, Col. 2.

If honesty in journalism is not a lost virtue the *Times* should not forget at this moment Lord Curzon, the real author of all the present unrest in India. Bengal was a peaceful Province three or four years ago. Since the partition which was effected in the teeth of the opposition of the people it has become a seething mass of discontent. But all the time that Lord Curzon was in India the *Times* and the Anglo-Indian press in general have been inciting and encouraging him on in his career of folly. His Lordship is now at home posing as a great authority on Indian affairs. He is now a leader of his party hoping, apparently, to become Prime Minister of England. But in India the people are reaping the fruit of his regime, and Lords Morley and Minto have had no rest since they came into their respective office. In India itself the Anglo-Indian press, with a few exceptions, have begun a campaign of vilification as if the people of India had anything to do with the revolutionaries in Bengal. Bnt we sincerely hope that better counsel will prevail. Let the law-breakers be dealt with according to law. But no action should be taken the effect of which will be to retard progress and injure permanantly the interests of the people at large.

Ex. D 29.

PUNJABEE—May 9, P. 3, Col. 1.

It is a suggestive commentary on the influences of European methods in India tc find that it should have converted a cerain section of the flower of the Indian population into sycophants or anarchists—mercenary agents of an alien Government, or the ferocious harbingers of such deadly ideas as lead to dastardly deeds like the one lately committed at Muzaffarpore. May we ask the Brstish statesmen to ponder, if there is anything inherent in their system of Government in India which crushes the spirit of manliness and encourages instead thereof either a spirit of abject dependence or one of cowardliness? Why should there be a sense of helplessness which drives people to these undesirable extremes, either on the side of the Government or against it? It is just these two types which are at present attracting attention in India, we mean the sycophant or the bomb-thrower. There are highly educated men in the ranks of both—men who could be the pride of their country and ornaments of their society if they could command a free scope for the proper employment of those talents with which nature has gifted them and education has fitted them. Surely there must be something abnormal and unnatural in the social conditions of India under which men of rare parts and good social environments should either take to mercenary sycophancy or blood-thirsty anarchism.

Ex. D 30.

TRIBUNE—May 19, P. 4, Col. 1, 2.

But at the same time we are not very much impressed with the theory that their mental aberrations have been due to the unbridled license of the Bengalee vernacular press. We maintain our view that in this matter any legislation for gagging the press may perhaps prove even a worse remedy than the disease and that in such matter the thing needful can be best done by the authorities and the leaders of the people co-operating towards the right solution. But we must point out that it will not do to lay hold merely at one end of the wedge. It is no use pouring your vials of wrath upon disreputable sheets in the vernacular press while letting the Anglo-Indian fire-eaters like the *Asian* scot free. It may be said that the latter sheet has not prompted any person to commit any violence. That may be so but still it has to be admitted that the red-hot extremist paper is the natural counter-part of the fire-eating Anglo-Indian Journal from which it derives its cue. And if any measure is taken against the one, it must fairly and squarely apply against the other, although for ourselves, we are of opinion that this is a matter where the leaders of the public in both communities should co-operate with the Government in putting a stop to this fire-eating business.

Ex. D 31.

PATRIKA—May 5, P. 6, Col. 1, 2.

The Anglo-Indian papers, we are surprised to find, are acting the part of an enemy and not a friend. By their inflamatory and malignant writing they are trying to poison the minds of the Government against the people of the country. For instance, the "Statesman" which owes its birth and growth to Indian money and Indian patronage, and daily eats Indian salt, thus seeks to connect the Mozufferpur outrage with Indian Nationalism :—"The terrible outrage perpetrated at Mozufferpur and the revelation of a wide-spread criminal conspiracy to which it has led, are indications only too plain that Indian Nationalism has entered upon a new and portentous phase, the ultimate significance of which it is impossible at present to guage. Since the partition of Bengal, the crowning folly of Lord Curzon's regime, a different spirit has manifested itself, whose weapons are apparently to be bombs and dynamite." The above is a gross distortion of facts, and its sole object is to rouse the worst passions of

Government against the rising national feeling of the Indians. It is a big lie to say that bombs and dynamite are the weapons of those who have agitated and are yet agitating—against the partition measure. If tens and hundreds of thousands of anti-partitionists had turned Fenians and resorted to infernal machines, the country would have presented quite a different aspect. As every body knows, what they did when Bengal was partitioned was simply to hold thousands of public meetings and adopt resolutions praying for justice. But their prayer was treated with contempt. It was then that they sought to give up begging and rely on their own resources, as far as that was possible, in order to improve their economic and domestic condition. They would not have abandoned the mendicant policy if the rulers had shown them some consideration ; but they trampled the sentiments and views of a whole nation under foot, and left the latter no alternative but to preach and practise, to some extent, self-reliance as regards economic and domestic matters.......We trust, responsible rulers will not be influenced by such writings. In the cause of peace and order, they must, of course, take all necessary measures, but they will serve no useful purpose by giving play to their tiger qualities, because of the foul acts of some irresponsible Indian youths. The "Statesman" very pertinently characteries the partition of Bengal as "the crowning folly of Lord Curzon's regime." There is no doubt that it is measures like the Partition of Bengal and severities which rendered Mr. Kingford's criminal administration in Calcutta so conspicuous, which unhinge the minds of a certain class of people and impel them to commit dreadful things. One of the best means to prevent such dastardly deeds is, therefore, for the Government and its officers to avoid measures and acts which outrage public opinion and tend to give birth to fanaticism.

Ex. D 32.

PATRIKA—May 6, P. 5, Col. 1, 2.

The " Hindoo Patriot, " the organ of the British Indian Association, makes some excellent suggestions in connection with this affair. Our contemporary says :—

" But coolly discussed, the recent events would point to the urgency of finding out the root-causes of the turbulent spirit and to the advisability of removing them without delay. To regret or condemn, or to give way to passion and angry feelings is somewhat conventional. The pratical and statesman-like course is to tackle the incidents in the right spirit and clear up the misunderstandings and misgivings on which the anarchist ideas are feeding. The proper remedy for the nihilist spirit is a popular form of Government—both being often assumed to be foreign to the genius of the people of this country—for which the demand is strong and widespread. While it is necessary that the perpetrators of the outrage should be exemplarily dealt with, according to the law, it is hoped that the reforming hand will not be arrested, but will courageously complete what it has taken up and move faster. " With every deference to the " Empire ", which does not like the above sentences, we think the " Hindoo Patriot " has done a public service, by bringing this aspect of the situation prominently to the notice of the Government while yet the outrage is quite fresh in the minds of all. For, the authorities may forget all about it as soon as the culprit has been punished. The case has certainly been very clearly put by the "Hindoo Patriot". Condemn the dastardly deed as indignantly as you can; mete out condign punishment to the culprit according to law; but the first duty of Government is to finger the real plague-spot and remove it with a strong hand. It is now admitted on all hands, official and non-official, that the prevaling discountent in the country owes its origin to the partition of Bengal and some other measures of the Curzon Government. Mr. Morley, or rather Lord Morley of Blackburn, instead of removing it, has fostered its growth by introducing or sanctioning other repressive measures. The Government of Sir Andrew Fraser again not only regarded with indifference, the draconian severity which marked the administration of criminal justice by Mr. Kingsford, but increased his pay, though he had been shocking the susceptibilities of humanity—nay, of Mr. Morley himself—by awarding brutal punishment to a number of boys belonging to respectable families, merely on political grounds. Where is the wonder that by brooding upon these matters and reading Nihilist literature, some young men would get their mind so unhinged as to be fired with the ambition of imitating the devilish examples of their Nihilist "Gurus" in Europe? The best policy of Government is to govern the country in such a way as not to give any opportunity to Indian youths to convert themselves into fanatics and commit blood-curdling acts.

Ex. D 33.

PATRIKA—May 7, P. 5, Col 1.

By "respectable people" we mean those who have a stake in the country. These men unless their minds have been thoroughly unhinged, can have nothing to do with a campaign of destruction which is bound to be as disastrous to themselves as to those against whom the same may be directed. If disorder and lawlessness are established in the country by a body of anarchists, who will suffer more than these very respectable people? It is also evident that, in order to make bombs and carry on missionary work large funds are not requir ed. A few thousand rupees would be sufficient to purchase a large number of revolvers and manufacture a good many bombs. The money-question, on which the Chowringhi paper builds its theory, has thus no bearing on the Indian anarchist movement.

Ex. D 34.

BENGALEE—June 13, P. 8, Col. 1.

Sir Harvey Adamson was particularly clear and explicit in his pronouncement. "We have" said he, "striking examples of how they (newspapers of the type of the *Yugantar*) "have converted the timid Bangali into the fanatical *ghazi* and they are not to be ignored. The difference between the East and the West in this respect is the difference between dropping a lighted match on stone floor and dropping it in a powder magazine." It is recognized on all hands that the character of the Bengalee has undergone a great change. Even Sir Charles Elliott, wedded to the old world views, is constrained to admit that there must be a reconstruction of English ideas with regard to the submissiveness of the Bengalee. What then has brought about this strange transformation? The inflammatory writings of a few vernacular newspapers have not converted the timid Bengali into the fanatical Ghazi. The inflammatory writings (which we strongly condemn) are the product of the self-same political conditions which have created the Bengalee Ghazis. If these political conditions did not exist, those writings would not have appeared; and if they did, nobody would have paid the smallest attention to them and no press law would have been necessary. For more than half the life-time of a generation, a reactionary policy has been in the ascendant; public grievance upon grievance has been piled; the voice of public opinion has been treated with open contumely; the faith of the people in constitutional agitation has been subjected to the severest strain, and when at last the expected hour of relief came by the installation of a Liberal Government in power, salvation was not found. Have we not here a condition of things calculated profoundly to stir the popular mind and drive the most excitable to desperate and foolish measures, to violent writings and to deeds still more violent and foolish? This is the legitimate explanation of the change in that aspect of the national character which we are now considering. Do not lay the responsibility upon the wrong shoulders.

Ex. D 35.

BENGALEE—May 20, P. 5, Col. 1, 2, 3.

Now it is a curious fact that the inflammatory writings of certain Indian periodicals have received condign punishment, whereas certain Anglo-Indian papers, despite their inflammatory tone at a crisis of the nation's affairs have escaped unpunished. To our mind there are two ways of stirring up sedition, one by preaching violence to the people, another by preaching violence against the people. If it be true, as we are so often told, that certain Indian journals are determined to embitter race against race, it is certainly time for Englishmen to consider if there be nothing in their own actions and in the utterances of certain of their press, calculated to cause a permanent estrangement between race and race. If there be anti-racial feelings among the Indians, they have learnt them from people who consider themselves their betters. All the schemes of the Government will come to nothing if the supercillious and insolent tone adopted by certain Englishmen towards Indians is allowed to go unpunished. All its measures of reform will be worthless, unless it can control the actions and utterances of those who, coming from the same race as itself, do and say things utterly repugnant to the spirit of the race. It is time for the Government, if we are to have any real measure of peace, prosperity or reform. any real trust between the people of India and its governors, to punish not only the delinquencies of Indians, but also the delinquencies of Anglo-Indians and Anglo-Indian journals which have done much to bring about the present state of affairs.

Ex. D 36.

PATRIKA—May 31, P. 3, Col. 2, 4.

Attacks bureaucracy and says that they are all Kings in India.

Ex. D 37.

INDIAN SPECTATOR—May 9, P. 361, 362.

And what shall we say about the innocent victims of the diabolical crime at Muzaffarpur ? We always deprecate the habit of importing into a discussion or denunciation of such crimes any consideration which may savour of racial animus. It is as unreasonable to call upon the whole population of India to put on sackcloth and ashes for the crimes of a few dynamiters in Bengal, as it is to ask the whole Anglo-Indian community to expiate for the indifference of a European soldier for the life of a cooly, or the assault upon an Indian lady by a white rascal. But there is a difference between crimes which are the offspring of pure selfishness, and crimes which are professedly undertaken in the interests of a larger or smaller class of a beneficiaries. The dynamiters of Bengal imagine that they are doing a service to their country, and hence it may, not unreasonably, be expected by some that the intended, but unwilling, beneficiaries of the crimes would do more than express their profound sympathy for the victims of the outrage. The funeral of the two ladies is said to have been attended by Natives as well as Europeans. The reason, perhaps, was not only that Mr. Kennedy is popular with the Native community of the place, but also that that community wished to disclaim all sympathy with the excesses of the criminals. Nothing like a movement seems to be on foot as yet to condemn the conspiracy detected by the police. Some people seem to have suspected that bombs were on their way to Poona and to Tuticorin simultaneously with their despatch to Muzaffarpur. Heaven be praised if the friendly gifts of the Bengali manufacturers, to be used in the up-to-date political Kindergarten, have not reached their destination, or have deteriorated during the journey.........We must be slow, on such an occasion, to accept the single version of this or that party. The reports alleged to have been made by the Police, and the allegations of certain excited Anglo-Indian writers, need to be carefully sifted. The authorities and the Courts will doubtless do this. But we feel constrained to say, at the very threshold of the inquiry, that the theory of a widespread conspiracy, shared in by well known and respectable citizens, seems untenable. Nor can we get over the fear that the innocent many will suffer with the guilty few, if the local Police are allowed to have their own way in the investigations that must follow. The situation is too serious to need the importation of official prejudice or racial passion. How to improve it is the question of prime importance for the statesman. As hinted above, this can be best done by the authorities and the natural leaders of the province co-operating towards the right solution. If an untoward development of the situation embarrasses the Government, it will also prove disastrous to the permanent interests of the community itself. The Bengalis need settling down—to become true to themselves and their traditions of love of peace and reverence for authority. Whoever seduces them from loyalty to these traditions is the worst enemy, not only of the people of Bengal, but of the whole country. The love of independence is innate in mankind, and the literature of the West and political agitation within the country are only influences which favour the development of that aspiration into seditious conspiracies. The reported discovery of Russian literature with the Calcutta seditionists was scarcely expected. It cannot be suggested that Russian spies have been at work on the north-west frontier and in

Bengal; the importation of Russian literature must be attributed to the scientific methods which educated men have been taught to apply to all their undertakings.

Ex. D 38.

INDIAN SPECTATOR—May 16, P. 381, Col. 1-2.—Playfully deals with the situation.

The chemistry of the weapons with which these deluded "saviours of the country" are fighting their "battles" is itself some proof of imitation; but the imitation is not all of the West. Portions of the confessions cannot fail to convince those who have read Bakim Chunder Chatterji's *Anandamatha* that, while the physical weapons are borrowed from the last, the spirit comes from the graves of the Sanyansi rebels whose war-cry "Bande Mataram" plays such a prominent part in modern politics. The cry itself is innocent, and Sir Andrew Fraser once responded to it in the street by respectfully taking off his hat. But the song expresses a faith in the possibility of the millions of doughty arms devoted to the service of the Motherland driving out foreign rulers. The song was directed against Muhammadans by the Sanyasis of old; it must be suggestive of a different class of foreigners to the young political Sanyasis of to-day.

Ex. D 39.

GUJRATHI—May 17, P. 707, Col. 1, 2, 3; P. 705, Col. 2, 3; P. 706, Col. 1, 2, 3.

Investigates into the causes of unrest and holds Government responsible for the same.

Ex. D 40.

GUJRATHI—May 31, P. 779, Col. 1; P. 777, Col. 1. 2; P. 778, Col. 1, 2, 3.

Charges Government and Anglo-Indian Papers with sowing seeds of discontent.

Ex. D 41.

GUJRATHI—June 14, P. 858, Col. 2.

A humourous skit on God Bomb. Says :—'Bomb will make his name permanent if he will bring in political reforms.'

Ex. D 42.

INDU PRAKASH—May 5, p. 7, Col. 2-3. Says that Terrorist movements are the product of particular kinds of rule.

अनार्किस्ट लोकांच्या भयंकर उपायांचा अवलंब करण्यास रशिया, पोलंडसारख्या देशांतलेच लोक तयार होतात. इंग्लंडसारख्या सुव्यवस्थित राज्यव्यवस्था असलेल्या देशांत अनार्किझमूचें बीं सहसा रुजूं शकत नाहीं. सोशालिझमूसारख्या चळवळीही जर्मनीसारख्या लष्करी बाण्याच्या व विशेषशी लोकसत्ता नसलेल्या देशांतच बळावतात. अर्थात् परिस्थिति व असल्या चळवळी यांचा बराच निकट संबंध असल्याचें इतर देशांतल्या उदाहरणावरून सिद्ध होतें.

Ex. D 43.

INDU PRAKASH—May 8, P. 2, Col. 5, 6.

It is just at this moment, however, that statesmanship and wise counsels ought to prevail with our Anglo-Indian friends. If they also lose their head and say and write sensationally on the basis, merely of wild speculations and unproved datas, and thereby hurt the minds of all loyal citizens, the matter will without doing any good cause pain and irritation fraught in itself with no small danger. As instances in point, we may refer to the hint dropped by one paper about the adoption of lynch law, and the wholesale abuse of Indians in general, indulged in by another. Some of these are now trying to connect these untoward incidents with the writings in the newly started journals of Calcutta, and advocate *pucca bandobast* about them. Now really speaking this is a mistaken or at least a very partial view. Anarchism or Nihilism is never the direct result of writings or speeches of the kind referred to. Both are manifestations of different results produced by one cause. A spark at one place dies out, at another produces a little fire and smoke and at another an explosion. To say that the Bomb outrages are the outcome of the writings in these papers is to say that the horse trots onward because it has a cart behind. I am inclined to connect these outrages not so much with the articles in question, as with the general discontent caused by repressive Government measures and more specially with the campaign of police high-handedness, and the indiscriminate and rankerous persistency with which the Bengal Press was harassed last year.

Ex. D 44.

DNYAN PRAKASH.—May 19, p. 2, Col. 6. Says merere-pression will not kill the terrorist movement or the general unrest.

अपराध्यांना कडक शासन खुशाल करा, त्याबद्दल कोणी दोष देणार नाहीं; परंतु अपराध्यांस शिक्षा केली ह्मणजे अस्वस्थताही लयास जाईल, असा समज करून घेतल्यास तो चुकीचा ठरेल. लोकांच्या तीव्र असंतोषाचीं कारणें दूर झालीं ह्मणजे तीं पुन्हां पेट घेण्याची भीति रहाणार नाहीं. मुद्रणस्वातंत्र्यावर घाव घालून पत्रें चिरडून टाकलीं व भाषणस्वातंत्र्य संपुष्टांत आणून लोकांचीं तोंडें बंद केलीं ह्मणजे क्रांतिकारक चळवळीचें उच्चाटण होईल, व लोकांतील अस्वस्थता मोडेल अशी सल्ला अँग्लो-इंडियन पत्रें सरकारास देत आहेत. परंतु असल्या उपायांनीं असंतोष नाहींसा होईल अशी कल्पना करणें चुकीचें आहे.

Ex. D 45

DNYAN PRAKASH.—May 26, p. 2, col. 5. Says outrages are the venomous fruit of the poison-tree planted by Lord Curzon.

परंतु ज्या कारणांमुळें ही प्रक्षुब्ध स्थिति अस्तित्वांत आली आहे, व जिच्या योगानें अगदी तरुण व होतकरू लोक जिवावर उदार होऊन साहसी कृत्यें करूं लागले आहेत त्यांचा शांतपणें विचार करून तीं कारणें निर्मूल करण्याचा सरकाराकडून प्रयत्न होईल अशी आह्मांस आशा आहे, लोकमताचा अव्हेर करून बंगालच्या फाळणीनें विषवृक्षबीजारोपण करण्यांत आलें. फुल्लर व कर्झनसाहेबांच्या उद्दाम वर्तनानें हा वृक्ष

जोमांत येऊन त्यांचीं जहर फळें बंगाल्यांत दिसूं लागलीं आहेत. या विषवृक्षाचा निर्मूल उच्छेद करणें हाच एक हल्लींच्या संकटांत खात्रीचा उपाय आम्हांस वाटत आहे. जुलमी शासनपद्धतीमुळें लोकांत संताप उत्पन्न होतो; हा संताप तोंडावाटें बाहेर पडतो. जुलुमाचा अतिरेक झाला ह्मणजे दारूण कृत्यें करण्याची मनुष्याची प्रवृत्ति होते. खरी मुत्सद्देगिरी ज्या कारणांनीं प्रजेंत असंतोष वाढतो तीं नाहींशीं करण्यांत आहे, हें सरकारानें ध्यानांत ठेविलें पाहिजे.

Ex. D 46.

DNYAN PRAKASH.--May 30, p. 2, col. 3, 4, 5. Says, that failure of constitutional agitation only produces the terrorist–movement.

परंतु ज्यांचीं मनें पूर्वग्रहानें दूषित झालीं आहेत, हिंदुस्थानांतील अनियंत्रित सत्तेच्या वातावरणाच्या संपर्कामुळें ज्यांचे उन्नत विचार विकृत झाले आहेत, किंवा स्वभावतःच ज्यांचीं मनें वक्र आहेत, अशा लोकांस सरळ गोष्टीही वांकड्या भासाव्या, व शुद्ध विचारांतही कांहीं काळेंबेरें असल्याचा संशय त्यांच्या मनांत डाचूं लागावा हें त्यांच्या स्वभावास, शीलास व ब्रीदास अनुरूप असेंच आहे. राज्यकर्त्यांकडून हिंदी लोकमताचा उपमर्द व मनोवृत्तींचा अपमान होतो, ह्या जाणीवेमुळें उत्पन्न झालेल्या असंतोषानें व निराशेनें अदूरदर्शी हिंदी लोकांची अराजक पंथाकडे प्रवृत्ति झाली आहे, ही गोष्ट ॲंग्लो इंडियनांस लपवून ठेवावयाची आहे व ह्मणूनच हिंदुस्थानांतील असंतोषाचें निदान ठरविणारे निस्पृह व स्पष्टवक्ते चिकित्सक ॲंग्लो-इंडियनांच्या डोळ्यांत सलतात. 'कॉन्स्टिट्यूशनल' चळवळ कितीही केली, तरी तिजपासून कांहीं फलप्राप्ति होत नाहीं, व सरकार आपलें ह्मणणें ऐकत नाहीं, अशी मनाची पक्की खात्री झाल्याखेरीज सत्ताविध्वंसक मताचा उद्भवच होऊं शकत नाहीं.' असें आम्हीं दोन आठवड्यांपूर्वीं एका अग्रलेखांत ह्मटलें होतें.

Ex. D 47.

DNYAN PRAKASH—June 7, p. 2, col. 3, 4, 5.

अधिकाऱ्यांच्या अनियंत्रित सत्तेला आळा घालण्यास वर्तमानपत्रांतील टीका हेंच एक अप्रत्यक्ष साधन लोकांच्या हातीं आहे; आणि लोकांतील अस्वस्थता व असंतोष आंतल्या आंत धुमसत रहात नाहीं, ह्याचें कारण हा असंतोष बाहेर पडण्यास लेखनस्वातंत्र्यामुळें वाव मिळत आहे हें होय, ही गोष्ट व्हाइसरायसांहेबांनीं लक्षांत घ्यावयास पाहिजे. हल्लींच्या अस्वस्थतेची जबाबदारी सर्वस्वी देशी पत्रांच्या माथीं मारून त्यांच्या मुसक्या आवळून टाकल्या कीं, तेवढ्यानें असंतोष दूर होईल अशी कल्पना करणें चुकीचें आहे. अलीकडे कित्येक महिने सरकारानें दाबदडपीचें धोरण अंगिकारिलें आहे. हद्दपाऱ्या, वर्तमानपत्रांवरील खटले, सभाबंदीचा कायदा, असे अनेक उपाय योजून असंतोष दाबून टाकण्याचा सरकारानें प्रयत्न केला, परंतु त्यापासून इष्ट हेतु सिद्धीस गेला नाहीं. लोकांतील असंतोषाचें मूळ काय आहे, त्यांच्यावर निराशेनें पगडा कां बसविला आहे, ह्याचा बारकाईनें व शांतपणानें विचार करणें, हें अधिकाऱ्याचें कर्तव्य आहे; परंतु त्या दिशेनें असंतोष नाहींसा करण्याचा प्रयत्न न होतां तो दडपून टाकण्याचीं साधनें निर्माण करण्यांत येत आहेत. मूळ रोगावर औषधच जर पोंचलें नाहीं, तर नुसत्या दाबदडपीनें तो नाहींसा कसा व्हावा?

Ex. D 48.

CHIKITSAK—May 27. p. 3, col. 3. Says, that responsible leaders of the people warned Government that the young generation was getting out of hand : but Government did not heed the warning.

हिंदी प्रजेच्या मनःक्षोभाचीं कारणें यांहून अगदीं भिन्न आहेत. कायदेशीर राजकीय चळवळीस यावें तसें व नितकें यश न आल्यामुळें उत्साही तरुणांची निराशा विकोपास जाईल, व त्याजकडून प्रस्तुतच्या सारखे अत्याचार घडून येतील अशी पूर्व सूचना जबाबदार लोकधुरीणांनीं सरकारास कधींच दिली होती. आपलें हें भविष्य खरें झालें म्हणून या मंडळीस सखेद आनंद वाटेलच. पण हातीं धरलेल्या राजकीय प्रगतीच्या धोरणास यामुळें धोका बसेल, या भीतीनें त्यांचीं मनें अस्वस्थ झालीं आहेत.

Ex. D 48A.

CHIKITSAK.—May 13, p. 2, Col. 1, 2. Calls Anglo-Indian papers the pet-dogs of Government.

लोकमतास पायांखालीं तुडवून सुलतानी अमलाचा जयजयकार करण्याचा अघोर प्रयत्न जर लॉर्ड कर्झनसाहेबांनीं केला नसता आणि जन्मभर लोकपक्षीय, उदार व उदात्त तत्त्वें जोरानें, कळकळीनें व निर्भीडपणें प्रतिपादणारे मि. (नव्हे, चुकलों–लॉर्ड) मोर्ले लाटसाहेबांचे कट्टे पुरस्कर्ते बनले नसते, तर कदाचित बंगाली लोक हल्लींच्या बौद्धिक व नैतिक स्थितीस पोहोंचण्यास कित्येक वर्षें लोटलीं असतीं. मुजफरपूरच्या घोर कृत्यानें व त्या निमित्तानें उघडकीस आलेल्या एकंदर गोष्टींनीं सरकाराचीं, तशींच लोकांचीं, मनें निरनिराळ्या मनोविकारांनीं व विचारांनीं क्षुब्ध होऊन राहिलीं आहेत. सरकारचे लाडके कुत्रे हिंदी लोकांवर पुनः स्वैरपणें भुंकून आपल्या धन्यास राक्षसी मसलती देत आहेत.

Ex. D 48B.

CHIKITSAKA—May 20, p. 2, col. 1. Attacks Anglo-Indian press as idiotic relations on the wife's side (शालक) of Government, who are cruel, deceitful, silly, vain, worthless, and hiding behind the tail of Imperial lion.

समर्थांचा म्याडपणा.

आंग्लोइंडियन वृत्तपत्रकारांच्या मानसिक अवस्थेचें स्थूलमानानेंही परीक्षण केल्यास मृच्छकटिक नाटकांतील शकाराच्या स्वभावरचनेची आठवण होते. ब्रिटिश साम्राज्यसिंहाचे हे शालक जसे म्याड, तसेच क्रूर, जसे धूर्त तसेच भोळसट, जसे गर्विष्ट तसेच गचाळ होत, असें आजवरच्या त्यांच्या चरित्रक्रमावरून सिद्ध झालें आहे. मेहुण्याच्या जीवावर हवी तीं दुष्ट कृत्यें करण्यास शकारास ज्याप्रमाणें एक प्रकारचा उपजत हक्क होता, त्याप्रमाणें या साम्राज्यशालकांचीही समजूत दिसते. साम्राज्यसिंहांच्या शेपटीच्या आड राहून सुरक्षितपणें प्रतिपक्षांवर भुंकण्यास व प्रसंग साधून त्यांचीं चौंवा घेण्यास हीं समर्थांचीं श्वानें सदा तयार असतात.

Ex. D 49.

INDIA—May 8, P. 231, Col. 2; p. 232, Col. 1. 2; p. 533, Col. 1.

Expresses English opinion on the situation (Vide Ex. D. 56).

Ex. D 50

INDIA—May 15, 1908 p. 243.

THE INDIAN PORTENT (FEOM THE "NATION.")

Our indifference to the normal life of the greatest dependency in the world is an old scandal, but it will be widely disturbed by the news of the outbreak of a form of political violence hitherto almost unknow to it. From our neglect of India sprang the Swadeshi movement; for it was hoped that a boycott on English goods might make our people listen to the grievance of Bengal. We suppose that the party which has meditated these recent deeds of extreme and savage outrage was partly influenced by the same motives. If they could wreck the train of a fairly popular Lieutenant Governor of Bengal, as was attempted last November, or assasinate a magistrate who had made himself notorious by flogging political offenders, as was attempted a week ago, then, they thought, the people of our country might at last be compelled to realise the character of the crisis in India's history. Much of our news from Calcutta is untrustworthy, and confessions merely extorted by native police from Indian prisoners awaiting trial ought not to be admitted as evidence. But it seems probable that a conspiracy for violent and isolated outrages, similar to the methods of the Russian terrorists, existed in the capital.

Outbreaks of political violence may arise from one cause or another. But they certainly do occur under a system of political repression such as we have adopted in various parts of India since the "chapel bell" motive, the desire to attract attention to grievances, when legitimate means fail. But we also, think, that in the case of India, they are the answer to the hard doctrine which Lord Morley disavowed a year ago, that "we won India by the sword and must keep it by the sword." Neither clause in that doctrine is true, but it is repeated as a form of ritual by nearly every English newspaper in India, and many newspapers and other authorities at home. The idea of violence is thus promulgated throughout the Indian Empire, by a Press which incorrectly represents the best aspects and tendencies of British rule. Indians are falsely taught by many of our representatives to believe that there is no relation between us and them, but the military advantage of ruler over ruled. For generations it has been the fashion for Anglo-Indians to laugh at the submissive spirit in native India. If Indians are found to meet the taunt of cowardice with cruel outrage, we are not altogether free from blame, for we have supplied the retort which ill-balanced natures readily supply when they defend or half defend, political murder. In a far happier vein runs the advice of a member of Lord Morley's India Council, quoted in the "Westminster Gazette" of last Tuesday (May. 5). He warns the Viceroy not to listen to those who insist too much on "stern repressive measures." "Wherever you get the spread of education," he says, "there also you find agitation and discontent. Do we not see this here in England? And what would happen if, instead of arguing these matters quietly you were to fine and imprison your labour agitators and leaders of independent thought?"

But, serious as outbreaks of violence are, it is the ultimate cause at the back of violence to which we must look. From the Extremist party, Indians hear the counsels of despair—despair of England's justice, of her belief in self-government, of her zeal for liberty. The question of all others before us now is whether, by a wise and generous reform or enlargement of our Indian administration, we will cut the ground from under the Extremists' feet. We shall not content them. But, as Lord Morley said at Arbroath last October, it would be the height of political folly to refuse to do all we can to rally the Moderates to our cause. And if it be said, as it is now being said every day that Orientals do not understand concessions, and believe in no power except the sword, we would reply with a passage from the same speech, one of the most courageoue of recent reflections on Indian government :—"We are not Orientals. This is the root of the matter. We are representatives, not of Oriental civilisation, but of Western civilisation, of its methods, its principles, its practices, and I, for one, will not be hurried into an excessive haste for repression by the argument that Orientals do not understand this toleration." The views of men like Mr. Gokhale, the leader of the largest and most powerful reform party among his people, represent a line of contact between Lord Morley's principles and the native movement in India. They include a practicable modification of the Partition of Bengal, perhaps a re-arrangement of the whole country into seven governorships, certainly the admission of Indians upon the Executive Councils, and the concession of real power to the elected Indian members of the Legislative Councils, especially in finance. They open up a scheme of universal education, gradually extending to the villages, and an essential reform of the police—the black spot in Indian administration. Reforms such as these are at least vital and full of hope. We wish we could say the same of the changes proposed by Simla last year for criticism, and now again submitted, we believe, together with the remarks of Sir Herbert Risley, unhappily one of the least sympathetic of Anglo-Indian officials on the Viceroy's Council. Surely at such a moment it is our business to listen to the counsels of hope and moderation, to lead native India away from the dangerous spirits which are beginning to misdirect her, and back to a faith in the capacity and generosity of our own Government.

Ex. D 51

INDIA—May 22, 1908, P. 258.

INDIA'S TROUBLES—AND THE REMEDY-A FRENTH VIEW OF THE CRISIS.

[SPECIALLY TRANSLATED FOR "INDIA."]

Some months ago (writes the Paris "Temps" in a leading article on affairs in India) we ventured in the most friendly manner (need it be said?) to take stock of the difficulties which England was in our judgment being called upon to encounter in *India*. Several London newspapers accused us thereupon of pessimism and "parti pris." Nothing would have caused us greater satisfaction than to admit that they were correct in their estimate of the situation, and that we were wrong. Unhappily, the course of events since that time has only too completely justified the apprehensions to which we gave expression.........Since the first meeting of the National Congress at Bombay, in 1885, political gatherings have become more and more numerous An organisation has been created, which has, its ranks of workers and its organs in the Press. Among the three hundred million inhabitants of India, the number of politicians is not considerable. But the action of a portion of the whole is not always to be measured by its numerical force. Add the absenteeism which finds favour more and more with English officials, the tendency which they display more markedly every day, to stand aloof from the people of the country, the increasing difficulty in finding recruits for an Indian administrative career. Bear in mind also the calamities of nature; famine and plague which Englishmen have done their utmost to forestall, but the ravages of which, up to the present, have been greater than all the precautions taken and which have been aided by ill-will and superstition. You will, if you unite all these facts, have arrived at some perception of the profound causes of the insecurity which exists—an insecurity which is assuredly far from menacing British domination yet a while, but which calls for the urgent consideration of necessary reforms.........The situation is further complicated by sins of commission. The one to which reference has been made above, and which is concerned with the administrative division of Bengal, could have been remedied without difficulty. But instead of remedy, aggravation was induced by prohibition of meetings and the proscription of the Bengal national song.......The crisis which is enveloping India is a crisis of native politics. In the case of Algeria and Tunis, France has encountered similar crisis; and she has disposed of them by liberal measures. We do not presume to give advice to a friendly Government. We confine ourselves to recalling what experience has taught us. The arbitrary system of colonial administration, which in days gone by was necessary and fruitful, would seem to have served its time. Liberal England is certainly capable of inspiration by a new spirit which shall reconcile her interests with those of the populations among whom prevails the Pax Britannica.

Ex. D 52.

INDIA—May 29, 1908. P. 260.

The Paris "Temps" published on Sunday last (May 26) an interview, which its London correspondent has had with Mr. Romesh Chandra Dutt, member of the Indian Decentralisation Committee. Mr. Dutt is reported, in the summary supplied by Reuter, to have said, that the recent bomb outrages and conspiracies in India showed that discontent of certain classes of Indians had reached a dangerous point. The Anglo-Indian police somewhat exaggerated the conspiracies, but the facts were, nevertheless, calculated to inspire grave anxiety; discontent was increasing, and the Government must grant reforms and give the Hindus a larger share in the administration of the country. Specifying the reforms required, Mr. Dutt is represented to have said, they were: First, legislative councils with Indian representation from every district; second an executive council for every province, including at least one Hindu represenutive; third, a more equitable share for Indians in the Civil Service. These reforms could be easily realised, and would yield satisfactory results. Mr. Dutt admitted that the present Government was actuated by the best intentions.

THE LESSON OF THE BOMBS.

The following letter from Captain Arthur St. John also appears in the current number of the "Nation" :—Perhaps there is no more urgent duty for all of us at this moment than to realise the present situation in India and how it has come about. When the Indian National Congress was started, it raised hope, and secret societies dwindled away, I have been told. During the last few years, when hope has failed, confidence in British Government and official has largely diminished if not disappeared, and Indians and Anglo-Indians have been becoming more and more estranged, secret societies seem to have been springing up again, and now we have bombs.........Obviously more repression will not mend matters. The wise thing surely is to consider the causes and deal with them. Hope must be revived, confidence restored, and estrangement stopped. It is just possible that this can yet be done, though it will want more faith, courage, and good sense than would appear to be easily found amongst our rulers and officials. The Indians, who have confidence of the Indians, must be consulted, and Europeans and Indians must be joined together in a wholehearted and sustained effort for the good of India, with the sincere aim of gradually enabling Indians to manage their own affairs. But if we meet outrage with mere repression, as the blind leaders of the blind are now urging us to do, without recognising our own responsibility for the present most deplorable state of affairs, then we shall be courting further disaster, and things will go from bad to worse......Let me repeat :—India is suffering from loss of hope, want of confidence in, and estrangement from, her rulers. Her rulers are suffering from lack of faith, of courage, and of good sense, and perhaps of accurate information. Truly a great task is before us calling for the cooperation of all Indian and British men and women who can recognise it.

Ex. D 53.

INDIA—June 5, 1908. P. 280.

THE TRUTH ABOUT THE BOMBS. NO INDIAN SUPPORT FOR TERRORISM.

The Indian newspapers continue to discuss the recent bomb outrage with unabated interest, dealing exhaustively both with its causes and its probable results (writesthe Calcutta correspondent of the "Manchestor Guardian" in a letter dated May 14). After the first outburst of horror, a number of journals, and conpicuously the "Amrita Bazar Patrika" have begun to urge the view that the real responsibility for what has occurred rests with the rulers, who have oppressed the people and imposed heavy sentences on political offenders. Never, we are told, has the country been so misgoverned as during the th last twenty-five years. The "Indian Nation," an admirably written weekly, challenges this method of handling so grave a theme. "Nothing," it says, "can be more unfortunate, ill-timed, and perverse than to moralise on the shortcomings of the Indian Administration, in view of the fearful dis closures of the last few days; to observe, for instance, that there would have been no secret machinations if there had been no repressive measures." The "Indian Nation" goes on to justify the order prohibiting schoolboys from attending political gatherings and defends the suppression of public meetings in disturbed areas......The Conservative Anglo-Indian papers for the most part see in the outrage the fruits of bitter and unscrupulous agitation. The "Englishman" upbraids

Lord Minto for his leniency, and hints that the strong hand has been wanting since a Liberal Ministry came into office in England. The "Pioneer," in an article on "The Cult of the Bomb," includes among the mischief-makers the smooth Legislative Councillor, the Congress Moderate, and the "more candid" Extremist, and argues that they have, one and all, contributed to the conditions which produce Terrorists. In another issue it urges that vigorous measures should be taken against seditious writings and violent oratory. Some of the baser sort of journals read by Anglo-Indians advocate free shooting by Europeans. The "Asian," a sporting weekly, has offered this very remarkable advice to Mr. Kingsford, the Session-Judge, for whom the bombs at Mozufferpore were intended. The "Englishman" reproduced the inflammatory effussion, and while dissenting from its suggestion of shooting at sight, does so on the ground that it believes the Government to be sincere in the intention of protecting the community against outrage. But there is a growing conviction that the outrages have not the significance which was at first attributed to them, and that the outbreak of terrorism is an isolated freak. It is absolutely certain that the bulk of the people have no sympathy with outrages or the policy which they represent. This is abundantly clear from the language of the newspapers, the tone of public speeches, and, I may add, from the remarks of every Indian whom one meets. Everywhere one is told that mad acts of violence of the kind planned by the Terrorists are utterly abhorrent to every self-respecting Indian.

Ex. D 54

INDIA—June 12, p. 593, Col. 2; p. 295, Col. 1.

Expresses English opinion on the Bomb-outrage.

Ex. D 55.

ADVOCATE OF INDIA.—June 19, P. 7, Col. 4.

The Bishop of Lahore, speaking at the annual festival of the Southwork Diocesan Board of Missions, said that they were faced with a great crisis in India at the present time. They were all much dismayed by certain recent occurrences, and a thrill of horror had gone through the country at the revelation of the state of affairs in Calcutta, such as he should never have dreamed to exist there when he left three months ago. He did not feel that the maintenance of order was the very first duty that we owed to that great land. But almost more urgently he would say, do not let us think that we can stop there. Do not let us suppose that all we have to do is to sit on the safety-valve, to repress disorder, to smite upon the head any who attempts to take up a prominent position. That would not serve in the long run. What we needed to do was to realise that a new life was coming to the birth in India. We had to do not merely with the agitator with local outbursts, and the like; there was a position of extraordinary interest and wonderful possibilities of development, such as no country has been faced with before all down the pages of the world's history. A new life was indeed coming to the birth. Had we not been trying to bring in new thoughts, new standards, new ideals of life, new conceptions of God and and of society? And were we to expect all that to go on endlessly, producing no result, no craving for larger and fuller and stronger life?

Ex. D 56.

MAHRATTA—May 24, 1908, P. 246, Col. 1 and 2.

OPINION ON THE SITUATION IN BENGAL.

"Some of the statements from India regarding the plot at Calcutta are of a very alarmist character; but one may judge that many of the stories are pure gossip of the camp."

The Western Daily Mercury.

"The development was the natural outcome of the policy now being pursued in India." *Keir Hardie M. P.*

"It is not because, but in spite of, the Congress that the bomb has been resorted to. We have bred a gang of seditious youths, who have been goaded by the infliction of floggings for political offences into this kind of crime." *Sir Henry Cotton M. P.*

"The English extremists cannot divest themselves of a grave responsibility. They have encouraged sedition by wild talk in Parliament and elsewhere, which has been telegraphed to India and served to inflame the animosity in that country. * * * The vast majority of the Indian peoples are still orderly, law-abiding, and filled with respect for British rule, but the disaffected minority is growing in numbers and audacity." *Daily Mail.*

"It is doubtless the offspring of the more constitutional reform movement which is also as unquestionably the result of the faulty system of education we have introduced into India." *Liverpool Courier.*

"The murders and the subsequent discoveries are startling evidence that the agitation in the Eastern Province has entered upon a dangerous phase. It is unnecessary to assume however that the Bengal anarchists represent a large element in the population." *The Dundee Advertiser.*

"The people mostly to be feared are not the agitators in India who would soon collapse if left alone; but the people in England who support and encourage them. It is certain that the worst foes of England to-day are the English People." *Nottingham Guardian.*

"It is the National Congress which has kept alive the belief in constitutional methods and restrained the enthusiasts who might have had recourse to conspiracy and revolutionary violence. * * * It is most unfortunate that the Indian authorities, instead of recognising their real friends, put their trust in a secret police, notoriously untrustworthy, and persist in a policy of repression which is the direct parent of the outrage we deplore." *Sir William Wederburn.*

"Order must be maintained, cruel homicide must be punished. But the Government and Home Government will fail utterly in their responsibility if they content themselves with enforcing the penalty and do not proceed first to ascertain and then to remove the causes of a novel and unprecedented offence." *Morning Leader.*

"Sedition is a word of moods and tenses; but regarding it at its worst, few methods are more unpromising in the way of a cure than to take men of education and refinement and flog them judicially." *Yorkshire Observer.*

"The real danger in India does not lie in the Anarchist conspiracy which has been laid bare. It must be sought in the policy which makes such conspiracies possible in a country in which nothing has been more remarkable than the fidelity of the educated Indian to the English ideal of constitutional political agitation. If this fidelity has lately shown some signs of weakening, on whose shoulders must the blame be put?" *India.*

"We have to face the fact that the Indian of to-day is not even the same as the Indian of twenty years ago. It is no longer possible to treat India as a purely oriental country." *Daily Graphic.*

"I do not believe the Propaganda of sedition is being carried on by more than a comparatively few. Wherever you get the spread of education, there also you find agitation and discontent. Do we not see this here in England? And what would happen if instead of arguing these matters quietly you were to fine and imprison your labour agitators and leaders of independent thought? I hold that any repressive measures should be carried out as judiciously as possible." *An 'India Office' official.*

"The Extremist party will continue to gain power until it makes our position in India almost impossible, unless we give Moderate leaders like Gokhale and Lajpatrai such generous and effectual measures of reform as they can point to with hope. * * *

If they are losing influence over minds excited and kept in continual irritation by our policy for the last four years, the fault is ours." *H. W. Nevinson.*

" How is it to be brought home to the British people that they and their representatives in India are mainly responsible for the manufacture of the bombs in India ? Shall we have the courage to adopt the obviously sensible and manly course of restoring confidence by timely measures for consulting the will and the feelings of the Indian peoples in their own affairs and restoring the old aim of letting them to learn to govern themselves ? " *Captain Arthur St. John.*

" It is a logical but unforeseen outcome of the civilizing work of which the British people are rightly so proud. " *Journal Des Debats (Paris).*

India like Egypt, has to-day its nationalist party, which by means different from those employed in the latter country, is resolved to attract the attention of the people of Great Britain. The *Temps* thinks that mistakes have been made, and points to the administrative partition of Bengal as one of them which might have been easily avoided. The article concludes thus :—" Whether it be in Algeria or in Tunis, we have known similar crisis, and we have disposed of them by liberal measures We don't presume to give advice to a friendly Government. We confine ourselves to recalling what experience has taught us. The abitrary system of colonial administration which in days gone by was necessary and fruitful, would seem to have served its time. Liberal England is certainly capable of adopting a new spirit with a view to reconciling her interests with those of the populations among whom prevails Pax Britannica.— The Paris *Temps.*

" We imagine however, that Lord Morley will refuse to apply to India a policy whose failure he has brilliantly exposed in Ireland." The *Nation.*

Our rule is strong and just but it is not sympathetic ; and the more impregnable in a material sense our position in India becomes the more likely are we to be confirmed in the egotistical methods of scholastic, literary and artistic education, and of religiou-proslytism, we have so strenuously enforced on its many-languaged and its many-relid gioned peoples. We are destroying their faith and their literature and their arts, ans the whole continuity of the spontaneous development of their civilisation, and their great historical personality ; in a word, we are destroying the very soul of the nation. This is the cause of the restlessness that—by those who have eyes to see and ears to hear—is to be found every where fretting into the very hearts of the English educated classes in India." *Sir George Birdwood.*

Ex. D 56. A.

THE MAHRATTA.—June 28, 1908; P. 304, Col. 1, 2.

The meaning of the words " an incitement to an act of violence " is, we think, plain enough. But in the dictionary of politics any words may bear any sense, and it is not too much to suppose that some newspapers will have to be victimised in India before any thing like a definite sense of the words could be pronounced upon judicially. With the passing of an Act of law only the riddle or the conundrum of the legal Sphynx is framed. Its oracular solution really lies with the court of law; and in critical times and times of unrest we have but to expect that newspaper writers will be unconsciously led into being the means of attempting that solution. So far as the executive Government is concerned it will willingly interpret the words in question as " any words that may suggest to any one the idea of any kind of use of force by any one to any one at any time and at any place." We may only hope that the law courts will not allow themselves the latitude assumed in the above interpretation. The *Hindu* of Madras has stumbled over a reference to these very words in Hansard's reports of Parliamentary debates; and curiously enough there we have a pronouncement on the words by no less a person than Mr. Gladstone. Says the *Hindu* :—

" In 1884, in consequence of riots provoked by the opposition of the House of Lords in England to the question of electoral reform, Mr. Joseph Chamberlain, then President of the

Board of Trade, had hinted that a hundred thousand men might well march from Birmingham to London, and Lord Salisbury had treated this remark as incitment to violence. Mr. Gladstone, then Prime Minister, in taking up the defence of his colleague in the sitting of October 30, 1884, in the House of Commons, gave as his opinion that it was very well to say to the people, " Love order and hate violence, " but that it would not do to say that and nothing more. " But while I exclude violence, " he added, " I cannot—I will not adopt that effeminate method of speech which is to hide from the people of the country, the cheering fact that they may derive some encouragement from the recollection of former struggles, from the recollection of the great qualities of their forefathers and from the consciousness that they may possess them still. Sir I am sorry to say that if no instructions had ever been addressed in a political crisis to the people of this country except, to remember to hate violence, and love order and exercise patience, the liberties of this country would never have been obtained." (Hansard, Parl. Debates. Vol. 293, Page 643.)

* * *

The struggle that is going on in Persia at this moment is interesting from more than one point of view. It is perhaps the first struggle in the east between a Monarch and the Parliament of the country. The birth of the Persian Parliament was hailed with joy by the lovers of the democratic power all over the world; and they need not allow their sentiments to undergo a change simply because that new birth has been soon followed by what looks like a revolution. We may frankly say that we have not as complete a knowledge of the merits of the struggle as would justify us in passing an opinion as to who is right and who is wrong. But there are signs about the passing events which clearly indicate that the struggle is one for popular liberty more than for any thing else. The Shaha may have heroically declared tha t he can not relinquish his power without an appeal to the sword with which his ancestors had won the kingdom. But the appeal has no newness about it. The Shaha could not have remembered the course of the history of the nations of the world when he was making that declaration. The sword or its equivalent is not the monopoly of a Monarch ; and when time is bent on fighting against Monarchs, it sharpens tha popular sword with an edge which does not tu rn even on adamant.

Ex. D 56 B.

MAHRATTA—March 15, 1908; *P. 126. Col. 2.*

MR. TILAK'S EVIDENCE BEFORE THE DECENTRALISATION COMMISSION.

The question of centralisation or decentralisation of the powers of the administrative machinery involves the considerations of uniformity, smoothness and regularity of work, general efficiency, economy of time, work and money, popularity &c ; and speaking broadly these may be classed under three different heads : (1) Efficiency, (2) Economy, and (3) Popularity.

As regards the first, I do not think it is seriously contended that the efficiency of administration has suffered merely owing to over-centralisation. On the contrary it is urged that it is worthwhile making the administration a great deal more popular even if it would become a trifle less efficient by decentralisation. But the cry for decentralisation has its origin in the desire of the local officers to have a freer hand in the administration of the areas committed to their care. They believe that their life has been made rather mechanical or soulless by over-centralisation ; and having naturally attributed to the same cause the growing estrangement between themselves and the people they have proposed decentralisation as an official remedy to remove this admitted evil. I do not think the people, looking from their own standpoint, can accept this view. The general public is indifferent whether efficiency and economy are secured by more or less official decentralisation. It is entirely a matter between higher and lower officials, between the secretariate and the local officers, or between the supreme and the local governments. The people still believe that centralisation secures greater uniformity and regularity, and reduces the chances of the conscious or unconscious abuse of power resulting from unappealable authority being vested in lower officers, and would rather oppose decentralization in this respect. The only complaints, so far as I know, against the existing centralisation or decentralisation hitherto raised by the people are (1) The combination of the Executive and the Judicial functions in the same officers, (2) Financial centralisation in the Government of India as evidenced by the Provincial Contract System, (3) Partition of Bengal and (4) Excessive growth of departmentalism encroaching upon popular rights. But these, excepting the second, do not from the subject of the official grievance against over-centralisation.

My knowledge of the internal working of the different departments of administration is too limited to make definite proposals regarding the redistribution of power and authority between various officials so as thereby to make the administration more economical than at present. I shall, therefore, confine my remarks mostly to the popular aspect of the question and to the four complaints noted above.

It is idle to expect that the adoption of the loose and irregular system of earlier days would remove the present estrangement between officers and people. It is true that in earlier days the relations between officers and people were more cordial : but this was not due to the looseness of the system then in vogue. In days when the system of British administration had yet to be evolved and settled, the help of the leaders of the people was anxiously sought by officers as indispensable for smooth and efficient administration of a new province. The officers then moved amongst the people and were in touch with them, not as a matter of mere goodness or sympathy but a matter of necessity, as they themselves had yet many things to learn from these leaders ; and this much satisfied the people at that time, as new aspirations were not as yet created. That state of things has ceased to exist. The creation and gradual development of the various departments, the framing of rules and regulations for the smooth working thereof, the settlement of all old disputes, the completion of the revenue survey, the disarmament of the people, the gradual waning of the influence of the old aristocracy including the higher class of watandars, the compilation of the works of ready reference on all matters embodying the experience of many years for the guidance of the officers, and other causes of the same kind, joined with the facilities for communication with the head-quarters of Government, have all tended to make the local officers more and more independent of the people and so lose touch with the latter. Overcentralisation may, at best, be one of such causes ; but if so, it is to my mind very insignificant. No amount of decentralisation by itself can therefore restore that cordiality between the officers and the people which existed in the earlier days of the British rule as a necessity of those times ; and though the present officers may by nature be as sympathetic as their predecessors, it is not possible to expect from them the same respect for growing popular opinion as was exhibited by their predecessors in older days. Under these circumstances such further decentralisation as would tend to vest greater powers in the lower officials will only make the system unpopular by encouraging local despotism which the people have justly learnt to look upon with disfavour. The only way to restore good relations between the officers and the people at present is, therefore, to create *by law* the necessity of consulting the people or their leaders, whom the old officials consulted, or whose advice they practically followed, as a matter of policy in earlier unsettled times. This means transfer of authority and power not between officials themselves, but from officials to the people, and that too in an ungrudging spirit. The leaders of the people must feel that matters concerning public welfare are decided by officials in consultation with them. The officers did it in earliear days as a matter of necessity, and the necessity which was the result of circumstances in those days must, if we want the same relations to continue, be now created by laws granting the rights of self-government to the people, and thus giving to their opinion and wishes a duly recognised place in the affairs of the State. I do not mean to say that this could be done at once or at one stroke. We must begin with the village system the autonomy of which has been destroyed by the growth of departmentalism under the present rule. The village must be made a unit of self-government, and village communities or councils invested with definite powers to deal with all or most of the village questions concerning Educations, Justice, Forest, Abkari, Famine Relief, Police, Medical Relief and Sanitation. These units of self-government should be under the supervision and superintendence of Taluka and District Boards which should be made thoroughly representative and independent. This implies a certain amount of definite popular control even over Provincial finance ; and the Provincial Contract System will have to be revised not merely to give to the Provincial Government a greater stability and control over its finances, but by further decentralisation to secure for the popular representative bodies adequate assignments of revenue for the aforesaid purposes. This will also necessitate a corresponding devolution of independent legal powers on the popolur bodies whether the same be secured by a reform of the Legislative Council or otherwise. Mere Advisory Councils will not satisfy the aspirations of the people, nor will they remove the real cause of estrangement between the officers and the people. The remedy proposed by me, I know, is open to the objection that it means a surrender of power and authority enjoyed by the bureaucracy at present, and that the efficiency of the administration might suffer thereby. I hold a different view. I think it should be the aim of the British Administration to educate the people in the management of their own affairs, even at the cost of some efficiency and without entertaining any misgivings regarding the ultimate growth and result of such a policy. It is unnecessary to give any detailed scheme regarding the organisation of Village, Taluka or District Councils proposed above, for if the policy be approved and accepted there will be no difficulty in framing a scheme or making alterations therein to meet difficulties and objections as they occur in practice. As regards other complaints referred to above against the present centralisation or decentralisation of powers amongst officials, I think it is high time that the combination of Judicial and Executive functions in the same officers should be discontinued. In Judicial functions I include those judicial powers that are granted to revenue officers in the matter of land revenue, pensions, Inams and Saramjams, except, such as are necessary for the collection of revenue. There is no reason why these powers should be retained by executive officers if they are to be divested of jurisdiction in criminal matters. It is needless to say that this reform pre-supposes complete independence of judicial officers. Unnecessary growth of departmentalism is well illustrated by the latest instance of the partition of the Khandesh District. The partition of Bengal is the worst instance of the kind. These are objectionable even from an economical point of view, and in the case of the partition of Bengal the policy has deeply wounded the feelings of the people. The revenues of the country are not inelastic; but the margin, soon as it is reached, is swallowed up by the growth of departments at the sacrifice of other reforms conducive to the welfare of the people. In this connection I may here state that I advocote a re-arrangement of Provinces on considerations of linguistic and ethnological affinities and a federation thereof under a central authority. To conclude: the mere shifting of the centre of power and authority from one official to another is not in my opinion, calculated to restore the feelings of cordiality between officers and people, prevailing in earlier days. English education has created new aspirations and ideals amongst the people; and so long as these national aspirations remain unsatisfied, it is useless to expect that the hiatus between the officers and the people could be removed by any scheme of official decent tralisation, whatever its other effects may be. It is no remedy,—not even palliative,—agains, the evil complained of, nor was it ever put forward by the people or their leaders. The fluctuating wave of decentralisation may infuse more or less life in the individual members of the bureaucracy, but it can not remove the growing estrangement between the rulers and the ruled-unless and until the people are allowed more and more effective voice in the management of their own affairs in an ever expansive spirit of wise liberalism and wide sympathy aiming at raising India to the level of the governing country.

B. G. TILAK

9th March 1908.

Ex. D 57.

TIMES OF INDIA—May 12, P. 7, col. 1

LONDON, May 11.

Mr. Gokhale was welcomed at Charing Cross by Mr. Nevinson and numbers of young Indins. He informed Reuter's representative that he hoped to see Viscount Morley in connection with reform schemes. Mr. Romesh Chunder Dutt, in the course of an interview, said :—" The development of anarchism in India has been foreseen. It is the result of a growing feeling among discontented Indians that the Government is not trying to solve the present-day political problems. Until a large measure of self-government is granted, crime is sure to increase. "

Ex. D 58.

ORIENTAL REVIEW—May 6, 1908; P. 131, col. 1 and 2.

But we put not the whole responsibility for such grave outrages on this party; for much of the present ill-feeling might have been checked, nay might not have risen at all if there had not been the regime of Lord Curzon. He it was who effected, in the very teeth of bitter opposition from all people as Mr. Morley even said, the partition of Bengal and gave a deep, never-to-be-forgotten insult to the cherished sentiments of the Bengalis. But even then all the later developments of a nation's anger might not have come to be if the Secretary of State for India had shown a little of statemanship, a little of that Liberalism of which he was considered the high priest up to this time. His famous pharse about "the settled fact of the Bengal Partition" dashed all hopes to the ground. The agitation carried on by the Bengalis and all over the country, though it may have sometimes lapsed into extremes, had not up to that time gone even an inch beyond strictly constitutional lines. But unfortunately the warnings of all the real patriots of this country and steadfast friends of the British Government were unheeded. The Hon'ble Mr. Gokhale plainly told at the time of the passing of the Seditious Meetings Act that agitation which would not be allowed above ground would be carried on underground—and underground agitation is the most dangerous. Anarchism is the child of dispair. It is only pessimists tired of the ways of the world, helpless fanatics who rush off to do such dark deeds, the why and wherefore of which they themselves do not know. Their life is one embodied doubt and this extends even to their deeds. They do not think that their actions will be followed by a tangible good. In fact this idea of final purpose is utterly foreign to their minds. They do them because they are filled with despair. British statemanship failed in uprooting this despair.

Ex. D 59.

TIMES OF INDIA—June 20, P. 8, Col. 1.

Mr Morley said :—

I am trying to feel my way through the most difficult problem, the most difficult situation that I think responsible Governments, you and I and all of us ever had to face. Of course I am dependent upon information. But as I read it, as I listen great Indian experts with large experience there is a certain view like, I hope it is so superficial estrangement and alienation. (Hear, hear.) Now that is the problem that we have to deal with. Gentlemen, I should very badly repay your kindness in asking me to come among you to-night if I were to attempt for a minute to analyse or to probe all the conditions that have led to this state of things. It would need hours and hours. This is not, I think. the occasion for that, nor is it the moment for it. Our first duty—the first duty of any Government—is to keep order. (Cheers). But first remember this. It would be idle to deny, and I am not sure that any of you gentlemen would deny, that there is at this moment, and there has been for some little time past, and very likely there will be for some time to come, a living moment in the mind of those people for whom you are responsible. A living moment, and movement forwhat! a movement for. objects which we ourselves have all taught them to think desirable objects. (Hear, hear.) And unless we somehow or another can reconcile order with satisfaction of those ideas and aspirations, gentlemen, the fault will not be theirs. It will be ours; It will mark the breakdown of what has never yet broken down in any part of the world—the breakdown of British statesmanship. That is what it will do. (Cheers) Now nobody, I think I do not believe anybody either in this room or out of this room—believes that we can now enter upon an era of pure repression. (Cheers.) You cannot enter at this date and with English public opinion mind you, watching you, upon an era of pure repression, and I do not believe really that any body desires any such thing. I do not believe so. Gentlemen, we have seen attempts in the lifetime of some of us here tonight, we have seen attempts in Continental Europe to govern by pure repression, and indeed in days not altogether remote from our own, we have seen attempts of that sorts. They have all failed. There may be now and again a spurious semblance of success, but in truth they have all failed. Whether we with our enormous power and resolution should fail, I do not know. But I do not believe anybody in this room, representing so powerfully as it does dominant sentiments which are not always felt in England—that in this room there is anybody who is for an era of pure repression. (Hear, hear.)

Ex. D 60.

BOMBAY GAZETTE—July 2, 1908. P. 7, Col. 1-2.

LORD CURZON'S DEBATE.

LORD MORLEY'S REPLY.

LONDON, JULY 1.

In the House of Lords last night, Lord Curzon moved the following motion :—

" To call attention to the state of affairs on the Frontier and in the interior of India ; to ask the Secretary of State whether he can give the House any information on the subject ; and to move for papers.

LORD MORLEY'S REPLY.

Viscount Morley, on rising to reply, admitted Lord Curzon's title to speak for India, but said that he failed to see his reason for concluding with an appeal to the Government to preserve order. He (Viscount Morley), during the last two and a half years, had not deviated one hair's breadth in any action from the policy which he thought order required. He was seriously disappointed in the tone of Lord Curzon's remarks on one or two points. Lord Curzon had made the remarkable statement that questions in the House of Commons were fatal and deleterious. Nobody had more reason than himself to dislike questions, but they had not the slightest significance or importance, and did anyone suppose that the democracy were going to be without their simpletons—perhaps, even the aristocracy had their simpletons. When Lord Curzon laid down the tremendous proposition that the Parliamentary system was incompatible with the maintenance of our power in India.—Lord Curzon (interrupting) declared that he did not say anything so absurd. He himself used to revel in asking questions in the House of Commons, and he only said that the duty of answering them imposed an unreasonable burden upon officers in India—Viscount Morley repeated that Lord Curzon had made the remark; and asked, if Lord Curzon disliked Parliamentary action, what we were going to do with the Parliamentary system. Lord Curzon apparently did not see that we were confronted with an immensely difficult problem and that the conditions were fixed. Referring to Lord Curzon's criticisms of the system of education, Viscount Morley said he felt sure that any Government or Viceroy going to the roots of the present conditions would devote the utmost power to the revision of the Educational system. Viscount Morley said that the refutation of the charges in connection with the Partition of Bengal appeared to be Lord Curzon's main object in raising a not very fruitful discussion. He (Viscount Morley) thought that the Partition was mistaken in its methods, but it was a settled fact. So far as he was concerned, he never could see why it was regarded as sacrosanct, but it was so, because it had become a test, and he was willing to abide by that test.

Viscount Morley said that he accepted Lord Curzon's reasons for the internal unrest in India, but Lord Curzon did not suggest the course that the Government should pursue. He said that Lord Curzon did not agree with the formula of "Martial law and no damned non-sense;" but everything that Lord Curzon said led to the assumption that we must decide without reference to Indian demands. Viscount Morley continued:—"I cannot sufficiently admire the manful courage with which the Viceroy—unyielding to panic on the one side, and to disgust at blind and reckless crimes on the other—has persisted in the path which I have marked out. Between no two servants of the Crown is there better understanding or fuller confidence than between Lord Minto and myself. Lord Minto's speech in introducing the Explosives and Press Act, in which he said that no crime would deter him from endeavouring to meet honest reformers, was a very fine utterance. We have no choice but to persevere in the path of reform: we cannot escape our own history. We cannot leave the course marked out by the conscience of Britain in dealing with alien races, and the longer the reforms are postponed the greater will be the ultimate difficulty. If we took our hand from the plough now, we should be exposed not merely to the blind verdict of the Extremists and the lamentations of the Moderates, but we should disappoint the great mass of Anglo-Indian opinion." Viscount Morley said that he believed that the report of the Hobhouse Commission would supply material; not for the reconstruction of the Indian Government, but for the improvement of the Administration, for the simplification of correspondence, and for giving to Indians some opportunities of handling some of their own affairs, which, he hoped, would be not merely advisory but some executive powers. He also hoped that it would limit excessive official interference, and would stimulate the formation of independent opinion in local District governments. He was not aware whether the scheme of reforms would necessitate legislation, but the Government would expect to receive the approval of Parliament, and he was confident that Parliament would not be blind and not deaf to reasonable demands. Viscount Morley concluded by emphasizing the importance of public men abstaining from anything calculated to make the people think that they were influenced by personal considerations, in view of the tremendous issues involved.

Ex. D 61.

GAZETTE OF INDIA—November 2, 1907, P. 164–165.—Dr. Rash Behari on Seditious meetings bill.

Whatever precautions you may take speeches will continue to be delivered. You cannot effectually gag one-sixth of the population of the world. I do not wish to indulge in well worn common places about the futility of coercion of the danger of sitting on the safety valve for instance which must be familiar even to men less gifted than Maculay's forward school boy. But I must remind the Hon'ble members that the Irish question yet remains to be solved. It has certainly not been solved by the numerous coercion Acts, fifty in number, which bulk so largely in the Statute Books in that unhappy country, the Isle of Destiny. Agitation has led to coercion, in its turn to a greater and more dangerous agitation but I am perhaps forgetting that Ireland is a cold country where a fur coat might be useful and therefore the analogy may not quite hold good. One thing however I may safely assert and that is that in Ireland as well as in India, the application of drastic remedies to skin diseases, which rapidly disappear under a mild treatment, always leads to serious complications. Is there any reason for thinking that this is not true of the body politic. Though therefore the measure now before the Council may secure for the time, outward quiet and drive sedition underground, its inevitable fruits will be, growing discontent and distrust which may, under repression, readily slide into disaffection. It will thus create more evils than it can possibly cure and this reminds me that the movement in the Punjab was mainly agrarian and was arrested by your Lordship's refusal to give your assent to the Colonisation Act and not by the Ordinance, the powerlessness of which to keep down unrest is shown by the fact that there are no signs of improvement in Eastern Bengal. We have no doubt whatever that in devising the present measure the Government have only the interests of peace and order at heart; but the authority which is compelled to be severe is liable to be suspected and when it seizes the rude weapons of coercion its motives are liable to be misconstrued. People are everywhere asking in fear and in trepidation what next and next. What is to be the end of this new policy? For the spirit of coercion is not likely to die for lack of nourishment, as it makes the meat it feeds on and trifles, light as air, are to it confirmations as strong, should I be wrong in saying, as an Indian Police report or a score of telegrams from "our own correspondents." I repeat that the situation is not in the least dangerous and an over-readiness to scent danger is not one of the notes of true statesmanship. But suppose I am wrong and the position is really critical, what does it prove? It proves, unless we are afflicted not merely with a double or even a triple but withal a quadruple dose of original sin, that the Government of the country is not the most perfect system of administration that some people imagine. My Lord, I began by saying that this Bill is an indictment of the whole nation. If however it is true and this can be the only justification of the measure that India is growing more and more disloyal this Bill is really an indictment of the administration. The positions will then be reversed—the Government and not the people will then be put on their defence. There is no escape from this dilemma. If there is no general disaffection you do not want this drastic measure. The prairie cannot be set on fire in the absence of inflammable materials to feed it. If on the other hand a spirit of disloyalty is really abroad, it must be based on some substantial grievance, which will not be redressed by coercive Acts. You may stifle the complaints of the people but beware of that dreary and ominous silence which is not peace but the reverse of peace. Even immunity from public seditious meetings may be purchased too dearly. It has been said that this Bill is a measure of great potency. I agree, but potency for what purpose?—for putting down sedition? I say no. It will be potent for one purpose—and one purpose only, for the purpose of propagating the bacilli of secret sedition. The short title of the Bill is.—A Bill for "the prevention of seditious meetings." I think and I venture to think the title requires a slight addition. It ought to be amended by the addition of the words—"and the promotion of secret sedition." Order may be kept, peace may reign in India, but this measure will produce the greatest disappointment among those by whom, though they are not the natural leaders of the people, public opinion is created and controlled. The logic of coercion, we all know, is charming in its simplicity, but its authors forget that they cannot coerce thought, they cannot make men loyal by an Act of Parliament.

Ex. D 62.

GAZETTE OF INDIA—9th June 1908, P. 1-4.—An act further to amend the law relating to explosive substances

ACT NO. VI OF 1908.

2. DEFINITION OF "EXPLOSIVE SUBSTANCE."—In this Act the expression "explosive substance" shall be deemed to include any materials for making any explosive substance; also any apparatus, machine, implement, or material used, or intended to be used or adapted for aiding in causing, any explosion in or with any explossive substance; also any part of any such apparatus, machine, or implement.

3. PUNISHMENT FOR CAUSING EXPLOSION LIKELY TO ENDANGER LIFE OR PROPERTY.—Any person who unlawfully and maliciously causes by any explosive substance an explosion of a nature likely to endanger life or to cause serious injury to property shall, whether any injury to person or property has been actually caused ornot, be punished with transportation for life or any shorter term, to which fine may beadded, or with imprisonment for a term which may extend to ten years, to which fine may be added.

4. PUNISHMENT FOR ATTEMPT TO CAUSE EXPLOSION OR FOR MAKING OR KEEPING EXPLOSIVE WITH INTENT TO ENDANGER LIFE OR PROPERTY—Any person who unlawfully and maliciously—(a) does any act with intent to cause by an explosive substance, or conspires to cause by an explosive substance, an explosion in British India of a nature likely to endanger life or to cause serious injury to property or (b) makes or has in his possession or under his control any explosive substance with intent by meano thereof" to endanger life, or cause serious injury to property in British India, or to enable any other person by means thereof to endanger life or cause serious injury to property in Britsh India; shall, whether any explosion does or does not take place and whether any injury to person or property has been actually caused or not be punished with transportation for a term which may extend to twenty years, to which fine may be added, or with imprisonment for a term which may extend to seven years to which fine may be added.

5. PUNISHMENT FOR MAKING OR POSSESSING EXPLOSIVE UNDER SUSPICIOUS CIRCUMSTANCES—Any person who makes or knowingly has in his possession or under his control any explosive substance, under such circumstances as to give rise to a resonable suspicion that he is not making it or does not have it in his possession or under his control for a lawful object, shall, unless he can show that he made it or hadit in his possession or under his controi for a lawful object, be punishable with transportation for a term which may extend to fourteen years, to which fine may be added, or with imprisonment for a term which may extend to five years, to which fine may be added.

6. PUNISHMENT OF ABETTORS.—Any person who by the supply of or solicitation for money, the providing of premises, the supply of materials, or in any manner whatsoever, procures, counsels, aids, abets or is accessory to, the commission of any offence under this Act shall be punished with the punishment provided for the offence.

7. RESTRICTION ON TRIAL OF OFFENCES.—No Court shall proceed to the trial of any person for an offence against this Act except with the consent of the Local Governor General in Council.

ACT No. VII OF 1908.

An Act for the prevention of incitements to murder and to other offences in newspapers.

3. POWER TO FORFEIT PRINTING PRESSES IN CERTAIN CASES.—(1) In caseswhere, upon application made by order of or under authority from the Local Government, a

Magistrate is of opinion that a newspaper printed and published within the Province contains any incitement to murder or to any offence unde rthe Explosive Substances Act, 1908 or to any act of violence, such Magistrate may make a conditional order declaring the printing press used, or intended to be used, for the purpose of printing or publishing such newspaper, or found in or upon the premises where such newspaper is, or at the time of the printing of the matter complained of was printed, and all copies of such newspaper, wherever found, to be forfeited to His Majesty, and shall in such order state the material facts and call on all persons concerned to appear before him, at a time and place to be fixed by the order, to show cause why the order should not be made absolute. (2) A copy of such order shall be fixed on some conspicuous part of the premises specified in the declaration made in respect of such newspaper under section 5 of the Press and Registration of Books Act, 1867, or of any other premises in which such newspapers is printed and the affixing of such copy shall be deemed to be due service of the said order on all person concerned. (3) In cases of emergency or in cases where the purposes of the application might be defeated by delay, the Magistrate may, on or after the making of a conditional order under sub-section (1), make a further order ex prate for the attachment of the printing press or other property referred to in the conditional order. (4) If any person concerned appears and shows cause against the conditioual order the Magistrate shall take evidence, whether in support of or in opposition to such order, in manner provided in section 356 of the Code of Criminal Procedure, 1898. (5) If the Magistrate is satisfied that the news paper contains matter of the nature specified in sub-section (1), he snall make the conditional order of forfeiture abssolute in respect of such property as he may find to be within terms of the said sub-section. (6) If the Magistrate is not so satisfied, he shall set aside the conditional order of forfeiture and the order of attachment, if any.

4. Power to seize.—(1) The Magistrate may bywarrant empower any Police-officer not below the rank of a Sub-Inspector to seize and detain any property ordered to be attacked under section 3, sub-section (3), or to seize and carry away any property ordered to be forfeited under section 3 sub-section (5), wherever found and to enter upon and search for such property in any premises—(a) where the newspaper specified in such warrant is printed, or published or (b) where any such property may be or may be reasonably suspected to be, or (c) where any copy of such newspaper is kept for sale, distribution, publication or public exhibition or reasonably suspected to be so kept. (2) Every warrant issued under sub-sec. (1) so far as it relates to a search shall be executed in manner provided for the execution of search warrants by the Code of Criminal Procedure 1898.

5. Appeal.—Any person concerned who has appeared and shown cause against a conditional order of forfeiture may appeal to the High Court within fifteen days from the date when such orders is made absolute.

6. Bar of Other Proceedings.—Save as proided in section 5, no order duly made by a Magistrate under section 3 shall be called in question in any Court.

7. Power to Annull Declaration Under Press and Registration of Books Act, 1867.—Where an order of forfeiture has been made absolute in relation to any newspaper the Local Government may, by notification in the local official Gazette, annul any declaration made by the printer or publisher of such newspaper under the Press and Registration of Books Act, 1867, and may by such notification prohibit any further declaration being made or subscribed under the said Act in respect of the said newspaper, or of any newspaper until it is the same in substance as the said newspaper,until such prohibition be withdrawn.

8. Penalty.—Any person who prints or publishes any newspaper specified in any prohibition notified under section 7 during the cotinuance of that prohibition shall be liable, on conviction, to the penalties prescribed by section 15 of the Press and Registration of Books Act, 1867.

Ex. D 63.

GAZETTE OF INDIA—June 13, P. 142, Col. 2.

Extract from Hon. Syed Mahomad's speech on Explossive Act quotting " Ethics of Dynamite " from " Contemporary Review "—This is also the view taken by many thoughtful men in England. Writing on the Ethics of Dynamite in the *Contemporary Review* in 1894 the Hon'ble Mr. Aubern Herbert admirably summed up the situation in the following words :—If the only effect upon us of the presence of the dynamiter in our midst is to make us multiply punishments, invent restrictions, increase the number of our official spies. forbid public meetings, interfere with the press, put up gratings, as in one country they propose to do, in our House of Commons, scrutinise visitors under official miscroscopes,request them as at Vienna and I think now at Paris, also to be good enough to leave their great coats in the vestibules, if we are in a word, to trust to machinery to harden our hearts and simply to meet force with force, always irritating, always clumsy and in the end fruitless, then I venture to prophesy that there lies before us a bitter and an evil time. We may be quite sure that force users will be force begetters. The passions of men will rise higher and higher and the authorised and unauthorised Governments—the Government of the majority and of written laws, the Government of the minority and dynamite—will enter upon their desperate struggle of which no living man can read the end. In one way, and only one way, can the dynamiter be permanently disarmed by abandoning in almost all directions our force and machinery, and accustoming the people to believe in the blessed weapon of reason, persuasion and voluntary service.

Ex. D 64.

THE ORIENTAL REVIEW—July 1, P. 239, col 1, 2. Quoting the letter of the Calcutta correspondent of the "Morning Leader"

No sane person will countenance this propaganda of violence, for a moment ; but it might have been foreseen, as, in fact, it has been foreseen, by everyone who has read history. If anything is responsible for it, it is the fatuous policy of the Government and the Yellow Press in England which has hounded it on to one act of repression after another. The Government has deliberately sat on all the safety-valves, an advice which can be only characterised as criminal ; and now that an explosion has taken place, it is surprised and shocked, and is considering the advisability of sitting on them again tighter than ever. I daresay it will do so. and I venture to predict that the effect will only be to aggravate the situation. The one hope lies in the natural gentleness of the Indian character, which may well be said to have endured all things. Now that the Bengalees, who are the gentlest of all the Indian races, have taken to dynamite, it is at least probable that the other races will not be less drastic in their methods. The bomb-thrower having established himself, has come to stay, and the first thing the Government has got to make up its mind to is that rocky fact. All the deportations and Press prosecutions in the world will not dislodge him; they will only intensify his malignant activity. On the other hand, it must be frankly recognised that display of moderation by the Government, and no concession short of a complete British exodus, will now get rid of him, on the " killing by kindness " principle. Such is the upshot of three years of repression. There was no more loyal people th an the Indian people ten years ago. Lord Curzon and Lord Minto between them have managed to squander this rich heritage, until to-day the dynamiter only puts into practice what practically every Indian feels inclined to preach.

Ex. D 65.

CONTEMPORARY REVIEW,—May 1894, p. 578 and onwards,—

Article on Ethics of Dynamite.

Ex. D 66.

KESARI—June 16, P. 4, Col. 3.—Discusses the definition of ‘explosives.’

पहिला कायदा (१९०८ चा ६ वा) ज्वालाग्राही पदार्थांच्या बद्दलचा होय; आणि तो हिंदुस्थानांत आणि हिंदुस्थानाबाहेर अथवा नेटिव संस्थानांत राहणाऱ्या इंग्रज सरकाराच्या प्रजेस लागूं केलेला आहे. या कायद्याचा उद्देश असा आहे कीं, बाँबसारख्या एकदम पेट घेणाऱ्या भयंकर अस्त्राम लागणारें सामान ज्याच्यापाशीं सांपडेल अथवा जो अशा प्रकारचीं तात्काल अपघात करणारीं भयंकर अस्त्रें तयार करील त्यांस कडक शिक्षा व्हावी; मग त्याच्या योगानें प्राणाची हानी होवो वा न होवो. हल्लींच्या कायद्याप्रमाणें अशा अपराधास पाहिजे तितकी कडक शिक्षा देतां येत नसल्यामुळें हा नवा कायदा करावा लागला आहे. १८८३ सालीं इंग्लंडांत एका मनुष्याजवळ बाँबला लागणारें नायस्ट्रो-ग्लिसरीन, पिक्रिक असिड, वगैरे सामानाचा भरपूर पुरवठा जेव्हां अकस्मात् पोलिसाला सांपडला, तेव्हां पार्लमेंट सभेनें सर वुइल्यम हॉरकोर्ट यांच्या सूचनेवरून एकाच बैठकींत अशा प्रकारचा कायदा पास करून टाकला असा दाखला आहे. या पार्लमेंटाच्या कायद्याचेंच हिंदुस्थान सरकारनें अनुकरण केलें आहे. इतकेंच नव्हे तर सर हार्वे ॲडमसन यांनीं सिमल्यास हा कायदा कायदे कौन्सिलापुढें मांडतांना जें भाषण केलें आहे तेंही सर वुइल्यम हॉरकोर्ट यांच्या भाषणाची बहुतेक अक्षरशः नक्कल आहे, असें म्हणण्यास हरकत नाहीं. उघडच आहे कीं, एकदां विलायतच्या पार्लमेंटामध्यें कोटिक्रम ठरल्यावर तो किंवा त्यांतील शब्द तरी बदलण्याची सर हार्वे ॲडमसन यांनीं काय म्हणून तकलीफ घ्यावी ! परंतु पार्लमेंट सभेंत हा कायदा जरी बैठकींत पास झाला होता तरी त्यांतील पांचव्या कलमाबद्दल पार्लमेंटाच्या कांहीं सभासदांनीं तेव्हांच हरकत घेतली होती. ज्वालाग्राही पदार्थांच्या व्याख्येंत घासलेट तेलसुद्धां येऊं शकेल, इतकेंच नव्हे तर बाँबगोळा तयार करण्यास लागणारे लोखंडी खिळे वगैरे सामान किंवा सदर गोळा पेट घेणाऱ्या वाती अथवा इतर ज्वालाग्राही पदार्थांबरोबर मिश्रण करण्याकरितां लागणारा भुसा किंवा कोळसा अगर माती यांचा देखील समावेश केलेला आहे; आणि अशा प्रकारचा ज्वालाग्राही पदार्थ त्याच्या ताब्यांत असेल त्याच्या हेतूबद्दल पोलिस किंवा माजिस्ट्रेट यांस शंका आल्यास, सदर पदार्थ कायदेशीर ःकामाकरितां आपल्या संग्रहीं आहेत हें पुराव्यानें सिद्ध करण्याचा बोजा सदर इसमावर या कायद्याच्या पांचव्या कलमाप्रमाणें ठेवलेला आहे.

Ex D 67.

MAHRATTA—1st September 1907 P. 411–2.

In 1734 Cosby was the Governor of New York, appointed by the British Crown. He had purposed a high-handed and tyrannical policy subversive of those principles of liberty for which, even at that early date, the people of New York had long contended, and his acts were receiving keen and unsparing satarical treatment in one of the two New York public prints, the *Weekly Journal*. On November 17th Peter Zenger, the publisher of that paper, was arrested, charged with having published seditious libels, thrown into prison, and denied the use of paper, pen and ink. His friends procured a writ of *Habeas Corpus*, but being unable to furnish the extravagant bail demanded—some 7,000 Rupees—(the ways of tyranny have been the same in all ages and in all parts of the earth)—the efforts in his behalf were for the time unavailing. He, however, continued to edit his paper, giving directions to his assistants through chinks in the door of his place of confinement. The grand Jury having refused to find an indictment, the attorney general, on the 23th of January 1735, adopted the star-chamber procedure of filing an information without an indictment, charging Zenger with false, scandalous, seditions and malicions libel. Smith and Alexander, eminent barristers, were retained as his counsel. They began by taking exception to the commissions of Chief Justice DeLansy and Judge Philipse of the Court, because these commissions ran during the pleasure of the Crown, instead of during good behavior, the usual formulæ always insisted on by the American Colonies, and had been granted by the Governor without the advice or consent of his Council. The Court refused to entertain the plea, and to punish the audacity of Counsel for offering it, ordered their names to be struck from the list of barristers. As there were at that time but three lawyers of eminence in New York, one of those being already in the retainer of the Government for the case Zenger was left destitute of any able counsel. This was precisely what the court had foreseen and desired. Determined to thwart this ingeniously concerted intrigue, Zenger's friends secretly engaged the services of the venerable Andrew Hamilton of Philadelphia, then eighty years of age, but in full possession of his faculties, and one of the most distinguished barristers of the day. Hamilton was imbued with the principles that were fast springing up in America, and had shown himself earnest in opposing the despotic tyranny which England was beginning openly to exert over her colonial possessions. A more able or eloquent advocate could hardly have been found and the scheme, which had been designed by the enemies of Zenger to ensure his ruin, ultimately proved the means of his salvation. On the 4th of August 1705, the court assembled for the trial of the prisoner. The court room was crowded to excess, and the unexpected appearance of the eloquent Hamilton as a counsel for Zenger filled the opposite party with astonishment and dismay. The trial came on in the supreme court, with Delancy Acting Chief Justice, Philipse as second judge, and Bradley as Attorney General. The published articles complained of were read, and Hamilton boldly admited responsibility for them for his client. "Then the verdict must be for the king" exclaimed Bradley in triumph. Hamilton quietly reminded him that printing and libelling were not synonymous terms, and was proceeding to prove the truth of the charges contained in the alleged libels, when he was interrupted by the Attorney General, on the plea that the truth of a libel could not be offered in evidence as a defence. This contention was made at length by the Prosecution in which he was sustained by the court, which declared that a libel was all the more dangerous if true, and that therefore the truth of the statements contained in the articles could by no means be considered in the case. Hamilton was therefore unable to put in his evidence, but he made a brilliant address to the jury, ridiculing with biting sarcasm the decision of the court, that truth only made a libel the more dangerous and insisting that the jury were judges both of the law and the fact, he adjurred them to protect their own liberties, now threatened to the person of the persecuted Zenger In his definition of libel the Attorney—General has declared—" Whether a person defamed be a private or a magistrate whether living or dead, whether the libel be true or false, or the party against whom it is made be of good or evil fame, it is nevertheless a libel and as such must be dealt with according to law" ; and he had gone on to demonstrate that Zenger had been guilty of a gross offence against God and man in attacking by words and innuendoes the sacred person of royalty through its representative, the Governor. Hamilton in his address turned these remarks, with infinite keenness and wit against the state. " Almost anything a man may write ", said he, "may, with the help of that useful term of art called an innuendo and be construed to be a libel, according to Mr. Attorney's definition of it; whether the words be spoken of a person of public character or of a private man, whether dead or living, good or bad, true or false, all make a libel.........If a libel is understood in the large and unlimited sense of Mr. Attorney there is scarce a writing that I know of, that may not be called a libel, or scarce any person safe from being called to account as a libeler ; for Moses, meek as he was, libeled Cain, and who is it that has not libeled the devil ; for, according to Mr. Attorney, it is no justification to say that one has a bad name.........I sincerely believe that were some persons to go through the streets of New York now-a-days and read a part of the Bible, if it were not known to be such, Mr. Attorney with the help of his innuendoes, would easily turn it into a libel. As, for instance, the 16th verse of the 9th chapter of Isaiah ' The leaders of the people (innuendo, the Governor and Council of New York) cause them (innuendo, the people of this province) to err, and they (meaning the people of this province) are destroyed (innuendo, are deceived into the loss of their liberty, which is the worst kind of destruction) " " Or, if some person should publicly repeat, in a manner displeasing to his betters, the 10th and 11th verses of the 55th chapter of the same book, then Mr. Attorney would have a large field for the display of his skill in the artful application of his innundoes. The words are : ' His watchmen are blind, they are ignorant, they are greedy dogs that can never have enough.' But to make them a libel, no more is wanting than ' His watchmen (innuendo, the Governor, Council and assembly) are blind, they are ignorant (innuendo, will not see the dangerous designs of his Excellency); yea, they, (meaning the Governor and his Council) are greedy dogs which can never have enough (innuendo, of riches and power.)" After dwelling on the fact that laughable as these illustrations might be, they were strictly anagolous to the charges against his client, and urging the jury to judge for themselves of the truth or falsehood of Zenger's article and to render their verdict accordingly, the eloquent barrister thus concluded his remarks:— "I labour under the weight of many years and am borne down by many infirmities of body; yet, old and weak as I am, I should think it my duty, if required, to go to the utmost part of this land, where my service could be of any use in assisting to quench the flame of prosecutions set on foot by the government to deprive a people of the right of remonstrating (and complaining too) against the arbitary attempts of men in power. Men who injure and oppress the people under their administration provoke them to cry out and complain, and then make that very complaint, the foundation for new oppressions and prosecutions. I wish I could say there were no instances of that kind. But to conclude, the question before you, Genlemen of the jury, is of no small or privte concern; it is not the cause of a poor printer, nor of new York alone, which you are trying. No! It may in its consequence affect every freeman that lives under the British Government on the mainland of America. It is the best cause; it is the cause of liberty; and I make no doubt but that your upright conduct this day will not only entitle you to the love and esteem of your fellow-citizens, but every man who perfers freedom to a life of salvery, will bless and honour you, as men who baffled the attempts of tyranny, and by an impartial and incorrupt verdict, have laid a noble foundation for seruring to ourselves, our posterity and our neighbours, that, to which nature and the laws of our countary have given us a right—the liberty of both exposing and opposing arbitrary power in these parts of the world at least by speaking and writing the truth" The orator concluded amidst a burst of applause. Every eye in the Court room glistened with admiration and every heart forgot the dead letter of the law in the living inspiration of truth and patriotism. Wholly borne down by this torrent of eloquence Bradley attempted but a brief reply and Delancy vainly charged the Jury that they were Judges not of the law only of the fact, and that the truth of a libel was a question beyond their Jurisdiction. Reason and common sense prevailed for once over technicality and the Jury withdrew and returned, after a few minutes deliberation, with a unanimous verdict of "not guilty." The Court-room rung with huzzas which the disappointed Judges vainly endeavored to suppress, and Hamilton was borne from the Hall by the exultant crowd to a splendid entertainment which had been provided for his reception.

Ex. D 68.

SUDHARAK—May 11, P. 2. Col. 2.—Saying bomb was fortold by Hon. Gokhale in 1905.

वंगभंगामुळें बंगाल्यांत उत्पन्न झालेल्या चळवळीमुळें लोकांत एक प्रकारचा असंतोष उत्पन्न झाला आहे; त्या असंतोषांत खरा जोम नाहीं, ही केवळ वरकांती खटपट आहे असें स्टेट सेक्रेटरींनीं बोलून दाखविल्यानें त्या चळवळीस वरचेवर अधिक अधिक जोर येत गेला. लोकांत एक नवीन जागृती उत्पन्न झाली आहे, आणि तीमुळें पारतंत्र्य अधिक टोंचूं लागलें आहे. लोकांत नव्या तृष्णा आणि आकांक्षा उत्पन्न झाल्या आहेत, त्यांची तृप्ति योग्य मार्गांनीं झाली नाहीं तर भलतेच प्रसंग गुजरल्यावांचून राहणार नाहींत, असा इशारा १९०५ सालीं ना० गोखले यांनीं विलायतेंतील लोकांस आपल्या व्याख्यानांत दिला होता. त्याचा अनुभव इतक्या लवकर अशा प्रकारें येईल असें फारच थोड्या लोकांस वाटलें असेल. एका अर्थी

बंगाल्यांत हल्लीं उत्पन्न झालेला अनर्थ परिस्थितीचें फल आहे. जीं बिचारीं अल्पवयी आणि अविचारी मुलें हल्लींच्या विपरीत मार्गानें प्रसिद्धीस आलीं आहेत, तीं त्या परिस्थितीस बळी पडलीं आहेत, त्यांजवर सर्व राग काढण्यापेक्षां दया करणेंच अधिक श्रेयस्कर आहे, हें थोड्या शांत चित्तानें विचार केल्यास कबूल करावयास पाहिजे. या मुलांचा अपराध शब्दव्यूहानें झांकून टाकण्याचा आमचा हेतु नाहीं; परंतु त्यांच्या हातून घडलेल्या अपराधाचा सर्वच दोष त्यांचा नाहीं. यांतील पुष्कळ वांटा त्याहून अधिक समंजस लोकांकडे वस्तुतः आहे, आणि त्यांत सरकाराकडेही कांहीं भाग येत नाहीं असें नाहीं, हें या प्रसंगीं सरकारी अधिकाऱ्यांनीं लक्षांत वागवावें हें बरें!

Ex. D 69.

SUBODH PATRIKA—May 10th 1908, P. 9, Col. 2.

The bomb outrage at Mujafferpur to which one innocent syce and two European ladies fell victims is another indication of the undesirable way in which Bengalees are training themselves. The law will have its course and the perpetrators of the crime will get their meads. But this disgraceful incident must not blind the rulers to the fact that disaffection is spreading in the country in an alarming degree. After the frenzy which has taken hold of every Anglo-Indian head is over, we trust, Government will do its utmost to find out the causes of the disaffection which is more or less of its own creation and will try to remove them. Something must be done to make such outrages impossible and the only statesmanlike way to do it is to remove the causes that lead to them.

Ex. D 70.

SUBODH PATRIKA—May, 17th 1908. p. 2, col 2.

As might have been expectsd the "Bomb Outrage" has created an unprecedented stir in the Anglo-Indian, and the Indian world as well. Newspapers of the type of the *Englishman* and the *Pioneer* have been as it were set a-raving by the bomb. They are all talking of hanging natives by the dozen for every European killed and they have put forth many other suggestions with a view to secure the safety of the Europeans in India. We need hardly say that no real Indian can have any sympathy with such outrages and the perpetrators of them, but at the same time we cannot but condemn the virulent writings of the Anglo-Indian press which has the one pernicious effect of exciting racial animosities between His Majesty's subject races in this country. Our impression is that anti-Indian writings in the Anglo-Indian press of the rabid type are as much responsible for the breaking of law and order by young men as are the writings in the scurrilous vernacular press of the land. Could not Government who has been prosecuting the Calcutta newspapers so persistently see its way to deal in a deserving manner with the Anglo-Indian press also? If it did, it would be removing half the cause of the discontent prevalent in our midst. The policy of repression was sure to result in anarchism. This was foreseen by men like Mr. R. C. Dutt and Mr. Gokhale, the latter giving Government a warning against making fanatics of people by continuing to follow the policy any longer. Unfortunately what these men foresaw has come to pass. Now at least will not Government stop to consider whether the times do not demand a change in their methods of work? Some people say bombs are the outcome of *Swadeshi*. If so *Swadeshi* is the outcome of the Partition of Bengal. It follows therefore, that bombs and the like are the result of that ill-advised measure for the non-modification of which Government is wholly responsible. The real statesmanship of the present moment is to undo that most hated measure and to remove the root of the discontent altogether. It is never too late to mend. Nothing can become a *settled fact* even if Viscount Morley may have declared the Bengal partition to be one, from his seat in Parliament. We appeal to Government to codsider the situation calmly and not to turn Bengal into another Ireland by continuing the hated and the repressive measures any longer.

Opinion on the Tilak Case.

(*1*) *English Opinion.*

H. E. A. Cotton in the 'New Age'

Irishman—not even of the half-blood—requires to ask the meaning of the two words. "Thiggin Thu ?" ("Do you understand ?") which form the burden of one of T. D, Sullivan's most famous national songs:—

Oh ! freedom is a glorious thing;
Even so our gracious rulers say;
And what they say I sure may sing,
In quite a legal proper way,
They praise it up with all their might
And praise the men that seek it too,
—Provided all the row and fight
Are out in Poland:—Thiggin Thu !

A profound comprehension of the Englishman's character is exhibited in these lines. As Emerson discovered, there is in his brain a valve that can be closed at pleasure as an engineer shuts off steam. And one may despair of making him grasp the true inwardness of the events which have, under the "most perfect" and "most just" administration of India, relegated the Parnell of Indian Nationalism for six years to the society of murderes and forgers and professional thieves, unless he can be induced to imagine a man of his own race standing in the dock lately illumined by Mr. Tilak with a burning eloquence and a noble courage which would have earned for him the plaudits of the Empire-if he had not been an Indian. Fortunately, an example is at hand. * * * *

We may pass over the presence on the Bench of the Parsee Judge who was Mr. Tilak's counsel in the former trial of 1897, and who by an irony of fate has now condemned his old client to what is virtually a life sentence in the Andamans. There is a Hindu Judge of the Bombay High Court whose services were available; But Mr. Justice Davar's impartiality may be willingly conceded, although the terrible sentence he has passed may not help some of us to appreciate his sense of proportion. What of the Jury however ? The articles which have brought about the conviction of Mr. Tilak were written neither in English nor in the mother tongue of the Parsees, but in the Marathi language. There are dozens of Marathi-speaking Hindus on the special Jury-list of the High Court. Why were all such so rigidly excluded from the jury which was made up of seven Englishmen and two Parsis, and which went against the accused, as has been said, in exactly that proportion of seven to two ? In the course of his six days address, Mr. Tilak strongly denounced the inaccuracy of the official translations of the offending articles. They would, he said, make anything seditious and could only be compared to distorting mirrors. He demanded either new translations or a complete acquittal. He obtained neither, but a verdict of guilty from a jury of whom it is safe to say that seven of the nine were not able to read a single word of the articles in their original Marathi.

And what is the result? Prior to his arrest, Mr. Tilak was but the leader of a party. He is now a national martyr and a popular hero. When he was taken before the Magistrate some four weeks ago there occurred the most violent display of anti-British feeling that Bombay has known for years. The news of his conviction was followed by the closing of the markets and shops in the so-called "native" quarter. It may be that independent causes must be sought for the strike of the mill-hands and the rioting and bloodshed which have followed so close upon the heels of the trial; but at any rate the co-incidence is remarkable. There can be no doubt that Bombay has been thrown into a ferment, even a Madras has been stirred by the savage sentences of ten years' transportation and transportation for life passed upon the accused in a "sedition" case at Tinnevelly.

The Manchester Guardian.

The nature of the sentence passed upon Mr. Tilak will be interpreted throughout India as a proof that the Government had resolved by hook or by crook to remove him from their path. He has been condemned on his "general record"—which being interpreted means that he has been punished because he can and does stir up to higher things the emotion of a multitude that understands him.

Mr. Tilak is fifty-two. He will never return from the penal settlement to which he has been consigned. But the memory of his trial and his conviction will serve for many a long day to prevent that amelioration of race bitterness and that restoration of confidence and mutual understanding without which the good government of India by Englihmen is entirely impossible, and without which all "reforms" will be completely futile.

The London Times.

The real importance of Mr. Tilak's conviction lies in the fact that he is the acknowledged and undisputed leader of the Extremists' movement in India. That he had guilty knowledge of the darker developments of that movemet is not of course suggested. Mr. Tilak remained at the moment of his conviction the most conspicuous politician in India and among large sections of the people he has enjoyed a popularity and wielded an influence that no other public man in the Dependancy could claim to equal. The Extremists' movement in its open manifestations, both within and outside the Congress, was almost entirely his conception."

The India. (London.)

We do not know if the trial and sentence will be described in any quarter as a triumphant illustration of the imparatiality of British Justice. It certainly does not strike us in that light and those who have set the engine of the law in motion after this fashion may rest assured, that they have dealt a staggering blow to the cause of constitutional reform in the Western Presidency. The acquittal of Mr. Tilak after the admissions made by him in his address, would have meant the death of the form of " Extremism " with which his name is associated. His conviction is likely to drive many hundreds of recruits into the ranks of that still more dangerous " third party " which, Sir Herbert Roberts, rightly pointed out on one day constitutes the real danger to British rule in India.

The Star.

It appears that Mr. Tilak's articles were not direct incitements to the use of bombs. His language was vague and veiled. He indulged in subtle hints and delicate insinuations. Now, we all know that nothing is easier than to fasten upon the rhetoric of a politician in critical times a darker meaning than it would sustain in times of peace. The leading case of Parnell and the Invincibles must always be remembered. There was a period during which few Englishmen believed in Parnell's innocence, and his speeches were ransacked for phrases which could be intepreted in a sinister way. If India were Ireland, it is possible that Mr. Tilak might have been able to persuade a Jury that his language, though dubious, was not intended to stimulate the business oi bomb—throwing, he denounced bomb-throwing as "horrible." This, of course, is another remarkable parallel to the case of Parnell, for Parnell denounced the Phoenix park murders. It is to be hoped that the Judge and the Jury were alive to the necessity of making assurance doubly sure before convicting and sentencing Mr. Tilak. It would be a pity if he turned out to be a Parnell. Mr. Tilak's language during his address to the Jury, which lasted six days, appears to have been modelled upon the language of English reformers. After the verdict he " maintained that there were higher powers over ruling the destinies of men and nations. It may be the will of Providence that the cause I represent will profit more by my suffering than by my presence here." These words are not unworthy of an honest and a noble cause, and even if the guilt of Mr. Tilak be greater and graver than the Jury and the judge held it to be, the responsibility that lies upon the Government is also great and grave. It is for Lord Morley and his colleagues to see that political reform is pushed on without delay and without dread. Reform is the best answer to the bomb.

The Manchester Guardian.

Published a letter from an Anglo-Indian correspondent on the " sources of Mr. Tilak's influence in India" from which we take the following extract. By a constant series of prosecutions the Government has made him, what he is, a martyr and without a rival in Eastern India. Such being the case a wise Government recognizing the danger of such adversary would have taken to avoid providing him with a further grievance; but the Bombay Government was not wise * * * * He is beyond question the most powerful and astute of living Indians. He combines a brilliant and versatile intellect with a personality that appeals irresistibly to the multitude. Unlike the majority of Indian political leaders he has escaped the suspicion attaching to Western influences.

The Scotsman.

The closing of the markets is perhaps of graver import than the riots, as it serves to show that the feeling of the largest and wealthiest, if not also the most intelligent and enterprising community of Indian-merchants and financiers, is on the side of Mr. Tilak. The fact makes it the more important to know the precise nature and full extent of the offence for which the ideal patriot of Western India has been sent to the Andaman Islands. Mr. Tilak has been for many years the acknowledged leader of the Nationalist agitation among the Mahratta people of the west of India. His influence was not confined to the Bombay side of the Empire. As the leader of its more extreme section he holds a commanding position among the bolder agitators throughout India. He is a man of scholarship and great intellectual ability, an eminent pleader standing by reputation high above the coarser and more violent-type of demagogue. The serious aspect of the situation is that all Native Bombay, from mill worker to merchant, seems to sympathise with the convict. The feeling is certainly proof of the supreme popularity of the man.

The Nation.

The punishment of Mr. Tilak is serious for he represents the Left Wing of the native movement in India, and stands to the agitation in much the same relation as Mr. Parnell occupied to the physical force party in Ireland and America. Part of Mr. Tilak's article seems to us to put crudely the arguments of all reformers that force used against national movements is no remedy, but the other part is certainly revolutionary declaring that the use of bombs in India was on all fours with their use in Russia and hinting that they might prove a more powerful anti-British weapon than muskets and guns. The article, like one or two of Mr. Parnell's speeches, hovered between constitutional doctrine and condonation of violence.

Reynold's Newspaper.

Mr. Tilak, the Indian editor, has been found guilty of publishing seditious articles, and has been sentenced to six years' transportation to the Adaman Islands: Let us try to realize, before we turn over this page in Indian history, what the episode means. In the first place Mr. Tilak is the leader of the "popular" party. When they heard the sentence the mob broke out into rioting, and workmen went on strike. Already he is a martyr, and we have been taught by history to believe that the blood of the martyrs is the seed of the Church.

H. M. Hyndman in the London Times.

With its usual fairness in the matter of news the *Times* is the only newspaper which has given its readers the opportunity of forming a reasonable judgment on the prosecution and conviction of the Mahratta Brahmin, Mr. Tilak. I am quite sure that an unprejudiced Englishman reading the evidence which you have adduced from the journals edited by Mr. Tilak, will come to the conclusion that, if articles of that character are to earn the writer six years' transportation to the Andaman Islands then we may just as well at once state plainly that no free criticism of our rule is to be permitted in India at all. I defy any one to point to a sentence in Mr. Tilak's articles which incites to bomb-throwing or violence; and I cannot understand how Englishmen, who have always supported peoples struggling for freedom in other countries, and are doing so to-day in regard to Russians or Turks can resort to such measures of repression as those which Lord Morley and Lord Minto, both nominally Liberals, are applying in India.

What, however I am specially anxious that you should allow me to call attention to is the manner in which this trial has been conducted. According to our law in Great Britain, a man prosecuted as Mr. Tilak has been prosecuted is entitled to be tried by a Jury of his peers, and they must render a unanimous verdict as to his guilt before sentence can be passed. The Jury which tried Mr. Tilak consisted of nine persons, seven of them being Europeans and two Parsis, Mr. Tilak himself being, as I said, a Mahratta Brahmin of the highest position. This Jury so empanelled was not even agreed as to Mr.Tilak's guilt. The voting was seven for conviction and two against, and I do not think I can be very far wrong supposing that the seven Europeans voted in the majority and the two Indians in the minority. I ask, Sir, whether that is a verdict which justifies a Judge, nominated and paid by the foreign rulers, in sentencing the leader of the Indian national party to six year's transportation. Mr. Tilak is not a young man, and as he said this sentence may not make much difference to him but surely justice is justice all the world over; and I at any rate intend during the coming autumn and winter to denounce this trial as utterly contrary to the whole spirit of English equity and to call upon my countrymen in all our great cities to enter their protest against such shameful deeds being done in their name.

Keir Hardie in the Labour Leader.

There is no man in India who has such a hold upon the working class as Mr. Tilak, and the result of his conviction will be more far reaching than that of any single individual which has yet taken place. I spent three days in his company when visiting Poona less than a year ago. His life history has been a record which marks him out as one of those men of whom most nations are proud. As a scholar he has a worldwide reputation, and was the founder of the Fergusson College, where for years he was a professor. He is a man of means, and some years ago resigned his position in the college that he might be free to devote himself to the interests of his people. Since then he has been the leading figure in the advanced section of Indian reformers, and was, nominally at least, mainly responsible for the break-up of the Congress at Surat last year. His standing in literature is on a par with that of Tchaikovsky, the Russian who is in prison without trial in Russia, or with our own Alfred Russel Wallace, in science. I mention these things that it may be understood who and what Mr. B. G. Tilak is. The conclusion I formed concerning him was that his temperament had been soured by long, weary years of disappointed waiting, but that whilst he advocated extreme measures of agitation he would be satisfied with moderate reforms provided they were genuine and indicated a real desire to improve the condition of India. His sympathy with the peasantry was intense, and some of his journals were published in the native vernacular and circulated extensively throughout the country districts of the Bombay presidency. This stirring up of the peasantry has been, I believe, the bedrock of his offence.

The Manchester Guardian.

The arrest of Mr. Bal Gangadhar Tilak, the Nationalist leader of Poona, is by far the most serious and sensational step so far taken by the Government of India in the campaign against sedition. It would be impossible to exaggerate its significance. Mr. Tilak is a Mahratta Brahmin of remarkable ability and of unique standing among his countrymen. He has a personal following larger and more devoted than any other popular leader in India commands. This is not his first experience of a sedition charge. His is the astutest brain so far placed at the service of the Nationalist cause. He edits two weekly newspapers—the *Mahratta* in English and *Kesari* in the vernacular. Both have for years waged uncompromising warfare against the administration, though the *Kesari* has been more down right in policy and expression than the *Mahratta* Sir George Clarke, in deciding upon the arrest of Mr. Tilak, has doubtless realised that the Government could not consistently prosecute the smaller fry without striking at the most powerful revolutionary in the country, a man by comparison with whom such persons as Bepin Chandra Pal and even Lajpat Rai are inconsiderable.

The Daily News.

The *Daily News*:—An Anglo-Indian correspondent write : No step which the Indian Government could have taken in the present campaign against sedition could for a moment compare with the arrest of Mr. Tilak, the ablest, subtlest and most powerfull popular leader in the country. Since his condemnation for sedition eleven years ago, Tilak has been the high-priest of the extremist Nationalism. His creed is taught chiefly in his two papers—the *Mahratta* (English) and the *Kesari*, a vernecular weekly. It will be noted that, acording to Reuters summary, the article, on which the charge of sedition is based, contains no incitement to violence. The question suggests itself : " If this is the worst that M. Tilak has written since the bomb-outrages (which he condemned), has the Government of Bombay not made a grave mistake in committing itself to an action calculated to arouse an unprecedented storm ? "

The Morning Leader.

There are very few people in England in a position to realise what the arrest of Mr. Bal Gangadhar Tilak, the Nationalist leader of Poona, actually means in India. His personal power is unapproached by any other politician in the country; he dominates the Deccan, his own country, and is adored with a kind of religious fervour by every extremist from Bombay to the Bay of Bengal, The break-up of the National Congress at Surat was his doing; his is the mind that conceived, his the pen that expressed, and his the force that has directed the extraordinary movement against which the bureaucracy is now calling up all its resources. Bal Gangadhar Tilak is a Maratha Brahmin—thinker and fighter in one. He was sentenced for sedition in 1897, and since that time has felt the weight of the Government's hand in a series of prosecutions, from which he emerged triumphant and with a personal prestige that made him the most dangerous opponent of the Government's policy. He edits two newspapers in Poona–the *Mahratta* in English and the *Kesari* in the vernacular. Although he has lately published an expression of regret for the bomb-outrages, he has evidently been driven to bay by the new Press Act. But, it will be noted, he has been proceeded against under the regular clause of the Penal Code. Assuming that Reuter's summary of the offending article is passably correct, the Government obviously could not deal summarily with the editor, for there is here nothing like an incitement to violence. This, however, is a minor matter. The point of overwhelming importance is that Sir George Clerke has taken a step calculated to open the floodgates of popular fury. It may have been necessary; but if so, the question still remains, who is to be held responsible for so desperate a condition of affairs?

(2) *Indian Opinion.*

TheIndian Spectator (Bombay.)

The Tilakolatry of the shopkeepers and the mill-hands and of other classes even in a city like Bombay must have struck Government as a remarkable sign of the times and as an unmistakable indication of the political bias of the people. The political atmosphere of Bombay is, indeed, very different from that of Poona. Society here is so heterogeneous, and so free from the influence of the Poona Brahman, that not one of the ten persons who sat in judgment upon Mr. Tilak—one Judge and nine Jurymen—belonged to his own community. Yet even in the political atmosphere of this city, Tilakolatry flourishes to an extent which could not have failed to impress Government in the course of last week. Many have worked themselves into a state of mind which may without exaggeration be described as a frenzy of disconsolation. "Let us have a look at Tilak Maharaj" was the demand with which the populace greeted the advice of that sympathetic and devoted friend of the citizens of Bombay—Mr. S. M. Edwardes. And they were not Poona Brahmans. Why do we call attention to this phase of the political tendency of the time ? Not because we wish to suggest that Government should be afraid of dealing with sedition or should treat popular leaders differently from obscure journalists. The law should, indeed, be no respecter of persons. But as the object of punishing sedition is preventive and reformatory, the temper and the bias of the classes likely to be influenced by seditious writings should not be lost sight of.

The Mahratta (Poona.)

It is true that Mr. Tilak was allowed to have a patient and an uninterrupted hearing in his defence. But that is not the whole essence of a fair trial. The unfairness of the trial commenced with the dragging of Mr. Tilak to Bombay. The articles were in Marathi and he should have been tried at Poona by the Sessions Court with the aid of Marathi knowing jurors or assessors who would be able to know not only the spirit of the writings but of the effect likely to be produced upon the general class of the readers of the *Kesari*. Then again it was quite unfair that Mr. Tilak was not released on bail, as he was thus deprived of the opportunity and the means of making even a more satisfactory defence than he actually did. The next thing in the same connection is that a Special Jury was ordered to be empanelled instead of a Common Jury. The latter would have contained more Marathi-knowing Jurors than the former; and notwithstanding the assurance, given by Mr. Justice Davar, that he hoped that the arrangements about summoning Jurors would be so made that the different communities would be fairly represented on the panel, an overwhelming majority of those summoned, or at any rate of those whose names were picked out from the ballot-box turned out to be Europeans. The Jury actually empanelled contained only two Indians. Then, again, the joinder of three charges arising out of two articles separated in point of time by about four weeks was evidently calculated to prove prejudicial to the Defence; and the Judge allowed it even without recording an acquittal on the fourth charge, which he could not legally allow to be joined but which he was not unwilling to allow to be kept hanging on Mr. Tilak's head. The Advocate-General made a passionate speech full of rank abuse and offence and quite against the traditions of the office of the Counsel for the Crown who is expected not to unduly press any point against an accused person, especially when he makes his own defence. About the unfairness of the Judge we shall speak presently; and about the majority of the Jury who convicted Mr. Tilak on all the three charges we need say nothing for obvious reasons.

Having obtained a Special Jury for trying Mr. Tilak, Government seemed to be confident that they might go to sleep over the prosecution. And they were probably engaged during the week the trial lasted only in making due provision for further dealing with Mr. Tilak as a convict. On the last day of the trail the whole government praty appeared to be nearly off their guard and displayed a wonderfully prophetic vision in getting the closure, as it were put upon the trial which threatened to be prolonged into another day. The Judge himself seemed to divine something about the exigencies of finishing the trial a day before the Budget debate in the Parliament, when he asked the Jury at 2-30 P. M. on Wednesday to return at 3 P. M. and, in asking the Advocate General how long he would take, assured him significantly that he did not want to hurry him up unnecessarily. At about 5 P. M. mysterious movements and consultations among the Government party began, and the whole Court house was taken by surprise when it learnt that the Judge had decided to finish the case that day however long it might take them into the night. Mr. Branson was only reasonable. After the brief recess between 5-30 and 6 P. M. he most agreeably collapsed into brevity; and bringing his address to a somewhat unnatural termination, he ungrudgingly left the whole field to the Judge and the Jury. Nor was the Judge himself behind hand. He was quite ready with his written charge to the Jury and the Jury did not waste more than an hour and a quarter in trying to be unanimous. So the whole blessed thing was finished by 10 P. M., and the official party could go home in time if not for dinner, at any rate for sleeping the sleep of righteous men. To Mr. Tilak, however, the want of a prophetic vision, the lack of a rich imagination made a world of difference. He was under the reasonable belief that the case could not be finished before Thursday

It even looked like that till 5-30 P. M. on Wednesday, till the usual hour for adjournment, when the beginning of the end of Mr. Branson's speech was not in sight. Mr. Tilak had paobably thought of having a talk with his friends and relations that evening and the next morning in view of the eventuality of his conviction. But the net was woven around his life surreptitiously in the closing vesper hours of that memorable day. When the Judge rose after passing sentence all rose with him, and in the twinkling of an eye, Mr. Tilak was spirited away by the Police so that those who would have liked to have a conscious look of him before his exile for six years, perhaps the last conscious look, were denied even that consolation.

But if Mr. Tilak suffered on both the occasions by the verdict of a European majority among the Jury, we do not blame the European Jurymen therefor. They could not understand the language of the writing. They could not possibly divest their mind of the knowledge with which they entered the Jury box to the prejudice of Mr. Tilak. They probably believed it to be as patriotic a duty to convict Mr. Tilak as Mr. Tilak himself believed it to be to write his articles. The fault in the situation is the fault of the system. In India we have merely the mockery of a trial by Jury. The name is the same in India as in England. But the actual conditions of the trial by Jury we have here are materially different. In England an accused person has necessarily a Jury made up of his own countrymen and his peers. In India European British subjects enjoy nearly the same privilege under the guarantee of Statute law. The Indians in India, however can not claim that privilege, and in the City of Bombay more than half of the members of the Special Jury list must be Europeans. There is hardly any Indian newspaper which cannot be technically said to be published in Bombay. And every newspaper prosecution is sure to be treated as an important case and a case for a Special Jury. It necessarily follows, therefore, that in every newspaper prosecution in Bombay the accused must be tried by men who do not know the language of the incriminating writing who must be prejudiced against Indian editors generally, and that the accused must be, therefore, convicted. The fault of the system clearly—as we have said. We may, however, deal with the subject at length later on at leisure.

And what shall we say of the Judge who tried the case? It goes without saying that Mr. Justice Davar gave Mr. Tilak a very patient hearing. We know also that under the law he was entitled to express his own opinion upon the case in his charge to the Jury, and we for one shall never blame him for expressing an adverse opinion if he honestly thought that Mr. Tilak had transgressed the limits of the law as he understood and interpreted it. We ought not to expect every Judge to see eye to eye with ourselves in every case; but while we cannot allow Mr. Justice Davar to claim credit for showing misplaced leniency to Mr. Tilak by passing a sentence of transportation for six years, we must express our disapprobation of the affectation of which he was guilty in his charge to the Jury and must strongly and positively condemn some of the words he used towards Mr. Tilak in passing a severe sentence upon him. The influence of those words, though uttered at the end of the trial, could not but relate back; and hence we are inclined to put a meaning of our own upon some of the words he uttered in the earlier stages of the case. Thus it was observed that whenever any question arose for a ruling by the Judge, it was invariably found that his Lordship had considered it " most *anxiously*" too. So also whatever his Lordship did, was in the interest of the Defence itself. If Mr. Tilak was not released on bail, it was in his own interest that it was so ! If a Special Jury was ordered to be empanelled the same consideration, viz. the interest of the accused, was present to the Judge's mind ! The Judge in fact showed a paternal solicitude for the accused as he was undefended ! But when the moment for the charge to Jury had arrived, every thing was to be changed. As soon as the Judge found his liberty of speech he made every point against the accused; and only repeated at stated intervals the ridiculously meaningless formula that the Jury might decide the matter as they thought and set aside his view unhesitatingly. Towards the commencement of the charge it looked as if the Judge would content himself with explaning the law, and would leave the merits to the Jury. In fact he said so, remarking that as Mr. Tilak had expressed his confidence in the Jury he would only add to their responsibility by leaving the whole thing to them. But apparently the temptation of the exercise of his privilege proved too great; and Mr. Justice Davar took it upon himself not only to bestow a one-sided and an adverse treatment on the incriminating articles, but tried to make the case for Prosecution more complete than the Advocate-General himself had done by ferreting out hidden words, and hidden inuendoes which were never touched by the Counsel for the Crown.

But the worst is yet behind. And it is that which causes us the utmost pain. We have so far noticed things which might be regarded as judicially done and against which we could not legitimately complain. We have no quarrel with Mr. Davar the Judge, but we must express our sense of disgust at some of the words which he used towards Mr. Tilak and for using them we must blame Mr. Daver the gentleman. The bushel with which Mr. Davar the Judge may have been endowed to deal out justice may be a small one. That we do not regard as his fault. It may be he is wrong in holding him to be innocent. But there cannot be two views, two opinions about the insult he gave to Mr. Tilak,standing helpless in the dock, by branding him as a man with a diseased mind, and worse still, by daring to talk of Mr. Tilak as professing to love his land, his country! Mr. Tilak's diseased mind! Surely the very meaning of words must have changed since Mr. Davar was elevated to the Bench. But may there not be in the human world may more categories of mental disease than medical quacks in red robes are aware of or would agree to admit ? For how else shall we describe a Judge who takes advantage of his position to cruelly libel an accused in the dock before him? And as for saying that Mr. Tilak only *professed* to love his country, meaning that he did not really love it, we think Mr. Justice Davar might well have spared Mr. Tilak the pain and himself the ignominy of that heartless white lie ! It is unkind, it is cruel, it is mean, it is cowardly. Mr. Tilak's enemies, even those who may be privileged enough to sit on the Bench, might, if they like, call him, indiscreet, or reckless, or obsinate, or misguided, but anything except 'a man only *professing* to love his country.' Oh! the shamefulness of the accusation: it only grows wtih repetition ! We had known of the glow-worm, holding his torch to the Sun, being talked of as a good illustration of impudence. But we had never realised its force or its pithiness before we actually heard one man, who had probably done nothing except earning money all his life, cruelly taunting another man with only *professing* to love his country-a man who, if he had so chosen, would have, as a High Court Judge, ranked senior to Mr. Justice Davar, but deliberately chose the path of self-sacrifice at the parting of the ways and expended his life-bloold in serving his country and in giving his fellow countrymen political education of a difficult but much needed type.

The Indu-Prakash, (Bombay.)

The great case under Sections I24A. and I53A, of which the tryingly slow progress and development was so anxiously watched not only by united Bombay in a manner belying for once at least her character for too exclusive an absorption in the pursuit of Mammon and the resulting sobriety and apathy in politics, but also by India, and as the papers brought by the last mail show, by England too,—that great case has at last come to an end. × × × × The trial, conviction and sentence in a case of a political offence, created by law and having none of the immoral complexion of ordinary crimes, against a unique personality like Mr. Tilak, cannot but be one of those infrequent occasions when the reason refuses to be bound by mere technicalities and legalities or even by the needs of the day, when it takes account of past and future and of human strength and weaknesses and looks to far off consequences as well as present results—when in short, the reason declines to act without her inseparably associated partner,-human feeling. The undoubted ability and attainments of Mr. Tilak, his simplicity, his indomitable energy and ceaseless activity, the purity of his private life, his single minded dedication of all that was his to public life, explain the hold and influence he has been able to gather round him like an irresistible and surging tide, and the admiration he extorts from opponent no less than friend. What human being could withstand the irresistible call for deep sympathy which is made to the heart at the spectacle of a man like this being led by honest convictions into a course provoking chastisement from Government in spite of both having at heart the common aim of the good of the people, and of his coming on that account under the clutches of the law and having to go into an immurement from the world for 6 years—an almost death—like sentence on a man of 53, suffering long since from diabetes ! ! ! + the constitutionalist must feel the present policy of the Government of Bombay to be a sore grievance with him. The men of this party know full well the differences that separate their methods and ideals from those of the Nationalists, but we think we are not inaccurate in expressing this to be their almost unanimous conviction that the right and efficacious remedy for the present crisis consists in Government's strengthening their hands by material concessions to the demands for constitutional progress of the day and then to leave them to fight their fight with their opponents.

The Indian Social Reformer (Bombay.)

We have differed from Mr. Tilak's aims and methods of public controversy for the last fifteen years and more. But—and we say it with full deliberation—we have never for a moment believed him to be capable of such a political propagandism as appears to have actuated the originators and abettors of the Muzafferpur crime. This is still our belief. The views expressed in the *Kesari* in connection with that outrage have little in common with those that we have expressed in these columns, but in the absence of proof that the writer had intended them to be the starting point of a similar propagandism, we are unable to think that that was his intention. Would anybody say that the comments of the *Pioneer* on the bomb-outrages in Russia, meant that the writer of them was or intended to be a manufacturer of bombs himself? The card with the two names of books on explosives written on it, which was produced with much solemnity, was explained in a perfectly satisfactory manner by the accused, and the learned Judge very properly directed the Jury not to attach too much importance to it. He might have said that they should discard it altogether from their minds. A book is not a bomb, much less so, the name of a book, and the prosecution, we think, should never have used it as it did. What other evidence was there to show that the articles were anything more than the outcome of intellectual perversity and of a certain moral purblindness which affects many persons, not exclusively of Indian nationality, in dealing with subjects of this nature? How can we justify the extremely severe sentences passed on the accused.

× × × ×

We have, therefore, no exception to take to the policy of prosecuting seditious writings and we must express our satisfaction that in the two more important prosecutions Government saw fit to change the venue from the Magistrates' to the High Court. But it is obvious that the system, under which a Jury composed largely of men not acquainted with the language in which the writings complained against are composed, can be found trying a fellow subject for an offence punishable with transportation for life, hardly comes up to the ideal of judicial rightness which it should be the aim of every Government to appropriate. Any one who has at all to explain in a vernacular language ideas political can well understand Mr. Tilak's plea that the terminology of political controversy in Marathi is not fixed and has to be eked out, often on the spur of the moment, by more or less approximate adaptations from that general reservior of most of the Indian languages, Sanskrit.

In the case of a writer like Mr. Tilak, this defect of the present system is apt to press with more than ordinary hardship because, whatever we might think of him as a politician or a a social reformer, it must be admitted that, in relation to the Marathi language, he represents in the words of Waltur Pater, "that living authority which language need" and which "lies in truth in its scholars, who recognising always that every language possesses a genius, a very fastidious genius, of its own, expand at once and purify its very elements, which must needs change along with the changing thoughts of living people."

× × × ×

In reviewing the proceedings of this trial, we have tried to point out where the Prosecution seems to us to have fallen short of that scrupulous fairness which should be expected in all prosecutions by the Crown. We have also pointed out what we conceive to be the weak points in Mr. Tilak's defence. We do not believe him to be capable of organising a movement of assassination and his evidence before the Decentralization Commission shows that he is not an apostle of anarchy. These, however, are not necessary elements in the offence of sedition and our feeling is one of deep regret that a gentleman of his ability and scholarly attainments should have followed a course leading to the Jail. We do not conceive it to be our duty, and we should be ashamed of ourselves if we felt any inclination, to trample upon the prostrate form of one who, after all is, as a contemporary gracefully says of him, " a citizen and a scholar," and is not a coward.

The Gujarathi Punch (Ahmedabad.)

The news came upon us with the tragedy of a thunderbolt. It will be no exaggeration to say that it has completely paralysed our pen. The whole thing looks like a nightmare, an evil dream. It is, alas ! but too true. The tumult created in our heart by the dread fate which has overtaken one of India's greatest and most remarkable sons makes it impossible for us to write of the trial and the conviction. We will not make the attempt. But we cannot conclude without expressing for Mr. Tilak our heartiest and sincerest sympathy. He made a noble, the grandest possible fight for the liberty of the Native Press. He has failed. But the memory of the trial and of what he has had to suffer will ever be green in the hearts of his countrymen. The magnificent defence made by him has truly earned the admirition of even his enemies. The last scene in the terrible tragedy concluded at Bombay on Wednesday last was a historic one, worthy the brush of a great painter. Or rather it requires no canvass, for it will be imprinted on the heart of every one of Mr. Tilak's countrymen, a picture which death alone will efface from the tablets of memory. The prosecution of Mr. Tilak may be legally justifiable, but it was under the circumstances not expedient. Before we conclude, however, it is our sacred duty te express our heartiest sympathy for M. Tilak and that we do without the least hesitation. Mr. Tilak's last words in the dock were worthy of the occasion and the man, and but clearly depicted the grandeur and indomitability of the hero.

The Gujarathi (Bombay.)

It is difficult to concede that the present system of selecting special jurors for the trial of sedition cases can be looked upon as altogether satisfactory. On the face of it it looks not a little strange that European jurors not knowing a word of Marathi or any other vernacular should be called upon to sit in judgment upon the seditious character or otherwise of any writings or speeches in vernacular. The anomaly becomes the more glaring when the accuracy of the English translations is challenged, as was the case in Mr. Tilak's trial, by the defence. We do not think Englishmen who enjoy very valuable safeguards against unjust conviction for sedition in their own country will ever consent to submit to any trial under similar circumstances. Nor do we believe that impartial Englishmen will seriously maintain that the present system is either satisfactory in itself or calculated to command the implicit confidence of the public at large. The vernaculars of the country are in a state of growth. The political vocabulary is slowly growing with the growing political thought of the country. The varying shades of thought and feeling embodied in particular English words or phrases can, if at all, be expressed with very great difficulty through the medium of vernulars, and conversely there is experienced a corresponding difficulty in rendering vernacular expressions into English. Out of the nine gentlemen composing the jury in Mr. Tilak's trial, six were Europeans, one a Jew and two Parsees. Is it altogether fair or satisfactory that men who do not know Marathi and are unacquainted with the political vocabulary of the Deccan should be required by law to give their opinion on matters on which they themselves must feel great difficulty and decide the question of guilt or otherwise on the strength of translations the accuracy of which is vehemently challenged. The present system is unfair to the prosecution, the defence and even to the Court. It may be admitted that with all its defects the Jury does arrive at a correct decision in particular instances. But on principle it can scarcely be pronounced to be satisfactory. The machinery of trial must not only be satisfactory in itself, but what is of still greater importance in the trials of political offences the whole machinery and procedure must bear upon their very face the stamp of scrupulous fairness, so far as the people at large are concerned. We do not think an Englishman would like to be tried by Greeks or Russians innocent of all knowledge of English even with the help of translations for writing a seditious article in English and it would be a strange misconception of human nature and the principles of justice, if one were to suppose that in this country alone the cause of justice, law and order demanded or justified the application of different considerations.

The Phœnix (Karachi.)

An erudite scholar, a cultured journalist, a man of sterling independence—decidedly he was a terror to the bureaucracy. He was the recognised leader of the Nationalists. When he saw that the bureaucracy did not heed to the prayers and the protests of the Moderate Party, when he saw that the rulers flouted the Indian public opinion as in the case of the partition of Bengal, his was the brain that organised the Nationalist Party, his was the pen that advocated passive resistance. Now he is transported to the great disappointment of his followers and the jubilation of the mighty bureaucracy. Indeed, this is a great blow to the Nationalist Party. Though he wrecked the Indian National Congress, we cannot but deplore the fate and sympathise in the troubles under which the Great Mahratta leader has fallen. This much is certain that the entire country from Dan to Beersheba, watched with admiration the able and elaborate defence which he made; and the way in which he, without the aid of the lawyers, conducted his own case, had added greatly to the estimation and love in which Mr. Tilak is held by many of his countrymen. We widely differ from Mr. Tilak as regards his political views. We have often taken him to task for his Extremist propaganda. All the the same, we hold that Mr. Tilak has suffered for *not loving his country wisely but too well*. We pertinently ask our English friends whether these sedition trials and the punishment of popular leaders would check the present unrest and the discontent in the country or whether it would make the British rule more and more unpopular among the masses. Certainly, the feeling that has been excited about this trial at Bombay and in Deccan clearly indicates the direction in which the wind is blowing.

The Khalsa Advocate (Amritsar.)

The Tilak case is at an end and the great Marhatta leader has been transported for six years. His honesty of purpose, his straightforwardness, his erudite learning and his noble patriotic zeal are acknowledged even by his worst enemies. One may not agree with his line of action or his opinion bnt every patriotic Indian will be proud to possess a spark even of that fervour with wiich that great man has attempted to work (though in his own way with which every body may not agree) for the good of his country. Mr. Tilak is above 50 now and to be sent adrift in this old age is extremely unfortunate. We would devoutly wish that such eminent men should not give any occasion to the other side to bring them under the clutches of law and heartily sympathise with the noble scholar in his trouble.

The Telegraph (Calcutta.)

The unprecedented hour up till which the Court sat in judgment, the suddenness with which the trial came to a close,the hurry in which he was removed to the steamer, and the readiness with which he was received there—have left the people agape with wonder and surcharged with a heavy feeling of uneasiness in their breasts. The people were quite unprepared. The suddenness and the heaviness of the sentence have descended upon them like a bolt from the blue. They were listening with wrapt attention to his masterly defence from day to day, they were struck with his brilliant address to the Jury, they were expecting every moment an honourable acquittal— and all on a sudden their hopes were dashed to pieces. An illustrious man whose noble figure towered high above all in his country,—a man whose vast erudition and scholarly habit won admiration from even the proud Westerners,—a man who devoted his whole life-time in the service of his countrymen and motherland—a man whose fervent piety, purity of character and intense religiousness even the tongue of calumny of enmity never dared to impugne-a man who banished all thoughts about his self when he served the plague patients of his country—such a man sentenced to serve in a penal settlement among thieves and murders! Though our heart is surcharged, though our thoughts lie toe deep for words, though our heart may break through the fullness of sorrow—we should bear in patience and silence; sufferance is the badge of the tribe-for to suffer in silece is what is enjoined by our Shastras.

The Panjabee (Lahore.)

SJ. Tilak appealed to a higher Power than any earthly Government in his reply to Justice Davar's question if he had any thing to say before sentence was passed. He said "There were higher powers that ruled the destinies of men and nations and it might be that the cause he represented might be benefited more by suffering than by his freedom." This sentiment reveals to us the intensely spiritual character of our eminent publicist. He has been supported in all his trials and tribulations by the faith that the work he has to do is sacred and that the blessing of God is upon it. Trust in mere earthly instruments and resources cannot inspire a man with the fine moral fervour which is discernible in Sj. Tilak's public utterances. He does not look upon politics as a mere game of chance or as the art of haggling for a bargain between two countries. He believes in the future destiny of his country and feels that the power that guides and controls the Universe is devising means and methods for the speedy realisation of that destiny. And let all workers in the country's cause remember the lesson conveyed in Sj. Tilak's pregnant words. If we do not believe in the great Moral Law which governs the fate of nations, we shall wreck our glorious movement on rocks of materialism and pessimism. Truth is great and shall prevail that should be our motto, and our watchword in the struggle on which we have entered. Governments are strong in the strength of armaments and irresponsible authority. But there is something stronger far than any human Government, more enduring then the most cunningly woven fabric of Empire that the world may yet see. And that some thing is the unconquerable Spirit of the Righteous Man, the Moral Power of a soul devoted to the highest ends. No earthly potentate can in the long run oppose the advance of a movement founded on the eternal basis of Truth and Justice. The Moral Law alone endures; all else is consumed and transformed as the Law works itself out. If we put our shoulders to the wheel in the spirit of earnest apostles of the religion of Patriotism, we must succeed in the end, even though dangers and difficulties may sorely try our faith and mock our enthusiasm. Politics in India have been regarded as mere matters of administration, which are trivial in themselves and meaningless in so far as they are not brought under some general law of progress. But Sj. Tilak has raised politics to the level of religion, he has shown that we are called to spend and be spent in a great cause, which is indeed a Divine Dispensation for this nation at the time of her greatest need. Let us cast out all fear of the deities of clay whom the world adores: and let us obey the voice of our conscience, which calls us to go forth and sacrifice ourselves for the Motherland.

× × ×

For ten days last the country has been all ears to hear the end of Sj. Tilak's trial. For a time all sense of danger was lost in the pride which the country felt from one end to the other in the masterly defence which the eminent prisoner in dock was making. Every one felt as if Sj. Tilak was making hisiory.

× × ×

The present verdict, we are afraid, given by seven Europeans on a prosecution started by the Government, is not likely to be accepted as a Judicial pronouncement of any value by the country at large. The country would look upon it as if the Prosecution sat in judgment over their own case. Coming to the sentence we wish Justice Davar had spared the accused the pain which he was inflicting upon him by trying to palliate the severity of the sentence which he was proposing to give, by his sweet compliments to the ability of the accused. Sj. Tilak required no certificate from him. His abtlity and influence are acknowledged by his worst enemies; and even the English Press in commenting upon his arrest and the action of Government in prosecuting him has given him the position of the greatest living Indian. As such we think Justice Davar only added insult to injury by talking of his abilities and influence when he had made up his mind to transport him for a term of six years. It was still more preposterous for him to say that he was transporting him out of considerations for his age. A ferocious sentence like that after a defence like the one Sj. Tilak made, on a man of his position cannot certainly be called a lenient one. It was practically sealing his fate, because a man of his age suffering from a fatal disease like diabetes cannot be expected to survive it and return to his country after serving his term.

× × ×

For over 25 years continuously Sj. Tilak has been serving the country. He has been devoting to the cause of the motherland his admittedly high abilities, his phenomenal energies and everything else which was at his command. He has been one of the most prominent leaders of that school of politics which has been represented by the Congress, and though some of our countrymen did not entirely agree with some of his methods of work, there was not one among them who did not unreservedly admit the selfless devotion and the disinterested spirit with which he carried on the work of political education. In his thorough knowledge of the circumstances of his country, in his grasp of our political situation and in applying proper remedies to improve that situation, he, in our humble opinion stood head and shoulders over our political leaders, though we do'nt mean to say that he never made mistakes.

× × ×

People belonging to he moderate and anti—Congress school of Indian Politics do not, of course agree with Mr. Tilak in his political views, but there are no two opinions with regard to Mr. Tilak's high intellectual attainments, ardent patriotism, moral courage and boldness. The arrest and trial of such a man has, undoubtedly, produced a great sensation troughout India and the sentence which has now been passed on him is sure to shock his admirers. With the transportation of Mr. Tilak the extremists have lost their guide and the country one of its selfless and devoted workers. Mr. Tilak conducted his own case in the High Court and defended himself. The defence was indeed most learned and dignified. He remained as undaunted at the bar as he was on the Congress platform in the month of December last.

United Burma (Rangoon.)

Coming to the prosecution, procedure and the punishment which even his worst enemy has pronounced it to be "heavy," one shudders and sighs. Heavy as it is his merciful enemies are happy and justify the sentence. They think that the majesty of the law is vindicated. The people, on the contrary believe that the whole procedure was not quite free from bias and that the articles that form the subject-matter of the prosecution were only bonafide criticism of the acts of the bureaucracy. Even if there was a doubt he ought to have been first tried at Poona, wherefrom he had a chance of an appeal to the High Court. Even in Bombay he should have been allowed a Marathi-knowing jury, a jury composed mostly of his own countrymen and not one consisting mostly of different race, feelings and sentiments if not of active bias, as they were quite ignorant of the Language in which the articles were written especially so, when the sole question to be decided was whether the spirit conveyed by the language was seditious or not. The punishment awarded is extremely severe if not harsh and vindictive and the way in which he is transported looks as if everything was not so innocent as is made to appear. The whole country is stunned to hear that Mahraja Tilik is transported and breathe heavy sighs at so dramatic a trial and transportation though every man from the commencement of the trial anticipated that he will be severely punished, if not transported for life. Justice Davar inspite of the mildness of language and sympathy for accused has been compared to Pinhey of the Tuticorin trial. Maharaja Tilak might go as many have gone before him but there is not the slightest doubt that he is the real leader of men. He is known as "the uncrowned king of the Deccan" and king real he has been and well wears the crown because he weilds tremendous influence amongst the people deeper than any leaders of India. We may not agree with all his views but we admire the man and bow at his feet.

The Rangoon Standard (Rangoon.)

With due respect for the opinions of Mr. Justice Davar, we beg to state that we have read the articles in the language in which they were written and they never struck us as 'seething with sedition.' The impression they left on our mind was that the anarchist trouble owed its origin to the flouting of public opinion and that the real remedy was to appease the minds of the public by extending to them some real substantial rights. Mr. Tilak's paper is looked upon by those who understand the Marathi language as one giving ample information and offering straight-forward though strong comments on the current topics. He appeared to express what were the uppermost thoughts in the minds of his readers. If such a paper is closed people will be deprived of the best paper in Marathi journalism.

Bande Mataram (Calcutta.)

We are after all human and cannot press back our tears when high-souled patriotism is reported to be rewarded with a convict's fate in a penal settlement. Solemn thoughts may afterwards previal, strength may afterwards come to pull up the sinking heart but the keen anguish of the hour when the stuning news of a great patriot's fate is flashed by the wire for time, is too real to be glossed over with the admonitions of proud philosophy. This morning, we have actually seen three or four old men flinging away the newspaper that brought them the terrible news and taking to mournful musings. Such chastening sorrow has its noble use. It is that one touch of nature which will make us all kin and add to the credit side of the account.

× × ×

We all have not the stuff of Tilak in us and cannot but indulge in this human frailty. But the hero has himself left us a spell to secure us against the effect of this fearful act of persecution. The brilliant address to the jury which will for ever enrich our patriotic literature was not ment for his own defence but only to put heart into his countrymen. Where is the Indian, nay, the cultured being who, after reading his address to the jury and watching his conduct in the dock can help exclaiming, "here was a man, take him for all in all, we shall not look upon his like again."

× × ×

Go, Tilak, whether yon may be sent to crush your body. Your example will hover around us all unimprisoned and unexiled. The canker of the chains will not only eat into your limbs but also into every heart of the country to stir it up to its duty. Nearer the God, nearer the fire. He places his good soldiers in the very thick of the battle. You have fulfilled your mission,—you have taught your people to bear tortures rather than deny their country, you have staratled the deep slumber of false opinions, you have thrilled a pang of noble shame through callous consciences. And into the next age, if not into your own, you have flashed an epidemic of nobleness. What else have patriots, heroes and martyrs done?

The Amrita Bazar Patrika (Calcutta.)

The composition of the jury was a guarantee against Mr. Tilak's escape. The seven European jurors who found him guilty and whose verdict was accepted by the Judge had no help in the matter.

× × ×

The wonder, is that Mr. Justice Davar, who did not understand high-flown Mahratti was absolutely sure of the seditious character of the articles. How could the Judge then conscientiously convict the accused and pass practically a death sentence upon him when he had no evidence before him to show the effect which the original articles in the "Kesari" had or could have produced upon Mahratti knowing people?

× × ×

The greater wonder is that the Judge could reject with a light heart the verdict of the other two jurors who, being children of the soil, presumably knew the Marathi language and were thus better competent than their European colleagues to understand the real drift of the articles.

× × ×

If Mr. Tilak were tried in England, and two jurors were in his favour the presiding Judge would not have accepted the verdict of the majority but would have ordered a re-trial; and the accused would not have been convicted till the jury were unanimous. What then could have led Mr. Justice Davar to follow a procedure which no Judge in England would venture following?

The Bengalee (Calcutta.)

The country has received this news with a sense of profound sorrow and disappointment, and in this feeling the personality of Mr. Tilak does not at all enter It depends entirely upon the merits of the case and the extraordinary sentence passed by the presiding Judge. The public will not enter into legal or complicated technicalities, but there is the broad fact that the verdict was not a unanimous one and that two of the jurors who sat to try him brought in a verdict of not guilty. And let it be remembered that among the jurymen there was not a single Hindu or Deccani Brahman and that the Indian element was represented by only two Parsees, When there was such a differenee of opinion among the jurors, the public would naturally conclude that there were at least doubtful, that there were at least two honest and capable men who, after a conscientious examination of facts, doubted the guilt of the accused and that, therefore, he was entitled to the benefit of the doubt. This is a commen sense view—apart form all legal technicalties, the force of which it is impossible to resist. At any rate, the fact that there was this difference of opinion regarding the guilt of the accused among the jurors ought to have determined the case. The presiding Judge ought to have determined the measure of punishment inflicted in the case. The presiding Judge ought to have realised the fact that strong as might have been his own view of the matter, there were honest and capable men who had formed a different opinion which he was bound to respect, if not by accepting it, at any rate, by recognising it as a factor in the determination of the punishment to be inflicted. With all respect for the Judge, we regard the sentence as monstrous—as utterly out of proportion to the offence alleged to have been committed, and as one which will be universally condemned by our countrymen and all right-thinking men.

× × ×

The result, after all, is that Mr. Tilak is convicted of sedition not by his own peers but by some foreigners who are not only ignorant of the language in which the incriminating articles were written, but whose political views are diametrically opposed to those of the accused. Although the Advocate-General, addressing the Jury, resented Mr. Tilak's references to the political character of the trial, yet both he and the entire public know that it is on account of his politics that Mr. Tilak has been punished. Mr. Justice Davar practically admitted this when he said that it was desirable that the accused should be banished from the country for half-a-dozen years in the interests of peace. In short something like a death sentence-for, considering his age and the state of his health Mr. Tilak is not likely to survive six years' transportation—has been passed on him, because he proved dieagreeble to the ruling classes for his political views. This may not, of course, be the opinion of his prosecutors or the Judge, and Jury who tried him but, we believe. such is the view of his countrymen at large.

The Mussalman (Calcutta.)

The ability with which Mr. Tilak defended himself and the explanation that he gave in regard to his alleged seditious writings led many people to believe that he will be acquitted. If it was the intention of the Government to give the accused a fair trial we think the Jury should not have been constituted in the manner in which it was. The jury had of course no hand in the sentence passed by the presiding judge and we think his Lordship has gone too far in inflicting such a heavy punishment. It is unfortunate that courts in the land, both high and low, are becoming more or less devoid of sense of proportion in inflicting punishments in cases of a political nature. Level-headedness on the part of the authorities is never more desirable than under the present circumstances.

Reis and Rayyet (Calcutta.)

Sir George Sydenham Clarke has got rid of the most turbulent, the most influencial and the most formidable leader of one of the political parties in his Presidency. It was only a few months ago that Mr. Tilak was invited by the Governor to inspect the plague research laboratory. To-day Mr. Tilak is an exile in a foreign country, alone and friendless. Only his indomitable spirit is with him. Moderate or extremist, the news will shock all!